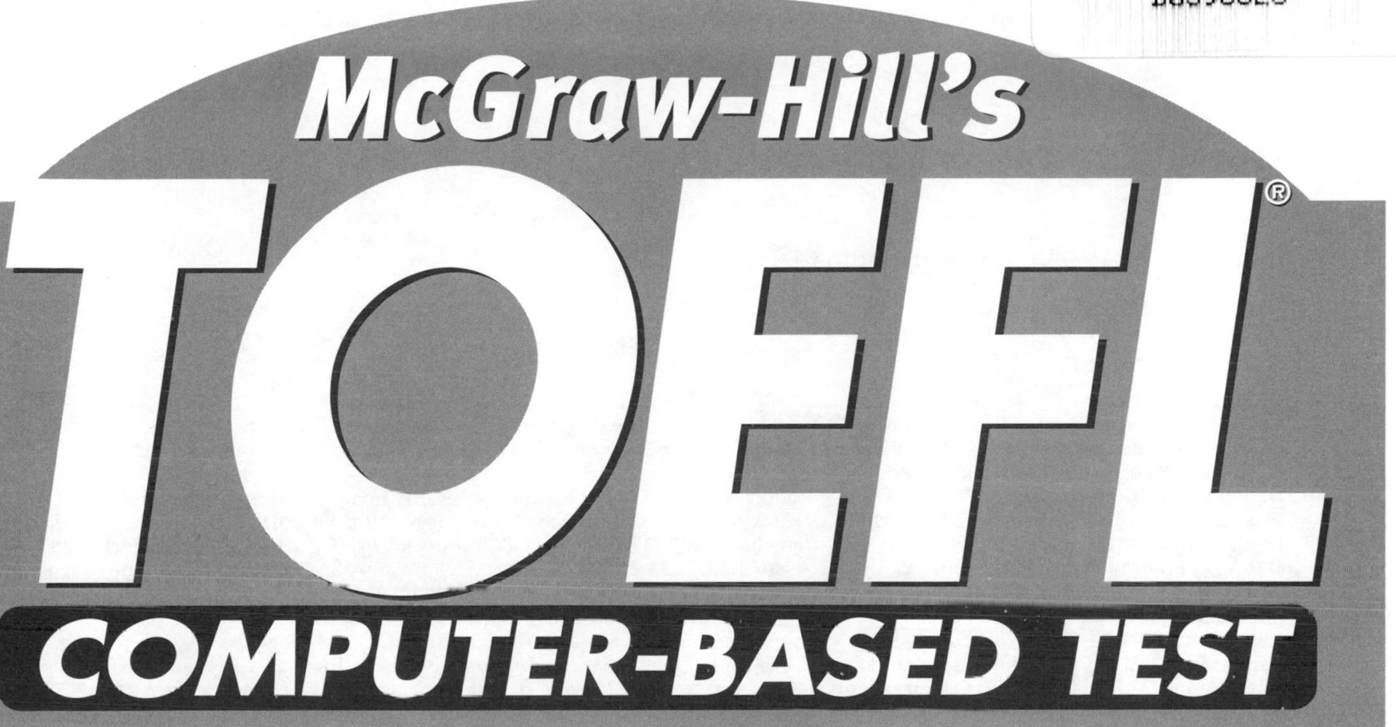

with 2 Audio CDs

ROBERTA STEINBERG

McGraw-Hill
New York Chicago San Francisco Lisbon London Madrid Mexico City
Milan New Delhi San Juan Seoul Singapore Sydney Toronto

1 2 3 4 5 6 7 8 9 0 QPD/QPD 0 9 8 7 6 5

ISBN 0-07-145194-3 (book with audio CD)

Interior design: NK Graphics
Art: NK Graphics
Photo credits:
4 *(top to bottom)* © Masterfile Royalty Free/Masterfile; © Roger Ressmeyer/CORBIS; © Bananastock/Robertstock.com; © Michael Goldman/Masterfile; © Mark Richards/Photo Edit **5** *(top to bottom)* © Bill Aron/Photo Edit; © Royalty-Free/CORBIS; Stockbyte/ PictureQuest; © Royalty-Free/CORBIS; © PhotoDisc/Getty Images **6** © PIXTAL/AGE Fotostock **8** *(top to bottom)* © Digital Vision/Getty Images; © PIXTAL/AGE Fotostock **9** *(both)* © Andrew Wakeford/Getty Images **11** *(both)* © Digital Vision/AGE Fotostock **13** *(both)* © PIXTAL/AGE Fotostock **18** © Ryan McVay/Getty Images **19** © PhotoDisc/Getty Images **20** © Digital Vision/AGE Fotostock **22** © PhotoDisc/Getty Images **25** © PIXTAL/AGE Fotostock **27** © T. Stewart/Zefa/Masterfile **28** © Royalty-Free/CORBIS **30** © Comstock Images/Getty Images **33** © HIRB/IndexStock Imagery **35** © Sonda Dawes/The Image Works **37** © BananaStock/PictureQuest **39** © PhotoDisc/Getty Images **41** © Michael Goldman/Masterfile **42** © BananaStock/AGE Fotostock **44** © Seth Joel/Getty Images **45** © Royalty-Free/CORBIS **47** © IndexStock/Alamy **51** *(top to bottom)* © Cindy Charles/Photo Edit; © IT Stock Free/Alamy **52** *(top to bottom)* © Vicky Kasala/Getty Images; © BananaStock/Alamy **53** *(top to bottom)* © Lonnie Duka/IndexStock Imagery; © PhotoDisc/Getty Images **54** *(top to bottom)* © David Young Wolff/Photo Edit; © Doug Menuez/Getty Images **55** *(top to bottom)* © James Marshall/The Image Works; © BananaStock/PictureQuest **56** *(top to bottom)* © Royalty-Free/CORBIS; © Comstock Images/Getty Images **58** *(top to bottom)* © Tom Stewart/CORBIS; © Royalty-Free/CORBIS **59** *(top to bottom)* © Sally A. Morgan; Ecoscene/CORBIS; © Kennan Ward/CORBIS; © Kevin Schafer/CORBIS; © Buddy Mays/CORBIS **62** *(top to bottom)* © Sally A. Morgan; Ecoscene/CORBIS; © Kevin Schafer/CORBIS; © Kennan Ward/CORBIS; © Buddy Mays/CORBIS **68** *(both)* © Cindy Charles/Photo Edit **70** *(left, top to bottom)* © PhotoDisc/Getty Images; © Paul Almasy/CORBIS; *(right, top to bottom)* © Cooperphoto/CORBIS; © Bill Stormont/CORBIS; © PhotoDisc/Getty Images **71** *(closewise, from top right)* © Paul Almasy/CORBIS; © Bill Stormont/CORBIS; © Cooperphoto/CORBIS **72** *(left, top to bottom)* © Royalty-Free/CORBIS; © Thomas A. Heinz/CORBIS; ; *(right, top to bottom)* © Farrell Grehan/CORBIS; © G.E. Kidder Smith/CORBIS; © G.E. Kidder Smith/CORBIS **73** *(left, top to bottom)* The Frank Lloyd Wright Foundation, Scottsdale, Arizona; © Peter M. Wilson/CORBIS; *(right)* © Royalty-Free/CORBIS **75** *(both)* © Patrick Clark/Getty Images **77** *(both)* © Doug Menuez/Getty Images **79** *(both)* © PhotoDisc/Getty Images **81** *(both)* © Comstock Images/Alamy **83** © Patrick Clark/Getty Images **87** *(top to bottom)* © Mauritius/AGE Fotostock; © David Urbina/Photo Edit; © PhotoDisc/Getty Images; © Royalty-Free/CORBIS; © Digital Vision/PictureQuest **88** *(top to bottom)* © Bananastock/Robertstock.com; © Mark Richards/Photo Edit; © PhotoDisc/Getty Images; © PhotoDisc/Getty Images; © Masterfile Royalty Free/Masterfile **89** © Royalty-Free/CORBIS **91** *(top to bottom)* © Jeff Maloney/Getty Images; © Royalty-Free/CORBIS **92** *(left, top to bottom)* © Scott T. Baxter/Getty Images; © Francis G. Mayer/CORBIS; *(right, top to bottom)* **The Art Institute of Chicago; The Art Institute of Chicago**; © Asian Art & Archaeology, Inc./CORBIS; © Doug Menuez/Getty Images **93** *(top both)* © Christie's Images/CORBIS; *(bottom, left to right)* © Lester V. Bergman/CORBIS; © Alexander Burkatovski/CORBIS **94** *(both)* © PhotoDisc/Getty Images **96** *(both)* © RubberBall Productions/Alamy **331** *(top to bottom)* © Royalty-Free/CORBIS; © T. Stewart/Zefa/Masterfile; © James Marshall/The Image Works; © Digital Vision/AGE Fotostock; © BananaStock/ PictureQuest **332** *(top to bottom)* © PhotoDisc/Getty Images; © Patrick Clark/Getty Images; © Masterfile Royalty Free/Masterfile; © Scott T. Baxter/Getty Images; © Dave Robertson/Masterfile **333** © PIXTAL/AGE Fotostock **335** *(top to bottom)* © Doug Menuez/Getty Images; © Royalty-Free/CORBIS **336** *(both)* © PhotoDisc/Getty Images **338** *(both)* © Royalty-Free/CORBIS **339** *(left, top to bottom)* © Leonard de Selva/CORBIS; © CORBIS SYGMA; *(bottom, left to right)* © CORBIS SYGMA; © Bettmann/CORBIS **340** *(both)* © PIXTAL/AGE Fotostock **347** *(top, left to right)* © Archivo Iconografico, S.A./CORBIS; © Hulton Archive/Getty Images; *(bottom, left to right)* © CORBIS; The Granger Collection, NY **357** *(top to bottom)* © Bananastock/Robertstock.com; © PhotoLink/Getty Images; © CORBIS; © PhotoDisc/Getty Images; © PIXTAL/AGE Fotostock; © Chabruken/Getty Images **358** *(top to bottom)* © PhotoDisc/Getty Images; © PIXTAL/AGE Fotostock; © PIXTAL/AGE Fotostock; © IndexStock/Alamy; © Royalty-Free/CORBIS **359** © Dave Robertson/Masterfile **361** *(top to bottom)* © Comstock Images/Getty Images; © Royalty-Free/CORBIS **362** *(left, top to bottom)* © Andrew Wakeford/Getty Images; © Bettmann/CORBIS; © CORBIS **363** *(top, left to right)* © The Corcoran Gallery of Art/CORBIS; © Bettmann/CORBIS; *(bottom, left to right)* © Bettmann/CORBIS; © CORBIS **364** *(both)* © Tom Stewart/CORBIS **366** *(both)* © Patrick Clark/Getty Images

This book is printed on acid-free paper.

TABLE OF CONTENTS

ACKNOWLEDGMENTS

This textbook is dedicated to my former TOEFL/TWE students at Harvard University Extension, whose test-taking anxiety motivated my rethinking of TOEFL/TWE instruction.

Thank you to the following:

The essayists for this project as well as their instructors/coordinators: Brandeis University Summer School students, Barbary Levy, instructor; EmbassyCESL/Lasell College students, Kathy Buruca, instructor; CELOP/Boston University, Bruce Rindler, Director; and my students at SMA/MIT and Mount Ida College.

Donna Lee Kennedy and Jennifer Monaghan for encouraging me to undertake this project.

Thomas Healy at McGraw-Hill.

The following, whose advice, comments, and suggestions during the writing of this text is greatly appreciated:

Jamie Beaton	Boston University/CELOP
Shira Fischer	National Academy of Science, Institute of Medicine
Christine Root	ESL Ink
Sloan Sable	The Winsor School
Christine Seashore	The Winsor School
Doree Shafrir	University of Pennsylvania

and Michael Shafrir for his help with college conversation topics and dialogues.

Finally, special thanks to Judith Dileo for her inspiring material and Liz Kelley and Diana Renn for their exceptional editorial advice.

The publisher and the author would like to thank the following individuals who reviewed *McGraw-Hill's TOEFL® Computer-Based Test* during the development of the series and whose comments and suggestions were invaluable in creating this project.

Elizabeth Kelley	University of California at San Diego
Tammy Gilbert	
Jody Stern	University of California at San Diego
Kathleen Makanani Randall	San Francisco Institute of English
Arden Collier	Intrax English Institute San Francisco
Kelly Smith	English Language Programs, UCSD Extension
Charlotte Currie	San Francisco Institute of English

INTRODUCTION AND GENERAL INFORMATION ABOUT THE TEST

The TOEFL test evaluates the English ability of those whose native language is not English. More than 2,400 colleges and universities in the U.S. and Canada as well as many agencies and licensing boards require the TOEFL test. Each school and board decides on its acceptable score. The computer-based TOEFL (CBT) test, the only test offered by ETS in the U.S., is now used in most of the world. All four sections of the test are mandatory.

HERE ARE ANSWERS TO MANY OF YOUR QUESTIONS ABOUT THE TOEFL TEST:

1. *What's tested on the TOEFL test?*

There are four sections to the test, all of which you must do.

- Listening
- Structure
- Reading
- Writing

You must write an essay in order to receive a total score.

2. *What does computer adaptive mean?*

On the CBT, the Listening and Structure sections are "computer adaptive." That means that questions are chosen from a very large bank of questions that are organized by difficulty and content. The questions are chosen by the computer based on how you answered the previous question. The first question will be of "average" difficulty. If you get the question wrong, the next question will be easier. If you get the question right, the next question will be harder. All students have the same number of questions. In these two sections, you will be able to change your answers as often as you wish until you make your final choice and confirm it, moving on to the next question. However, you will NOT be able to go back to a previous question. Adjustments in scoring are made according to the difficulty of the questions.

The Reading section is NOT adaptive. That means you can leave out answers, go back to earlier questions, and change your answers. Questions don't change as you take the test.

In the Writing section, the computer will assign you a topic from a pool of topics. See pages 27–32 in the TOEFL test bulletin for the list of topics. You will have the choice of typing or handwriting your answer.

3. *How can I pay for the test?*

Today the TOEFL test costs $110.00. If you need to change the date once you make an appointment, the charge is $40.00. There are many ways to pay. If you register by phone or fax, you must pay with a credit card. If you register by mail, you can use a credit card OR use a check or money order. Fees are subject to change without notice.

4. *How often can I take the test?*

You can take the test once every calendar month.

5. *How do the scores compare to the paper-based test (PBT)?*

Although the scores of the CBT and the PBT are not directly comparable, ETS has published a table that many institutions use to compare the two.

PBT TOTALS	CBT TOTALS
660–677	287–300
640–657	273–283
620–637	260–270
600–617	250–260
580–597	237–247
560–577	220–233
540–577	207–220
520–527	190–203
500–517	173–187
480–497	157–170
460–477	140–153
440–457	123–137
420–437	110–123
400–417	97–107
380–397	83–93
360–377	70–80
340–357	60–70
320–337	47–57
310–317	40–57

6. *How long is the test?*

The entire test session is approximately four hours long, including tutorials which teach different computer skills. You must complete the tutorials even if you are very familiar with computers. The average test-taker spends 40 minutes on the tutorials.

Each test includes additional questions for research only. These items will not be scored; however, you will not know which questions these are as they are inserted randomly throughout the test. The total amount of time allowed for a section is stated in the directions. The time allowed to respond is displayed at the beginning of a section. Look at this information before you begin.

The current question number, the total number of questions in a section, and the time remaining in the section are displayed on the title bar. Use this information so that you can finish each section before time runs out.

Listening has between 30 and 49 questions.
Structure has between 20 and 25 questions.
Reading has between 44 and 55 questions.

Because the number of questions changes, the amount of time you are given to answer the questions changes. In the Listening section, you will be given 15 to 25 minutes to answer the questions. That time does NOT include when you are listening to conversations and talks. The actual time to complete the section is about 40 to 60 minutes. In the Structure section, you will have between 15 and 20 minutes to complete the questions. In the Reading section, you will have between 70 and 90 minutes to finish, including time spent reading the passages and answering the questions. Everyone's score is based on the same number of questions, but you may have some additional questions which are being evaluated. You will not know which test items are being counted in your score.

You must write the essay and you must write only on the topic you are given. You will have 30 minutes to write your essay. Turn to the Writing the Essay section of this book for preparation.

7. *I know how to use a computer. Will I have to do the computer tutorials?*
Yes. Everyone MUST do the tutorials.

8. *I'm not really comfortable using a computer. Will I get a bad score?*
Everyone will complete non-scored computer tutorials the day of the test. Before you take the test you will learn

- how to use the mouse
- how to scroll
- how to use the testing tools

In addition, you will practice how to answer the questions for each of the sections of the test. Practice the tutorials on the ETS web site at www.toefl.org.

9. *When will I get my scores?*
If you handwrite the essay, the scores will be mailed to you about five weeks after you take the test. If you write the essay using the computer, you can expect the mailed scores in approximately two weeks.

10. *Can I leave during the test?*
There will be one MANDATORY five-minute break during the test. At that time you must leave the testing room. Other than that short break, you CANNOT leave the room.

11. *How do you suggest I prepare for the test?*
Read the following strategies carefully before you begin working in this book.

TOEFL TEST-TAKING STRATEGIES

1. **Know what the test looks like.** Learn what you need to know about using a computer. Decide BEFORE you take the test if you're going to type or handwrite your essay.
2. **Go to the ETS website and practice the computer tutorial section.** If you need to push the HELP button once the test begins, you will lose valuable test-taking time.
3. **Do the Practice Tests just like a regular TOEFL test.** Do not stop in the middle. Finish an entire test in one sitting. Do not take notes during the Listening section because you will not be able to during the test. Take one complete TOEFL test from the back of the book before you begin the exercises in the book, and do the second one after you have finished the book. You will then be able to decide which section is your weakest and strongest.
4. **Give yourself enough time to prepare.** Work through this book and pay attention to areas that are difficult for you.

I wish you all good luck on the test, and please e-mail me with your comments, questions, and suggestions.

Roberta (Robby) Steinberg
rgsteinberg@mountida.edu

SECTION ONE

LISTENING

In this section, a Pre-Test will first acquaint you with the Listening section of the TOEFL test. This is followed by an overview of the Listening test and strategies for tackling different types of questions. These strategies are accompanied by illustrative exercises. Finally, a Post-Test will allow you to test your understanding and chart your progress. In addition, you will find two full-length practice tests, covering all four sections of the TOEFL test, including Listening, in Appendixes C and D.

In all tests and exercises, Listening questions are designed to replicate the style of the TOEFL Computer-Based Exam. On the page you will see question numbers, answer options, and often accompanying computer screens, but you will not see the audio portion of the questions, which includes a passage and occasionally the related question. For a transcript of these audio elements, turn to Appendix E. If these passages are being read to you, a pause of about ten seconds should be allowed between questions. The inclusion of dialogues means that, ideally, three speakers should participate in the reading.

The answers to all tests and exercises appear in the Answer Key at the back of the book.

LISTENING PRE-TEST

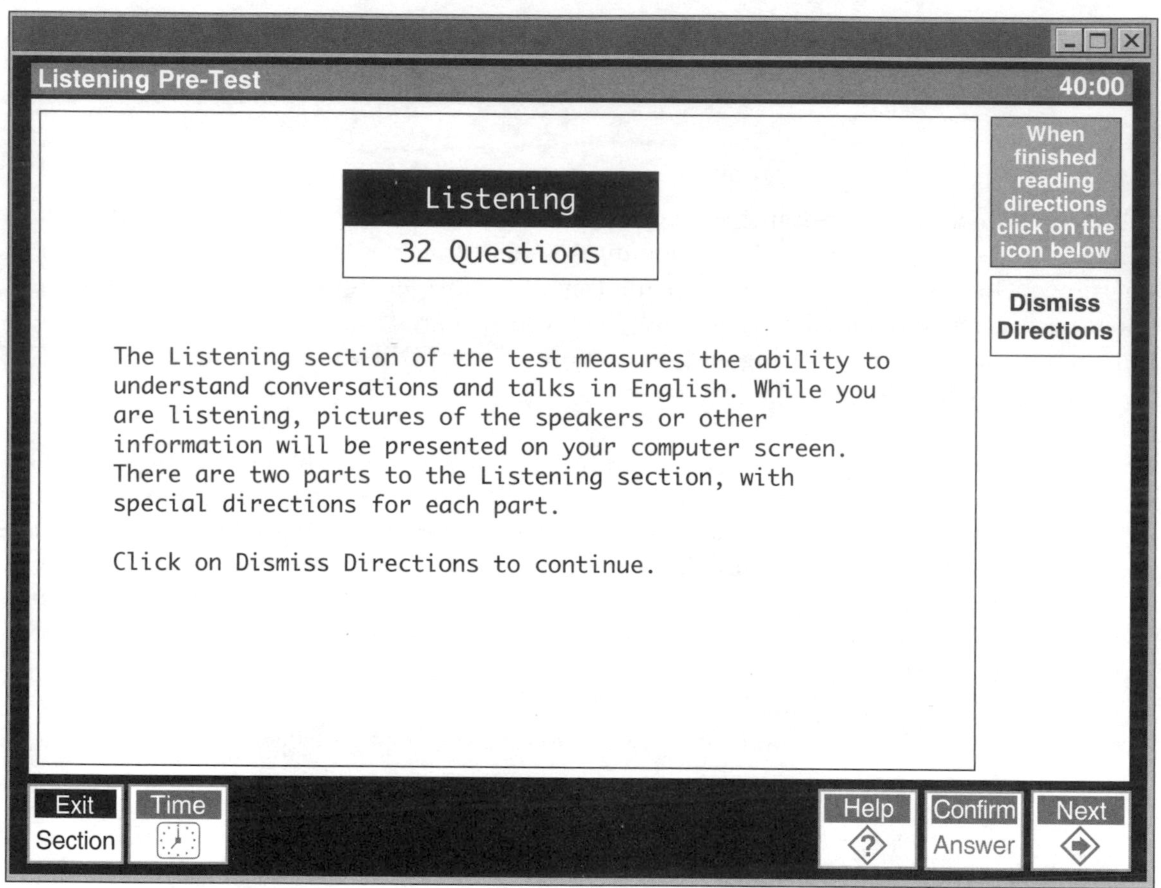

Listening Pre-Test
40:00
Listening
32 Questions
The Listening section of the test measures the ability to understand conversations and talks in English. While you are listening, pictures of the speakers or other information will be presented on your computer screen. There are two parts to the Listening section, with special directions for each part.
Click on Dismiss Directions to continue.
When finished reading directions click on the icon below
Dismiss Directions
Exit Section
Time
Help
Confirm Answer
Next

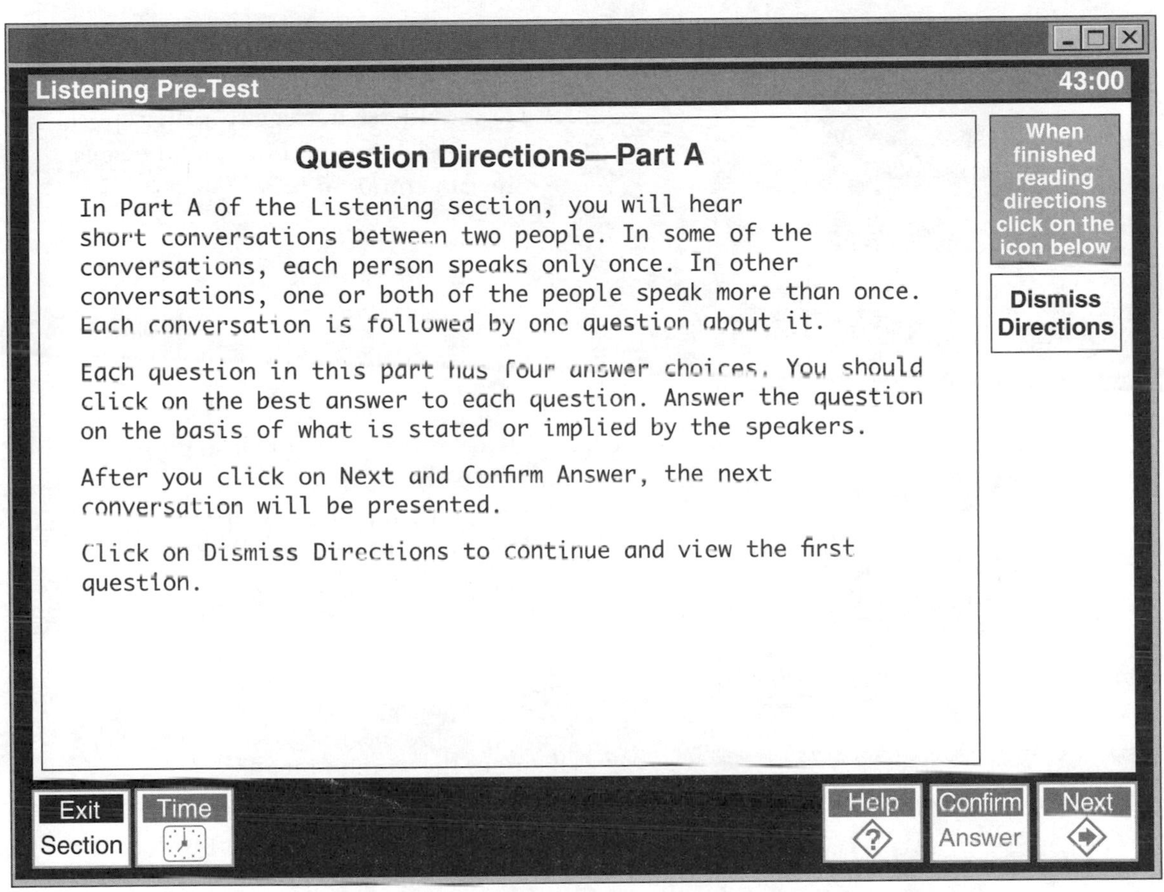
Listening Pre-Test
43:00
Question Directions—Part A
In Part A of the Listening section, you will hear short conversations between two people. In some of the conversations, each person speaks only once. In other conversations, one or both of the people speak more than once. Each conversation is followed by one question about it.
Each question in this part has four answer choices. You should click on the best answer to each question. Answer the question on the basis of what is stated or implied by the speakers.
After you click on Next and Confirm Answer, the next conversation will be presented.
Click on Dismiss Directions to continue and view the first question.
When finished reading directions click on the icon below
Dismiss Directions
Exit Section
Time
Help
Confirm Answer
Next

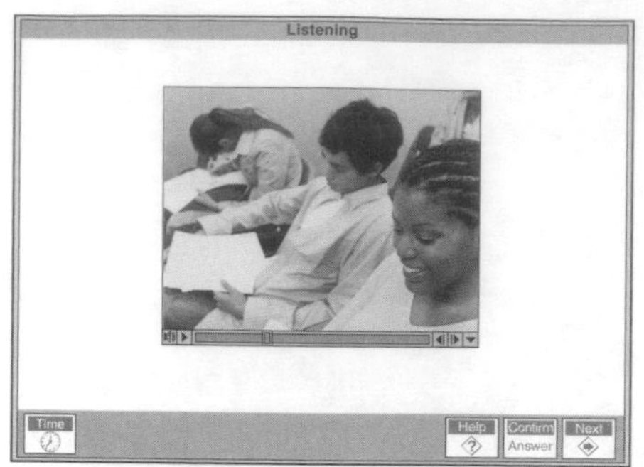

1. What does the woman mean?
   - He can see some plays during his vacation.
   - He forgot about his performance.
   - He'll soon have time to get ready.
   - He can perform during the vacation.

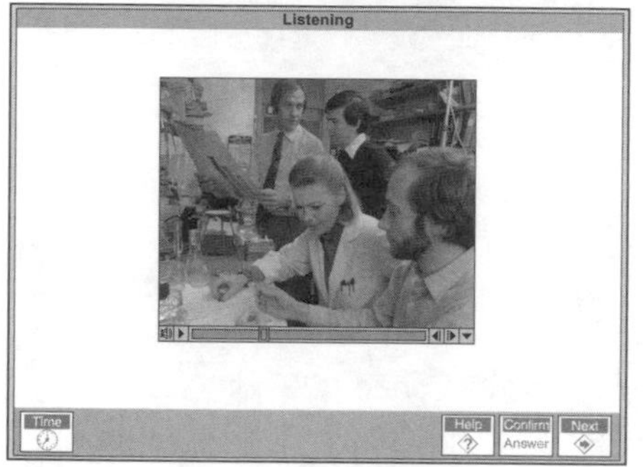
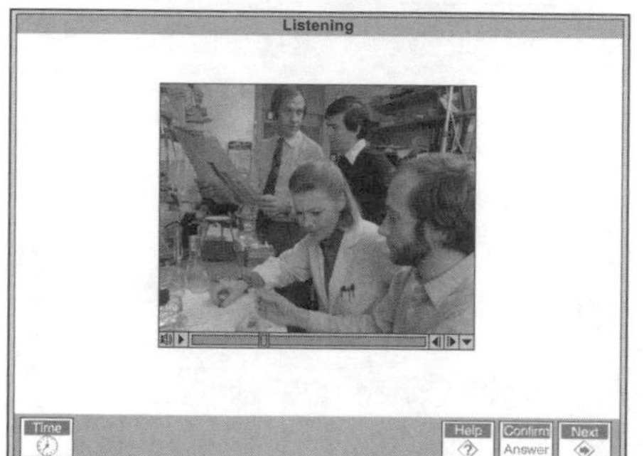

2. What does the woman imply?
   - She wouldn't rely on Dan.
   - He should use her eggs for the report.
   - That basket may not hold all the eggs.
   - She can count on him.

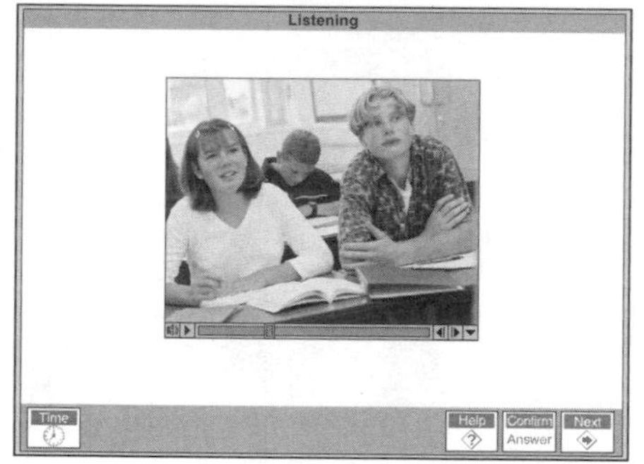

3. What does the man imply?
   - He'd rather not divide into groups.
   - There's not enough time for group work.
   - He's not going to participate.
   - He's going to give the professor his opinion.

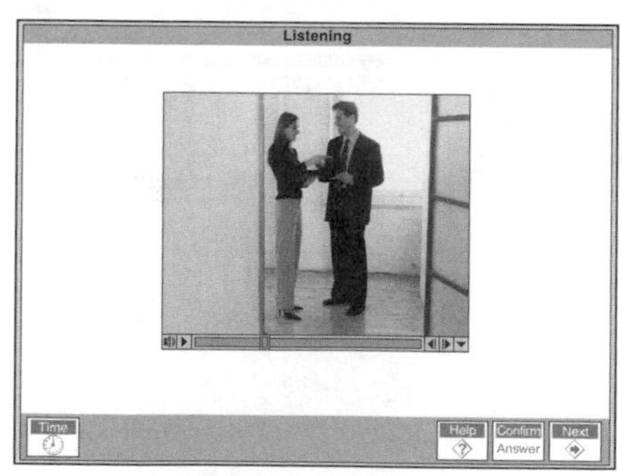

4. What does the woman mean?
   - The taxi will come as soon as they call it.
   - They should call Joyce and Kenny.
   - They should have called the taxi earlier because now they'll be late.
   - To avoid being late, it's best to call for a taxi immediately.

5. What does the man imply?
   - He doesn't know where she'll find a machine like her old one.
   - He'd like to help her find the part and fix the machine.
   - It will be cheaper to find the broken part than to buy a new machine.
   - Replacing the machine would cost less than repairing the old one.

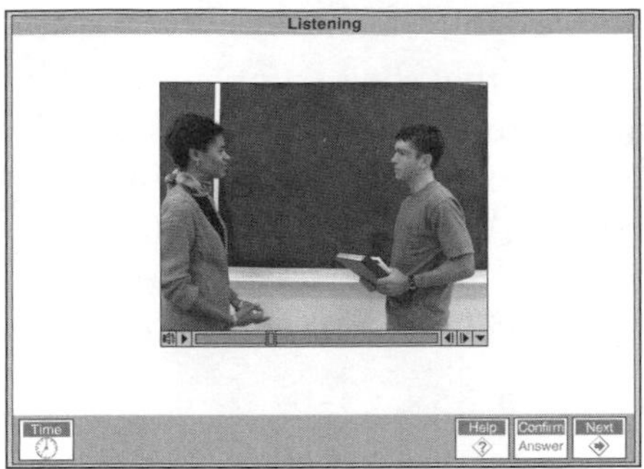

6. What can be inferred from this conversation?
   - ⬭ The man's improvement hasn't been steady.
   - ⬭ The man agrees with the woman's recommendation.
   - ⬭ The man doesn't want to repeat the course.
   - ⬭ All the students will be repeating the course.

7. What does the woman mean?
   - ⬭ She went to the dentist to have her tooth fixed.
   - ⬭ Her tooth cracked on the way to see the dentist.
   - ⬭ After seeing the dentist, she broke her tooth.
   - ⬭ She still hasn't gone to see the dentist.

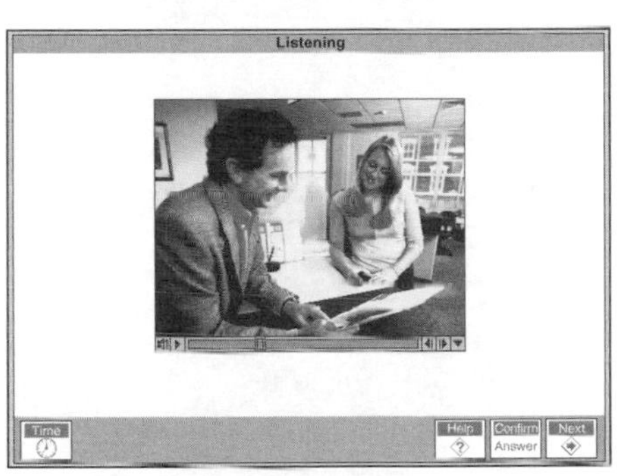

8. Where does this conversation probably take place?
   - ⬭ At an airport
   - ⬭ At a hotel
   - ⬭ At a travel agency
   - ⬭ At a computer store

9. What does the woman imply?
   - ⬭ She'll probably miss the chancellor's welcome.
   - ⬭ She doesn't see a meal plan.
   - ⬭ She may be signing up for a cafeteria meal plan.
   - ⬭ If she goes to the cafeteria tonight, she'll miss the president's speech.

10. What does the woman imply?
    - ⬭ She's lucky her classes aren't in the special classrooms.
    - ⬭ The art classes are held in Shaw Hall's smart classrooms.
    - ⬭ She's crazy about her classrooms.
    - ⬭ Her classrooms aren't up to date.

11. What does the man imply?
   - He's surprised that she's completed all but the final chapter.
   - He'd like to see her table of contents.
   - Her thesis won't be complete without a bibliography.
   - The graphics will take her more time to finish.

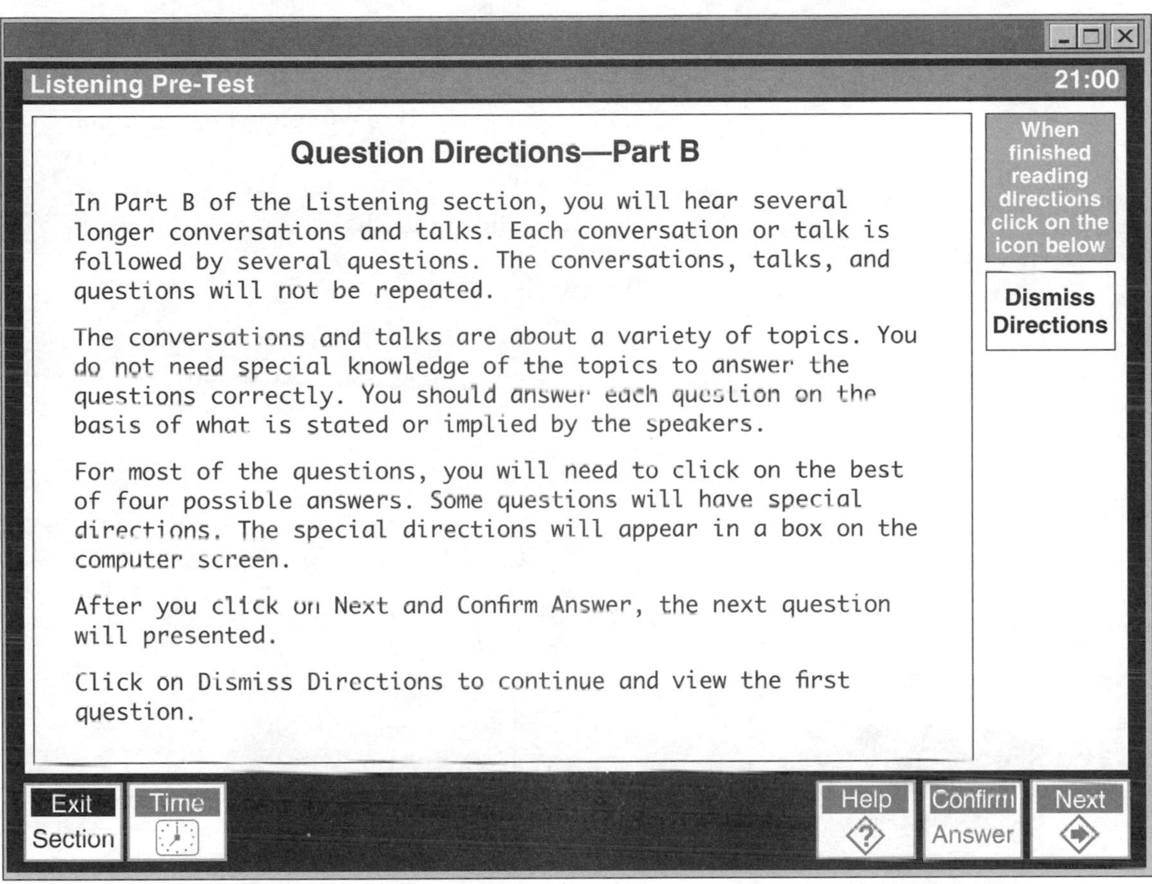
Listening Pre-Test
21:00

Question Directions—Part B

In Part B of the Listening section, you will hear several longer conversations and talks. Each conversation or talk is followed by several questions. The conversations, talks, and questions will not be repeated.

The conversations and talks are about a variety of topics. You do not need special knowledge of the topics to answer the questions correctly. You should answer each question on the basis of what is stated or implied by the speakers.

For most of the questions, you will need to click on the best of four possible answers. Some questions will have special directions. The special directions will appear in a box on the computer screen.

After you click on Next and Confirm Answer, the next question will presented.

Click on Dismiss Directions to continue and view the first question.

Questions 12–14

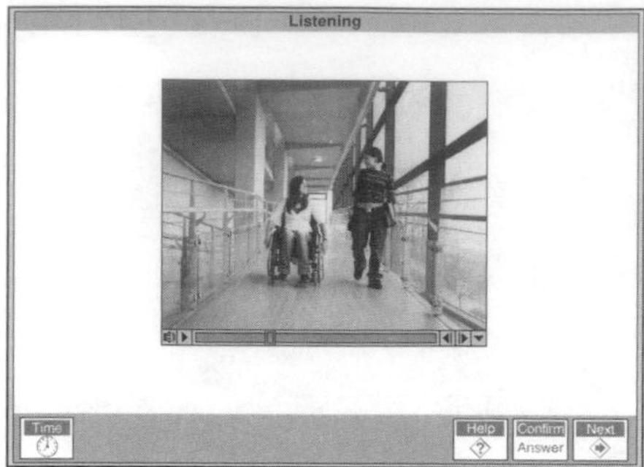

12. What can be inferred from the passage?
    - ⬭ Tammy will go to the mall later, without Sarah.
    - ⬭ Sarah will buy something for Tammy at the mall.
    - ⬭ It isn't 4 o'clock yet.
    - ⬭ Tammy and Sarah have just gotten out of class.

13. Why can't Tammy go to the mall with Sarah?
    - ⬭ She needs to complete her assignment.
    - ⬭ She has to meet a friend at the library.
    - ⬭ Her paper needs to be edited.
    - ⬭ She doesn't like the mall.

14. What is Sarah likely to do at 4?
    - ⬭ Meet her boyfriend at a party
    - ⬭ Go to the mall
    - ⬭ Wait for Tammy at the library
    - ⬭ Give Tammy a call

Questions 15–17

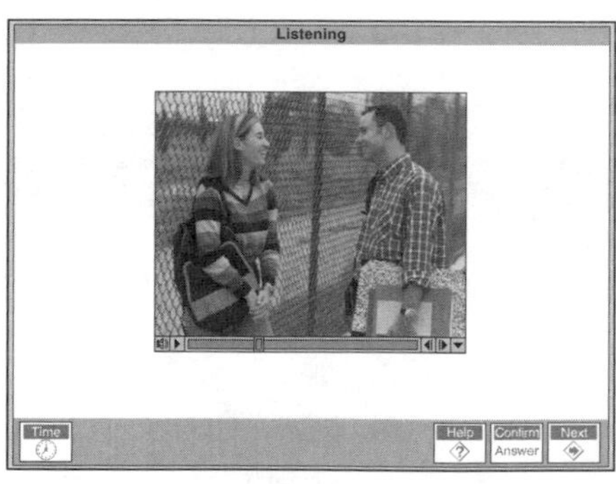

15. Where will the performance likely be held?
    - ⬭ The student center
    - ⬭ The cafeteria
    - ⬭ The auditorium
    - ⬭ The gymnasium

16. What will Danielle probably do next?
    - ⬭ Go to the gym
    - ⬭ Tell a friend about Adam Sandler's performance
    - ⬭ Get a ticket for the performance
    - ⬭ Watch the a cappella concert

17. What can be inferred from the passage?
    - ⬭ Adam Sandler sings a cappella.
    - ⬭ The man will be going to hear Adam Sandler.
    - ⬭ The auditorium is bigger than the gym.
    - ⬭ There are still tickets left to see Adam Sandler.

Questions 18–22

Listen to a lecture in an anthropology class on the development of speech.

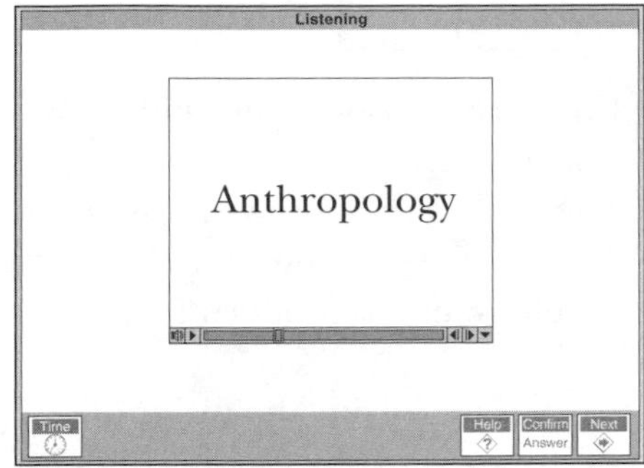

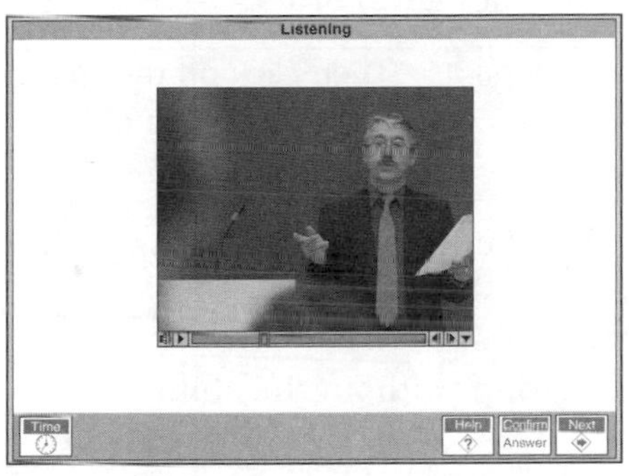

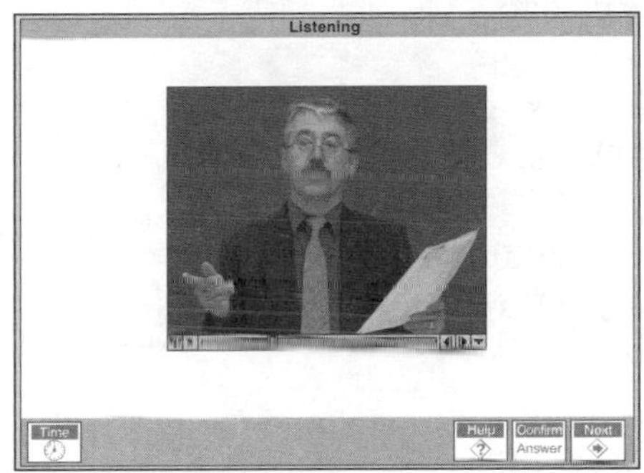

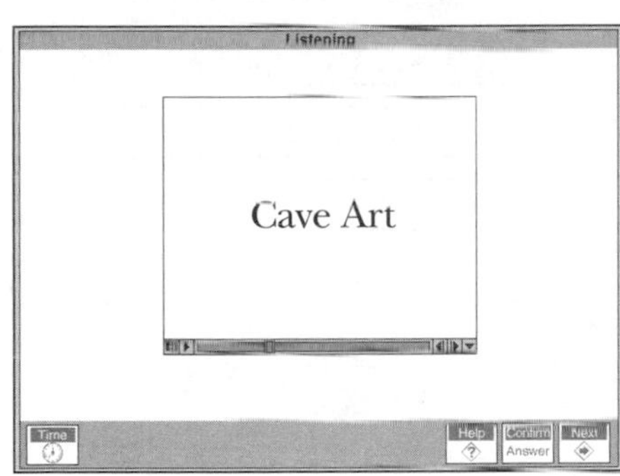

18. What is one of the most important differences between animals and humans?

- ⬭ Humans live in social groups.
- ⬭ Humans have the capacity for speech.
- ⬭ Scientists have studied the skulls of humans.
- ⬭ Animals have a canal at the back of the skull.

19. Approximately how long ago did cave art begin to appear in Europe and Africa?

- ⬭ 4,000 years ago
- ⬭ 40,000 years ago
- ⬭ 400,000 years ago
- ⬭ 4,000,000 years ago

20. Where is the canal that scientists have been studying to learn more about very early speech?

- ⬭ In the tongue
- ⬭ In the nerves
- ⬭ In the skull
- ⬭ In the muscles

21. Which of the following support the belief that man was able to speak 40,000 years ago?

Click on 2 answers.

- ☐ Evidence of cooperative behavior
- ☐ The appearance of cave art
- ☐ The discovery of human fossils
- ☐ Same nerve/tongue/muscle development as modern man

22. The professor explains the order of each of these occurrences. Put them in their chronological order.

Click on a phrase. Then click on the space where it belongs. Use each phrase only once.

The first skulls with canals the same size as modern skulls
The appearance of cave art
Social groups without the ability to speak
The study of fossil anatomy

1. ______
2. ______
3. ______
4. ______

Questions 23–27

Listen to a discussion in a fashion design class. The discussion is about weaving.

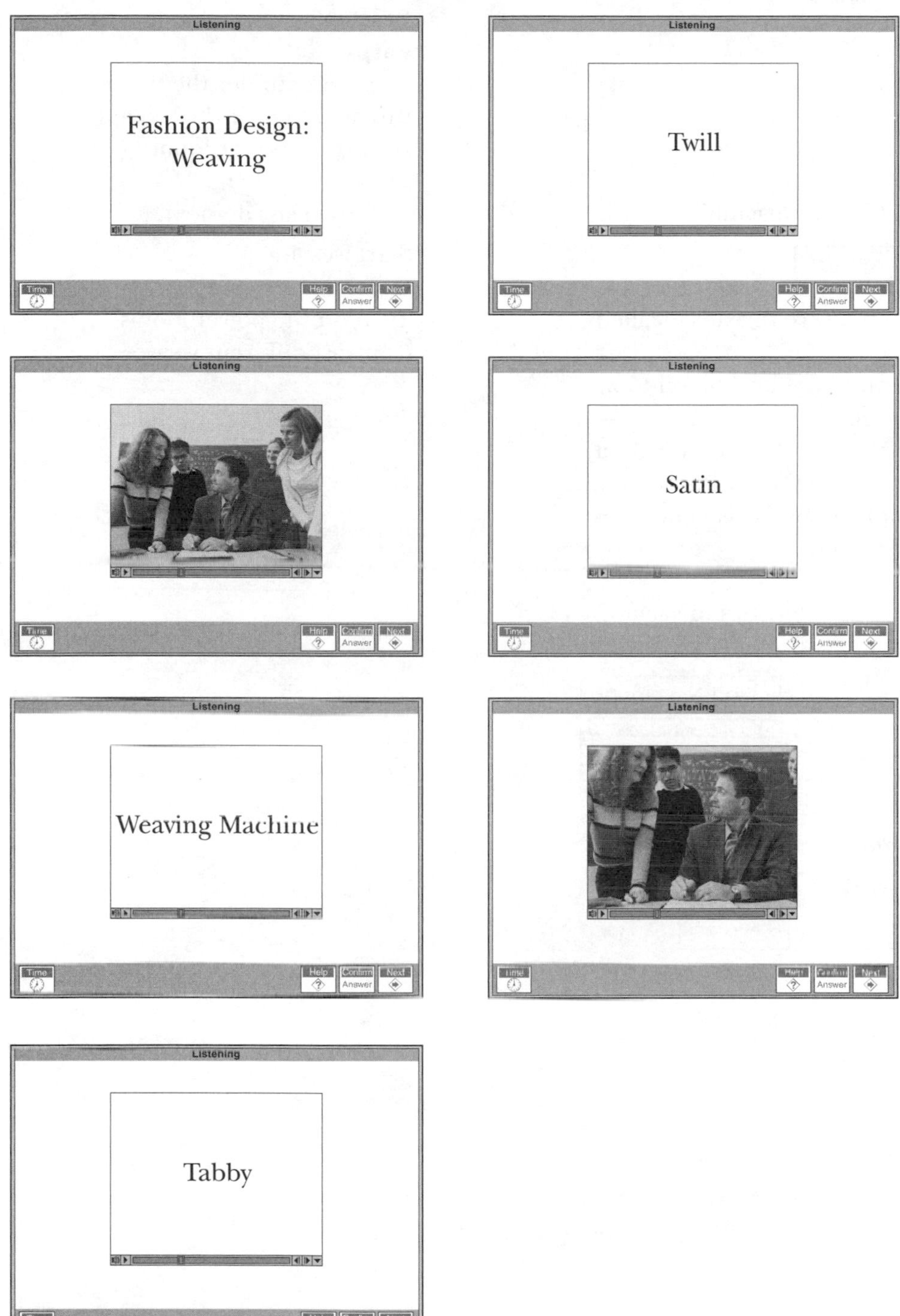

23. According to the discussion, which of the following is commonly woven?

Click on 2 answers.

- ☐ Rugs
- ☐ Furniture
- ☐ Clothing
- ☐ Quilts

24. What is stated about weaving?

Click on 2 answers.

- ☐ A set of crosswire threads is called the warp.
- ☐ Both hand looms and power looms can be used.
- ☐ Crossing 2, 3, or 4 warp threads at a time creates extra width.
- ☐ The simple weave is also known as the twill weave.

25. What are the characteristics of each of these types of weaves?

Click on a word. Then click on the empty box in the correct column. Use each word only once.

tabby	**twill**	**satin**
sturdy	glossy	simplest
☐	☐	☐

26. How does the satin weave create a smooth finish?

- ⬭ By creating raised, diagonal lines
- ⬭ By each weft spanning up to 12 warps
- ⬭ By passing under the first warp thread and over the second
- ⬭ By using a power loom

27. What will the class do next?

- ⬭ Start weaving
- ⬭ Get the looms ready
- ⬭ Turn on the power looms
- ⬭ Contrast different weaves

Questions 28–32

Listen to a lecture in an American history class. The professor is talking about the settlement of Roanoke.

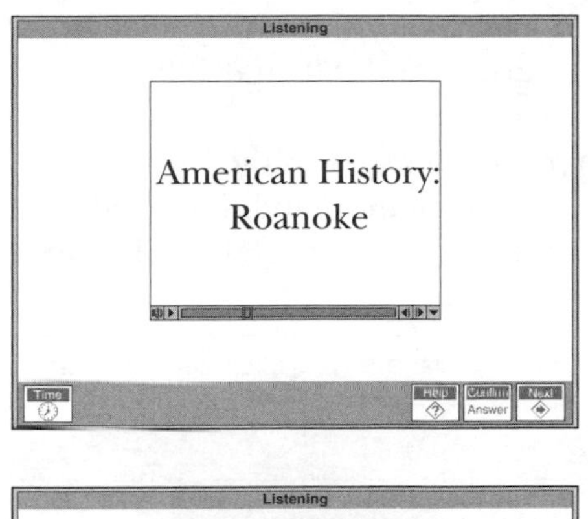

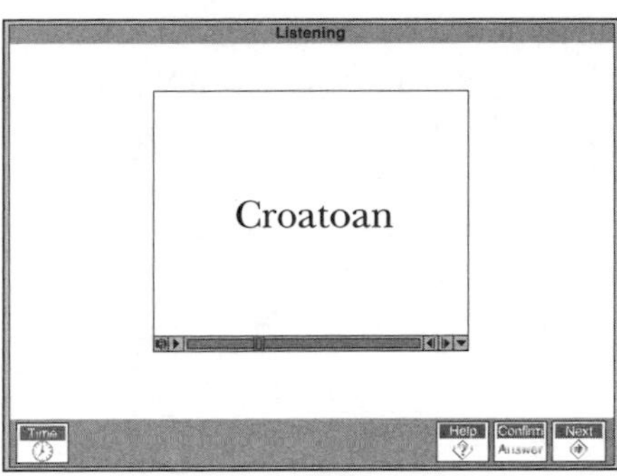

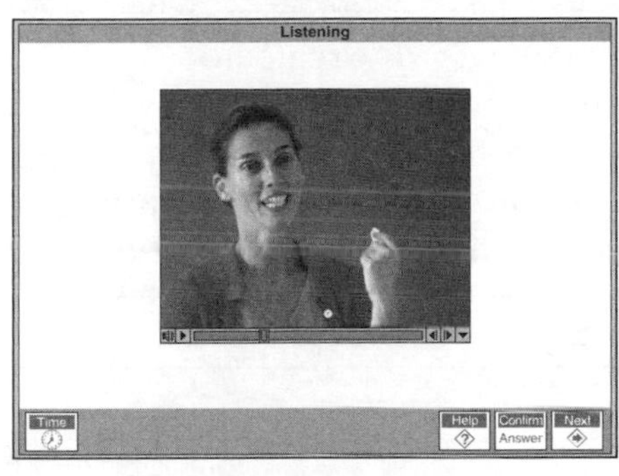

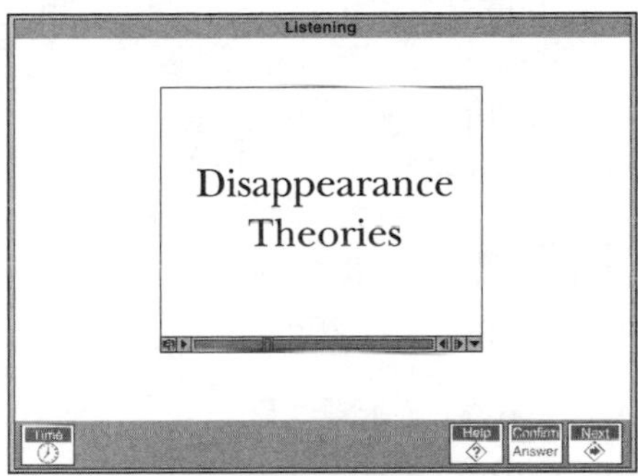

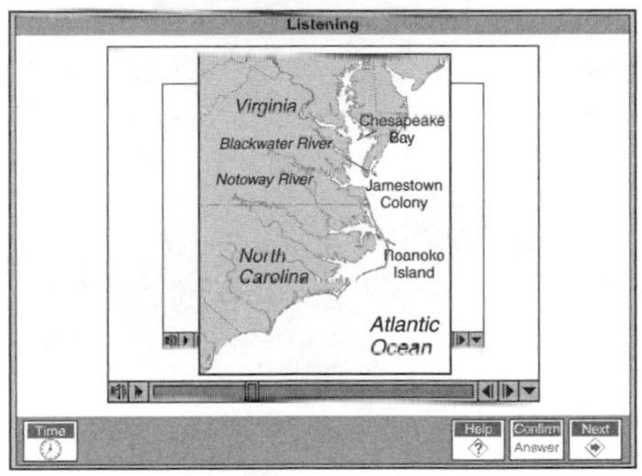

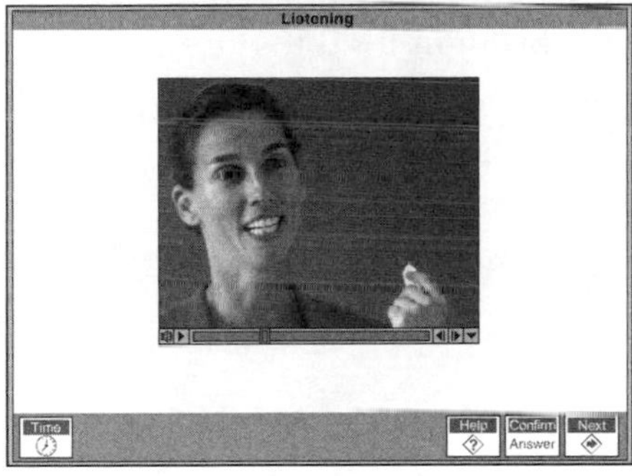

28. Why did the leaders of the settlers return to England?
   - ⬭ To get arms to defend the group against the Croatoans
   - ⬭ To get more supplies
   - ⬭ To fight the Spanish Armada
   - ⬭ To give the settlers an opportunity to live off the land

29. How soon after landing at Roanoke did the leaders of the group return to England?
   - ⬭ Four days later
   - ⬭ After a few months
   - ⬭ The following year
   - ⬭ Three years later

30. What might have happened to the settlers who disappeared from Roanoke?

   Click on 2 answers.

   - ☐ Maybe they fought with the Indians.
   - ☐ Maybe they followed the Croatoans south.
   - ☐ Maybe they went back to England.
   - ☐ Maybe they brought food to the Croatoans.

31. When did the Roanoke area suffer a terrible drought?
   - ⬭ 800 years ago
   - ⬭ Before the settlers landed at Roanoke
   - ⬭ In the late 16th century
   - ⬭ During the 1980s and 1990s

32. The professor explains the history of the Roanoke settlers and their leaders. Put these occurrences in their chronological order.

   Click on a phrase. Then click on the space where it belongs. Use each phrase only once.

   Finding the word "Croatoan"
   Leaders returning to England
   Arriving in 1587
   Taking British ships for the Spanish Armada

   1. ____________
   2. ____________
   3. ____________
   4. ____________

LISTENING

The Listening section of the test measures your ability to understand conversations, talks, and lectures in English. You will use headphones. While you listen, pictures of the speakers or other information will appear on the computer screen. The visual information does NOT provide information necessary for answering questions. There are two parts to the Listening section, with special directions for each part.

- The section has 30 to 50 questions and lasts from 40 to 60 minutes.
- The amount of time you have to answer all the questions will appear on the computer screen.
- The time you spend listening to speakers will not be counted.
- You can take as much time as you need to answer a question, but remember the test is timed. Therefore, work as quickly as you can.
- You will NOT be allowed to take notes or have any paper, pencils, or pens with you. You will hear the questions before the answer choices appear.
- The listening material and questions will be presented only one time.
- You may change any answer before you press CONFIRM ANSWER. After you press CONFIRM ANSWER, you will not be able to return to the question.
- This section is **computer adaptive,** which means if you get a question wrong, your next question will be an easier one. If you get a question right, the next question will be a harder one.
- You can adjust the volume of the sound before you begin. Once you begin, you can change the volume only during question directions, not while someone is speaking.

PARTS A AND B OF THE LISTENING SECTION

The Listening section is divided into two parts.

PART A: Short Dialogues

These are two to four line conversations between two people. You will see a picture on the screen that tells you generally where the conversation takes place. This picture will NOT help you answer the question. Then you will hear a conversation between the speakers followed by a question. You will hear the question before it appears on the screen with its answer choices, which are not read aloud. There will be between eleven and seventeen short conversations, each followed by one question.

PART B: Longer Conversations, Academic Discussions, and Lectures

There are three different kinds of talks in this part of the Listening test.

LONGER CONVERSATIONS

- The conversations are five to seven lines long and approximately thirty to ninety seconds long.
- These conversations are similar to short conversations, just longer. As with the shorter conversations, there are two speakers. You will see a picture on the screen which tells you who the speakers are and where they are talking. These pictures do NOT help you answer the questions.
- The topics are informal and related to college life.
- After you hear the conversation, you will hear and see each question before the answers appear.
- On each test there will be two to four longer conversations with two or three questions each.

ACADEMIC DISCUSSIONS

- Longer than the longer conversations, these are discussions among three or four people that last anywhere from 120 to 150 seconds.
- The topics are academic and are more formal than conversations.
- Sometimes the speakers interrupt one another.
- There will be a series of context-related pictures and visuals for each discussion, followed by three to six questions.
- There will be one or two discussions per test.

LECTURES

- Each lecture is 120 to 150 seconds.
- These talks are similar to classroom lectures given in a university course and are formal in tone.
- There is only one speaker, usually a professor.
- There will be a series of context-related pictures and visuals for each discussion, followed by three to six questions.
- There will be two or three lectures per test.

GENERAL STATEGIES FOR THE LISTENING SECTION

1. **Study the directions and question types for each listening part BEFORE you take the test.** Then you can click on DISMISS DIRECTIONS as soon as you start. The time begins as soon as the directions appear. The directions never change.
2. **Watch the time carefully in this section.** Although you can take as long as you want to answer a question, you will have only forty to sixty minutes for the whole section. Watch both the clock icon, which tells you how much time you have left, and the item number in the upper right corner of the screen, which tells you how many items you have done and how many items there are in the entire section.
3. **Never spend too long on any one question.** Focus on the question you are answering and try to forget previous questions.
4. **Always guess, except at the very end of the test.** Try to eliminate choices that are clearly wrong and then guess. If you have NO idea, just guess quickly instead of rereading

choices. Because this section is computer adaptive, don't guess at the end of the section if time is running out. These incorrect answers will hurt your score.

5. **Understand the meanings of "imply" and "infer."** Many questions use these words. A speaker *implies* something without stating the point directly. *When the governor said that he would not rule out a tax increase,* ***he*** *(the governor)* ***implied*** *that some taxes might be raised.* A reader *infers* a meaning from what the speaker says even if the point isn't stated directly. *When the governor said that he would not rule out a tax increase,* ***we*** *(the readers)* ***inferred*** *that he had been consulting with new financial advisers, since his old advisers were in favor of tax reductions.*

STUDY TIPS

1. While preparing for this part of the test, listen to recordings of English speakers as often as you can.
2. Although watching television is helpful in general, it does not prepare you for the test as you do not see the speakers' lips move on the test. If you watch television with Closed Captioning, you also SEE what is spoken. On the TOEFL test, you cannot see what is spoken.
3. Listen to the radio, especially programs with multiple speakers. Listen to online lectures.

PART A SHORT DIALOGUES

In Part A of the Listening section, you will hear short conversations between two people, usually a man and a woman. In most of the conversations, each person speaks only once. However, in other conversations, one or both people speak more than once. Each conversation is followed by one question about it.

Each question in this part has four answer choices. Click on the best answer to each question. Answer the question on the basis of what is stated or implied by the speakers. After you click on NEXT and CONFIRM ANSWER, the next conversation will be presented. **There will be between eleven and seventeen questions in this part of the test.**

Format

The first Listening section consists of short conversations between two speakers. Each dialogue is accompanied by a photograph of the two speakers. Although the photograph gives the general context, it will NOT help you answer the questions that follow the dialogue.

The conversations appear in the following forms:

DIALOGUE FORM 1

WOMAN (or MAN) says something or asks something
MAN (or WOMAN) responds

NARRATOR asks a question about the conversation. The question and the answer choices then appear on the screen.

EXAMPLE:

On the computer screen, you will see:

You will hear:

(Woman) Do you understand which courses are open electives?

(Man) My advisor explained to me that an open elective is any course other than those required for your major.

You will then see and hear the question before the answer choices appear:

What does the man mean?

- ⬭ Each major requires its own open electives.
- ⬭ She should speak to her advisor to determine which courses to take.
- ⬭ She must finish all her prerequisites before she can take open electives.
- ⬭ Open electives are those courses not mandatory in one's major.

To choose an answer, you will click on an oval. The oval next to that answer will darken.

The correct answer is indicated below.

What does the man mean?

- ⬭ Each major requires its own open electives.
- ⬭ She should speak to her advisor to determine which courses to take.
- ⬭ She must finish all her prerequisites before she can take open electives.
- ⬬ Open electives are those courses not mandatory in one's major.

The man said *an open elective is any course other than those required for your major. Required* and *mandatory* are synonyms.

DIALOGUE FORM 2

WOMAN (or MAN) says something or asks something
MAN (or WOMAN) responds
WOMAN (or MAN) responds

NARRATOR asks a question about the conversation. The question and the answer choices then appear on the screen.

EXAMPLE:

On the computer screen, you will see:

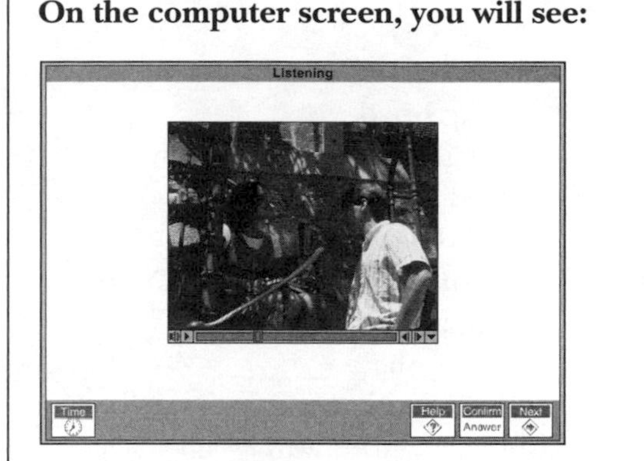

You will hear:

(Woman)	Did I see you yesterday at the football game?
(Man)	Wasn't me. I was in the library studying for my midterms.
(Woman)	Well, there's someone on campus who looks just like you.

You will then see and hear the question before the answer choices appear:

What does the woman imply?

- ◯ She met the man's twin.
- ◯ She's glad she saw him at the football game.
- ◯ She saw someone who resembles the man.
- ◯ She's looking for someone on campus who looks like the man.

To choose an answer, you will click on an oval. The oval next to that answer will darken.

The correct answer is indicated below.

What does the woman imply?

- ◯ She met the man's twin.
- ◯ She's glad she saw him at the football game.
- ⬤ She saw someone who resembles the man.
- ◯ She's looking for someone on campus who looks like the man.

The woman said she saw someone who *looks just like* the man at the game. *Looks like* and *resembles* are synonyms.

DIALOGUE FORM 3

WOMAN (or MAN) says something or asks something
MAN (or WOMAN) responds
WOMAN (or MAN) responds
MAN (or WOMAN) responds

NARRATOR asks a question about the conversation. The question and the answer choices then appear on the screen.

EXAMPLE:

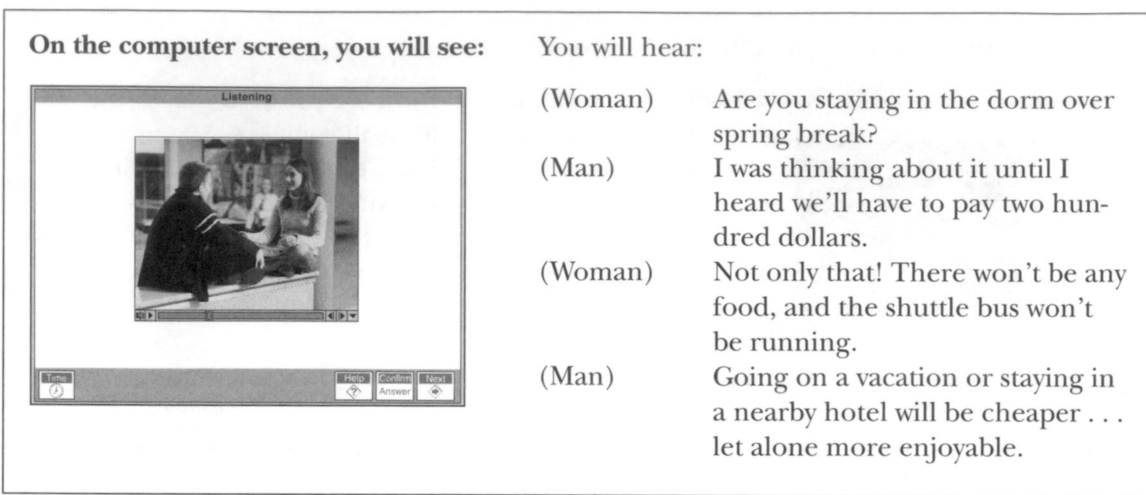

On the computer screen, you will see:

You will hear:

(Woman) Are you staying in the dorm over spring break?

(Man) I was thinking about it until I heard we'll have to pay two hundred dollars.

(Woman) Not only that! There won't be any food, and the shuttle bus won't be running.

(Man) Going on a vacation or staying in a nearby hotel will be cheaper . . . let alone more enjoyable.

You will then see and hear the question before the answer choices appear:

What does the man mean?

- ⬭ He doesn't have the two hundred dollars to pay for the dorm.
- ⬭ He needs to decide whether going away or staying in a local hotel will be cheaper.
- ⬭ He wouldn't have a good time staying in the dorm.
- ⬭ He'd like the woman to go on vacation with him over spring break.

To choose an answer, you will click on an oval. The oval next to that answer will darken.

The correct answer is indicated below.

What does the man mean?

- ⬭ He doesn't have the two hundred dollars to pay for the dorm.
- ⬭ He needs to decide whether going away or staying in a local hotel will be cheaper.
- ⬬ He wouldn't have a good time staying in the dorm.
- ⬭ He'd like the woman to go on vacation with him over spring break.

The man said *going on a vacation or staying in a nearby hotel . . . would be more enjoyable* than staying in the dorm. These ideas are better than staying in the dorm.

These conversations involving each speaker speaking two different times are VERY RARE.

Topics

Almost all conversations are between two students or between a student and a professor. The conversations take place on or near a North American college campus.

Topics include:

- registering for classes
- talking to instructors
- clarifying assignments
- finding apartments
- students' extracurricular life, such as planning parties, going to restaurants, taking vacations, getting jobs, and going shopping

Tone

The conversations are all natural. For example, you will hear *gonna,* not *going to, wajasay,* not *what did you say,* and *wanna,* not *want to.*

Language

You will hear many idioms and phrasal verbs in these conversations.

STRATEGIES FOR SHORT DIALOGUES

1. **Listen carefully.** The dialogue is spoken only one time.
2. **Listen carefully to the last speaker.** The answer is ALMOST ALWAYS a paraphrase (NOT the exact words) of something you hear in the last line. The earlier speaker will provide content but not the answer.
3. **When you see an exact word or phrase in an answer, you can be sure that it is incorrect.** NEVER pick an answer because it sounds like something you heard.
4. **Don't worry about the pictures.** You will see a picture of the speaker which will help you focus on the location of the conversation, but it will NOT help you answer the question.
5. **The question is spoken and written on the screen.** You have a few seconds to predict an answer before the choices appear. The answer choices appear on the screen as well.
6. **If you are unsure, try to find an answer that has a restatement of something you hear in the last line.** Guess even if you have no idea. Do not worry about misunderstanding any conversation.
7. **Focus ONLY on the question you have in front of you.** Try to forget previous conversations, and don't worry about answers you already chose.
8. **You cannot change your answer once you click** NEXT **and** CONFIRM ANSWER. The next question appears **immediately. You will NOT be able to return to a previous question.**
9. **Try to work quickly in this section, which is the easiest Listening section.** You will need more time for the harder sections to follow. Remember this section is timed.
10. **Be familiar with the directions so you can click on** DISMISS DIRECTIONS **as soon as you can.** The time begins as soon as the directions appear.

Types of Short Dialogues

Listen for the following types of dialogues. These dialogue types are frequently combined, meaning a conversation and the answers may include more than one type.

1. DIALOGUES WITH IDIOMATIC EXPRESSIONS

Idiomatic expressions appear often in short conversations.

An idiomatic expression (or simply, an idiom) is a group of words that does not have the same meaning as any of the individual words in the group. For example, the expression *learn by heart* means *to memorize.* It has nothing to do with the word *heart. On the other hand* means *however.* It has nothing to do with the word *hand.* There are thousands of idioms in English. There are always idiomatic expressions on the Listening section in general, and in the short conversations in particular.

STUDY TIPS

1. As you learn more English, you will learn more idioms.
2. Suggested references: NYC American Idioms, www.eslcafe.com then click on IDIOMS.
3. In order to learn idioms, you must first learn to recognize when a group of words does not mean what the words mean literally. Try to guess the meaning from the conversation. Then find out the idiom's meaning, write it down, and learn it by heart.

The idioms in these exercises are not specifically TOEFL test idioms. There is no exact list of idioms the TOEFL test uses. There is no way to prepare by memorizing a certain list because the idioms on the test constantly change.

EXAMPLE:

On the computer screen, you will see:

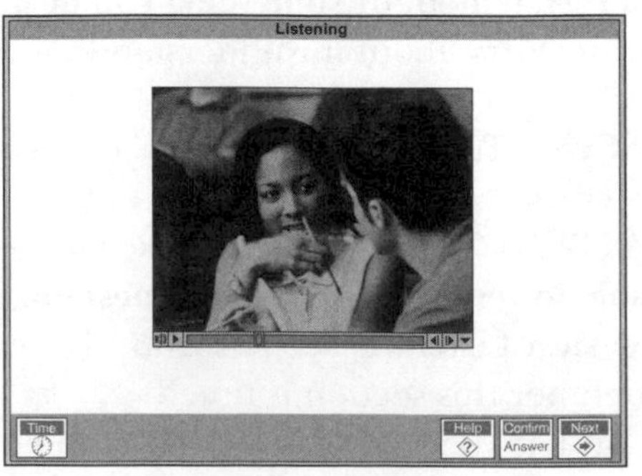

You will hear:

(Woman) Josh should run for office.
(Man) He's organized and a good speaker.
(Woman) Student council could use some new blood.

After the dialogue is complete, the question and answer choices appear on the computer screen as the narrator states the question.

On the computer screen, you will see:	**You will hear:**
Listening What do they think about Josh? ⬭ He'd make a suitable candidate. ⬭ He should run to his office. ⬭ He should organize the office. ⬭ He should donate some blood. Time · Help · Confirm Answer · Next	(Narrator) What do they think about Josh?

In the example there are two idiomatic expressions: *run for office* and *new blood*. Answer (B) confuses *run for office* with *run to his office*. Answer (C) confuses *he's organized* with *organize the office*. Choice (D) confuses *new blood* with *donate some blood*. The correct answer almost always uses a synonym, rather than exact words of the speakers. Even if you do not know that *run for office* means *be a candidate* and that *new blood* means *someone who hasn't been involved before*, Choice (A) is the only choice that doesn't recycle the speakers' words.

EXERCISE 1: In this exercise, listen carefully to the short dialogue and question on the tape. Then choose the best answer to the question. (See Appendix E, pages 384–85, for a transcript.)

1.
- ⬭ Registration
- ⬭ When the line breaks
- ⬭ How long the line is
- ⬭ People who don't wait their turn

2.
- ⬭ Kate made it by hand.
- ⬭ Kate gave it to her grandmother.
- ⬭ Kate's grandmother used to wear it.
- ⬭ Kate's grandmother made it.

3.
- ⬭ That her head hurts
- ⬭ That her application was mailed ahead
- ⬭ That she thinks the man hit her on the head
- ⬭ That she agrees with the man

4.
- ⬭ Don't push me around
- ⬭ Let's go inside
- ⬭ Don't hit that tree
- ⬭ Get right to the point

5.
- ⬭ The man's glasses are falling off his head.
- ⬭ The glasses have nice curves to them.
- ⬭ The man is fashionable.
- ⬭ The man should shop only in Europe.

6.
- ⬭ He wants her to make him go.
- ⬭ He needs a hand with some things.
- ⬭ He wants to walk to class hand in hand.
- ⬭ He wants her to drive him to class.

7.
- ⬭ She slipped on the way to the dentist.
- ⬭ She forgot all about it.
- ⬭ She wouldn't mind going at 10.
- ⬭ She completed the appointment earlier.

8.

- ⬭ There have been dogs and cats all over the place.
- ⬭ It's been pouring.
- ⬭ It's never going to be sunny again.
- ⬭ She'd like a change.

9.

- ⬭ The man should stop talking to his cat.
- ⬭ The man's tongue hurts.
- ⬭ The man finds it hard to speak.
- ⬭ The man is worried about his cat's tongue.

10.

- ⬭ She wants to learn how to dance.
- ⬭ They need to cooperate.
- ⬭ She needs to find a new partner.
- ⬭ She can teach him how to do the tango.

11.

- ⬭ The rehearsal was perfect.
- ⬭ The rehearsal was pretty rocky.
- ⬭ The lights went off during the rehearsal.
- ⬭ The rehearsal took place without a director.

12.

- ⬭ Dr. Springer was speaking informally.
- ⬭ Dr. Springer seemingly has a cough.
- ⬭ Dr. Springer rolled up his cuffs.
- ⬭ Dr. Springer made the cuff links.

13.

- ⬭ Susan's apartment building has stones thrown on it.
- ⬭ Susan lives close to the student union.
- ⬭ Susan can throw stones at the student union from her house.
- ⬭ There's a stone path from Susan's apartment to the student union.

14.

- ⬭ She speaks slowly.
- ⬭ She is surely enjoying Spanish class.
- ⬭ The best way to progress in Spanish is to study it slowly.
- ⬭ Her Spanish is gradually getting better.

15.

- ⬭ He couldn't understand what the lecturer said.
- ⬭ He missed the train.
- ⬭ He got lost going to the presentation.
- ⬭ He was trying to follow the lecturer to the train.

16.

- ⬭ Her headache isn't getting better.
- ⬭ It looks like her headache is stopping.
- ⬭ When she goes away, she gets headaches.
- ⬭ She's stopped getting headaches.

2. DIALOGUES WITH PHRASAL VERBS (2 AND 3 PART VERBS)

Phrasal verbs appear often in short conversations.

A phrasal verb is a combination of a verb and one or more adverbs or prepositions that together have a single meaning. Phrasal verbs are idiomatic, which means that even if you know what all the words in the phase mean individually, you may not understand the meaning of the words as a unit. For example, *look up to* means *respect, look over* means *check, look back on* means *reminisce, look forward to* means *anticipate,* etc.

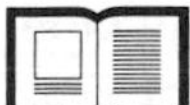

STUDY TIPS

1. Just as with idioms, there are thousands of phrasal verbs.
2. You must learn to recognize that when you hear a verb + preposition(s) or verb + adverb(s), the meaning is going to be different from what the verb alone means.
3. The correct answer will NOT be one that includes the verb alone. As with idioms, try to guess the meaning from the conversation.
4. A phrasal verb may appear only as an answer choice and NOT in the conversation.
5. Sometimes the correct answer choice may be a different phrasal verb than the one heard in the dialogue.
6. Keep a phrasal verb dictionary, adding new phrasal verbs and their meanings.

EXAMPLE:

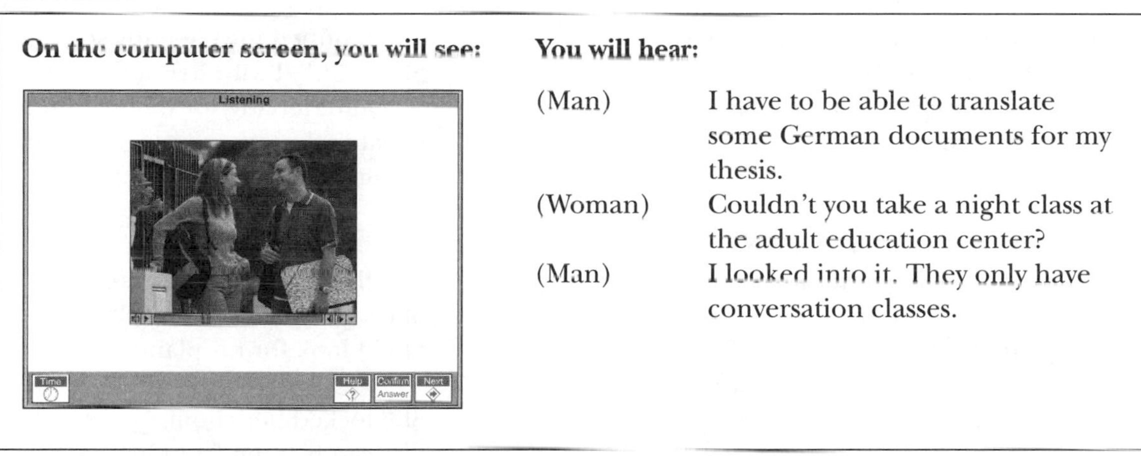

On the computer screen, you will see:

You will hear:

(Man) I have to be able to translate some German documents for my thesis.

(Woman) Couldn't you take a night class at the adult education center?

(Man) I looked into it. They only have conversation classes.

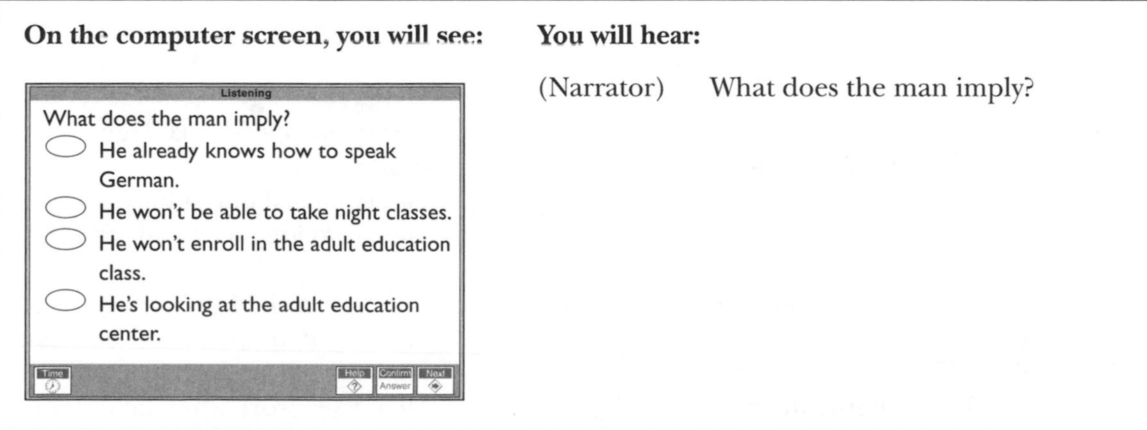

On the computer screen, you will see:

Listening
What does the man imply?
He already knows how to speak German.
He won't be able to take night classes.
He won't enroll in the adult education class.
He's looking at the adult education center.
Time
Help
Confirm Answer
Next

You will hear:

(Narrator) What does the man imply?

Look into means *investigate* or *check out.* He learned that the adult center has only conversation classes, which he doesn't need, so answer (C) *He won't enroll in the adult education class* is correct. (A) and (B) are incorrect, and (D) confuses *look into* with *look at.*

EXERCISE 2: In this exercise, listen carefully to the short dialogue and question on the tape. Then choose the best answer to the question. (See Appendix E, page 385, for a transcript.)

1.
- ◯ Two hundred eleven passengers called about the flight.
- ◯ Flight 211 was called off.
- ◯ Flight 211 was announced.
- ◯ The flight was delayed.

2.
- ◯ He bought a new red car.
- ◯ He went out of business.
- ◯ He closed for the day.
- ◯ He sold Kathy a new red car at full price.

3.
- ◯ He's in a hurry.
- ◯ He never finishes assignments early.
- ◯ He wants to be done with the assignment before Friday.
- ◯ He'll complete the assignment soon.

4.
- ◯ He has a better idea.
- ◯ It would be better if Julie would come with him.
- ◯ He thinks Julie's idea is the best.
- ◯ Julie should come up with a better idea.

5.
- ◯ Jeremy's efforts have been worthwhile.
- ◯ He hasn't been building for long.
- ◯ He's been working hard on his building.
- ◯ Jeremy has paid a lot of money for his reputation.

6.
- ◯ The softball team took the gift with them.
- ◯ She went away with the gift.
- ◯ She'll be bringing the gift to the party.
- ◯ She contributed money to a gift.

7.
- ◯ She's thinking about getting paid in the future.
- ◯ She's eagerly awaiting getting her money.
- ◯ She's looking for where to get paid.
- ◯ She's looking for her money.

8.
- ◯ They have forty children.
- ◯ They put their children with forty others.
- ◯ They postponed having a family.
- ◯ They lost contact with their children until they were in their forties.

9.
- ◯ She bumped into her advisor.
- ◯ She collided with her advisor.
- ◯ She and her advisor were running to catch the subway.
- ◯ She missed the subway.

10.
- ◯ She'll look into his office.
- ◯ She'll take care of his plants.
- ◯ She's going on vacation.
- ◯ She'll look for his plants.

11.
- ◯ She locked her room.
- ◯ She can be seen from her room.
- ◯ She doesn't have the key to her room.
- ◯ She stared out of her room.

12.
- ◯ Henry didn't go to college.
- ◯ Henry dropped his college diploma.
- ◯ Henry passed out in history class.
- ◯ Henry no longer attends college.

13.
- ◯ He wants to join the others.
- ◯ He will catch up with the others later.
- ◯ He missed work when he caught a cold.
- ◯ He is behind in his work.

3. DIALOGUES WITH WISHES AND THE CONDITIONAL

Wishes and the conditional appear often in short conversations.

A **wish** means something that is desirable is impossible; it can't or didn't happen.

PRESENT UNREAL	SOMETHING IS NOT TRUE NOW, BUT YOU WOULD LIKE IT TO BE
Wish + simple past *I wish I* ***had*** *a sharp pencil right now.* Wish + would + base form (when talking about someone else) *I wish you* ***would walk*** *the dog for once.*	 (I don't have one, however.) (You never do.)
PAST UNREAL	**SOMETHING IS NOT TRUE IN THE PAST WHICH YOU REGRET**
Wish + past perfect *I wish I* ***had studied*** *harder for the test.*	 (But I didn't.)

EXAMPLE:

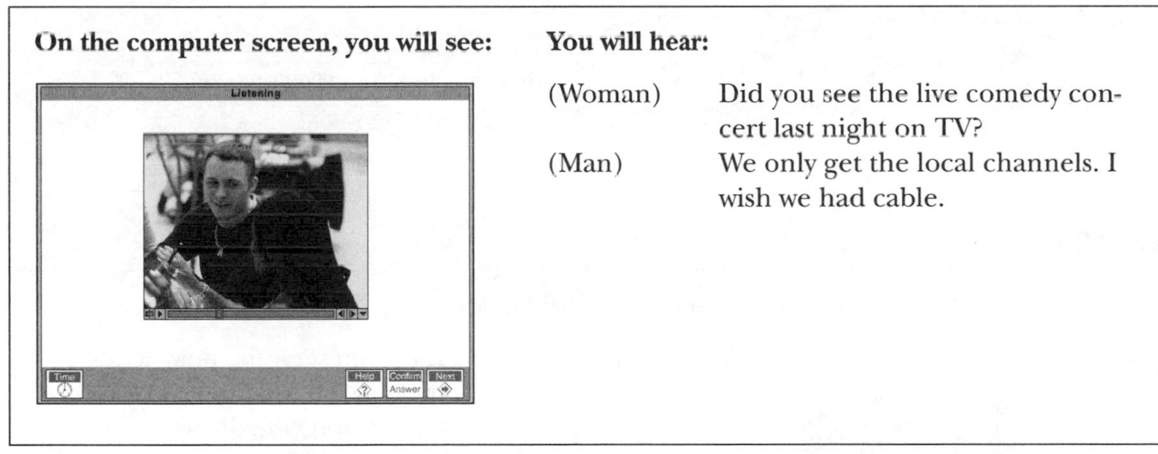

On the computer screen, you will see:
Listening
Time
Help
Confirm Answer
Next
You will hear:
(Woman) Did you see the live comedy concert last night on TV?
(Man) We only get the local channels. I wish we had cable.

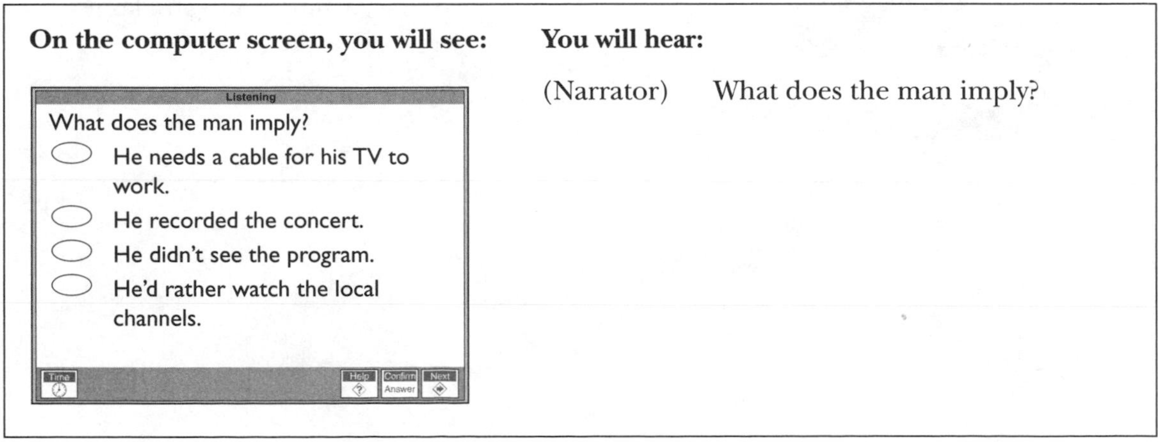

On the computer screen, you will see:
Listening
What does the man imply?
He needs a cable for his TV to work.
He recorded the concert.
He didn't see the program.
He'd rather watch the local channels.
Time
Help
Confirm Answer
Next
You will hear:
(Narrator) What does the man imply?

The correct answer is (C), he didn't see the program because his TV doesn't get the cable channels. He wishes he could have seen the program. (A), (B), and (D) are factually incorrect.

The **conditional** uses *if, even if,* and *unless (if you don't)* to describe a possibly real or unreal situation.

DEPENDENT CLAUSE	INDEPENDENT CLAUSE
1. *Future Possible Real (Something may happen in the future)*	
If + simple present /present continuous	*command, future, or modal + base form, or present continuous.*
If it **rains** tomorrow,	**take** an umbrella. *(command)*
	I'll take an umbrella. *(future)*
	I **might take** an umbrella. *(modal + base form)*
	I'm taking an umbrella. *(present continuous)*
Unless you **take** an umbrella,	you**'ll get** wet. *(future)*
2. *Present Real (The idea of whenever)*	
If + simple present	*simple present*
If I **get** a headache,*(whenever I do)*	I **lie** down.
3. *Present Unreal (Not possible at present/but wish it were)*	
If + simple past	*will/would + base form*
If I **had** a million dollars, *(but I don't)*	**I'd give** you some.
4. *Past Unreal (Didn't happen in the past/but wish it had)*	
If + past perfect	*would have + past participle*
If I **had gotten** to the store before six o'clock,	I **could have bought** computer paper.
(But I didn't get there before six, so I couldn't buy the paper.)	

EXAMPLE:

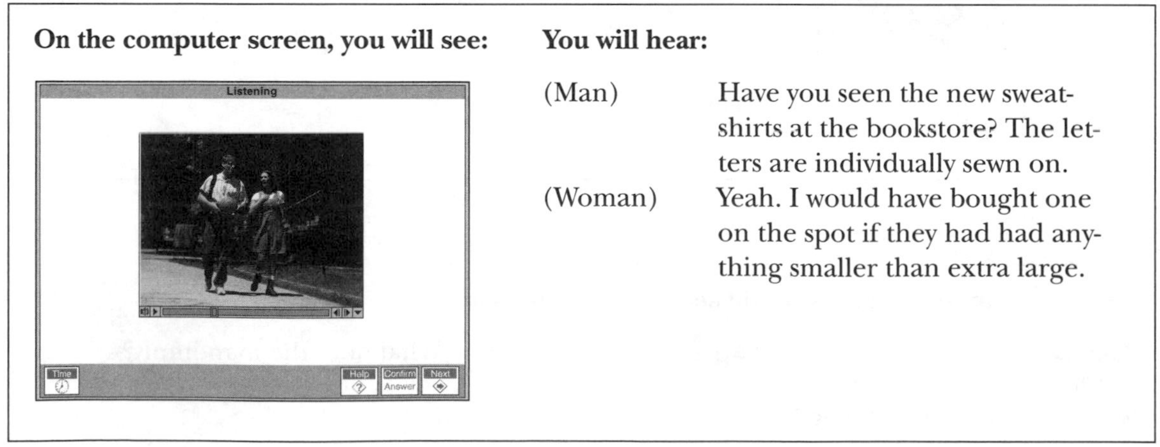

On the computer screen, you will see:

You will hear:

(Man) Have you seen the new sweat-shirts at the bookstore? The letters are individually sewn on.

(Woman) Yeah. I would have bought one on the spot if they had had anything smaller than extra large.

On the computer screen, you will see:	You will hear:
Listening What does the woman imply? ◯ She's going to buy one on the spot. ◯ They were all out of extra large ones. ◯ The bookstore doesn't have any more sweatshirts. ◯ The sweatshirts they have are all too big. Time Help Confirm Answer Next	(Narrator) What does the woman imply?

The correct answer is (D), she wears a smaller size than the ones they have, which are only extra large. She wishes they had smaller ones, but they didn't, because she wanted to buy one when she saw them. (A), (B), and (C) are factually incorrect.

EXERCISE 3: In this exercise, listen carefully to the short dialogue and question on the tape. Then choose the best answer to the question. (See Appendix E, pages 385–86, for a transcript.)

1.
- ◯ No one has a friend like Michael.
- ◯ Everyone is Michael's good friend.
- ◯ The man feels lucky to have Michael as a friend.
- ◯ The woman doesn't like many of the man's friends.

2.
- ◯ Last July the house was sold.
- ◯ The house has been for sale since July.
- ◯ They went to the market in July.
- ◯ They marked down their house last July.

3.
- ◯ Because he already has vacation plans
- ◯ Because he goes to a beach house each August
- ◯ Because he won't be able to take a vacation
- ◯ Because he didn't know the woman's intentions

4.
- ◯ He learned more in his section.
- ◯ He's sorry he didn't stay in Judy's class.
- ◯ His section was too hard for him.
- ◯ He can't remember why he transferred out.

5.
- ◯ Take the subway
- ◯ Skip the conference
- ◯ Hurry to the conference
- ◯ Get on a bus

6.
- ◯ Get the waitress's attention
- ◯ Put the tip on the credit card
- ◯ Tell the waitress about the tip
- ◯ Look for the tip

7.
- ◯ Withdraw the form
- ◯ Meet with the man the next day
- ◯ See the man's books in the afternoon
- ◯ Sign him up for another appointment

8.
- ◯ They'll have to see what Sunday looks like.
- ◯ Only if the sun is shining will graduation be outside.

- Graduation will be outside no matter the weather.
- People won't come if it's raining.

9.

- Speak to one of the professor's students.
- He won't get into the class because it's full.
- He can't get in if he doesn't try.
- If he goes to see the professor, she'll let him in.

10.

- Why she picked Dr. White in the first place
- If she can choose a different advisor
- If Dr. White is an expert in the woman's field
- Why he's unhappy with her thesis advisor

4. DIALOGUES WITH SURPRISE

Elements of surprise appear often in short conversations.

The following words and phrases indicate that the speaker has been surprised by something he or she heard:

- I'm surprised.
- Oh
- It's hard to believe./I can't believe
- Wouldn't you know it.
- I was wrong. (can be preceded by *Guess*)
- That explains why./That's why.
- Why, yes./Why, no.
- Wow!
- What?
- That's all?
- What a shame/relief/surprise.
- What are you talking about?

The following question indicates that the speaker is surprised that the person he/she's speaking with does not know something.

- Don't/Didn't you know?

EXAMPLE:

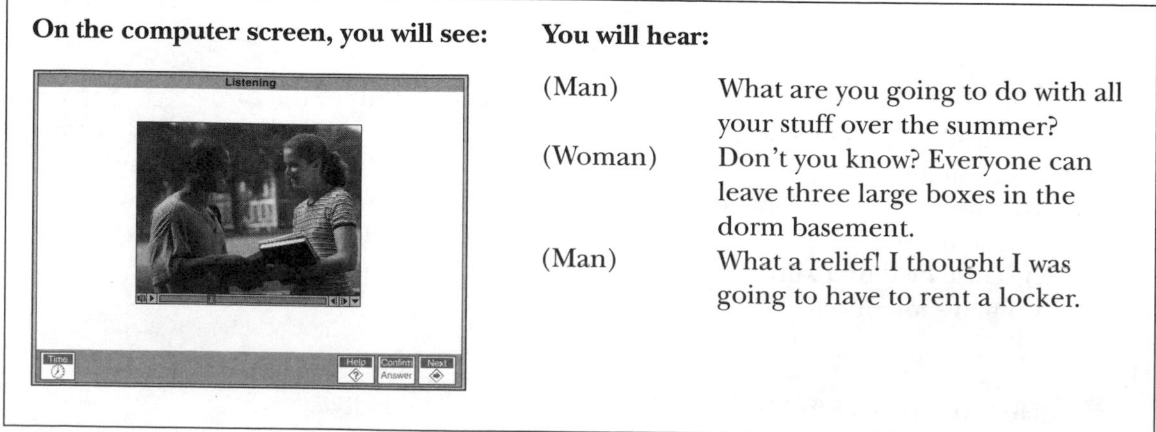

On the computer screen, you will see:

You will hear:

(Man) What are you going to do with all your stuff over the summer?

(Woman) Don't you know? Everyone can leave three large boxes in the dorm basement.

(Man) What a relief! I thought I was going to have to rent a locker.

On the computer screen, you will see:

Listening

What will the man probably do?

- Rent a ladder
- Store some of his things in the dorm
- Take his stuff home over the summer
- Fit all his belongings into three boxes

Time | Help | Confirm Answer | Next

You will hear:

(Narrator) What will the man probably do?

The correct answer is (B) *Store some of his things in the dorm.* She is surprised that he didn't know that dorm policy, as she begins her comment with *Don't you know?* He is relieved to learn of the policy and then most likely will do what she tells him, *leave three large boxes in the dorm basement.* Answers (A) and (C) are factually incorrect. Although he will leave three boxes, it doesn't mean that all his belongings will fit into three boxes, making choice (D) incorrect.

EXERCISE 4: In this exercise, listen carefully to the short dialogue and question on the tape. Then choose the best answer to the question. (See Appendix E, pages 386–87, for a transcript.)

1.
- David is the best student in the class.
- David's ability is surprising.
- David is going to be a movie star.
- David didn't pass the exam.

2.
- Missed her friends
- Worked over the weekend
- Made up a story
- Timed her job

3.
- He owns a dairy.
- He teaches at a college.
- He raises sheep.
- He spins wool.

4.
- She needs to finish her language sequence.
- She's going to change her major.
- She's a science major.
- She's going to drop her language courses.

5.
- He wants to kick her off his mailing list.
- He had the wrong e-mail address for her.
- He'll keep forwarding her e-mails.
- He thought she enjoyed what he sent her.

6.
- She didn't know Bill played hockey.
- When she saw Bill, she didn't know what was wrong.
- She didn't know Bill was back in health services.
- Bill didn't see her at health services.

7.
- She needs to listen to him.
- She is surprised who he is.
- She couldn't hear his conversation.
- She needed help to hear him.

8.

- ⬭ That her work has really improved
- ⬭ That the exhibition is far away
- ⬭ That it won't be long until he can look at her graphics
- ⬭ That she should come see him right away

9.

- ⬭ She hasn't talked to the Millers in over a year.
- ⬭ She doesn't know who he's talking about.
- ⬭ The Millers come for dinner once a year.
- ⬭ It's been a very long time since the Millers visited.

10.

- ⬭ She doesn't know if her professor will give her a note.
- ⬭ It's impossible to look at the rare manuscripts.
- ⬭ She needs to do some research using the manuscripts.
- ⬭ She thought it would be really difficult to get authorization.

5. DIALOGUES WITH AGREEMENT AND DISAGREEMENT

The following statements of agreeing and disagreeing appear often in short conversations.

AGREEMENT

- Me too.
- The same thing
- Yeah
- Also
- Good idea.
- No problem.
- Why, yes.
- Isn't that the truth?
- You can say that again!
- Has it ever!/Does it ever!
- So do I./I do too.
- Neither do I./I don't either.
- I know.
- OK

DISAGREEMENT

- It's not that
- What do you mean?
- What are you talking about?
- That's not true/right.
- I don't agree.
- I don't think so.
- I beg to differ.
- That's nothing.

We can agree with a positive statement *Man: It's so cold today. Woman: Yeah. I know what you mean.* **as well as with a negative statement.** *Man: It's never going to stop raining. Woman: Isn't that the truth?*

EXAMPLE:

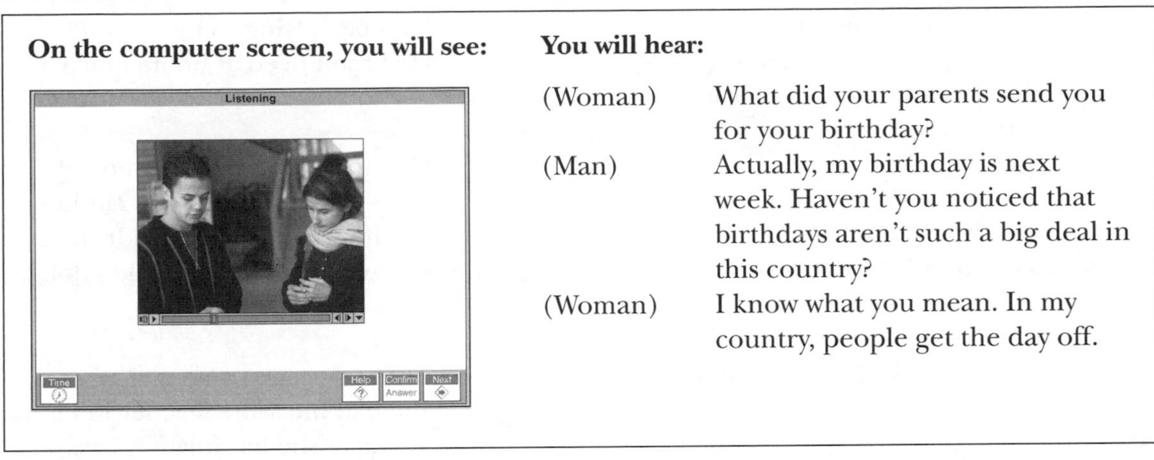

On the computer screen, you will see:

You will hear:

(Woman) What did your parents send you for your birthday?

(Man) Actually, my birthday is next week. Haven't you noticed that birthdays aren't such a big deal in this country?

(Woman) I know what you mean. In my country, people get the day off.

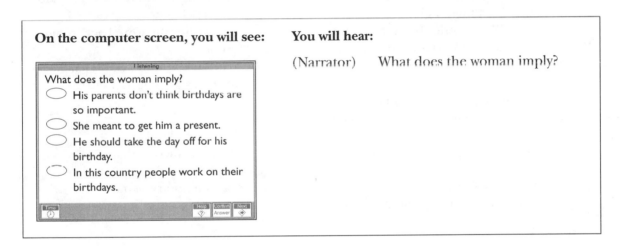

On the computer screen, you will see:

Listening

What does the woman imply?

- ◯ His parents don't think birthdays are so important.
- ◯ She meant to get him a present.
- ◯ He should take the day off for his birthday.
- ◯ In this country people work on their birthdays.

Time | Help | Confirm Answer | Next

You will hear:

(Narrator) What does the woman imply?

The correct answer is (D) *In this country people work on their birthdays.* When she says *I know what you mean,* she's agreeing with him that birthdays aren't such a big deal in this country. Answer (A) confuses the man with his parents. Answers (B) and (C) are factually incorrect.

EXERCISE 5: In this exercise, listen carefully to the short dialogue and question on the tape. Then choose the best answer to the question. (See Appendix E, page 387, for a transcript.)

1.
- ◯ She's busy now.
- ◯ The operator did the same thing to her.
- ◯ If the operators are busy, he should dial later.
- ◯ She can't reach the operator either.

2.
- ◯ He felt sleepy during the seminar.
- ◯ He disagrees with the woman about the seminar.
- ◯ He fell asleep at two.
- ◯ He found the seminar dazzling.

3.
- ◯ The man and woman want to go downtown.
- ◯ The woman wants to go to the park, but the man doesn't.
- ◯ The man doesn't know where to park the car.
- ◯ The man wants to find out where the park is located.

4.

- ⬭ You should believe everything you read.
- ⬭ The man thinks the book is excellent.
- ⬭ The woman wonders which newspaper the man reads.
- ⬭ Reactions to the book have been varied.

5.

- ⬭ They should decide by Friday.
- ⬭ They have another week to decide.
- ⬭ They must tell the professor their topic on Friday.
- ⬭ They don't have to debate in class.

6.

- ⬭ She'd like to borrow his glasses.
- ⬭ She doesn't need glasses.
- ⬭ She'd like to order from the menu.
- ⬭ She doesn't like dark restaurants.

7.

- ⬭ Jennifer and Jessica don't act alike.
- ⬭ Jennifer and Jessica live in the same apartment.
- ⬭ Jennifer and Jessica are looking for each other.
- ⬭ Jennifer and Jessica's apartment looks out on the common.

8.

- ⬭ He has lost all of her messages.
- ⬭ He should get an answering machine.
- ⬭ He's been lying to her.
- ⬭ He hasn't been at home much.

9.

- ⬭ She doesn't have much money.
- ⬭ She's always washing her clothes.
- ⬭ She moved into the laundromat.
- ⬭ The washing machine takes dollar bills.

10.

- ⬭ She had the same teacher in high school as she has now.
- ⬭ She really enjoyed her high school history class.
- ⬭ She wishes she were back in high school.
- ⬭ Her high school history teacher wasn't as good as her current one.

11.

- ⬭ Finish the book
- ⬭ Wait for the due date
- ⬭ Find the book
- ⬭ Pay the library penalty

6. DIALOGUES WITH NEGATIVES

Negative phrases appear often in short conversations.

Listen for the following words and phrases that indicate a negative response:

NEGATIVE WORD(S)	EXAMPLE
• Nothing	• What's bothering you? *Nothing.*
• Never	• *I've never been to Alaska.*
• Nope/No	• Are you going home for break? *Nope/No.*
• Neither . . . nor	• *Neither Diana nor Latoya is taking the test today.*
• Can't	• *I speak French, but I can't speak Spanish.*
• Couldn't	• Did you have time to look at my paper? *Sorry, I couldn't.*
• Don't	• Should I take Exit 13? *Don't.* Exit 12 is better.
• Didn't	• I should have listened. *I didn't take Exit 13,* and I got there late.
• Hasn't/Haven't	• *I haven't had time to register this morning.*
• Nobody/No one/None	• Was anyone at the review session? *No one/Nobody but me.*
• Wouldn't	• *I wouldn't wait too long.*
• Shouldn't	• *You shouldn't drink anything before the blood test.*

Usually a negative in the conversation will have a positive paraphrase in the response and vice versa.

EXAMPLE:

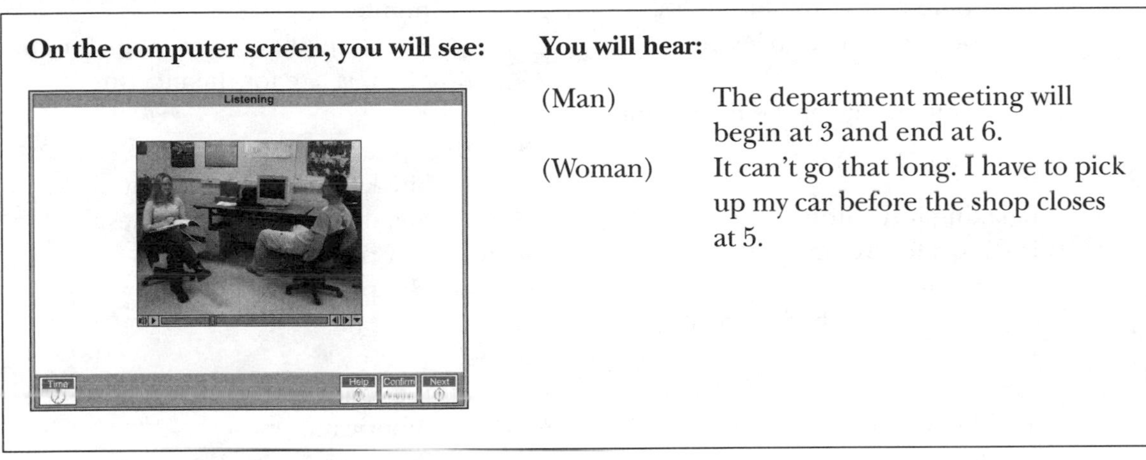

On the computer screen, you will see:

You will hear:

(Man) The department meeting will begin at 3 and end at 6.

(Woman) It can't go that long. I have to pick up my car before the shop closes at 5.

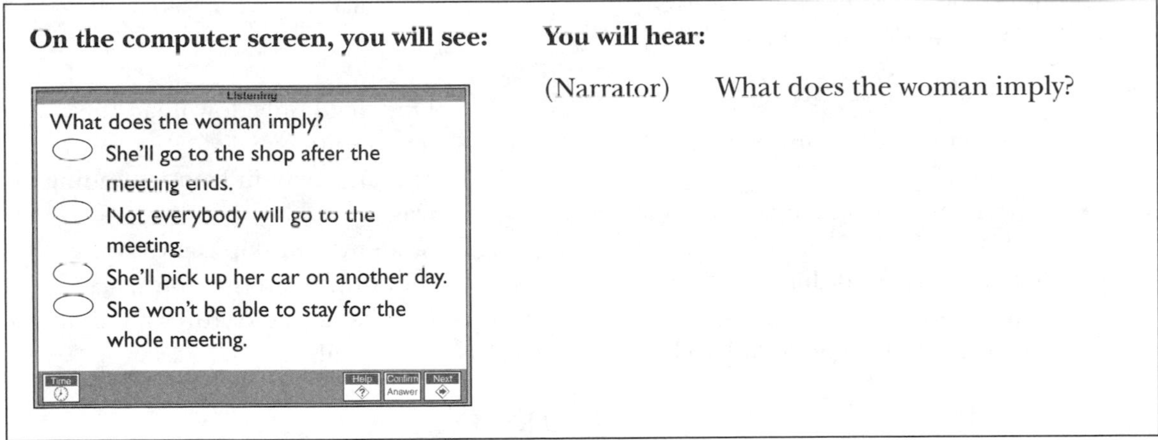

On the computer screen, you will see:

You will hear:

(Narrator) What does the woman imply?

The correct answer is (D) *She won't be able to stay for the whole meeting.* Since she has to be at the car shop by 5:00, she won't be able to stay for all of the meeting. Answer (A) is factually incorrect because if she waits until 6:00, the shop will be closed. Answer (B) is not mentioned, and Answer (C) is incorrect because she has to pick up her car before 5:00 today.

EXERCISE 6: In this exercise, listen carefully to the short dialogue and question on the tape. Then choose the best answer to the question. (See Appendix E, pages 387–88, for a transcript.)

1.
- ⬭ It was nice of him to lend someone his notes.
- ⬭ Next time he can use her notes.
- ⬭ It's not a good idea to let others use your notes.
- ⬭ He should study for the next exam.

2.
- ⬭ Relaxing just a little
- ⬭ Having a festive time
- ⬭ Exercising
- ⬭ Getting her health spa into shape

3.
- ⬭ She'd like to have the store send it to save time.
- ⬭ She'll take it with her because she's in a hurry.
- ⬭ It will be mailed to her in a bag.
- ⬭ It must be shipped quickly.

4.
- ⬭ The man couldn't understand what she said.
- ⬭ All the noise inside made him want to leave.
- ⬭ He was surprised that she didn't want to stay.
- ⬭ He wants to be able to talk to her.

5.
- ⬭ The new players win every time.
- ⬭ She thinks the football team will win.
- ⬭ She doesn't want to discuss the game.
- ⬭ The new players haven't played well.

6.
- ⬭ She must have done well on the tests.
- ⬭ She's worried about her average.
- ⬭ She'll still need to take the final exam.
- ⬭ She is glad she took calculus after all.

7.
- ⬭ She went running this morning.
- ⬭ She didn't have his phone number.
- ⬭ She didn't have time to meet him.
- ⬭ She was late for the meeting.

8.
- ⬭ She knows nothing about birds.
- ⬭ She doesn't like vegetables.
- ⬭ Her parents have a bird.
- ⬭ Her parrot can't talk.

9.
- ⬭ It doesn't seem possible that she's American.
- ⬭ She seems to be American.
- ⬭ He didn't believe she's American.
- ⬭ He's surprised that she was born in America.

10.
- ⬭ One need only download the lecture notes.
- ⬭ Students benefit from attending class.
- ⬭ Students can skip class as long as they download the notes.
- ⬭ Discussing the lectures after class is beneficial.

11.
- ⬭ She shouldn't have missed the deadline.
- ⬭ Nothing could have improved her grade during the term.
- ⬭ She's planning to hand in her extra credit when it is due.
- ⬭ She has until Friday to hand in the last extra credit project.

12.
- ⬭ They're excited about it.
- ⬭ They can wait a while to see it.
- ⬭ They want to read some more about it.
- ⬭ They're going to see it on Sunday.

7. DIALOGUES WITH SUGGESTIONS, REQUESTS, OR OFFERS

Suggestions, advice, offers of help, or requests appear often in short conversations. Pay attention to which speaker is asking for what and which speaker is offering what:

SUGGESTIONS
- You should
- You can/could
- I think you should/could
- Let's
- Why don't
- Why not
- It would be better/best
- I suggest/recommend

REQUESTS
- Do you have
- I'd appreciate it if
- Would it be OK?
- Would you mind?
- Could I/you

OFFERS
- I can/could
- Follow me
- Help yourself.
- Here's
- Be my guest.
- Do you want to

> Imperatives can be used for suggestions, with or without signal phrases. The suggestion *Let's call your parents* is a more polite way of suggesting *Call your parents.*

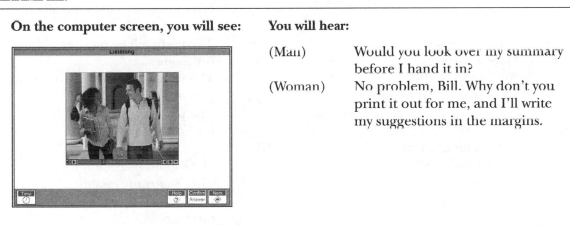

EXAMPLE:

On the computer screen, you will see:

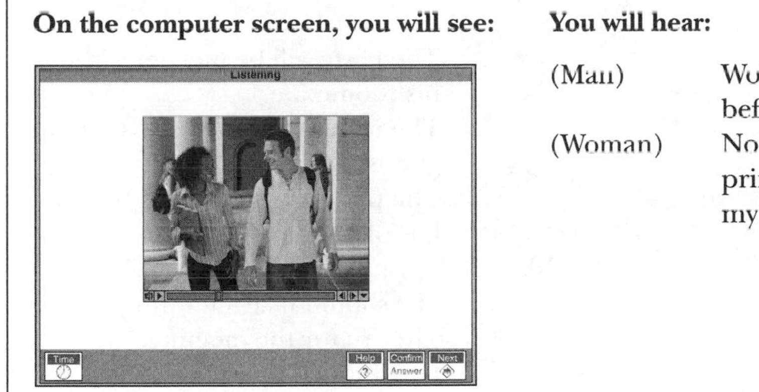

You will hear:

(Man) Would you look over my summary before I hand it in?

(Woman) No problem, Bill. Why don't you print it out for me, and I'll write my suggestions in the margins.

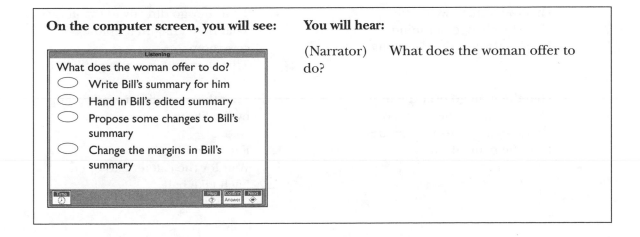

On the computer screen, you will see:

Listening

What does the woman offer to do?

- ◯ Write Bill's summary for him
- ◯ Hand in Bill's edited summary
- ◯ Propose some changes to Bill's summary
- ◯ Change the margins in Bill's summary

Time Help Confirm Answer Next

You will hear:

(Narrator) What does the woman offer to do?

The correct answer is (C) *Propose some changes to Bill's summary.* She offers to *write suggestions* for change *in the margins.* Bill has already written the summary, so answer (A) is incorrect. Answers (B) and (D) are factually incorrect.

EXERCISE 7: In this exercise, listen carefully to the short dialogue and question on the tape. Then choose the best answer to the question. (See Appendix E, pages 388–89, for a transcript.)

1.
- ◯ That she help herself to some food in the kitchen
- ◯ That he'll call her office for her
- ◯ That he'll help her use the phone
- ◯ That she feel free to make a call

2.
- ◯ Guard her apartment for her
- ◯ Move to the new high rise downtown
- ◯ Be on the lookout for an apartment for her
- ◯ Show her an apartment in the high rise

3.
- ◯ Like his friends
- ◯ Have a party
- ◯ Arrange everything
- ◯ Take care of his friends

4.
- ◯ At his summer school
- ◯ At his brother's home
- ◯ In Boston
- ◯ At his forwarding address

5.
- ◯ That it makes no difference
- ◯ That the woman wear blue
- ◯ That she change her mind
- ◯ That they select the color blue

6.
- ◯ That the man go over the lecture
- ◯ That they meet the next day
- ◯ That the man miss the lecture
- ◯ That the man take a bus

7.
- ◯ The woman has an extra umbrella.
- ◯ The man should borrow her umbrella.
- ◯ The woman needs to use an umbrella.
- ◯ The man can leave his umbrella upstairs.

8.
- ◯ Go ahead of the woman
- ◯ Go with her to the test
- ◯ Look for Building 10 later
- ◯ Help the woman with the placement test

9.
- ◯ His roommate will be the life of the party.
- ◯ The party will be merrier without his roommate.
- ◯ The man needs to find even more guests to bring.
- ◯ The party will be more fun with lots of people.

10.
- ◯ She should take a muffin.
- ◯ They're for the meeting.
- ◯ Don't touch them before the meeting.
- ◯ He'd like her to be his guest.

11.
- ◯ That they go directly to the library
- ◯ That they straighten up the classroom
- ◯ That they walk in a straight line to the library
- ◯ That the most direct way is going by the library

12.
- ◯ Eat something
- ◯ Wait for the cafeteria to open
- ◯ Each take half
- ◯ Go to the track

13.
- ⬭ She take out her writing
- ⬭ She find a perfect space
- ⬭ She take the old desk up to the attic
- ⬭ She do her writing at home

14.
- ⬭ Many people on campus are sick with a virus.
- ⬭ Try not to go near anyone who's sick.
- ⬭ There has been a rash of car crashes on campus.
- ⬭ Don't try to get on the college website.

8. DIALOGUES WITH ALTERNATIVE RESPONSES, SUGGESTIONS, OR OFFERS

Alternative responses/suggestions/offers are often heard in short conversations. When one speaker makes a suggestion/request/offer, the other speaker answers with an alternative plan or an indirect refusal. Similar, if not identical, phrases as in Section 7 are sometimes used. The difference is the last speaker has an alternative idea. Listen carefully to the words of the last one to speak. Additional words or phrases you might encounter include:

- It all depends.
- I thought
- Actually
- I was hoping
- Ahhh

EXAMPLE:

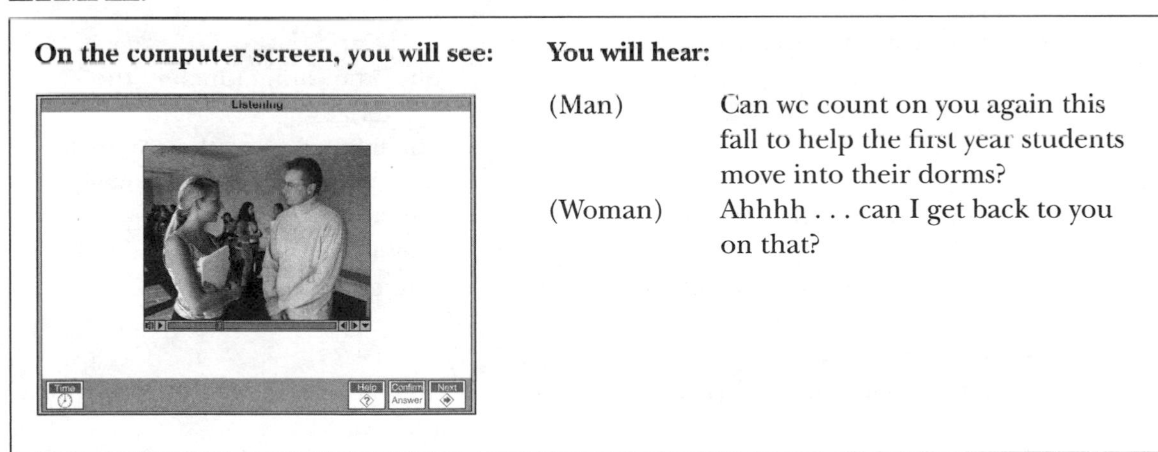

On the computer screen, you will see:

You will hear:

(Man) Can we count on you again this fall to help the first year students move into their dorms?

(Woman) Ahhhh . . . can I get back to you on that?

On the computer screen, you will see:	**You will hear:**
Listening What will the woman probably do? ◯ She might contact him later. ◯ She's not moving into her dorm. ◯ She'll be a freshman this fall. ◯ She's counting how many freshmen will live in dorms. Time Help Confirm Answer Next	(Narrator) What will the woman probably do?

The woman does not agree immediately to the man's request. Instead, she "puts him off" by asking *Ahhhh . . . can I get back to you on that?,* which makes answer (A) *She might contact him later* correct. There is no mention of the woman living in a dorm, Answer (B). Answer (C) is incorrect because the woman is being asked *again* to help the first year students, so we understand she is not a new student. Answer (D) confuses *count on,* meaning rely on, with *count.*

EXERCISE 8: In this exercise, listen carefully to the short dialogue and question on the tape. Then choose the best answer to the question. (See Appendix E, page 389, for a transcript.)

1.
- ◯ Not every composer likes music.
- ◯ Composers like things other than music.
- ◯ Composers like to listen to music a lot.
- ◯ Composers usually like CDs.

2.
- ◯ The woman lost Dana's phone number.
- ◯ The man needs to get a cell phone.
- ◯ The man doesn't have Dana's phone number yet.
- ◯ Dana used to live in California.

3.
- ◯ Fix the pipes
- ◯ Check the weather forecast
- ◯ Take the train to work
- ◯ Complete her current project

4.
- ◯ Go home
- ◯ Make up a story
- ◯ Wait until the morning edition comes out
- ◯ Continue working

5.
- ◯ She'll be eating lunch in the cafeteria.
- ◯ She'll be going to the eye doctor.
- ◯ She'll be supervising the new employees.
- ◯ She'll keep the workers in the cafeteria.

6.
- ◯ To wait a while after finishing the report
- ◯ To drink coffee before this meeting
- ◯ To take a coffee break
- ◯ To have coffee later

7.
- ◯ She wanted to take the 6:00 flight.
- ◯ She made a reservation for the 7:00 flight.

- ⬭ She made a reservation for the 6:00 flight.
- ⬭ She changed the reservation.

8.
- ⬭ Rush to class
- ⬭ Arrive before class starts
- ⬭ Leave class early
- ⬭ Meet in front of the auditorium

9.
- ⬭ She knows she shouldn't go.
- ⬭ She'll review her notes before the movie.
- ⬭ She'll take the midterm and then see the movie.
- ⬭ She has her midterm tonight.

10.
- ⬭ Call the bursar's office
- ⬭ Write out a check
- ⬭ Look up the office location
- ⬭ Check into Angell Hall

11.
- ⬭ Join the group
- ⬭ Complete the paper
- ⬭ Go to work
- ⬭ See the members for an hour

9. DIALOGUES WITH INFORMATION

Sometimes you need to listen for and remember specific information in short conversations. Usually the information can be found in the words of the last one to speak. The questions will usually include the words *what* and *where*.

QUESTION WORD	QUESTION
• Where	Where does this conversation take place?
• What	What are the speakers doing?

In trying to determine *Where does this conversation take place?* listen for key words in the conversation. However, sometimes seemingly key words can be distracters. The speakers may be discussing *tickets* and *schedules* but may not be at a train station.

EXAMPLE:

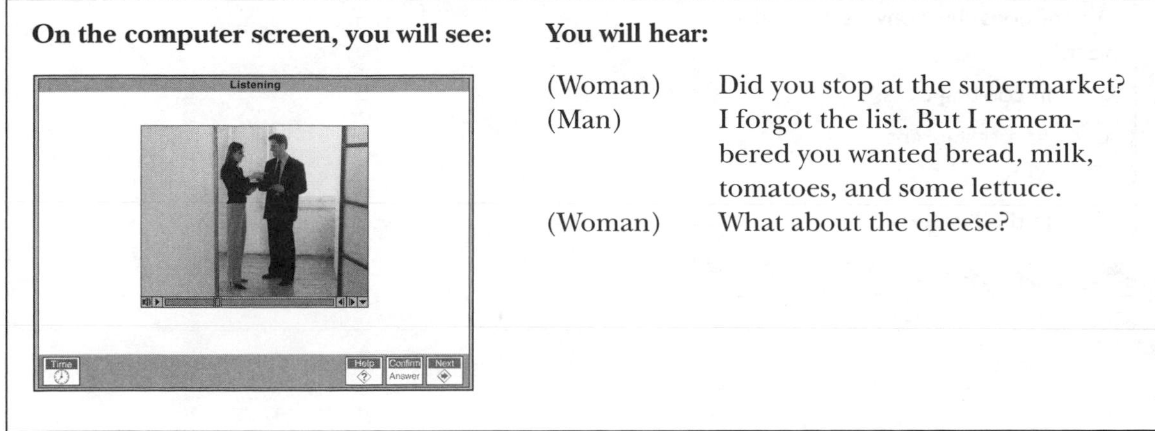

On the computer screen, you will see:

You will hear:

(Woman) Did you stop at the supermarket?
(Man) I forgot the list. But I remembered you wanted bread, milk, tomatoes, and some lettuce.
(Woman) What about the cheese?

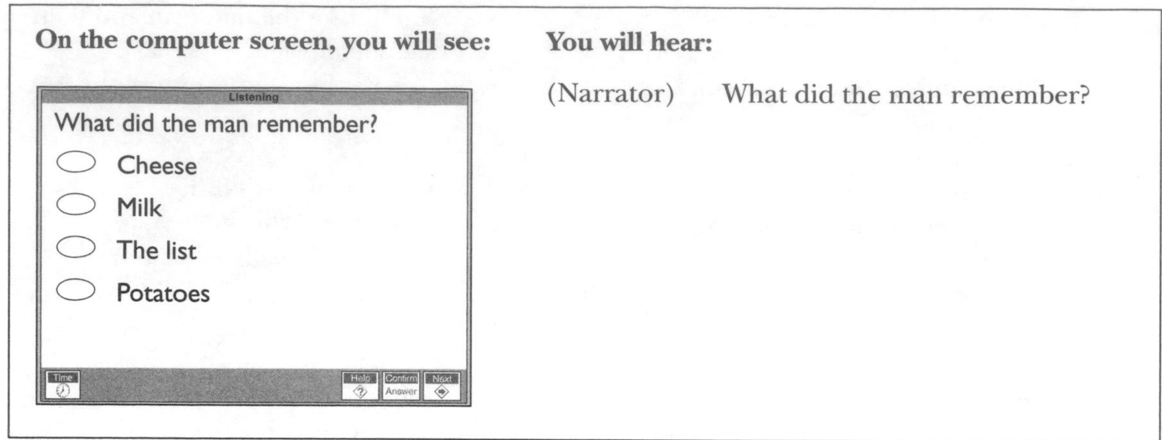

The correct answer is (B); he remembered *milk.* He forgot both the *cheese* (A) and *the list* (C). Answer (D) confuses *tomatoes* with *potatoes.*

EXAMPLE:

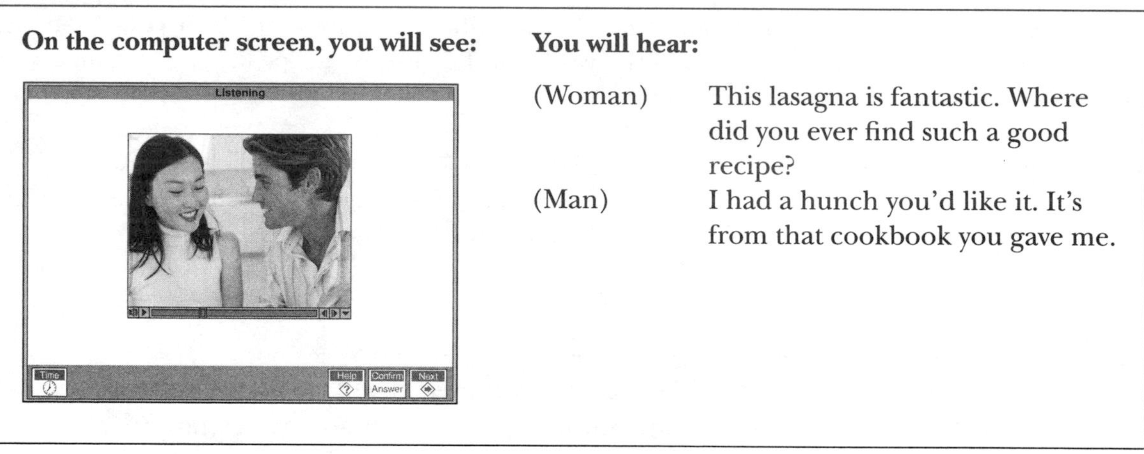

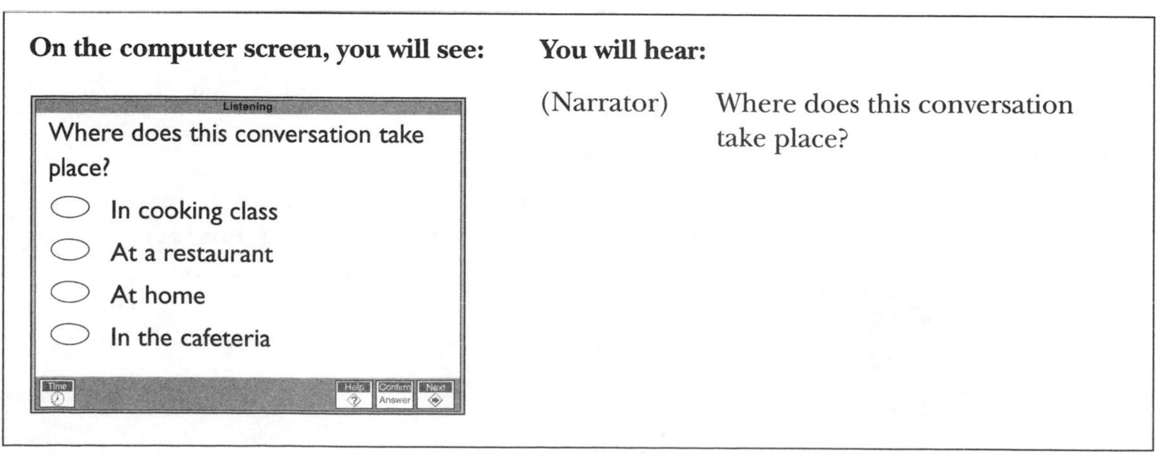

The correct answer is (C), *at home.* The man has made the meal himself, from a *cookbook,* so answers (A), (B), and (D) could not be correct.

EXERCISE 9: In this exercise, listen carefully to the short dialogue and question on the tape. Then choose the best answer to the question. (See Appendix E, pages 389–90, for a transcript.)

1.
- They're married.
- They're brother and sister.
- They're presidential speechwriters.
- They're colleagues.

2.
- Looking for the right floor
- Buying a present
- Giving directions
- Returning a gift

3.
- She imagined herself skiing.
- She went on a skiing trip.
- She looked at Rob's pictures with the man.
- She took some pictures of herself skiing.

4.
- Ann was relatively generous.
- Ann was quite generous to a relative.
- Ann received money from a relative.
- Ann heard about a lot of money.

5.
- An appointment
- School hours
- The museum schedule
- A part-time job

6.
- She'd better write down the change back to Thursday.
- Recitation classes will be alternating between Tuesdays and Thursdays.
- He thought she had forgotten to go to class.
- The next recitation will be on the regular day.

7.
- His schedule will vary.
- He'll work however much he wants.
- He won't need to work.
- He depends on the job.

8.
- She'll be paying for dinner.
- They need to get some money.
- The cash machine is closed.
- He can get money at dinner.

9.
- If it's possible to change advisors
- How to download the change of advisor form
- Who her new advisor will be
- Where she'll take her completed form

10.
- At an airport
- At a movie theater
- In a supermarket
- At a hotel

11.
- She made it herself.
- She had an old one remade.
- She bought it from the tailor.
- She borrowed an old skirt and jacket.

12.
- At a party
- At a restaurant
- At a bakery
- At someone's house

10. DIALOGUES WITH UNCERTAINTY AND CONCLUSIONS

Voicing uncertainty and drawing conclusions are often heard in short conversations. A speaker is unable to make a decision or, on the other hand, is able to conclude something based on what is learned from the other speaker. Many of these dialogues contain modals (may, must, should have, could, etc.):

UNCERTAINTY
- Well
- I forgot why
- I'm not sure
- I don't know whether
- I hesitate to
- Could/Could have
- Might/May
- Might have/May have

CONCLUSIONS
- You/he must
- It must have
- I should have
- Oh
- Now
- Oh, that's why
- Certainly

Usually the conclusion, or deduction, is heard in the last line. Listen carefully for modals. The speaker deduces *It must have rained last night* from seeing water on the ground and not from seeing it actually rain.

EXAMPLE:

On the computer screen, you will see:

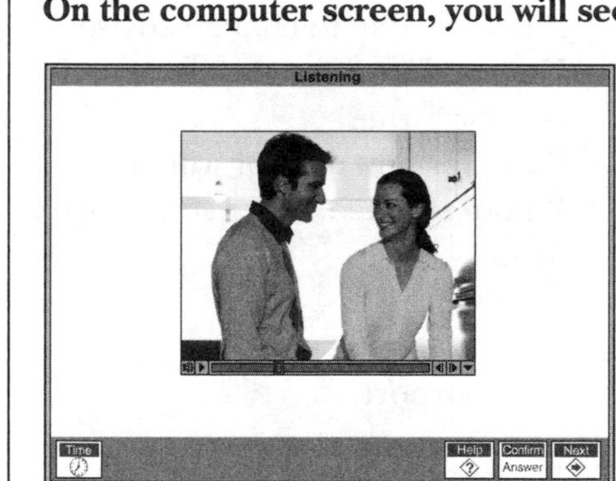

You will hear:

(Man) I forget why I'm looking through my file cabinet.

(Woman) Remember? You were going to show me an article you thought I'd enjoy.

On the computer screen, you will see:

Listening

What does the woman imply?

- The man had planned to clean up his file cabinet.
- The man had been searching for something of interest.
- She was enjoying the article he had filed for her.
- She will find the article.

Time | Help | Confirm Answer | Next

You will hear:

(Narrator) What does the woman imply?

The correct answer is (B) *The man had been searching for something of interest.* She says to him *Remember?* she is reminding him what he has forgotten. Answer (A) confuses *looking through* with cleaning up. Answers (C) and (D) are factually incorrect but distracting because they include *file* and *article,* words used in the dialogue.

EXAMPLE:

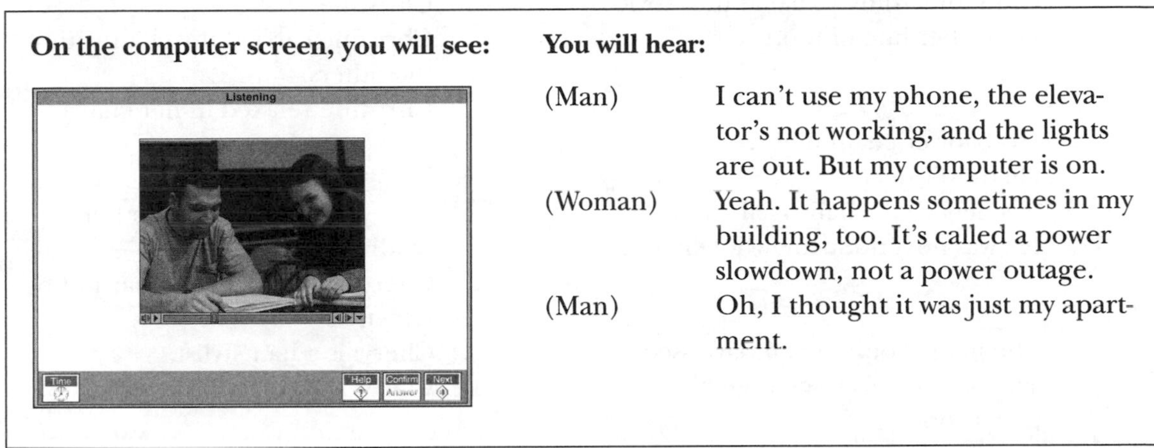

On the computer screen, you will see:

You will hear:

(Man)	I can't use my phone, the elevator's not working, and the lights are out. But my computer is on.
(Woman)	Yeah. It happens sometimes in my building, too. It's called a power slowdown, not a power outage.
(Man)	Oh, I thought it was just my apartment.

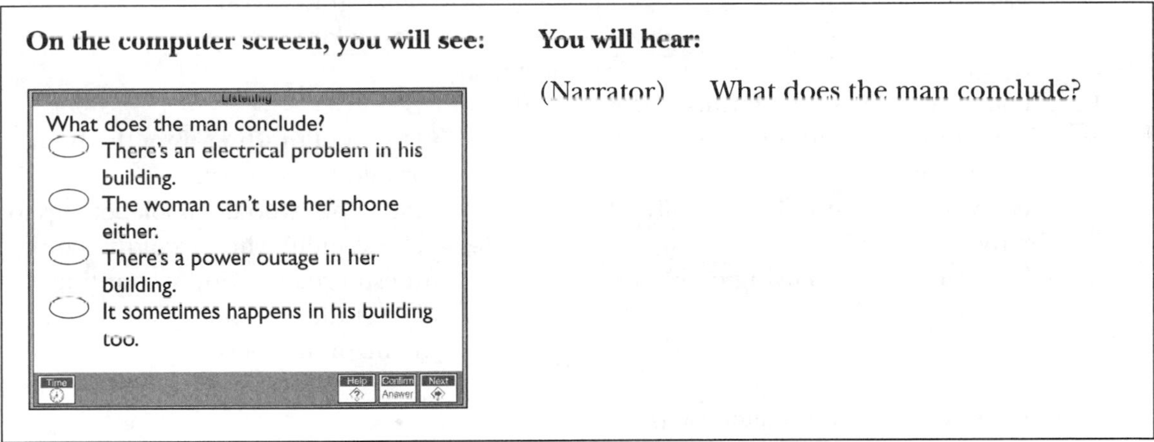

Listening
What does the man conclude?
There's an electrical problem in his building.
The woman can't use her phone either.
There's a power outage in her building.
It sometimes happens in his building too.
Time
Help
Confirm Answer
Next

On the computer screen, you will see:

You will hear:

(Narrator)	What does the man conclude?

The man learns from the woman (A) *There's an electrical problem in his building.* Answers (B) and (C) are factually incorrect. It does happen in her building as well, but until they spoke he thought it was just in his apartment. Answer (D) therefore confuses *his* with *her.*

EXERCISE 10: In this exercise, listen carefully to the short dialogue and question. Then choose the best answer to the question. (See Appendix E, pages 390–91, for a transcript.)

1.
- ◯ Eat before the film
- ◯ Eat after the film
- ◯ Grab something to eat at the movie
- ◯ Finish her bite of food

2.
- ◯ His baby cried all night.
- ◯ He didn't sleep.
- ◯ His neighbor's baby is ill.
- ◯ He was next door the whole night.

3.
- ◯ The man should be embarrassed.
- ◯ The man needs to change his paper topic.
- ◯ No one else can read the man's paper.
- ◯ The man has to go home before class.

4.
- ◯ The woman lives on a farm.
- ◯ The woman should walk instead of taking the bus.
- ◯ The woman must wake up really early.
- ◯ The woman thinks living on North Campus is a joke.

5.
- ◯ Not listening to her teacher was a mistake.
- ◯ She will always do what her teacher tells her.
- ◯ She should have her ears examined.
- ◯ Her teacher will tell her what to do.

6.
- ◯ The Jackson boys have striped shirts.
- ◯ That boy resembles other Jacksons.
- ◯ That Jackson boy has to wear striped shirts.
- ◯ That boy must be Jack's son.

7.
- ◯ There won't be enough chairs.
- ◯ Someone took the chairs from Christine.
- ◯ Christine carried the chair with the others.
- ◯ Christine relaxed in her chair.

8.
- ◯ Cheryl looks for proof in her reading.
- ◯ Cheryl's proofreading may not be effective.
- ◯ Cheryl is a hair stylist.
- ◯ Cheryl's reading has style.

9.
- ◯ Work for a small company
- ◯ Be independent
- ◯ Delay graduation
- ◯ Start a large company

10.
- ◯ The student who forgot the book should be an artist.
- ◯ She knows who the book belongs to.
- ◯ The student who forgot the book doesn't really enjoy accounting.
- ◯ The student should put his or her name on the book.

11.
- ◯ Going to the supermarket or his apartment will necessitate cooking.
- ◯ The supermarket is between the union and the cafeteria.
- ◯ There's nothing to eat in the man's apartment.
- ◯ She'll meet him at either the union or the cafeteria.

12.
- ◯ He'll have to buy the paper if he wants to get it.
- ◯ He thought he'd be getting the paper free for longer than twelve weeks.

- If he buys the textbook, he'll get a free paper every day of the term.
- He'll have a busy twelve weeks.

13.
- She didn't know when the audition was.
- She needs to try out for the musical.
- She may be too scared to audition.
- She tries too hard.

14.
- Emily won't be going to the concert.
- Emily's willing to take a loss.
- He'd like the woman to go with him.
- Emily isn't sure she wants to sell the ticket.

PART B LONGER CONVERSATIONS, ACADEMIC DISCUSSIONS, AND LECTURES

There are three different types of listening passages in Part B. They are presented in random order, which means you may hear a longer conversation, then an academic lecture, and then an academic discussion or any combination of the three. Usually there are two lectures, two longer conversations, and one academic discussion, but this combination can vary.

Longer Conversations

Like short conversations, longer conversations involve two speakers. Instead of two to four lines, these talks are five to seven lines long. You will see a picture of the speakers as you listen to their conversation, which is followed by two or three multiple-choice questions. The test will have two or three such conversations.

EXAMPLE:

On the computer screen, you will see:

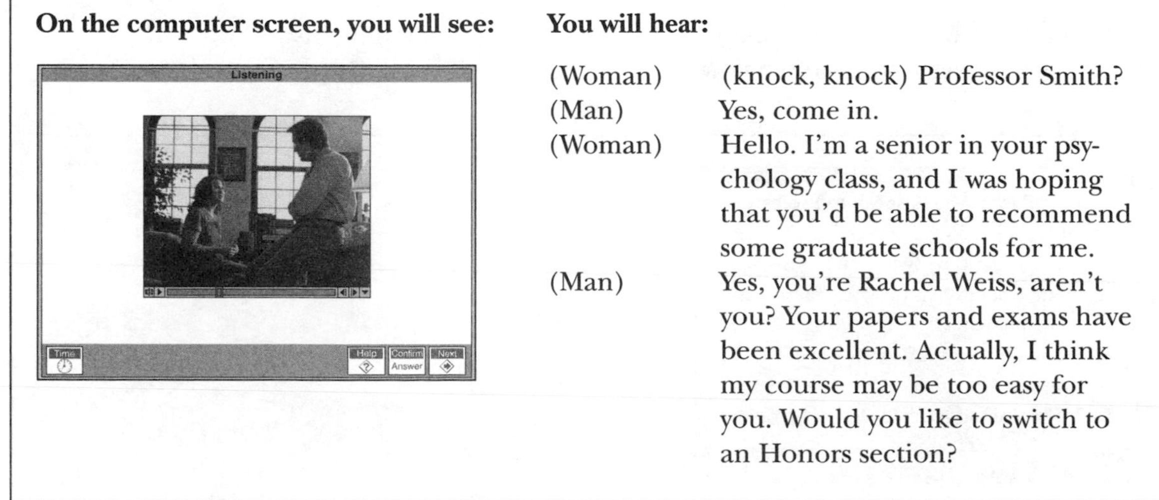

You will hear:

(Woman) (knock, knock) Professor Smith?
(Man) Yes, come in.
(Woman) Hello. I'm a senior in your psychology class, and I was hoping that you'd be able to recommend some graduate schools for me.
(Man) Yes, you're Rachel Weiss, aren't you? Your papers and exams have been excellent. Actually, I think my course may be too easy for you. Would you like to switch to an Honors section?

(Woman)	Yes, but I really didn't come here to talk about switching sections. In addition to recommending graduate schools, would you kindly suggest some essays for me in the field of child development? I'm quite interested in this field.
(Man)	No problem. You know, there's an excellent childcare center on campus you might be able to observe. Here's a reading list, and I'll put together a list of some graduate schools by next Tuesday. Come back then, OK?
(Woman)	Thanks so much for your time.

You will then see and hear the question before the answer choices appear:

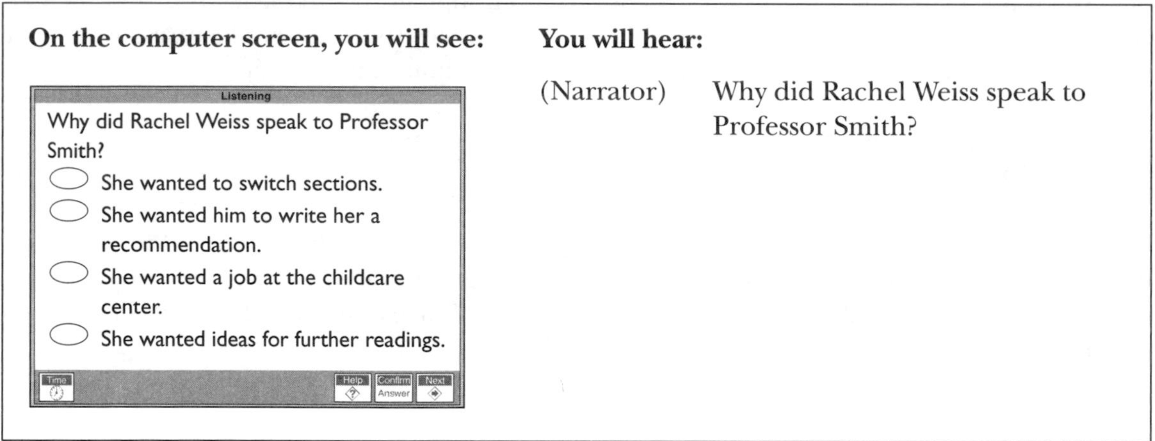

To choose an answer, you will click on an oval. The oval next to that answer will darken. The correct answer is indicated below.

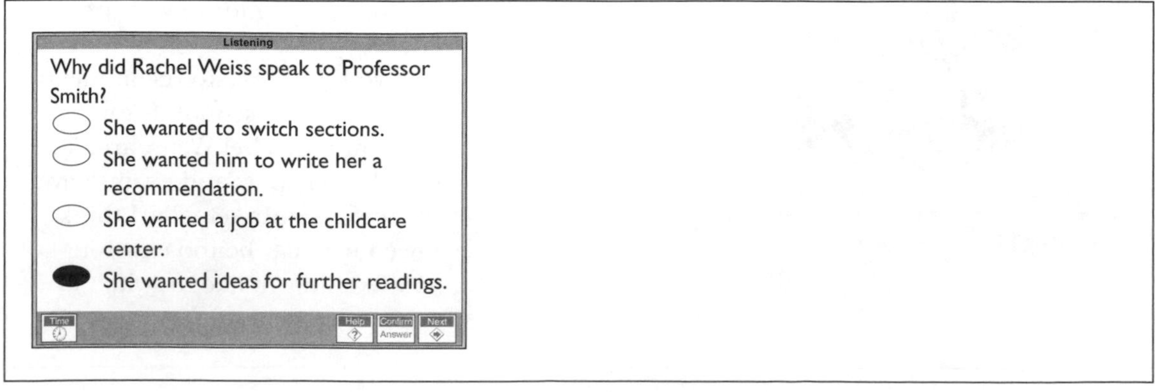

In the conversation, the woman asks the professor if he would suggest *articles for me in the field of child development. Articles* means *a type of reading material.* Although she wants his recommendation of graduate schools, she did not ask him to write a recommendation.

When you finish, the next question is spoken.

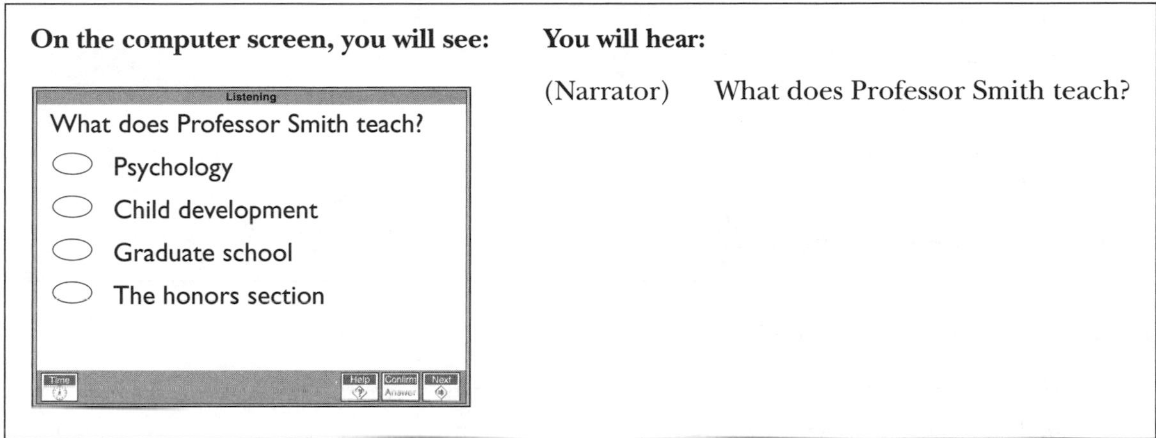

The correct answer is indicated below.

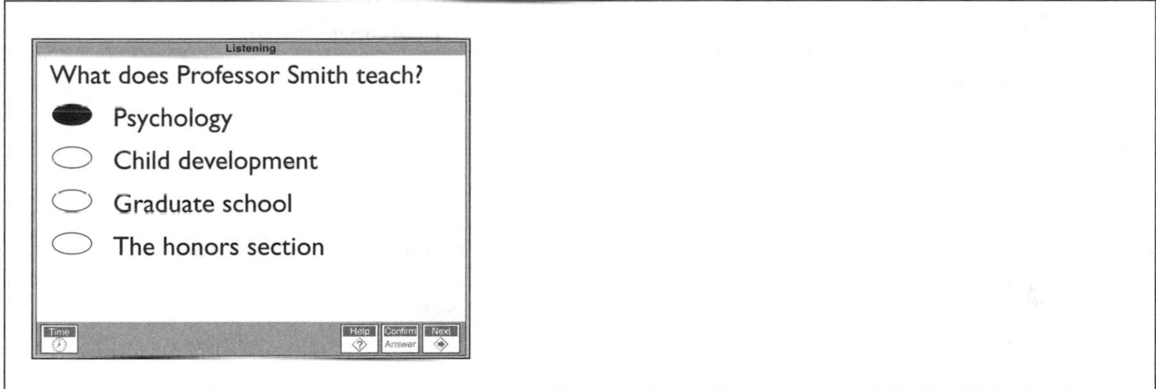

Rachel says to Professor Smith that she's *in his psychology class.* Although he teaches an honors section, he does not teach "the" only section. Rachel wants recommendations for graduate school and child development readings; it does not mean he teaches graduate school or child development.

When you finish, the next question is spoken.

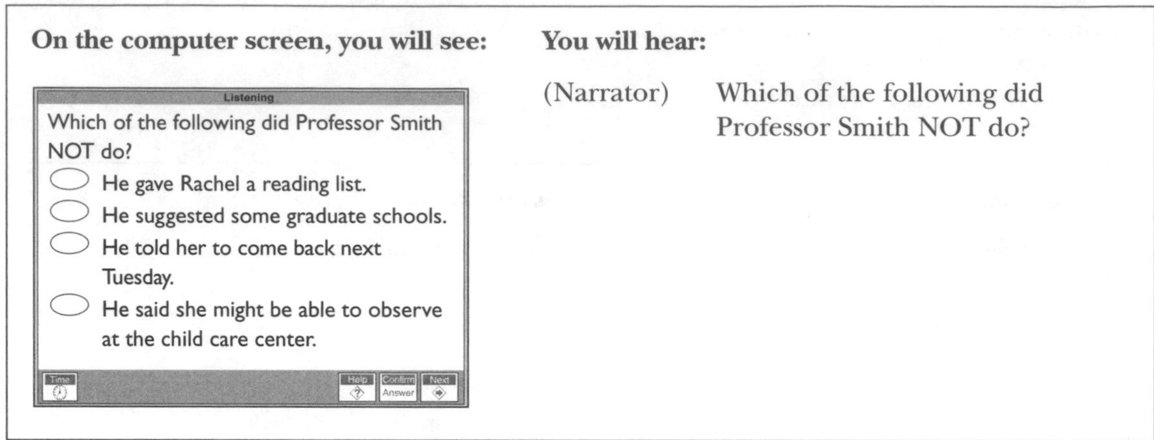

The correct answer is indicated below.

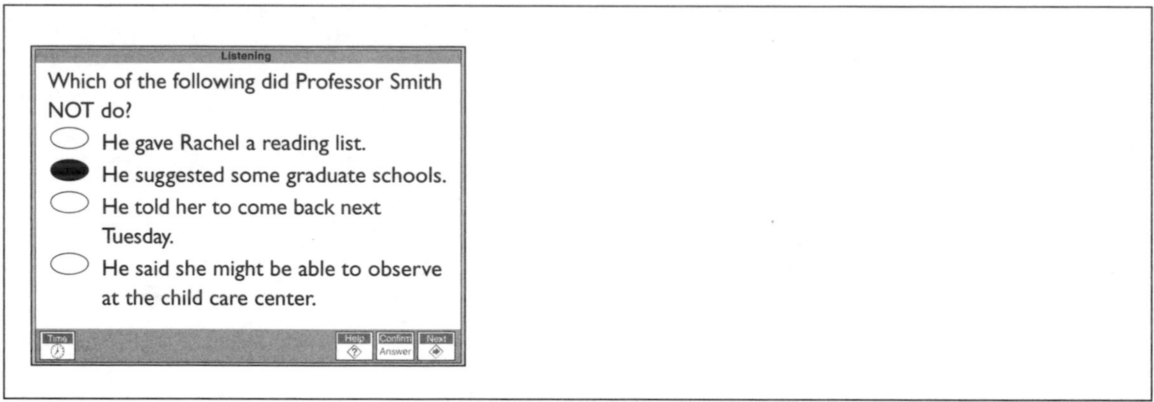

He told her that he would *put together a list of some graduate schools by next Tuesday,* so he did NOT yet *suggest some graduate schools.*

STRATEGIES FOR LONGER CONVERSATIONS

1. **Listen carefully.** The conversation is spoken only one time.
2. **Unlike the shorter conversations that focus frequently on the meaning of an idiom, phrase, or vocabulary word, you need to focus on the overall meaning.**
3. **Listen carefully to the first line.** You may be able to determine the main topic. Try to imagine the situation/setting/context by listening to key words.
4. **Unlike shorter conversations, some answers may be directly stated in the conversations.**
5. **Answer the question even if you don't remember or understand everything you have heard.**
6. **Eliminate answer choices that are clearly incorrect.** Then guess without taking too much time.
7. **Then click on NEXT and CONFIRM ANSWER and be ready to hear a new talk.**
8. **Be familiar with the directions, so you can click on DISMISS DIRECTIONS as soon as you can.** Time begins as soon as the directions appear.

EXERCISE 11: Look at ONLY the picture as you listen to each longer conversation. **On the test, you will not be able to see the questions or answer choices during the conversation.** (See Appendix E, pages 391–94, for a transcript.)

Questions 1–3

1. Why did Mark arrive early?
   - His car pool arrived an hour before the test began.
   - He planned to review with the woman.
   - He wanted to find out what would be on the test.
   - He wanted to go over his notes.

2. What subject is the exam testing?
   - Biology
   - Composition
   - Economics
   - History

3. What does Mark advise the woman?
   - To review her notes
   - To be very specific
   - To change her major
   - To answer the easy questions first

Questions 4–6

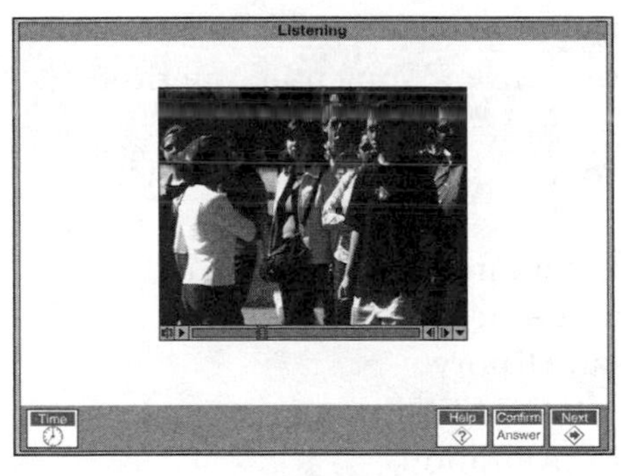

4. Why does the man want to see the student center?
   - It's part of the campus tour.
   - He's between classes.
   - He might be spending time there.
   - He's not feeling comfortable.

5. Why did the tour NOT go inside the student center?
   - It's closed.
   - It's open only to students.
   - It's not included in the visit.
   - It would take too long.

6. What will the man probably do after the tour?
   - He'll stay late at the student center.
   - He'll buy a meal at the cafeteria.
   - He'll make sure he likes the student center.
   - He'll study at the library.

Questions 7–8

7. Why does the woman sell her books to the bookstore?
   - ⬭ She gets good money there.
   - ⬭ It's in a good location.
   - ⬭ It's near the post office.
   - ⬭ That's where she buys them.

8. What will the woman probably do next?
   - ⬭ Go to the bookstore
   - ⬭ Check out the site the man mentioned
   - ⬭ Go to the post office
   - ⬭ Compare selling prices at the bookstore with the Internet site

Questions 9–11

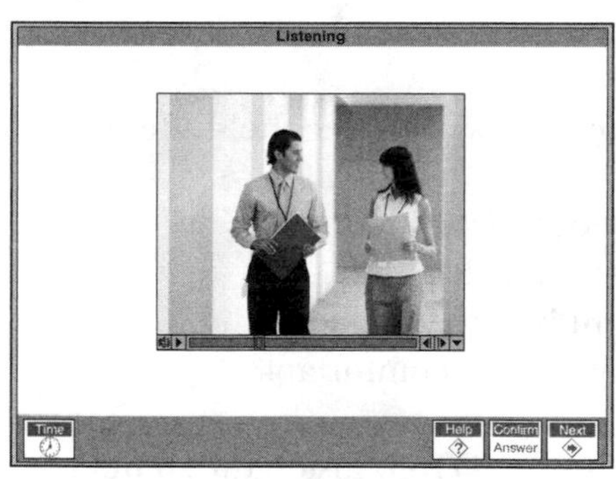

9. What will the woman probably do next?
   - ⬭ Contact Professor Halpern
   - ⬭ Speak to Brian
   - ⬭ Teach sections of Women in American History
   - ⬭ Get in touch with the department chair

10. What did the man most recently teach?
    - ⬭ Women in American History
    - ⬭ American History
    - ⬭ Twentieth Century Europe
    - ⬭ Ancient Civilizations

11. Why doesn't the woman want to teach the same course again?
    - ⬭ She's tired of the subject.
    - ⬭ She wants to explore other fields.
    - ⬭ She knows Brian wants to teach it.
    - ⬭ She'll be writing her dissertation.

Questions 12–14

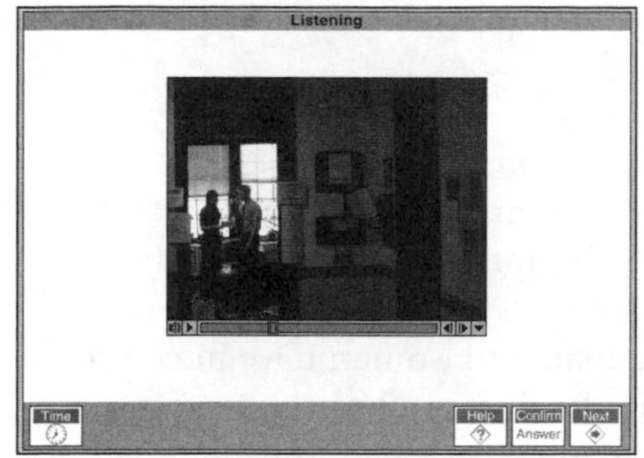

12. What does Dr. Martin think the man should do next?
    - ⬭ Stay for the spring term
    - ⬭ See her in November
    - ⬭ Get catalogues from other schools
    - ⬭ Register for upper level courses

13. When will the man probably transfer?
    - ⬭ In the spring
    - ⬭ Next fall
    - ⬭ After completing all the introductory courses
    - ⬭ When the term ends

14. What does Dr. Martin imply?
    - ⬭ He'll get credit for any course if he transfers.
    - ⬭ Transfer policies vary from school to school.
    - ⬭ He should wait another term before transfering.
    - ⬭ She'll consider whether or not he should transfer.

Questions 15–17

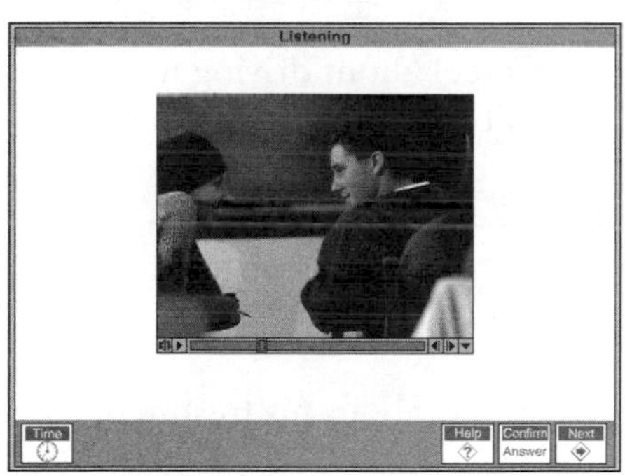

15. What will the man probably do next?
    - ⬭ Buy some exotic seeds and plants
    - ⬭ Attend Dr. Roberts' retirement party
    - ⬭ Get in touch with everyone in the class
    - ⬭ E-mail Dr. Roberts

16. What is the university planning for Dr. Roberts?
    - ⬭ A memorial garden
    - ⬭ A faculty luncheon
    - ⬭ A large party
    - ⬭ A donation

17. What does the woman say about Dr. Roberts?
    - ⬭ He'd like the students to attend his reception.
    - ⬭ He informed the class of his hobby.
    - ⬭ He suggested the students buy him some plants.
    - ⬭ Everyone in the class knows of his retirement plans.

Questions 18–19

18. What will the man probably do over Thanksgiving?
    - He has no idea.
    - He'll stay in the dorm.
    - He'll accompany the woman.
    - He'll see his family.

19. What do the man and woman have in common?
    - Talkative family members
    - No place to go for Thanksgiving
    - Being dorm residents
    - A love of football

Questions 20–22

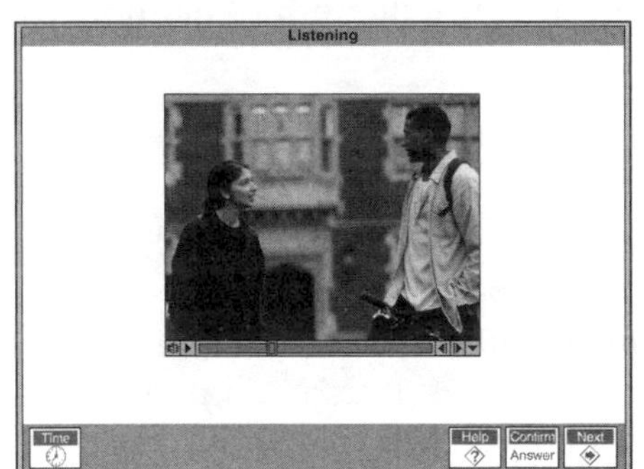

20. What will the man probably do next?
    - Go to Chicago
    - Drive himself home
    - Check out the ride listings
    - Compare bus and plane prices

21. How does the man feel about driving with someone he doesn't know?
    - Somewhat scared
    - Relieved
    - Confident
    - Extremely excited

22. What does the man say about his freshman roommate?
    - He went to Chicago for Thanksgiving.
    - He got home quicker than if he had taken a bus.
    - He was a little bit nervous to use the ride board.
    - He got a ride from someone he didn't know.

Questions 23–24

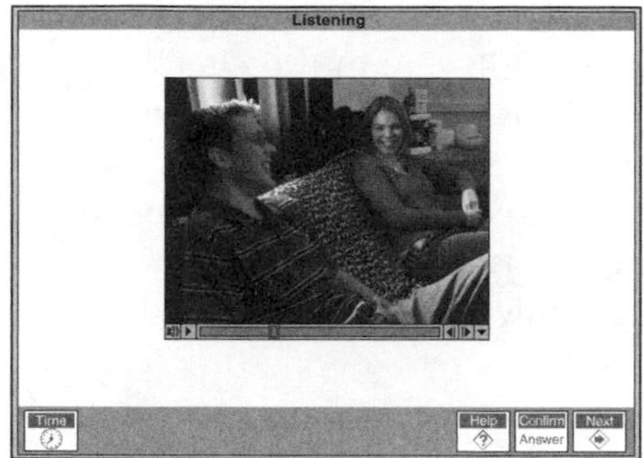

23. Why does the man stop by Carly's room?
    - To inform her of the new policy
    - To make sure her room isn't so noisy
    - To find out who has been making noise in C-305
    - To ask her to turn down her CD player

24. What did the man do?
    - He went to the wrong room.
    - He thought Carly was someone else.
    - He already complained three times to Carly.
    - He removed Carly's CD player and TV set.

Questions 25–27

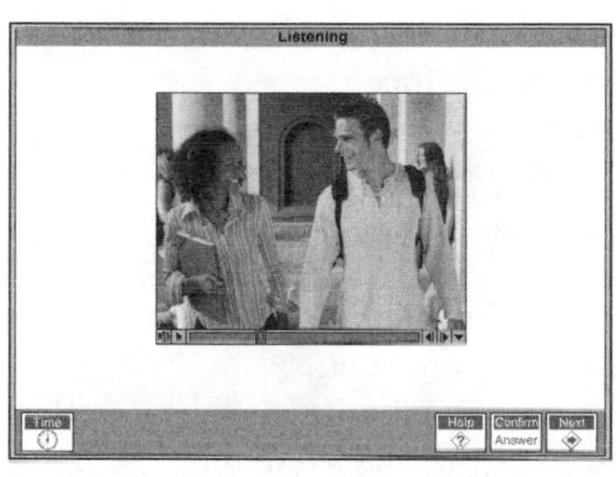

25. When should the woman go to practice?
    - At six
    - At three
    - From four to six
    - After she finishes her school work

26. Why is the woman unsure about swimming again?
    - It's difficult to go to school and swim.
    - She's not sure she could make the team.
    - The roster is full.
    - She hadn't contacted the coach.

27. What does the coach want the woman to do next?
    - Tell him about her swimming
    - Contact him
    - Come to practice
    - Be honest with him

Questions 28–29

28. What is the problem?
    - ⬭ The man's family sent in two checks.
    - ⬭ The school has no record of his family's having paid.
    - ⬭ The school's records need to be updated.
    - ⬭ The man needs to get documentation from his family.

29. What will the man probably do next?
    - ⬭ Register on line
    - ⬭ Bring his paperwork to the bursar
    - ⬭ Contact his parents' bank
    - ⬭ Pay the $4,000 he owes

Questions 30–32

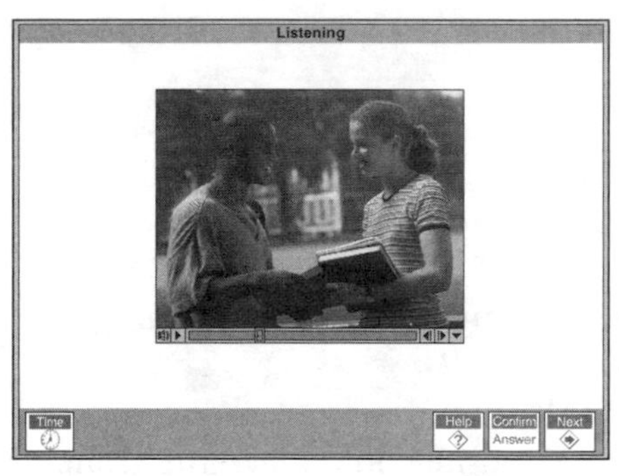

30. What is the woman looking for?
    - ⬭ The admissions office
    - ⬭ The library
    - ⬭ The place that repairs computers
    - ⬭ The student handbook office

31. What can you say about the directions?
    - ⬭ They had to be repeated.
    - ⬭ The man made a mistake.
    - ⬭ They were easy for the woman to remember.
    - ⬭ The woman found them in the guidebook.

32. Where is the place that fixes computers?
    - ⬭ Next door
    - ⬭ Next to the admissions office
    - ⬭ Right in the library
    - ⬭ At the computer lab

Academic Discussion and Lectures

Academic discussions and lectures take place in the classroom. You will see a series of visuals that explain what is being discussed. **In this section, the visuals are important, both for comprehension and for answering the questions to follow.** Each discussion or lecture is two to two and a half minutes long. Each test will have one or two discussions and usually two lectures.

In addition to multiple-choice questions, the discussions and lectures are followed by four other types of questions.

TYPES OF QUESTIONS

1. **Multiple-Choice Questions with One Correct Answer.** This standard question type typically asks for the main idea of the passage/lecture.
2. **Multiple-Choice Questions with Two Correct Answers.** Based upon the information in the discussion, you must select two correct answers out of the four choices. You CANNOT continue until you have chosen two answers. The questions may ask about the main idea, details, or what you can infer from the passage.
3. **Graphics Questions.** This type of question comes in two varieties. One has a graphic with four letters on it. You click on the correct letter. The other has four graphics, and you choose the correct one. These questions are usually about specific details from the passage.
4. **Matching Questions.** These questions ask you to match three categories with three items or examples from those categories.
5. **Ordering Questions.** These questions ask you to put four pieces of information in the correct order—either chronologically (in time order) or procedurally.

The five question types appear following the discussion.

EXAMPLE:

On the computer screen, you will see:

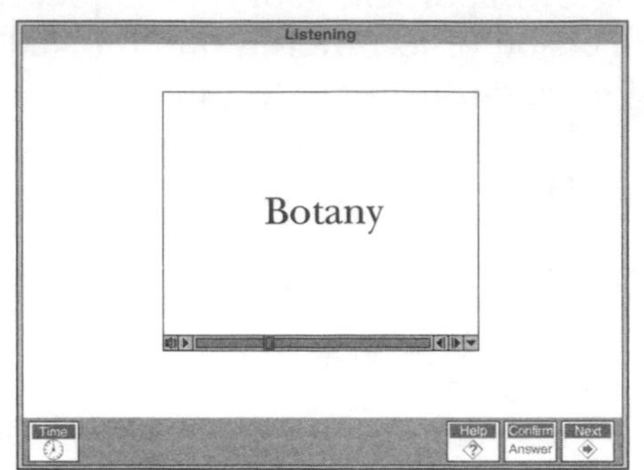

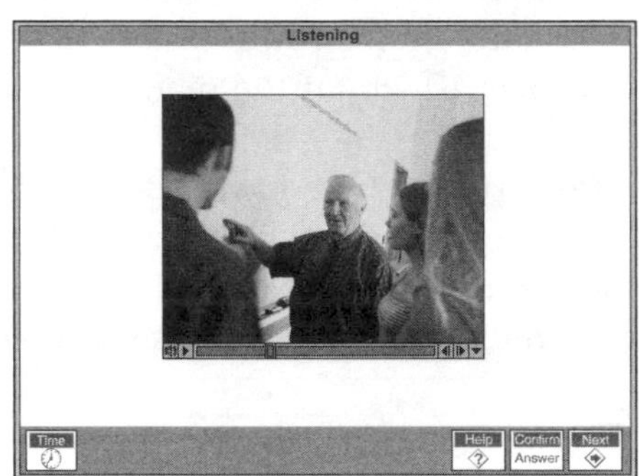

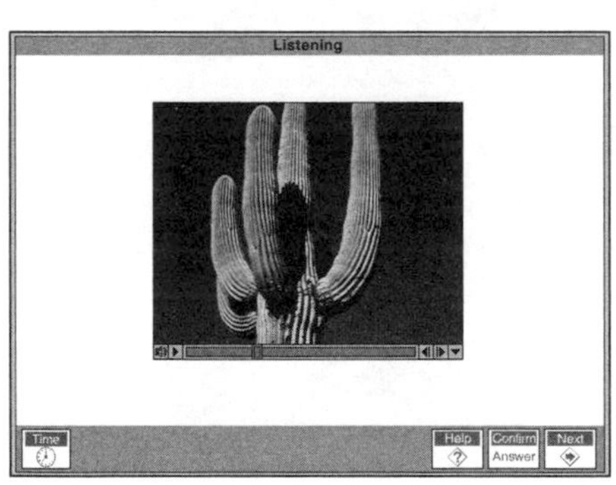

You will hear:

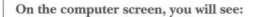

(Narrator)	Listen to a discussion in a botany class.
(Instructor)	Today we're moving on to plants of the Southwest. For those of you from the Northeast, I'm sure cacti are quite exotic. But for those of us from near-desert communities, the cactus is an ever-present symbol of beauty and uniqueness. Has anyone ever touched a cactus?
(Leah)	Ouch! Why are they so prickly?
(Instructor)	Good question. They weren't always that way. Scientists believe the first cacti, which appeared millions of years ago, had leaves and branches like trees. Most species became shorter and then the leaves developed into spines. Lastly, the woody stem became softer, enabling it to absorb water in the desert.
(Tyler)	Are they found only in deserts?
(Instructor)	Today most cacti are found in hot dry regions, especially in the southwestern U.S. and Mexico.
(Felicia)	What do they have in common? I've seen pictures of lots of different ones.
(Instructor)	They all produce flowers. Most grow very slowly. They live from 50 to 200 years. They are important to animals and people.
(Leah)	Do people eat them?

(Instructor) Yes. They provide food for both animals and people. People eat their peeled fruit or grind their seeds into cakemeal. Animals feed on their stems and flowers and may hide from their enemies in their stems. Let's look at four different varieties.

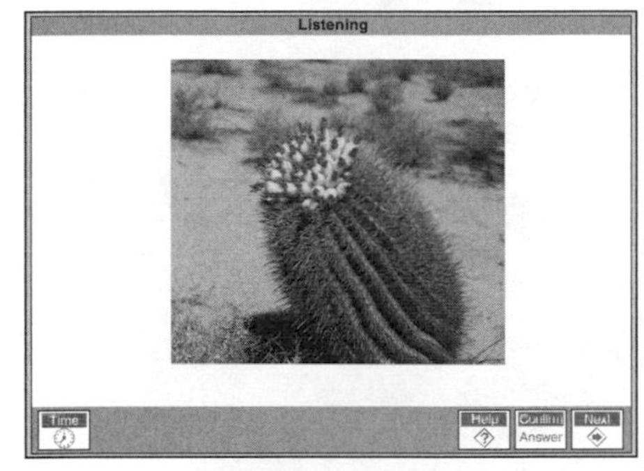

The barrel cactus has the same shape as its name. Indians once used their curved spines as fish hooks. Its juicy pulp has saved the lives of many thirsty travelers in the desert.

This cactus has stems that look like pipes of an organ. Some people enclose their properties with rows of these cacti that form a fence.

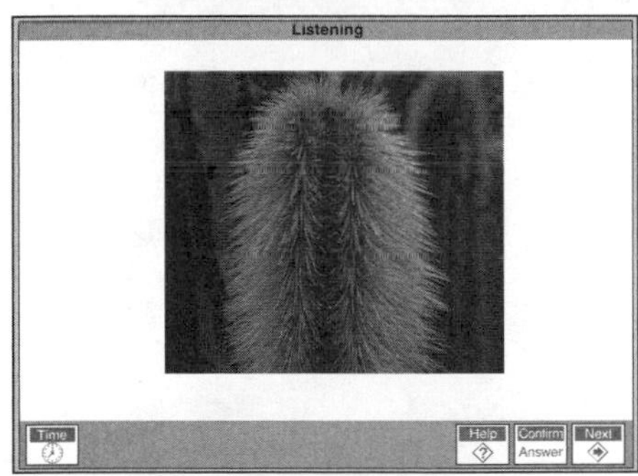

This old man cactus has a coat of white hair and no thorns! Its hair protects it from the sun.

This prickly pear cactus has thorny leaf-like stems. The plant bears pear-shaped fruit that is good to eat.

A problem is the popularity of cacti as house plants. People dig the plants out of natural areas to sell. Certain species are becoming so rare they are in danger of becoming extinct.

For tomorrow, read chapters 10 and 12 and be prepared to discuss evergreen plants.

After the discussion finishes, the first question and answer choices appear on the computer screen as the narrator states the question.

MULTIPLE-CHOICE QUESTION WITH ONE CORRECT ANSWER

Choose the one best answer.

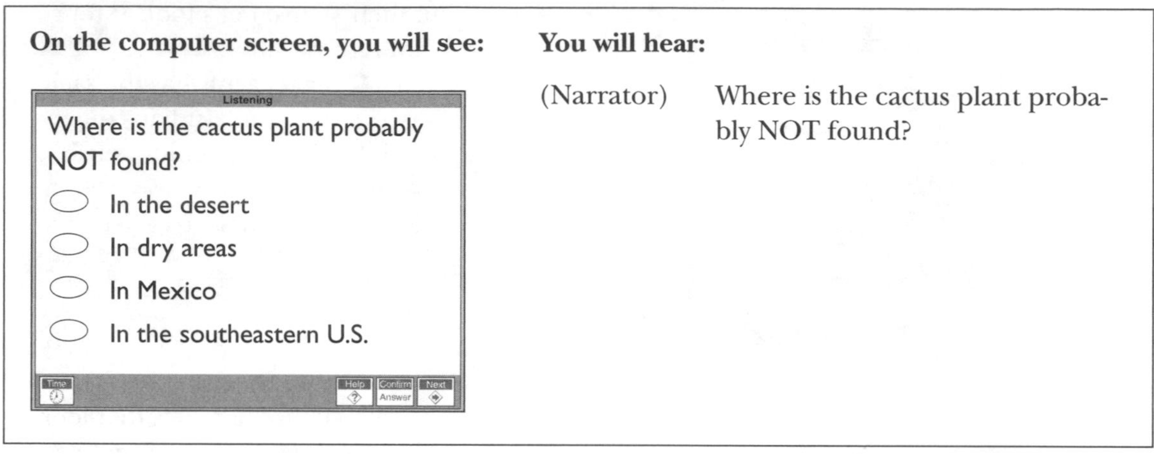

On the computer screen, you will see:
Listening
Where is the cactus plant probably NOT found?
In the desert
In dry areas
In Mexico
In the southeastern U.S.
Time
Help
Confirm Answer
Next
You will hear:
(Narrator) Where is the cactus plant probably NOT found?

The instructor said cacti are found *in the southwestern U.S.*, not the southeastern U.S. So the last answer is the best answer to this question. Click on *In the southeastern U.S.*

MULTIPLE-CHOICE QUESTION WITH TWO CORRECT ANSWERS

Click on the two correct choices.

On the computer screen, you will see:

What is stated about all cacti?

Click on 2 answers.

Listening

- ☐ They produce flowers.
- ☐ They don't absorb water.
- ☐ They don't live long.
- ☐ They are important to people.

Time | Help | Confirm Answer | Next

You will hear:

(Narrator) What is stated about all cacti?

In the discussion, the instructor said *they all produce flowers* and *they are important to people.* So the first and last answers are correct. You MUST click on both answers.

GRAPHIC QUESTION WITH FOUR LETTER CHOICES

Click on the right letter choice.

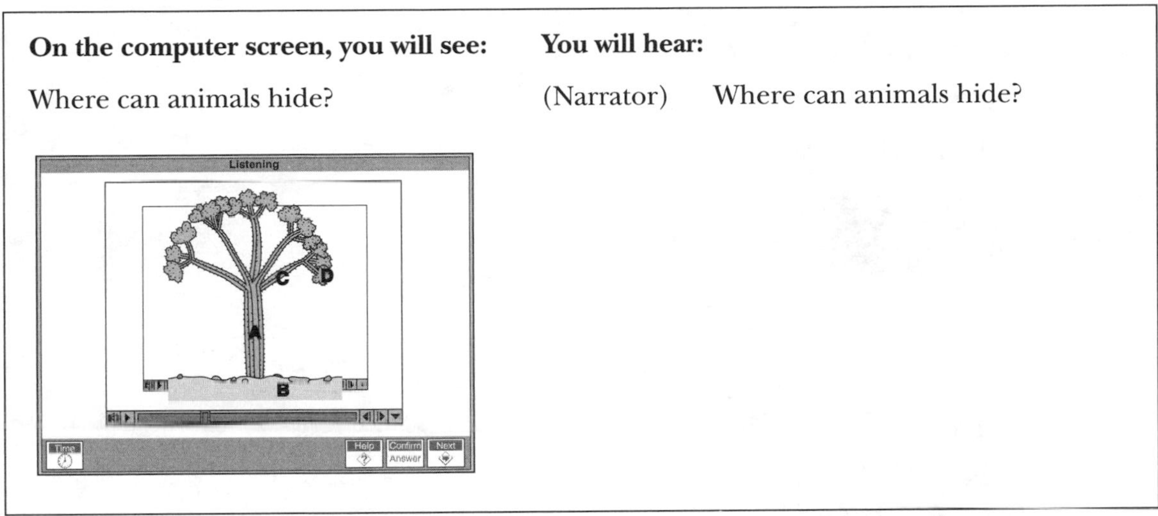

On the computer screen, you will see:
Where can animals hide?
You will hear:
(Narrator) Where can animals hide?
Listening
C
D
A
B
Time
Help
Confirm Answer
Next

In the discussion, the instructor said *animals may hide from their enemies in their stems,* so the correct answer is letter A, the stem.

MATCHING QUESTION

Click on each of the words and then click on the box where it belongs.

On the computer screen, you will see:	**You will hear:**
How is each of these described in the discussion?	(Narrator) How is each of these described in the discussion?

Click on a phrase. Then click on the empty box in the correct column. Use each phrase only once.

Barrel cactus	**Old man cactus**	**Organ pipe cactus**
Hair protects it from the sun	Used as fences	Indians used for fish hooks

The narrator states that the barrel cactus was once used by *Indians as fish hooks,* the old man cactus *has a coat of white hair* that *protects it from the sun,* and the organ pipe cactus is used by *some people* to *form a fence* on *their properties.*

GRAPHIC QUESTION WITH FOUR GRAPHICS

Click on the graphic that answers the question.

On the computer screen, you will see:	You will hear:	
Which of these is the old man cactus?	(Narrator)	Which of these is the old man cactus?

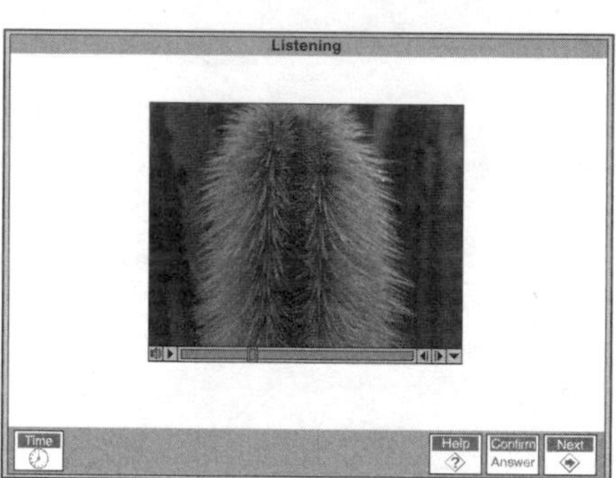

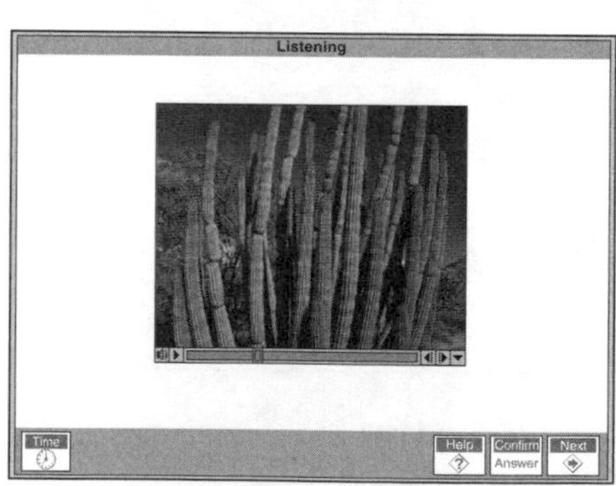

In the discussion, the instructor says the old man cactus *has a coat of white hair* and *no thorns,* so the picture in B most clearly resembles this description.

ORDERING QUESTION

Click on each of the sentences and then click on the box where it belongs.

On the computer screen, you will see:	You will hear:	
In the discussion, the history of the cactus is discussed. Put the stages in correct chronological order.	(Narrator)	In the discussion, the history of the cactus is discussed. Put the stages in correct chronological order.

Click on a sentence.
Then click on the space where it belongs.
Use each sentence only once.

Cacti became shorter.
Cacti had leaves and branches.
Cacti leaves developed into spines.
Stems of cacti became softer.

1.
2.
3.
4.

In the discussion, the instructor says *the first cacti had leaves and branches. Most became shorter and then the leaves developed into spines. Lastly, the stem became softer.*

The correct order is:

Cacti had leaves and branches.
Cacti became shorter.
Cacti leaves developed into spines.
Stems of cacti became softer.

VOCABULARY

Analysis of academic texts has determined which words are used most often. The most frequently used words appear below in five lists compiled by Averil Coxhead of the University of Victoria, Wellington, New Zealand. The words on these lists may or may not appear on your TOEFL test. The words appear here because they are important for your academic studies, and you should be familiar with many of them.

STUDY TIP

Read through each list with a highlighter. Highlight the words you can define. Write them alphabetically with their meanings in your own dictionary. Then use them in sentences. Read through the lists every two weeks, checking to see if you know any new words. Try to use new words in your speaking and writing.

SUBLIST 1 OF ACADEMIC WORD LIST

This sublist contains the most frequently used words.

analysis
approach
area
assessment
assume
authority
available
benefit
concept
consistent
constitutional
context
contract
create
data
definition
derived
distribution
economic
environment
established
estimate
evidence
export
factors
financial
formula
function
identified
income
indicate
individual
interpretation
involved
issues
labor
legal
legislation
major
method
occur
percent
period
policy
principle
procedure
process
required
research
response
role
section
sector
significant
similar
source
specific
structure
theory
variables

SUBLIST 2 OF ACADEMIC WORD LIST

This sublist contains the next 60 most frequently used words.

achieve
acquisition
administration
affect
appropriate
aspects
assistance
categories
chapter
commission
community
design
distinction
elements
equation
evaluation
features
final
focus
impact
injury
institute
potential
previous
primary
purchase
range
region
regulations
relevant
resident
resources
restricted

complex
computer
conclusion
conduct
consequences
construction
consumer
credit
cultural
investment
items
journal
maintenance
normal
obtained
participation
perceived
positive
security
sought
select
site
strategies
survey
text
traditional
transfer

SUBLIST 3 OF ACADEMIC WORD LIST

This sublist contains the next 60 most frequently used words.

alternative
circumstances
comments
compensation
components
consent
considerable
constant
constraints
contribution
convention
coordination
core
corporate
corresponding
criteria
deduction
demonstrate
document
dominant
emphasis
ensure
excluded
framework
funds
illustrated
immigration
implies
initial
instance
interaction
justification
layer
link
location
maximum
minorities
negative
outcomes
partnership
philosophy
physical
proportion
published
reaction
registered
reliance
removed
scheme
sequence
sex
shift
specified
sufficient
task
technical
techniques
technology
validity
volume

SUBLIST 4 OF ACADEMIC WORD LIST

This sublist contains the next 60 most frequently used words.

access
adequate
annual
apparent
approximated
attitudes
attributed
civil
code
commitment
communication
concentration
conference
error
ethnic
goals
granted
hence
hypothesis
implementation
implications
imposed
integration
internal
investigation
job
parallel
parameters
phase
predicted
principal
prior
professional
project
promote
regime
resolution
restrained
series

contrast
cycle
debate
despite
dimensions
domestic
emerged
label
mechanism
obvious
occupational
option
output
overall
statistics
status
stress
subsequent
sum
summary
undertaken

SUBLIST 5 OF ACADEMIC WORD LIST

This sublist contains the next 60 most frequently used words.

academic
adjustment
alter
amendment
aware
capacity
challenge
clause
compounds
conflict
consultation
contact
decline
discretion
draft
enable
energy
enforcement
entities
equivalent
evolution
expansion
exposure
external
facilitate
fundamental
generated
generation
image
liberal
license
logic
marginal
medical
mental
modified
monitoring
network
notion
objective
orientation
perspective
precise
prime
psychology
pursue
ratio
rejected
revenue
stability
styles
substitution
sustainable
symbolic
target
transition
trend
version
welfare
whereas

STRATEGIES FOR ACADEMIC DISCUSSIONS AND LECTURES

1. **Listen carefully.** The discussion or lecture is spoken only one time.
2. **The first visual will help you focus on the topic.** It shows you how many people are talking. In a discussion, there can be two to five people talking and interrupting each other. In a lecture, only the professor speaks.
3. **Individual vocabulary is not tested;** try to focus on the overall topic. The words in the five lists may help you focus on words used in academic discourse in universities.
4. **In this section, the visuals are necessary.** The visuals are related to the topic being discussed and go in order. The visuals alone will NOT enable you to answer the questions, so listen carefully.
5. **Answer each question as quickly as you can.**
6. **You may NOT take notes as you would in a real lecture, so try to remember important details that you think will be asked.**
7. **Pay attention to the organization features: categorical (division with similar items), chronological (time order), and spatial (organization by space).**
8. **Guess even if you have no idea.** Try to eliminate answers that are clearly wrong, and go on.

9. **You cannot change your answer once you click on NEXT and CONFIRM ANSWER.** The next question appears immediately.
10. **You will not be able to return to a previous question.**
11. **Do not worry about misunderstanding one talk.** Be ready to hear a new one.

STUDY TIP

The following websites have actual academic lectures from American universities to be used for practice:
www.hti.umich.edu/m/micase
web.pdx.edu/~mooredr/LectureVideoShowcase.html
videocast.nih.gov/PastEvents.asp
Search the Web to find other lecture websites for practice.

EXERCISE 12: Academic Discussions

Look at ONLY the words, pictures, and maps as you listen to each academic discussion. On the test, you will not be able to see the questions or answer choices during the discussion. (See Appendix E, pages 394–97, for a transcript.)

Questions 1–5

Listen to a discussion in a philosophy class on Brook Farm.

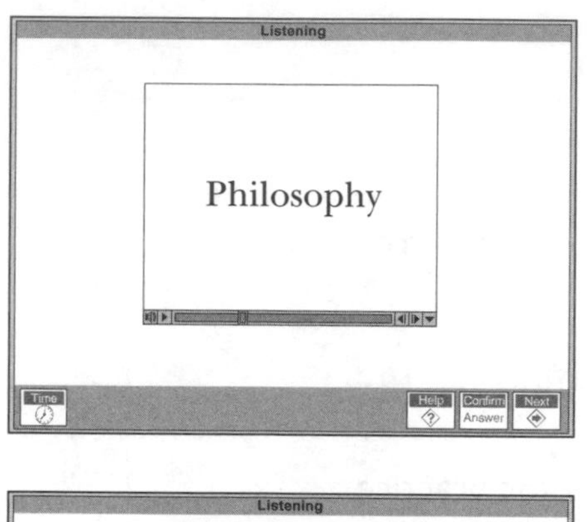

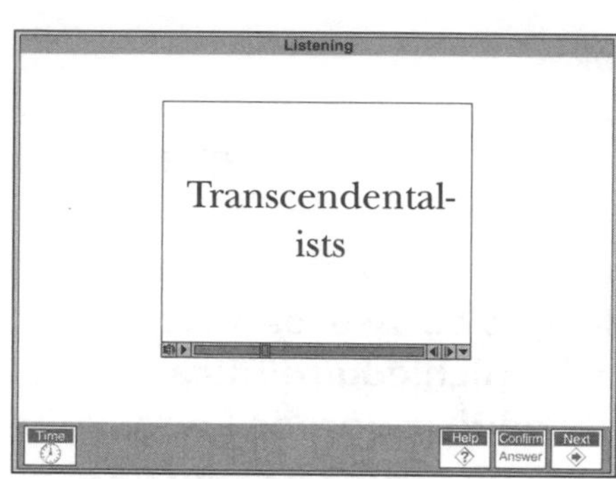

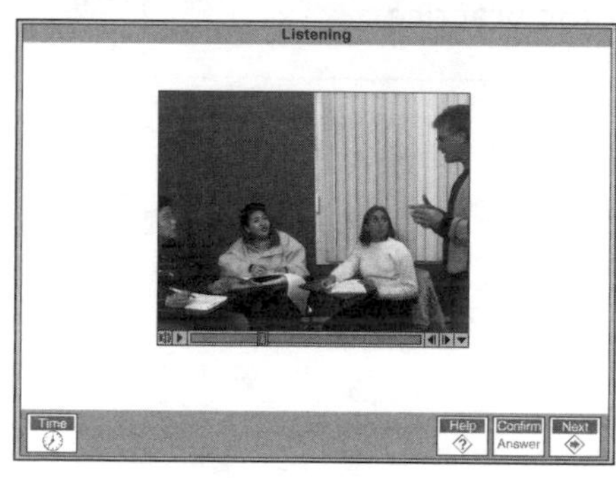

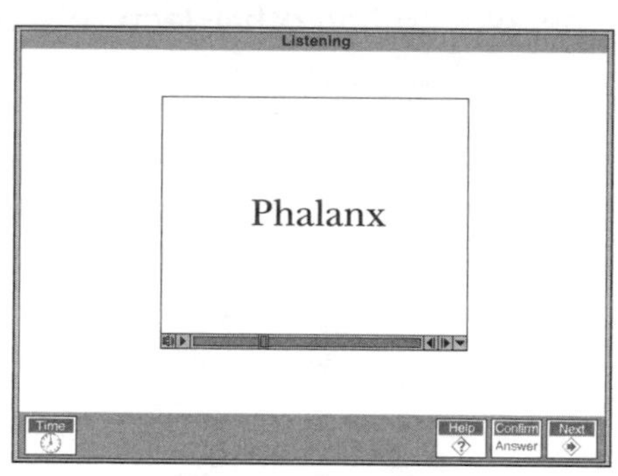

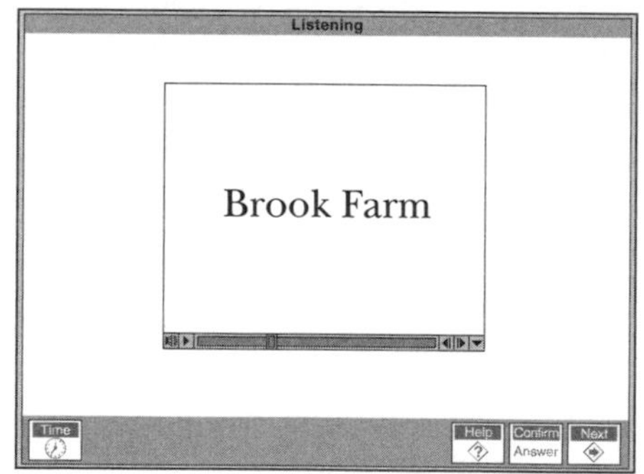

1. What is the discussion mainly about?
   - ⬭ A typical day in the life of a Brook Farm resident
   - ⬭ The Brook Farm Utopian experiment
   - ⬭ Whether or not the students should take the field trip
   - ⬭ Why the Brook Farm experiment failed

2. What is stated in the discussion about Nathaniel Hawthorne?

   Click on 2 answers.

   - ☐ He was a famous American novelist.
   - ☐ He was the most celebrated Brook Farm member.
   - ☐ He lived at Brook Farm in the 1840s.
   - ☐ His house is located in Salem.

3. According to the discussion, which of the following is NOT mentioned as characteristic of the Brook Farm philosophy?
   - ⬭ Literary
   - ⬭ Political
   - ⬭ Social
   - ⬭ Religious

4. What are the numbers of each of the following?

   Click on a number. Then click on the empty box in the correct column. Use each number only once.

a phalanx	Brook Farm's acreage	the greatest number of residents
120	1800	200
☐	☐	☐

5. The events which occurred at Brook Farm were discussed. Put them in the correct chronological order.

   Click on a sentence. Then click on the space where it belongs. Use each sentence only once.

   The central building burned down.
   Brook Farm closed.
   Brook Farm incorporated as a phalanx.
   Brook Farm opened.

   1. ☐
   2. ☐
   3. ☐
   4. ☐

Questions 6–10

Listen to a discussion in an engineering class. The discussion is on windmills.

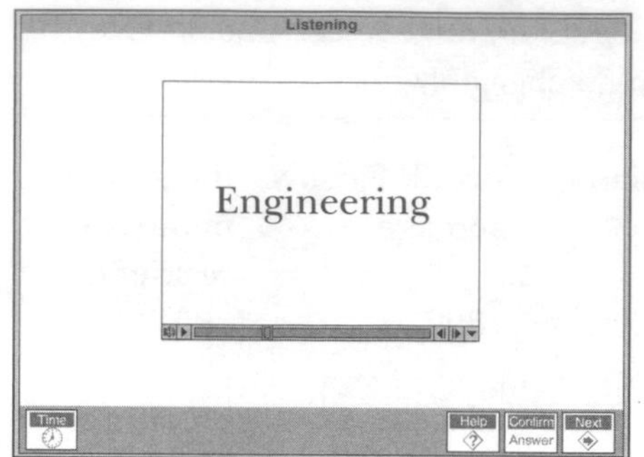

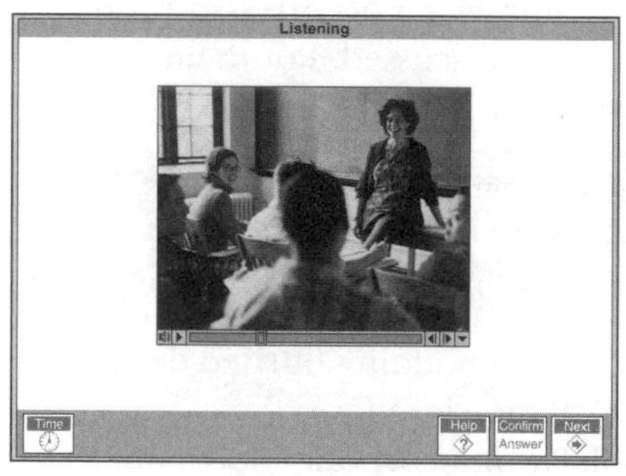

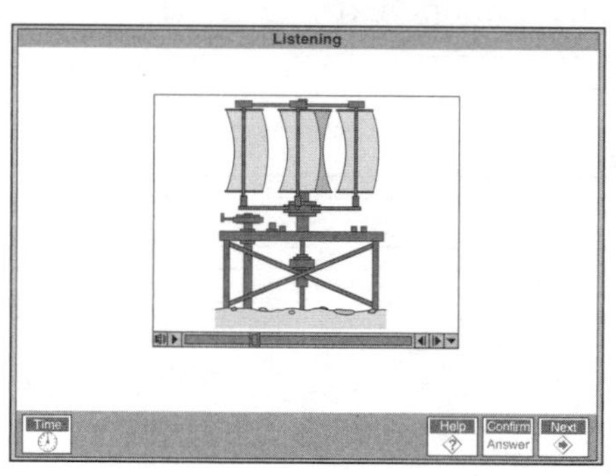

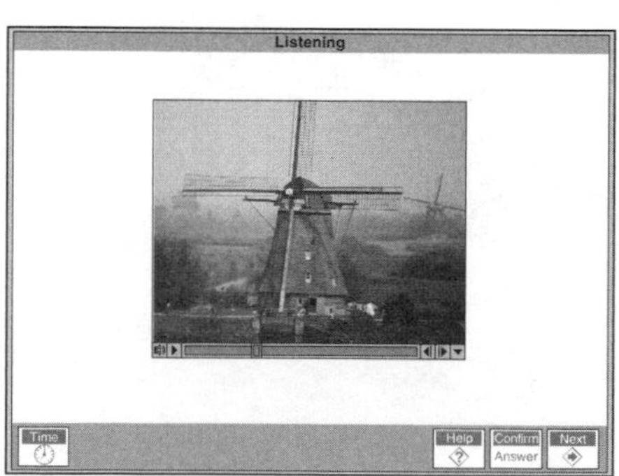

6. What does the professor mainly talk about?

   ⬭ The arguments for using wind power as a primary energy source
   ⬭ The evolution of windmills
   ⬭ The development of wind turbines
   ⬭ An explanation of wind power

7. Identify which picture represents a Dutch windmill.

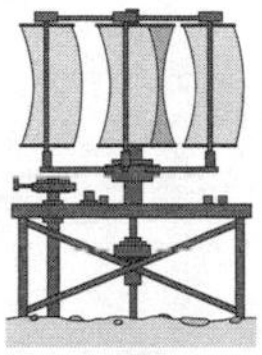

8. Based on the professor's description, classify each of the following descriptions.

   Click on a word or phrase. Then click on the box where it belongs.

Iranian windmills	**Dutch windmills**	**American windmills**
four long arms	sails	curved blades of wood or steel

9. The professor explains the order in which countries developed windmills. Put these countries in their historical order, from first to most recent.

   Click on a country. Then click on the space where it belongs. Use each country only one time.

   New Zealand
   U.S.A.
   Iran
   Netherlands

   1.
   2.
   3.
   4.

10. What is the assignment for the next class?

    ⬭ To research the history of windmills
    ⬭ To predict the future of windmills development
    ⬭ To analyze windmill usage where it is most popular
    ⬭ To identify where wind power would be most productive

Questions 11–15

Listen to a discussion about the architect Frank Lloyd Wright.

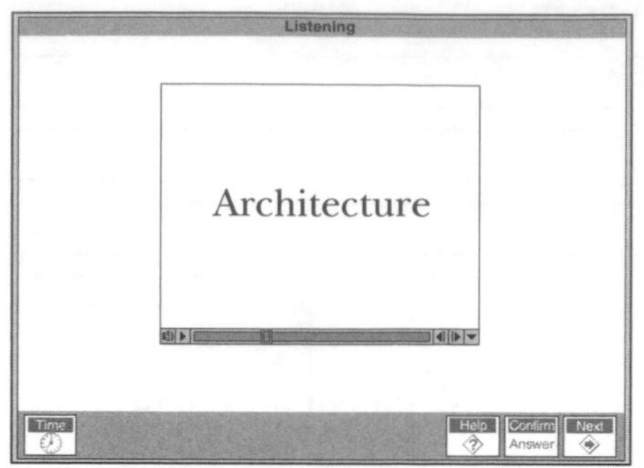

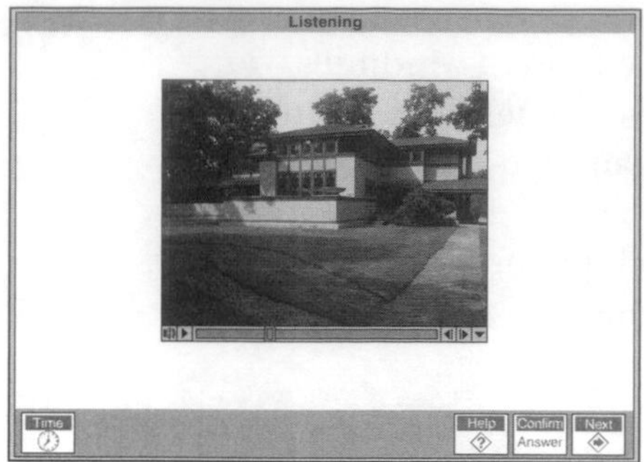

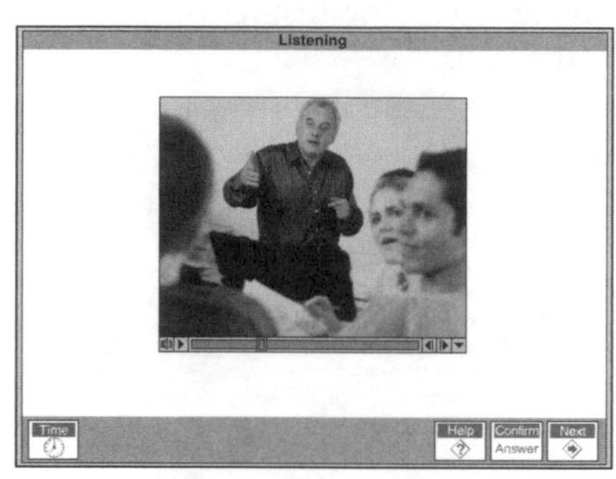

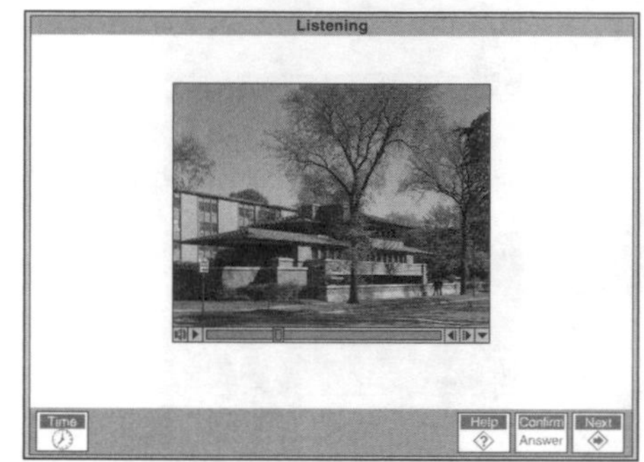

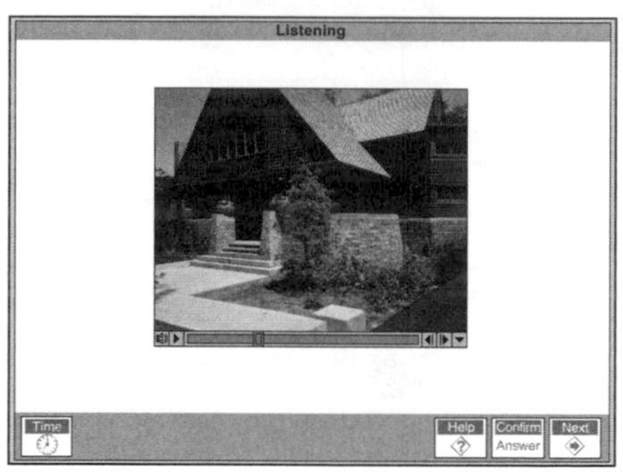

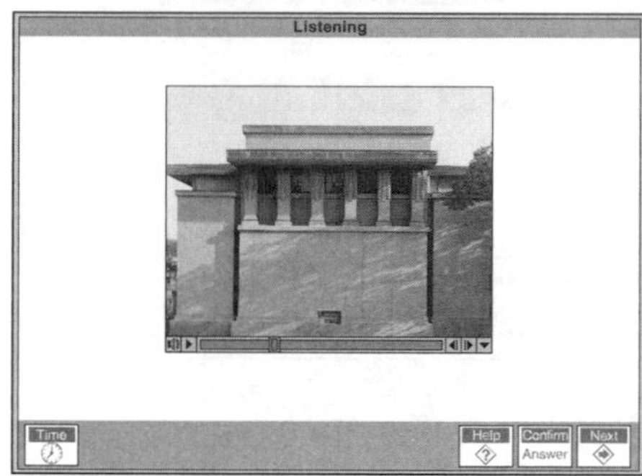

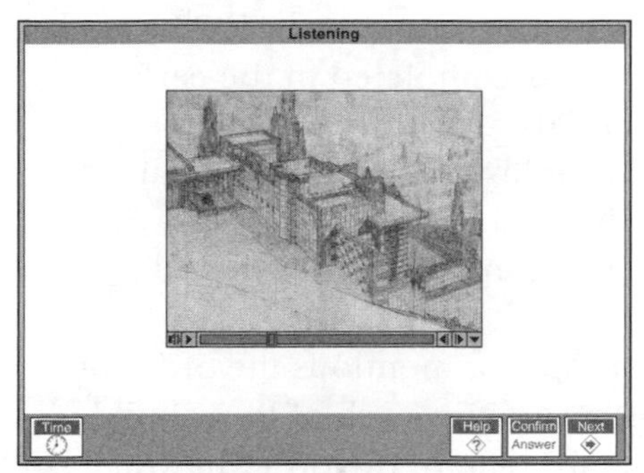
Listening
Time
Help
Confirm
Answer
Next

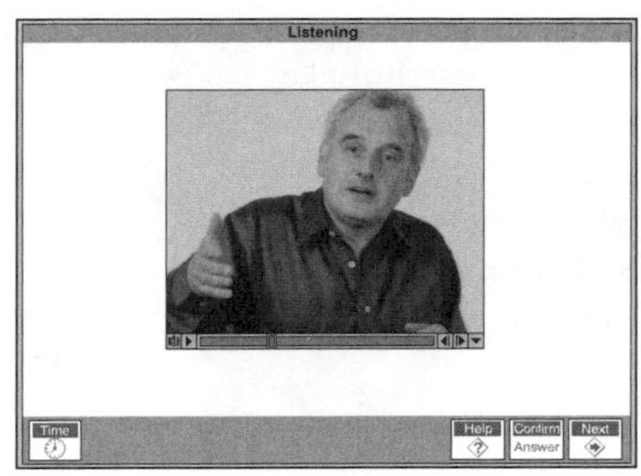
Listening
Time
Help
Confirm
Answer
Next

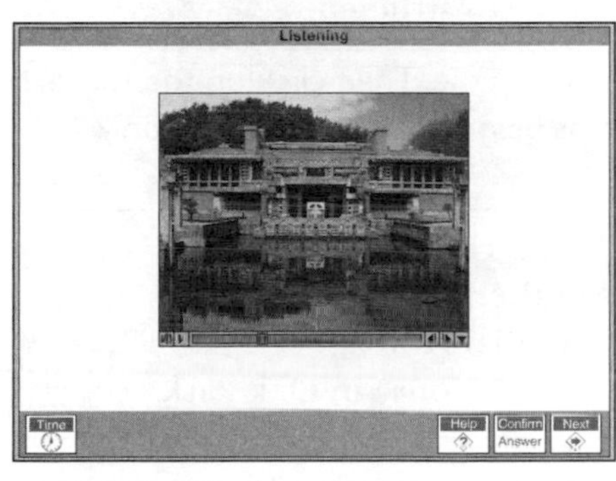
Listening
Time
Help
Confirm
Answer
Next

11. According to the professor, what is characteristic of the Prairie Style?

Click on 2 answers.

☐ It can withstand earthquakes.
☐ The homes seem to grow out of the ground.
☐ It is Wright's first unique style.
☐ Prairie Style homes were built in Southern California.

12. What is characteristic of each of these buildings?

Click on a phrase. Then click on the empty box in the correct column. Use each phrase only once.

Wright's house	**Robie House**	**Unity Temple**
low, horizontal form	shingles and brick	poured concrete
☐	☐	☐

13. What is stated about Southern Californian Wright houses?

Click on 2 answers.

☐ They are made of precast concrete blocks.
☐ There are different block patterns on each house.
☐ The textiles used in furniture design vary.
☐ The concrete is covered with other materials.

14. What is NOT stated about the Imperial Hotel?

⬭ It was severely damaged in the Tokyo earthquake of 1923.
⬭ It was completed in the early 1920s.
⬭ Its lobby was reassembled in Nagoya.
⬭ It is constructed of soft lava.

15. The professor mentions the order of construction for each of these buildings. Put them in the order in which they were constructed.

Click on a name. Then click on the space where it belongs. Use each name only once.

The Robie House
The Southern California houses
The Imperial Hotel
The Wright House in Oak Park

1. ☐
2. ☐
3. ☐
4. ☐

Questions 16–20

Listen to a discussion in an American history class. They are discussing the American flag.

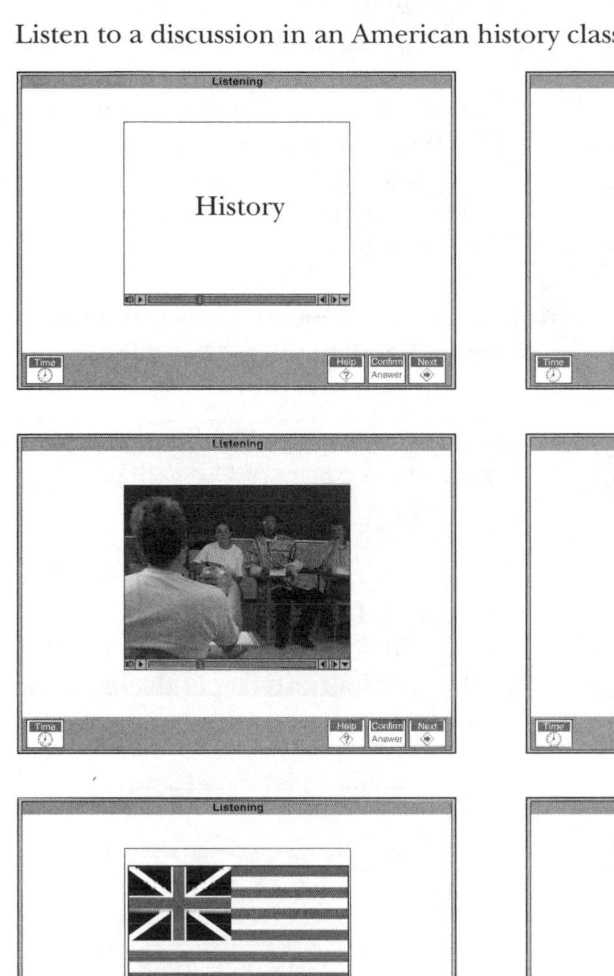

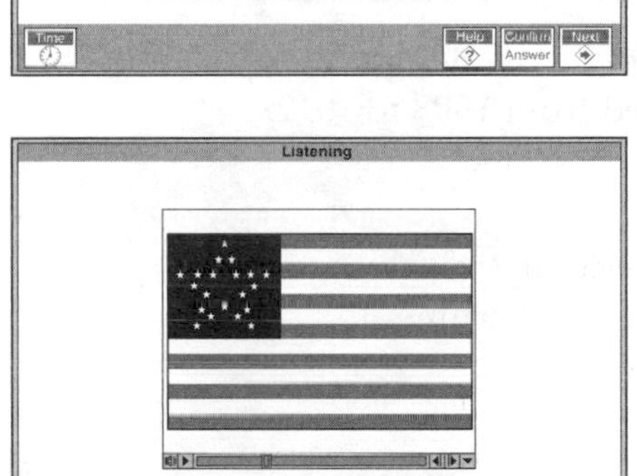

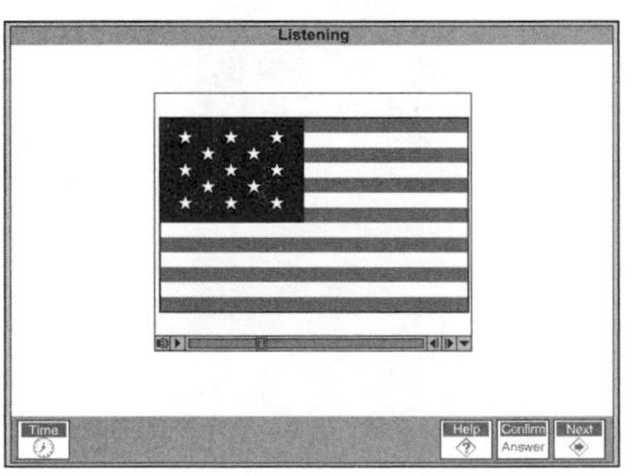

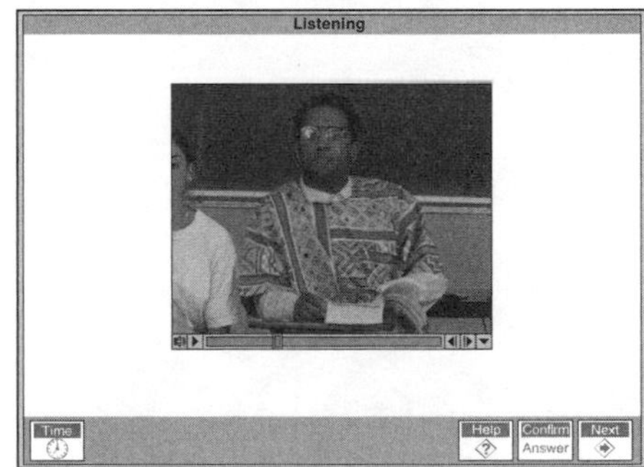

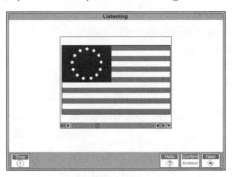

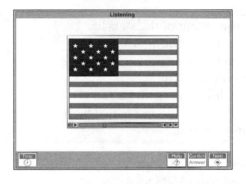

16. What is the discussion mainly about?
    - ⬭ How the *Stars and Stripes* got its name
    - ⬭ The Betsy Ross controversy
    - ⬭ Arranging and rearranging the American flag
    - ⬭ Determining the color choices for the U.S. flag

17. What is stated in the discussion about the American flag?
    - ⬭ During the Civil War the southern states removed their stars from the U.S. flag.
    - ⬭ The positioning of the stars has had numerous configurations.
    - ⬭ At one time there was a star and stripe for each state.
    - ⬭ The original American flag and national anthem were created by the same person.

18. Who decided on the design of the 46-star flag, used from 1908 to 1912?
    - ⬭ The Army and Navy
    - ⬭ The Congress
    - ⬭ The President
    - ⬭ No one in government

19. When does a new star get added to the American flag?
    - ⬭ Once the president gives the order to do so
    - ⬭ When a new state joins the union
    - ⬭ Whenever Congress decides to add a star
    - ⬭ On the July 4 after a state enters the union

20. The professor mentions several different flag configurations. Put these events in their historical order.

Click on a flag design. Then click on the space where it belongs. Use each phrase only once.

A flag with 13 stars in a circle
A flag with 15 stripes
A flag with 20 stars in a five-pointed star
A flag with a British flag in the upper left-hand corner

1. __________
2. __________
3. __________
4. __________

Exercise 13: Lectures

Look at ONLY the words, pictures, and maps as you listen to each lecture. On the test, you will not be able to see the questions or answer choices during the discussion. (See Appendix E, pages 397–400, for a transcript.)

Questions 1–4

Listen to part of a lecture in a biology class.

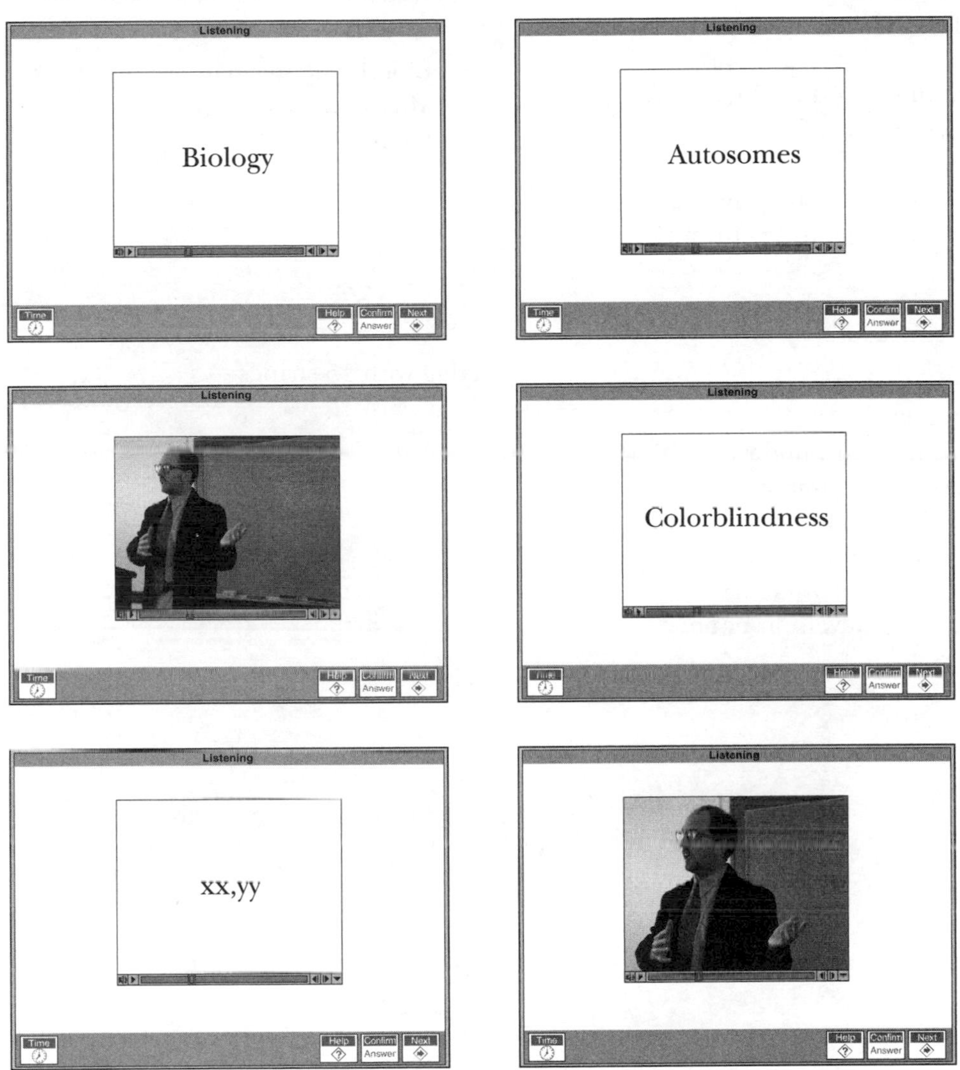

1. What does the professor mainly talk about?
   - ◯ The relation of the sex chromosome to some disorders in men
   - ◯ How the XX and the XY chromosome affect men and women differently
   - ◯ An explanation of why colorblindness is different in men and women
   - ◯ The evolution of the 23 pairs of chromosomes

2. What will happen when mutations occur in one of the regular 22 chromosomes?

   Click on 2 answers.

   - ☐ Men will develop more disorders than women.
   - ☐ Men and women will develop disorders at the same rate.
   - ☐ Women will develop more disorders than men.
   - ☐ Other possible factors may influence the development of disorders.

3. What causes colorblindness?
   - ◯ A mutation on the X chromosome
   - ◯ A cell is missing a gene
   - ◯ Not having two X chromosomes in the 23rd pair
   - ◯ A mutation on the Y chromosome

4. Which of these disorders is NOT mentioned as a disorder linked to the sex chromosome?
   - ◯ Blood type mismatches
   - ◯ Muscular dystrophy
   - ◯ Hemophilia
   - ◯ Colorblindness

Questions 5–9

Listen to part of a lecture in a criminology class.

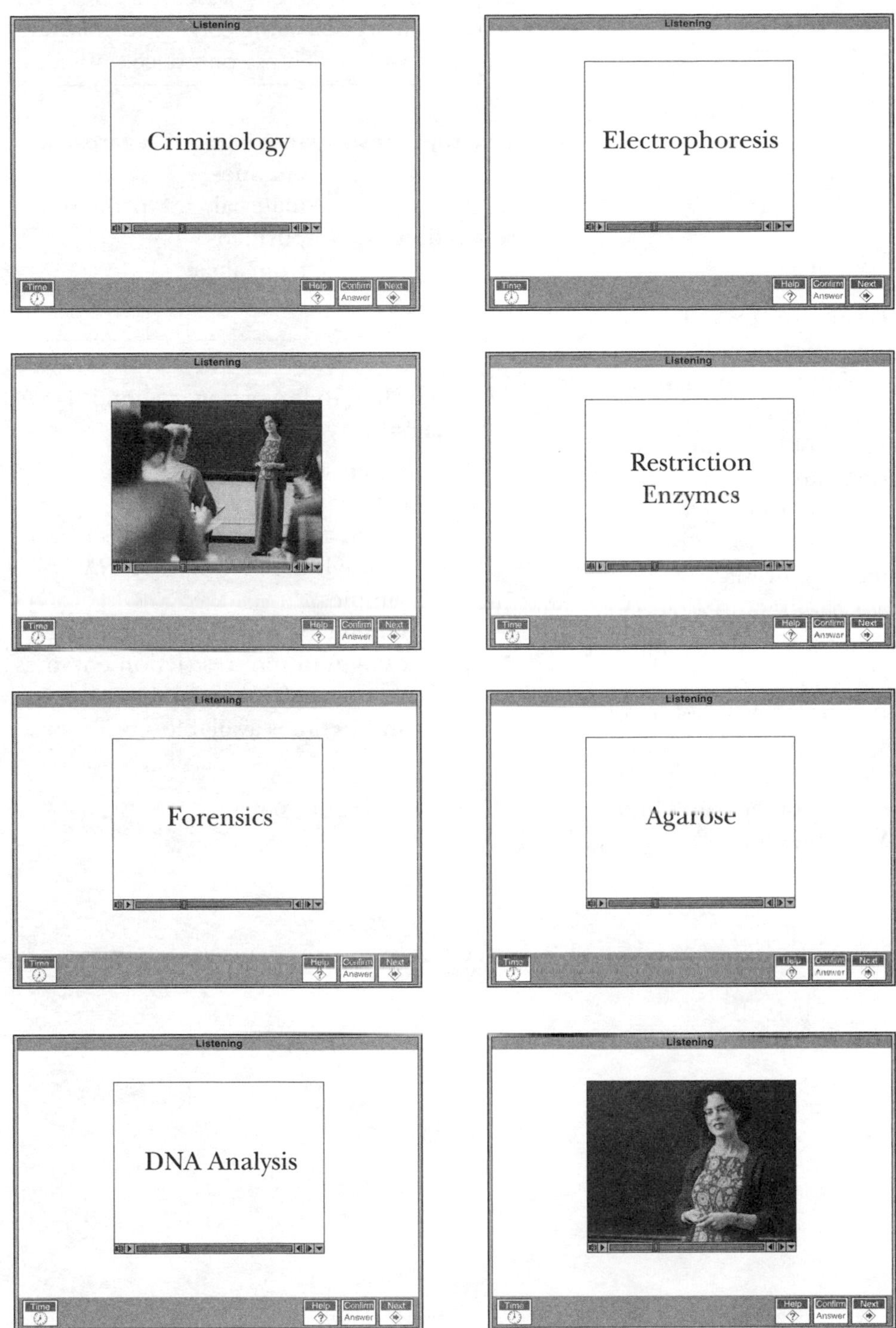

5. What does the professor mainly talk about?

   ⬭ The discovery of DNA
   ⬭ The new tool of forensics
   ⬭ The DNA processes used in crime solving
   ⬭ The limitations of DNA in forensic science

6. What is true about DNA?

   Click on 2 answers.

   ☐ Scientists can use DNA to determine a person's identity.
   ☐ Smaller DNA pieces move more slowly through gel.
   ☐ Several drops of blood are needed to provide a sample.
   ☐ DNA is negatively charged.

7. What is gel electrophoresis?

   ⬭ The use of science and technology
   ⬭ The division of fragments utilizing an electric field
   ⬭ The cutting of DNA samples from both the crime scene and the suspect
   ⬭ Mixing restriction enzymes into the DNA fragments

8. What are the characteristics of each of the following?

   Click on a word or phrase. Then click on the empty box in the correct column. Use each word or phrase only once.

electrophoresis	**restriction enzymes**	**agarose**
fragment separation	material purified from algae	proteins
☐	☐	☐

9. According to the passage, when is DNA analysis very accurate?

   ⬭ When scientists and police collaborate
   ⬭ When an electric current is run through the cuttings of DNA samples
   ⬭ When electrophoresis is repeated using different restriction enzymes
   ⬭ When the DNA from the suspect and victim is available

Questions 10–14

Listen to part of a lecture in a meteorology class. The professor is talking about the El Niño weather pattern.

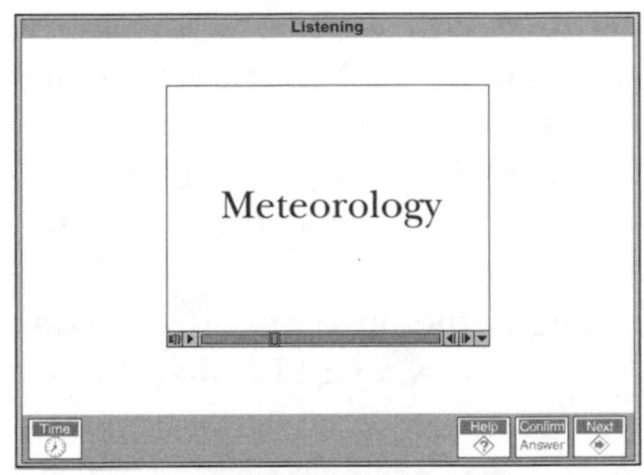

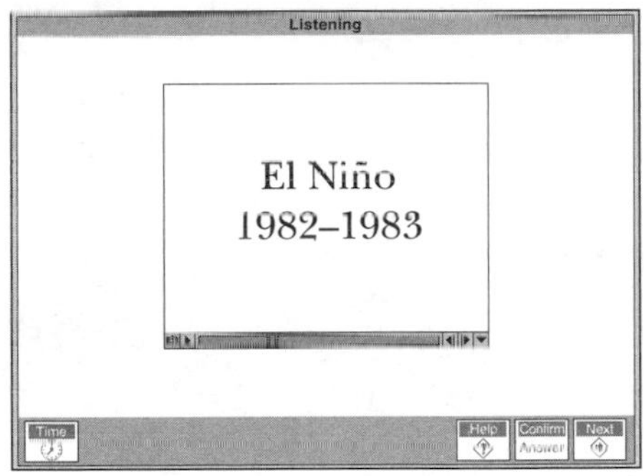

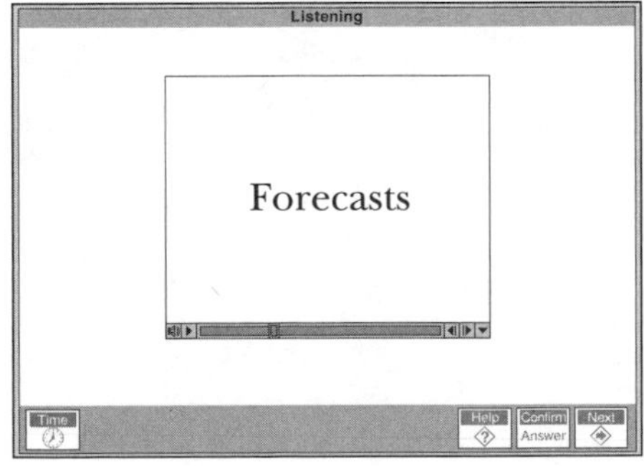

10. What does the professor mainly talk about?

- ⬭ Forecasting El Niño
- ⬭ Crops in Northern Peru
- ⬭ Statistical forecasting
- ⬭ How El Niño got its name

11. What does the term El Niño mean to-day?

- ⬭ The dropping of sea surface temperatures
- ⬭ Periods of warm weather coupled with much rain
- ⬭ Flooding preceded by draughts
- ⬭ The Christmastime season

12. What is true about Peruvian El Niño forecasts since the 1983–1984 season?

- ⬭ Forecasts are based on wind observations and water temperatures.
- ⬭ Forecasts have enabled maximization of overall yields.
- ⬭ Forecasts are completed each year in November.
- ⬭ Forecasts use previous years as models.

13. Which of the following have the highest probability of occurring according to forecasts?

- ⬭ Cooler than normal waters offshore, with higher than normal chance of drought
- ⬭ A full blown El Niño with flooding
- ⬭ Near normal conditions
- ⬭ A weak El Niño with a slightly wetter than normal growing season

14. According to the professor, what might Peruvian farmers do if El Niño is fore-cast?

- ⬭ Delay the sowing of crops until May or even June
- ⬭ Plant more rice and less cotton
- ⬭ Decide on alternative crops to sow
- ⬭ Plant more cotton and less rice

Questions 15–19

Listen to part of a lecture in an anatomy class. The professor is discussing the left-brained, right-brained theory.

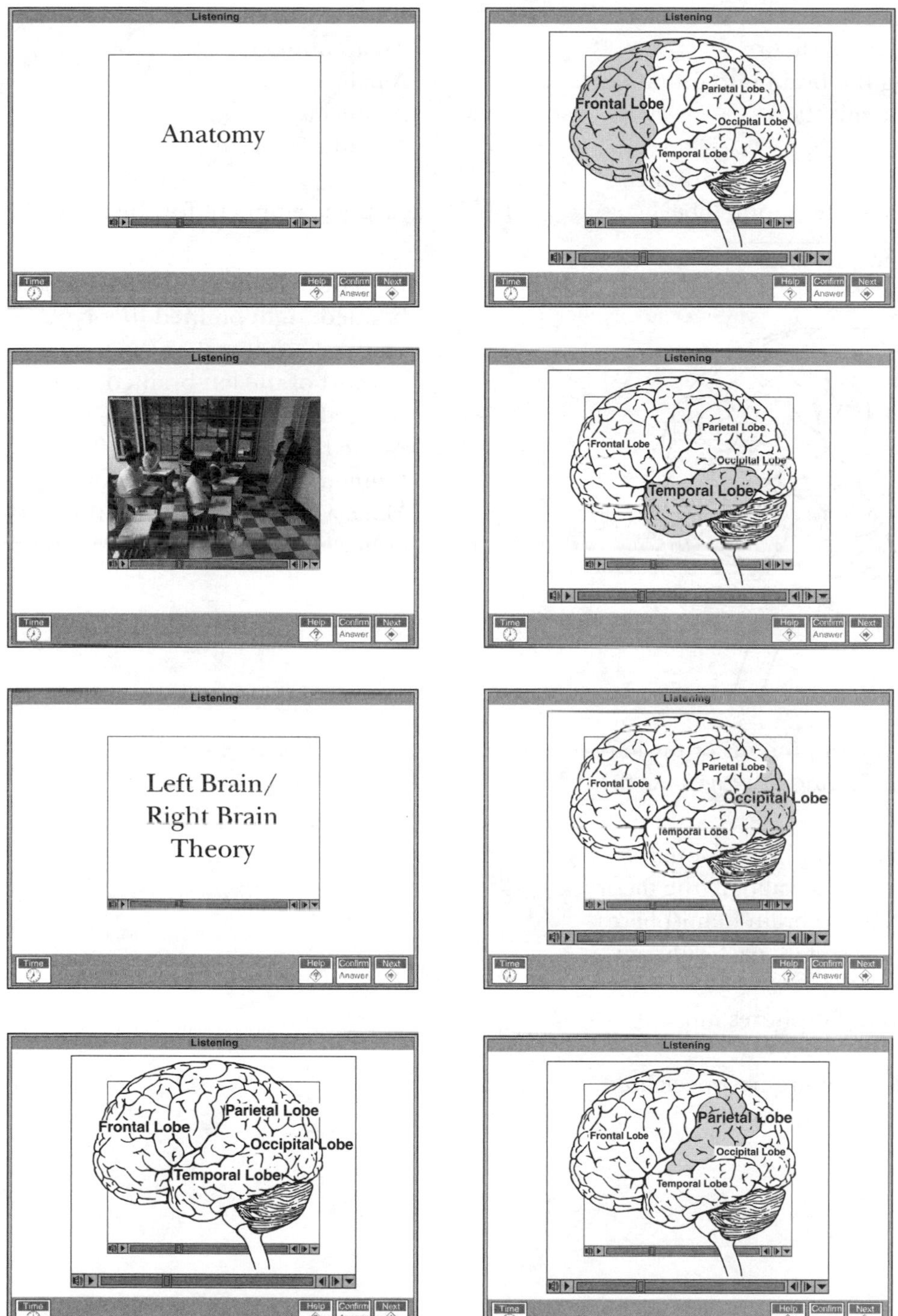

15. What is the lecture mainly about?
   - ⬭ Defining which functions are right or left brained
   - ⬭ The functions of the four brain lobes
   - ⬭ Demythologizing the left-brained, right-brained theory
   - ⬭ Dividing the brain into four lobes or two hemispheres

16. Which of the following parts of the illustration is the temporal lobe?

   Click on the correct letter.

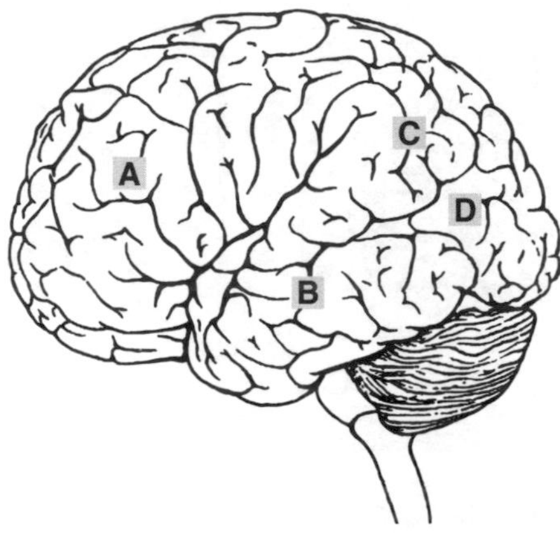

17. On what do the opponents of the left-brained, right-brained theory base their arguments?
   - ⬭ There have not been enough experiments to validate the theory.
   - ⬭ When the two brain hemispheres are disconnected, each side can still function.
   - ⬭ The two hemispheres must integrate activities.
   - ⬭ Each hemisphere has specialized and unique functions.

18. According to the left-brained, right-brained theorists, which of the following professions would be considered left-brained?

   Click on 2 answers.

   - ☐ An accountant
   - ☐ A painter
   - ☐ A dancer
   - ☐ A mathematician

19. What is the assignment for the next class?
   - ⬭ Prepare arguments against the left-brained, right-brained theory
   - ⬭ Find experimental or theoretical support of the left-brained, right-brained theory
   - ⬭ Argue for or against the left-brained, right-brained theory
   - ⬭ Make a list of occupations that are either left-brained or right-brained

LISTENING POST-TEST

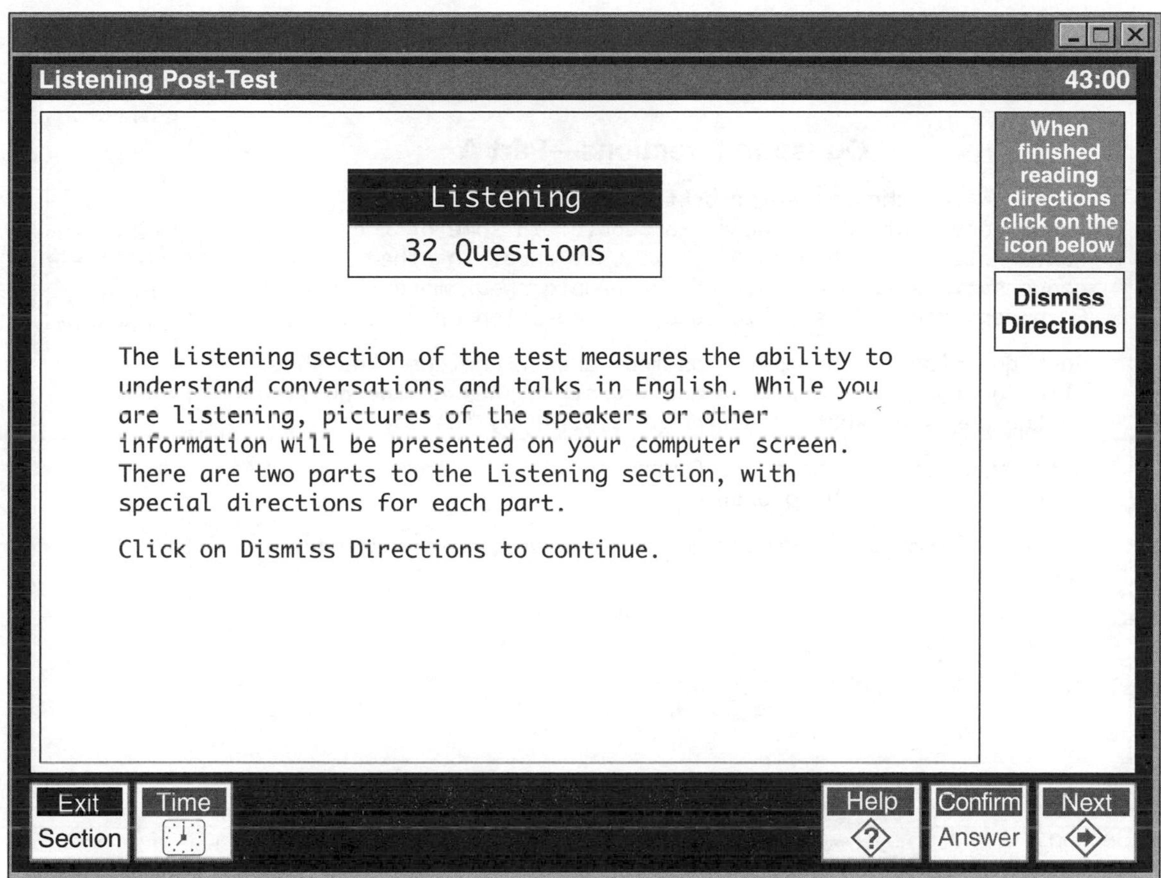

Listening Post-Test
43:00
Listening
32 Questions
The Listening section of the test measures the ability to understand conversations and talks in English. While you are listening, pictures of the speakers or other information will be presented on your computer screen. There are two parts to the Listening section, with special directions for each part.
Click on Dismiss Directions to continue.
When finished reading directions click on the icon below
Dismiss Directions
Exit Section
Time
Help
Confirm Answer
Next

See Appendix E, pages 400–403, for the transcript of the audio passages for this Post-Test.

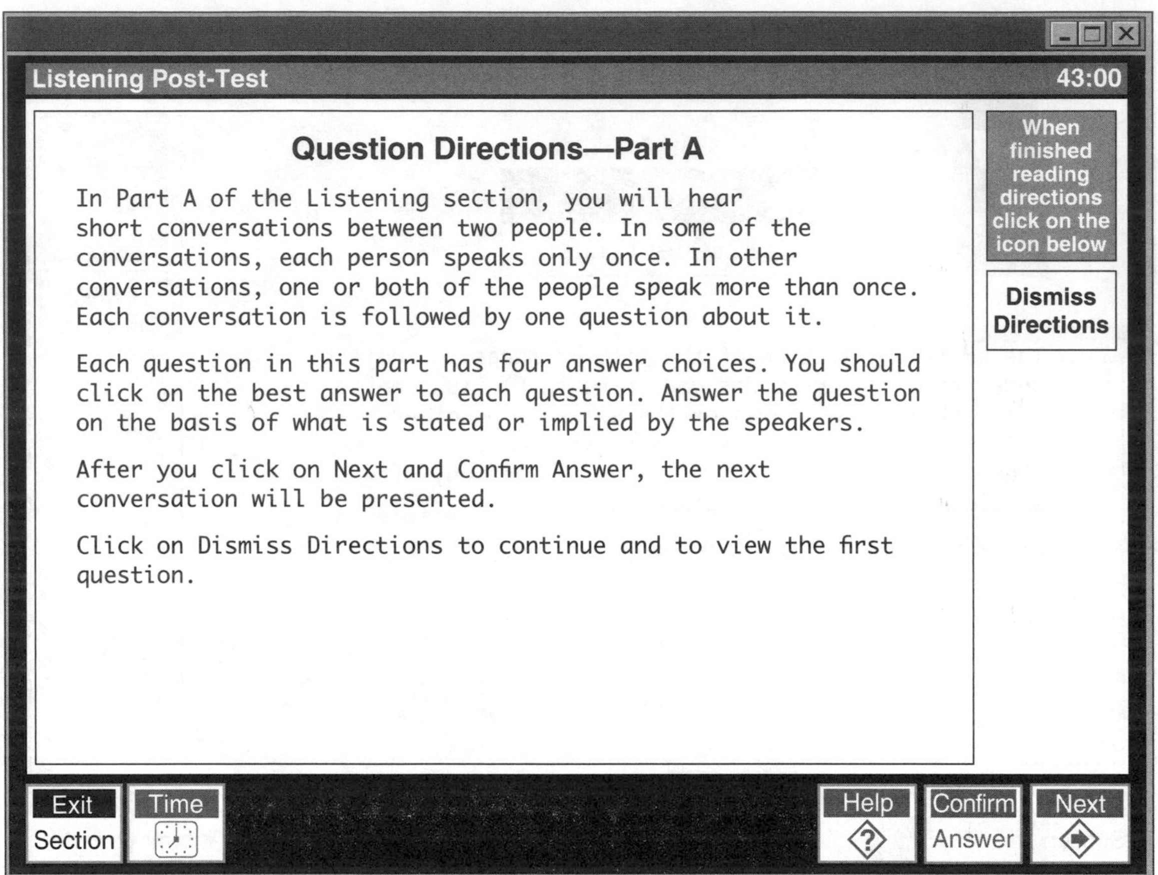
Listening Post-Test
43:00
Question Directions—Part A
In Part A of the Listening section, you will hear short conversations between two people. In some of the conversations, each person speaks only once. In other conversations, one or both of the people speak more than once. Each conversation is followed by one question about it.
Each question in this part has four answer choices. You should click on the best answer to each question. Answer the question on the basis of what is stated or implied by the speakers.
After you click on Next and Confirm Answer, the next conversation will be presented.
Click on Dismiss Directions to continue and to view the first question.
When finished reading directions click on the icon below
Dismiss Directions
Exit Section
Time
Help
Confirm Answer
Next

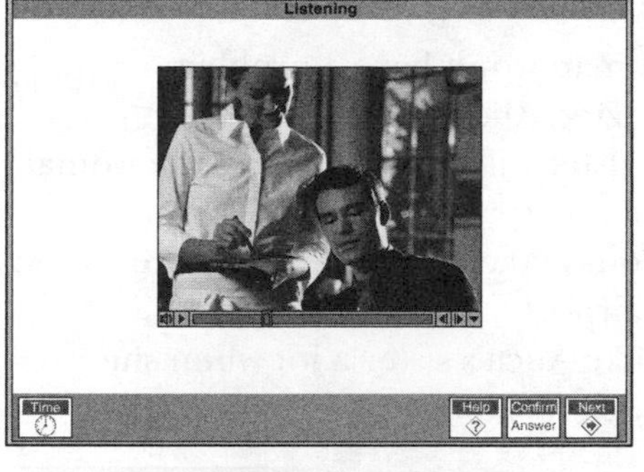

1. What will the man probably do?
   - Order the cheesecake
   - Order both desserts
   - Skip dessert after all
   - Get his car out of the alley

2. What does the man mean?
   - The computer store blew up.
   - He got the printer for a good price.
   - He never shops downtown.
   - The computer store sold all its printers.

3. What does the man mean?
   - He'll share the driving with the woman.
   - It'll be a treat to go with her.
   - He'll go with her if it'll be cheap.
   - He'll give her money for gas.

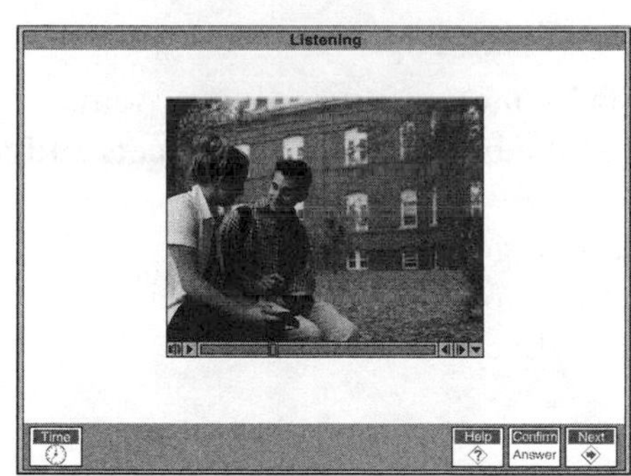

4. What does the man imply?
   - The woman should be in his literature class.
   - The history class has nothing due this week.
   - He has much more work for his literature class.
   - The man didn't do his history assignment.

5. What does the woman imply?
   - It's not her paper, so she can't give it to him.
   - The man should feel free to read the paper.
   - He should wait to see who the paper belongs to.
   - She'll be leaving soon, so he can sit on the chair.

6. What does the man imply?
   - ⬭ The woman won't have a problem recognizing Alice's sister.
   - ⬭ Alice's sister will be looking for the woman in the airport.
   - ⬭ She should take the picture of Alice's sister to the airport.
   - ⬭ She'll like Alice's sister a lot when she meets her.

7. Where does this conversation take place?
   - ⬭ At a swimming pool
   - ⬭ At a movie set
   - ⬭ At a camera shop
   - ⬭ At a movie theater

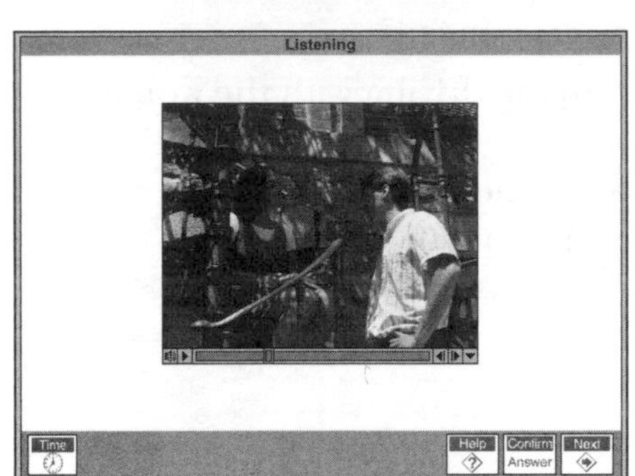

8. What does the man imply?
   - ⬭ He'll be the only one doing the internship.
   - ⬭ He's worried about swimming without a lifeguard.
   - ⬭ He's afraid to be on his own the whole time.
   - ⬭ If he's going to make it, he'll do it by himself.

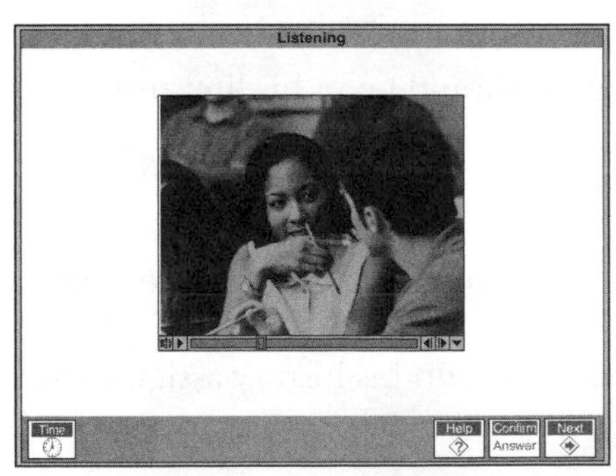

9. What does the woman imply?
   - ⬭ She won't be moving into a dorm room.
   - ⬭ She's glad she brought her own sheets and blankets.
   - ⬭ She'll have to get bedding.
   - ⬭ She wasn't supplied with an adequate number of sheets.

10. What does the man imply?
   - ⬭ Although he didn't get a letter, he'll be taking the assessment.
   - ⬭ He must be a good writer.
   - ⬭ He won't be taking the writing test.
   - ⬭ He's waiting for his letter to arrive.

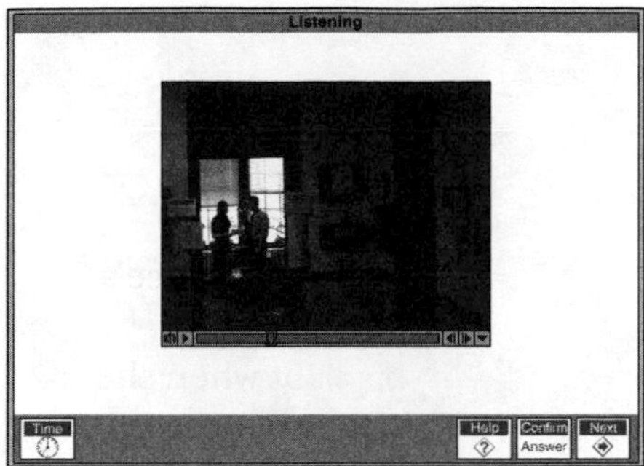

11. What's the man's problem?
    - ⬭ He can't see his application.
    - ⬭ His undergraduate application is incomplete.
    - ⬭ He wants to copy his high school transcript.
    - ⬭ He doesn't know how to get an official record.

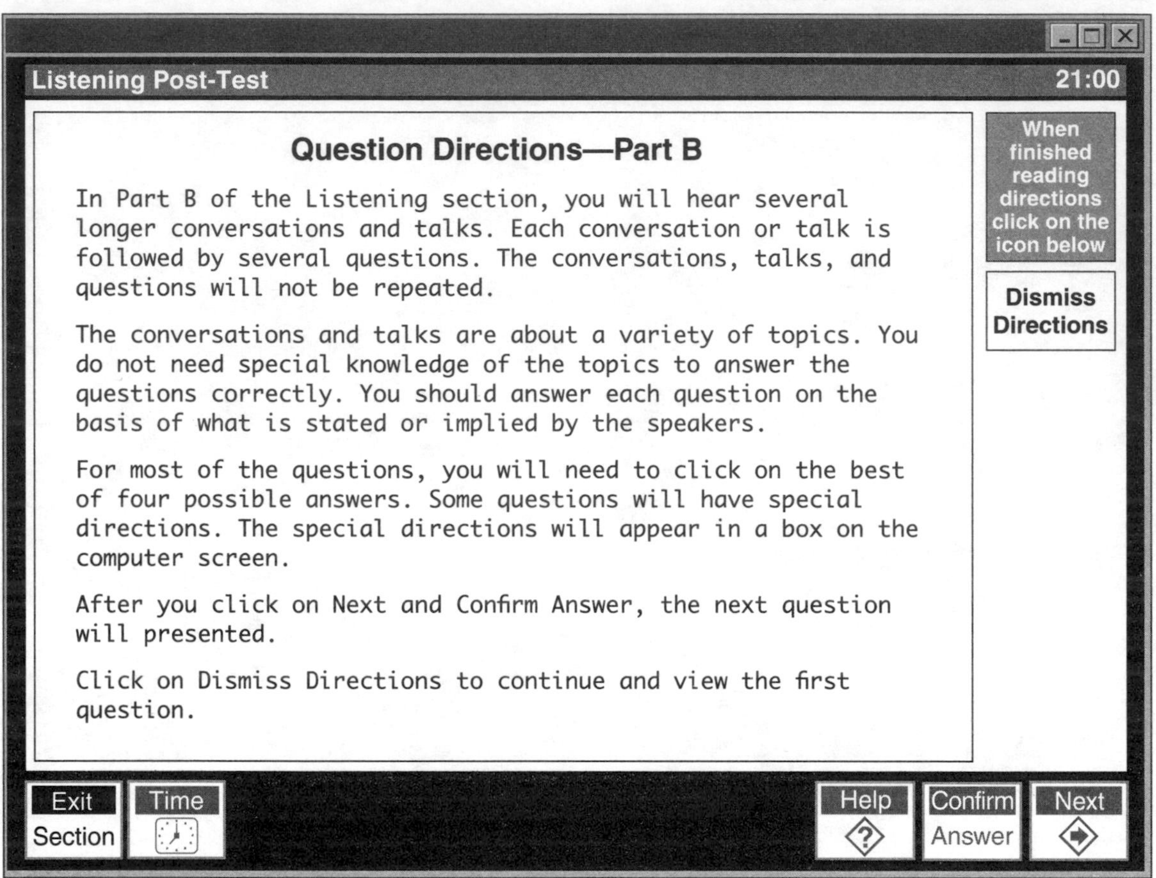
Listening Post-Test

21:00

Question Directions—Part B

In Part B of the Listening section, you will hear several longer conversations and talks. Each conversation or talk is followed by several questions. The conversations, talks, and questions will not be repeated.

The conversations and talks are about a variety of topics. You do not need special knowledge of the topics to answer the questions correctly. You should answer each question on the basis of what is stated or implied by the speakers.

For most of the questions, you will need to click on the best of four possible answers. Some questions will have special directions. The special directions will appear in a box on the computer screen.

After you click on Next and Confirm Answer, the next question will presented.

Click on Dismiss Directions to continue and view the first question.

Questions 12–14

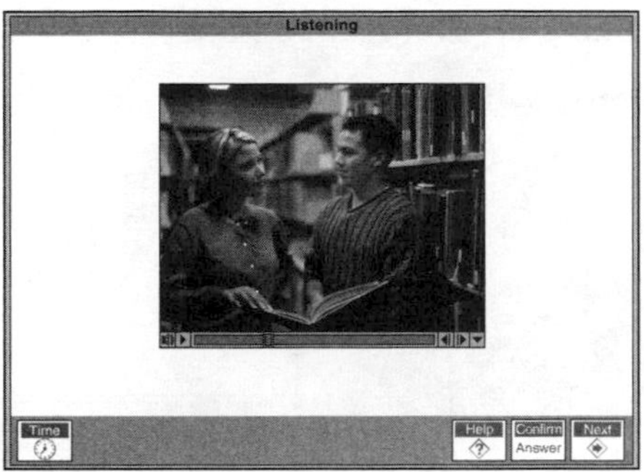

12. What will Charlotte probably do next?
    - Watch the football game on TV
    - Pick up a ticket to the game
    - Ask another student to go with her
    - Play football

13. What can be inferred about Tim?
    - He's been to football games before.
    - He goes to Penn State.
    - He doesn't care who wins the league championship.
    - He works at the stadium.

14. Why does Tim suggest getting to the game early?
    - He wants to hang out with Charlotte.
    - The game might start before 2 o'clock.
    - Charlotte might have trouble getting a ticket.
    - People enjoy themselves at the stadium then.

Questions 15–17

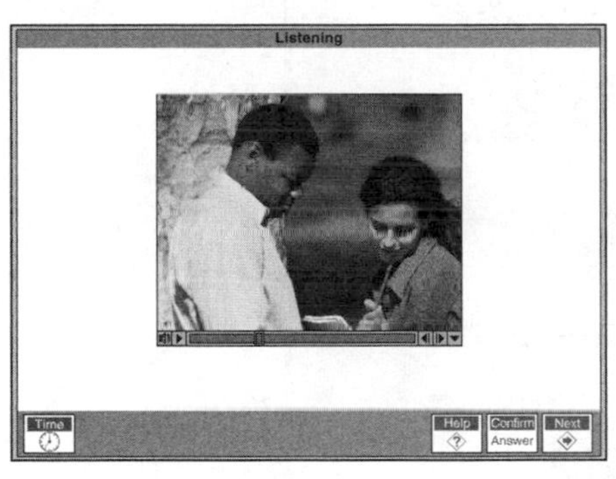

15. Why did Alison do better on the quiz than Craig?
    - Alison is smarter than Craig.
    - Alison is majoring in the subject.
    - Alison has a philosophy tutor.
    - Alison took the class last semester.

16. What is Craig's major?
    - Economics
    - Physics
    - Chemistry
    - Psychology

17. What does Alison advise Craig to do?
    - Drop the class
    - Study harder for the next quiz
    - Get a chemistry tutor
    - Stop by the Academic Success Center

Questions 18–22

Listen to a lecture in an art history class. The professor is talking about Mary Cassatt.

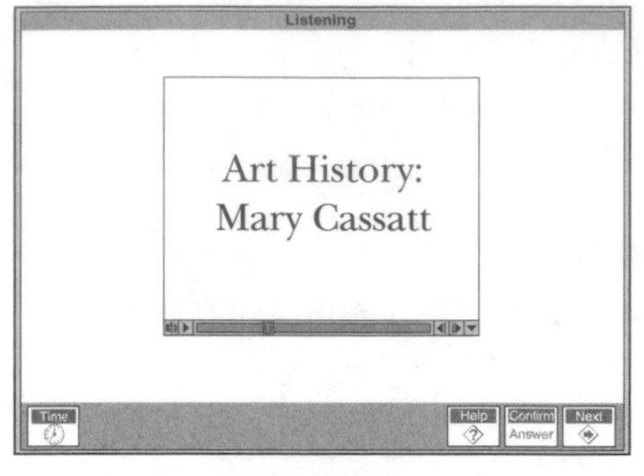

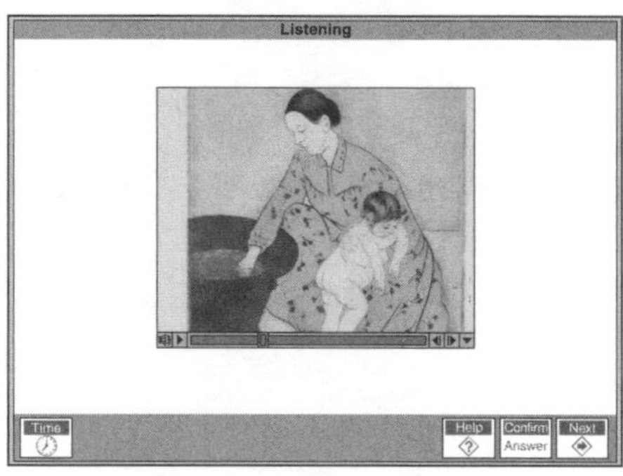

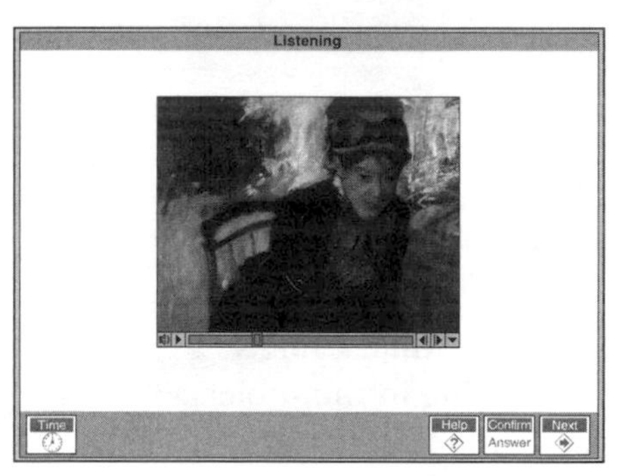

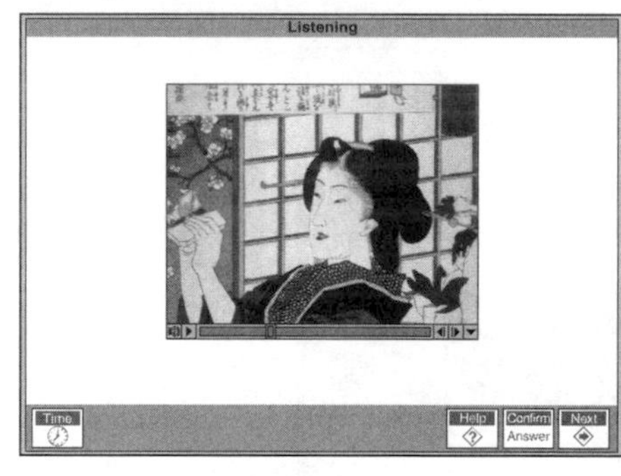

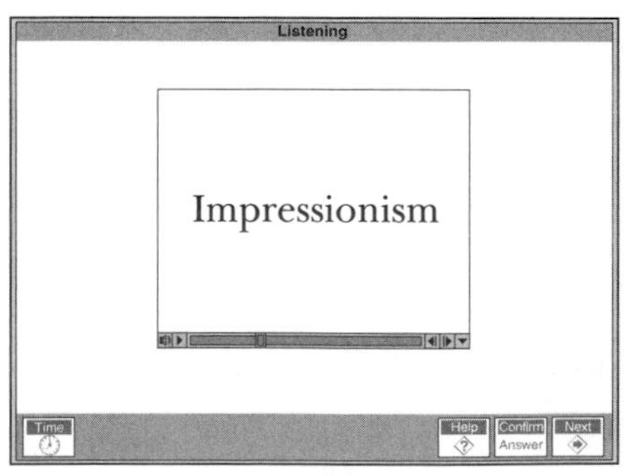

18. What is stated about Mary Cassatt's family?

Click on 2 answers.

- ☐ They were extremely wealthy.
- ☐ They were opposed to her decision to become an artist.
- ☐ They were middle class.
- ☐ They lived in France.

19. When did Mary Cassatt decide to become an artist?

- ○ When she met Impressionist painters in Paris
- ○ When she was traveling in Europe
- ○ When she was at the Pennsylvania Academy of Fine Arts
- ○ When she was still a child

20. What is typical of Impressionist painting?

Click on 2 answers.

- ☐ Invisible brushstrokes
- ☐ Use of dark colors
- ☐ Day-to-day subject matter
- ☐ Use of light colors

21. What kind of people did Mary Cassatt paint?

Click on 2 answers.

- ☐ Other artists
- ☐ Her family
- ☐ People from long before her time
- ☐ The people of her day

22. Which work of art is probably by Mary Cassatt?

Click on a painting.

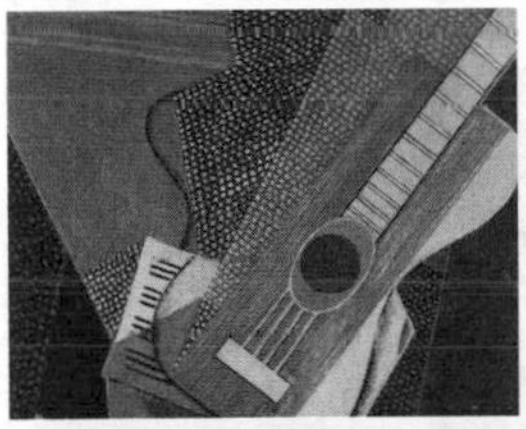

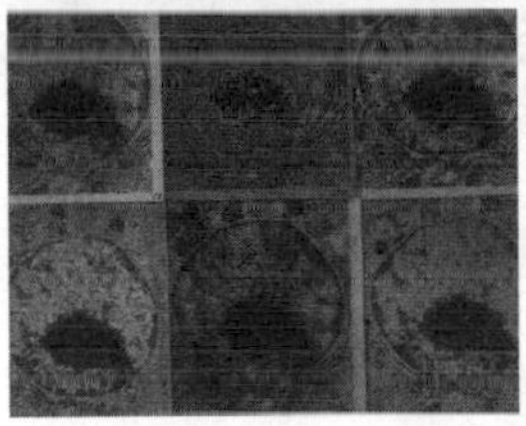

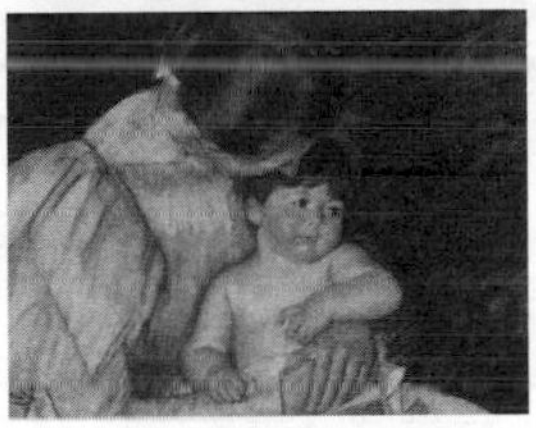

Questions 23–27

Listen to a discussion in a history class. The discussion is about the Great Depression.

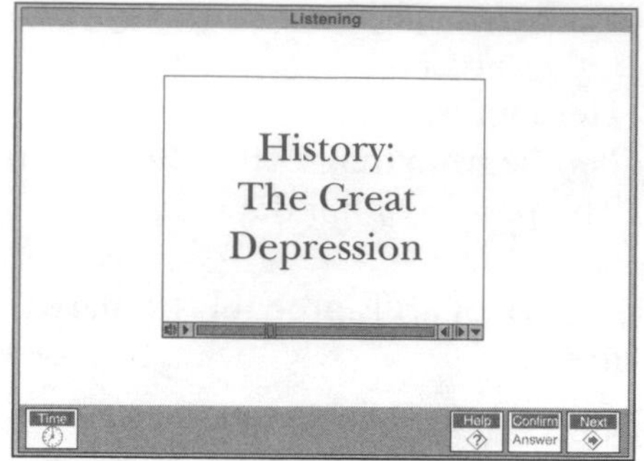

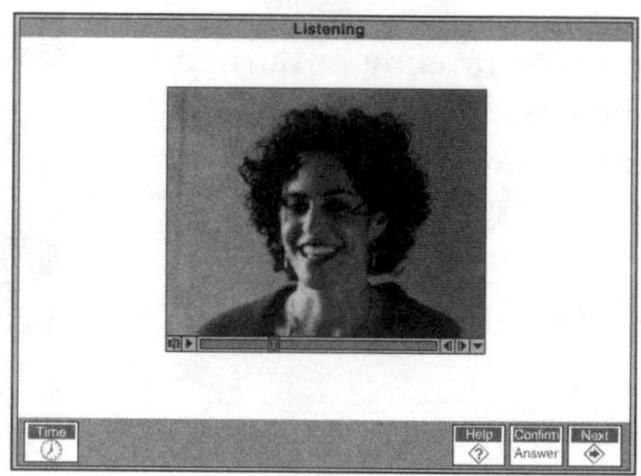

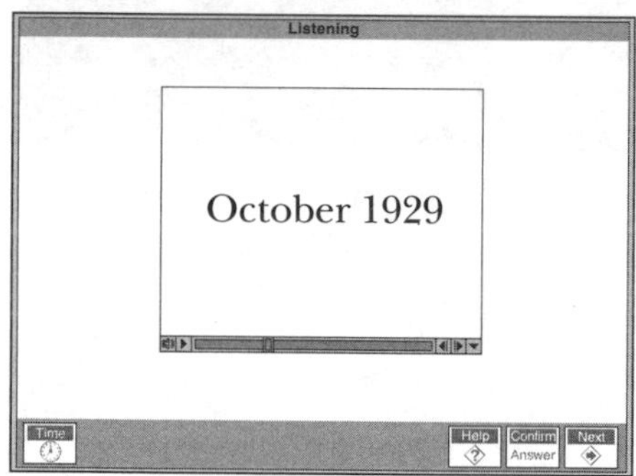

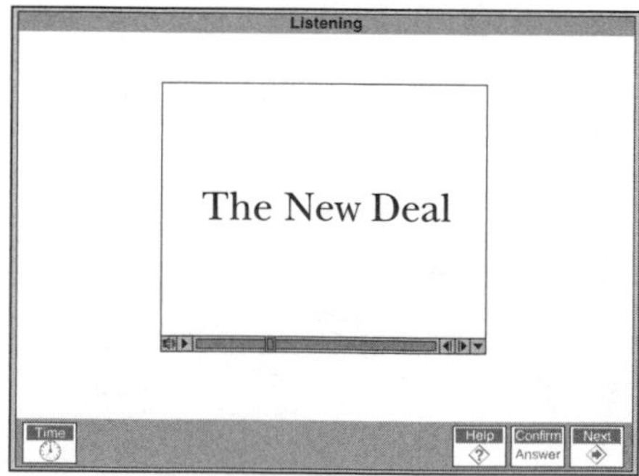

23. What is the assignment for Friday?
    - ◯ To find WPA sponsored projects
    - ◯ To prepare for the quiz
    - ◯ To read pages 35–70
    - ◯ To stay on topic

24. Which of the following is mentioned as being built by the WPA?

    Click on 2 answers.

    - ☐ Golf courses
    - ☐ Art museums
    - ☐ Soup kitchens
    - ☐ A bath house

25. The professor mentions a series of events. Put them in their chronological order.

    Click on a phrase. Then click on the space where it belongs.

    Use each phrase only once.

    Election of Franklin Delano Roosevelt
    Great Depression
    Stock market crash
    Establishment of Works Project Administration

    1. ______
    2. ______
    3. ______
    4. ______

26. According to the professor, what were the effects of the Great Depression on the American economy?

    Click on 2 answers.

    - ☐ Millions of people were out of work.
    - ☐ New works of art weren't commissioned.
    - ☐ People lost their savings.
    - ☐ Unemployed construction workers produced murals.

27. What are the characteristics of each of these terms?

    Click on a phrase. Then click on the empty box in the correct column. Use each phrase only once.

New Deal	**WPA**	**Black Thursday**
Stock Market crash of Oct. 1929	Plan to help Americans affected by the Depression	Sponsored projects for the unemployed

Questions 28–32

Listen to part of a talk in a genetics class.

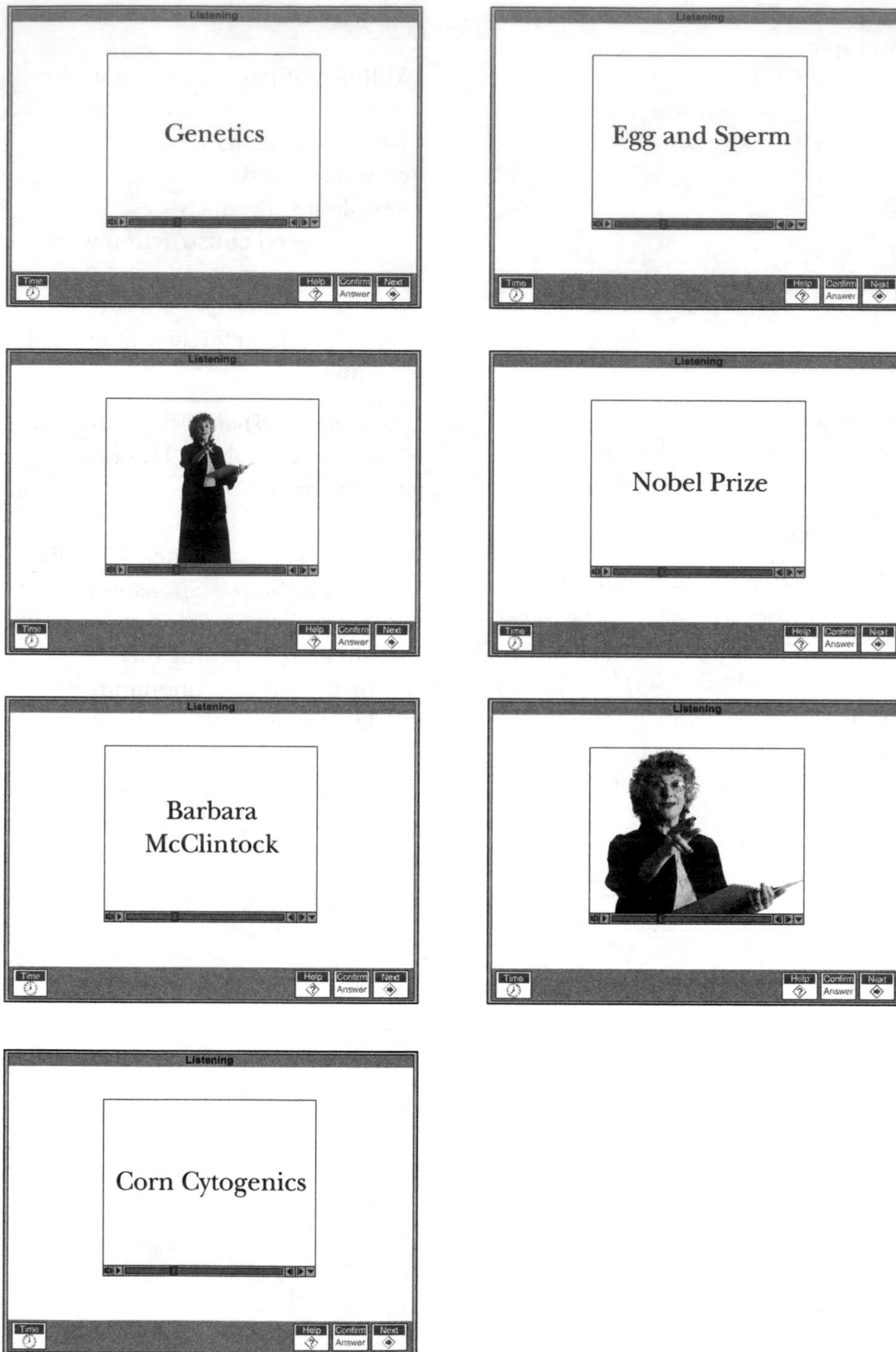

28. What does the professor mainly talk about?
   - ⬭ The great nineteenth-century co-discoverer of radioactivity, Marie Curie
   - ⬭ The discovery of mobile genetic elements
   - ⬭ The unusual properties and gene formation of corn plants
   - ⬭ The lifework and accomplishments of Barbara McClintock

29. What is stated in the lecture about Barbara McClintock?

   Click on 2 answers.

   - ☐ She co-discovered radioactivity.
   - ☐ She decided to become a scientist while in college.
   - ☐ She was the first woman to receive a Nobel Prize.
   - ☐ She pioneered the field of maize cytogenetics.

30. According to the lecture, what did McClintock study?

   Click on 2 answers.

   - ☐ The way corn inherits its traits
   - ☐ How chromosomes break and join together
   - ☐ The existence of DNA
   - ☐ Radioactivity

31. What can be inferred about corn plants?
   - ⬭ Inheritance of traits is unpredictable.
   - ⬭ The number of gene combinations is constant.
   - ⬭ The mobile gene's location on a chromosome can vary.
   - ⬭ Mobile genes do not affect nearby genes.

32. The professor discusses a series of events. Put the events in their chronological order.

   Click on a sentence. Then click on the space where it belongs. Use each sentence only once.

   McClintock receives the Nobel Prize.
   McClintock attends Cornell University.
   McClintock announces her discovery of mobile genetic elements.
   McClintock shows that chromosomes can break and join together differently.

   1. ☐
   2. ☐
   3. ☐
   4. ☐

SECTION TWO

STRUCTURE AND WRITING THE ESSAY

STRUCTURE PRE-TEST

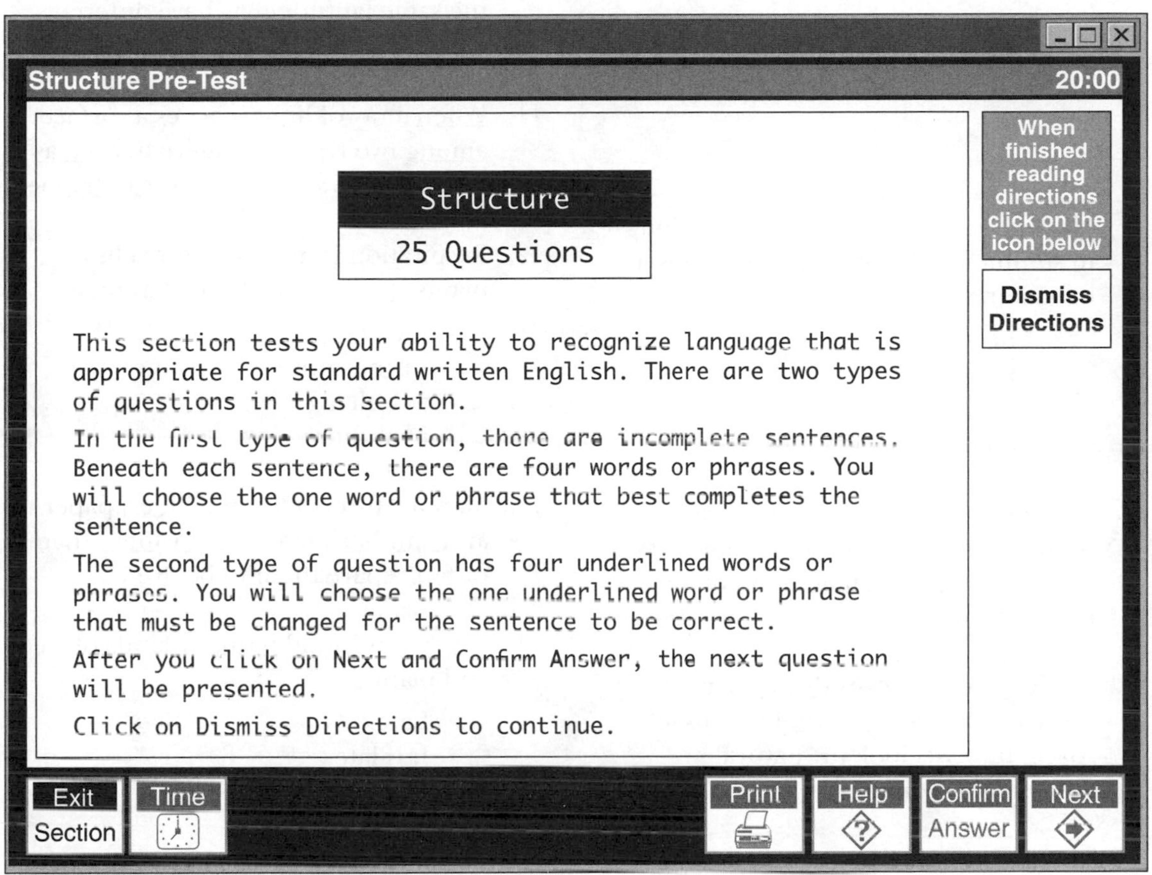

1. Much retired people move to Miami from other parts of the United States because of the healthful climate of southeastern Florida.

2. Until the ninth century, written words were not actually separated, _____ in some literary writing, dots or points were used to indicate divisions.

   - ◯ in spite of
   - ◯ contrary
   - ◯ contrast to
   - ◯ but

3. _____ 1830s, the working day in Lowell, Massachusetts, was thirteen hours long in summer and from sunrise to sunset in winter.

   - ◯ The
   - ◯ In the
   - ◯ It was in the
   - ◯ When in the

4. A letter of credit is issued by a bank, permitting an individual or a business firm drawing up a stated amount of money from that bank.

5. While some scientists drafts plans for intricate vehicles to carry humans to space, futurists look to "natural" spaceships—comets.

6. The ostrich is ________ of all living birds.

   - ◯ the largest
   - ◯ the largest that is
   - ◯ the larger
   - ◯ larger than

7. The Mormons built both a thriving city, Salt Lake City, or an efficient irrigation system with which they made the desert bloom.

8. Jerusalem artichokes are ________ in the production of levulose sugars, which people with diabetes can eat.

   - ◯ special value
   - ◯ of a value especially
   - ◯ especially valuable
   - ◯ valuably especially

9. Cotton has been one of the most usefulest materials for more than five thousand years.

10. Despite of the importance of latitude in determining climate, two places at the same latitude may have different climates.

11. When a ray of light reaches a surface among two types of materials, such as air and gold, several things can happen.

12. Respiration is necessary for cells of plants _______ for those of animals.

    - ◯ including
    - ◯ furthermore
    - ◯ as well as
    - ◯ in addition

13. Manufacturers bleach textiles, paper, and another materials to whiten them or to prepare them to be dyed.

14. _______ is found in many kinds of trees and plants.

    - ◯ Latex
    - ◯ It is latex
    - ◯ Since latex
    - ◯ That latex

15. People who enjoy collecting rocks and minerals as a hobby _________ rock hounds.

    - ◯ themselves call
    - ◯ called
    - ◯ call themselves
    - ◯ they are called

16. Nancy Kassebaum was the first woman elected to a full term in the United States Senate ___________ her husband in either the Senate or the House of Representatives.

    - ◯ who succeeded
    - ◯ succeeded
    - ◯ who was succeeded
    - ◯ she didn't succeed

17. The largest silver nugget ever finding in North America was discovered in Aspen, Colorado, in 1894.

18. With long slender legs, necks, and bills, both the male and female crane are looking like their young.

19. Although most people wear contact lenses because they believe they do not look good in glasses.

20. The fine furniture early Shaker communities produced _________ after today as collectors' items.

- ⬭ are highly sought
- ⬭ is highly seeking
- ⬭ are highly seeking
- ⬭ is highly sought

21. In order to fly, honey bees must to maintain their flight muscles at a temperature of at least 30 degrees Celsius.

22. Francis Cabot Lowell, an American textile manufacturer, founded the first mill that carried through the entirety cotton-manufacturing process from raw material to finished cloth.

23. The New Frontier, _________, got off to a slow start.

- ⬭ the name of the program which John F. Kennedy gave
- ⬭ the name John F. Kennedy gave to his program
- ⬭ John F. Kennedy named his program
- ⬭ while the program named by John F. Kennedy

24. ___________ in the United States Senate, regardless of population, is equally represented.

- ⬭ Each state
- ⬭ Where each state
- ⬭ Each state that is
- ⬭ For each state

25. Chain stores can save money by sharing operational costs in such areas as accountant and advertising.

STRUCTURE

This section measures your ability to recognize language that is appropriate for standard written English. The Structure section of the test is **computer adaptive**. This means that the first question you see will be of medium difficulty. If you get this question correct, the next question will be harder. If you get this question wrong, the next question will be easier. All students have approximately the same number of questions.

THE STRUCTURE QUESTIONS

Two types of questions in this section are presented interchangeably: sentence completion questions and error identification questions.

Sentence Completion Questions

In approximately half of the questions, there are sentences to complete. In this book, these are referred to as sentence completion questions. Beneath each sentence are four words or phrases. You choose the correct word or phrase.

EXAMPLE:

Click on the one word or phrase that best completes the sentence.

___________ made after English settlers came to Jamestown was a map of Virginia by John Smith, the famous adventurer.

- ⬭ The first map
- ⬭ It was the first map
- ⬭ That the first map
- ⬭ There was a first map

Clicking on a choice darkens the oval. The correct answer is shown below.

> ____________ made after English settlers came to Jamestown was a map of Virginia by John Smith, the famous adventurer.
>
> ● The first map
> ○ It was the first map
> ○ That the first map
> ○ There was a first map

After you click NEXT and CONFIRM ANSWER, the next question will be presented.

Error Identification Questions

In approximately half of the questions, sentences have four underlined words or phrases. In this book, these are referred to as error identification questions. You choose the one underlined word or phrase that is **incorrect** and must be changed for the sentence to be correct.

EXAMPLE:

Click the one underlined word or phrase that must be changed for the sentence to be correct.

> Since the 1940s, creativity in modern dance has centered on both U.S. dancers or dance companies.

Clicking an underlined word or phrase will darken it. The correct answer is shown below.

The sentence should read: *Since the 1940s, creativity in modern dance has centered on both U.S. dancers and dance companies.*

After you click NEXT and CONFIRM ANSWER, the next question will be presented. **You do NOT need to supply the correct answer.**

- Some grammar points are tested PRIMARILY in sentence completion questions.
- Some grammar points are tested PRIMARILY in error identification questions.
- Some grammar points are tested in BOTH sentence completion questions and error identification questions.

GENERAL STRATEGIES FOR THE STRUCTURE SECTION

1. **Do not spend time reading the directions.** This section is timed. The questions are always of the two types described above.
2. **Press DISMISS DIRECTIONS as soon as you see the icon.** By doing so, you will have more time for the questions. Time starts as soon as you see the directions.
3. **If you do not know the answer to a question, first eliminate any obvious wrong choice before making a guess.**
4. **Always read a question and all the answers completely before you answer it.** Read everything even if you think the first choice is definitely the right one.
5. **Quickly confirm your answer when you are ready to go on to the next question.**
6. **Keep moving.** Don't spend too much time on any one question.
7. **Watch the time bar on the computer screen.** It will tell you how much time you have left, how many questions are in the section, and what number question you are now answering.
8. **Don't answer the remaining questions randomly if you do not have time to finish.** Because this section is computer adaptive, your score will be lower. You cannot skip questions or go back and change answers.
9. **Remember that your essay will count for HALF of the structure score.** The multiple-choice questions will count for the other half.

Structures and Strategies

Questions about the following grammatical structures commonly appear in the Structure section of the TOEFL test. You should become familiar with the rules of these structures and the types of errors that can occur.

1. VERBS

In both the sentence completion questions and the error identification questions, there are many different types of verb errors. As you read a sentence, find the verb and make sure it is in the correct form, tense, and voice.

A. VERB FORMS

Each verb has five forms: **the base form** (the infinitive form without *to*), **the present tense, the present participle, the past tense,** and **the past participle**. We refer to the following forms when we discuss verbs:

BASE FORM	PRESENT TENSE	PRESENT PARTICIPLE	PAST TENSE	PAST PARTICIPLE
go	go(es)	going	went	gone
fly	fly(ies)	flying	flew	flown
teach	teach(es)	teaching	taught	taught
see	see(s)	seeing	saw	seen
look	look(s)	looking	looked	looked

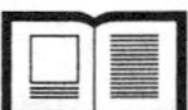

STUDY TIP

Make sure you memorize all of the common irregular verb forms. See Appendix B.

Errors with irregular verb forms appear on the TOEFL test.

EXAMPLES:
Homing pigeons have been know to fly more than one thousand miles in two days.

The correct verb form is *known,* not *know.*

Some art historians have say that too many artists have tried only to imitate previous painting styles.

The correct verb form is *said,* not *say.*

B. VERB TENSES

Make sure you examine a sentence carefully to decide what tense the verb should be. Watch out for time phrases and other verbs in the sentence that will help you determine the tense.

Simple Present Tense

The simple present tense is used in the following situations:

- for a generally known fact: *Water evaporates in the sun.*
- for a state of being: *He is sick today.*
- for a habitual occurrence: *The sun rises in the east.*
- for a scheduled event in the future: *The bus leaves at noon tomorrow.*
- for summaries/explanation of a written text: *Faulkner eloquently describes life in the American South.*

The simple present tense is formed with the base form and agrees with the subject.

Subject	Base Form	
The girl	*writes*	*her parents once a week.*
The girls	*write*	*their parents once a week.*

EXAMPLES:
Stalagmites are produced when water to drop directly to the floor of a cave.

The sentence should read: *Stalagmites are produced when water drops directly to the floor of a cave.* Because the information is factual, the verb should be in the simple present, *drops,* not the infinitive.

A Raisin in the Sun, the highly acclaimed Broadway play by Lorraine Hansberry, dealing with the serious and comic events in the life of a black family in modern America.

The sentence should read: *A Raisin in the Sun, the highly acclaimed Broadway play by Lorraine Hansberry, deals with the serious and comic events in the life of a black family in modern America.* Because the information is factual, the verb should be in the simple present, *deals*, not the present participle.

Simple Past Tense

When there is a specific time or date in the sentence, use the simple past.

EXAMPLES:

Johnny Appleseed was the name given to John Chapman, a pioneer who has planted large numbers of apple trees along the early frontier from 1797 to 1845.

The sentence should read: *Johnny Appleseed was the name given to John Chapman, a pioneer who planted large numbers of apple trees along the early frontier from 1797 to 1845.* Because the specific time is given, *from 1797 to 1845,* the verb should be in the simple past, *planted,* not the present perfect, *has planted.*

During the 1940s, science and engineering had an impact on the way music reaches its audience and even influenced the way in which it was composed.

The sentence should read: *During the 1940s science and engineering had an impact on the way music reached its audience and even influenced the way in which it was composed.* Because the time is *the 1940s,* the verb *reach* should be in the simple past, *reached,* not the present tense, *reaches.*

EXERCISE 1: These questions focus on the simple present and simple past tenses. There are 25 questions, and you have 20 minutes.

1. Abraham Lincoln delivers his most famous address at the dedication of the soldiers' cemetery in Gettysburg in 1863.

2. A narcotic is a substance that was having a strong depressant effect on the human nervous system.

3. Princess Grace of Monaco was a famous American motion-picture actress before she ______ Prince Rainer III of Monaco in 1956.
   - ⬭ marries
   - ⬭ married
   - ⬭ marrying
   - ⬭ has married

4. Typically, ________ in meadows or damp woods and bloom in the spring.
   - ⬭ wild violets grow
   - ⬭ wild violets growth
   - ⬭ growing wild violets
   - ⬭ the growth of wild violets

5. A Norway rat weighed about one pound, and its body is between eight and eighteen inches long.

6. The poet Marianne Moore was initially associated with the imagist movement, but later develops her own rhyme patterns and verse forms.

7. With affection and humor, poet Phyllis McGinley ________ of ordinary life.
   - ⬭ praises the virtues
   - ⬭ the virtues praises
   - ⬭ praising the virtues
   - ⬭ the virtues praised

8. The Jay Treaty, signed in 1794, addressed disputes that _______ between the

United States and Great Britain after the Revolutionary War in America ended.

- arise
- arose
- are arising
- have been arising

9. The barnacle has been described as a shrimplike animal that stands on its head in a limestone house and kicking food into its mouth with its feet.

10. The Hawaiian alphabet, introduced by missionaries in the 1820s, _______ and only seven consonants.

- the five vowels consist of
- consisting of five vowels
- that consisted of five vowels
- consists of five vowels

11. A great aviation pioneer, Amelia Earhart was already famous when she sets out on her ill-fated attempt to circle the globe in 1937.

12. Working like a telescope, ____ the size of objects at great distances.

- which magnifies a telephoto lens
- a telephoto lens magnifies
- a telephoto lens which magnifies
- and magnifying a telephoto lens

13. President Lyndon Johnson _______ as a janitor in the late 1920s to help pay his college expenses.

- will be working
- is working
- works
- worked

14. Sound eaves entering the ear and change into nerve signals that are subsequently sent to the brain.

15. Paul Revere designing the metal plates on which the first paper money in the United States was printed.

16. The early work of Edith Wharton _______ the relationship between the individual and the community.

- focuses attention on
- focusing the attention on
- the attention is focused on
- is the attention and focus

17. When the Civil War has begun in 1861, Mathew Brady felt the conflict must be photographed as completely as possible.

18. Large advertising agencies generally _______ a team of persons from the various departments of the agency to handle all of the advertising for a specific advertiser.

- assigning
- to assign
- assign
- to be assigned

19. Maine _____ more than 5,000 rivers and streams.

- had
- which has
- has
- having

20. Tabby cats to be symmetrically patterned with stripes and blotches of a dark color on a lighter background.

21. Margaret Fuller was not active in the women's rights movement, but she asking for a fair chance for women in her book, *Woman in the Nineteenth Century*.

22. The process of heredity _____ among all living things—human beings, animals, plants, and even bacteria and other microscopic organisms.

- been occurring
- occurring
- occurs
- are occurring

23. The flow <u>of</u> electricity <u>through</u> metals, alloys, and <u>other</u> conductors <u>generated</u> heat.

24. General Douglas MacArthur ____ the Inchon landing, a surprise move that turned the tide of war in the Allies' favor in September, 1950.
    - ⬭ lead
    - ⬭ led
    - ⬭ had led
    - ⬭ is leading

25. Since the consumer <u>considers</u> the best fruit to be that which is the most attractive, the grower <u>must provide</u> products that <u>satisfying</u> the <u>discerning</u> eye.

Present Progressive/Continuous Tense

This tense is used to express:

- an action happening during a specific time: *I am reading this book now.*
- an event that is taking place temporarily: *We're staying in a hotel until I can find an apartment.*
- an event that is taking place in the near future: *My bus is leaving in ten minutes.*

It is formed with **is, am,** or **are** and the **present participle**: ***I am trying*** *to print the essay right now.*

Linking verbs (be, seem, appear, remain) use only the simple present and not the present progressive, even if they refer to the moment of speaking: ***I like*** *my roommate this semester. You* ***seem*** *tired right now.*

EXAMPLE:

Scientists <u>finding</u> out that the universe <u>is</u> even <u>larger</u> and more complex than anyone has ever <u>imagined</u>.

The sentence should read: *Scientists are finding out that the universe is even larger and more complex than anyone has ever imagined.* The verb *finding* is missing its auxiliary, *are.*

Common TOEFL test errors are a verb missing its auxiliary or a progressive form after a linking verb.

Present Perfect Tense

The present perfect tense is used to express the duration of an event that began at a definite time in the past, has continued to the present, and probably will continue into the future: *The United States has been an independent country since July 4, 1776.* Often, **for** and **since** are used. **For** is used for an amount of time: *for two hours, for three weeks.* **Since** is used for a specific time: *since Tuesday, since 1977.*

The present perfect tense is formed with **has** or **have** and the **past participle**: *We have flown domestic airlines for twenty years.*

Common TOEFL test mistakes confuse the uses of the simple past and present perfect tense and incorrectly form the verb. Make sure the subject agrees with the verb: *we have flown*, NOT *we has flown*.

EXAMPLE:
The *Aeneid* was the greatest achievement in the golden age of Latin literature, and it does continued to influence poets through the centuries.

The sentence should read: *The Aeneid was the greatest achievement in the golden age of Latin literature, and it has continued to influence poets through the centuries.*
The verb, *continue,* should be in the present perfect because the influence of the *Aeneid* started in the past, happens now, and will probably continue.

Past Perfect Tense
The past perfect tense is used to express an event that occurred before another in the past time: *By the time the bus came, I had already called a taxi.* It means *I called the taxi BEFORE the bus came.*

It is formed with **had** and the **past participle**.
I had taken ten practice tests before I took the real TOEFL.

In conversation, you will often hear "I took ten practice tests before I took the real TOEFL." It is correct also. With time words, such as *before* and *after,* we don't need to use the past perfect since the relationship between the two events/times is clear.

EXAMPLE:
By the time Neil Armstrong and Edwin Aldrin, Jr., *walked on* the moon in July, 1969, there will have been many space expeditions.

The sentence should read: *By the time Neil Armstrong and Edwin Aldrin, Jr., walked on the moon in July, 1969, there had been many space expeditions.* By 1969 there had been many space expeditions.

The past perfect tense does not often appear on the TOEFL test.

Future Perfect Tense
The future perfect tense is used for an event that precedes another in the future: *By the time I graduate, I will have lived (OR will have been living) in Chicago for ten years.*
It is frequently used with **by the time** and **when**.

It is formed with **will have** and the **past participle**: *When I see you next summer, I will have gotten married.*

The future perfect tense does not often appear on the TOEFL test.

EXERCISE 2: These questions focus on the perfect and the simple past tenses. There are 12 questions, and you have 10 minutes.

1. Under the guidance of choreographers Martha Graham and Jerome Robbins, American dance ________ new levels of artistic achievement.

   ○ reaching
   ○ has reached
   ○ reach
   ○ have reached

2. Some art historians have say that too many artists have tried only to imitate previous painting styles.

3. Although meteorologists begun recently to unravel the mysteries of frontal systems and even tornadoes, thunderstorms have stubbornly clung to their secrets.

4. Armies ______ bugles for hundreds of years to sound battle calls.

   ○ been using
   ○ are using
   ○ have used
   ○ are being used

5. The construction of the homes and buildings in which people live and work is being a major industry ever since early human beings first made huts of sticks, mud, and rocks.

6. Human beings has greatly affected what scientists call natural communities.

7. Wealthy Philadelphians have restored hundreds of 200-year-old homes in the Society Hill section for 1976, and many blocks look much as they did in colonial times.

8. In 1709, Bartholemmeo Cristofari, an Italian who built musical instruments, ________ a keyboard instrument with strings that were struck by hammers.

   ○ has invented
   ○ had been invented
   ○ was inventing
   ○ invented

9. During the 1950s and 1960s, many poets have used frankly autobiographical material in their works.

10. The study of political science __________ greatly with the growth and spread of democracy during modern times.

    ○ have increased
    ○ has been increased
    ○ is being increased
    ○ has increased

11. For answers to the questions of the world and reality, people have relied on magic, superstition, and religion before the Greek philosophers sought answers by studying nature.

12. By the year 2076, the United States will be independent for three hundred years.

ESSAY EXERCISE 1: Correct these student sentences from TOEFL test essays. Find verb tense errors.

1. When I was in junior high, I often clean our bathroom.
2. When I am study by myself, I may never know the answer.
3. If you're learn boxing, it's always better if there's a teacher with you.
4. Requiring hard work has made me be responsible when I was in high school.
5. Moving to the countryside last year enabling us to enjoy nature.
6. When I was in high school, I listening to my friends' advice.
7. In 1995, I will have decided to visit China.
8. I enjoy when a large number of my family be in the same place.
9. I think when all my dreams come true, I going to be happy.

10. In my country, everybody has to go to school since sixteen years.
11. I heared there are a lot of beautiful places in China.
12. I think no matter who you're being with, the most important thing is to have fun.

C. VOICE: ACTIVE/PASSIVE

Action verbs are in either the ACTIVE VOICE or the PASSIVE VOICE. Voice is the form of a verb that indicates whether the subject of the sentence is doing or receiving the action of the verb.

ACTIVE VOICE means that the person or thing doing the action (**the doer**) in the sentence is the subject of the sentence.
PASSIVE VOICE means that the **direct object**, which receives the action, is the subject of the sentence.

	Doer		**Direct Object**
Active	*The mailman*	*delivers*	*the mail.*
	Direct Object		**Doer**
Passive	*The mail*	*is delivered*	*by the mailman.*

Often the doer is not important, so the *by* . . . phrase is not included, as in the sentence *Rice is grown in Japan. By farmers,* the doer, is understood. Sometimes the doer is important, especially when the doer is emphasized: *That book was written by Stephen King, not by Philip Roth.*

The passive voice can be formed in all verb tenses.

	ACTIVE	PASSIVE (DOER UNDERSTOOD)
Simple Present	The tenant *pays* the rent.	The rent *is paid.*
Simple Past	The tenant *paid* the rent.	The rent *was paid.*
Future	The tenant *will pay* the rent.	The rent *will be paid.*
Present Perfect	The tenant *has paid* the rent.	The rent *has been paid.*
Present Modal	The tenant *can pay* the rent.	The rent *can be paid.*
Past Modal	The tenant *should have paid* the rent.	The rent *should have been paid.*

Active/Passive Strategies

1. **In the passive, the main verb ALWAYS uses the past participle form.** Only the helping verb changes. It shows the tense and must agree with the subject.

EXAMPLES:
The experiments **were conducted** in the lab/The experiment **was conducted** in the lab.

2. **Figure out who the doer is and who/what the object is, so you can decide if the sentence should be active or passive.** If the sentence does not have a direct object, or the verb is not an action verb, the sentence cannot be passive.

EXAMPLE:
Franklin Pierce **died** in Concord, New Hampshire in 1869.

The verb, *died,* is not an action verb (intransitive), and there is no direct object, so the sentence cannot be made into a passive one.

3. **Be careful of deletions in dependent clauses. See page 122.**

EXAMPLE:

The house which was built by my father is no longer standing can become *The house* **built** *by my father is no longer standing.*

4. **Intransitive verbs cannot be made passive.** These verbs, also known as linking verbs include *be* (when it's the only verb), *seem, appear, remain, become, like, die, lie, rise, sit, come* and *smell, taste, look,* and *feel* when no action is involved. The dog *feels* (=*is*) sick. However, in the sentence *The doctor felt my arm carefully* the verb, *felt,* is an action verb because the doctor is performing an action. Therefore, the sentence could be passive: *My arm was felt carefully.*

EXAMPLES:

Fine handmade lace is traditionally making of linen thread.

The sentence should read: *Fine handmade lace is traditionally made of linen thread.* It's a passive sentence; the object, *fine handmade lace* is the subject, and the doer is understood. The verb should be in the past participle form, *made.*

Modern dance can teached in the same kinds of studios as ballet.

The sentence should read: *Modern dance can be taught in the same kinds of studios as ballet.* It's a passive sentence with a modal, *can.* The direct object, *modern dance,* is now the subject; the doer, by teachers, is understood. The modal *can* takes the form *be,* and the verb must be in the past participle form, *taught.*

Red clover, the state flower of Vermont, was the leading leguminous hay crop of the northeastern region of the United States until it surpassed by alfalfa.

The sentence should read: *Red clover, the state flower of Vermont, was the leading leguminous hay crop of the northeastern region of the United States until it was surpassed by alfalfa.* It is a passive sentence; the pronoun *it* is the subject of the passive dependent clause. *By alfalfa* is the doer. The verb *surpassed* is missing its auxiliary, *was.*

Only sentences with action (transitive) verbs can take the passive voice.

ACTIVE/PASSIVE EXERCISE 1: Make the following active sentences passive (if possible). In some cases a by-phrase is optional.

1. One of the servants stole the jewels.
2. They could have written more letters to their parents.
3. We feed the animals twice a day.
4. We drove to Las Vegas during our winter vacation.
5. She invited us to the movies.
6. The airplane flew over our house.
7. We took the test on Friday.
8. One of the students sang the song.
9. Professor Scott teaches literature in the fall.
10. The grocer freezes the meat every day.

ACTIVE/PASSIVE EXERCISE 2: Make the following passive sentences active.

1. The prisoners were captured by the enemy.
2. The exercises are being done by the class.
3. The homework could have been done by him in ten minutes.
4. The lesson is taught by the teacher on Fridays.
5. The museum is not used by people who live outside the city.
6. The students spoke Creole before they came to Miami.
7. Meetings are held by our club on Fridays.
8. Romans no longer speak Latin.
9. The key is always forgotten by my roommate.
10. My application had already been filled out by the time I was called.

EXERCISE 3: These questions focus on the passive. There are 25 questions, and you have 20 minutes.

1. Because soapstone is not affected by high temperatures, ________ in laboratories for tabletops, sinks, and some chemical equipment.
   - ◯ it uses
   - ◯ it is used
   - ◯ is it used
   - ◯ is used

2. The old statehouse in Annapolis, Maryland, __________, overlooks the quiet streets that radiate from it like the spokes of a wheel.
   - ◯ in 1772 they built
   - ◯ built in 1772
   - ◯ it was built in 1772
   - ◯ in 1772 it was built

3. Tattooing <u>is done</u> by <u>pricking</u> small holes in the skin with a sharpened stick, bone, or needle that <u>has dipped</u> in pigments with <u>natural</u> colors.

4. The tenor drum is used primarily in military bands and ________ with small felt sticks.
   - ◯ is normally play
   - ◯ is normally played
   - ◯ has normally played
   - ◯ normally plays

5. Detroit, Michigan _________ the automobile capital of the world.
   - ◯ called
   - ◯ is called
   - ◯ has called
   - ◯ is call

6. Sheep yield wool, meat, and leather and _______ in all parts of the world.
   - ◯ raised
   - ◯ is raised
   - ◯ are raising
   - ◯ are raised

7. Transformational grammar is a system of <u>precisely</u> describing the rules that <u>determine</u> all the sentences that <u>can</u> possibly be <u>to form</u> in any language.

8. Mack Sennott, a pioneer motion-picture director and producer, _____ and spent his early years in Quebec, Canada.
   - ◯ is born
   - ◯ bore
   - ◯ was born
   - ◯ who was born

9. Playwright Lillian Hellman _________ for the mixture of strength and sensitivity she gave to her female characters.
   - ◯ was noted
   - ◯ been noted
   - ◯ had noted
   - ◯ being noted

10. The earthworm _____ in moist, warm soil in many geographical areas.
   - ⬭ finds
   - ⬭ is found
   - ⬭ are found
   - ⬭ found

11. Archaeologists know that ________ 35,000 years ago, but it is still unclear for precisely what purpose.
   - ⬭ drawing being practiced
   - ⬭ the practice of drawing
   - ⬭ drawing was practiced
   - ⬭ drawing is practice

12. The industrial heartland of Canada is locate along the Great Lakes and Saint Lawrence waterways, situated in the province of Ontario.

13. A theory developed by a scientist cannot be accepted as part of scientific knowledge until it _________ by the studies of other researchers.
   - ⬭ is verifying
   - ⬭ will verify
   - ⬭ verifies
   - ⬭ has been verified

14. The Heisman Trophy is award annually to the most outstanding college football player in the United States.

15. Arthroscopy allows joint problems _______ by a physician.
   - ⬭ examining
   - ⬭ to be examined
   - ⬭ to examine
   - ⬭ to have examined

16. Volcanoes are divided into three main groups, based on the type of material they ___________ and their shape.
   - ⬭ is made of
   - ⬭ made of
   - ⬭ are made of
   - ⬭ are making of

17. The grasslands of all continents support populations of grazing animals feed on the grasses.

18. The nineteenth century feminist leader Susan B. Anthony became increasingly aware through her work in the temperance movement that ________ the same rights as men.
   - ⬭ women were not granted
   - ⬭ women didn't grant
   - ⬭ women are not granted
   - ⬭ women is not granted

19. The knife is probably the most useful of all the simple tools ever devising.

20. Seaweed nurtures numerous communities of living things, which is protected under the wet coverings of the weeds while the tide is out.

21. When the focus of a pair of binoculars is adjusted, _____ into view.
   - ⬭ bringing distant objects
   - ⬭ distant objects can be brought
   - ⬭ distant objects can bring
   - ⬭ distant objects can be bringing

22. Diffraction explains why sound can heard around a corner even though no straight path exists from the source to the ear.

23. Electrostatic photocopying ___ in 1938 by Chester F. Carlson, an American physicist.
   - ⬭ was invented
   - ⬭ invented
   - ⬭ was being invented
   - ⬭ was to be invented

24. Precisely because photographs are producing by mechanical devices, a camera's images now seem to some artists the perfect means for expressing the modern era.

25. With the incorporation of jazz history into current academic curricula, leading jazz musicians are now founding on the faculties of several universities.

ESSAY EXERCISE 2: Correct these student sentences from TOEFL test essays. Find passive and past participle errors.

1. I was grown up in the countryside.
2. I have spend a lot of time with only one or two close friends.
3. Traditional schools are base on the idea that learning with a teacher is best.
4. Cities where universities are founding usually have a higher standard of living.
5. Only good students have admitted to universities in my country, so many students don't have a chance to improve their lives.
6. Changes are making to my university.
7. If a new university built in my hometown, students will have good and bad experiences.
8. England is used English.
9. Medical schools and dental schools are applied to high level students.
10. If I study with a teacher, I can be understood my problems.

2. INDEPENDENT CLAUSES

A group of words containing a subject and a verb and expressing a complete thought is called a sentence or an **independent clause**. Do not confuse clauses with phrases. A **phrase** is a group of words that lacks either a subject or a verb.

A **simple sentence** has one independent clause, with one subject and one verb. The subject may have more than one noun or pronoun, and the predicate (rest of the sentence) may have more than one verb.

Sometimes an independent clause stands alone as a sentence. Sometimes two or more independent clauses are combined into one sentence. When we connect two independent clauses with a coordinating conjunction, the sentence is a **compound** sentence. We can remember coordinating conjunctions by the first letter of each word, or **FANBOYS**—

- ***for*** (introduces a reason)
- ***and*** (introduces another point)
- ***nor*** (introduces a negative idea)
- ***but*** (introduces a contrast)
- ***or*** (introduces an option)
- ***yet*** (introduces an opposite idea)
- ***so*** (introduces a conclusion)

EXAMPLES:
I like black, **and** I wear it a lot.
I like black, **but** I never wear it.

Many sentences have a subject + action verb + an object.

Subject	**Action Verb**	**Direct Object**
Deirdre	*won*	*the prize.*
Virginia	*has examined*	*the dog.*

Sentences with linking (intransitive) verbs are followed by nouns or adjectives.

Subject	**Linking Verb**	**Noun or Adjective**
Jerene	*is*	*a doctor.*
Meghan	*looks*	*unhappy.*

A sentence should have only one subject. A pronoun renaming the subject cannot come between the subject and the verb. You may hear people say, "My cousin, she lives in Chicago." But this sentence is INCORRECT when used in writing. It has two subjects: *My cousin* and *she.* It should have only ONE. The correct sentence should read: *My cousin lives in Chicago.*

EXAMPLES:

With neither hat nor topcoat in the 22 degree Fahrenheit chill, the youthful John F. Kennedy _______ a stirring inaugural address on January 20, 1961.

- ⬭ he delivered
- ⬭ was delivered
- ⬭ who was delivering
- ⬭ delivered

The sentence should read: *With neither hat nor topcoat in the 22 degree Fahrenheit chill, the youthful John F. Kennedy delivered a stirring inaugural address on January 20, 1961.* The sentence needs a verb in the simple past because the action took place in 1961. The first choice repeats a subject, *he.* The second choice uses the wrong verb tense. The third choice uses a dependent clause.

Macadamia trees ___________ to Hawaii in the 1800s, and today the nuts are an important crop there.

- ⬭ bringing
- ⬭ when brought
- ⬭ were brought
- ⬭ brought

The sentence should read: *Macadamia trees were brought to Hawaii in the 1800s, and today the nuts are an important crop there. Were brought* is the correct form of the verb. The passive is needed in this sentence. *Macadamia trees* is the object. The subject, *by traders,* is understood. The first choice is an incomplete verb; the second choice is a deleted adjective clause, not a main verb, and the fourth choice is the active form.

- Make sure the sentence has a SUBJECT and a VERB.
- Make sure the DIRECT OBJECT follows the ACTION VERB.
- Make sure a NOUN or an ADJECTIVE follows a LINKING VERB.

EXERCISE 4: These questions focus on incomplete independent clauses. There are 25 questions, and you have 20 minutes.

1. The Freedom Trail _______ in the state of Massachusetts.
   - ⬭ which is
   - ⬭ being
   - ⬭ is
   - ⬭ which is being

2. Missionaries _______ in establishing contact between whites and Indians in what became the United States.
   - ⬭ the way led
   - ⬭ the way was led
   - ⬭ led the way
   - ⬭ the way did lead

3. The name "Arkansas" ______ from an Indian word that means land of downstream people.
   - ◯ will have come
   - ◯ comes
   - ◯ is coming
   - ◯ it comes

4. The <u>human</u> brain <u>it</u> is <u>so highly</u> developed that it makes people different <u>from</u> all other living things.

5. ________ several years for bamboo seeds to grow into plants suitable for commercial use.
   - ◯ Taking
   - ◯ It takes
   - ◯ By taking
   - ◯ Although taking

6. During courtship, ________ displays his green and gold upper tail feathers.
   - ◯ the crested peacock who
   - ◯ crested peacock it
   - ◯ the crested peacock is
   - ◯ the crested peacock

7. Bernard Baruch <u>he</u> <u>was</u> often <u>consulted</u> by Presidents Harding, Coolidge, and Hoover on <u>economic</u> matters.

8. In blank verse, __________ of ten syllables, five of which are accented.
   - ◯ line consists of each
   - ◯ consists of each line
   - ◯ each line consists
   - ◯ it consists of each line

9. By the 1950s, Mahalia Jackson's joyous gospel music had brought her ________.
   - ◯ and she had an international reputation
   - ◯ with an international reputation
   - ◯ which was her international reputation
   - ◯ an international reputation

10. Mace ______ a highly flavored spice used in foods.
    - ◯ which is
    - ◯ is
    - ◯ as
    - ◯ is being

11. David G. Farragut _______ to become an admiral.
    - ◯ the first American was an officer
    - ◯ the first officer was an American
    - ◯ was the first American officer
    - ◯ the first American officer was

12. Louis Armstrong, <u>a trumpet player,</u> <u>he</u> <u>was</u> the first <u>internationally</u> famous soloist in jazz.

13. Wild chickens _______ any of their own chicks that lack specific color patterns.
    - ◯ destroying
    - ◯ will destroy
    - ◯ being destroyed
    - ◯ will be destroyed

14. Swamps and marshes __________ in almost every country throughout the world.
    - ◯ they find
    - ◯ are to find
    - ◯ are finding
    - ◯ are found

15. Andy Warhol, famous for his silk-screen soup cans, was _________ in the Pop Art Movement.
    - ◯ that one of a leading figure
    - ◯ a leading figure
    - ◯ leading figures
    - ◯ who leads figures

16. ___________ a twelve-member Supreme Court.
    - ◯ The United States has
    - ◯ Having the United States
    - ◯ Because the United States has
    - ◯ That the United States has

17. _______ established his reputation as a portrait painter and is best known for his dashing portrayals of fashionable subjects.
   - ◯ John Singer Sargent
   - ◯ It was John Singer Sargent
   - ◯ John Singer Sargent was
   - ◯ When John Singer Sargent

18. _______ may relieve doctors of various routine duties, such as examining patients.
   - ◯ Nurses they with special training
   - ◯ For nurses with special training
   - ◯ Nurses have special training
   - ◯ Nurses with special training

19. Natural resources of Massachusetts <u>they</u> include thick forests, <u>hundreds of</u> miles of rivers and streams, and <u>coastal</u> waters filled <u>with</u> sea life.

20. Nutritionists ______ goat milk to be rich, nourishing, and easily digestible.
   - ◯ consider
   - ◯ is considered
   - ◯ are considered
   - ◯ considering

21. ___________ ranks as one of Jefferson's greatest achievements.
   - ◯ It is the Louisiana Purchase
   - ◯ Because the Louisiana Purchase
   - ◯ That the Louisiana Purchase
   - ◯ The Louisiana Purchase

22. The need <u>for</u> a dam on the Colorado River <u>it</u> <u>has been</u> apparent <u>since</u> the early 1900s.

23. In most of his nearly 300 works of fiction, O. Henry ___________ of mechanical plots, which build up to sharp, unexpected endings.
   - ◯ showed his mastery
   - ◯ his mastery showed
   - ◯ was showed his mastery
   - ◯ his mastery did show

24. Since <u>the</u> early eighteenth century, people in many parts of the world <u>developed</u> <u>an interest in</u> pottery making <u>as</u> a hobby.

25. The plastic industry <u>is</u> uses the word *plastics* in the plural form <u>to refer</u> to such things <u>as</u> plastics products and plastics materials in order <u>to avoid</u> confusion with the term *plastic.*

3. DEPENDENT CLAUSES

Some clauses contain a subject and a verb, but they do not express a complete thought and therefore cannot stand alone as a sentence. Such word groups are dependent on something else in the sentence to complete their meaning. Therefore, they are called **dependent clauses**. Any clause beginning with a subordinating word like *what, that, who, which, when, since, before, after,* or *if* is a dependent clause. Dependent clauses function as nouns, adjectives, and adverbs in the sentence. There are three kinds of **dependent clauses**.

A. NOUN CLAUSES

Noun clauses usually begin with **introductory** or **trigger words** such as *that, what, whatever, why, whether, who, which,* and *how.* Like nouns, they can be the subjects, direct objects, and objects of the prepositions in a sentence. In a noun clause, the **subject** and then the **verb** immediately follow the **trigger words**. Noun clauses can be replaced by the word "it."

TYPE OF NOUN CLAUSE	CLAUSE EXAMPLE	QUESTION WORD ORDER
Subject	*Why I know the answer is surprising.*	*Why do I know the answer?*
Direct Object	*I hate what you're wearing.*	*What are you wearing?*
Object of the Preposition	*I'm interested in how you came to America.*	*How did you come to America?*

> Do not use question word order in noun clauses. Don't let a question word (*what, who, how,* etc.) make you think the sentence is a question.
> Noun Clause: *I haven't decided what dorm I should choose.*
> Question: *What dorm should I choose?*

NOUN CLAUSE EXERCISE Make a question using a question word from the given sentence. The words (in parentheses) should be the answer to the question you make. Then change the sentence to a noun clause.

1. She is transferring (*because she wants to be a doctor*).
Question: ____________________?
Noun Clause: Please tell me ____________________.

2. Her friend lives (*in Wingate Hall*).
Question: ____________________?
Noun Clause: Please remind me ____________________.

3. Rose's mother has (*a Macintosh*) computer.
Question: ____________________?
Noun Clause: Do you know____________________?

4. (*David Lee*) is Tom's roommate.
Question: ____________________?
Noun Clause: I don't know ____________________.

5. That textbook cost (*$100.00*).
Question: ____________________?
Noun Clause: Tell me ____________________.

B. ADJECTIVE CLAUSES

Adjective clauses modify a noun or pronoun that they immediately follow.
Dependent adjective clauses usually begin with **relative pronouns** or **trigger words** such as *who, whom, whose, which, that,* and relative adverbs like *where, when,* and *why.* The adjective clause is NOT a sentence by itself; it needs an independent clause to become a complete sentence.

Adjective Clause Rules

1. An adjective clause is used to combine what could be two sentences.

EXAMPLES:
My class has twenty students, **many of whom** live in the dormitory.

If the adjective clause were a sentence, there would be two sentences: *My class has twenty students. Many of them live in the dormitory.*

I have two books for English class, **both of which** are heavy.

If the adjective clause were a sentence, there would be two sentences: *I have two books for English class. Both of them are heavy.*

2. If the adjective clause is relative pronoun + subject + verb, the relative pronoun may be omitted. WHOSE can never be omitted.

EXAMPLES:
I took the class **that you recommended**.

I took the class that you recommended can also be *I took the class you recommended.*

My brother, **whose son attends Columbia,** works downtown.

The relative pronoun, *whose,* cannot be omitted. The sentence CANNOT read: *My brother son attends Columbia works downtown.*

3. After a preposition in an adjective clause, only WHOM or WHICH may be used. [*both of whom, many of whom, for which,* etc.]

EXAMPLE: Marie Curie discovered radium, **for which** she won the Nobel Prize.

4. Adjective clauses that have a subject pronoun—WHO, WHICH, or THAT—can be reduced to form adjective phrases. If the clause contains the BE verb (as in is talking below), omit the pronoun and the BE verb.

EXAMPLE:
The man **who is talking** to you is my professor.
The man **talking** to you is my professor.

If the clause does NOT contain the BE verb, it is sometimes possible to omit the subject pronoun and change the verb to the *-ing* or past participle form.

EXAMPLES:
The movie **that begins** at nine will end at eleven thirty.
The movie **beginning** at nine will end at eleven thirty.

Beginning is active; the movie is doing the action.

The chair **that was broken** by the student is in the corner.
The chair **broken** by the student is in the corner.

Broken is passive; the chair was broken by someone else.

5. Adjective clauses can have the same meaning as nouns or noun phrases called **appositives**. Appositives rename the subject. Appositives are words or phrases, not clauses.

EXAMPLE:
Thomas Jefferson, **who was secretary of state under President George Washington,** became the third president.

The part of the sentence *who was secretary of state under President George Washington* is an adjective clause.

Thomas Jefferson, **secretary of state under President George Washington,** became the third president.

The part of the sentence *secretary of state under President George Washington* is an appositive.

> Common TOEFL test errors are a sentence that uses an incorrect trigger word or an adjective clause missing a subject or a verb. Adjective clauses, like all clauses, must have both a subject and a verb. The relative pronoun can be the subject.

EXAMPLES:
Watercolor, ____ allows extraordinary free brushwork, provides a brilliant transparency and freshness.

- ◯ during
- ◯ which
- ◯ whose
- ◯ for which

The sentence should read: *Watercolor, which allows extraordinary free brushwork, provides a brilliant transparency and freshness. Which* is the correct relative pronoun, modifying *watercolor. During* is a preposition, and must be followed by a noun. The relative pronoun *whose* must be followed by a noun. *For which* must be followed by a subject + verb.

Alfalfa plants flourish in fertile, well-drained soil _______ neutral or slightly alkaline.

- ◯ which
- ◯ is that
- ◯ is
- ◯ that is

The sentence should read: *Alfalfa plants flourish in fertile, well-drained soil that is neutral or slightly alkaline. That is* is the correct adjective clause form, relative pronoun + verb. The first choice is missing a verb. Both the second and third choices begin with verbs, which is incorrect.

<u>Raspberries</u> <u>contain</u> salicylic acid, <u>whose</u> is the <u>active compound</u> in common aspirin.

The sentence should read: *Raspberries contain salicylic acid, which is the active compound in common aspirin.* The correct relative pronoun should be *which,* not *whose.*

ADJECTIVE CLAUSE EXERCISE: Find and correct the errors in the following sentences:

1. Doree went to see a friend that his father is the president of the college.
2. Montpelier is the capital city of Vermont has six months of winter.
3. I had an interesting talk with two students, both of them are from Turkey.
4. In my house I have all kinds of paintings, most of them are from the twentieth century.
5. Friends are people which choose to spend time together.
6. The exam began at ten will end at midnight.
7. My economics professor will let me take my final exam after vacation for that I am very grateful.
8. I would never marry a man that his religion is different from mine.

C. ADVERB CLAUSES

Adverb clauses function exactly like adverbs.

Adverb: He ate *quickly. Quickly* modifies the verb, *ate,* explaining *how* he ate.

Adverb Clause: He ate *so that he could leave. So that he could leave* modifies the verb, *ate,* explaining why he ate.

Adverb clauses can modify a verb, an adjective, or an adverb. They show time, place, cause, purpose, result, condition, concession, manner, or comparison. The introductory words of these clauses are called **subordinating conjunctions.**

FUNCTION OF ADVERB CLAUSE	TRIGGER WORDS	EXAMPLE
TIME	as, when, before, since, while, after, until, as soon as, whenever, as long as	I will stay home **until I feel better.**
PLACE	where, wherever	**Wherever you go,** I will go also.
CAUSE	because, since, as	**Because I was afraid to be late,** I woke up an hour early.
PURPOSE	in order that, so that, that	I bought this TOEFL book **so that I could do better on the exam. (so that** must be followed by subject + *can, could, will,* or *would*)
RESULT	so . . . that, such . . . that	He was **so tall that** he couldn't find pants.
	so . . . that	
	so + adjective + that	The flower was **so pretty that** I bought it.
	so + adverb + that	He ran **so quickly that** he won the race.
	so + few, little, many, much + that	I have **so many pens that** I decided to give you one.
	such . . . that	We're **such good friends that** we write every day.
	such + (a) adjective + noun	
CONDITION	if, unless (Use **unless** to state a negative condition: It means **if . . . not**)	**If it rains tomorrow,** I'll take my umbrella. **Unless you come to class,** you won't be able to pass this course. **If you don't come to class,** you won't be able to pass this course.
CONCESSION	although, though, even though	We decided to play tennis **even though it was raining.**
MANNER	as, as if, as though	She looked **as though she wanted to laugh.**
COMPARISON	as, than	She is older **than her sister.** I tried **as** hard **as I could.**
CONTRAST	while, whereas	Michael is poor, **whereas his sister is rich.**

Adverb clauses CANNOT stand alone; they need an independent clause to be a sentence.

Correct:	I got a dog *so that I could feel safe.*	*Because I'm tall,* I play basketball.
Incorrect:	*So that I could feel safe.*	*Because I'm tall.*

How to Change Adverb Clauses to Phrases

Adverb clauses, like adjective clauses, can become phrases. Clauses beginning with *after, before, while, when,* and *since* can be changed to phrases.

1. If there is a form of the **be** verb, omit the subject and the **be** verb:

EXAMPLE:
While I **was waiting** for the bus, I saw an accident.
While **waiting** for the bus, I saw an accident.

2. If there is no **be** verb, omit the subject and change the verb to an *–ing* form if active.

EXAMPLE:
Before I **did** my homework, I checked my e-mail.
Before **doing** my homework, I checked my e-mail.

3. If there is no **be** verb, omit the subject in the phrase and change the verb to a **past participle** form if passive.

EXAMPLE:
Once the bathing suits **are worn,** they cannot be exchanged.
Once **worn,** the bathing suits cannot be exchanged.

4. Clauses beginning with *after, before, while, when,* and *since* can be changed to phrases only if the subject in the independent clause is the same as the subject in the adverb clause.

INCORRECT: After barking all night, the owner bought earplugs.
The owner was not barking all night; it was the dog. The subject of the independent clause must be *the dog, who was barking all night.*

DEPENDENT CLAUSE STRATEGIES

1. **Make sure the correct trigger word/relative pronoun/subordinating conjunction is used.**

EXAMPLE:
______ Georgia's early days, most of the school buildings were cabins built by local farmers.

- ◯ Nevertheless
- ◯ Among
- ◯ Although
- ◯ During

The sentence should read: *During Georgia's early days, most of the school buildings were cabins built by local farmers. During* is the preposition that is needed to precede the noun, *days. Although* would introduce a dependent clause. *Nevertheless* would be followed by a subject + verb. *Among* is a preposition but is used for space, not time.

2. **Be careful of connectors that have the same meaning as dependent clauses.** Although some prepositional phrases have the same meaning as dependent clauses, the grammar is different.

Because of and **due to** are phrasal prepositions and so must be followed by a noun.

EXAMPLES:
I made the dean's list because I got good grades.
I made the dean's list *because of (due to)* **my good grades**.

Despite and **in spite of,** which both mean *although,* are prepositions and must be followed by a noun or noun phrase.

EXAMPLES:
Although the book was long, I decided to read it.
Despite (In spite of) **its length,** I decided to read the book.

In spite of the fact that and **despite the fact that** are followed by a subject + verb. **[See Commonly Confused Words, page 145]**

3. **Make sure the word order is correct,** especially following subordinating conjunctions and prepositions.

4. **Make sure no part of the clause is missing.**

5. **Do not use two connectors (subordinating conjunctions, coordinating conjunctions, or two subordinating conjunctions) in the same sentence.**

6. **Do not confuse *although (a subordinating conjunction)* with *however (a transitional adverb)*.** *Although* must introduce a dependent clause indicating an unexpected result. *Although I was sick, I went to class.*

   However means *on the other hand* or *nevertheless* and does NOT introduce a dependent clause. It can appear in several places in a sentence. *I did poorly on the reading section; however, I did well on the listening section.* OR *I did poorly on the reading section; I did well, however, on the listening section.*

ADVERB CLAUSE EXERCISE: Finish these sentences with a dependent clause, paying attention to the change in subordinating conjunctions.

1. She lived in France so that____.
   because ____.
   whereas____.

2. I sold all my furniture even though ____________________________________.
   as soon as ____.
   after____.

3. They're going to take the TOEFL test if ________________________________.
   wherever____.
   ______ many times that________________________________.

4. I'm going to the party in order that ____________________________________.
   before____.
   unless____.

EXERCISE 5: These questions focus on dependent clause errors. There are 25 questions, and you have 20 minutes.

1. Some psychologists believe what even when a person suffers from amnesia, some memory remains in the subconscious.

2. Costume jewelry is very popular because _____ allows for a great variety of styles.
   - its low price
   - of its low price
   - the price is low
   - the price is being low

3. ________, Jupiter spins on its axis, an imaginary line through the center.
   - As it orbits the sun
   - So that it orbits the sun
   - So it orbits the sun that
   - Whereas it orbits the sun

4. Isaac Bashevis Singer, __________ best-known tales are romantic or legendary rather than realistic, won the 1978 Nobel Prize for literature.
   - who
   - that
   - which
   - whose

5. Whichever they may differ widely in function, all cells have a surrounding membrane and an internal, water-rich substance called the cytoplasm.

6. Massasoit agreed that _________ his people would not harm the Pilgrims.
   - as long as he lived
   - though he lived
   - that he lived
   - he lived

7. The name "Minnesota" comes from two Sioux Indian words ________ "sky-tinted waters."
   - to mean
   - by meaning
   - meaning
   - it means

8. _________, it seems much larger than the stars and about the same size as the sun.
   - It is the moon so near the earth
   - Despite the moon so near the earth
   - Because the moon is so near the earth
   - The moon is so near the earth

9. __________ in modern living, algebra is studied in schools and colleges in all parts of the world.
   - Since its importance
   - Its importance
   - Because of its importance
   - Importance

10. However viewed as having a serious, sometimes pessimistic side, Mark Twain remains best known as a humorist.

11. ___________ is weak, certain aluminum alloys are as strong as steel.
    - Pure aluminum
    - Although pure aluminum
    - That pure aluminum
    - It is pure aluminum

12. The gray bark crypsis is typical of many moths _____ makes them seem to disappear when they rest on certain trees.
    - the coloring
    - which coloring
    - whose coloring
    - it is coloring that

13. Medical research indicates but large amounts of histamines can be responsible for colds, hay fever, and other respiratory reactions.

14. ________, asbestos can cause serious health problems if its dust is inhaled in large quantities.

- ◯ Even though its usefulness
- ◯ Despite it is useful
- ◯ In spite of its usefulness
- ◯ It is useful

15. Louisa May Alcott wrote *Little Women*, _______ classic of children's literature.

- ◯ it is a
- ◯ a
- ◯ that is a
- ◯ but a

16. Based on her studies of contrasting patterns of culture, Margaret Mead years ago came to the conclusion _________ extremely malleable.

- ◯ is human nature which
- ◯ which is that human nature
- ◯ is human nature
- ◯ that human nature is

17. Contemporary film directors, some of them write the scripts for, act in, and even produce their own motion pictures, are thereby assuming even more control of their art.

18. Farmers grow popcorn in much the same way ________ field corn.

- ◯ they grow
- ◯ that grow
- ◯ that they grow it
- ◯ do they grow

19. Although hazel trees are small, _____ branches are strong and flexible.

- ◯ and
- ◯ their
- ◯ so the
- ◯ but their

20. Lakes may dry up _____ a change in climate or a change in the course of the waters that feed them.

- ◯ when
- ◯ since
- ◯ because of
- ◯ while there

21. Beacon Hill, _________ cobblestone streets, is one of Boston's most charming historical sections.

- ◯ where Colonial brick houses line
- ◯ that Colonial brick houses line
- ◯ which Colonial brick houses line
- ◯ when Colonial brick houses line

22. As a result of _______ in physics and chemistry, scientists have been able to make important discoveries in biology and medicine.

- ◯ there is now knowledge
- ◯ what they now know
- ◯ knowing now that
- ◯ known now

23. Alloys that have a high copper content are almost as soft that pure copper.

24. Like other women ______ in the field of medicine, Sara Mayo found the beginning years difficult.

- ◯ who they pioneered
- ◯ they pioneered
- ◯ who pioneered
- ◯ pioneered

25. In his writing, John Crowe Ransom describes what ___ the spiritual barrenness of society brought about by science and technology.

- ◯ he considers
- ◯ does he consider
- ◯ considers
- ◯ considers it

4. CORRELATIVE CONJUNCTIONS/PAIRED WORDS

Paired words, also known as correlative conjunctions, come in pairs. Like coordinating conjunctions, they connect grammatically equal ideas in a sentence. Correlative conjunctions can connect clauses, phrases, or words.

The following pairs occur together:

- Either . . . or
- Neither . . . nor
- Not only . . . but also
- Both . . . and

EXAMPLE:

A striking feature of nearly all ballet companies today is their interest in either classical and contemporary works.

The sentence should read: *A striking feature of nearly all ballet companies today is their interest in both classical and contemporary works. And* is not an error choice; therefore, the pairing is *both . . . and.*

The connector error will be that one of the pairs is mismatched. Make sure the right connectors appear together.

EXERCISE 6: These questions focus on connector errors. There are 10 questions, and you have 8 minutes.

1. Horse raisers can breed a fast horse with a strong horse to produce an animal that has both speed or power.

2. The invention of the contact lens literally opened new vistas for people who _____wear glasses.
   - ◯ neither could or would
   - ◯ either could not nor would not
   - ◯ neither could nor would not
   - ◯ either could not or would not

3. Mimicry is the condition in which a living organism imitates ______ an animal or a plant.
   - ◯ both
   - ◯ either
   - ◯ instead of
   - ◯ neither

4. At the beginning of the Civil War, neither the North neither the South had a prepared strategy.

5. The American Civil Liberties Union has met with either success and failure in its work.

6. Married couples may volunteer for the Peace Corps if ____________have skills the corps can use in the same country.
   - ◯ not only the husband and the wife
   - ◯ both the husband or the wife
   - ◯ either the husband and the wife
   - ◯ both the husband and the wife

7. A primary election is considered closed when each voter must declare a choice of party, either when registering to vote and when voting.

8. Bacteria are either plants nor animals, but are single-celled organisms which reproduce most commonly through binary fission.

9. Studies of either vision and physical optics began almost as early as civilization itself.

10. Hawaii is world famous for both its beauty or its pleasant climate.

5. SUBJECT/VERB AGREEMENT

Every complete sentence has a subject and a verb. The verb in every independent or dependent clause must agree with its subject. Although there is usually no problem in finding the subject and making sure it agrees with its verb, there are several exceptions and rules to learn.

There are several subject/verb agreement topics tested on the TOEFL test.

A. PREPOSITIONAL PHRASES BETWEEN THE SUBJECT AND THE VERB

The verb is NOT affected by any prepositional phrase (*with, together with, along with,* etc.) that comes between the subject and the verb.

EXAMPLE: The test *along with the answers* **is** found at the end of the book.

The subject, *test,* is singular. It agrees with the verb *is. Answers,* the object of the prepositional phrase *along with,* has no effect on the verb.

B. SENTENCES BEGINNING WITH *THERE* AND *HERE*

In some sentences, the verb comes before the subject. Be sure to find the entire subject.

EXAMPLES:
There **is** a lot of pollution in many countries today.

The subject is a singular noncount noun, *pollution.* It agrees with verb *is.*

Here **are** a proposal, an outline, and a description.

The subjects are plural—*proposal, outline,* and *description. Here* means *they,* the subjects, and agrees with the verb *are.*

C. INDEFINITE PRONOUNS OR ADJECTIVES

The indefinite pronouns or adjectives *either, neither,* and *each* and the adjective *every* are always singular. So are compounds such as *everybody, everyone,* and *someone.*

EXAMPLE: *Every* student, teacher, and employee **is** required to attend graduation.

D. PLURAL NOUNS

Nouns that end in *s* usually require a singular verb. These nouns look plural, but they are singular in meaning.

CATEGORIES	EXAMPLE WORDS	EXAMPLE SENTENCES
Countries	Philippines, United States	The United States **has** fifty states. The Philippines **is** a FedEx hub.
School Subjects	mathematics, economics, statistics, physics	Mathematics **is** required. Physics **is** taught in the afternoon.
Diseases	mumps, AIDS, SARS, measles	SARS **has** recently been diagnosed. Mumps **is** no longer common.
Other Words	news, whereabouts	The news **is** on TV at 6:30 PM. His whereabouts **is** unknown.
Exceptions (words that end in *s* that are plural)	scissors, pants, glasses, jeans, gloves	My pants **are** too short. His glasses **are** from Korea.

E. TIME, DISTANCE, AND MONEY

Time, distance, and money take a singular verb because the amount is considered a single unit.

EXAMPLES:
Six hours **is** a long time to wait for the bus.
Eight dollars **is** all you'll need for lunch.
Two miles **is** a lot to run every day.

F. MATH FACTS

These facts take a singular verb.

EXAMPLES:
Two plus two **is** four.
Eight divided by four **is** two.
Six times seven **is** forty-two.
Ten minus three **is** seven.

G. GERUNDS AS SUBJECTS

Gerunds, nouns ending in *-ing,* always take a singular verb.

EXAMPLE:
Writing letters **is** no longer necessary.

H. THE NUMBER OF/A NUMBER OF

A number of means *a lot of* and takes a plural verb. *The number of* is used to give an exact amount and takes a singular verb.

EXAMPLES:
A number of teachers **are** sick today.
The number of days in a week **is** seven.

I. LANGUAGES/NATIONALITIES

Nouns of nationality that end in *ch* (French), *sh* (Polish), and *ese* (Vietnamese) can mean either a language or a group of people. When the noun refers to a language, the noun is singular. When the noun refers to a group of people, the noun is plural. Not all nationalities have these endings.

EXAMPLES:
Spanish **is** spoken in Mexico.
The French in my class **speak** French during lunch.

J. DETERMINING MODIFIERS

The nouns that follow the quantity words *some, all, part, most, fraction,* and *percent* determine the verbs. Don't be confused by the preposition *of.*

EXAMPLES:
Quantity **Noun**
Ten percent of the *students* **live** in apartments.
The noun *students* is plural, so the verb *live* agrees with it.

Quantity **Noun**
Some of the *money* **is** in the bank.
The noun *money* is singular, so the verb *is* agrees with it.

K. COLLECTIVE NOUNS

A collective noun names a group of people or animals. Although collective nouns do not end in *s,* they are plural and take a plural verb.

EXAMPLES:
The cattle **need** more grazing land.
The elderly **live** in nursing homes.
The rich **subsidize** this housing development.

Subject-verb agreement is frequently tested on the TOEFL test. Find the subject and find the verb in the sentence. Make sure they agree.

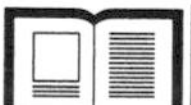

STUDY TIP

Memorize exceptions to subject-verb agreement rules.

SUBJECT/VERB AGREEMENT EXERCISE: Circle the correct form of the *italicized* verb.

1. Neither of the books that I ordered (*has, have*) come yet.
2. A number of students (*hopes, hope*) to graduate this June.
3. I can never remember if seven times eight (*is, are*) fifty-six or fifty-nine.
4. The president, with his wife, (*is, are*) planning to visit Hawaii.
5. Each of the students maintaining the required average (*is, are*) going to receive a scholarship.
6. Inside my pocketbook (*is, are*) my calculator, lunch, and keys.
7. Measles (*has, have*) reappeared among the kindergarten children.
8. The number of students in this year's freshman class (*is, are*) 212.

9. Eight miles (*is, are*) a lot to jog every day.
10. Indonesian (*is, are*) very difficult for Americans to learn.
11. The Dutch (*loves, love*) good bread.
12. The United States (*is, are*) more than two hundred years old.
13. Twenty dollars (*is, are*) a lot to spend for a pair of socks.
14. The news about the earthquake (*is, are*) surprising.
15. The police (*is, are*) exercising more nowadays.
16. Some of the students (*is, are*) taking an incomplete in the class.
17. Physics (*is, are*) taught by Dr. Roberts this term.
18. My scissors (*isn't, aren't*) sharp. Can I borrow yours?
19. Some of the light from the kitchen (*is, are*) shining in my room.
20. Completing all the exercises (*is, are*) a good idea.

EXERCISE 7: These questions focus on subject/verb agreement. There are 8 questions, and you have 8 minutes.

1. While some scientists drafts plans for intricate vehicles to carry humans to stars, futurists look to "natural" spaceships—comets.

2. When a crossword puzzle is completed, each square will contain a letter that help to spell a word.

3. The wings of an airplane extends outward from each side of the fuselage.

4. About two-thirds of the people of Nebraska lives in urban areas.

5. An increasing number of newspapers is using photographic type, which consists of photographic images of letters.

6. Dividing numbers with signs that are not alike gives a negative quotient, such as 24 divided by negative 3 are negative 8.

7. Knitting with two needles produce a flat fabric whereas knitting with three or four points can produce tubular pieces for socks and skirts.

8. Japanese are spoken in different styles according to social situations.

ESSAY EXERCISE 3: Correct these student sentences from TOEFL test essays. Find subject/verb agreement errors.

1. Trading products have different advantages than paying money.
2. A big city usually have a large population and serious pollution.
3. If half of the students chooses a traditional school, they won't have teachers.
4. Establishing new universities are not always a good thing.
5. Each of these ways are pretty good.
6. My sister together with my parents live in the countryside.
7. There are in Eastern European countries a serious problem: pollution.
8. In my country measles are still a big health concern.
9. The Chinese loves to visit their Great Wall.
10. I'd like to visit Argentina because Spanish are spoken there.

6. PLURAL FORMS

There are several plural form errors on the TOEFL test. Words may be singular when they should be plural, words may be plural when they should be singular, and the word may be incorrectly spelled.

A. IRREGULARLY SPELLED PLURALS

1. Words ending in y

If a vowel comes before a *y*, as in boy, add an *s*: *boys*.
If a consonant comes before the *y*, as in city, drop the *y* and add *ies*: *cities*.

2. Words to memorize

These are the commonly tested items (there are no rules for these words):

SINGULAR	PLURAL	SINGULAR	PLURAL
man	men	woman	women
child	children	tooth	teeth
foot	feet	mouse	mice
ox	oxen	goose	geese

3. Words ending in o

Sometimes we add *s* or *es* to words ending in o. All food words take *oes*: *mangoes, potatoes*. All music words take *s*: *pianos, altos, sopranos*. But in other cases, there are no rules; just memorize the spelling.

o	oes
zoos	heroes
videos	echoes
tattoos	

4. Words ending in *f* or *fe*

Some nouns ending in *f* or *fe* change to *ves* in the plural. Other nouns add *s*.

ves	s
knife-knives	roof-roofs
calf-calves	dwarf-dwarfs
shelf-shelves	chief-chiefs
thief-thieves	chef-chefs
wolf-wolves	belief-beliefs
life-lives	cliff-cliffs
loaf-loaves	
self-selves	
half-halves	

5. Words with the same singular and plural form

Some nouns have the same form in the singular and in the plural, including *deer, sheep, fish, series*, and *offspring*. Remember to change the verb if the meaning is plural: *One deer is living in town. Two deer were spotted yesterday.*

B. COUNT AND NONCOUNT NOUNS

Certain words in English do NOT take a plural form; they cannot be counted. There are many noncount nouns. They can be divided into categories:

CATEGORY	EXAMPLES
Collections of Items:	food, jewelry, equipment, luggage, clothing, etc.
Fluids:	water, tea, oil, grease, soup, etc.
Solids:	gold, bread, wood, cotton, cheese, etc.
Particles:	sand, rice, salt, sugar, dust, grass, hair, etc.
Languages:	Arabic, Thai, Hebrew, etc.
Fields of Study:	biology, sociology, physics, English, mathematics, etc.
Recreation/Sport:	bridge, swimming, lacrosse, football, music, etc.
Natural Phenomena:	sunshine, rain, snow, etc.
Abstractions:	love, hate, time, space, homework, grammar, luck, etc.

Count and noncount nouns are introduced by certain quantity words and articles.

Noncount ***(homework)***	**Count** ***(tests)***
some	some
a lot of	a lot of
(too) much	(too) many
(a) little	(a) few
a great deal of	a number of
hardly any	no
no	two, three (numbers)
	several
	hundreds, thousands (etc.) of

If the noun is a plural count noun, the number quantifier (before *of*) must be plural: *Hundreds of students, thousands of animals.* Don't confuse these with adjectives: *A hundred students, a thousand animals.*

EXAMPLES:

A cattle can be raised for beef or kept as dairy cattle.

The sentence should read: *Some cattle can be raised for beef or kept as dairy cattle.* The word *cattle* cannot be counted; we CANNOT say *a cattle.*

Even as he wrote copiously on such diverse topic as education, politics, and religion, Lewis Mumford remained active in city and regional planning.

The sentence should read: *Even as he wrote copiously on such diverse topics as education, politics, and religion, Lewis Mumford remained active in city and regional planning. Topic* is a count noun, and it should be plural, *topics* in this sentence because it is preceded by the adjective, *diverse,* meaning *different* and followed by a list of topics.

Helen Keller became both blind and deaf because of a fevers she contacted at nineteen months.

The sentence should read: *Helen Keller became both blind and death because of a fever she contacted at nineteen months. Fevers* should be singular, *fever,* because it is preceded by the singular article, *a.*

Check the verbs in the sentence. A singular verb takes a singular noun. A plural verb takes a plural noun unless the noun is a noncount noun.

STUDY TIP

Memorize irregular plural forms.

EXERCISE 8: These questions focus on irregular plurals. There are 20 questions, and you have 16 minutes.

1. A team of researchers from the University of Michigan extracted the back part of a skull and several teeths of a whale estimated to be 45 million years old.
2. The leafs of a cabbage plant grow close together to form a hard, round head.
3. There are hundred of kinds of cheeses, and they differ in taste, texture, and appearance.
4. When two ant meet, they "smell" each other with their antennae.
5. Winslow Homer settled on the coast of Maine, where he captured in much of his paintings the shifting moods of the Atlantic Ocean.
6. The spools in a telephone receiver contain many foots of wire, coiled up into a tiny space.
7. Institutions of higher learning get their funds from a variety of source.
8. The discovery of kerosene and the invention of the glass chimney made possible a greatly improved lamps.
9. Numerous professional associations have educational program for their members.
10. Some people are allergic to certain type of food, for example, strawberries or seafood.
11. Gauze is a thin, open-weave clothes made of cotton, silk, rayon, or synthetic fibers.
12. A swamp between two sea, the Okefenokee Swamp in Florida lies in a basin 120 feet above sea level.
13. Based on a 1990 survey of 7.4 million household, *The Lifestyle Market Analyst* reported that computer games had become the favorite pastime in some United States cities.
14. Although she is best known for her children's stories, Frances Hodgson Burnett also wrote novels for adult and articles for the popular press.

15. Geysers are spectacular features of thermal area, periodically erupting with explosive bursts of steam and hot water.

16. First incorporated in 1871, Dallas, Texas, had become the seventh largest cities in the United States by 1976.

17. Why certain plants contain alkaloids remains a mystery, although botanists have formulated a number of theory to explain it.

18. Sculptor Duane Hanson is noted for his many life-sized and realistic figure.

19. Every man, women, and child was evacuated from the village before the hurricane struck the island last September.

20. Pharmacist fill drug prescriptions, keeping records of the drugs their patients are taking to make sure that harmful combinations are not prescribed.

7. ARTICLES (*A*, *AN*, AND *THE*)

A and *AN* are indefinite (not specific) articles. *A* is used before words beginning with a consonant (*b, c, d, f, etc.*) sound (*a long test, a decision, a university*). *AN* is used before vowel (*a, e, i, o, u*) SOUNDS—not spelling (*an hour, an egg, an impossible result*). Make sure that a word beginning with a vowel sounds like a vowel. *THE* is a definite, or specific, article.

A. ARTICLE RULES

1. Articles with singular count nouns

An article is used with a singular count noun, meaning there is only one of something. When we are not talking about something specific we use *a* or *an*.

EXAMPLE: Give me **a** pen.

When we are talking about something specific, we use *the*. It is similar in meaning to *that*.

EXAMPLE: Give me back **the** pen I lent you yesterday.

The speakers understand which pen is being discussed.

The first time something is mentioned we use *a* or *an*. After that, we use *the*.

EXAMPLE: I saw **an** accident at noon. **The** accident was serious.

2. Articles and plural count nouns

Because a plural count noun refers to more than one, *a* or *an* cannot be used. However, indefinite adjectives, such as *some, any, several, many, few, a few,* and *fewer* may be used to show an indefinite number.

EXAMPLES:

I eat eggs.

I eat **some** eggs every week.

There aren't **many** eggs in the refrigerator.
I ate **fewer** eggs last year.

Articles are not used before plural nouns that refer to an entire group of persons or things.

EXAMPLES:
Oranges are good for you.
Students usually don't wear uniforms in the U.S.

When the plural count noun is specific, using *the* before it is similar to using *those.* Prepositional phrases can show that the noun is specific.

EXAMPLES:
The oranges *on the table* are from Florida.
The students *in my class* have a test on Friday.

3. Articles with noncount nouns

A and *an* are not used with noncount nouns because you can't have only one of these types of nouns. It is either *water* or *the water.* Indefinite adjectives such as *some, any, much, a little,* and *less* may be used with noncount nouns to show an indefinite quantity. **[See the noncount list in Section 6, page 135.]**

EXAMPLE: I'd like **some** homework. (NOT: *I'd like a homework.*)

4. Articles with proper nouns

A proper noun gives the name of a person or a particular place or time.

TYPE OF NAME	WITHOUT ARTICLE	WITH *THE*
Countries	France, Korea, Japan	the United States, the Dominican Republic
States, cities, counties, provinces	Boston, Suffolk County, New York City	the City of Boston, the State of New York, the Province of Quebec
Continents	Asia, Europe	
Geographical areas	Western Europe, Southern Florida	the North Pole, the Equator
Empires, etc.		the British Empire, the Ming Dynasty
Streets	Main Street, Memorial Drive	
Parks	Central Park, Hyde Park	
Islands, lakes, mountains	Singular: Coney Island, Lake George, Mount Fuji	Plural: the Great Lakes, the White Mountains
Oceans, seas, canals, deserts, forests	Sherwood Forest	the Atlantic Ocean, the Erie Canal, the Mohave Desert,
Universities, colleges, schools, institutes	Mount Ida College, Cornell University, Franklin Institute	the University of Michigan, the College of the Holy Cross
Museums, libraries, galleries		the Museum of Fine Arts, the Boston Public Library, the Tate Gallery
Buildings, auditoriums, halls, theaters, hotels	Mann Auditorium, Independence Hall, Carnegie Hall	the White House, the Plaza the RCA Building, the Strand Theater
Businesses	Polaroid, IBM, JCrew, Bloomingdale's, Sears,	the Polaroid Corporation, the Gap
Holidays	Ramadan, Christmas, Thanksgiving, Valentine's Day	the Fourth of July

5. Nationalities

When referring to an entire group of people, use no article if the name has a plural form.

EXAMPLES:
Americans like football.
Italians eat a lot of pasta.

The is usually used if the name does not have a plural form.

EXAMPLES:
The French drink a lot of wine.
The Danish often ski in the winter.

When the name of a nationality is used as an adjective, no article is used.

EXAMPLES:
Akihiro is **Japanese**.
Jean Paul's cousins are **Swiss**.

6. Specific uses of *the*

The is usually used with names of things that are known or familiar.

EXAMPLES:
Has **the** mailman come yet? (We know who usually brings the mail.)
I'm going to **the** beach tomorrow. (The beach is a familiar place.)

The is used with items in the universe that are always singular.

EXAMPLES: **the** sun, **the** Earth, **the** moon, **the** equator

The is used in certain time expressions.

EXAMPLES:
in **the** morning (afternoon, evening), in **the** middle of the week, **the** day after tomorrow

The is NOT used in other time expressions.

EXAMPLES:
at 9 o'clock, at noon, on Monday, in May, last week, next month, midnight

The is used when first, second, third, etc. precede a noun.

EXAMPLES:
He fought in **the** Second World War.
He fought in **World War II**.

Finish **the** third chapter by tomorrow.
Finish **Chapter 3** by tomorrow.

7. *A number of/the number of*

A number of means *several* and takes a plural verb: *A number of students were absent on Friday.*

The number of refers to a specific number and takes a singular verb: *The number of students in my chemistry class is thirty-five.*

Make sure that the correct article is used, that the sentence is not missing an article, and that there is not an unnecessary article.

ARTICLE EXERCISE: Circle the correct form in the following sentences. A "0" indicates no article is needed.

1. Many of (a/the) larger kinds of whales face (a/an) uncertain future.
2. West Virginia, in (an/the) Appalachian Highlands, has some of (a/the) most rugged land in (0/the) United States.
3. Almost all looms have (0/the) same basic features and weave fabric in much (a/the) same way.
4. No art form presents (a/the) more complete or clearer record of (0/the) development of human culture than sculpture.
5. Wind is (0/the) movement of air from (a/an) high-pressure area to (a/an) low-pressure area.
6. Water polo is (a/the) dangerous sport because players kick and wrestle or sometimes hold (a/an) opponent's head under (a/the) water, though such actions are against (0/the) rules.
7. Henry Ford established (0/the) Ford Motor Company, which revolutionized (an/the) automobile industry with its assembly line method of production.
8. Aldo Leopold, (a/an) American naturalist, won international fame as (0/an) authority on wildlife conservation.
9. Harold Lloyd, the silent motion picture comedian, appeared in (0/a) famous scene hanging from (0/a) clock atop (a/an) office building in *Safety Last* (1923).
10. (0/The) first two lines of (a/the) limerick, (a/an) humorous verse, rhyme with (a/the) fifth line.
11. (0/A) letter of credit, issued by a bank, permits (a/an) individual, (a/the) business firm, or a designated party to draw up to (0/a) stated amount of money on that bank.
12. A lichen is (a/an) organism that consists of an alga and (a/the) fungus living as (0/a) single unit.
13. The golden retriever is (a/the) medium-sized hunting dog which has won recognition as (a/an) intelligent, hard-working gun dog and as (0/a) guide for (0/the) blind.
14. The Golden Gate Bridge spans (0/a) channel at (0/the) entrance of San Francisco Bay.
15. Despite (a/the) length of its neck, (0/a) giraffe has only seven neck bones—(a/the) same number that human beings and most other mammals have.
16. Nonprescription glasses may be bought without (0/an) eye examination and are sold at (0/the) many stores.
17. Golf is (a/an) outdoor sport in which (a/an) player attempts to hit a small, hard ball into (a/an) hole in as few swings as possible.
18. The natural beauty of (0/the) Grand Canyon attracts about three million visitors (a/the) year.

19. A space station is designed so that many people can live and work in orbit for (0/a) longer time than they could in (a/an) ordinary, crowded spacecraft.
20. (0/The) animals have been kept as pets by people in all parts of (a/the) world for thousands of years.

EXERCISE 9: These questions focus on article errors. There are 20 questions, and you have 16 minutes.

1. During Coolidge's tenure in office, for the first time in the history of any nation the mass market developed for cars, radios, refrigerators, and vacuum cleaners.

2. Hibernation is a inactive, sleeplike state that some animals enter during winter.

3. Sometimes the impressionists painted the same subject in different atmospheric situations to show how colors and surface effect change at various times of a day.

4. A clam is a animal whose soft body is covered with a protective shell.

5. To make adobe, workers first mix sandy clay or loam with water and the small quantity of straw, grass, or a similar building material.

6. The American water spaniel, an hunting dog with a thick, curly coat, was developed in the United States to be of special help to pheasant and duck hunters.

7. The Fifth Amendment to the United States Constitution guarantees that people cannot be forced to testify against themselves in the criminal case.

8. Of all the Native Americans in the United States, the Navajos form largest group.

9. Tacoma, one of the largest cities in Washington, is a industrial and commercial center.

10. In general, humanistic theories tend to stress the significance of emotions in the learning.

11. In 1890 Kate Hurd-Mead became medical director of the Bryn Mawr School for girls, one of a first schools in the United States to initiate a preventive health program.

12. The hardness of mineral often gives a clue to its identity.

13. Booker T. Washington, an educational leader, worked throughout his lifetime to improve economic conditions for black people in United States.

14. Although rhubarb is technically the vegetable, people usually prepare it as a dessert food, often as pie fillings and sauces.

15. David Rittenhouse of Philadelphia was the leading astronomer, mathematician, and clockmaker who measured in 1769 the earth's distance from the sun.

16. Knute Rockne was a American college football coach who served as head coach at the University of Notre Dame from 1918 until his death in an airplane crash.

17. E.B. White was known chiefly as an essay writer, but he also wrote the poetry and children's books.

18. Great technical advances in aerial and satellite photography have been made since end of the Second World War.

19. Ballads were early types of poetry and may have been among a first kinds of music.

20. Oscillation is a electronic function that changes a direct current to the signal of desired frequency.

ESSAY EXERCISE 4: Correct these student sentences from TOEFL test essays. Find article errors. There are some sentences with no article errors. Some sentences have more than one error.

1. I agree with view that all students should have access to higher education.
2. I prefer to study following teacher's lectures.
3. I cannot understand what is good student.
4. If there is the poor man who is a genius, should the university accept him?
5. I prefer to have a teacher because if I just learn by myself, maybe I will make mistake.
6. When I was high school student, my hometown had only one university.
7. Children should learn how to use knives correctly.
8. As you know, Venezuela was an Spanish colony.
9. There is a saying that nature is teacher.
10. First, those who like to spend time with close friends can do many things in the short time.
11. I need to find job now, so I prefer to spend time with number of friends.
12. It is very important to me that everyone who is an expert give me an advice.
13. When I was a child, my mother always told me that I could not cook without adult supervisor.
14. They just want degree to enter some good company.
15. However, they had good grades in the high school.
16. My family decided to move because they wanted to give us better environment and larger space to enjoy ourselves.
17. If I do not know the answer to something, maybe I can find the book in order to help me.
18. The teacher will teach you if you're using wrong posture, or using wrong hand.

8. PREPOSITIONS

Prepositions are words that precede nouns or pronouns. Together the preposition and noun make a prepositional phrase, which generally shows time, location, and direction.

EXAMPLE: I like to swim *in the ocean on Sundays.*

In the ocean and *on Sundays* are prepositional phrases.

Here is a list of the most common prepositions:

about	before	despite	of	to
above	behind	down	off	toward(s)
across	below	during	on	under
after	beneath	for	out	until
against	beside	from	over	up
along	besides	in	since	upon
among	between	into	through	with
around	beyond	like	throughout	within
at	by	near	till	without

Prepositions can follow adjectives.

EXAMPLES: interested in, afraid of, married to, finished with

Certain prepositions can be combined with verbs to create new verb meanings.

EXAMPLES:
You should **look** before you leap.
Here *look* means *see.*

Look up the word in the dictionary.
Here *look* with the preposition *up* means *search for and find,* as in a book.

STUDY TIP

These combinations, sometimes called **phrasal verbs** or **idioms,** are also found in the listening section. There are many, many phrasal verbs in English. It is a good idea to keep an alphabetical notebook of these verbs and their meanings.

A. IMPORTANT PREPOSITION RULES

1. On/In: Time

In dates, *on* is used before days of the weeks or before the month + the day of the month; *in,* before months not followed by the day and before numbers indicating the year.

EXAMPLES:

On Sunday	**In** May
On May 21	**In** 1950
On May 21, 1950	**In** May, 1950

2. On/In: Place

In general, *in* means *beneath the surface, on* means *touching the surface.*

EXAMPLES:
I don't know how I got a hole **in** my sweater.
There's a red pen mark **on** my computer screen.

On is used with the name of the street; *at* with the house number + name of the street.

EXAMPLES:
I live **on** Commonwealth Avenue.
My school is **at** 1010 Commonwealth Avenue.

3. At/In

In referring to location, *at* usually means *in or in front of place; in* means *within a location,* inside a house, building, city, country, etc.

EXAMPLES:
Let's meet **at** the public library **in** the lobby.
He's now living **in** Australia.

4. Since/For/During

For refers to a period of time, usually expressed in terms of the number of hours, days, weeks, etc, or in expressions such as *for a long time, for a few minutes,* etc. *During* also refers to a period of time, usually stated as a block of time: *during the summer, during the semester, during my vacation. Since* refers to a period of time from a point in time in the past to the present or to another point in time in the past.

EXAMPLES:
I've taught English **since** *1971.*
We haven't seen him **for** *two or three weeks.*
We saw each other five times **during** *semester break.*

5. On time/In time

On time means *on schedule. In time* usually means *before a specified time with time left over.*

EXAMPLES:
You must be **on time** for the test.
I get to school **in time** to have a cup of coffee before class begins.

6. Between/Among

Between is used for two things; *among* for more than two.

EXAMPLE:
Sarah is sitting **between** Josh and Allison.
I know my passport is somewhere **among** all the papers on my desk.

B. THE FOUR MOST COMMON PREPOSITION MISTAKES

1. The wrong preposition is in the sentence.

EXAMPLE:
An electronic game is a game controlled on a tiny computer called a microprocessor.

The preposition *on* should be *by.*

2. The preposition is missing.

EXAMPLES:
Simple heat transfer takes place when a colder substance comes in contact a warmer substance.

It should read *in contact with.*

Professional recognition came to Ida Hyde in 1902 when she was elected the American Physiological Society, its first woman member.

The sentence should read: *Professional recognition came to Ida Hyde in 1902 when she was elected to the American Physiological Society, its first woman member. Elected* should be *elected to.*

June is the sixth month of the year according the Gregorian calendar, which is used in almost all the world today.

The sentence should read: *June is the sixth month of the year according to the Gregorian calendar, which is used in almost all the world today.*

3. The wrong word form follows the preposition.
After a preposition, use a gerund (a noun ending in *–ing*).

EXAMPLES:
Animal researchers have identified many behavioral patterns associated with selection a place to live.

It should read *with selecting.* Since nouns follow prepositions, gerunds (which are nouns) can also follow a preposition.

4. Commonly confused words are used.
(Like/unlike/alike, despite/except, after/afterwards, because/because of)

i. *Like* and *unlike* are prepositions and therefore come before nouns. *She looks like her mother. Unlike last semester, this semester we will have a final examination.* Don't confuse *unlike* with *alike. Alike* can be either an adjective as in *She and her sister look alike,* or an adverb as in *She and her sister dress alike.*

Look closely at the words surrounding *alike, like,* and *unlike* to determine if you need to use a preposition (*like, unlike*) or an adjective or an adverb (*alike*).

EXAMPLES:
Alike traditional choreographers, Twyla Tharp includes ballet, various social dances, and tap dancing in her work.

The sentence should read: *Unlike traditional choreographers, Twyla Tharp includes ballet, various social dances, and tap dancing in her work.* A preposition instead of *alike* is needed before the noun *choreographers.*

The Hudson River is sometimes called the Rhine of America because some sections of its beautiful shores look alike the shores of the Rhine.

The sentence should read: *The Hudson River is sometimes called the Rhine of America because some sections of its beautiful shores look like the shores of the Rhine.* A preposition is needed before the noun, *shores.*

ii. *Despite* and *except* are both prepositions. *Despite* means *in spite of. Except* means *other than. Despite the fact that* and *In spite of the fact that* are NOT prepositions and must be followed by subject + verb.

EXAMPLES:
Despite the rain, we had a picnic.
Despite the fact that it was raining, we had a picnic.
Everyone **except** Jane can leave at 2:30.

iii. *After* is a preposition. *Afterwards,* an adverb, means *at a later time.*

EXAMPLES:
After the test, we'll meet for coffee.
Let's go out for coffee **afterwards**.

iv. *Because of* is a preposition followed by a noun or a noun phrase. *Because* is a subordinating conjunction which introduces a dependent clause and is followed by a subject + verb.

EXAMPLES:
Dogs are able and willing to learn a wide variety of tasks because of they are intelligent and devoted to their owners.

The sentence should read: *Dogs are willing to learn a wide variety of tasks because they are intelligent and devoted to their owners.* The mistake is *because of.* It is followed by *they* (subject) and *are* (verb), so *because* should be used.

New housing construction fell to inadequate levels during World Wars I and II because a lack of building materials.

The sentence should read: *New housing construction fell to inadequate levels during World Wars I and II because of a lack of building materials.* The mistake is *because.* Since it is followed by a noun phrase and not a subject and verb, it needs to be *because of.*

PREPOSITION EXERCISE: Circle the correct preposition in the following sentences.

1. A thorough study of mythology requires familiarity (with/for) the properties of plants and trees, and the habits (of/in) wild birds and beasts.
2. Will Rogers was widely recognized (in/for) his daily newspaper column, in which he humorously criticized and commented (in/on) the politics of his time.
3. The discovery of gold in California (in/at) 1848 brought more than 40,000 prospectors there (by/in) two years.
4. The Van de Graaf generator, an electrostatic machine used (in/of) nuclear physics to study transformation (at/in) subatomic particles, produces powerful electric currents.
5. Observation (in/of) the sun, moon, and stars has enabled humans to determine both the seasons and the time (from/of) day.
6. Average world temperatures have risen (by/on) half a degree Celsius (for/since) the mid-nineteenth century.
7. Telepathy is the communication of thoughts, feelings, or knowledge (by/from) one person to another (across/without) the use of the senses of hearing, sight, smell, taste, or touch.
8. Tape recordings can easily be edited (by/in) cutting out the unwanted sections and then joining the ends (at/of) the tape.
9. Bones are held in place at the joints (by/from) strong ligaments that fasten to the bones (above/during) each joint.
10. Geochemists have theorized that the Earth may have begun as part (from/of) a huge cloud (of/upon) dust and gases.
11. Duke Ellington is considered (by/beyond) many to be the most important figure in the history (around/of) jazz.
12. Common amphibians, salamanders are found worldwide (despite/except) in Australia and the polar regions.

13. (After/Afterwards) some modest victories (against/through) outdoor air pollution, scientists now find that the air indoors, laden with potentially deadly chemicals, can be far worse.
14. Some paintings reflect (of/on) the historical period (during/among) which they were created.
15. (In/On) November, 1860, the Pony Express carried news of President Abraham Lincoln's election from Fort Kearny, Nebraska, (by/to) Fort Churchill, Nevada.
16. (Because/Because of) the drought, water will be rationed his summer.
17. The twins look (alike/unlike), but you look just (alike/like) your father.
18. I'm living in an apartment (because/because of) I like to cook for myself. (Because/Because of) my getting a scholarship, I don't have to work this summer.
19. Usually the Northeast has lots of snow. This snowless winter is (like/unlike) any we can remember.
20. I won't be able to take that course (because/because of) the prerequisites. (Because/Because of) the reading list is so long, I really didn't want to take it anyway.

EXERCISE 10: These questions focus on preposition errors. There are 25 questions, and you have 20 minutes.

1. Deer are the only animals with bones called antlers on top their heads.

2. Cubism began on 1907 and became one of the most influential movements in modern art.

3. Benjamin Silliman, who founded the American Journal of Science in 1818, graduated in Yale University in 1796 and became Yale's first professor of chemistry and natural history.

4. Hormones serve as a means of communication among the brain and the pituitary gland.

5. Cancers are identified scientifically according of the type of body tissue in which they originate.

6. In addition works created for his own company, Alvin Ailey has composed dances for ballet and opera companies.

7. In an arboretum, plants are arranged based in the relationship to others of the same species.

8. A person can develop an allergy from any time, but in most cases, the first symptoms appear during childhood.

9. Alike crocodiles, alligators have a much broader snout and are much less vicious.

10. The standard paper used in finger painting is large and has a glazed side, at which the paint is applied.

11. The Earth can be divided to two parts, or hemispheres, according to the meridians of east and west longitude.

12. The Straits of Mackinac is a crucial link in the water route that leads during Lake Michigan to the Atlantic Ocean.

13. The United States needs lower vehicle-operation costs and better roads, capable in carrying more traffic with greater safety and speed.

14. Rock videos are shown for commercial and cable television stations, and at some dance clubs.

15. In March 12, 1933, President Franklin Roosevelt gave the first of his famous "fireside chats," speaking to the nation by radio.

16. Saccharin has been widely used in place sugar by people dieting to lose weight and by people with diabetes.

17. The tadpole stage may last from ten days to more than two years depending the species of frog or toad.

18. Tangelo is a mandarin citrus fruit that results from crosspollination among a tangerine and a grapefruit.

19. The Tasmanian devil, a fierce animal, is active mainly in night and spends the day in a cave, a hollow log, or some other shelter.

20. Like other woven fabrics, tapestries consist in vertical threads which make up the warp, and horizontal threads which form the weft.

21. The ease of solving a jigsaw puzzle depends the number of pieces, their shapes and shadings, and the design of the picture.

22. Plants range in size to tiny, single-celled, blue-green algae, invisible to the naked eye, to giant sequoias, the largest living plants.

23. The giant panda closely resembles the bear, but account of certain anatomical features it is classified in the raccoon family.

24. Wind may blow so fast and hard that it smashes buildings, pushes throughout large trees, and blows away soil from farmland.

25. Yo-yos, small toys that have been popular in the United States for the 1930s, consist of two round, flat pieces of wood or plastic joined at the center by a small peg.

ESSAY EXERCISE 5: Correct these student sentences from TOEFL test essays. Find preposition errors. There are some sentences with no preposition errors.

1. I think that information technology is useful two reasons.
2. Human beings have become skillful people by listening many things.
3. Because new students will come to my community, people living in my community may interact these new people.
4. When I was a child, I grew up the countryside.
5. I think children should be required to help with household tasks as soon as they are able because parents can give their children to some knowledge.
6. For my experience, when I was in junior high, I often cleaned our bathroom.
7. In order to establish a new university, the government has to look about areas to build the necessary buildings.
8. In my community there are two educational institutions in a high level.
9. Both spending time with one's family and spending time with friends have advantages.

10. When you are with a large number of friends, you can do many activities together, like going in a trip.
11. I used to always be with two of my friends. Do you think I was happy that time?
12. We need to belong a society.
13. They can speak each other all the time.
14. I like to share my happiness in this special day.
15. I always had fun in my birthday parties.

9. VERBALS (GERUNDS, INFINITIVES, AND PARTICIPLES)

Verbals may look like verbs because they have verb forms inside them, but they are NOT verbs. Make sure you don't confuse verbals with the verb in the sentence. Verbals include gerunds, infinitives, and participles.

A. GERUNDS

Gerunds are nouns that end in *–ing*. They are NOT the verb in the sentence.

They can be the subject of the sentence.	**Skiing** is fun.
They can be the direct object.	I enjoy **skiing**.
They can be the object of a preposition.	I am afraid of **skiing**.
The gerund form should follow prepositions.	After **skiing** all day, I'm tired.

DON'T confuse gerunds with verbs. **I was skiing** *last weekend when you called.* (*Was skiing* is a verb, not a gerund.) **Skiing** *is dangerous.* (*Skiing* is the gerund/noun subject and *is* is the verb.)

Certain verbs must be followed by the gerund form.

admit	feel like	postpone
avoid	finish	quit
can't help	give up (stop)	recall
consider	imagine	recommend
delay	keep (continue)	regret
discontinue	look forward to	report
dislike	mind (object to)	suggest
enjoy	miss	understand

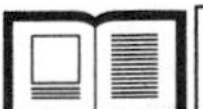

STUDY TIP

Memorize verbs which must be followed by a gerund. See Appendix A for a complete list.

B. INFINITIVES

Infinitives are *to* + base verb form. They are NOT the verb in the sentence.

They can be a noun.	I like **to ski**. (direct object) **To ski** is fun. (subject)
They can modify an adjective.	That's a good place **to ski**.
They can modify an adverb.	He ran quickly **to ski** before sundown.

Certain verbs must be followed by the infinitive form.

agree	decide	pay
allow	expect	prepare
appear	hope	promise
ask	learn	refuse
begin	need	want
can't wait	offer	wish
choose		

Certain verbs must be followed by an object and the infinitive.

advise	force	remind
allow	forbid	require
cause	hire	teach
convince	invite	tell
enable	order	urge
encourage	permit	warn
forbid	persuade	

EXAMPLE:		**Verb**	**Object**	**Infinitive**	
	I	**hired**	**her**	**to paint**	the house.

STUDY TIP

Memorize verbs which must be followed by an infinitive or an object + infinitive. See Appendix A for a complete list.

Certain verbs can be followed by the gerund or the infinitive.

begin	intend	remember *
can't stand	like	start
continue	love	stop *
forget*	love	try *
hate	regret *	

* These verbs change their meaning based on their taking a gerund or an infinitive.

EXAMPLES:

I stopped **smoking**. (gerund)	=	I quit smoking.
I stopped **to look** in the window. (infinitive)	=	I paused to look in the window.
I remember **meeting** Alyce Curtis. (gerund)	=	I remember something that happened in the past.
I always remember **to feed** the fish. (infinitive)	=	I remember to perform an obligation.
I often forget **to take** my keys. (infinitive)	=	I forget to do something.
I'll never forget **seeing** him for the first time. (gerund)	=	I won't forget something that happened in the past.

The form of the verbal may be incorrect: *I want to going home*. The sentence should read: *I want* to go *home*.

STUDY TIP

Memorize verbs which can be followed by either the gerund or the infinitive. See Appendix A for a complete list.

GERUND/INFINITIVE EXERCISE: Circle the correct form.

1.	I enjoy	(swimming/to swim).	
2.	He persuaded	(me to go/to go).	
3.	Where did you learn	(to play/playing)	bridge?
4.	I can't stand	(waiting/to wait)	for my clothes to dry.
5.	Before	(to cross/crossing)	the street, look both ways.
6.	Where would you like	(living/to live)	next semester?
7.	Who taught	(them to speak/to speak them)	French?
8.	I miss	(being/to be)	able to go next door for a pizza.
9.	I hate	(arriving/arrive)	late.
10.	My roommate doesn't recall	(giving/to give)	me her key.
11.	I wouldn't mind	(repeating/to repeat)	this exercise.

EXERCISE 11: These questions focus on gerund/infinitive errors. There are 10 questions, and you have 8 minutes.

1. The purpose of inductive logic is to inferring general laws from particular occurrences that seem to occur frequently.

2. Giraffes have eyes that allow them seeing in all directions without twisting their heads.

3. Until the 1910 formation of the National Hockey Association in Canada, professional and amateur teams were encouraged to playfully as well as to compete together.

4. The energy needed for animals grow is derived primarily from carbohydrates and fat.

5. A number of general farm organizations work to advancing the interests of farmers and to coordinate the sharing of machinery.

6. When inflation is rampant, many families no longer enjoy to spend as much money as they used to do.

7. Mercury is so small and so near the sun that one must use a telescope to see it although one can imagine to visualize it with the naked eye.

8. John Marshall felt that creating a strong central government, rather than enabling states to be self-sufficient, could best help the United States growing safe and strong.

9. Mathematics is necessary in design bridges, buildings, tunnels, and other architectural and engineering projects so that engineers can avoid miscalculating basic dimensions.

10. During World War I, the success of American movie companies enabled producers spending money on extravagant costumes and set designs.

C. PARTICIPLES

Participles are adjectives that end in *–ing* or are the past participle form, commonly *-ed.* They are NOT the verb in the sentence.

1. *-ing* Adjectives

Participial adjectives end in *–ing,* (the present participle) if their meaning is ACTIVE.

EXAMPLES:

The **boring** teacher is in Room 222.
The teacher is doing the action. The teacher is causing other people to feel bored.

The **crying** baby finally fell asleep.
The baby was crying.

2. *-ed* Adjectives

Participial adjectives end in *–ed,* sometimes *–en,* (the past participle) if their meaning is PASSIVE.

EXAMPLES:

The **bored** student fell asleep.
The student was bored by someone else.

The **broken** window is on the second floor.
The window was broken by someone else.

Common Participles:

amusing/amused	boring/bored	breaking/broken
confusing/confused	exhausting/exhausted	frightening/frightened
interesting/interested	surprising/surprised	tiring/tired

EXAMPLES:

A registering cow is one whose family history has been recorded with the appropriate breed association in its register.

The sentence should read: *A registered cow is one whose family history has been recorded with the appropriate breed association in its register.* A cow is registered BY someone official.

A worked camel cannot wear a bit and bridle, as a horse does.

The sentence should read: *A working camel cannot wear a bit and bridle, as a horse does* because the camel is doing the work.

STUDY TIP

Find the subject in the sentence. Is the subject causing (ACTIVE) the action or feeling, or is the subject experiencing (PASSIVE) the feeling? *The interesting professor* is causing the students to feel interest. *The interested student* is experiencing an interest in the subject because of someone or something.

PARTICIPLE EXERCISE: Decide if the active or passive participle form is needed.

EXAMPLE: Robin Williams amuses people.
amusing Robin Williams amused people

1. Copley Place satisfies customers.
___________Copley Place ___________customers
2. Clowns sometimes frighten children.
_____________children _____________clowns
3. Races exhaust swimmers.
____________swimmers ____________ races
4. The article bored the students.
The _________ article The _______ students
5. The new traffic patterns confuse drivers.
The ________ new traffic patterns The _________ drivers
6. The recipe interests the cook.
The _________ recipe The _________ cook
7. The fire damaged the forest.
The _________ forest The _________ fire
8. The trip tired the hikers.
The ________ hikers The ________ trip
9. The score surprised the test taker.
The _________ test taker The ________ score
10. The conversation distracted the professor.
The __________ professor The _______ conversation

EXERCISE 12: These questions focus on participle errors. There are 15 questions, and you have 10 minutes.

1. Woody Allen has written, directed, and starred in many comic films in which he portrays a witty but confused man troubling by modern society and his relationships with women.

2. The Statue of Liberty is one of the most celebrating examples of repousse work, a process of hammering metal inside a mold.

3. Physical anthropologists study differences among human beings, included blood types, skin colors, and inherited diseases.

4. There is an increasing demand for architects who can recondition existed buildings of artistic or historical value.

5. Millions of tourists who are interested in boating and fishing visit Arkansas every year to enjoy the sparkled lakes.

6. John Ashbery, an American poet, writes poems which have no realistic beginning, middle, or end, imitated instead the fluidity of thought.

7. Twinkled stars are actually an illusion caused by moving layers of air in the earth's atmosphere.

8. In black humor, authors insert moments of hilarity into novels and stories that deal basically with depressed topics and abused loved ones.

9. The author most closely associating with surprising endings is O.Henry, the pen name used by William Sydney Porter.

10. Although Maya Angelou's giving name was Marguerite, she acquired her current name from her brother, who nicknamed her Maya as a child.

11. The plan connected the Hudson River with Lake Erie by a canal was first proposed in the waning years of the eighteenth century.

12. To gild china and pottery, a paint is mixed with gold powder and applying with a brush.

13. Wool, silk, and animal skins dying with the orange-red dye henna are sold and sought after around the world.

14. The medium of television helped John F. Kennedy greatly during his four televising debates with Vice President Richard Nixon.

15. As early as 3500 B.C., craftworkers discovered that gold heating with fire could be pounded into thin sheets and then shaped.

ESSAY EXERCISE 6: Correct these student sentences from TOEFL test essays. Find gerund, infinitive, and participle errors.

1. I'm interesting in the evolution of those people.
2. Studying without a teacher would be bored.
3. I really miss to be with my close friends in my country.
4. Children should be required helping with the household tasks.
5. It is locating in the center of town.
6. I can't wait returning to see my hometown's new university.
7. If I could visit a country for two weeks, I'd visit Thailand because I've been hoping going there for many years.
8. I enjoy to live in a university town.
9. When I stopped to wear my school uniform every day, I felt like an adult.
10. I can't wait visiting Spain because I want to see a bullfight.

10. MODALS

A modal is an auxiliary (*can, could, may, might,* etc.) + the base verb form or the past participle form. It changes the meaning of the verb. Modals can express that the speaker feels something is necessary (*MUST*), recommended (*SHOULD*), possible (*CAN*), or preferable (*WOULD RATHER*).

A. PRESENT MODALS
MODAL + BASE FORM
(I CAN SING.)

Can
Could
Can
May
Might
Must
Ought to
Should
Will
Would

B. PAST MODALS
MODAL + *HAVE* + PAST PARTICIPLE
(I COULD HAVE SUNG.)

Could have
Should have
Had to have
Must have
Would have
May have
Might have
Ought to have
Was supposed to have
Would rather have

C. PHRASAL MODALS
PHRASAL MODAL + BASE FORM
(I'M ABLE TO SING.)

Be able to
Be going to
Be supposed to
Have got to
Used to
Have to
Had better

STRATEGIES FOR MODALS

1. **Make sure *to* is NOT inserted between the modal auxiliary and the base form.**

EXAMPLE:
Today a person can to take a picture simply by aiming the camera and pressing a button.

The sentence should read: *Today a person can take a picture simply by aiming the camera and pressing a button.*

2. Make sure *to* is necessary.

EXCEPTIONS:

- the modals *have to* and *have got to* meaning *must*
- *used to,* meaning something no longer done
- *supposed to,* meaning expectation
- *able to,* meaning ability

EXAMPLES:

I **used to** play piano.
I am **supposed to** meet my advisor at noon.
I'm **able to** speak Arabic.

3. Make sure the base form doesn't change.

INCORRECT: She should studies. She should studied.
Both sentences should read: *She should study.*

EXERCISE 13: These questions focus on modal errors. There are 10 questions, and you have 8 minutes.

1. Birds such as the raven and the pigeon can to solve simple counting problems.

2. A liquid does not have reach its boiling point to evaporate completely.

3. The ease with which houseplants can grown causes them to be popular among amateur horticulturists.

4. Scientists believe that the jumping motion of the jumping bean helps scare away birds and other animals that might to try to eat the seeds.

5. Karate students may advanced through various ranks of achievement, each of which is designated by a belt of a different color.

6. For kindergarten students, a trip to the post office can leading them to build a post office with blocks or to pretend that they are collecting and delivering the mail.

7. During the Middle Ages, hunters used to using their knives for eating as well as hunting.

8. Knitted clothes are popular because they can to stretch and then return to their original shape.

9. At night the desert floor radiates heat back into the atmosphere and the temperature may be drop to near freezing.

10. After his trips to the West between 1869 and 1872, Ralph Albert Blakelock would often painted American Indian encampments on brown-and-yellow toned canvases.

ESSAY EXERCISE 7: Correct these student sentences from TOEFL test essays. Find modal errors.

1. If I had the opportunity to visit any country in the world, I would probably chose Spain.
2. Education should be remain as an undergraduate major.
3. My mother told me that I could not cook without adult supervision because I would burned myself.
4. Not being able to pay the tuition might be affect my studying.
5. We could easily understood each other.
6. I must to graduate next spring.
7. Sometimes I would like just be with one or two of my friends.

11. PRONOUNS

Pronouns are words that take the place of nouns or noun phrases. They refer to people or things previously mentioned in the sentence or understood from the context. Pronouns can serve different functions in a sentence. For example, they can serve as subjects or objects. The form of the pronoun usually changes depending on its function.

Recognize the function of the pronoun in the sentence. Be sure it is in the correct form.

SUBJECT PRONOUNS	OBJECT PRONOUNS	POSSESSIVE ADJECTIVES	POSSESSIVE PRONOUNS	REFLEXIVE PRONOUNS
		(must be followed by a noun)		
I	me	my	mine	myself
you	you	your	yours	yourself
he	him	his	his	himself
she	her	her	hers	herself
it	it	its	*no form*	itself
we	us	our	ours	ourselves
you	you	your	yours	yourselves
they	them	their	theirs	themselves

EXAMPLES:
The pronghorn resembles an antelope. **It** has small forked horns.
It, the subject pronoun, refers to the pronghorn in the previous sentence. If the pronoun is the subject of the sentence, use a **subject pronoun**.

The horns are curved. Most animals are afraid of **them**.
Them, the object pronoun, coming after the preposition *of,* refers to the horns. If the pronoun is the object in the sentence, use an **object pronoun**.

The job **itself** isn't so difficult. Carol lives **by herself**.
These pronouns are **reflexive pronouns,** pronouns used when subjects and objects of a sentence refer to the same people or things. In the first sentence, *itself* refers to the preceding noun, *job.* In the second sentence, *by herself* means *without any help* or *alone.*

A. PRONOUN RULES

1. **A pronoun must agree in number (singular or plural) with the noun it refers to.**

EXAMPLES:
By 1923, the average wage of industrial workers was twice what they had been in 1914.

The sentence should read: *By 1923 the average wage of industrial workers was twice what it had been in 1914.* The subject is *wage,* a singular noun, and the pronoun, *they,* should be singular.

The kangaroo rat is so good at storing its seed supply in an underground burrow that farmers may someday borrow their method.

The sentence should read: *The kangaroo rat is so good at storing its seed supply in an underground burrow that farmers may someday borrow its method.* The incorrect pronoun *their* is referring to the kangaroo rat, which is singular.

2. **Pronouns must be in the correct form.**

EXAMPLES:
The Double Helix is James Watson's notoriously personal account of the scientific feat that won himself and Frances Click the Nobel Prize in 1962.

The sentence should read: *The Double Helix is James Watson's notoriously personal account of the scientific feat that won him and Frances Click the Nobel Prize in 1962.* The pronoun should be the object form, not the reflexive form.

The telescopes of the late 1600s magnified objects thirty-three times theirs original size.

The sentence should read: *The telescopes of the late 1600s magnified objects thirty-three times their original size.* The pronoun should be in the possessive adjective form, not the possessive pronoun form.

STUDY TIPS

1. Recognize differences between spoken and written English.
2. Although you may hear native speakers say, "Me and my sister are applying to graduate schools," the subject pronoun is needed. The sentence should read: *My sister and I are applying to graduate schools.* (The pronoun comes after the named subject.)
3. Make sure you use object pronouns after prepositions. You may hear native speakers say, "What I'm telling you is just between you and I." The sentence should read: *What I'm telling you is just between you and me.*

3. **If a sentence has a subject, it doesn't need a second one.**
A pronoun is often used as an incorrect double subject.

EXAMPLE:
Puritan settlements they grew marvelously, as fur trading, fishing, and shipbuilding blossomed into important industries.

The sentence should read: *Puritan settlements grew marvelously, as fur trading, fishing, and shipbuilding blossomed into important industries.* The sentence has a subject, *settlements.* It cannot have a second subject, the pronoun *they.*

Make sure the pronoun is in the correct form and that it agrees with the noun that precedes it.

PRONOUN EXERCISE: Circle the pronouns. Draw arrows to the noun references. Then correct the errors.

1. Abraham Lincoln delivered its most famous address at the dedication of the soldiers' cemetery in Gettysburg.
2. The poet Marianne Moore was initially associated with the imagist movement, but later developed her own rhyme patterns and verse forms.
3. Many narcotic plants and its products, such as nicotine, are effective in controlling insects.
4. Farming becomes more expensive when farmers are forced to apply greater quantities of costly fertilizers to sustain its yields.
5. The metaphors we use routinely are the means by which we describe one's everyday experiences.
6. If they are prepared skillfully, soybeans they can be appetizing as well as nutritious.
7. Studies of both vision and physical optics began almost as early as civilization themselves.
8. James Whitcomb Riley, the "Hoosier Poet," wrote much of his work in standard English, but himself wrote his most popular poems in the dialect of his home state, Indiana.
9. A traditional Halloween decoration is a jack-o-lantern, which is a hollowed-out pumpkin with a scary face cut into them.
10. In the homeopathic remedy called proving, various substances are administered to healthy people and its effects carefully observed.

EXERCISE 14: These questions focus on pronoun errors. There are 25 questions, and you have 20 minutes.

1. The men and women who pushed the frontier westward across America probably never thought of them as brave pioneers.

2. The human brain it is so highly developed that it makes people different from all other living things.

3. The bottom of a valley is called their floor, and usually slopes gradually in one direction.

4. Most kinds of mollusks, including clams and oysters, have a hard, armorlike shell that protects its soft bodies.

5. The largest crowds come to New Orleans for the annual Mardi Gras celebration, with their spectacular parades and other merry festivities.

6. Most bottom-dwelling creatures, considered part of the plankton, drift with the currents during the early stages of its development.

7. Porcelain, characterized by its whiteness and delicate appearance, is a type of ceramic highly valued for their beauty and strength.

8. Manufacturers of consumer goods often change the styles of them products.

9. Inventor Granville Woods received him first patent on January 3, 1984, for a steam boiler furnace.

10. Tent caterpillars get its name because most species spin loose, white, tentlike webs in the forks of trees.

11. To form a silicate glass, the liquid from which it is made must be cooled rapidly enough to prevent it crystallization.

12. By distinguishing himself as a judge in Arizona, Sandra Day O'Connor caught President Reagan's attention and was appointed the first woman justice on the Supreme Court.

13. The Postal Service has modernized their operations to increase the speed of mail handling.

14. Petroleum it is composed of a complex mixture of hydrogen and carbon.

15. Archaeological investigations indicate that control of fire is an extremely old technical attainment, though the time, place, and mode of his origin may never be learned.

16. The hardness of minerals often gives clues to his identity.

17. Taconite is so hard that ordinary drilling and blasting methods cannot be used to obtain them.

18. In the winter, New Hampshire skiers race down snow-covered slopes and then warm them near crackling fires in friendly ski lodges.

19. Gorillas are the most terrestrial of the great apes because their bulky size makes it ill suited to dwelling in trees.

20. United States senators were elected by state legislatures until 1913, when the Seventeenth Amendment to the Constitution required that them be chosen by popular election.

21. Snails travel on roadways that they make them by producing a sticky liquid.

22. Tarragon is widely cultivated for their leaves and young shoots, which are used as a flavoring for vinegar.

23. Seeds need oxygen for the changes that take place within theirs during germination.

24. The two sides of the heart relax and fill, and then contract and empty them at the same time.

25. Profit is the amount of money a company has left over from the sale of their products after it has paid for all the expenses of production.

ESSAY EXERCISE 8: Correct these student sentences from TOEFL test essays. Find pronoun errors.

1. It helps people to get rid of something they don't want instead of throwing them away.
2. Everybody has to do what they are told to do.
3. In some countries, teenagers have jobs while themselves are students.
4. Between you and I, it's not a good idea to build a high school in my community.
5. I think universities should give more money to its libraries than to sports.
6. My best friend watches television all the time and doesn't spend enough time on hers homework.
7. I thought I knew a lot about the United States because I had seen many of their advertisements.
8. If I were to choose my roommate by myself, I might pick someone just like myself.
9. The invention of the telephone, it has enabled people in very remote areas of my country to feel less isolated.
10. Me and my best friend went to ten countries together last summer.

12. *TAKE, MAKE, DO*

The following verb + noun combinations cause problems for many students. Although these combinations may not always appear on the TOEFL test, studying them will help your essay writing. Also, the following expressions are used frequently in spoken English. Often these verb + noun relationships don't translate well from other languages into English.

TAKE	MAKE	DO
care	a mistake	homework
a picture	friends	well
your time	a deposit	research
an airplane	a suggestion	exercises
medicine	a reservation	a good job
a chance	a speech	an experiment
a trip	a bet	housework
a turn	progress	a favor
a good look	money	a project
a bath	a promise	your own thing
charge	an effort	or die
effect	a recommendation	your best
exception	a comparison	
five	arrangements	
place	an appointment	
the heat	your bed	
sides	a face	
stock	believe	
the heat	fun of	
one's breath away	ends meet	
hold	do	
	a model	
	clothes	

> Make sure the nouns that follow *TAKE, MAKE,* and *DO* are used correctly.

***TAKE/MAKE/DO* EXERCISE:** Circle the correct verb.

1.	How often do you	make/take	medicine?
2.	We have to	do/make	all the exercises by Friday.
3.	You can	do/make	a reservation on the Internet.
4.	That comedian is always	doing/making	fun of his wife.
5.	Your picture	did/took	my breath away.
6.	Let's see if we can	do/make	the housework by noon.
7.	Don't	make/take	sides.
8.	Will you	do/make	me a favor?
9.	I'm not sure you'll	do/make	money selling your books.
10.	Can I ask you to	do/take	a picture of our class?
11.	If I	do/make	a good job, I'll be happy.
12.	We can use Lab 212 to	do/make	the experiment.
13.	Please don't	do/make	a face in the class photo.
14.	The general	made/took	charge of the operation.
15.	Try and	make/take	a good look.
16.	Are you going to	make/take	a trip over spring break?
17.	It's easy for her to	do/make	friends wherever she goes.
18.	Just	do/make	your best.
19.	I hope the implant will	make/take	hold.
20.	Do you want to	make/take	a bet?

EXERCISE 15: These questions focus on *take/make/do* errors. There are 10 questions, and you have 8 minutes.

1. Because terra cotta can be molded easily, many sculptors have used the materials to take preliminary models of their work.

2. Honey is the sweet, thick fluid did by bees from flower nectar, which is thin and watery.

3. Doing clothing was an important task in most colonial households.

4. The remarkable plasticity of clay does it an especially responsive medium for amateur potters.

5. When doing a speech, the speaker should select a familiar topic and do the necessary research.

6. Engineers thoroughly test new airplane prototypes before they do the planes into the sky.

7. In 1944, the International Monetary Conference did place at Bretton Woods in the White Mountains of New Hampshire.

8. While making research, a researcher makes a list of key words in the field and of authors who have written on the subject.

9. Proper lighting and a comfortable, supportive chair help one to make homework more effectively.

10. One can take an appointment by fax, on the Internet, by phone, or in person from nine to five.

13. PARALLELISM/WORD FORM/WORD ORDER

What appears most often on the TOEFL test are items testing parallelism or word form. To make sure items are parallel, meaning *in the same form,* check lists of words/phrases, or words on either sides of coordinating conjunctions to be sure that they have the same form. In error identification questions, for example, the underlined word might be an adjective when it should be a noun. In sentence completion questions, the item will ask you to identify which word, phrase, or clause is parallel to something else in the sentence.

STUDY TIP

Understanding parallelism, word form, and word order is also important for writing the essay. See the Essay Writing section, pages 209–217, for more detailed explanations and numerous exercises.

A. PARALLELISM/WORD FORM/WORD ORDER RULES

1. Adjectives always come BEFORE nouns and compound nouns

EXAMPLES: impressionist painters, reserved places, football stadium, a contented cow
(**NOT** noun before adjectives: *painters impressionist, places reserved, stadium football, a cow contented*)

2. Adverbs come before adjectives

EXAMPLES: very fast, extremely good
(**NOT** adjectives before adverbs: *fast very, good extremely*)

3. Nouns or adjectives come after linking verbs

EXAMPLES: Elizabeth is a doctor. She seems tall.
(**NOT** adverbs after linking verbs: *Elizabeth is quickly.*)

4. Nouns or adverbs come after action verbs

EXAMPLES: The family ate supper. The dancer performed beautifully.
(**NOT** adjectives after action verbs: *The family ate happy. The dancer performed beautiful.*)

EXAMPLES:
With a dictionary, a person can a word look up quickly, discover what it means, and learn how it is pronounced.

The sentence should read: *With a dictionary, a person can look up a word quickly, discover what it means, and learn how it is pronounced. A word look up* is not in the correct order. The direct object, *word,* should come AFTER the phrasal verb, *look up.*

Ants as well as honeybees have queens that lay all the eggs, and workers that food gather for the colony.

The sentence should read: *Ants as well as honeybees have queens that lay all the eggs, and workers that gather food for the colony. Food gather* is not in the correct order. The direct object, *food,* should come AFTER the verb, *gather.*

The Mark Twain Home and Museum in Hannibal, Missouri, is the ____________ of the writer.

- ⬭ restored childhood home
- ⬭ home restored of childhood
- ⬭ home where childhood restored
- ⬭ restored home of his childhood

The sentence should read: *The Mark Twain Home and Museum in Hannibal, Missouri, is the restored childhood home of the writer.* The correct order of the phrase is *restored childhood home. Childhood home* is the compound noun, meaning these two ideas, like *tennis court* or *bus driver,* act as one, preceded by the adjective, *restored.*

Plantations developed in colonies _______ by growing a single crop for export.

- ⬭ where people lived the majority
- ⬭ where lived the majority of people
- ⬭ where the majority of people lived
- ⬭ where did the majority of people live

The sentence should read: *Plantations developed in colonies where the majority of people lived by growing a single crop for export.* The correct order of the adjective clause is *where the majority of people lived.* The correct word order is relative pronoun, *where,* subject, *the majority,* verb, *lived.*

Buffalo Bill, whose real name was William Frederick Cody, was a frontiersman rugged and noted sharpshooter of the American West.

The sentence should read: *Buffalo Bill, whose real name was William Frederick Cody, was a rugged frontiersman and noted sharpshooter of the American West.* The adjective, *rugged,* should come before the noun, *frontiersman.*

Parallelism/word form/word order errors are very common on the TOEFL test. Check each word to make sure it is in the correct form. Check that words or phrases are parallel with each other. Check that words are in the correct word order.

STUDY TIP

Make sure you are able to recognize nouns, verbs, adjectives, and adverbs from their form/endings. Make sure you know the word order these parts of speech follow in clauses.

EXERCISE 16: These questions focus on word order errors. There are 20 questions, and you have 16 minutes.

1. In the three decades after 1950, the population of the North increased at half only the rate of the South and West.

2. Hazel is any one of about fifteen trees and shrubs that grow in the climates temperate of Asia, Europe, and North America.

3. Baby's breath is the common name applied to several World Old plants with blossoms that are delicate in fragrance and appearance.

4. A computer receives individual pieces of data, changes the data into more useful information, and then tells the operator _______.
   - ◯ the information is what
   - ◯ what is the information
   - ◯ isn't it the information
   - ◯ what the information is

5. The metaphors we use routinely are the means which by we describe our everyday experiences.

6. Clarence Day's works *Life with Father* and *Life with Mother* provide _______________ in New York City during the late 1800s.
   - ◯ an upper-class picture life entertaining
   - ◯ a picture entertaining of upper-class life
   - ◯ upper class life's entertaining picture
   - ◯ an entertaining picture of upper-class life

7. The primary aim of science horticultural is to develop plants of the highest quality that offer the promise of high yields.

8. A solar day is the _________ the earth to turn around once with respect to the sun.
   - ◯ length the time it takes
   - ◯ time that it takes the length
   - ◯ length of time that it takes
   - ◯ takes the length of time

9. It was after shortly microscopes were introduced at the beginning of the seventeenth century that microorganisms were actually sighted.

10. Many of the trees native to Maine yield woods useful, a number of which are of high market value.

11. Seismology has not reached yet the stage where earthquakes can be foretold with a great deal of accuracy.

12. The factory system was introduced in New Hampshire in early the 1800s, and mills sprang up where rivers furnished water power and transportation.

13. In blank verse ______ of ten syllables, five of which are accented.
    - ◯ line consists of each
    - ◯ consists of each line
    - ◯ each line consists
    - ◯ it consists of each line

14. In the 1960s, a singer named Marni Nixon famous became in the United States for supplying the singing voice for prominent movie actresses.

15. The recent discovery of a novel by Harriet Wilson, published in 1859, ________ a landmark in Black American literature.
    - ◯ has brought to light
    - ◯ light to brought has
    - ◯ brought to light has
    - ◯ has light to brought

16. Coral reefs owe their brilliant colors to algae that live in symbiosis with polyps coral.

17. Exciting tales of cowboy life, cowboy sad songs, and colorful cowboy language have all become part of American folklore.

18. After the great blizzard of 1978 in the northeastern Unites States, it took some ________ the snow away from their homes.
    - ◯ days to shovel people several
    - ◯ people several days to shovel
    - ◯ several days people to shovel
    - ◯ people to shovel several days

19. John Singleton Copley, whose superb portraits capture the character of Americans in settings of everyday life, is generally considered the greatest painter portrait in colonial America.

20. __________ of a newspaper nor the number of pages in an edition has ever been standardized.
    - ◯ The page size is neither
    - ◯ Neither is the pages size
    - ◯ The page size, neither
    - ◯ Neither the page size

EXERCISE 17: These questions focus on parallelism, word form, and word order errors. There are 20 questions, and you have 16 minutes.

1. On foot, on horseback, and going by boat, William Clark and Meriwether Lewis led an expedition from 1804 to 1806.

2. The University of Kentucky has colleges of agriculture, architecture, business, economics, dentistry, education, legal, and pharmacy.

3. An abacus can be used to add, subtract, multiply, for dividing, and calculate square roots and cube roots.

4. The revolutionary Eugene O'Neill great influenced the theater with his realistic themes and daring stage techniques.

5. More than 33 billions dollars is spent on advertising in the United Sates each year.

6. Neil Simon has become the most commercial successful playwright in the history of American drama.

7. The invention of the reaper, the thresher, and the steel plow encouraged the development of farm in the well-irrigated eastern part of the prairies.

8. Holography is a method of making three-dimensional images on a photographically plate or film.

9. Many states and local governments have laws regulating the conditions under which dairy farmers can produce and _____ milk.
    - ◯ sold
    - ◯ sell
    - ◯ selling
    - ◯ sale

10. The first elevated railroad cars were elaborate, with mahogany woodwork, carpet floors, and plush seats.

11. The immune system produces substances that are ____________ designed to fight a particular invading substance.
    - ◯ specific
    - ◯ specification

- specifically
- special

12. A hiccup is an abrupt, involuntarily intake of air caused by a spasm of the diaphragm.

13. American musical comedy has inspired some of the most _____ dances ever created.
    - imagination
    - imagine
    - imaginative
    - imagined

14. The juicy of one orange provides the minimum daily requirement of Vitamin C.

15. Unlike swimming, diving emphasizes technique rather than endurance or _____.
    - sped
    - speeding
    - speedy
    - speed

16. Gerald R. Ford, the thirty-eighth president of the United States, had a calm, friendly manner and an unquestioned reputation for honest.

17. Dogs provide _______ for people of all ages.
    - companion
    - companionable
    - companionship
    - companies

18. The major of bees are solitary insects, as each female provides for her own offspring.

19. The first dolls manufactured in the United States were ___________ made by Izannah F. Walker of Central Falls, Rhode Island.
    - probing
    - probability
    - probably
    - probable

20. The city of Toronto, in the Canadian province of Ontario, has one of the world's safest, cleaning, and most efficient subway systems.

EXERCISE 18: These questions focus on parallelism, word form, and word order errors. There are 20 questions, and you have 18 minutes.

1. Libraries play a vital role in the education, working, and recreation of millions of people.

2. Technological information has become _________ of many nations.
    - the importance of a concern
    - a concern of important
    - the importance concerning
    - an important concern

3. The future of lands from Nebraska to western Texas depends on an underground water supply, a naturally treasure called the Oglala Aquifer.

4. Since World War II, the pace of medical discoverer has quickened, spurred by billions of dollars in federal aid.

5. The technological advances of the first half of the nineteenth century contributed significant to naval design.

6. The luster of the fabric damask depends on length of fibers, closeness of weave, and ___________.
    - yarns of the uniformity
    - uniformity yarns
    - yarns uniformity
    - uniformity of yarns

7. In the United States, petunias are cultivated widely as annually garden flowers.

8. The tent caterpillar has a row of ____________ along its back.
   - ◯ spot of yellow
   - ◯ yellow in spots
   - ◯ yellow spots
   - ◯ yellow spotted

9. Most psychiatrists and ____________ still consider dreams to be psychologically meaningful.
   - ◯ psychological
   - ◯ psychologically
   - ◯ psychology
   - ◯ psychologists

10. A computer can handle vast amounts of facts and figures and solve complicated problems at incredible high speeds.

11. Most American Indian groups handed down their folk tales and poets by word of mouth for centuries.

12. Idaho's natural resources include fertile soil, minerals deposits, thick forests, and abundant water.

13. The cottage industry was an economic system wide used during the Industrial Revolution.

14. Cotton buys and sellers judge cotton on the basis of samples cut from the bales.

15. U.S. cattle owners have worked to improve breeds and increasing milk and beef production.

16. Parrots are sociable, noise birds that live chiefly in forested areas in lowlands and mountains.

17. Thomas Jefferson favored a ________ that would pay more attention to the common citizen.
   - ◯ government
   - ◯ govern
   - ◯ governess
   - ◯ governmental

18. Oliver Wendell Holmes was an American writer who achieved famous for his essays and poems.

19. Dogtooth violet is an ____ spring wild flower of the Eastern United States.
   - ◯ attractive
   - ◯ attraction
   - ◯ attract
   - ◯ attracted

20. Billie Holliday was admired for the uniquely bittersweet quality of her vocal and for phrasing that had much in common with the solos of the great improvising jazz musicians.

14. INVERTED SUBJECT + VERB ORDER

In English, the most common word order of a sentence is subject + verb + object.

Subject	**Verb**	**Object**
I	read	the book.

There are a few special situations in which this word order is reversed, or **inverted**. Instead of subject + verb, it's verb + subject. In many cases, only the auxiliary (or helping) form of the verb (*do, did, have, has,* etc.) comes before the subject, and the main verb comes after the subject. This auxiliary has to be added.

You are already familiar with inverted word order in question form.

Auxiliary Verb	**Subject**	**Verb**
Did	you	read the book?
Should	we	meet after class?

However, questions NEVER appear on the Structure section.

Inverted word order sentences have two patterns.

• Auxiliary Verb	Subject	Main Verb
• Other Structure	Verb	Subject

A. PATTERN I

Auxiliary Verb **Subject** **Main Verb**

1. Conditional sentences (present and past unreal without *if* or *unless*)

Regular Word Order	**Inverted Word Order**
Present Unreal **If I were** tall, I would play basketball.	Present Unreal **Were I** tall, I would play basketball.
Past Unreal **If I had known** your phone number, I would have called you.	Past Unreal **Had I known** your phone number, I would have called you.

2. Comparisons ending with *so have/has, so will, so do/does, did, neither, than*

Regular Word Order	**Inverted Word Order**
John eats a lot, and **I do** too.	John eats a lot, and **so do I**.
Trevor will resign, and **Chuck will** too.	Trevor will resign, and **so will Chuck**.
Neither Katie nor Jenny finished the book.	Katie didn't finish the book, and **neither did** Jenny.
I read more pages than **Kevin read**.	I read more pages **than did Kevin**.

3. *Only* and time expressions (*only once, only after, etc.*)

Invert the subject + verb in the main clause.
Only once **have I had** such a wonderful class.

Only after I moved to California **did I learn** to surf.

Only since I came to Boston **have I had** lobster.

B. PATTERN II

Other Structure **Verb** **Subject**

1. Negative beginnings (*hardly ever, rarely, never, nowhere, no, at no time, scarcely, not only*)

When a negative word or phrase begins a sentence, the subject and verb are inverted. (This usage is uncommon in speech, but in writing, it emphasizes the point.)

Regular Word Order	**Inverted Word Order**
I have never taken such a hard test.	**Never have I taken** such a hard test.
It has seldom rained this summer.	**Seldom has it rained** this summer.
You will never find me doing laundry.	**At no time will you find me** doing laundry.
I skipped breakfast and lunch.	**Not only did** I skip breakfast, but I also skipped lunch.

2. Introductory prepositional phrases

These phrases have an intransitive verb and a state of location.
If the prepositional phrase is NECESSARY to complete the idea, the subject and verb are inverted.

Regular Word Order	**Inverted Word Order**
The essays are on my desk.	On my desk **are the essays.**

The prepositional phrase *on my desk* is necessary to complete the sentence.

If the prepositional phrase is NOT necessary to complete the idea, the subject and verb are not inverted.

I swim in the ocean in the summer.
The prepositional phrase is NOT necessary, so the subject and verb (*I swim*) do NOT invert.

3. Sentences beginning with *here* or *there*

The verb must agree with the subject that comes after it.

Here **is** the answer **key**.
Singular verb, *is,* agrees with singular noun, *key.*

There **are** our **keys**.
Plural verb, *are,* agrees with plural noun, *keys.*

INCORRECT: There is the test, the book, and the papers you requested.
The sentence should read: *There are the test, the book, and the papers you requested.*
Think of the sentence rewritten as *The test, the book, and the papers you requested are there.*

INVERTED WORD ORDER EXERCISE: Rewrite the following sentences. Explain the reason for the inversion.

1. Nowhere we find such unusual gifts.

___

2. In the drawer the pencils are.

___

3. Here the final numbers are.

___

4. If you were prepared, you wouldn't worry about the test.

___

5. More planes take off from the Boston Airport than those do from the Providence Airport.

____

6. On the test questions were about the Civil War.

____

7. Only once I answered all the questions.

____

8. Neither Steve nor I have an interest in going.

____

9. Rarely it snows in October along the East Coast.

____

10. There my students are in the back of the cafeteria.

____

EXERCISE 19: These questions focus on inverted word order. There are 10 questions, and you have 8 minutes.

1. Only recently ________ possible to separate the components of fragrant substances and to determine their chemical composition.
   - ◯ it becomes
   - ◯ it has become
   - ◯ has it become
   - ◯ becomes it

2. Seldom __________ been of practical use in playing real games.
   - ◯ mathematical theories of games
   - ◯ are the mathematical theories of games
   - ◯ has the mathematical theory of games
   - ◯ the mathematical theory of games has

3. Probably no man had more effect on the daily lives of most people in the United States _________ Henry Ford, a pioneer in automobile production.
   - ◯ as was
   - ◯ than was
   - ◯ than did
   - ◯ as did

4. Not only _________ faster than mechanical switches, they are also free of arcing and mechanical wear.
   - ◯ electronic switches are
   - ◯ do electronic switches
   - ◯ are electronic switches
   - ◯ the electronic switches

5. ______ advance and retreat in their eternal rhythms, but the surface of the sea itself is never at rest.
   - ◯ Not only when the tides do
   - ◯ As the tides not only do
   - ◯ Not only do the tides
   - ◯ The tides do only

6. Beneath the streets of a modern city _____ of walls, columns, cables, pipes, and tunnels required to satisfy the needs of its inhabitants.
   - ◯ where exists the network
   - ◯ the existing network
   - ◯ the network exists
   - ◯ exists the network

7. The impact of Thoreau's "On the Duty of Civil Disobedience" might not have been so far-reaching __________ for Elizabeth Peabody, who dared to publish the controversial essay.
   - ◯ it not having been
   - ◯ it is not being
   - ◯ had it not been
   - ◯ is it not being

8. Sandstone in general is more easily cut and shaped than ____ such as granite.

- ⬭ are hard rocks
- ⬭ rocks as hard
- ⬭ rocks are hard
- ⬭ they are hard rocks

9. __________ the American pioneers not been so resourceful, they never would have survived.

- ⬭ Had
- ⬭ If
- ⬭ Would
- ⬭ Have

10. Only in the last 200 years __________ domestic sheep primarily for their meat.

- ⬭ have developed breeders
- ⬭ developed breeders have
- ⬭ breeders have developed
- ⬭ have breeders developed

15. *OTHER/THE OTHER/ANOTHER/THE OTHERS*

Other, the other, another, and *the others* can be confusing.

	ADJECTIVE	PRONOUN	MEANING
Singular	*another* book (is)	*another* (is)	Indefinite
	the other book (is)		Definite
Plural	*other* books (are)	*others* (are)	Indefinite
	the other books (are)	*the others* (are)	Definite

A. *OTHER/THE OTHER/ANOTHER/THE OTHERS* RULES

1. Make sure you don't use the word *others* before a noun. Adjectives NEVER end in *s*.

EXAMPLES:
Superior to all others wood for shipbuilding, teak is also used for furniture, flooring, and general construction.

The sentence should read: *Superior to all other wood for shipbuilding, teak is also used for furniture, flooring, and general construction.* Before the noun, *wood,* an adjective is needed. *Others,* ending in *s,* is not an adjective.

California covers a larger area than all others states except Texas and Alaska.

The sentence should read: *California covers a larger area than all other states except Texas and Alaska.* Before the noun, *states,* an adjective is needed. *Others,* ending in *s,* is not an adjective.

2. Make sure a noun is a singular count noun if *another* is used.

EXAMPLE:
The ancient Hopewell people of North America probably cultivated corn and another crops, but hunting and gathering were still critically important to their economy.

The sentence should read: *The ancient Hopewell people of North America probably cultivated corn and other crops, but hunting and gathering were still critically important to their economy. Crops* is plural, so *another* cannot be used.

EXERCISE: Fill in the blanks with *other, the other, another,* or *the others.*

1. Judy reads the *Boston Globe* every day. She doesn't read any ________ paper.
2. Some people like coffee. __________ like tea.
3. Only two students failed the test. All of ____________ passed.
4. Two countries border the U.S. One is Canada; __________ is Mexico.
5. There are thirty-three majors to choose. One is graphic design; ____________ is computer programming.
6. There are twelve students in my class. One is from Russia. __________ is from Cape Verde. __________ is from Taiwan. _____________ are from Korea. __________ are from Haiti, and ___________ are from Japan.

16. COMPARATIVE/SUPERLATIVE

Comparative forms compare two things. Superlative forms compare three or more things.

A. COMPARATIVE/SUPERLATIVE RULES

1. Most adjective rules follow this pattern:

ADJECTIVES	COMPARATIVE	SUPERLATIVE
1-SYLLABLE ADJECTIVES	ADD +ER	ADD +EST
small, tall	*smaller, taller*	*smallest, tallest*
2-SYLLABLE ADJECTIVES THAT END IN -Y	DROP -Y, ADD +IER	DROP -Y, ADD +IEST
crazy, pretty	*crazier, prettier*	*craziest, prettiest*
MOST 2-SYLLABLE ADJECTIVES	more + adjective	most + adjective
crowded	*more crowded*	*most crowded*
ALL 3+ SYLLABLE ADJECTIVES	more + adjective	most + adjective
talented	*more talented*	*most talented*

Some Exceptions

ADJECTIVE	COMPARATIVE	SUPERLATIVE
bad	worse	the worst
far	father/further	the farthest/the furthest
good	better	the best
little	less	the least
many	more	the most
much	more	the most

2. **To make an equal comparison, use *as* + (adjective/adverb) + *as*.** *He is* ***as tall as*** *his older brother. She runs* ***as quickly as I do.***

3. **If there's a number (*sixth*) before the superlative (*tallest*),** *the* ***sixth tallest building,*** **the noun (*building*) is in the singular.**

4. **Use *the* + comparative form of the adjective + *the* + comparative form of the adjective to show a cause and effect relationship.** ***The older*** *I get,* ***the more*** *I forget.*

EXAMPLES:

During hot summer months, cows are happiest and productivest when they are kept cool.

The sentence should read: *During hot summer months, cows are happiest and most productive when they are kept cool.* The superlative form of the three-syllable word productive is *the most productive.*

An adult human must take eight steps to go _______ as a giraffe does in one stride.

- ⬭ as far
- ⬭ the farther
- ⬭ how far
- ⬭ farther

The sentence should read: *An adult human must take eight steps to go as far as a giraffe does in one stride.* The equal comparison form is *as . . . as.*

> ☞ **Make sure that the comparative/superlative forms are correct. Make sure you recognize exceptions.**

COMPARATIVE/SUPERLATIVE EXERCISE: Circle the correct form.

1. She runs faster/more fast than her sister.
2. The test was difficulter/more difficult than I expected.
3. That was the baddest/worst tomato I've ever eaten.
4. I have less/littler time to see you this week.
5. Which of the two test sites is farther/more far from your house?
6. I don't think I did as well/so well on this test as I did on the last one.

EXERCISE 20: These questions focus on comparative/superlative errors. There are 5 questions, and you have 4 minutes.

1. Horses once provided the fastest and most sure way to travel on land.

2. The activities of the international marketing researcher are frequently much broader than ______.
   - ⬭ the domestic marketer has
   - ⬭ the domestic marketer does
   - ⬭ those of the domestic marketer
   - ⬭ that which has the domestic marketer

3. The greater an object's mass, _________ it is to speed it up or slow it down.
   - ⬭ the more it is difficult
   - ⬭ difficult
   - ⬭ the difficulter
   - ⬭ the more difficult

4. Coral reefs have always been __________ hazards to ships sailing in tropical seas.
   - ⬭ one of the greatest
   - ⬭ the greatest ones
   - ⬭ ones greatest
   - ⬭ the greatest were

5. The province of Newfoundland has ___________ than any other region of North America in which the first language is English.
   - ⬭ its longer history
   - ⬭ a longer history
   - ⬭ the longer the history
   - ⬭ the history is longer

EXERCISE 21: These questions focus on missing words, *other/the other,* commonly confused words, wrong words, and comparative/superlative errors. There are 24 questions, and you have 20 minutes.

1. Lillian Gilbreth was one of the leading engineers of the twentieth century as well a pioneer in the field of scientific management.

2. A mineral is made up substances that were never alive.

3. A striking feature of nearly all ballet companies today is their interest both classical and contemporary works.

4. "S" is about the eighth most frequently used letter in books, newspapers, and others printed materials in English.

5. Much retired people moved to Miami from other parts of the United States because of the healthful climate of southeastern Florida.

6. Alike most natural fibers, manufactured fibers are produced in long, continuous lengths, called filaments.

7. Meadowlarks are about the same size as robins, but they have more heavier bodies, shorter tails, and longer bills.

8. Rabbits and hares look much like and are often mistaken for each other.

9. Humus, a substance found in soil, is soft and spongy and enables plant roots to send out tiny hairs through that they absorb water and food.

10. Bowling is one of the most oldest and most popular indoor sports in which more Americans compete than in any other sport.

11. Marlon Brando ranks among the most famousest American actors to appear in the second half of the twentieth century.

12. While in the seventeenth century, South Carolina was the leading cultivator of rice in the American colonies.

13. Absolute zero is the theoretical temperature at which the atoms and molecules of a substance have the less possible energy.

14. Shirley Temple, the most popularest child motion-picture star of the 1930s, made her movie debut at the age of three and became a star in the 1934 film musical, *Stand Up and Cheer.*

15. The most worst economic reversal of the twentieth century, the Great Depression of the 1930s, began in the United States and spread abroad.

16. President Hoover said in his inaugural address that in no nation were the fruits of accomplishment more securer.

17. Seattle is the larger city in Washington and an important manufacturing, trade, and transportation center of the Pacific Northwest.

18. Scientists finding out that the universe is even larger and more complex than anyone has ever imagined.

19. Woody Herman ranks with Duke Ellington and Count Basie as one of three most durable figures in the history of big-band jazz.

20. Many engineers prefer a girder bridge to a truss bridge because a girder bridge is more attractive and more easy to construct and maintain.

21. Though smaller than our solar system, a quasar, which looks like an ordinary star, emits more light as an entire galaxy.

22. Making model ships is a fascinated hobby for both children and adults.

23. Underneath the direction of Charles Scribner, Sr. and that of his son, the firm of Charles Scribner's Sons published works which helped to make many authors famous.

24. In most countries, tea ranks as the more popular drink of all beverages.

ESSAY EXERCISE 9: Correct these student sentences from TOEFL test essays. These sentences have errors with wrong words, *other/the other,* missing words, comparative/ superlative, and commonly confused word errors. Some of the sentences have more than one error. There may be more than one way to correct some sentences.

1. And other thing is many special experiences from school.
2. I agree with children to grow up in the countryside.
3. Maybe it's because of we have different opinions.
4. Despite I live in a big city, I like the quiet of the countryside.
5. I prefer to spend time with number of friends.
6. Others choose to spend time a large number of friends.
7. Usually I like to enjoy activities that do not involve a lot of time to prepare. Then it is easy to commit one or two people.
8. I enjoy spending time with one or two close friends lifelong.
9. People are not same each other.
10. In China there are a lot of people speak Mandarin.
11. If I have good teachers, they can help me my problems.
12. We need to belong a society which we call school and we also need to communicate.
13. However it was not an advanced course, I learned a lot.
14. Now I'm a student alike my children.
15. When children can help to do tasks, they will learn that what responsibilities are.
16. They don't have a good time together because her roommate complains her all the time.
17. People living in my community may interact these new people, and social relations may increase.
18. But, on the other hand, my community has a high grow rate.
19. If the community were more big, we would feel better.
20. What happens to you may be totally different that what happens to your family or friends.

STRUCTURE POST-TEST

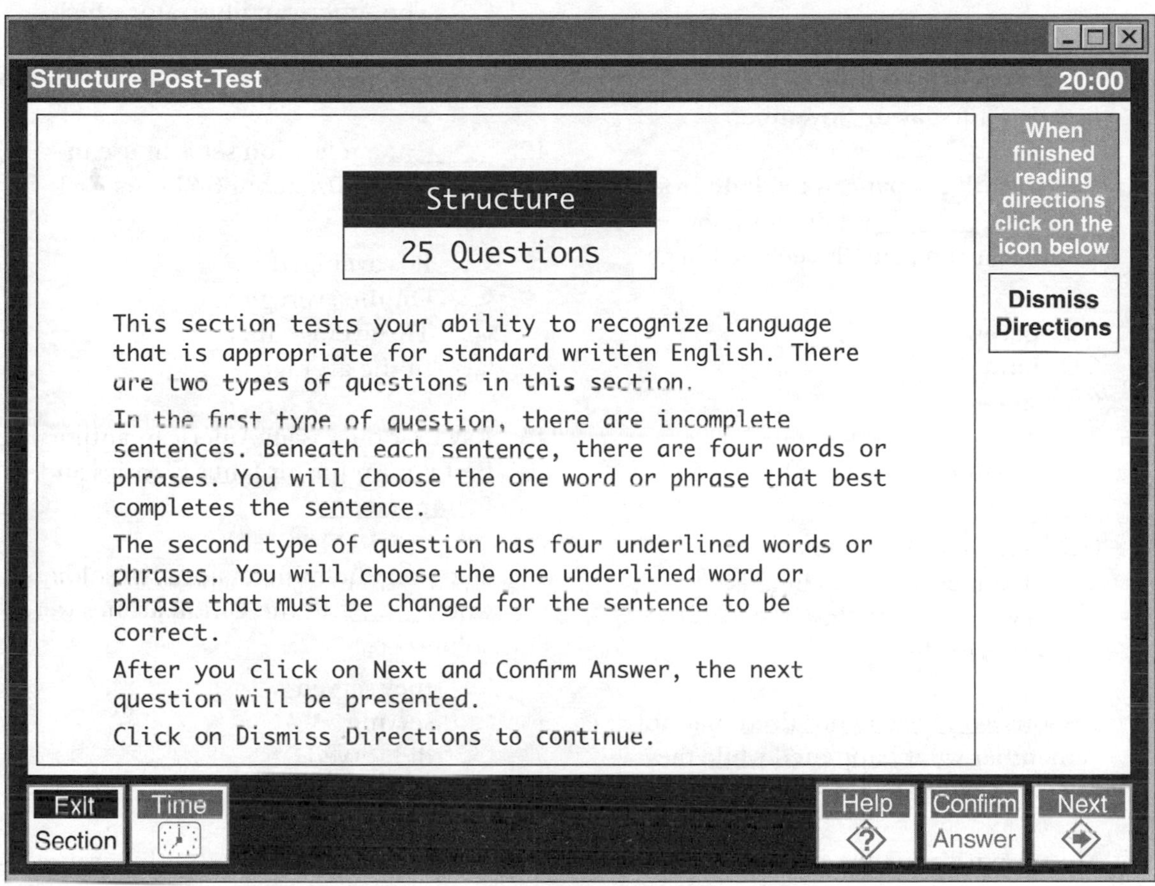

1. The telephone ______ was the invention of Alexander Graham Bell.
   - ◯ as is known by us
   - ◯ as do we know it
   - ◯ as we know it
   - ◯ as we know

2. Milk is <u>a</u> important part <u>of</u> most <u>people's</u> <u>diets</u>.

3. <u>Thanksgivings</u> feasts are celebrated <u>with</u> big dinners and <u>joyous</u> reunions <u>on the</u> fourth Thursday in November.

4. We know that a bat can tell light from darkness, _______ we do not know whether it can actually see anything.
   - ◯ as
   - ◯ because
   - ◯ but
   - ◯ since

5. Ants are most numerous in regions __________.
   - ◯ have a warm climate
   - ◯ that have a warm climate
   - ◯ a warm climate has
   - ◯ a warm climate

6. Persons <u>who have hypnotized</u> may not remember <u>what happened</u> <u>while</u> they were in <u>a</u> hypnotic trance.

7. Most Americans <u>have</u> <u>a great deal</u> of leisure time and they spend <u>them</u> in a <u>variety</u> of ways.

8. Art deco <u>featured</u> a look of sleek <u>elegant</u> that was <u>associated with</u> wealth and <u>sophistication</u>.

9. Each working day commuter trains carry _________ of suburban residents to and from work in large cities such as Chicago and New York City.
   - ◯ a thousand
   - ◯ a hundred thousand
   - ◯ hundreds of thousands
   - ◯ hundreds and thousands

10. The <u>earliest</u> descriptions of colonial life were <u>wrote</u> <u>to tell</u> Europeans about the settlements in the <u>New World</u>.

11. ________, Norman Rockwell painted everyday people and situations that usually tell stories, often humorous ones.
    - ◯ He was an American illustrator
    - ◯ An American illustrator
    - ◯ The American illustrator which
    - ◯ He was an illustrator who is American

12. _______, a television set is in use in every home for about 6½ hours each day.
    - ◯ It is averaged
    - ◯ On the average
    - ◯ The average that
    - ◯ In the average

13. Ray Bradbury is an American author best <u>known</u> <u>for</u> his <u>fantasy stories</u> and <u>fiction science</u>.

14. The overwhelming majority of soldiers who _______ in the Union armies were volunteers.
    - ◯ they served
    - ◯ serving
    - ◯ did served
    - ◯ served

15. A dam <u>may harm</u> certain <u>fish</u> <u>because of</u> it changes the flow of a river, causing <u>less</u> water to travel downstream.

16. Corn is _______ that botanists have only recently been able to track down the wild ancestors from which the Indian plant breeders developed it.
    - ◯ such civilized a plant
    - ◯ such a plant civilized
    - ◯ such a civilized plant
    - ◯ a so civilized a plant

17. The first national park at the world—Yellowstone National Park—was established in 1872 to preserve the area's unusual features and scenic beauty.

18. Geographers _______ where people, animals, and plants live and their relationship with the Earth.

- ⬭ they study
- ⬭ study
- ⬭ studying
- ⬭ are study

19. Nellie Bly was the pen name of Elizabeth Cochrane Seamon, an American journalism famous for her daring exposés.

20. Plane geometry is ________ kind of geometry studied in school.

- ⬭ first the
- ⬭ a first
- ⬭ the first
- ⬭ the one first

21. When a beam of sunlight passes through a specially shaped glass object called a prism, the rays of different wavelengths are bent at variety angles.

22. Plantations developed in colonies ________ by growing a single crop for export.

- ⬭ where people lived the majority
- ⬭ where lived the majority of people
- ⬭ where the majority of people lived
- ⬭ where did the majority of people live

23. Relative humidity is the amount of water vapor the air contains at a certain temperature compared with the amount _______ at that temperature.

- ⬭ hold
- ⬭ it could hold
- ⬭ it is holding
- ⬭ is held

24. Most businesses need management workers to plan and administer company activities and policies as well as to train and supervise others employees.

25. Fluorescent lamps have limited use in homes, but they are wide used in offices, schools, and stores.

WRITING THE ESSAY

Although you will write your essay at the end of the TOEFL test, after you complete the Reading section, this book includes the Essay section with the Structure section. You will need to know structure rules in order to write a good essay. The score you receive on the essay will be one half of your Structure score.

After you finish the Reading section of the test, you will write a short essay. You will need to generate and organize ideas, as well as support those ideas with evidence or examples, and compose in standard written English a response to an assigned topic.

The essay topic will be given to you. You will have thirty minutes to write on that topic, and that topic only. If you write on any other topic, you will receive a score of "0." Before you see the topic, you must choose whether to type your essay on the computer (which does NOT have a spellcheck) or to handwrite your essay on the paper essay answer sheet provided. You can click on Next and Confirm Answer to end the Writing section at any time. At the end of 30 minutes, the computer will automatically end the session. The essay topic will appear on the computer screen and will look like this one:

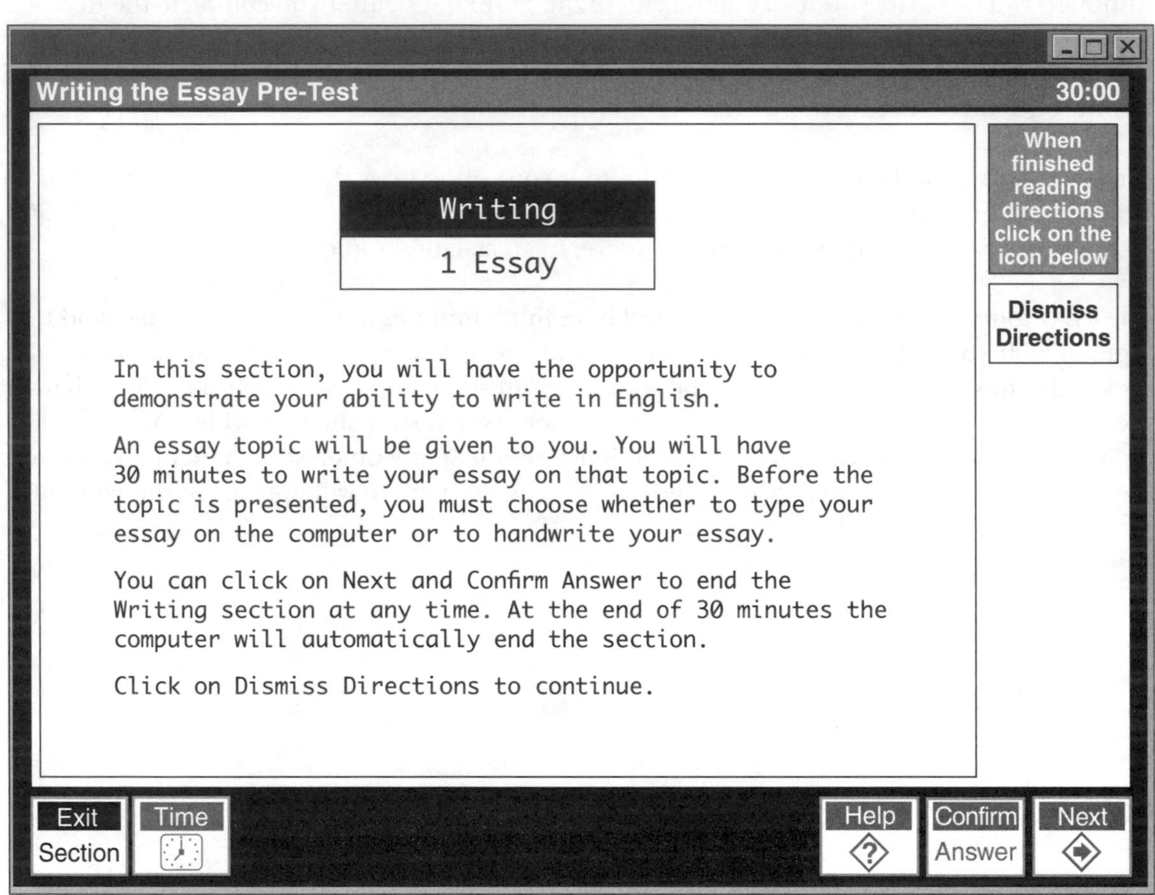
Writing the Essay Pre-Test
30:00
Writing
1 Essay
In this section, you will have the opportunity to demonstrate your ability to write in English.
An essay topic will be given to you. You will have 30 minutes to write your essay on that topic. Before the topic is presented, you must choose whether to type your essay on the computer or to handwrite your essay.
You can click on Next and Confirm Answer to end the Writing section at any time. At the end of 30 minutes the computer will automatically end the section.
Click on Dismiss Directions to continue.
When finished reading directions click on the icon below
Dismiss Directions
Exit Section
Time
Help
Confirm Answer
Next

Some people believe that university students should be required to attend classes. Others believe that going to classes should be optional for students. Which point of view do you agree with? Use specific details and reasons in your answer.

Read the topic and then make any notes that will help you plan your response. Begin typing your response in the box at the bottom of the screen, or write your answer on the answer sheet provided to you.

At the end of 30 minutes, the computer will automatically end the session. You MUST plan, write, and edit in 30 minutes.

ESSAY TOPICS

ETS publishes a list of writing topics, one of which will probably appear on the actual test (see current TOEFL test bulletin). ETS may add topics to or delete topics from this list at any time. Remember, you must write only on the topic that has been assigned to you.

The most recent bulletin includes four different types of essays, which are explained below.

Compare/contrast; agree/disagree

(89 such topics listed in Bulletin, or 67% of all questions)
In this kind of essay, you will be asked to compare how two thoughts, ideas, or proposals are similar or how they are different. You can do either or both. You will need to choose which idea you agree with or which one you think is better. In the response to the following question, you could talk about someone you know whose pet has brought them much happiness. Or you could discuss the fact that although people may treat their pets in a ridiculous manner, spending much money on dog clothes and expensive toys, sometimes people have a better life because of a pet.

EXAMPLE:
Many people have a close relationship with their pets. These people treat their birds, cats, or other animals as members of their family. In your opinion, are such relationships good? Why or why not? Use specific reasons and examples to support your answer.

Describe something

(21 topics, or 16% of all questions)
In this type of essay, you are asked to describe something. Although the question does not ask you to compare anything, sometimes a comparison helps to make your point. In response to the following question, you could discuss one country's films and what you learned about the country from them. Or you could contrast how another country's films were so different from your country's films because that other country is so different from your own.

EXAMPLE:
Films can tell us a lot about the country in which they were made. What have you learned about a country from watching its movies? Use specific examples and details to support your answer.

Choose among several choices

(20 topics, or 15% of all questions)
In this kind of essay, you will have several different ideas to consider. You will need to choose which one you think is best/most important. In response to the following question, you can choose one feature and write your essay on only that (such as location is the most important feature), or you can discuss several different choices before picking the most important one.

EXAMPLE:
When choosing a place to live, what do you consider most important: location, size, style, number of rooms, types of rooms, or other features? Use reasons and specific examples to support your answer.

Make one change to something

(3 topics, or fewer than 1% of all questions)
In this type of essay, you will need to analyze the changes you would make to something such as a town, school, or organization. This question is asking you to spend the essay talking about only one choice.

EXAMPLE:
If you could change one thing about your hometown, what would you change? Use reasons and specific examples to support your answer.

ESSAY RATING

The essay you compose in the Writing section of the test will be rated according to the scoring guide and procedures explained below. In the computer-based test, your essay rating will be incorporated into the Structure/Writing scaled score, with the rating of the essay constituting one-half of the Structure/Writing scaled score. The rating will appear on your score report under the heading "Essay Rating." It is provided as a service to help you and your institution better understand your Structure/Writing score.

The essay you compose in the Writing section will be scored by two readers using the Writing Scoring Guide explained below. Neither reader will know the rating assigned by the other. Your essay will receive the average of the two ratings unless there is a discrepancy of more than one point; in that case, a third reader will independently rate your essay. Thus, your essay will receive a final rating of 6.0, 5.5, 5.0, 4.5, 4.0, 3.5, 3.0, 2.5, 2.0, 1.5, or 1. A score of 0 will be given to papers that are blank, simply copy the topic, are written in a language other than English, consist only of random keystroke characters, or are written on a topic other than the one assigned.

Writing Scoring Guide

6 An essay at this level

- effectively addresses the writing task
- is well organized and well developed
- uses clearly appropriate details to support a thesis or illustrate ideas
- displays consistent facility in the use of language
- demonstrates syntactic variety and appropriate word choice

Although it may seem as though only a native speaker can write a 6 essay, a 6 essay can have some errors. However, this essay is almost error-free, uses many specific examples, is well developed in numerous paragraphs, and uses many different English structures. Its length is always considerable.

5 An essay at this level

- may address some parts of the task more effectively than others
- is generally well organized and well developed
- uses details to support a thesis or illustrate an idea
- displays facility in the use of the language
- demonstrates some syntactic variety and range of vocabulary

This essay is not as developed as a 6, has more errors, but is still a well-written, well-argued piece of writing.

4 An essay at this level

- addresses the writing topic adequately but may slight parts of the task
- is adequately organized and developed
- uses some details to support a thesis or illustrate an idea
- demonstrates adequate but possibly inconsistent facility with syntax and usage
- may contain some errors that occasionally obscure meaning

An essay 4 writer may one day write a 5 or 6 essay, but for the moment, this writer is clearly less proficient than those who can write a 5 or a 6. There are many areas of weakness: underdeveloped paragraphs or arguments, phrase or word choices that confuse the reader, and numerous grammatical errors.

3 An essay at this level may reveal one or more of the following weaknesses

- inadequate organization or development
- inappropriate or insufficient details to support or illustrate generalizations
- a noticeably inappropriate choice of words or word forms
- an accumulation of errors in sentence structure and/or usage

A 3 essay is usually very short. Although it may have some bright spots (good arguments, good vocabulary, etc.), overall, it's dramatically less coherent and filled with many more errors than a 4 essay.

2 An essay at this level is seriously flawed by one or more of the following weaknesses

- serious disorganization or underdevelopment
- little or no detail, or irrelevant specifics

- serious and frequent errors in sentence structure and usage
- serious problems with focus

Sometimes differentiating between a 2 and a 3 essay is difficult. The 2 essay is generally shorter and much more incomprehensible than a 3.

1 An essay at this level

- may be incoherent
- may be undeveloped
- may contain severe and persistent writing errors

This essay is a step up from a 0 in the sense that the writer tried to answer the question, but the writer's English is too limited to express any thoughts.

0 An essay will be rated 0 if it

- contains no response
- merely copies the topic
- is off-topic, is written in a foreign language, or consists only of keystroke characters

This description is self-explanatory.

GENERAL STRATEGIES FOR THE ESSAY

- **Remember to brainstorm specific points/examples BEFORE you start writing.**
- **Never start writing the essay on the scrap paper with the idea of "copying it over."**
- **Decide BEFORE you take the TOEFL test if you'll be handwriting or typing.** Remember to use a 14–16 word a minute typing test to help you decide.

STUDY TIP

Get a copy of the TOEFL test bulletin and study the writing prompts. Set aside a half hour each day for at least a month. Write in response to a different prompt each day. After a short time, you should notice that you're able to write more in 30 minutes than you initially could. Have a native English speaker read some of your essays and talk about them with you.

PREPARATION FOR WRITING THE ESSAY

This section is divided into three parts: A: The Structure and Writing of the Essay; B: Specific Areas for Grammar Review and Editing; C: Sample Student Essays (that have been scored by official readers).

The Structure and Writing of the Essay

1. ESSAY FORMAT

The **format** of an essay is how it looks on a page or a computer screen. It is important to use the correct format in the Writing section of the TOEFL test.

A. MARGINS

Margins are the empty columns at the sides of a page. They make the essay appear more polished, and you should leave approximately one inch on both the left and right side of the paper. If you use the computer, the margins automatically appear.

B. INDENTATIONS

The first line of all paragraphs must be **indented**. That means you must leave an inch space on the left-hand side of the margin. When using a regular computer, you can press "Tab" and the computer automatically indents, or goes in, five spaces. When you use the computer for the exam, however, you will have to hit the space bar five times because the tab key does not work in this program. Another suggestion is to leave two lines between paragraphs without indenting.

C. PARAGRAPHS

A **paragraph** is a group of sentences that are about one topic. They are connected to the **topic sentence** (see Part 5 on page 195). There should be no unrelated sentences, examples, or ideas in each paragraph. The last sentence of a paragraph should bring it to a logical end. As a general rule, a paragraph should be at least four sentences. If your paragraphs are too long (more than ten sentences), the reader can lose interest.

A standard essay should have at least four paragraphs: one, the introduction and thesis statement; two, the first main point and examples; three, the next major point and its examples; and four, a conclusion.

Sometimes the essay can have five paragraphs if you have another major point with its supporting specifics. But in 30 minutes you probably won't have enough time to write five developed paragraphs. If you do not divide your essay into paragraphs, even if you include all of the points listed above, you will be penalized in the grading of your essay because it does not look like a typical American essay.

2. BRAINSTORMING

The word **brainstorming** comes from the words "brain" and "storm." As you can guess, the meaning of this word is to quickly generate many ideas (like an unexpected storm). In order to come up with some ideas quickly before you begin writing, you will need to get good at brainstorming.

STUDY TIP

Plan to spend 2–4 minutes brainstorming BEFORE you begin to write.

For example, suppose the question is as follows:

Some high schools require all students to wear school uniforms. Other high schools permit students to decide what to wear to school. Which of these two school policies do you think is better? Use specific reasons and examples to support your opinion.

Maybe you don't have an opinion about whether or not to require school uniforms when you read this question. So, while brainstorming, make two columns and start to think:

FOR	AGAINST
• Cheap—don't need many outfits	• Look like everyone else
• Quicker in AM	• Can't show originality
• No competition	
• Promotes equality	

If you have trouble thinking of reasons not to have uniforms, your thesis statement and essay will be something about how it's better to wear uniforms. You may decide to argue only for wearing uniforms, or you may decide to combine both sides (a more sophisticated essay). Combining opposing ideas will be discussed later. At least now you know what your main points are, and you can begin to think about the examples and stories that will support your points. The key is to decide QUICKLY what side you're taking (even if it's not something you really believe), so that you can begin finding examples and start to write.

A. BRAINSTORMING STRATEGIES

- **Once you see your question, plan to brainstorm for 2–4 minutes before you write your essay.**
- **Some students close their eyes while thinking of specific points. Others immediately write down words that come into their minds.**
- **DO NOT write down entire sentences; this time should be used only for MAIN IDEAS.** Write words or phrases.
- **The purpose of this time is to come up with enough specific points and examples that will prove what your essay is arguing (your thesis statement).** Without supporting details, you cannot prove your thesis statement.
- **Never begin to write without thinking and writing down key ideas first.** You will be given scrap paper to use for brainstorming and planning the essay.

BRAINSTORMING EXERCISE: For each question, spend 2–4 minutes coming up with main points.

1. **Some people prefer to spend most of their time alone. Others like to be with friends most of the time. Do you prefer to spend your time alone or with friends? Give reasons to support your answer.**

(You can either pick one and see how many points you can find, or you can look at both choices and then see which list is longer.)

ALONE	WITH FRIENDS
1.	1.
2.	2.
3.	3.

2. **A gift (such as a soccer ball, a camera, or an animal) can contribute to a child's development. What gift would you give to help a child develop? Why? Use reasons and specific details to support your choice.**

(This question is asking you to pick only one, so quickly choose one of the choices and find reasons why that one is good.)

SOCCER BALL	CAMERA	ANIMAL
1.	1.	1.
2.	2.	2.
3.	3.	3.

3. **Imagine that you have received some land to use as you wish. How would you use this land? Use specific details to explain your answer.**

(There is no choice in this question, so once you choose what you want to do with the land, write down some benefits for this choice).

Land use: ________________
Why it's a good choice:
1.
2.
3.

4. **People behave differently when they wear different clothes. Do you agree that different clothes influence the way people behave? Use specific examples to support your answer.**

(If you said people don't behave differently, you'd have no essay. List different situations that people act differently in, depending on what they're wearing. Find at least two different situations in which people act differently, and then find specific examples.)

SITUATION 1:__________
1.
2.

SITUATION 2:____________
1.
2.

5. **The 21st century has begun. What changes do you think this new century will bring? Use examples and details in your answer.**

CHANGES
1.
2.
3.

(To make your point, think of specific examples BEFORE you start to write. It's always best to use specific examples whenever you can.)

3. INTRODUCTIONS/THESIS STATEMENTS

The **introduction** is probably the most important part of the essay. Readers need to decide very quickly what score to give the essay, so they are greatly influenced by what they read first.

A. INTRODUCTORY PARAGRAPH STRATEGIES

- Make sure it's a paragraph and not just one sentence.
- Give a general introduction to the main points you will bring up later in your essay without going into specifics.
- Think about **sentence variety,** for the introduction is the place to impress the reader. For example, you can ask a question.
- As you are writing the **introduction,** DO NOT rewrite any part of the question. If you do so, the reader judges that you are a beginning writer and cannot write your own ideas.
- The introduction should be neither too specific nor too general.
- End the introduction with your **thesis statement**. (see below)

An essay must have a **thesis statement**. The thesis is the one sentence which tells the reader your point of view about the topic. The reader will be convinced that your **thesis** and essay are good once all of your evidence and specifics are read. As a general rule, put the **thesis statement** last in the opening paragraph. The next two paragraphs will prove your thesis.

B. THESIS STATEMENT STRATEGIES

- A thesis should make the reader want to read the essay.
- A thesis must express an idea with which it is possible to disagree.
- A thesis must express a judgment, an observation, OR a question which the essay will go on to prove.
- A thesis statement could briefly mention the supporting points that will be discussed in the essay.

Here is a question:

> **Some people think they can learn better by themselves than with a teacher. Others think that is it always better to have a teacher. Which do you prefer? Use specific reasons to develop your essay.**

When writing a comparison/contrast essay, try to avoid a thesis statement such as *There are many advantages to learning by oneself.* It restates *learn* and *by themselves/oneself* which are in the question and it uses *advantages.* Many students write *There are many advantages* or *There are many disadvantages.* Readers get tired of reading the same reused question words again and again.

STUDY TIP

Practice different ways of writing thesis statements.

1. Use the comparative form of the adjective: *Learning by oneself is more beneficial (or productive, satisfying), than learning with a teacher.* Or, depending on the point, you may also use the comparative form of the adverb as well: *Learning by oneself regularly rather than with a teacher eliminates the need to go to school.*
2. When you are combining opposing points you can use *although: Although it may seem that learning by oneself is better than with a teacher, it may not always be true.*

THESIS STATEMENT EXERCISE: Try to write thesis statements for these questions using comparatives:

1. Do you agree or disagree with the following statement? Playing a game is fun only when you win.

   ____

2. Would you prefer to live in a traditional house or in a modern apartment building?

   ____

3. Do you agree with the following statement? A zoo has no useful purpose.

   ____

4. Do you agree or disagree with the following statement? All students should be required to study art and music in high school.

   ____

5. People listen to music for different reasons and at different times. Why is music important to many people?

   ____

6. People recognize a difference between children and adults. What events (experiences or ceremonies) make a person an adult? Use specific reasons and examples.

   ____

7. Imagine that you have received some land to use as you wish. How would you use this land? Use specific details to explain your answer.

   ____

INTRODUCTION EXERCISE: Look at this question:

> **Do you agree or disagree with the following statement? Playing games teaches us about life. Use specific reasons and examples to support your answer.**

What are some of the problems with the following introductions?

1. I agree with the statement that playing games teaches us about life. My essay will explain why I agree.

___

2. I have always played lots of games, both in school and with my friends. I agree that playing games teaches us about life because it teaches us cooperation, teamwork, and problem-solving skills.

___

3. When I was in high school I played soccer every day. I had to learn how to get along with my teammates and balance my homework with practice. I couldn't go to parties on the weekends, couldn't smoke, and had to watch my diet.

___

What makes this introduction different?

> There are many kinds of games. For some people, participating in athletic games is a major part of their lives whereas other people spend hours every day playing video games or board games. Others like doing word games such as crossword puzzles. Playing games can take up a lot of time, but can playing games teach us something? Playing soccer has taught me life lessons that I would not have learned otherwise.

___

INTRODUCTION AND THESIS STATEMENT EXERCISE: Look at these questions and write introductions and thesis statements for them.

> **Some people say that advertising encourages us to buy things we really do not need. Others say that advertisements tell us about new products that may improve our lives. Which viewpoint do you agree with? Use specific reasons and examples to support your answer.**
>
> **What is the most important animal in your country? Why is this animal important? Use reasons and specific details to explain your answer.**
>
> **Choose a building that has special meaning for you. Explain why this building is important to you. Support your explanation with specific details.**

4. CHOOSING ONE SIDE OR COMBINING AGREE/DISAGREE

Since 67% of all questions ask you to agree or disagree with a statement, you should spend time thinking about how you want to write about this kind of essay. Many say that it's easier to pick one side in a prompt and write the essay only arguing for that point. For example, look at this question:

Some people believe that students should be given one long vacation each year. Others believe that students should have several short vacations throughout the year. Which viewpoint do you agree with? Use specific reasons and examples to support your choice.

It may seem that you need only decide whether you prefer one long or several short vacations. You certainly could write a well-argued essay for one choice. But carefully consider looking at both sides. Because there isn't a right/wrong answer, often a more sophisticated essay is able to include a discussion of BOTH options and explain why the decision isn't simply one or the other. There may be times when you would want several short vacations and another time you would like one long one. If you decide to choose only one side, the reader may be left feeling you haven't carefully thought about the question.

Your thesis statement could look something like this:
Although I appreciate the sense of relaxation a long vacation can give me, several short vacations are very much needed during a stressful academic year.

One paragraph would discuss how great it is to have a long vacation, using a specific long vacation that you took and how great it made you feel. The next paragraph would talk about the benefits of several short vacations during the year, again using some personal stories that demonstrate the value of this type of vacationing.

Here's another question which asks you compare and contrast two different ideas. It may seem that you are being asked to choose only one idea. But by incorporating both sides into an argument, you are creating a more advanced essay.

It has been said, "Not everything that is learned is contained in books." Compare and contrast knowledge from experience with knowledge gained from books. In your opinion, which source is more important?

First brainstorm both sides:

FROM EXPERIENCE
- What friends/family have been through
- Learning on my own (riding a bike)

FROM BOOKS
- Technical info couldn't get elsewhere
- "How to books" info from experts

Since there are arguments for both sources, the thesis statement could be something like this

I have learned many things from books; however, sometimes what I have learned from my own experiences has been just as important.

One paragraph would be about all the technical things you learned from books: how to install computer programs, how to prepare for the TOEFL test, how to make lasagna. The next paragraph would detail what you learned from your own and others' experiences: how to ride a bike, how to hold a baby, how to do some task at a job. The conclusion would incorporate both ideas: a lasagna recipe you found, but only through your own experience of cooking it and speaking to others who cook it were you able to perfect it.

A. COMBINING AGREE/DISAGREE STRATEGIES

- **Brainstorm each prompt, making sure you have points for both sides.**
- **Make sure your thesis statement includes a transition word that shows contrast.**
- **Your thesis statement can clearly state that you agree with a combination of both sides or under certain circumstances you agree with each side.** Then one paragraph will look at one side; the next will look at the other.
- **Alternatively, you may use both paragraphs to combine the ideas (a little bit harder to do).**
- **Make sure the conclusion restates why and in what circumstances you agree with both sides.**

COMBINING AGREE/DISAGREE EXERCISE: Look at these prompts. Brainstorm for a few minutes, then write a thesis statement that includes both sides, using a transition that shows contrast.

1. **Some people prefer to spend time with one or two close friends. Others choose to spend time with a large number of friends. Compare the advantages of each choice. Which of these two ways of spending time do you prefer? Give reasons to support your answer.**

ONE OR TWO FRIENDS	A LARGE NUMBER OF FRIENDS
1.	1.
2.	2.
3.	3.

Thesis statement: ____

____.

2. **Some people believe that college or university education should be available to all students. Others believe that higher education should be available only to good students. Discuss these views. Which view do you agree with? Explain why.**

ALL STUDENTS	GOOD STUDENTS ONLY
1.	1.
2.	2.
3.	3.

Thesis statement: ____

____.

3. **Some people prefer to spend their free time outdoors. Other people prefer to spend their leisure time indoors. Would you prefer to be outside or would you prefer to be inside for your leisure activities? Use specific reasons and examples to support your choice.**

OUTDOORS	INDOORS
1.	1.
2.	2.
3.	3.

Thesis statement: ____
____.

4. Do you agree or disagree with the following statement? People should sometimes do things that they do not enjoy doing.

SHOULD DO	SHOULDN'T DO
1.	1.
2.	2.
3.	3.

Thesis statement: ____
____.

5. Some items (such as clothes or furniture) can be made by hand or by machine. Which do you prefer—items made by hand or items made by machine? Use reasons and specific examples to explain your choice.

BY HAND	BY MACHINE
1.	1.
2.	2.
3.	3.

Thesis statement: ____
____.

5. TOPIC SENTENCES/SUPPORTING DETAILS

Paragraphs include topic sentences and supporting details, examples, or ideas. Both parts of the paragraph help to prove the thesis.

A. TOPIC SENTENCES

The topic sentence directs the reader by telling what the paragraph is trying to argue/prove. Each of the two paragraphs in the body of your essay should have a topic sentence. Although a topic sentence can come anywhere in the paragraph, it often is the first sentence in the paragraph because it makes it clear to the reader what will follow. Briefly state the main idea of the paragraph. The idea will be more fully developed in the paragraph with examples and specifics. In addition, the writer can keep looking back to make sure that all the sentences in that paragraph are related to that sentence.

Topic Sentences Strategies

- **If you put your topic sentence at the beginning, you can quickly look up as you write to remind yourself what your focus is.** Checking the topic sentence as you write helps keep you from putting in ideas that are not connected.
- **The topic sentence should be the main idea of the paragraph, not the specifics.**
- **Try not to make it too general because it needs to state the focus of the paragraph.**
- **The ideas in the topic sentences come from the thesis statement.**

For example, if your paragraph is discussing salaries of athletes and movie stars, a topic sentence could be *Many athletes and entertainers make more than doctors, lawyers, and even presidents.* You could then go on to contrast some specific people, their salaries, and their responsibilities.

If your paragraph is describing the benefits of wearing a uniform, a topic sentence could be *Wearing a uniform made my life in high school easy.* You would then discuss the specific ways it helped you.

If you are discussing the benefits of zoos, your topic sentence could be *Many animals would now be extinct if we didn't have zoos.* You would then name several species that are not extinct because zoos have protected them, enabling them to reproduce.

B. SUPPORTING DETAILS

The supporting details prove and support what your topic sentence claims. When you brainstorm, you write down specific examples or experiences that you can use. These supporting details are ideas for the paragraphs, just like the paragraphs are supporting ideas for the thesis.

Supporting Details Strategies

- The supporting details often include your own experiences and observations.
- The TOEFL test essay assumes you'll be talking about yourself. These personal experiences and stories make your writing richer and can prove your point. Don't worry if these points seem too conversational.
- Each supporting idea needs several sentences to develop, so the first sentence after the topic sentence can introduce the specific example/story you're about to write.

TOPIC SENTENCE/SUPPORTING DETAILS EXERCISE 1:
Part I. Remember an earlier question:

Read and think about the following statement: People behave differently when they wear different clothes. Do you agree that different clothes influence the way people behave? Use specific examples to support your answer.

Brainstorming phrases could look like this:

DRESSED UP
- Act differently
- Feel more grown up
- Doing something special

WEARING A UNIFORM
- Behave differently
- Commands respect
- Can instill fear

A thesis statement could look like this:
Whenever I'm wearing clothes that I don't usually wear, such as formal clothes or a uniform, I behave differently and people act differently around me.

For each pair of sentences, decide which is the better topic sentence and which is the better supporting point.

1. A. Wearing a uniform makes the wearer feel different.
   B. When I put on my school uniform, I know I'm going to school.

2. A. People act differently when they see people wearing uniforms.
   B. When I see a policeman in uniform, I get scared.

3. A. Wearing a long dress and high heels makes me feel glamorous.
   B. Getting dressed up can change how I act and feel.

4. A. In my country, people get dressed up on special occasions.
   B. Every birthday party my friends and I celebrate by wearing our best clothes.

5. A. I didn't think that how I dressed made a difference.
   B. Our speech teacher made us dress up on speech days to make us feel more professional.

6. A. By studying Farsi, you will be able to learn about an entirely different people and history.
   B. Once you are able to read Farsi poetry, you will understand the Persian people's struggle for independence.

7. A. A movie theater would give people of all ages a place to go for entertainment.
   B. My hometown doesn't have a movie theater.

8. A. Whenever I'm feeling sad, I put on a CD and listen to Chopin.
   B. Music can change my moods.

9. A. A dog can help any child feel better about herself.
   B. My parents got me a dog when I was eleven.

10. A. Some people don't understand how a pet can be like a family member.
    B. Every year we have a party for Moomoo, our pet parrot.

Part II. Find two or three points that can support the following topic sentences. Write complete sentences:

1. Some people think young children should spend most of their time playing.

•
•
•

2. Some people think that children should begin their formal education at a very early age and should spend most of their time on school studies.

•
•
•

TOPIC SENTENCE/SUPPORTING DETAILS EXERCISE 2: A common problem is using details that don't really support, or logically follow, your topic sentences. In the following exercise, choose and explain which set of details (A) or (B) more logically support the topic sentence.

1. Topic Sentence: The 21st century will bring many medical changes.

(A) There will be cures for diseases such as AIDS and cancer.
Doctors will rely more on computers to treat and diagnose patients.
Better medical care will result in people living longer.

(B) There aren't enough doctors in my country.
Most people can't afford to buy the pills they need to take.
The hospitals don't have enough supplies to treat their patients.

2. Topic Sentence: I would buy a business rather than a house.

(A) I would love to live near the ocean.
Houses aren't as expensive in my country as they are in the U.S.
Having my own business will take up all my time.

(B) If my business is successful, I would be able to buy a house one day.
It's not so important to me where I live.
I've always dreamed of having my own business.

3. Topic Sentence: Once I had to borrow money from a friend in order to pay my rent.

(A) I thought my best friend would lend me the money.
I knew my friend was worried I wouldn't pay him back.
I didn't want to lose this friend, so I quickly paid him back.

(B) My rent is due on the first of the month.
I have many friends who have lots of money in the bank.
It's cheaper to live in an apartment than in the dorm.

4. Topic Sentence: Music is important to me because it helps me relax.

(A) I've always loved to sing.
I listen to the radio when I'm studying.
Some of my friends borrow my CDs because I have so many good ones.

(B) After a hard day, I put on the radio and feel better.
When I have a headache, I listen to Bach.
It's hard to explain, but listening to music makes me forget my problems.

6. TRANSITIONS

Transitions are words that join one idea to another idea. We use transitions *within* a paragraph as well as *between* paragraphs. Transitions help the reader follow from one idea to the next. These words are also known as **connectors, markers**, or **signal words**.

To Show Addition	• Positive: and, as well, also, too, moreover, furthermore, in addition • Negative: neither . . . nor, nor, neither • Series: first (ly) . . . second(ly), next, lastly, finally
To Show Example	• for example • such as • for instance
To Show Similarity	• similarly • likewise • in the same way • as . . . as • as in, as with, as was etc.

To Show Cause or Reason	• because (of) • due to • on account of • thanks to
To Show Effect or Result	• as a result • consequently • thereby • thus
To Show Conclusion/Summary	• therefore • hence • in conclusion • thus • to sum up • at last • finally • all in all
To Show Contrast	• in contrast • on the contrary • in fact • however • yet • although • on the one hand . . . on the other hand • nevertheless/nonetheless • whereas • unlike • despite • in spite of • even so
To Show Emphasis	• clearly • evidently • obviously • actually • in fact • indeed • surely • above all • certainly
To Show Purpose	• so that • so as to • in order to
To Show Restatement/Repetition	• that is • in other words • to put it differently • to repeat • namely

A. PUNCTUATION RULES FOR TRANSITIONS

1. Sentences with coordinating conjunction (*for, and, nor, but or, yet, so*)

You can remember all of these words by taking the first letter of each word and making it into the word "FANBOYS."

If you have an independent clause (a subject + verb that can stand alone) that is connected to another independent clause with a FANBOYS word, put a (,) before the FANBOYS word.

EXAMPLE:
Colleges should give money to students' sports activities, **but** they should spend the same amount on their libraries.

2. Sentences can begin with **transitional** (or **conjunctive**) **adverbs** (*however, therefore, nonetheless, nevertheless, moreover, in fact, hence, consequently, in addition, thus*). But if these words connect two independent clauses, the punctuation is (;) transitional adverb (,).

EXAMPLE:
I think it's a good idea for students to evaluate teachers**; however,** I think most students would be afraid to write what they really think.

3. Sentences that begin with **adverbial clauses** (*if, because, although,* time words such as *when, after, before* etc.) need a comma after the clause. There is no comma if the clause is at the end of the sentence.

EXAMPLE:
If a shopping center were built in my neighborhood, I'd be really happy.
I'd be really happy **if a** shopping center were built in my neighborhood.

B. TRANSITION STRATEGIES

- **It's generally a good idea to introduce new paragraphs, especially the conclusion, with a transition.**
- **Recognize the grammatical structure required by the choice of the transition word.** For example, *due to* is a preposition and must be followed by a noun or noun phrase.
- **Choose the best transition to show the relationship between ideas (contrast, addition, etc.)**

TRANSITION EXERCISE 1: Finish these sentences.

1. Some people prefer to spend most of their time alone. However,
____.
2. A zoo has no useful purpose. In other words,
____.
3. Playing games encourages cooperation, teamwork, and problem-solving skills. Therefore,
____.
4. Students should evaluate their teachers so that
____.
5. Building a shopping center in my neighborhood would cause many problems. For example,
____.
6. I learn better with a teacher due to
____.
7. Advertising encourages us to buy things we really do not need. Furthermore,
____.
8. The most important class I ever took was my ESL class. Consequently,
____.
9. I would prefer to live in a modern apartment building. Similarly,
____.
10. All students should be required to study art and music in high school. Indeed,
____.

TRANSITION EXERCISE 2: Choose the correct transition for each sentence.

1. ____________ my high school teacher, I applied to study in the United States.
   a. Namely b. As well c. Thanks to d. All in all

2. Some athletes make millions of dollars every year for playing games a few hours a week. ____________, some doctors who trained for years and years make much less.
   a. In contrast b. Despite c. Likewise d. Even so

3. The most important animal in my country is the camel ________ it can carry loads for many miles without much water.
   a. because b. because of c. thus d. that is

4. First, the kitchen is where I eat. _______, the kitchen is where I do my homework.
   a. Obviously b. Second c. In the same way d. Finally

5. I began studying English as a very young child. _________, it has been easy for me to become fluent.
   a. As a result b. On the contrary c. Even so d. Next

TRANSITION EXERCISE 3: Combine the following sentences into ONE sentence using one of the transition words below. Although some words could be used in more than one sentence, others can only work in one sentence. Be careful of punctuation.

moreover **hence** **and** **although** **whereas**

1. My favorite class I ever took was my writing class last semester. I had to get up at 6:30 in the morning to get to it on time.

____

2. My writing teacher always gave homework. My reading teacher never gave homework.

____

3. I had to take three buses. I had to walk half a mile to campus.

____

4. The writing teacher helped me more than any other teacher I've ever had. I signed up to take another class with her next semester.

____

5. I really loved writing essays. I'm thinking about becoming an English major.

____

7. CONCLUSIONS

The conclusion is the fourth and final paragraph of your essay. It gives an ending to your essay, so the reader knows you have finished. Your conclusion should include a rewording of your thesis statement, so the reader can determine that you have proved what you set out to prove.

Many people say the closing paragraph of an essay is just as important as the opening one. But the TOEFL test is somewhat different. By the time the reader has gotten to your conclusion, he or she has probably decided on what score to give. In general, the conclusion is extremely important because it's the last picture the reader has of your essay. But for the TOEFL test, concentrate more on the introduction. That does not mean that you can leave out a conclusion, but spend more time thinking about what you're going to write in the introduction and how you're going to write it.

A. CONCLUSION STRATEGIES

- **Briefly summarize the main points.**
- **Make sure you restate your thesis statement in light of your arguments.** However, don't just copy your thesis statement; use different words to say the same thing. This skill is called paraphrasing.
- **Make it a full paragraph and not just a single sentence.** Give yourself five minutes, which will also include time for **editing** (Section 10, page 206), to make sure you don't run out of time.
- **Remind the reader of the key points from the essay and don't be too vague or over-general.**

CONCLUSION EXERCISE: Restate these thesis statements using different words.

EXAMPLE:

Thesis statement:	Although it may seem that many people listen to and care about the opinions of famous people such as rock stars, actors, and athletes, what these people have to say is usually not very important.
Rewrite:	Nowadays, we hear on television, read in the paper, and see on the Internet what famous singers, movie stars, or athletes think about important issues. I suggest that we listen to and care about what more experienced, educated people have to say.

1. Depending on my mood, I sometimes find reading fiction to be more enjoyable than watching movies.

____

2. When choosing a place to live, I consider the number of rooms to be most important factor.

____

3. Although there are many countries I would like to visit, I would visit Australia if I had the opportunity.

____

4. Some people are satisfied with what they have; however, others always want something more or something different.

____

5. I've probably seen a million advertisements in my lifetime, but the one that I believe is most effective is the Sony Walkman ad that uses a famous Japanese monkey.

____

6. If I could change one thing about the school I attended, it would be the dress code.

____

7. I know that in the United States some high schools allow students to study what they want, but I think that students shouldn't make those decisions.

____

8. Due to my family's sense of humor, we have all survived some very difficult situations.

____

9. Whenever I move to a new country, I follow the advice "When in Rome, do as the Romans."

____

10. What keeps old people young is what they can learn from young people.

____

8. SENTENCE VARIETY

Using a variety of sentence structures will make your writing more advanced and enjoyable to read. You may be writing sentences that are grammatically correct but boring because they all sound and look the same. As you look over your essays, do many of your sentences begin with *I* + a verb? Do you often connect clauses within your sentence only with *and*? As you concentrate on improving your writing, try to change the types of sentences and sentence structures that you use.

For example, look at these two simple sentences.

I cooked every night at home. I hoped to become a great chef.

You could instead begin with a gerund phrase.
By **cooking** *every night at home,* I hoped to become a great chef.

Or you could use a participial phrase.
Cooking *every night,* I hoped to become a great chef.

Or you could use an infinitive phrase.
My only hope of becoming a great chef was ***to cook*** *every night.*

Or you could begin with a prepositional phrase.
With *nightly homecooked meals,* I hoped to become a great chef.

Or you could use an appositive phrase.
I decided there was only one way to become a great chef: *nightly homecooked meals.*

Or you could use a question.
How could I become a great chef? I could begin by cooking at home every night.

Or you could use connectors.
Compound Sentence: I cooked every night at home, **for** I hoped to become a great chef.
Complex Sentence: I cooked every night at home **because** I hoped to become a great chef.

A. SENTENCE VARIETY STRATEGIES

- **Use an occasional question.**
- **Make sure you're not beginning all sentences the same way, such as *I* + a verb.**
- **Don't write all simple sentences.** Look at your writing to see where you could connect two simple sentences into one compound or complex sentence.
- **Use the above-mentioned phrase variations.**

SENTENCE VARIETY EXERCISE: Rewrite and combine these sentences to make them more interesting. Feel free to add words and related ideas.

1. I wore a uniform every day. I hated it.

___

2. I've lived in five countries. I tried to dress and act like the native people.

___

3. I've learned many things on my own. I learned how to ride a bicycle by riding one, not by reading about it.

____

4. In my country, university students don't have to go to class. Teachers don't care whether or not students come.

____

5. I played soccer in high school. My team never won one game.

____

6. I have many friends and go out with them on the weekend. I like to be alone during the week.

____

7. I grew up in a modern twenty-two-story apartment building. I want to live in a traditional house.

____

8. I would like to visit Australia. I could never afford to go there.

____

9. Some people listen to music when they are sad. Some people listen to music when they are in a good mood.

____

10. I live in a very boring small town. I wish we had a movie theater in town.

____

9. INCLUDING A TITLE

You may choose to give your essay a **title**. Writers often choose the title once the essay is finished. An interesting title makes your essay special and makes the reader want to read it. Don't just say **Uniforms** but something such as **Another Day, Another Blue Jumper**. Instead of **Soccer**, try something like **Soccer: Not Just a Game**. Instead of **Films in the U.S.**, try using a question such as **Is America Really Like Its Movies?**

A. PUNCTUATION RULES FOR TITLES

1. Do not use quotation marks.
2. Always capitalize the first word.
3. Do not capitalize articles (*a, an, the*), coordinating conjunctions (*for, and, nor, but, or, yet, so*) or prepositions (*in, on, at,* etc.) UNLESS these words are the first word in the title.
4. Capitalize all major words such as nouns, pronouns, verbs, adjectives, and adverbs.
5. It's OK to ask a question, followed by a question mark.
6. It may be safer to omit a title, rather than writing a grammatically incorrect one.

You do not have to include a title, but if you decide to use one, do not simply repeat the question or a part of it.

For example, imagine that your question is

> **Some people prefer to eat at food stands or restaurants. Other people prefer to prepare and eat food at home. Which do you prefer? Use specific reasons and examples to support your answer.**

A bad choice of a title would be **Eating at Restaurants**. It only repeats part of the prompt.

A title should create some interest in the essay. Better choices would be

- Let's Eat Out
- Nothing Beats Home Cooking
- Pizza Again?
- What's for Supper?

All of these choices make the reader want to read the essay.

TITLE EXERCISE 1: From the following prompts choose the better title and explain why it is better.

1. **Schools should ask students to evaluate their teachers. Do you agree or disagree? Use specific reasons and examples to support your answer.**

Which title do you prefer and why?
a. Should Students Evaluate Teachers?
b. Fear of Teacher Retaliation

2. **Do you agree or disagree with the following statement? A person's childhood (the time from birth to 12 years of age) is the most important time of a person's life. Use specific reasons and details to support your choice.**

Which title do you prefer and why?
a. My Life Began at Thirteen
b. The Most Important Years

3. **Think of the most important class you have ever taken. Why did you enjoy this class so much? Use specific reasons and details to explain your answer.**

Which title do you prefer and why?
a. The Most Important Class
b. Why I Was Never Absent

4. **You want to persuade someone to study your native language. What reasons would you give? Support your answer with specific details.**

Which title do you prefer and why?
a. A Whole New World
b. You Should Study Farsi

5. **Many people have a close relationship with their pets. These people treat birds, cats, or other animals as members of their families. In your opinion, are such relationships good? Why or why not? Use specific reasons and examples to support your opinion.**

Which title do you prefer and why?
a. My Dog Moomoo
b. You're Invited to Moomoo's Birthday Party

TITLE EXERCISE 2: Without first writing an essay, try to create an interesting title that connects to an essay you would write. Be able to explain what makes your title interesting.

1. **Do you agree or disagree with the following statement? Universities should give the same amount of money to their students' sports activities as they give to the university libraries.**

____

2. **It has recently been announced that a shopping center may be built in your neighborhood. Do you support or oppose this plan? Why? Use specific reasons and details to support your answer.**

____

3. **What do you consider to be the most important room in a house? Why is this room more important to you than any other room? Use specific reasons and details to support your opinion.**

____

4. **In general, people are living longer now. How will this change affect society? Use specific reasons and examples to support your opinion.**

____

5. **If you were asked to send one thing representing your country to an international exhibition, what would you choose? Why? Use specific reasons and details to explain your choice.**

____

6. **Do you agree or disagree with the following statement? A person's childhood (the time from birth to 12 years of age) is the most important time of a person's life. Use specific reasons and details to support your choice.**

____

7. **Think of the most important class you have ever taken. Why did you enjoy this class so much? Use specific reasons and details to explain your answer.**

____

8. **You want to persuade someone to study your native language. What reasons would you give? Support your answer with specific details.**

____

9. **Many people have a close relationship with their pets. These people treat birds, cats, or other animals as members of their families. In your opinion, are such relationships good? Why or why not? Use specific reasons and examples to support your opinion.**

____

10. EDITING

Try to leave five minutes at the end of the essay—before you write the conclusion—so you can write a conclusion and look over the essay. At this time, add a title, or quickly notice if you've used one word several times in a paragraph (such as *interesting* or *therefore*) and then change these words. But don't start rewriting the essay or try to add entirely new sentences. If you have only five minutes left and you haven't written a conclusion, it's more important to write one than to reread your essay. Specific editing strategies will be discussed in the next section.

STUDY TIP

Think about these clocks as you write your essay. Spend approximately 2–4 minutes brainstorming, 20 minutes writing the essay, and 5 minutes editing the essay.

Brainstorming
(2–4 minutes)

Writing
(20 minutes)

Editing
(5 minutes)

Specific Areas for Grammar Review and Editing

1. FRAGMENTS AND RUN-ON SENTENCES

In writing, two common mistakes are **fragments** and **run-on sentences.**

A. FRAGMENTS

A **fragment** is an incomplete sentence that does not express a complete thought. It may be missing a subject, a verb, or part of the verb. The fragment can also be a dependent clause that needs an independent clause.

INCORRECT: Because I came to America.
This dependent clause is NOT a sentence because it needs an independent clause to complete its meaning.
CORRECT: *Because I came to America, I met many Americans.*

INCORRECT : More students going to school.
This sentence contains an incomplete verb, which also creates a sentence fragment.
CORRECT: *More students are going to school.*

INCORRECT : So for me is very easy to understand Argentinean people.
This sentence is missing a subject.
CORRECT: *So for me it is very easy to understand Argentinean people.*

INCORRECT : A class that is enjoyable.
This dependent clause is NOT a sentence because it needs a verb to complete its meaning.
CORRECT: *A class that is enjoyable makes me interested in the subject.*

B. RUN-ON SENTENCES

A **run-on** error is two or more sentences joined without a word to connect them or a punctuation mark to separate them. If you put a comma between them, it is still incorrect. This error is called a **comma splice**.

INCORRECT: Sometimes I like to be with one or two friends sometimes I like to be with a large group of friends.

There are five ways to correct this run-on.

1. Make two sentences.
Although your sentences will be grammatically correct, this way is not the best. It creates two choppy simple sentences instead of one complex one.
CORRECT: *Sometimes I like to be with one or two friends. Sometimes I like to be with a large group of friends.*

2. Use a coordinating conjunction (*for, and, nor, but, or, yet, so*).
CORRECT: *Sometimes I like to be with one or two friends, but sometimes I like to be with a large group of friends.*

3. Use a semicolon (;).
You can use a semicolon between two closely related sentences. Be careful not to overuse this punctuation.
CORRECT: *Sometimes I like to be with one or two friends; sometimes I like to be with a large group of friends.*

4. Use a transitional adverb (*however, therefore, consequently, etc.*).
Be careful of the punctuation. Subject + verb **; transitional adverb,** subject + verb.
CORRECT: *Sometimes I like to be with one or two friends; however, sometimes I like to be with a large group of friends.*

5. Make one a dependent clause.
CORRECT: *Although sometimes I like to be with one or two friends, sometimes I like to be with a large group of friends.*

SENTENCE ERROR EXERCISE 1: Label the following as Sentences (S), Fragments (F) or Run-ons (RO). If sentences are F or RO, correct them.

_____ 1. For example, if you're going to buy a watch.
_____ 2. Learning English is not easy, it takes up your time and energy.
_____ 3. A good roommate who is quiet.
_____ 4. Getting out of the city for a camping trip.
_____ 5. My problem is the irregular verbs.
_____ 6. I spent three months looking for an apartment I couldn't find anything under $1000 a month.
_____ 7. Twelve required courses in math and statistics.
_____ 8. What is your major?
_____ 9. A two-week vacation is a very short time to experience another country.
_____ 10. She couldn't understand the directions, she asked her friend for help.

SENTENCE ERROR EXERCISE 2: From these student sentences, label the following as Sentences (S), Fragments (F), or Run-ons (RO). If sentences are F or RO, correct them.

_____ 1. First who like to spend time with close friends can do many things in a short time.

_____ 2. I think children should be required to help with household tasks as soon as they are able to do so because parents can give their children some knowledge and include them as family members.

_____ 3. Second, when you are with a large number of friends.

_____ 4. Let me give an example, when I was in the first year of university, I always used to be with two of my friends.

_____ 5. Well, those are my basic points of wanting to go there, I hope that now you understand my desire.

_____ 6. I would probably choose Spain I think that this choice may create confusion with the readers, but I will give my reasons.

_____ 7. Regardless of gender, age, religion, and nationality, a teacher's role in learning is enormous because a teacher is a guide who will help open my eyes to some specific field which is totally unknown.

_____ 8. I prefer to have a teacher because if I learn by myself, maybe something mistake.

_____ 9. Sometimes when I have problems.

_____ 10. Two reasons.

_____ 11. Are teacher better computers?

_____ 12. When I was a child, I grew up in the countryside, I think it is a nice place for children's education.

_____ 13. When I saw a fire in the kitchen.

_____ 14. Through their personal experiences such as training.

_____ 15. If I don't have experience with it.

_____ 16. After having explained the advantages of having had a lifelong best friend and the disadvantages of going out with a diverse group of friends, I prefer to spend time with one or two close friends than with a large number of friends.

_____ 17. No matter what you think.

_____ 18. Even though unrelated to their occupation in the future.

_____ 19. Because I am a person who can feel nature beautifully, who helps other people, and who knows social rules.

_____ 20. However, sometimes I would like just to be with one or two of my friends rather than with a large number of friends.

2. PARALLELISM

Construct a sentence making sure its parts are parallel, or the sentence will be off balance. Always try to balance similar structures, especially in lists, series, or around connecting words within your sentences. In addition, look for faulty parallel construction in the structure section. In order to make sure your writing is parallel, make sure you understand the following points:

A. CONNECT SENTENCE PARTS WITH COORDINATING CONJUNCTIONS

Use FANBOYS as explained in the Structure section, page 117 to help you remember the coordinating conjunctions. A good clause or phrase combines the same kinds of words, phrases, or clauses. Combine a noun with a noun, not a noun with an adjective.

Words

Noun + Noun

Recession or **inflation** will lead to disaster.

Verb + Verb

The pharmacist **weighed** and **measured** the medicine.

Adjective + Adjective

The child was **little** yet surprisingly **strong**.

With three or more items in a series, use commas. *The play was **funny, enjoyable,** and **short**.*

Adverb + Adverb

He ran **quickly** but **carefully**.

Phrases (groups of words that lack either a subject or a verb)

A(n) + Adjective + Noun

He is **a serious student** but a **hilarious comic**.

Verb + Adverb

Karen **swims quickly** yet **talks slowly**.

Prepositional Phrase + Prepositional Phrase

David eats **in the morning** and **in the afternoon**.

Clauses (groups of words that include a subject and a verb)

Adjective Clause + Adjective Clause

Peter is a colleague **who teaches math** and **who conducts the orchestra**.

Noun Clause + Noun Clause

I know **that you are smart** and **that you are nervous**.

There are many other types of words, phrases, and clauses that you can use in your writing. These are just some examples.

B. CONNECT SENTENCES WITH PAIRED CONJUNCTIONS

Instead of writing two short sentences, always try to combine sentences. One good way to connect similarly constructed sentences is with paired conjunctions. The pairs are:

<u>Both . . . and</u> (takes a plural verb)

Both Susan **and** Jenny speak Chinese.

Not only . . . but also
Monique **not only** jogs **but also** lifts weights.

Either . . . or
Either the idioms **or** the phrasal verbs are my biggest problem.

Neither . . . nor
Neither the football players **nor** the soccer players can take afternoon classes.

The subjects that come after *but also, or,* and *nor* determine the verb.
Either the teacher or the students **erase** the blackboard every day. (*Students* is plural, so the verb *erase* agrees.)
Either the students or the teacher **erases** the blackboard every day. (*The teacher* is singular, so the verb *erase* agrees.)

When these pairs are used, they must be followed by parallel types of words, phrases, or clauses.

EXAMPLES:
Here are two simple sentences. They use parallel construction, but they are choppy.

I want to go to Mexico. I want to go to Brazil.

These sentences can be combined into one:
I want to go to **both** Mexico **and** Brazil.

INCORRECT: I want both to go to Mexico and to Brazil.

Here are two more simple sentences:

I swim in the morning. If not, I swim at night.

These sentences can be combined into one:
I swim **either** in the morning **or** at night.

INCORRECT: I swim in either the morning or night. (because *night* takes *at* not *in*)

Here are two more sentences which can be easily combined:

She knew what to say. She knew when to say it.

These sentences can be combined into one:
She knew **not only** what to say **but also** when to say it.

INCORRECT: She not only knew what say but when to say it. (*not only* refers to *what to say,* not to *knew*)

C. DO NOT OMIT NECESSARY WORDS

Omitted articles, auxiliaries, and prepositions often affect parallel structure.

Be careful of changing verb tenses within a sentence.
INCORRECT: I always have and always will eat breakfast. (Although you may hear this sentence, it is incorrect in writing.)
CORRECT: I have always eaten and will always eat breakfast.

Be careful of changing articles within a sentence.
INCORRECT: Mark gave me an apple, pear, and oranges.
CORRECT: Mark gave me an apple, a pear, and oranges.

Be careful of changing prepositions.
INCORRECT: I was interested and surprised by the story.
CORRECT: I was interested in and surprised by the story.

As . . . as and *than*
When these two connectives introduce comparisons, you must be sure that the things compared are similar.
INCORRECT: The population of Japan is greater than Korea. DON'T compare a population with a country.
CORRECT: The population of Japan is greater than that of Korea.
INCORRECT: Joanne is as tall if not taller than her sister. (Although you may hear this sentence in conversation, don't forget the second "as.")
CORRECT: Joanne is as tall as if not taller than her sister.

D. RECOGNIZE WORD FORMS/WORD ENDINGS

In order to make sure the parts of your sentence are parallel, you will need to know what part of speech a word is by its ending.

- A NOUN is a person, place, or thing (*Robby, university, friendship*).
- A VERB is either transitive, showing action (*study*), or intransitive, indicating a state of being (*seem, be*).
- An ADJECTIVE describes a noun (*tired* baby, *two* universities), answering the questions What kind of? or How many?
- An ADVERB can describe a verb (ran *quickly*), adjective (*very* tired), or another adverb (*so* capably).

By memorizing suffixes (word endings), you will be able to know if a word is used incorrectly.

Memorize the following chart and add in your own examples of words with these suffixes:

NOUN ENDINGS	EXAMPLES	YOUR EXAMPLES
ness	happiness	________, ________
(i)ty	community	________, ________
th	width	________, ________
sion, tion	position	________, ________
ism	Buddhism	________, ________
ure	architecture	________, ________
(*ure* can also indicate a verb)		
ment	repayment	________, ________
(*ment* can also indicate a verb)		
ude	gratitude	________, ________
ence, ance	independence	________, ________
ship	friendship	________, ________
ery, ary	cemetery	________, ________
hood	neighborhood	________, ________
phy, gy, try	philosophy	________, ________
inct/ct	precinct	________, ________
ess	address	________, ________
(*ess* can also indicate a verb)		

PEOPLE NOUN ENDINGS		
ist, yst	chemist	________, ________
er,or	doctor	________, ________
ess	hostess	________, ________
ian	librarian	________, ________
ic	medic	________, ________
(*ic* can also indicate adjectives)		
eur	voyeur	________, ________
ant, ent	correspondent	________, ________
ect, ict	suspect	________, ________
(*ect* can also indicate verbs)		

VERB ENDINGS		
ize (yze)	criticize	________, ________
ate, ete	refrigerate	________, ________
(*ate* can also indicate adjectives)		
ify	identify	________, ________
uish, ish	distinguish	________, ________
(*ish* can also indicate adjectives)		
en	lengthen	________, ________
ute	dilute	________, ________
ure	endure	________, ________
ose	oppose	________, ________
ine	determine	________, ________
ulge	indulge	________, ________
ict	predict	________, ________
erse	converse	________, ________
end, ond	pretend	________, ________
use	enthuse	________, ________

erve	deserve	________, ________
uce	produce	________, ________
ess	address	________, ________
uade, ade	persuade	________, ________
ote	promote	________, ________
ave	behave	________, ________
age	encourage	________, ________
ect	reflect	________, ________
ame	inflame	________, ________
ment	experiment	________, ________
oy	destroy	________, ________

ADJECTIVE ENDINGS

ly	lovely	________, ________
(usually *ly* signifies an adverb, but some nouns + *ly* = adjectives)		
less	careless	________, ________
ful	useful	________, ________
al	usual	________, ________
ish	foolish	________, ________
y	crazy	________, ________
ary	scary	________, ________
ic	heroic	________, ________
ble, ible, able	incredible	________, ________
ive, tive	passive	________, ________
ant, ent	dependant	________, ________
ing, ed	interesting	________, ________
ous, ious	religious	________, ________
ate, ete, ute	ornate	________, ________

WORD FORM EXERCISE: Fill in the missing part of speech: The NOUN form indicates the "thing" form. The PERSON WHO category is another noun form of the word, used for people.

NOUN	PERSON WHO . . .	VERB	ADJECTIVE
________	________	create	________
symbol	XXXXXX	________	________
________	________	________	communicative
art	________	XXXXX	________
________	________	predict	________
________	________	execute	________
correspondence	________	________	________
________	________	________	suspicious
therapy	________	XXXXX	________
________	analyst	analyze	________
diagnosis	________	________	________
________	________	________	educational
manipulation	________	________	________
________	scientist	XXXXX	________
development	________	________	________
________	________	compete	________
________	immigrant	________	XXXXX
________	XXXXX	popularize	________

E. RECOGNIZE BASIC WORD ORDER IN SENTENCES

If you learn some basic English word order patterns, you will be able to recognize if a word is not in the correct form.

ACTION VERBS (AV) are followed by NOUNS (N) and ADVERBS (ADV), but never ADJECTIVES.
I **ran quickly**.
AV ADV
I **eat breakfast** in the morning.
AV N
The direct object (breakfast) should always come right after the action verb.
INCORRECT: I eat in the morning breakfast.

LINKING VERBS (LV): *be, seem, appear, become,* etc. are followed by NOUNS and ADJECTIVES (ADJ)
She **is** a **doctor**.
LV N
She **appears intelligent**.
LV ADJ

ADJECTIVES come before NOUNS
I read a **good book**.
ADJ N

ADVERBS OF INTENSITY (answering *To what degree?*) come before ADJECTIVES
I read a **very good** book.
ADV ADJ

ADVERBS OF MANNER (answering *How?*) come after ACTION VERBS
She **swims gracefully**.
AV ADV

ADVERBS OF FREQUENCY (answering *How often?*) come before ACTION VERBS
She **never repeats** the instructions.
ADV AV

PARALLELISM EXERCISE 1: Make the following sentences parallel. In some cases, there may be more than one correct answer.

1. The apartment was beautiful, expensive, and had a lot of space.
2. If you're going to use this recipe, you'll need a pepper, onion, and tomato.
3. Our teacher is interesting: she plays piano, writes poetry, and is a painter of watercolors.
4. I always have and always will sing in the shower.
5. Please turn down the television, or will you go to sleep?
6. Michael hopes his dedication, ability, and that he is considerate will help him get the job.
7. Daniel is a happy child and sleeps soundly.
8. Jodie Foster is a great actress and directs movies well.
9. The books on the top shelf are older than the bottom shelves.
10. At the University of Pennsylvania, morning classes are far more popular than the afternoon.

PARALLELISM EXERCISE 2: Complete each of the following sentences by adding words, phrases, or clauses that are parallel to the italicized words. There are many possible answers.

1. I was in favor of either *painting the walls purple* or ______________________________.
2. Matt found what he needed in the desk: *a ruler, a pen,* and ________________.
3. The square was crowded with young tourists *studying their guidebooks, eating lunches from backpacks,* and ______________________________.
4. Moving to a new apartment means I'll have to *decide what to keep, what to give away,* and ____________________.
5. During our coffee break we ate blueberry muffins that were *small* but ________.
6. The hats and coats were piled everywhere: *on the bed, on the chairs,* and even ________________.
7. Bonnie knew neither *what to say in her letter of application* nor ________________.
8. *Either the government will ban smoking in public buildings* or ________________________.
9. Molly walked *across the square* and __________________.
10. In the morning newspaper I *read that plans for a second airport are being considered* and ______________________________.

PARALLELISM EXERCISE 3: Correct student errors from TOEFL test essays, making the sentences parallel.

1. Life is more simple and people are more convenient than people who lived in the past.
2. I think neither spending time with one or two friends nor a large number of friends is preferable to being alone.
3. Some people say it is easy to get into but difficult to graduate U.S. colleges or universities.
4. If the community were bigger, it would be more comfortable and convenience.
5. A teacher can tell you what wrong is or which better way is.
6. I like to visit a lot of different foreign countries and spending my time with the people there.
7. It helps people to get rid of something they don't want instead of throwing it away but give it to someone who needs and wants it.
8. I don't have to worry if the goods are both damaged or not worth anything.
9. The boss either must decide to hire new employees or retrain the current ones.
10. The unemployment figures for those under twenty-five in Manila is larger than Singapore.

PARALLELISM EXERCISE 4: Make the following sentences parallel. In some cases, there may be more than one correct answer.

1. After a day at the beach, the children came home tired, sunburned, and hunger.
2. Larry Bird was a quick, skillful, and energy basketball player.
3. A good writer edits her work slowly, carefully, and regular.
4. The English composition course contains short stories, a novel, and poetic.
5. When you write an essay, you should check each verb for agree, tense, and form.
6. The airline allows passengers to take one, two or third suitcases.
7. My mother has been a waitress, a secretary, and taught school.
8. My uncle spoke in a humorous way and with kindness.
9. I am hot, dirty, and need something to drink.
10. The flavor of the strawberry yogurt is better than the peach.

PARALLELISM EXERCISE 5: Make the following sentences parallel. In some cases, there may be more than one correct answer.

1. We want to have a flower garden, but we don't know where to begin, how to proceed, or the flowers we should plant.
2. The summer of 1950 was as hot, if not hotter than any other in the last century.
3. I neither know what kind of computer he uses nor where he bought it.
4. I am afraid and excited about taking the TOEFL test.
5. Jared has sent resumes both to graphic design firms in Taipei and Hong Kong.
6. Chris is an affectionate husband, a dutiful son, and kind to his kids.
7. The shape of the rock, how long it is, and the color reminds me of a small elephant.
8. He danced gracefully, rhythmically, and with ease.
9. Judy is a gifted woman: a biologist, does carpentry, and she can cook.
10. Your job consists of arranging the books, cataloging the new arrivals, and brochures have to be alphabetized.

3. PUNCTUATION

Although punctuation is NOT directly tested in the structure section, it's a good idea to know some basic punctuation rules for your essay writing. An essay with numerous, significant punctuation errors will receive a lower score.

A. BASIC PUNCTUATION RULES

1. Never begin a sentence or a new line with a punctuation mark.

INCORRECT: ?Where are you from?

2. Write out numbers. Don't write 10 and 6. If a number is in the millions, you can use numbers. You can also write years in numbers.

EXAMPLE: Only ten pages of the 6,790,500 pages I wrote in 1992 remain.

3. Use a colon (:) only after a complete sentence and before a list.

EXAMPLE: I took many things to the beach: a blanket, suntan lotion, and lunch.

4. Capitalize the first word in a sentence and the following proper nouns:
People *(Thomas, Americans)*
Places *(the Panama Canal, Singapore)*
Months *(May)*
Days *(Sunday)*
Holidays *(Hanukkah, Ramadan, Valentine's Day)*
Languages/Nationalities *(Swahili, Swedish)*

EXAMPLE:
Justin visited Doree at the Hilton Hotel in Capetown last Sunday, April 5.

B. COMMA RULES

1. Do not use commas (,) between two sentences (see run-on sentence section, page 207).

2. Use commas before coordinating conjunctions (*for, and, nor, but, or, yet, so*) if there is a subject and a verb before and after the conjunction.

EXAMPLE:
I like black and wear black clothes a lot.
I like black, and I wear black clothes a lot.

3. If you have three adjectives, verbs, or nouns in a row, separate them with commas.

EXAMPLE: I like black, brown, and turquoise.

4. Transitional adverbs (*however, therefore, consequently,* etc.) have a semicolon (;) before them and a comma after them if there is a subject and a verb before and after.

EXAMPLE:	**Subject**	**Verb**	**Subject**	**Verb**
	I	like	black; therefore, I	wear it a lot.
Also correct:	**Subject**	**Verb**	**Subject**	**Verb**
	I	like	black; I,	therefore, wear it a lot.

5. If an adjective clause comes after a person's name, you can set it off with commas. These clauses are called **nonessential clauses**. By using commas, the reader knows the information is NOT essential to the meaning of the sentence.

EXAMPLES:
Jeff Brown, who lives next door to me, works in my office.
The man who lives next door to me works in my office.

In the second sentence we do not know who the man is, so we don't use commas. In the first sentence, the adjective clause is EXTRA information about Jeff Brown.

INCORRECT: Students, who arrived on time, can leave early.
We don't mean ALL students, we mean *only those who arrived on time,* so we cannot use commas. The sentence should have no punctuation: *Students who arrived on time can leave early.*

For more information about adjective clauses, see pages 121–123.

6. Use commas to set off introductory adverbial clauses. If the clause is NOT at the beginning, don't use a comma.

EXAMPLE:
Because I was sick, I stayed home.
I stayed home **because I was sick**.

PUNCTUATION EXERCISE: Insert the necessary punctuation. If the sentence is correct, write **C**.

1. Although Yutaka was absent she e-mailed me for the homework.
2. There are three sections on the TOEFL exam listening structure and reading.
3. I improved my writing ability because I wrote 2 essays a day.

4. I got autographs from my three favorite movie stars Meryl Streep Jodie Foster and Robin Williams.
5. Jean-Claude has taken several English classes therefore he is confident about his writing ability.
6. Luis Carlos a mexican didn't want to take a class with 7 other mexicans.
7. Maria Paula who comes from Colombia explained in her essay why she prefers to live in a dorm.
8. Carmen's daughter was sick so Carmen took her to the doctor.
9. I've been teaching for thirty-two years but have never had a student from Laos or Mali before this semester.
10. Faisal was worried about the midterm and thought about it during the break.
11. After Diana came to one class she never appeared again.
12. Luis speaks several languages Portuguese Spanish English and Italian.
13. I arrived on time for the test however I forgot my passport.
14. Classes which meet on Monday evenings will meet an additional time during exam week.
15. !Bravo! If I call your name you passed the entrance examination.

C. Student Essays

In this section, you will find authentic essays written by non-native English speakers. They are in their original form; nothing has been corrected, added, or deleted. The purpose of this section is for you to get a sense of what a 0, 1, 2, 3, 4, 5, or 6 essay can look like. Two official readers read each essay. In the Answer Key are an official score for each essay, comments from the official scoring guide that explain each score, and *comments in italics by Roberta Steinberg, the author of this text.*

How to use this section:

- Read the essays one topic at a time.
- Order them from worst to best.
- Decide which score you would give each essay, based on the ETS scoring guide. There may be several of the same score in each topic.
- Compare your scores with the readers' scores (in the Answer Key), paying attention to the criteria comments.
- Remember, scoring is NOT an exact science, but these essays have been scored by more than one official essay scorer.
- For added practice, correct what you can on the essays, paying attention to grammar, spelling, organization, sentence structure, and overall clarity.

TOPIC 1

Some people prefer to spend time with one or two close friends. Others choose to spend time with a large number of friends. Compare the advantages of each choice. Which of these two ways of spending time do you prefer? Use specific reasons to support your answer.

#1/A

Each of these ways are pretty good.
If you spend time with a large number of friends probably you will get more fun and learn out something new from them and so on.

But I prefer to spend time with several close friends. We know and understand each other, have the same interests, feelings.
When I am with my close friends I feel more comfortable and more freely than with a large company.

This is my first experience to study abroad.
In my opinion it is very difficult to mane a lot of friends. For me it takes a long time usualy. Maybe it's because of we have different mind or I am not active. Also my English is not good. I can't explaine all my thoughts.

So I really miss my close friends in my country.

#1/B

Some people prefer to spend time with one or two close friends. Other choose to spend time a large number of friends. Through my personal experience, I think both of them are fine. Sometimes, I may want to spend time with a group of friends. Sometimes, I feel that I want to be alone or just with one or two friends. I think spending time with either one or two friends or a large number of friends is fine.

I always like to celebrate my birthday with a large number of my friends. I think it's fine to celebrate my birthday, which only once a year, with a group of my friends. I like to share my happiness in this special day. In my birthday, I don't like to be alone or just with one or two of my close friends. I always had fun in my birthday party. Beside, if I involved many friends. I could get a lot of gift too. Therefore, I always have big birthday party.

However, sometimes I would like just be with one or two of my friends rather than a large number of friends. Being with one or two of my friends, I can tell them my secret. When I was in high school, I always went to one of my close friend's house and spent my weekend over there. We always laid on her bed and shared each other's secret. At that time, the bed and the time were just belone to two of us. We didn't want to let anyone else join with us. I think it was sweet to being with one or two friends.

I thin no matter who you're being with or how many people you're being together, the most important thing is to have FUN! You can celebrate something special with a large number of friends. Sometimes it's also sweet to being one or two friends.

#1/C

Some people prefer to spend time with one or two close friends, but others prefer to spend time with a large number of friends. I prefer to spend time with a small number of close friends because of two following reasons.

One of the two reasons is that it is easy to decide where to go. For example, if I go out with ten friends who are not so close to me, I may not know where they want to go because I am not so familiar with them, and because it's a large amount of people, their preference may not be same. But if I go out with one or two close friends, each person knows each preferance and our favorite may be same, because we are close friends. It's easy to decide where to go.

The other reason is that the conversation will be easy and interesting if I go out with one or two close friends. For example, a conversation with a large number of people would be difficult, because ten people, for example, have ten opinions or thoughts, it's going to be very hard to think all of their opinions or thoughts. But, on the other hand, if it's a small number of people, the conversation between us will be very easy and interesting, because each person has his or her friends' basic informations. I don't have to start conversation from the beginning such as "what do you like to do?" or "Which kind of movie do you like?" but I am able to ask or know deep thinking of my friends. To know basic informations about them makes the chat easy, and to know deep feeling or idea is very interesting.

In summery, I prefer to spend time with one or two close friends, because it's easy to decide where to go and the conversations is very interesting.

#1/D

Spending time is an important and necessary issue to think about nowadays. As time is a priceless asset in our lifes; we have to plan how to spend or invest time, especially when we decide to share and spend that time involving other people.

If we decide to spend time with friends, what the best choice could be, maybe spend time with one or two close friends or with a large number of friends.

Spending time with one or two close friends, it could be the best choice when you like to make stronger friendships. The fewer quantity of time you have, the best quality of attention you like to give; then it is easy to organize a meeting with two friends and keep a deep conversation with them than trying to do the same with a large group of friends.

Spending time with a large number of friends is good since diversity of people offer a diversity of characters and personalities, which give you more alternatives of enjoying free activities. A large number of friends is great to enjoy excursions or discover new places.

After said the advantages of one or other choice and having the personal experience as example, I prefer to spend time with one or two close friends than with a large number of friends. Usually, I like to enjoy activities that do not involve a lot of time in preparing it then it is easy to commit one or two people. In addition it is easier to find restaurant tables, tickets, etc for three people than for big group.

#1/E

People like to spend time with one or two close friends, as well as a large number of friends. Both of types of spending time have advantages. People who prefer to spend time with close friends is good to do easily and people who prefer to spend time with number of friends is good to get information.

Frist who likes to spend time with close friends can do many thin during the short time. When I want to go shopping or movie theater I usually go with my best friend. We made a list which we want to buy and we spent one or two hours to shopping. We also like same kind of food and movie, so we don't need to think for a long time to each watch. In addition, we really enjoy taking a trip. We are same university student so we don't need to make a plan before more two week. Thoes reasones can save my time.

In conclusion. Both of types of spending time have good ways. However I need to find job now, so I prefer to spend time with number of friends. It give to me a lot of advantage even though I want to go travel. I hope that some of meeting get in the special place to play and relex.

#1/F

Some people spend time with one or two close friends, and others spend time with a large number of friends.

Spending time with one or two close friends makes indeed friends. They can speak each other a lot of times, so they can know each other well. It makes strong believe each other. Therefore, They are going to become a real friend.

Spending time with a large number of friends gives you a lot of different experiences. People is not same each other, so you can have many kinds of experience when you meet many kind of people. I am sure what kinds of experience you have, but it helps you when you meet a new person.

Both ways of spending time with friends are good, but I prefer to spend time with one or two close friends because I want to get a real friend.

#1/G

The time in our life and we decide how to spend it, and in the end the time in our days and years, so some people spend the time with one or two others spend it with a large number of friends, any way in my opinion is better, these what I will discuse through this easy.

In my opinion spend time with a large number of friends is better for many reasons. First, with a large number of friends, there are different personality, and these will give varity in the time and will change from hour to onther. Second, when you are with a large number of friends. You can do many activities together, like going in a trip, playing soccur, make a big team to any kind of sports, or make a party. also, with a large number of friends you will find different experiences and different happits, so these as I think will give chance to do and know different things with this group.

Let me give an example when I was in the first year university, I used to be always with two of my friends, and we used to spend alot of time toghther and to go to every place toghther. Do you think I was happy that time? yes. I was happy because there was less argument where we could go, or what could we talk about it, and I knew my friends very well and so they did. and we could easily understood each other and did the best thing for every body, in addition we couldn't spend more time waiting or staying so really in that time I could do many activities with them. but after a year and a half I was with alarge number of friends and gradually I understood how much love, experiences, different personality, more knolwedge and more injoyable time with a large number of good friends.

#1/H

Friendship is an extremely important component in one's life. Spending time with either two friends or a large number of friends have their advantages as well as their disadvantages. There are different opinions of how many friends one should have and how much happier one would be depending on the amount of friends they have. However, I feel that it is more important to have two close friends rather than a large, foreign group of friends.

Spending time with a large number of friends has its advantages. There is more of a chance that you will actually do something with each other because you have more than two people to rely on. This means that if one person cannot spend time with you, you can always ask someone else. Also, spending time with a larger group opens up your mind to many new ideas and fun activities. There is more of a chance to have diversity in a larger group of friends, where you can learn about different cultures and perspectives. Another advantage is that to the outside world, you can appear happier because it looks as if you are surrounded by many loving friends. It makes people envy you because they think that you are happier than they are. However, this is not the only type of friendship you may have.

Having two close friends has its advantages, as well, which I believe benefit me more than having a large group of friends. Having a smaller amount of friends, I feel, is better because these are people you can always rely on for your personal dilemmas. They may not always be able to go watch a move with you, but they will always be there to make you feel good about yourself, on the inside. These are the friends that you will hold onto for a very long time, and sometimes, for your entire life. Having a small amount of close friends means deeper conversations and more one on one activities, where you can discover who you really are and learn to be comfortable with yourself. Having a few, close friends means a lot more bonding time where you can become a part of another person and they can become a part of you.

To conclude, spending time in either a large group of friends or a small group of close friends both have their advantages. However, I believe that spending time with a group of small, close friends is more beneficial to one's self than spending time with a large group of foreign people. Large groups leave you insatiable and craving a relationship, while smaller, closer friendships are undeviating and fill a gap in our lives.

#1/I

Should spare time be spent with many people or a few people? There are advantages and disadvantages to both. In a smaller environment, friendships are closer and in a large environment, friendships are not usually as close. But does this make it better to have a few very close friends than many close friends? Although a friendship may be closer in a smaller environment, the ideal environment is one that is larger.

There are many good reasons why spending time with smaller and closer friendships are good. For example, each person in these close-knit friendships knows the other extremely well. He knows the others likes and dislike. He knows the friend's personal history and knows the times that his friend has suffered or had fun. When there are fights in these close-knit friendships, the fights usually end quickly without bad things happening. It is easier to forgive and forget with someone who has been one of your best friends than someone who has not been as best a friend.

However, there is more fun to be had in a large group of friends. Usually in larger settings, it is nearly impossible to run out of things to do. Nearly everyone has an idea. Also in larger environments, games which take more people are enjoyable. It is more fun to play a basketball game with five on each team than it is to play a basketball game with a few players on each team. Games like capture the flag and such, can be played better with more friends. Video games are also fun to play with many people than a few people. Tournaments can be made and enjoyed with many people. There is also more diversity in a larger setting. It is possible to learn about other faiths and religions. In the end, the ideal setting is a larger one.

#1/J

It's good for us to have a large circle of friends. Different kinds of friends make one's life more miscillaneous. In other words, you may have different experience and views of lives. Moreover, when you spend time among a lot of friends, it helps to form a unique leadership spirit. However, I prefer to spend time with one or two close friends for several reasons.

First of all, I feel being neglected sometimes when I are among a large number of people. It's natural that it won't be possible to satisfy everyone's interests in those occasions. Unfortunately, I'm always among the "mute minorities". But when you are with only a few number of friends, this kinds of circumstance never happens, simply because two or three share the same interest. Thus, we all may enjoy our time better.

Another reason is that when I'm among a large circle of people, it's too noisy. One can do nothing but to chat with each other and laugh loud. This is not the only thing that I want to do with friends.

When I'm with only a small number of friends, I can change my mind with them and learn something special. For instance, I learned some details about renascaince in Europe from a roommate of mine when I was a freshman in my university and read some books You'll never have such a good mood to talk about it when you are among a large circle of noisy and garrulous crowd. Also, this kind of interaction helps both of my friends and are gain a broader view of life. Thus, there's an old saying in ancient China that "It's better to have only one but a really good friend than to have a large circle of friends who don't know you well."

Let's find a real friend and make it a better place for us to live in.

TOPIC 2

You have the opportunity to visit a foreign country for two weeks. Which country would you like to visit? Use specific reasons and details to explain your choice.

#2/A

If I have the opportunity to visit a foreign country for two weeks, I would have a difficult time to choose only one. I want to visit many places; for example, among them are France with it's barocco buildings, foggy England, hot Spain. However, now I am in the United States and I suddenly realized that this country can be the right choice for me. Let me explain why. First, I want to travel here; because U.S.A. is very big and policultural country. Many notions mixed here and produced special one, american nation. I think no one country in the world does not give an opportunity to see so many different cultures in one land. It would be interesting to know how people from different countries can communicate with each other, how they can survive in a new place. Second, if I choose the United States, I would have the opportunity to be in different climates and time zones. For example, people can travel by car from East coast of U.S.A. to west and see how the mixed forests can be changed by savannas and mountains. Third, I think that fact that people in the United States are very friendly can influence on my choice. Americans like to share their experience of live, because the american nation is the nation of immigrants, people visiting american feel themself at home. Even if foreign visitors do not speak a good English, americans can understand them and remain a patience at the same time.

To sum up, I think that U.S.A. is a right choice for me to visit it, because its people, culture, history, geographical environment are very attractive to people. We can get a different experience here!

#2/B

I think that if I have the oportunity to visit a foreign country for two weeks I'll choose Argentina because the politic situation, the second reason is because the language is the same like in my country, and the third reason is because that is a big country with a lot of diferents places to visit.

The first reason that I explain is the politic situation and that's because I'm a lawyer, and in my mayor I've been studing the governments of a lot of countries and how to grownup a bad economic situation. At the same time, now I think that travel around Argentina can be cheaper than before.

The second reason is the language. In Argentina people speak Spanish and I am Spanish, so for me is very easy understand the Argentine people. As important as this reason is that the Argentine people speaks with a very nice voice, similar as if they are sinning all the time.

The third reason, probably the most importan for all the tourist, is that Argentina is a very big country and you can find there a lot of different places like TIERRA DE FUEGO, a very cold place where all is ice and snow. Latter you can visit LA PAMPA, where you can do treeking. Other place really nice is Iguazu Falls, near Brasil. And you can't leave Argentina without visit Buenos Aires, the capital of the country. This city is very big and there you can hear a TANGO song and dance it.

I think that for all this reasons I would like to visit Argentina.

#2/C

If I had the opportunity to visit any country in the world I would probably chose spain, I think that this choice may create a confused reaction with the readers but I will give my reasons from which I made this chose.

First of all I'm going to say that my native country is Venezuela, may be your thinking "So, what does that have to do with wanting to go to Spain." As you know Venezuela was an Spanish colony, and I think that may be there's a cultural relation between these two nations, may be that trip would help me understand better the way that Venezeulan culture has been formed.

There's a saying in my country that says that "And old parrot never learn's to speak." So to say you are going to be what you've learned in the first stages of life, hence, I think that maybe Venezeula's failures maybe are because the Spaniards didn't lay a solid foundation for our country.

I also enjoy very much architecture and art, so i've heard Spain has very beautiful museums, such as "El museo del Prado", "Museo de Cordoba", where famous paintings are shown. Also Spain has a lot of history in her streets.

One of my main reasons to visit Spain it's because I'm a big soccer fan and right now their leagues is the best of the world, with high quality players and a lot of competiveness between all the teams that perform in this league. So one of my dreams is to see a soccer game there.

Well those are my basic points of wanting to go there, I hope that now you understand my desire.

#2/D

I would like to go to Italy because there are very beautiful, historical and fashionable country. Specially, Italy has very famous of food.

I like Italy but I have never been there. However I know Italy very well because I read many books and watched TV about Italy. I am interesting three things at Italy. Firstly, It is about fashion. Many famous brand companies are in Italy. For example, Armani, Prada, Gucci, and etc are. They are world wide companies and are making very nice clothes for women and men. Secondly, It is about food. Italian food is very famous around the world. For example pizza, lizotto, vine, hum and etc. They are very nice foods specially. French cooking is very famous in the world. However, the roots is Italian food. Italian king brought these foods to France. Finally, It is history. There are many historical places. Italy has north and south of part. North part has Filenze. South part has Rome and Napoli. Each part has very different cultures and caractors. However, both parts have very historical places also.

I would like to go to Italy. They are very fun to me. I can see and feel good in Italy. There is the best country for me.

#2/E

I would like visit Japan because it's an amazing country. It's culture is one of the most interesting around the world taking into account that even though Japanese people have a millenary culture and traditions, they a very opend minded about new productions methods and new forms to lead business and finance managements. It is for such reason that Japan is part of the community's countries developed. Thecnological development and the new discoveries that taught place in Japan have made change the world in very important aspects, for example in aspects like communications, transport, finance and computational science, Japan has been a the country leader. But not every thing in Japan is work and studing, one of the most famous international cussine is the Japanese, not only for it's high and exciting quality but for it's beautiful appearance. The qualities of the Japanese Cusine are part of the reach inheritance they have had and so them discipline and serious hard work make part of the Japanese culture.

Other important issue that constitutes a very importan element which makes Japan be one of the most attractive place in the world is its amazing architecture, the forms, color, textures of the traditionals buildingn makes an incredible but beautiful contrast with its modern buildings and perfectly describes the transition of the Japanese culture to the modern world with an interesting and valuable traditionar architecture.

#2/F

I would like to go to England. I like England very much because it was beautiful city. I want to go another city in London. I have roommate who from England. I am getting more and more attract about England.

If I go to England for two weeks. Frist one week, I stay in London. I go to see musium, and go to sightseeing, and shopping, and after them I go to another city around London. Probably I can speak English easily and fun.

#2/G

I would like visit Japan contry because, I think is the contry most interesting by the culture, the tradition, it's very different then mine, but the principal reason is the people, I have a very goods friends (of course Japanise friends) who teach me what kind of person are they.

I'm interesting in the evolution of that people because the lives in islend terretori and they have a lot of sources, for exaple they have rice, and very important industry, they are the best of the world in electronic industry, othe reason why I want go to Japan is structure of the contry, the houses streets the beuty of all construction.

In education way, I want learn the Japanise lenguage because I think that the future language same the English and I want learn to my major "Internatiol Commerce" and I know if I learn that two principal language, I gonna make a lot business and of course a lot of money.

I think when come true all my dream I gonna make happy and one of my principal drems is visit the "Gans Japan".

In two weeks I can make too many things in Japan, I know I can't learn Japaenisse or make business if I can know the people and know the culture at the same their tradition, and the principal is make come true one of my drems.

#2/H

If finance and time permit me to choose a favorite country to visit, my choice will surely be Italy although the communication is a big problem because of the difficult to learn italian. Three points encourage me to make a decision like that. They're following.

The first one is my strong admire to Italian soccer team. As a devout fan of Italy, I'm keeping the belif that Italy will win the champion when world cup comes every four years. Therefore, I hope to live see the series A of Italian soccer league to feel the sense of the true Italian soccer.

Then, the second one is supposed to be the beautiful natural scene in Italy. Someone ever told me that the most charming beach can be enjoyed in South Italy. More, I myself read some books and watched some introductions in TV which all tell the Italian nature scene as well as Italian long history. Ruins of Roma Empire and the holly church are full of attractive matters.

After that, it comes out my last point to support my trip to Italy. Italy is another country comparing with China, United States and Singapore. Italy has a long history unlike US and Singapore, as well as it's developed unlike China. The trip to Italy should be a very different experience for me. I'm looking forward to more by expericing difference from my familiar environment, because of my adventrous personality.

Frankly speaking, I've planned to travel throughout the world including the Africa, Antarctica. But Italy'll be my first stop during my rest of the global trip.

#2/I

If I have a change to visit a foreign country for 2 weeks, I will choose USA. Because there are a lot to see in USA, and the transportation is very convenient, so that you can travel to a lot of places within 2 weeks.

As a country with a large landscape, America has all kinds of sceneries to see. You can see white snow and ice in Alaska, enjoy the sunshine on the beach in Florida, and experience the Great Canyon in Colorado. Actually, you can experience all four seasons within 2 weeks in the lovely country.

On the other hand, America is the most developed country in the world. You can see a large variety of high-tech products and enjoy all kinds of high value-added services during your stay. Moreover, you can have some touch with a lot of cultures and races for US is an immigrated country.

Last but not least, America has a highly developed transportation system. You can reach every corner of the US by train, by bus or by plane and the fares are usually reasonable. Usually you can reach your destination safe and sound without being exhausted so that you can enjoy your trip.

A lot of us have US dreams, deam to see the Statue of Liberty, the White house, etc. So why not go to the US for traveling if you have 2 weeks time?

#2/J

If I get a chance to visit a foreign country for 2 weeks, I would like to go to India. India is always my dream land. It has a long history and colorful culture just like my country. It is so mysterious and wonderful. It attracts thousands and hundreds people like me from all over the world every year.

The begining of my knowledge about India is from those wonderful folk stories which my parents told me when I was still a child. Those colorful folklores reflect its colorful history and culture. From then on, my dream about India starts.

When I grew up, the more I knew about India, the more attractive I found it. There are many kinds of religions in India and it's the birthplace of Hinduism. So it is also a country of religions. You can find people with different religions live together harmonly. It will surely be interesting.

As I'm a person who want to experience different cultures by interacting with the local people, I wish to have a chance to see how people live with my own eyes and interact with them to feel their culture with my heart.

Although I have known a lot about India by books and TV, there are still pretty more interesting things about this old country waiting for me to explore when I get to this wonderful land.

TOPIC 3

Some people think that they can learn better by themselves than with a teacher. Others think that it is always better to have a teacher. Which do you prefer? Use specific reasons to develop your essay.

#3/A

I think it's always better to have a teacher. Maybe some people think that they can learn better by themself than with a teacher. However, if they have any question, there is no one can teach them.

There are many reasons that make me to think it's always better to have a teacher than studying by myself. For example, if I'm tring to solve a math problem, and I have no idea how to answer it. If there is a teacher, the teacher will tell me how to solve it in many ways. And the next time when I meet same kinds of question, I'll know how to do it. However, if I rather study by myself, I may never know the anwser. Maybe I can find the book in order to help me, but the book will just me the anwser. I won't know how to solve the same kind of question.

A teacher also can tell you if you're doing wrong. Sometimes you don't even know when you're making a mistake. People always make some mistakes, but they don't want to keep making same mistakes again and again. If you're learn boxing, it's always better if there is a teacher with you. The teacher will teach you if you're in wrong posture, or using wrong hand. It's very important to know whether you're right when you are doing sport, because any wrong posture many injure you.

A teacher can always teach you something and you can always keep asking question. After someone teachs you enough knowledge, you have to study and remember by yourself. A teacher can tell you what wrong is, or which better way is, but if you don't study, nobody can help you. Therefore, I think having a teacher is always better than studying by yourself. However, whether to learn or not is totally be descide by yourself.

#3/B

Besides parents, teachers are the most important people in our life. We have "Teacher" this word since long time ago. It must have reasons why the teachers exist in our socity.

If people just study by themself, they hard to solve the problems. When people study alone, they will always use the same way to think. They might have same problems again and again, but they will not notice that is wrong. If there is a teacher, he can see different point with you.

When the teacher beside us, he can watch us to make sure we are no lazy. For example, when I was in junior high school, almost every student study in school. I told my self, I can study by myself. So, I went home. However, I never studied, I just watched TV, and I fail the text.

No matter what you think. Teacher play a important role in each one's life.

#3/C

Regardless of gender, age, religion, and nationality, teacher's role in learning is enormous because a teacher is a guide who will help open my eyes to some specific field which is totally unknown to the student. Also, in broad meaning, old civilizations like Greek, Rome, Egypt and China, and different cultures from mine has been good teachers to the human being to achieve today's civilization.

First, imagine a society without school. That society may not have difficulties in food, housing and clothing which are most essential facts for survival, but it's impossible to expect civilization there. Teacher's role in school is to help students to shorten time for them to achieve the goal in life.

Secondly, there's a saying that nature is teacher. Not only geographically but also periodically different cultures provide human being good materials to learn. Nevertheless, it doesn't mean students don't need teachers. Only if teacher, student and good materials are harmonized, good learning conditions are available.

As a result, when students want to learn something, trying not to emphasize one fact only is essential. Harmony between student and teacher will provide the best condition.

#3/D

I prefer to have a teacher because if I just learn by myself maybe when I do or I learn something it mistrake. Sometime when I have problems. I can't find it out, how i can do it but if I have a good teachers, they can help me and maybe they can find out my problems and improve me to something it better. But if I just wait for my teacher help, I thing, I can't improve my English language and TOEFL TEST too much. That mean if I want to develop my English very well I want to help and learn by myself too. How I can develop very well? I think, it isn't just study in classroom and read books at home. I want to parktice listening and speaking by talking to many people, listening radios, watching TV or movies. How you can talk to other people if you just know grammar but can't use it to talk and

#3/E

When people learn, they must know how to study most efficiently. There are so many various people, so some people need teacher, and others are not.

In my case, I prefer to student following teacher's lectures. After taking lecture, I always review by myself.

I cannot study by myself. Also, I cannot belive why some people prefer to study alone. The question is remaining my head, so I will try to figure out against this problem.

This following is made hypothesis.

First of all, some people, they want to learn without teachers, have not ever met good teachers. They are so selfish that they could not adjust with their teacher's tempo. Secondary,

#3/F

Some people think that they can learn better by themselves than with a teacher, others disagree. I prefer to learn through experience, because I think that you can only learn by yourself.

In drivers education, a teacher lecture for 36 hours about driving, laws, and safety. I did not pay attention at all in the class, and I am a good driver; I am the only person I know that got a 100 percent on their drive test. My peers in drivers ed often paid more attention than me, but still did not get great scores on their drive tests. This is because they waisted time trying to learn from a teacher, I learned to drive by myself.

Throughout school, one has many teachers. Most are bad, and often not too smart. Since the first grade, I have had two good teachers. I think that I have learned alot; I can read, write, think, debate, and articulate my ideas. I did not learn this from my teachers; but on my own. In fourth grade, I had a despotic and moronic teacher who shall remain nameless. She used to punish me for reading in class. She didn't teach me, I had to teach myself, and she was upset and abusive because she knew that she couldn't help me.

The above two examples illustrate how people learn individually. They don't need the help of a teacher, just the will to accomplish on their own.

#3/G

The learning process may be stimulated by the presence of a teacher or by the self motivation of the student. This short paper will attempt to examine which way is preferable.

Learning with a teacher enables the student to have a structural environment. The teacher will determine the curriculum, the lesson plan and the homework. One needs only to follow the teacher and perform the work to benefit and learn the subject matter. The structure is also extended to the timing of the learning process. Classes are held at specific times and specific homework is assigned. This enables the student to methodically build his grasp of the subject.

Learning by one's self is not as structured and is dependent to a large extent on the motivation and self decipline of the student, the material studied, the time it is studied and the pace is entirely up to the student.

While studying with a teacher may seem more efficient, it may deprive the student of creative thinking and flexibility. Having to be in class at a certain time may be burdensome.

On the other hand, studying by one's self can lead to lack of regiment, slacking and motivation. I would personally prefer some kind of combination and integration of the two methods. A limited roll of the teacher, more as a facilitator and motivator, coupled with a large degree of flexibility afforded to the student, will be my preferred method.

#3/H

Some people think that they can learn better by themselves than with a teacher. Others think that it is always better to have a teacher. Which do you prefer? Use specific reasons to develop your essay.

#3/I

Regarding the ways of learning, everyone may has different point of view. Some people think they can learn better by themselves while the others think that have a teacher is better. I've come to my own conclusion. There are three reasons that I think learning with a teacher is better than by myself.

First reason is efficiency. Since the teachers have organized the informations that want to teach you, you can get the point more easily and quickly than learning by yourself. The second reason is interaction. While learning with a teacher, you can ask him/her to explain the parts that you can't understand immediately, and can discuss the questions or doubts you have. It's better than learning by yourself without others' help.

Most important of all, you can get some treasures that you can't find in the books from teachers. In my opinion, the most valuable things are not only the knowledges in the books, but also the ways that other people thinking, especially the ones who have more experiences than you. Besides, you may also get some new ideas when you interact with your teachers.

The reasons above show that's why I prefer to learn with a teacher than by myself. Although some people may have different point of view and disagree this, nevertheless, I think the reasons I've said are persuadable.

#3/J

It's true that one could not learn sth. very well without some important instructions from teacher. Teacher can often unwrap your puzzles, give you new idea, different ways to try out. However, it's also sufficiently imperative for all of us to culture the custom of learning by ourself. The is as follows"

First, one should spend enough independent time reviewing what he or she has learned, trying to figure out what's the proplems and how to solve it. I mean one should first think over the problem before asking teacher.

Second, Innovation should be very necessary part of the whole study framework. One should not follow exactly as what the teacher tell you. If we do so, the whole society may not progress any more. So we often look up the interesting things in the library, do the same problem from different angles and try to make a breakthrough on the former basis, etc.

Finally, different people have different ways of thinking. We may often be confused by teacher or someone else, although there is merely easy proplem. In that case, we must insist on what we think and try to "translate" the alien things into our own.

As I said previously, we also need help from our teachers, So we should be open but close. It's always possible that we may plunge ourself into the puzzleness and do not know what's wrong. Then, we can refer to teacher to seek for solution. Your teacher may see clearly what's the crucial points as he or she judges it in a general view.

In total, to my opion, it's better to combine two methods together and use it wisely. It's complementary to each other and should not be apart from each other, neglect one or the other. We also shall emphasize one but the other depending on different occasions. Only when we grasp the spirit of this organic integration can we do more better in life.

TOPIC 4

In the future, students may have the choice of studying at home by using technology such as computers or studying at traditional schools. Which would you prefer? Use reasons and specific details to explain your choice.

#4/A

I have been thinking about studying at home by using technology such as computers or television long time ago. If students can study at their home instead of going to school, they can study more comfortably.

At first, people can study with their computer screen, speaker microphone at home. They can also record something such as lectures, documents and whenever they want to review, they can use with their computer.

In my case, I took a lot of classes on internet.

Although it was not standard course, I felt comfort a lot.

Secondly, the more time is gone, the more students going to attend school. But my country is very small and environment for education is bad. If they can study at their home. We don't have to worry about those problems.
On the other hand, this way has some problems too. If people study at home, not only they can't make friends, but they will feel boring.
Lastly, people who want to study at home can study very easily because their computer has dictionary, calculator, encyclopedia, and so on.
I'm a student still now, but I also wish that a day which I can study at home easily will come as soon as possible.
For these reasons, I prefer studying at home by using technology than studying at traditional schools.

#4/B

Studying at home by using technology or studying at traditional school

In the present time, it is quite natural that students go to school to study. In the future, however; the system of studying at school will change completely; student may have choice of studying at home by using computer or television or of studying at traditional schools. If I assume that I'm a student in the future, I'm sure I'll choose studying at schools, even though I sometimes feel lazy to go to school.

Why do I choose studying at schools? Through my experiences as a student, I know it teachs us a lot of things; not only studying subject such as, English, history or math, but also society's rule and people's relationship. For example, if students go to school and attend the class, they will see many friends and teachers. Those students will enjoy having conversation with their friends. If teachers or friends have different opinions from them, they will be upset about that. However, those students will realize there are several kinds of people in the world and each person has each opinion.

On the other hand, if they don't have to go to school, they will have nobody to communicate with in addition to their family. Probably, it is very easy that they don't need to go to school, but when they have questions and need help, who does help? Even if computers or televisions can teach them, I can't imagine studying without my classmates, because studying with someone such as, teachers and classmates have helped me in several things. Sometimes, they encourage me, sometimes they comment on me and give me directions.

Therefore, I'm sure studying at schools gives students many things, and I believe experiences of studying at school will be unforgettable for students.

#4/C

Students have many choices of studying way in future. Basie on technology improve everyday. More knowledge we have to know. In my opinion, I bias to computers.

Undoubtly, each style of education has good side. But if students chose television. Maybe almost of them watch "funny show" or entertainment program instead. They couldn't be able to concentrate on their work. If chose traditional education. They must learn many subjects before that they never interested in. Even though unrelative with their occupation in future.

"Computer," it is a very important tool and we have to learn to operate. I can get more information from it. A lot of species I in the wide range. And it is very fast. In this society is focus on efficient. First come, first served. So I chose computer.

#4/D

I would like to prefer traditional school because if all of students chose computer or television to study, they can't make relationship. I think this is very big problem because, if you do not have relation ship you can't do everything and your maind is getting why, I think most of society is made by good relationship. And second reason, they will be getting fatter because they will stay at home almost one day, and they helth is getting bad, because they do not go out to play or something to do. When I was junior high school student, I always stayed at home to play video game and then I was getting fatter. And third reason, if all of student chose the way to study; then don't necessary teacher, may be most of teacher lost the job. If they lost the job, they can't get the money and who can't live any more so

#4/E

The introduction of communication technology may one day change the way we view schools. Staying at home connected to the internet or viewing courses on TV may render today's schools obsolete or force them to adopt to new realities.
This short papers will examine the choices confronting a student when selecting a traditional school versus one that uses technology that enables remote studying.

Information desseminatet via the internet can be presented in an more efficient way. Teachers and students can be more focused on the subject rather than in a classroom environment. On the other hand, the personal interaction between teacher and student and among students makes the discussion richer.

Cost of tuition can be a major factor. Traditional school, with its physical facility and staff is most likely more costly to run than one that uses remote studying.

Traditional school is more than just a conduit of information. Social life which is a major part of the traditional school is almost non existant in remote studying.

Studying on line can enable the student to have more flexible schedule than the rigid schedule at a traditional school. This may enable students to hold a job which they may not be able otherwise.

In conclusion, the adoption of a new technology can be incorporated into the structure of tradional schools. I would prefer to see traditional school using new technologies to make them more cost effective, more attuned to the individual needs of the students while, at the same time maintaining the vibrancy of the social interaction which make them an exciting place to be a part of.

#4F

I agree that students have the choice of studying at home by using technology such as something because for example. A man is sick now and he can't go to school. He can't study, but if he uses technology such as something, he can study. He may not go to school. Now. We can use Internet around the world. We can do something by Internet. The Information Technology improve every day. I think that Information Technology is useful. Two reasons. One is we can use it easy and if you know something we know almost to use Internet. The other is we use Internet.

#4/G

It is possible in the future that students may have the choice of studying at home. Their teachers will be the technology such as computers and TVs etc. But would it be a good choice for them? There are several reasons why I don't prefer studying at home.

First, we learn more than educational things in school. School is not just an education unit, it's more like a society. There are teachers classmates and rules in school. We learn How to behave and how to live with people, and also how to cooperate with others.

Second, Education is the matter of communication. But with the teachers like computers? It's an advanced way to communicate but still I don't think it's the best way. Exchange emotions and thoughts things like that are more important that knowledge itself

Last, it's a little bit of combination of these two things that I have mentioned, studying at home alone is not helpful to make a well-around person. We need to belong the society which we called school and we also need to communicate with people alive.

Studying at home and studying at school both has negative and positive sides. But no matter how the technology is getting into our lives deeply education should be remain as the field of human being and I don't want to lost the benefits that I can have from shooling

#4/H

"Why Be Social?"

At schools, children learn many things. Grammar, math, and science are all pressed upon a student throughout their school days. However, there are other elements of school that cannot be taught in the classroom. By going to school, children interact and become friends. If school was run at home by televisions and computers, then children would miss out on an outstanding social opportunity.

People need to interact. It is part of our nature. As a child, I mostly interacted at school. I made friends, we talked, and we got to know each other on better terms. By going to school, students not only learn to read and write, but they also learn from their peers about how to treat others. Without the social aspect of school, there would be no reason to stop hitting the snooze button.

In the future, children may be able to be educated by their televisions and computers. There are two problems with this. The first one is variety. All of the teaching programs would be the same and there would be no place for arguing or debating with the program. This aspect ties into the second problem, the lack of interaction. Students would not be able to communicate with, teachers, administrators, or fellow peers. They would be forced to interact with a computer program.

Spinoza once said, "Man cannot survive in solitary confinement." Having a program teach a student lessons is exactly that. There are no other children around to interact with. These programs may help our education but they will take away our ability to socialize with others.

#4/I

What's the purpose of school? Some people may say that school is the place to get knowledge, learn many different types of subjects. But many people also say that school is the place to make many friends. Which idea would you prefer?

When my mother was young, she was a teacher at kindergarten. Her students were often wrote letters to her about their primary school life. Many letters said that they got many friends at school and they were having exciting activities such as excursions. I also enjoyed such activities when I was in primary school. I visited famous parks, car factory, bread factory, museums. I am sure that all students enjoyed them.

Today's school style is changing now. Students can get education at their home without going school. Using computers and internet, sometimes phone too. I think this system is very useful for some students who live very far away from school. If students need 5 hours to get school that would be serious problems. And also transportation is big issue too. If they can't get any public transportation to go to school how can they get school? For those reasons I think this system is not bad. But would recommend it to you child? I guess that many parents say no. What's the reason? The reason is clear, they can't make friends.

For the first day of school how did you feel? Were you nervous? Worrying about making friends? Those experiences are very important when you become adult. When you work. And other thing is many special experiences from school. School offer many experiences for students, those may bring big interest for students. Maybe students think as their work after school.

I think school's main purpose is make many friends and get many experiences with other students. For all reasons I prefer to go to school.

#4/J

The opinion of the students may have the choice of studying at home by using technology such as computers or television or of studying at traditional schools is all alright, but it still depends on the person who wants to study, what they are going to study, and what is the purpose of the study itself.

I, if I am asked to choose, I think before I decide what my preference is. I would like to share you about my opinion since the three ways of studying have their own advantages and disadvantages. Firstly, studying by computers, nobody says that it is bad, but this kind of thing less human because we only see or get the knowledge from the packed material. Everything is already set up and we only sit, listen, and do the assigment. Indeed, we can have internet access, but still, if we are unclear about the material, we cannot ask directly eventhough we are allowed to ask the question exactly at that time, but, we seldom get the answer directly. And more, after one problem there can be the next and soon, and yet, we need the answer at that time.

Secondly, studying by television is similar to computer. There is a little bit difference: by computer, we can have on-line access but by television, it is merely a boring time. We are really treated like robots. We are merely asked to sit and listen and take a note. It is really not gorgeous way of studying. At the mean time, waiting for meeting teacher or the expert directly is really takes time eventhough sometimes this kind of thing offers us to ask questions or explanations directly by phone, but the problem is we have to race with other audiences too to have a chance for getting the answers or explanations of what we have asked.

Thirdly, studying at traditional schools is also not too bad. Perhaps we should limit the term of "traditional" here. Is it traditional in teaching method? for example; the way of teachers teaching is translation method? Of in terms of facility? Well, if we assume that it is limited on the facility, it means that the school doesn't have computer lab, language lab, or other sophisticated facility like internet. I think it is okay since the teachers are well educated, well trained, and good performance. These all things are more important that the electrical equipment because it is friendly and we can ask questions directly.

So, finally, I would like to say that studying by traditional schools is better because I like to communicate directly with the resource person and more friendly. And also I can discuss what subject should I take and what is the right choice for me. I think these all things are better by asking directly to the teachers like what traditional schools do.

TOPIC 5

It is better for children to grow up in the countryside than in a big city. Do you agree or disagree? Use specific reasons and examples to develop your essay.

#5/A

I prefer childern grow up in the countryside than in a big city. I would like to explain the reasons: Firstable, there's a place on your own where peaceful is great. As a second point, the nature has the answers for everything and it's marvellous to love it. As a last point, the creativity will be higher than if you're in a big city.

I'm trying to explain more widely: Peaceful, love and creativity are three key points to think where's the best place for children grow up.

I suggest another way: live in a big city and go on weekends to the countryside. This mix can be useful because children will have two perspectives: the life in a big city and the life in the countryside. They have to study in the city and at the same time they learn from the nature.

In past, I've seen the results in some kids and it works.

#5/B

Children are better to grow up in the countryside than in a big city. There are a lot of concerns for a child to grow up in a big city. A big city usually have large population and serious pollutions. If I have a child, I wouldn't bear him/her in a big city but the countryside.

The environment in the countryside is usually better in a big city. My family and I lived in a big city three years ago. The noise, the air pollution and the crowd made us very uncomfortable. My older sister always had problems with her breathing because the terrible air there. In terms of living in a big city, people couldn't own the space as big as they need. A lot of people have to either rent a place or live in a tiny apartment. My family decided to move because they want to give us better environment and larger space to enjoy ourselves.

We love to live in the countryside. You won't always feel a lot of people are around you. There are no pollution in the countryside. The river, the air, and the whole environment are extremely clean. It's the best place for living. If I were a child, I would like to live in the countryside. I would like to be beared in the place where has less pollution and noise. I would like to see clean river and enjoy large spaces.

#5/C

Many people might disagree, but I think it is better for children to grow up in the countryside than in a big city.

One of reason is that children learn many things from nature. For example, in summer they can go swimming in the sea and meet many fishes; while they can go to mountain and find plants and animals. They can learn many things by themselves. Second reason is that there are a few people, so they do not feel to stress out too much. In big city, children always have to compete to another children, so I think they stress out too much. In big city, children always have to compete to another children, so I think they stress out too much, while children who live in countryside do not compete many times. They can study with their friends and help each other.

Third reason is that countryside children have many times to talk their parents. I think to live city is so expensive. That is why their parents work until night, so their children eat dinner alone. Eventually, they can not learn from their parents. For example, social rules, mannars, greeting and habits. Countryside children can learn from their parents about them. Forth reason is that I grew up in country side, and then I feel it is right for me to grow up there. Because I am a person who can feel nature beautifully, who helps another people and who knows social rules. I think, thanks to my parents I can grow up this kind of person. They gave me many styles of education.

Finally, I think it is better for children to grow up in the country side than in a big city. To live in country side is good for their education. Children can study not only their school, but also nature.

#5/D

I agree with children to grow up in the countryside. I grow up in the countryside. My hometown in country. It is very beautiful place. This place has around mountain, and nice sinery. I think that children grow up place is better than town. When I was child, I always play in the beautiful natures with my brother. Now I remember for nice experience. I think country side is better, however I consider about children's education that big city is better than countryside. Countryside has a little schools. So big city has many schools. Children where live big city almost study very hard, becaus big city has many schools, and we can chose schools. The child getting more and more interested in about study. When I was high school student. My hometown had only one university. We have to go Tokyo, or we have to go this university. It is no choise.

My hometown's children not interested in about study. I think education is very important for children. Children have to study very hard.

If I have a child, I hope that I want to live countryside and grow up my child, because I like nature very much and when I was child, I grew up in countryside, I think where it nice place for children education.

I agree with this topic.

#5/E

It is better for children to grow up in the countryside. There are three reasons about that. First, there are many mountains in the countryside. Recently a lot of children are poor at sight so mountan's green color helps them from poor sights. Also in the city many people suffer from air pollutions. If children live in the countryside, they are much healthier than they live I the city.

Secondly, They can play outside in the countryside. They have enough space to play with their friends. If they do that, they can explore the nature. Thirdly, they can be optimistic in the country side. There are a lot of stressful things in the city. If they live in the country,

Above all I was grown up in the countryside. It was very helpful for me to live there. Children need the nature when they are growing up. That is why it is good for children to grown up in the countryside.

#5/F

As you walk down a street you feel the true experience of life all around you. There are huge skyscrappers covering the city, in which the sun reflects off of. The air is filled with noise pollution of honking cars and talkative people. This is what life should be like. Living in a big city is better for children to grow up in, rather than a countryside because of the wisdom they will learn, the atmosphere.

The wisdom a children will learn from growing up in a city, is one that could never be replaced. When one grows up in a city you get to learn about all different things. Small countryside areas tend to keep thing quiet, and secret, where as a big city is real and straight forward. Living in a big city myself I would never stop being greatful for the gift of knowledge I received.

The atomsphere of a big city is a great experience for someone to grow up in. A city up bigging is a lot about the streets and survival. The skills you gain, in a big city, you can use everywhere. If you can survive, in a city then you can survive anywhere. You learn to deal with traffic, subways, fast cars—everything. If someone from a countryside came into a city, they would be confussed. However, a city person would be able to make it in a countryside.

In conclusion, city life is the best. It helps to develop someone as a person and to grow up faster, thus becoming more mature. A country up bringing will not provide a children with the tools he or she will need to "make it" in the real world.

#5/G

I agree that it is better for children to grow up in the countryside. Because there are much opportunities to see another people who lives in the same area.

For example many parents who live in countryside pay attention for the children even if the children were not their children. While some parents who life in a big city doesn't care any children.

And again I think the children should touch nature, animals and plants. There exist a lot of nature in countryside. But the children who live in a big city can't touch nature so much times.

Off course There are some disadvantages in countryside, For example the problem of education.

Totally I agree that It is better for children to grow up in the countrysind than in a big city.

#5/H

I do agree that it is better for children to grow up in the contryside than in a big city.

Now, in a big city is very noise and populated while enroviment in countryside very frest and quieit. If children live in countryside, they can play outside in helthy enroviment, So it is good for their helth. In fact, children live in the countryside are often stronger than children live in a big city.

People live in countryside more friendly than people live in a big city, So it influence children personality, So children live in countryside often have good personality.

Many

#5/I

In my opinion, it's better for children to grow up in a big city, instead of countryside. There're many reasons for me to think so. And here I'll present some of them to you.

First, generally speaking, big cities have better education system than countryside. I can give you a example. In my hometown, a small countryside, there're only one school primary. After graduation, students have to transfer to other places for further education. What's more, the education quality there is not very high because of the poor hardware quality.

Second, countryside always don't have enough hospitals that are very important for the health of children. My childhood was spent in countryside. Each time I was ill, I had to big cities for a cure.

Third, the children in big cities have more clourful life. Because there're a lot of facilities in big cities, children can go to zoom weekend, visit museum in holiday, watch movies in night, and so on. I think such things are very important for the growth of children.

In addition there's still a lot of things playing a crucial important role in children's life in big cities.

So, I think that it's better for children to grow up in a big city.

#5/J

As the global economis increased this century, more and more people lived in the cities. A lot of people sugested that it's better for children to grow up in the countryside than big city. I agree with their opinion.

Firstly the children living in the big city will have chance to contact the high technology. There are lots of science museum and technical labs in the big city. They can go to the museum frequently to learn about the laws of nature and improve themselves. Some of them will be interested in science and become scientists in the future. If the children grow up in the countryside it's not easy for them to be close to the technology and develop a deep understanding in science.

Secondly, the life in countryside is quite simple and you know only a few persons even after you live in countryside for years. The children living in the countryside seldom learn about what happen around the world and have few chance to learn the new thing. One the other hand, the children growing up in big city have to face different kinds of people everyday and know more about the world. During the communication with the others, they can learn how to handle the life, how to get on well with all kinds of people and how to solve the problem they meet. And the children growing up in the countryside have to learn those things after they come to the big city. Their paces will be slower.

In conclusion, it's better for children to grow up in the big city than the countryside. They will know more and perform better.

TOPIC 6

Some people believe that college or university education should be available to all students. Others believe that higher education should be available only to good students. Discuss these views. Which view do you agree with? Why?

#6/A

Even though colleges or universities education in the US is comparatively available to all sorts of students rather than Japan, some people believe that higher education should be available only to good students. However, I don't understand why those people think so because I strongly agree with system that gives all students opportunity to get higher education rather than that of Japan.

Through my experience, I realized US colleges and universities have a lot of advantages to all students. Most schools in the US don't have very difficult entrance examination, but they require all students to study hard to graduate. Having easy requirement gives students many chances. For example, it is possible that the students who used to be not good students in their high school probably will be interested their study in their college or university students life. In addition, requiring hard work makes students being responsibility because if they don't study hard, they cannot graduate easily. Therefore, Japanese people say it is easy to get into, but it is difficult to graduate from US colleges or universities.

If the US higher education is available only to good students, some students won't have chance to get higher education. It is because they may will require students high grade in order to get just good students.

In conclusion, American higher educartion system gives our students alot of chance to study, and also it makes us strong and responsible because our grade and graduation depend on how much we study hard. I believe those students who used to have several opportunity to study and study hard will make good future.

#6/B

College or University education should be available to all students. In many countries the education is an economical and politicoil problem. Only a minimal part of population have access to universities or colleges, because the tuition is high. Many people cannot study because they don't have enough money to pay the tuition.
In this direction, I agree with education should be available to everybody. In academic item, the competition is stronger.
Only the best students will finish every program.
It isn't necessary to do that difference, because the academic system have the solution.
This way, to higher education arrive the best students from all program and from all countries.

#6/C

I agree with the view which is that university education should be available to all students.

First, I can't understand what is good student. Does good student have a lot of many, a lot of knowledge or kindness or everything? I can't understand this point. I want to be revealed it.

Next, for example, if there is the man who is poor, dosen't study hard and, but, he is geonias, should university education accept him. My opinion is yes. because it is high percentage that he gave benefits for society or world. I think it is failed that the person who have good talent of some part isn't accepted by society.

Society is constructed in the many kind of persons. We shouldn't refuse the person who is not much the society.

#6/D

I believe that higher education should be available only to good student. But there is one problem that what type of students are good or not.

For example, almost student never study before semester's exam after entering University or College in Japan. They just want degree to enter some good company. But They had good score at high school.

While there are some student's who couldn't get good score at high scool study hard at University or College.

Finally, when the judge of entering to University or College can be done correctly, I agr ee with the opinion which higher education should be available only to good student.

#6/E

"Joining in Real Life."

You have to work if you wanna be succesful in life. If you wanna be a doctor, you have to study human's body. You can not sit all your life and be a doctor. You have to go to high school, university then if you want to be more sure about your job you go to master.

University is a place where you seperate from your childhood and start to do decisions about your future. You choose your job, you learn how to do it, you work so that you can learn better. In these days people can not find a good job if they do not go to university.

I believe that every student have to go to college. It doesn't matter if a student is good or not. A student can not like chemistry or biology and won't be a good student but he or she can be succesful in college. High school and college are very different things.

In university you have more responsibility. You are alone, without your parents try to learn stuff so that you can be someone in future. Universities can accept students by their succes but it doesn't mean that bad student can not go to university.

If they accept only good students to college what happens to the other. You become an adult in university. You start to do your works, you take responsibility. University is a place where you join in real life, I do not think only good students can have this choice.

#6/F

Going to college is a very important stage in one's life. Some believe college should be available to only good students. However, I believe every person deserves the right to learn.

The top schools in the US such as, Harvard and Princeton are well known. Success in such schools requires very knowledgeable person. An unintelligent person may not be able to succeed in such a place, therefore a good school, especially in the Ivy league should only accept top of the line students.

Throughout the US there are many cheap public colleges. These colleges should accept all aplicants and when there is no more room there they should refer people to a different school. Everyone deserves a proper college education.

In the final analysis colleges should be open to all. It's not right to allow a person from having a full education. Everyone deserves the choice whether to go to college or not to.

#6/G

College or university education must be available to all students. There is no reason that only the good students have a chance to further their education. Most poor students need another chance to succeed in school. They need guidance. There is also an argument to the other side. People believe that students should be rewarded for their hard work while the other students should, in a sense, be punished. They believe that if the good students are put into an environment with other good students, they will all strive to the best, in turn helping them succeed.

Many poor students have not been guided correctly. They should not be punished for something they could not neccesarily handle. Most of these students just need another chance. Depriving them of a college or university education will only cause them to feel negative about themselves. Instead of being in school, these children will be in the streets getting into trouble. Since they have no other way to support themselves, they may possibly get involved with selling and buying drugs. These students must not be given up on. They must have a chance.

On the other hand, some people think the good students should be rewarded by giving only them a chance to have a good education. However, these people are wrong. These students can still be given a college education even if the poor students also have this opportunity. Why can't both groups of students have a university education available to them? Hence, while the good students should be rewarded for all their hard work, the poor students, too, should be given a chance to succeed in life.

#6/H

I think that college or university education should be available only to good students because it is important for them to keep quality of education and to have will which student want to study.

First, I think that college or university education should be available only to good students. If all students come to college or university, their quality of education would fall down. For example, Medical school and dental school are needed high level students because these have a lot of responsibility to grow good doctors.

#6/I

The availability of college education, to the better students or to all students (who say, graduate from high school) is controvertial. This short essay will examine the pros and cons and will attempt to reach a conclusion.

1) Resource allocation—making higher education available for the better students will allocate scarce resources more efficiently. The investment in higher education will be utilized more efficiently by the better students. College education for poorer students may become an inefficient resource allocation. On the other hand, larger school as a result of more universal education will operate more efficiently at the micro, or individual school level due to economies of scale.
2) Raising the skill level of society—college education raises the skill level of the individual as well as the society in general. However, the better students will likely benefit more than the poorer one since higher education may be more suitable to higher level. A less academic student may benefit more by attending a vocational school. Society may benefit more if education is matched to the academic level of the student.
3) Personal advancement—In a society which emphasizes college education the lack of one may be detrimental to the personal advancement of the individual. Lacking college degree may not give equal chance to various member of society.

In conclusion, higher education may open the door to all to advance in life. The availability of college education will make society more democratic as it will afford more equal opportunity to all. Despite the possible misallocation of resources the overall level of society will rise as more members are afforded college education, and hence, the benefit to society will far outweigh the additional cost to society.

#6/J

In these years, there is an argument about high education. Some people said all students in high schools should receive high education, say, in universities or colleges. But others disagreed with them. They said only the qualified students should get so.

In my opinion, I refer to the latter one. From the point of a biologist, everyone is not born the same with others. From another point of one social scientist, the background of each student is also different. So, these two factors determine someone would be good at researching, someone be good at hand-working, someone be good at sporting. That's just the need of a society which must arrange different groups of people at different positions.

In contrast, if we put all students no matter about someone are qualified or not into universities or colleges, what would be the result. To lower the level of textbooks, some excellent students would be common or be wasted just for the reason to make all students pass. To keep the same level as current level, lots of students would not get their diplomas. That's also a waste of time for them.

So, from the above two points, I think the exams for entrance into universities or colleges are necessary to ensure some qualified students would get their qualities in researching, art, and so on fully developed. The other students would find their favorite positions in the other fields. It's one good distribution of human power, I think.

TOPIC 7

Some people believe that the best way of learning about life is by listening to the advice of family and friends. Other people believe that the best way of learning about life is through personal experience. Which do you think is preferable? Use specific examples to support your preference.

#7/A

Some people believe that the best way of learning about life is by listening to advice of family and friends. Other people believe that the best way of learning about life is through personal experience. In my personal opinion, I think the best way of learning about life is combine the advice from your family and friends, and your personal experience.

When you take the advice from your family or friend, you can let youself never make same mistake as your family or your friend has made before. However, what happen to you or the situation may be totally different that what happened to your family or friends. Therefore, listening to the advice or family and friends is not enough for learning about life.

In your personal experience, you can always remember what you have done. You can remember how you made the mistake, and at the next time you won't made same kind of mistake again. However, when you're learning by yourself and never take the advice from your family and friends, you may need to spend some more time or money to make something done.

I think both of them have strong poing and shortcoming. If you can combine these two two together to learn about life, that will be

#7/B

When you Have to decide to choose one option about what it is the best way learing about life some people think about advice from other people. Other learn about life from their own experience, However I prefer to Have both options.

First of all. It is very Important to me that everyone, who knows perfectly about something, about live can give me an advice. For example when I was a child my mother told me so many times that I could not cook without adult supervisd because I would burned or something like that, well once I was cooking to myself. When I saw Fire in the kitchen. Nobody was at home, so I Had to call my Uncle who lived near to my House. Fortunally Nothing happened.

Second. Living your own experience is very important too. Something's you can not learn From other people. You Just have to live to learn. For example When I was 20 I began a relationship, with a person, who was, Jelous, selfish, and other kind of faults. I remember all of my Friends, who were worrying about the situation. They said to me that I Had to leave that guy. However I did not realize that they were right until. I felt in Jail myselft. Then I decided to broke with him

In conclusion, I can see for my personal experience that sometimes is Good. Listening people who know about, but others not.

#7/C

Each person think differace that they way for a some information.
We get many informations from TV, newspaper, book, listening and expierence.
I think that the best way is expierence.
I think the importentest is expierence. For me
But by the expierence, I got a little.
Because, My expierence has a limit.
So I get more by second way.
For example, They are TV, newspaper, book and listening
Although I get more information by second way, the expierence is more important for me.
For example, about one thing: many people have each opinion
They are a little bit difference.
It's difference about thinking for themselves.
I cann't get every opinions. If I get every opinionce that I will complex.
And I believe my expierance.
Sometimes that is wrong.
First I will choose by my expierance.
If I don't have expierance about it.
Second I will choose by second ways.

#7/D

Human being has become skillful person by listening many things from his family or friends or by learning through his personal experiences. I believe that it is useful that they become skillful person through their own personal experiences.

First of all, before I played tennis I had watched a lot of tennis match at courts and on TV. I believed that I could play tennis as good as a mature players who played very easily ways. And I went tennis court and began to play, but I could not hit the ball well. Then I realized that people could not do anything. Through their personal experiences such as training. It was not good for playing tennis that I had a lot of tennis knowledges.

Second of all, human being don't image their situation without their experiences. For example, I planned to go to US for studying English but I couldn't get image that I was in the U.S.

In conclusion, personal experiences are necessary for knowing everything which are useful for good living. Of course family and friends teaching are also important but people should get their skills by their personal experiences.

#7/E

Listening to people's advice to learn about life is beneficial, but is not effective unless the listener is able to experience what has become common knowledge on his own, and to incorporate other people's views, through these experiences, into his own philosophies. A symbiotic relationship, thus exists. A person who has been told everything all his life, but has never gone out on his own, will be completely foreign to the responsibilities necessary for self-reliance. In my situation, experience is more preferable.

I have been lectured all my life about being responsible and being careful of my possessions. I always lose things, nevertheless. It is experience that I need to finally begin to stop losing things, especially if I need them. I lost my calculator once, then borrowed one from the school, then lost that one, then got one from my friend. Since I wasn't faced with the problem of not owning a calculator, I never came to realize how much I needed one. My grandma yelled at me everytime I've lost something, but she never left me out in the cold without a calculator. I came to Brandeis Summer Odyssey and I lost my watch because I put it in a safe place and forgot about where I put it. I panicked so much because I needed the watch to know when classes started or when freetime was. Finding the watch in a safe place made me happy that I had known to keep it safe.

Back home I wasn't forced to do any chores like make the bed, but here I have to do them myself because otherwise I will live sloppily. I had to learn how to do the laundry because at home my grandma always yelled at me to do the laundry, but she'd do it for me anyway. She would teach me how to do it time and time again, but I never did it, so I kept forgetting. It is hard to forget how to do things if you have to do them, though.

Listening to people's stories are amazing and sometimes inspiring, but if it has no relevance to my life I cannot make my life into someone elses. People's success stories in how they achieved their dream cannot make me achieve my dream of playing basketball professionally. I have to take it upon myself to practice and work toward my dream. I have to overcome my own hardships, and find my own inner light. Yesterday I didn't play so well at basketball and it was because I was having a bad day. I need to find out how to make my game better, hence my day better.

I am inclined to believe that though both are necessary factors in people's lives, experiencing moments are much more effective lessons than simply hearing advice on how to live. One could not live without experience, locked up in a cave, hearing stories, because he will have never lived his own life. The best way for a person to get to know himself is to learn through his own experiences.

#7/F

"Around the Circle"

I'm seventeen years old, and I don't believe that I have learned about life by myself. That's because I'm a stranger on the world, trie to learn about life by listening people's advices or opinions. But I believe that after a certain time, when my parent won't be around, I will learn about life through my personal experience which is the best way.

My parents are my guardians. They don't want to be hurt by someone or something, however I'm aware that my parent won't be around one day. I'll be all by myself in this world. That'll be the time when I learn the life through my experiences. I will suffer the consequences, or sometimes be awarded. That will depend on me. I'll choose the Right or wrong. I will choose my own way where I will be happy. I Remember when I was a child, my father tells me not touch the oven, but I always sneak out of the Room and go to the kitchen. I was curious why oven is dangerous. And one day, my father let me touch the oven. Since that day, I understood that oven I dangerous which burns my hand. When I look back I know that inside of my mind I listen every word of my parents, Because they know the Right. But this way is preferable when your parents are around you.

As you grow, your opinions change very month or even every week. I'm going to be considered as an adult in two years and my parents or my friends are still giving me advices.

That's fine with me, but in some ways, I want to be free. I love my family or friends and I respect them. I listen and consider every word they tell me. My parents know better than me, because they experience the same situations before and know what's the correct way to deal with it. My friends also experience before unless they won't give me advices. I'm getting matured and I can see that listening the advices help me to get along with the problems.

This is like a circle. You start experiencing through your life and you give advices to your friend. Now I'm in a stage that I take advices and also learn about life through my personal experiences. I believe that I will be in a stage that I'll give advices depends on my personal experiences.

#7/G

I think that the best way of learning about life is by listening to the advice of family and friends. First, You can save money to go to school. If I want to learn it by myself, I need to study it in a school. If you ask your family or friends, it will be free for you. If you want to collect an information of learning about life alone, you need people who inform you. When you want to do it without any helping from people, you should have a burden. Finally, It's the best way to learn about life.

#7/H

I think the best way of learning about life is through personal experience. We have each our own values, so nobody understand other person's lives. Similarly, the way of learning about life is various for me, so we can only know the best way by each person.

Certainly if we can use the best way of learning abut life, we may find the answer than we exactly want to. We can touch the different values, experience of their own. In addition, this way is indirectly as safe.

However, the life is our own things. The responsibility of our life is depended by ourthelves. It is impossible for us not to suit for their values totally. It is important to recognize what is the best way of learning about life is the necessary in our life. Challenging and directing to know the best way is the first step of our way.

#7/I

How many times did you heare advices in your life? and How many timed did you make a good things or a bad things and learn from these bad or good things? to answer these questions, let me discuss what is the best way of learning in the life by listening to the advice of family and friends or from person experiences?

In my opinion the best way of learning in the life is through personal life, for many reasons and I will give my personal reasons. First, the advices can be forgotten quickly, How many advices we heard through our lives. And how many advices still in our minds, I think a few of them. In the other hand the mistakes which we have did it, impossible to forgetten. Because it is like traces in our days, mind and in deep experience. The people don't like to repete their mistakes or bad things because the felt the pain and tried the bad reaction for their fault so they learned by this way better than the advice.

Second, we we lesson to the advice we use only hearing, but in experiences all the tens like feeling, hearing, testing, thinking, touching and seeing are used, So the lesson will be strong and deep. As Aristo (Greek saintest) said "teach me, I will forget, but share me I will remember." for an example always my father advice me to be care when I'm driving my car, and he repet this advice every morning but I didn't be carful until I made an accident and me let was broken.

Third, The experience give the person chance to expiere his knowledge in different way. When you deal with people you discover different personalities, and you lern how to communicate with. let me give you these example, last month new employee came to our company he has strang personality, calm, silent and almost seem sad. Nobody could communicate with him or unless talk with him. But I could because I had wide experience in personalities, my friend told me she heared many advices about communication, but non of them help in this case. Also onther friend said, "I read 20 books about the personalities and that didn't help me, you experiences are the best"

In conclusion, advices are being heared, experiences are being learned, and every body use the Advice and the experince to paint a new life to herself or his self.

#7/J

Enjoying life during learning about life is most people's opinion to life. how can we learn about life? Some people believe that the best way it by listening to the advice of family and friends, while others prefer to learning through personal experience. My life tells me that the later is my favorite. The followings are some of my explanations.

Personal experience can give me a real view about life. When I try my best to know what life is by my own behaviors, I have to do a lot of things. Some times I suceed and sometimes I fail. Just during different successes and faliurs, I know what life is. Comparing with friend's advice, maybe some are even faults because of their good hearts, I prefer to learning about life by my own way.

Further more, personal experience can encourage me to fight for my goal. Someone once said, happiness exists during the process while not only at the end. I believe it. So I can not wait for others' advice during executing my plan. I do everything what I could to get near my goal and reach it at last. That I like to learning about life does not mean I neglect others' advice. Some good advice can help me avoiding many mistakes and to get success quickly.

In my opinion, enjoying life is the most important no matter the methods you use. So my advice about learning about life is try your best to feel, observe and execute your life.

TOPIC 8

The government has announced that it plans to build a new university. Some people think that *your* community would be a good place to locate the university. Compare the advantages and disadvantages of establishing a new university in your community. Use specific details in your discussion.

#8/A

Advantages and disadvantages of establishing new university

Establishing new university in my community will influence us many thing: both positive and negative thing. Some people may agree with that plan, others may not. Many reausons can be good point and at the same time, many facts can be bad point.

In my opinion, the plan of establishing new university in my community is good thing and I agree, even though I found some negative effect to our community after building new university. Because if new university would be established, it gives us a lot of positive things such as, community's growth and more opportunity to get higher education.

For preparation of finishing building university, our community need to develop everal things such as, city, institution and equipment in order to welcome the coming students. Our community should be great srounding for students, because those students' academic experience will be important for their near future. I believe these development will be positive influence for not only students but also citizens. If the community wold be more big, we will feel more convenience and many young people will feel they want to stay their hometown, these effect's related to make our community more enegetic.

On the contrary, some people may think making our community bigger because of establishing new university is not always good thing. After completion of building university, the population of our community will be grown and city will be more crowded then now. It my cause rising price, difficulty of finding place to live and environmental issues.

However, I still believe establishing new university brings us more good thing than bad things, because development of community makes citizens being like our sroundings and give great deal of experience, although those citizens don't go to outside.

#8/B

For a long time, my community has wanted the government to establish a new university in our city. Establishing a new university in our has some advantages and disadvantages.

One of the advantages in about the economy of the community. When a new university is established, because many new people, students, will come to study, their economic demand will increase economic activity and revenues of business and people in my community. Also, because new student will come to my community, people living in my community may interact these new people, and social relations may increase.

Besides its some advantages, establishing a new university in my community has some disadvantages. For one thing, in our city rents are already high. When new people come to community, rents will become higher. Secandly, in our city, roads are not enough under present circumtances, so traffic jam will be increase when a new university is established.

To conclude, establishing a new university in my community has some advantages and disadvantages. I think it is a good idea because nothing in the world has exact advantages without disadvantages.

#8/C

The university is the higher educational level. For this reason, in order to stablish a new one, the government has to look about some important features of the community to get the highest benefits.

In my community there are two education institutions of high level, which offer many different and attractive programs: one of them is public and the other one is private.

But, on the other hand, my community has a high rate of growing. The group of teenagers is very large a most of them are enrolled in the high school programs. Furthermore, there are three big factories which workers, young people, are interested in to improve their educational level.

In conclusion, the government and the community has to study and look for the best solution for the educational development of this population.

#8/D

There are several advantages as well as disadvantages to building a new university in my community. Building a university requires an immense amount of vast area. As a result, space must be found in my growing community. In addition, with a university, there are many new jobs, which may benefit people in my community who are currently searching for jobs. The new university may help the economy amelioriate. There are also many disadvantages that are encountered when building a new university. First of all, the population will rise. Secondly, the citizens in my community will have to pay more taxes.

Building the new university in my community may be beneficial. First of all, students will be encouraged to pursue their dreams by attaining a higher education because the university is close to home. Also, for the students that can't afford to go to the university, funding may be available for them because the university is in their town. Another advantage to my community would be that people may be able to find jobs easily. Due to the fact that my community is in a suburban environment, a number of citizens go to Boston for work. Boston is a half an hour commute, and as a result, many people are looking for jobs closer to home.

On the other hand, there are many disadvantages that come along with building a new university in my community. First of all, the government would require citizens to pay more taxes. Another disadvantage would be that because my community is continuously growing, we would have to stop the multiplying population to make room for the university. However, students who attend the university may live in my community, which would add to the population growth.

In conclusion, there are both disadvantages and advantages to building a new university in my community. Unwealthy students living in my community may be compelled to get a higher education because funds will be provided for them. On the other hand, creating space for the university will be an issue because my community is large and is continuing to grow.

#8/E

Ichigaya, it is located in center or Tokyo, is my hometown. There are some good and bad aspects to build a new university there.

First of all, it is located in center of Tokyo where is the capital of Japan. Almost all trains and metros pass this town. That works until midnight every day. However, whoever have to have lots of pain in the morning time because many people use this station.

Last of all, students can enjoy Tokyo very much. There are many theathers so they enjoy their private life. However, that is so expensive. It might be bothered students finances.

#8/F

Nowadays, Universities play quite important roles in the world. In fact, the human society can not develop without technology and science. However, to build a new university in a community may cause controversial disputes.

These people in our community who are on the opposite side of building the university will give out the following resons. First of all, they believe the existence of an university will change the lifestyle of the community. Since there are a large number of students and faculty in the university, the community might become crowded and noise. What's more, those who dislike the plan may insist on that the starting period of building an university would be orderless. Many buildings need to be constructed and a lot of facilities should be made. All these disadvantages can bring inconvience to the people living there.

However, in my opinion, the advantages brought by the existence of an university are of great value. I can give out strong evidences for my point. Since the university is always a place for people to learn knowledge and do research, it will definitely construct a nice environment for the whole community. As a matter of fact, the campus of an university is also very beautiful. People in the community can enjoy their lives there. Those facilites such as swimming pools, sports fields ect. can also be helpful for us to relax there. The most attractive point is that you can study in the university with you own family nearby. It is very convinient for you.

All these advantages given above weigh so heavy that I firmly believe the plan to build a new university will be of great value to our community.

#8/G

The Advantage and Disadvantage

Lots of people in my community disagree with the idea of building a university nearby. But, others consider it is a quite good idea. To my point of view, the plan has more advantages than disadvantages.

Firstly, the plan of setting up a university can stimulate the economy in our community, even our whole town. A large amount of investment will flow into this area definitely. Everybody living in our community will benefit from it. Obviously, the university will need lots of employee after it is built up. Therefore, it increase the employment and create new opportunities.

Secondly, the university will own a number of advanced facilities, including library, swimming pool, playground. These will open to us and provide serious entertainment. What's more, the university will attract more and more children to read books. This will decrease the crimes of the children.

However, some opposite will say that the new university harm the environment of our community, since at present our town is a quiet place to live in. But, I really think we can control the noise by more strict law. Also, we can invite the students in our house. Thus, they will live with us together compatibly.

From above points, we should conclude that setting up a new university is a wiser choice.

#8/H

I agree to establish a university in my community. Why not? There are so many advantages.

Firstly, University is a place where high technology exists. If it is located in my community, we can learn much more about the new high tech by reading the posters or attending their lectures. As I know, most of the Universities have free lectures. It is quite a great chance to catch up with the trend, isn't it?

Secondly, the students in the University can do much help to us. For example, we can find techers for our children more easily than before. And, we can hire them as part time engineers with relatively lower money. Yes, it's good to them as well because they need work expiriences and extra living expenses.

Thirdly, here comes another reason that the students can help improve our atmosphere by affecting our community. They are active, healthy and positive. We the residences will follow those always existing around us. Yes, the surrounding is very important for the children. I dare say the prospective university will increase the scores of our children inderectly.

Of course, there are also some disadvantages such as it will make the traffic more crowded and so on. But I think we should not worry about it because the government will sure to solve the problem for us.

Totally speaking, I hope the new university will be founded here.

#8/I

Recently, the government has announced that it is going to build a university in North Point, my community. Some think that its location to build the university I wonder why

North Point is one of the most crowded places in Hong Kong. How can they come up with a idea of building the proposed university in such a noisy place? One of the most important criteria of a university is it's peaceful and quiet environment whereby students is able to concentrate on their studies. Building a school in North Point is definitely not a wise idea.

Additionally, North Point is a small place and has limited space for building a university. One have to bear in mind that a university is a not short term project. Once it is built, it is going to be there for hundred years or even longer, so we should make sure there is enough space for the extension projects in the future. It would be better if it is location in a newly developed city in the rural part of Hong Kong which provides sufficient land for future use.

The only thing I can tell that is good to build the university in North Point is that it is convenience. It has a good transportation system and located in the middle of Hong Kong. Students will have no problem of getting to the school.

However, it is obvious that the downsides of building the proposed university in North Point overwhelmed it's advantages. By considering more thoroughly and wisely about such a big project which has profound influences on our community. Other better spots should be adopted.

#8/J

The recent announcement by the government of its intention to build a new university has created a stir in our community. Some local people believe that the best place for this new university is right here in out midst. This short essay will examine the advantages and disadvantages of such a move.

Access and transportation—while our town is located at a far end of the country, it enjoys excellent network of highways from major population centers of the country. This will enable students, parents and staff easy access. The local transportation, however, is another matter. The daily gridlocks, lack of parking and inadequate local streets will be made worse by the addition of thousand of people and cars.

Prestige and reputation—adding a new university will enhance the prestige and reputation of the community. This, however, will not be of the greatest importance since the area is replete with many highly ranked university.

Adding to the local economy—To the extent that most students will be from outside of the area, the local economy will benefit from the infusion of tuition paying population. This will enhance employment, add to the property values and create the multiple effect by supporting local businesses that will serve the new population. On the other hand, an influx of people will put a strain on the local services and infrastructure, such as water service, police, fire and social services.

The effect on non student population—The arrival of new, mostly young people in large numbers can change the fabric of the community. While, as previously mentioned, the economy may benefit, local residents may resent the aspects of student life, such as loud parties, excessive drinking and careless driving. In conclusion, while the community may benefit to a large extent from a new university, the adverse effect on local life should be carefully evaluated.

TOPIC 9

Do you agree or disagree with the following statement? Children should be required to help with household tasks as soon as they are able to do so. Use specific reasons and examples to support your answer.

#9/A

Teaching children to do household tasks is a training. They must know how to help their families as soon as they are able to do so.

When children can help to do tasks, they will learn that what responsibilities are. Parents give them jobs to do, and they should finish thoes completely. I have helped to wash dishes since I was ten years old. My sister and I did this job together. We knew if we didn't do it well, we had to use dirty dishes. We knew it's important to take a responsibility.

Every child will leave their parents someday. They will live alone or have their own family. They must learn how to do household stasks; however, they can't do those by themselves. I have a friend who lives in the dorm. She never help with household tasks at home because her parents didn't want her to spend more time on homework. Now, she lives with a roommate, and she still can't clean her room. Her roommate does all of the tasks. They don't have good time together because her roommate complains her roommate complains her all the time.

Parents should teach their children to help with household tasks as soon as they are able to do so. A good habit should be given when they are young, so they will keep this habit forever.

#9/B

I think the children should be required to help with household tasks as soon as they are able to do so because parents can give their children to some knowledge and to be found them as a family members.

First, the children should be required to help with household tasks as soon as they are able to do so because parents can give their children to some knowledge. For example, Parents can teach their children to cook some dishes. Children are going to learn how to use knife or how to bake or how to boil something.

Secondly, the children should be required to help with household tasks as soon as they are able to do so because Parents teach children who are the one of the family member. For example, If there were many household tasks, parents should separate and give some work to children. For my experience, when I was in junior high and high school student, I often clean our bathroom and clean the dishes after dinner.

In conclusion, I agree that the children should be required to help with household tasks as soon as they are able to do so because Parents can give education to their children. To work for family. It is good oppotunity for parents to educate children.

#9/C

"Children and Household Tasks"

One of the discussions that is going on about raising children in the right way is about whether or not children should be expected to take part in household tasks as soon as they are able to do it. Children should be required to help with the household tasks as soon as they are able to do so since they will learn to take responsibilities, how to live in a community and feel more confident because they can do something useful.

Helping with the household tasks as soon as they are able to do will help children while developing their characters. When a child is required to tidy his/her room, she/he will learn that he/she is responsible for keeping his/her own room tidy and will learn that she/he has to do it in the best way since its her/his responsibility. In addition to that, helping with the household tasks will give the family members the opportunity to do something together and the child will learn how to take part in a community, in his/her family which is the smallest unit of the society. A child who helps her/his mother to prepare the dinner will learn that he/she cannot expect others to do the things that she/her is responsible for. Moreover, tidying a room, helping someone to prepare a meal, or helping his/her parents in the garden will make the child feel and think that he/she can do something useful and a result the child will feel more confident.

As a conclusion, helping with the household tasks will help the development of a child since the child will learn feel more useful, gain self confidence and learn how to live in a society.

#9/D

"A Simple Task, A Simple Choice"

Children should be required to assist in household tasks as soon as they are able to do so because of the positive effects which result from working in a community, which they will have to do for the rest of their lives. Simple household tasks benefit the child more than the family in that it takes more time and effort of the parents to teach and nurture responsibility and life skills than it take the child to actually perform the task. Hard work also leads to the appreciation one feels for other people and all they do for you. When the process of accepting work, taking responsibility, and appreciating your own situation begins, then the ideas of sacrifice for the greater good and living in peace start to develop.

Responsibility is nurtured by the authority figure and forced upon a child at first, so eventually the child will realize how much taking responsibility for oneself is beneficial. Life skills such as cooking, cleaning, doing the laundry, taking out the trash, and doing the dishes will help and stay with the child throughout his/her life by becoming accepted as a part of life which is necessary for cleanliness, survival, and efficiency. The appreciation of others, of life, and of work is also encouraged and developed on a strong structure of self-respect which will help the child grow into a compassionate, yet well-rounded person. One choice to have a child take responsibility, develop pride, and work for the common good will always be remembered, appreciated, and lived.

#9/E

In china now, lots of families have only one child. So the special educations of the only child in a family become more and more important today. Among them, one big question is should children required to help with household task as soon as they are able to do it? In my opinion, I agree with it. I'll give you three reasons as following.

First of all, house work is good for children's health. In some meanings, Housework is also a kind of exercise. Especially for some light works, like wiping the floor or cleaning the table. They can help children get some exercise at the same time doing housework.

Second and especially important, leave some housework that just belong to the children themselves. It's a good habit for them to do their own things by themselves. They should learn of depending on themselves but not others from their childhood.

Last but not the least, housework makes children consider more of other people. If in a family, not only the mother or the father does the housework, but also the child does it, the child can actually feel how tough and hardworking it is. Later, the child will keep the floor and table clean when he is in home, because he knows it will cost his mother several minutes to clean it. Even more, the child will help his parents to do some housework, when he see them tired. It's really a good character for children to always consider others.

So, that concludes my opinion. I think it's better for children to do some housework which they are able to do, especially for the only child of their family.

#9/F

It's necessary that parents let their children help household tasks as soon as the children can do so.

First of all, doing household tasks is very beneficial for the kids themselves. Kids are usually curious about the world and want to try everything so why not give them a chance to try. With those practical work, children can know the outside world more quickly then just being isolated from those simple tasks.

Secondly, while doing housework children need communicate with parents. There comes another chance! Parents can know about their children more, then learn what the kids realy want, what are their preference. If you don't want your child to do anything, you will kill all of the chances to know him. We know a lot of kid are afraid of talking with their parents or unwilling to talk with their parents. This undeniably results from lacking of communication from the beginning. The less the communication, the more unwilling to communicate which leads to less and less understanding between parents and kids.

Thirdly, parents can also benefite a lot beyond understanding your kids! Why don't you think it's perfect that your housework is being reduced with days going on? Your children are growing up and doing more and more housework. One day, you can retire from kitchen! Isn't it a good plan? So try to let your kids do something they are able to do, if you don't like house work!

In conclusion, children doing houseworks can benefite both kids and parents.

#9/G

Nowadays, As the living standard of the people's life has been increased dramatically, the average people live a higher quality life, they're often busy on their work, and care a little about their housework. Some of them just hire cleaner for cleaning their house every week. It often happens that parents don't ask their children to do the housework for them, actually the children can do some of the housework. I do think that is a bad thing.

For one reason, and the most important reason supporting my opinion that children should do the housework as soon as they are able to so lies in the fact that housework really can improve their capability to deal with problems they can get a lot of practise and try to do the things in different ways, find out what's the best and most efficient way to solve problems they encountered while doing housework. That really contributed a lot to the children's imagination and creativity in the late days.

Secondly, Doing housework also shape children's character during the period of growth, that train children to be more independent to become people can stand on their own feet and with sense of liability, for example, many people in China only has one child. So they spoiled their children a lot and didn't ask them to do any housework in the home, they treated their children as the center of the whole family, but what happens is that all their efforts and goodwill didn't be rewarded with good results, the children are always relying on their parents to do all the things for them so, when they grow up they will become very dependent on someone else, that's too bad for a person don't has a ability to survive with himself.

Finally, I want to mention is children can really help their parents a lot while doing some housework for them. As we all known, the adults have a lot of work to do in the weekdays, if children can do them favor, that really help them a lot, then the whole family will be more harmonious and happier.

In one word, Doing housework really do a great good to children so children should take the liability to do the housework as soon as they are able to do so.

#9/H

I agree that children should be required to help with household tasks as soon as they are able to do so. There are three main reasons why they should do this.

The first reason is that it will make children independent. Independence is very crucial for every one of us. If someone always depends on others, he will achieve nothing in his own life. To help with household tasks teaches children they should do something for themselves, such as cleaning their own room and making fruit salad for themselves. It will be quite helpful to be independent before they leave their parents to fight his own future.

The second reason is that it will make children more responsible and more willing to help others. Children can learn that they should do something not only for themselves, but also for their families and even for the society. Helping their parents with the household tasks, such as washing everyone's dishes and cleaning the kitchen will offer them prize from their parents. Thus, they know that if you help others, what you do will be appreciated.

The third reason is that it will be physically good for children. When children help with household tasks, they get the chance to do some exercises, which will probably make them stronger.

In conclusion, it's not only physical benefits but also mental benefits children will get from helping with household tasks.

#9/I

Should children be required to help with household tasks as soon as they are able to do so? Definitely yes, In my opinion. Children should take part in household tasks as nearly as possible. It's very good for children's growth.

Many points can support this opinion. The first of all, children can learn many life-skills for their future life. No matter how young is a kid, he/she will live independently someday. At that time, he/she must do cleaning, laundry and cooking by himself/herself. That means, every child will have to do some household works after he/she chose to live independently. So, why we don't give them opportunities to learn to do it earlier. The earlier they learn to live independently, the earlier they chose to do it. Indepentent is an essential factor for adult person.

Secondly, children can experience cooperation when they do house hold task. Many household work, such as house cleaning, can't be completed by only one person, especially for kids. So, they have to cooperate with others. After a long time of such experience, they will be fit with cooperative work style. Cooperate is the fundament of our society. A child with such factor will tend to help others and be likely to finish his job with others' help. In short, a cooperative kid will become a kindly person.

Finally, sharing the household tasks will let the children know that, working is the basis method to live. In doing household work, kid will know that, no laundry then no clean clothes. So, they will know that it is working that gives them what they need for a happy life. After they grow up, we will meet a group of enterprising youth. From this way, our society can develop forward.

In conclusion, parents should enable kids to do household tasks as soon as they could. It's important not only for the children's growth, but also for the development of our society.

#9/J

Children as part of the family members are sometimes required to involve in the household tasks. This phenomena has bring both advantages and disadvantages to not only children themselves but also to our society.

Children should be required to help with household tasks as soon as they are able to do so because they should contribute to the family since they are a part of the family. Household tasks should not falls on the parents of a family only. Children should learn to appreciate the contributions of their parent and thus they should try to help with household tasks.

Besides, children should learn to deal with household tasks as they should be independent in the future. Therefore, this is a great opportunity for them as a starting point to learn with those tasks. Children should be independent and know how to take care of themselves because they are going to leave their family as they grow up.

On the other hands, there are some disadvantages if children are required to help with household tasks. As children are too childish and always careless dealing with household tasks, this might cause accidents to happen and therefore household tasks may be dangerous to children in this care.

In addition, children play an important role in our society children should gain as much as possible knowledge during school period. They should concentrate on their homeworks and not spending most of their time on the household tasks. Children may feel too tired after finished their tasks.

In conclusion, parents as the guide of children should compromise, so that the problem of children involve household tasks will be minimize.

SECTION THREE

READING

READING PRE-TEST

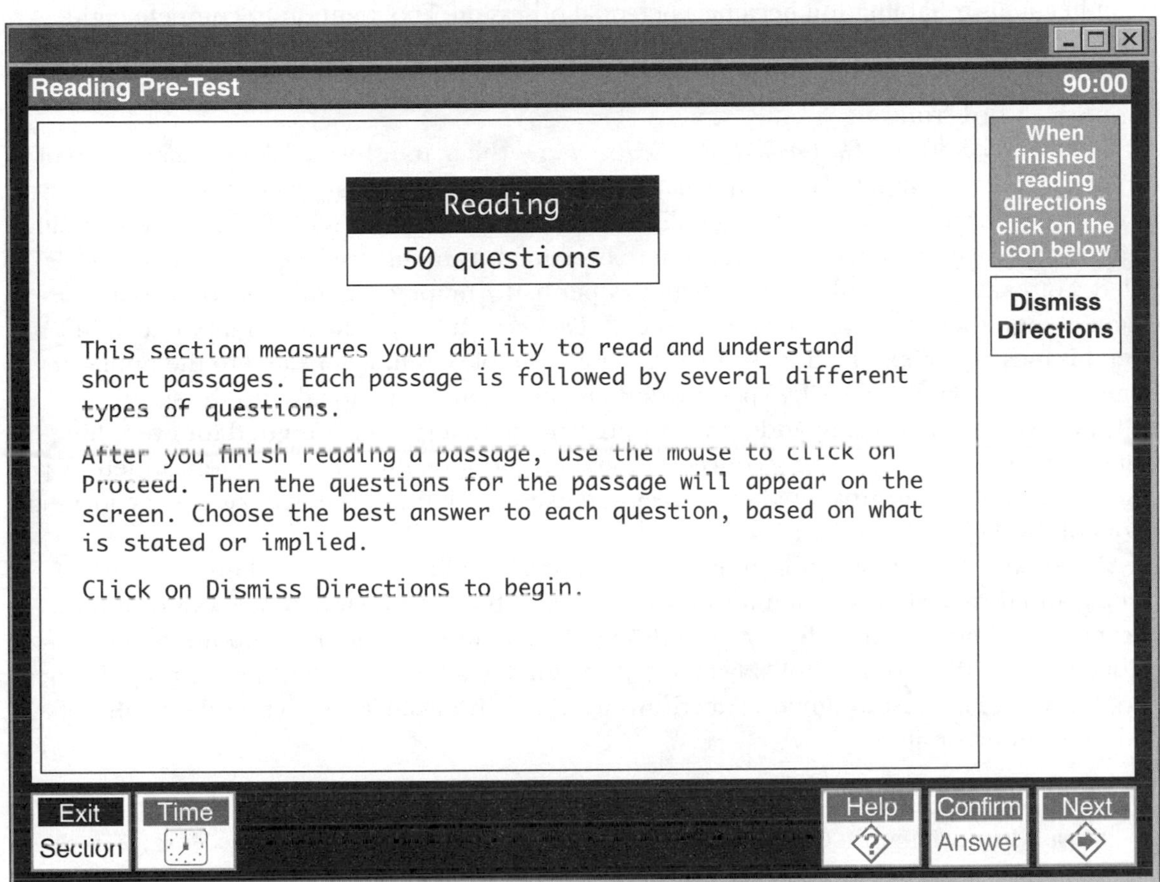

PASSAGE 1 Questions 1–13

At thirty-two years of age, Jim Fixx, an overweight, chain-smoking magazine editor from New York City, took up jogging. While playing weekend tennis, which was his only physical activity at the time, he pulled a calf muscle that then needed to be strengthened. As treatment for his pulled muscle, Fixx began jogging, exercising at a pace somewhat faster than a walk. What began as rehabilitation became a personal obsession. Fixx went on to compete eight times in the grueling Boston Marathon and to spearhead a national and international fitness craze. As jogging's popularity soared, the term jogging became synonymous with the more impressive word "running."

In 1977, Fixx wrote *The Complete Book of Running,* which transformed America's notion of fitness. Although competitive running dates back to the earliest Olympic Games, jogging began to catch on only in the 1960s among individuals seeking a new means of staying fit. Fixx's call to fitness appealed to a mass audience where his famous running predecessor's pleas had failed. For example, marathoner Kenneth Cooper had trumpeted regular exercise as an essential ingredient for good health in his text *Aerobics* in 1968, yet the general public didn't heed his message. Fixx's mantra, simple exercise in simple clothes, appealed to the public at large. The fact that no special, expensive equipment was necessary to take up the sport appealed to many people. In addition, Fixx proclaimed that jogging was good for everything from losing weight to increasing concentration. Furthermore, the success of large athletic-wear companies can also be attributed to sneaker and exercise clothing sales sparked by the jogging boom of the 1970s.

Paradoxically, Fixx recognized that runners, while physically fit, are still not immune to disease and death. He wrote about this issue in a later book. Unfortunately, Fixx's own life became a testimony to that theory. Even though he had lost sixty pounds and no longer smoked, at age fifty-two the unlikely fitness guru died of a heart attack while running. In the end, however, Fixx inspired many Americans to run for fitness. His impact on the health of a nation is immeasurable.

1. Which of the following would be the most appropriate title for the passage?
   - ○ How Running Became Jogging
   - ○ Jim Fixx and the Jogging Craze
   - ○ A New Line of Clothing
   - ○ Running the Boston Marathon

2. Look at the word pace in paragraph 1. The word is closest in meaning to
   - ○ determination
   - ○ speed
   - ○ passageway
   - ○ clumsiness

3. Look at the word grueling in paragraph 1. The word is closest in meaning to
   - ○ exhausting
   - ○ frightful
   - ○ fanatical
   - ○ widely known

4. Click on the phrase in paragraph 1 that indicates Fixx's means of exercise before he took up jogging.

5. Look at the word craze in paragraph 1. The word is closest in meaning to
   - ○ fad
   - ○ industry
   - ○ sound
   - ○ insanity

6. Look at the word which in paragraph 2. Click on the word or phrase in the paragraph that which refers to.

7. Look at the phrase catch on in paragraph 2. The phrase is closest in meaning to
   - entangle
   - take in
   - entrap
   - become popular

8. Click on the word or phrase in paragraph 2 that is closest in meaning to the word trumpeted.

9. The following sentence could be added to paragraph 2.

   Joggers, even presidents and movie stars, became familiar sights on jogging paths and highways.

   Where would it best fit into the paragraph? Click on the square to add the sentence to the paragraph.

   ☐ In 1977, Fixx wrote *The Complete Book of Running,* which transformed America's notion of fitness. ☐ Although competitive running dates back to the earliest Olympic Games, jogging began to catch on only in the 1960s among individuals seeking a new means of staying fit. ☐ Fixx's call to fitness appealed to a mass audience where his famous running predecessor's pleas had failed. For example, marathoner Kenneth Cooper had trumpeted regular exercise as an essential ingredient for good health in his text *Aerobics* in 1968, yet the general public didn't heed his message. ☐ Fixx's mantra, simple exercise in simple clothes, appealed to the public at large. The fact that no special, expensive equipment was necessary to take up the sport appealed to many people. ☐ In addition, Fixx proclaimed that jogging was good for everything from losing weight to increasing concentration.

10. Look at the word guru in paragraph 3. The word is closest in meaning to
    - practitioner
    - stickler
    - leader
    - healer

11. Which of the following is NOT true about Jim Fixx?
    - He designed a sneaker and exercise clothing line.
    - While exercising, he injured his leg.
    - Before jogging, his only exercise was tennis.
    - He universalized the sport of jogging.

12. It can be inferred from the passage that Jim Fixx
    - wrote more than one book
    - won the Boston Marathon
    - is the only well-known runner
    - smoked until he died

13. It can be inferred from the passage that
    - Kenneth Cooper and Jim Fixx were close friends
    - the words jogging and running are interchangeable
    - the jogging boom became less popular after Fixx's death
    - many joggers die of heart attacks

PASSAGE 2 Questions 14–25

Nowadays, children all over the world play with Danish Lego building blocks. However, in the early twentieth century, American children began playing with Erector sets, the mechanical predecessor of Lego. Erector sets contained metal nuts, bolts, gears, girders, and electric motors, enabling the construction of elaborate vehicles and structures.

The Erector set was the brainchild of A.C. Gilbert. In 1909, Gilbert founded the Mysto Magic Company, which marketed magic trick paraphernalia. Shortly thereafter, in 1913, Gilbert's Erector set debuted. The idea for the Erector set came to him one day when he was watching the electrification of the New Haven Railroad project. He focused in on the supporting girders, imagining their functionality in toy sets. Toy construction sets already in the marketplace, like the British Meccano, used strips of metal, bolts, and nuts that could be put together to build various small models. Gilbert was familiar with sets like these. He realized that by using miniature girders, gears, and motors like those he saw on the railway project, his product could be used for much more sophisticated designs. These ingenious additions quickly made Erector sets the exemplar of construction toys.

What made the Erector set so popular for the next 50 years was Gilbert's continued incorporation of cutting-edge technological advances. Even children who played with their Erector sets every day realized the number of building possibilities was limitless. The first sets Gilbert designed enabled their owners to assemble square girders, like those used for the construction of bridges and skyscrapers. In this way, Erector sets could imitate the engineering and architectural marvels of the day. In the 1920s, Gilbert added new features so that the sets could be used to construct trucks, Ferris wheels like those in the burgeoning amusement park industry, and zeppelins. In the 1940s, Gilbert introduced the Parachute Jump, which was based on World War II paratroopers. A lack of metal during the war resulted in several years of limited production. Back in full production in 1950, he came out with the Amusement Park set, which had an impressive merry-go-round.

Gilbert and his company produced toys until his death in 1961. By the end of the twentieth century, the company had been bought out twice, but the Erector name continues in production. Ironically, it is the Meccano Company which today markets Erector sets. Nostalgia surrounding the original Erector sets has made them highly collectible.

14. What is the main topic of this passage?
    - ◯ The construction toy industry
    - ◯ The history of the Erector set
    - ◯ Technological advances in the last century
    - ◯ The life of A.C. Gilbert

15. According to the passage, what did Gilbert do before he created the Erector set?
    - ◯ He performed as a magician.
    - ◯ He worked as an architect.
    - ◯ He set up a magic trick supply company.
    - ◯ He installed railroads.

16. Click on the sentence in paragraph 2 that explains what made Erector sets desirable.

17. Look at the word exemplar in paragraph 2. The word is closest in meaning to
    - ◯ ideal
    - ◯ representative
    - ◯ talent
    - ◯ influence

18. Click on the sentence in paragraph 3 that explains why those who used Erector sets were not bored.

19. Look at the phrase cutting-edge in paragraph 3. The phrase is closest in meaning to
    - ⬭ sharp
    - ⬭ precarious
    - ⬭ revolutionary
    - ⬭ borderline

20. Look at the word marvels in the paragraph 3. The word is closest in meaning to
    - ⬭ calamities
    - ⬭ surprises
    - ⬭ extremities
    - ⬭ achievements

21. The following sentence could be added to paragraph 3.

    Searching for other materials, Gilbert developed wooden girders.

    Where would it best fit into the paragraph? Click on the square to add the sentence to the paragraph.

    What made the Erector set so popular for the next 50 years was Gilbert's continued incorporation of cutting-edge technological advances. ☐ Even children who played with their Erector sets every day realized the number of building possibilities was limitless. The first sets Gilbert designed enabled their owners to assemble square girders, like those used for the construction of bridges and skyscrapers. In this way, Erector sets could imitate the engineering and architectural marvels of the day. ☐ In the 1920s, Gilbert added new features so that the sets could be used to construct trucks, Ferris wheels like those in the burgeoning amusement park industry, and zeppelins. ☐ In the 1940s, Gilbert introduced the Parachute Jump, which was based on World War II paratroopers. A lack of metal during the war resulting in several years of limited production. ☐ Back in full production in 1950, he came out with the Amusement Park set, which had an impressive merry-go-round. ☐

22. Which of the following pieces did Gilbert NOT produce?
    - ⬭ Ferris wheels
    - ⬭ Roller coasters
    - ⬭ The Parachute Jump
    - ⬭ Merry-go-rounds

23. According to the passage, when did Gilbert introduce the Erector Set?
    - ⬭ 1909
    - ⬭ 1913
    - ⬭ in the 1920s
    - ⬭ in the 1940s

24. Click on the paragraph that describes the various modifications of the Erector set.

25. It is implied in the passage that
    - ⬭ Erector sets were sold at amusement parks
    - ⬭ soldiers used Erector sets during World War II
    - ⬭ one cannot buy a new Erector set today
    - ⬭ original Erector sets have increased in value

PASSAGE 3 Questions 26–37

The house finch, a sparrow-like bird native to western North America, was originally a wild bird. In the seventeenth and eighteenth centuries, house finches made their homes in canyons and deserts, avoiding both forests and grassy regions without trees. Today, house finches can be found all over the United States, thanks to humans who changed the course of the birds' development. The wild populations of East Coast house finches provide an interesting case study of how birds adapt to their environments.

House finches first became popular as domestic birds in the mid-nineteenth century, when they were caught in their natural habitat and shipped from California to Hawaii, most likely as pets. The population of beautiful red and yellow birds, with their stunning singing voices, quickly spread to the other Hawaiian Islands. Starting around this time, Californian house finches, sold as "Hollywood" finches, were spread around the country because of market demand, particularly in major East Coast cities like Boston and New York.

The trade in house finches should have halted with the passage of the Migratory Bird Treaty Act of 1918, which forbade the sale of house finches as pets. This far-sweeping legislation prohibited the sale and transport of migratory birds in an attempt to protect dwindling bird populations. However, it was not until the summer of 1939 that the government finally began cracking down on the illegal sale of the so-called Hollywood finches in New York. People who sold the birds would have to pay a fine. Before they knew about the change in policy, pet store owners from Long Island had gone to Los Angeles to obtain finches to sell in New York. They did not learn of the policy change until they returned to New York with their birds. Instead of paying hefty fines, they released the birds into the city streets when confronted by law enforcement.

The finches ended up not only surviving in the wild streets of metropolitan areas but also breeding new populations. During the 1940s and 1950s, the population was mainly confined to New York City, but in the early 1960s, the birds' nesting sites started spreading. Twenty years later, house finches could be found throughout the U.S. and Canada. Their total number in North America is estimated at more than a billion, with a substantial percentage east of the Mississippi River.

26. Which of the following would be the most appropriate title for the passage?
    - ⬭ The Adaptation of the House Finch
    - ⬭ Spreading the House Finch to Hawaii
    - ⬭ The Migratory Bird Treaty Act
    - ⬭ Raising House Finches in New York City

27. Look at the word domestic in paragraph 2. Click on the word or phrase in paragraph 1 or 2 that is most nearly OPPOSITE the word domestic.

28. Look at the word they in paragraph 2. Click on the word or phrase in the paragraph that they refers to.

29. Look at the word stunning in paragraph 2. The word is closest in meaning to
    - ⬭ elusive
    - ⬭ impressive
    - ⬭ attacking
    - ⬭ shrill

30. It can be inferred from the passage that calling the birds "Hollywood finches"
    - ⬭ signified they had been in movies
    - ⬭ contrasted them with Hawaiian birds
    - ⬭ had glamorous appeal
    - ⬭ legitimized their nationality

31. Click on the sentence in paragraph 3 that describes how house finches once again became wild birds.

32. Click on the word or phrase in paragraph 3 that is closest in meaning to the word forbade.

33. Look at the phrase cracking down on in paragraph 3. The phrase is closest in meaning to

- ⬭ reporting
- ⬭ restraining
- ⬭ supervising
- ⬭ undermining

34. According to the passage, why were the finches trapped in Los Angeles?

- ⬭ To be released into the wild
- ⬭ To monitor their growth rate
- ⬭ To comply with the Migration Bird Treaty Act
- ⬭ To be sold in New York City

35. Look at the phrase case study in paragraph 1. The phrase is closest in meaning to

- ⬭ instructive example
- ⬭ syntactic relationship
- ⬭ precautionary tale
- ⬭ peculiar claim

36. The following sentence could be added to paragraph 3 or 4.

The birds experienced exponential growth in the wild because of the species' high fertility rate, which had decreased in captivity.

Where would it best fit into the paragraph? Click on the square to add the sentence to the paragraph.

□ They did not learn of the policy change until they returned to New York with their birds. □ Instead of paying hefty fines, they released the birds into the city streets when confronted by law enforcement.

□ The finches ended up not only surviving in the wild streets of metropolitan areas but also breeding new populations. □ During the 1940s and 1950s, the population was mainly confined to New York City, but in the early 1960s, the birds' nesting sites started spreading. Twenty years later, house finches could be found throughout the U.S. and Canada. □ Their total number in North America is estimated at more than a billion, with a substantial percentage east of the Mississippi River.

37. The paragraph preceding this passage most likely describes

- ⬭ what led to the signing of the 1918 Treaty Act
- ⬭ the accuracy of bird counting methodology
- ⬭ a different example of environmental adaptation
- ⬭ the physical characteristics of the house finch

PASSAGE 4 Questions 38–50

When English colonists first arrived in North America, they had no experience building homes from logs, large sections of tree trunks. Thus, these settlers built domiciles made of brush and bark until they could imitate the construction of frame houses, similar to ones back in England. On the other hand, colonists from forest-rich areas, including Germany, Switzerland, and Scandinavia felt right at home with the building materials at hand. They had all used logs, plentiful in North America, in constructing homes in their native lands.

Settlers from Sweden, who arrived in Delaware in 1638, assembled the first American log cabins. In Pennsylvania, the first log cabins, built by German immigrants, appeared in approximately 1710. However, log cabin construction did not begin in earnest until after 1720 when immigrants from Scotland and Ireland settled in the Appalachian Mountain area. By the 1770s, log cabins dotted the entire Western frontier landscape.

Although one could build a log cabin with relatively few basic tools, it was not a simple undertaking. An entire home could be assembled from three different types of logs: round, hewn on two sides, and squared. Most importantly, the logs had to be cut to about the same dimensions in order to fill the cracks between them easily with clay, mud, or moss. The logs could be fit together by cutting precise notches at the corner joints.

At first, the cabins had roofs made out of tree bark or foliage, such as reeds. Later, roofs were made from wooden shingles that had been sliced from logs. In most cases, residents could not afford to buy glass for windows, so they enclosed window frames with the skins of animals or paper covered in grease. Floor and doors, which hung on leather hinges, were constructed from logs slashed lengthwise. The majority of log cabins were one-story, containing either one or two rooms. More elaborate ones had lofts for sleeping and storage, accessible by ladders or by steps shaped into cabin walls.

Although the log cabin was a rather simple form of shelter, it has become a romantic symbol in American history. Being born in a modest log cabin and rising to a position of power is often used to illustrate the American dream. Abraham Lincoln was one famous American born in a log cabin. The belief that one may begin life humbly and become President of the United States still rings true.

38. Which of the following would be the most appropriate title for the passage?
    - Abraham Lincoln's Rise to the Presidency
    - The American Dream
    - The History of the American Log Cabin
    - Different Immigrant Group Contributions to the U.S.

39. Look at the word ones in paragraph 1. Click on the word or phrase in the paragraph that ones refers to.

40. Look at the word built in paragraph 2. Click on the word or phrase in the paragraph that is closest in meaning to the word built.

41. According to the passage, log cabins were built by settlers in which order?
    - Swiss, German, Scandinavian
    - German, Swedish, Scotch-Irish
    - Swedish, Scotch-Irish, German
    - Swedish, German, Scotch-Irish

42. Click on the phrase in paragraph 3 that indicates the various kinds of logs used.

43. Look at the word hewn in paragraph 3. The word is closest in meaning to
    - flat
    - cut
    - angled
    - smooth

44. Look at the word them in paragraph 3. Click on the word or phrase in the paragraph that them refers to.

45. According to the passage, what roofing materials were used?
   - ⬭ Mud
   - ⬭ Moss
   - ⬭ Bark
   - ⬭ Notched logs

46. According to the passage, why didn't most log cabins have windows?
   - ⬭ Glass was too expensive.
   - ⬭ Animal skins worked better.
   - ⬭ Tools weren't available.
   - ⬭ They were too difficult to build.

47. The following sentence could be added to paragraph 5.

   Daniel Boone and Andrew Jackson are others.

   Where would it best fit into the paragraph? Click on the square to add the sentence to the paragraph.

   ☐ Although the log cabin was a rather simple form of shelter, it has become a romantic symbol in American history. ☐ Being born in a modest log cabin and rising to a position of power is often used to illustrate the American dream. ☐ Abraham Lincoln was one famous American born in a log cabin. ☐ The belief that one may begin life humbly and become President of the United States still rings true. ☐

48. Look at the word modest in paragraph 5. The word is closest in meaning to
   - ⬭ unknown
   - ⬭ noble
   - ⬭ prototypical
   - ⬭ plain

49. According to the passage, all of the following are true EXCEPT
   - ⬭ most log cabins did not feature glass windows
   - ⬭ the early English colonists built the first log cabins
   - ⬭ precision was critical in assuring the proper fit of the logs
   - ⬭ an abundance of lumber made the log cabin a natural housing choice

50. It can be inferred from the passage that
   - ⬭ log cabins were built in England
   - ⬭ most presidents were born in log cabins
   - ⬭ animal skins were accessible to settlers
   - ⬭ most log cabins had two floors

READING

This section measures your ability to read and understand short passages similar in style and topic to those that students are likely to encounter in North American colleges and universities. This section contains reading passages and questions about them.

There are several different types of questions in this section. There are three different types of question-answer formats:

1. Multiple choice
2. Click on a word, phrase, sentence, or paragraph
3. Add a sentence

READING ON THE COMPUTER TOEFL TEST

In the Reading section, you will first have the opportunity to read the passage.

Reading

In his meteoric rise from poverty and obscurity, Alexander Hamilton was an American success story, yet Hamilton had little interest in wealth or social status. Instead, he had a strong desire to shape his adopted nation's future. Politics was his life, and he worked hard to achieve his goal of creating a dynamic and internationally respected nation.

As Secretary of the Treasury, Hamilton labored to establish sound national credit, a banking system, and programs to stimulate economic growth and expansion. He cared little for what the public thought of him or his politics. Thus, when news came in 1794 that farmers in western Pennsylvania had revolted against his whiskey tax, Hamilton wasted little time choosing a course of action.

Other Cabinet members saw the Whiskey Rebellion as justified civil disobedience to harsh or unfair legislation. Hamilton disagreed. He admitted that the tax—which was his brainchild—was a high one, requiring a 25% charge on all production of liquor. In addition, he knew that distilling was a critical home industry for many grain farmers whose crops might rot before reaching the market unless they were converted into whiskey. However, Hamilton cast the issue in dramatic political terms, arguing that the rebellion challenged the authority of the new constitutional government.

Time 23 Help Confirm Answer Next

You will use the scroll bar to view the rest of the passage.

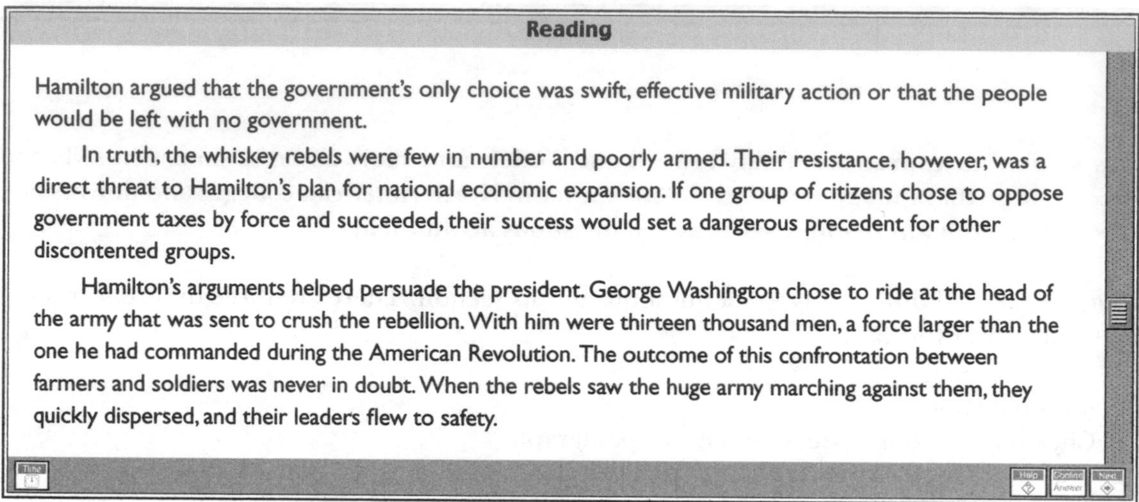
Reading

Hamilton argued that the government's only choice was swift, effective military action or that the people would be left with no government.

In truth, the whiskey rebels were few in number and poorly armed. Their resistance, however, was a direct threat to Hamilton's plan for national economic expansion. If one group of citizens chose to oppose government taxes by force and succeeded, their success would set a dangerous precedent for other discontented groups.

Hamilton's arguments helped persuade the president. George Washington chose to ride at the head of the army that was sent to crush the rebellion. With him were thirteen thousand men, a force larger than the one he had commanded during the American Revolution. The outcome of this confrontation between farmers and soldiers was never in doubt. When the rebels saw the huge army marching against them, they quickly dispersed, and their leaders flew to safety.

You will NOT see the questions until you click PROCEED. Then the questions will appear, one at a time.

Multiple-Choice Questions

Most of the questions will be multiple-choice questions. Answer all questions about the information in a passage on the basis of what is stated or implied in that passage. You will click on an oval to show your answer.

EXAMPLE:

With what topic is paragraph 1 mainly concerned?

- ◯ How Hamilton used his wealth to achieve success
- ◯ What influenced Hamilton's actions
- ◯ The fact that Hamilton was not born in America
- ◯ Hamilton's desire to achieve social status

When you click on a choice, the oval darkens to show which answer you have chosen. To choose a different answer, click on a different oval.

The correct answer is indicated on the screen below.

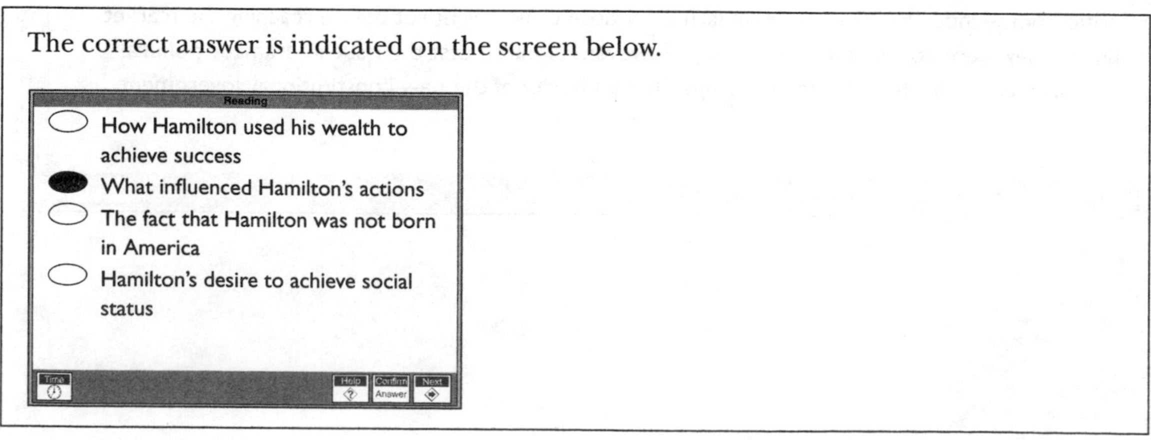

You will see the next question after you click NEXT.

Click on a Word, Phrase, Sentence, or Paragraph

To answer some questions you will click on a **word** in the passage.

EXAMPLE:

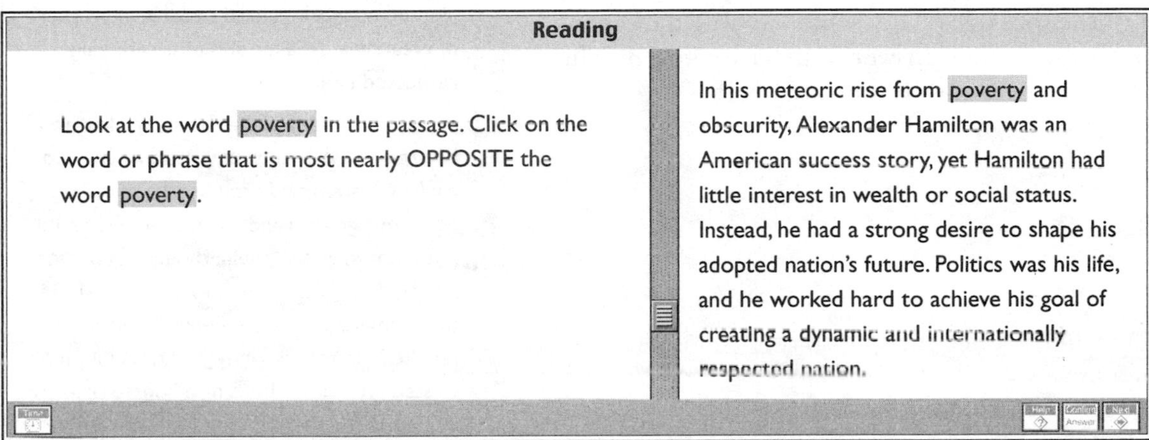

To answer, you can click on any word or phrase in the passage. You choice will darken to show which word you have chosen. The correct answer is indicated on the screen below.

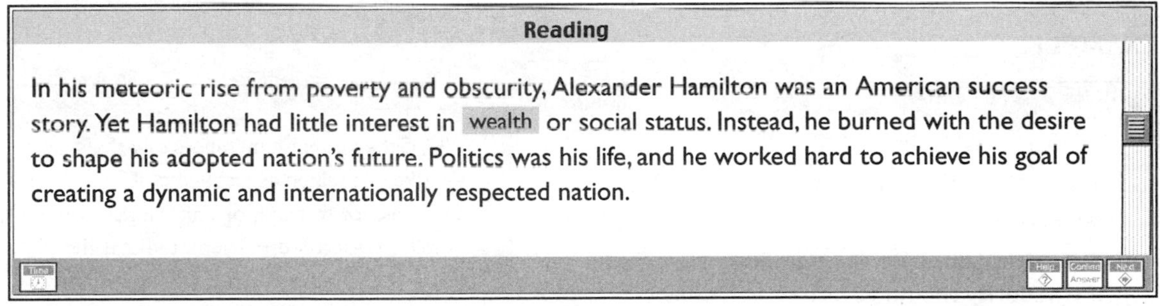

You will see the next question when you click on NEXT.

To answer some questions you will click on a **sentence** in the passage.

EXAMPLE:

Reading

Click on the sentence in paragraph 1 or 2 in which the author describes Hamilton's views on public opinion.

You can click on any part of the sentence in the passage. The sentence will darken to show which answer you have chosen. The correct answer is indicated below.

In his meteoric rise from poverty and obscurity, Alexander Hamilton was an American success story, yet Hamilton had little interest in wealth or social status. Instead, he had a strong desire to shape his adopted nation's future. Politics was his life, and he worked hard to achieve his goal of creating a dynamic and internationally respected nation.

As Secretary of the Treasury, Hamilton labored to establish sound national credit, a banking system, and programs to stimulate economic growth and expansion. He cared little for what the public thought of him or his politics .Thus, when news came in 1794 that farmers in western Pennsylvania had revolted against his whiskey tax, Hamilton wasted little time choosing a course of action.

Time | Help | Confirm Answer | Next

You will see the next question after you click on NEXT.

Add a Sentence

To answer some questions you will click on a square to add a **sentence** to the passage.

EXAMPLE:

Reading

The following sentence can be added to paragraph 3.

The critical question for Hamilton was whether the majority should govern or be governed.

Where would it best fit in paragraph 3? Click on the square ☐ to add the sentence to the paragraph. Paragraphs 2 and 3 are marked with an arrow.

☐ Other Cabinet members saw the Whiskey Rebellion as justified civil disobedience to harsh or unfair legislation. Hamilton disagreed. He admitted that the tax—which was his brainchild—was a high one, requiring a 25% charge on all production of liquor. ☐ In addition, he knew that distilling was a critical home industry for many grain farmers whose crops might rot before reaching the market unless they were converted into whiskey. ☐ However, Hamilton cast the issue in dramatic political terms, arguing that the rebellion challenged the authority of the new constitutional government. ☐ Hamilton argued that the government's only choice was swift, effective military action or that the people would be left with no government.

Time | Help | Confirm Answer | Next

When you click on a square, the sentence will appear in the passage at the place you have chosen. You can then read the passage to see if the sentence is in the correct place. If you want to change it, click on another square. The sentence will be added and shown in a dark box. The correct answer is indicated on the screen below.

Reading

Other Cabinet members saw the Whiskey Rebellion as justified civil disobedience to harsh or unfair legislation. Hamilton disagreed. He admitted that the tax—which was his brainchild—was a high one, requiring a 25% charge on all production of liquor. In addition, he knew that distilling was a critical home industry for many grain farmers whose crops might rot before reaching the market unless they were converted into whiskey. However, Hamilton cast the issue in dramatic political terms, arguing that the rebellion challenged the authority of the new constitutional government. The critical question for Hamilton was whether the majority should govern or be governed. Hamilton argued that the government's only choice was swift, effective military action or that the people would be left with no government.

READING SECTION INFORMATION

- The section contains four or five passages, with ten to fourteen questions about each passage.
- There are between 44 to 60 questions in the entire section.
- The passages average around 300 words each.
- This section is NOT computer adaptive; what you answer on one question does NOT change the level of your next question.
- You can go back and change a previous answer or look at a question again.
- Keep looking at the top left of the computer screen to see how much time you have left, and the top right to see which number question you are answering.

Topic Categories

The reading passages will include topics in the following categories:

1. **North American Culture**
   (geography, government, history, sports)
2. **Art and Architecture**
   (horticulture, literature, dance, drama, painting)
3. **Natural Science**
   (computers, medicine, biology, chemistry, geology)
4. **Social Science**
   (psychology, sociology, anthropology)
5. **Biography**
   (North American historical, political, artistic, scientific figures)

Question Types/Format

1. MAIN IDEA/PURPOSE

Look for questions such as these:

- The purpose of this passage is to
- Which of the following would be the most appropriate title for the passage?
- The passage is about
- What is the main topic of this passage?
- The passage mainly discusses
- With what topic is the passage mainly concerned?
- What is the author's main purpose in writing this passage?
- This passage would most likely be assigned reading in a course on
- With what topic is paragraph 2 mainly concerned?
- Which of the following best expresses the subject of the passage?
- The passage supports which of the following conclusions?

EXAMPLE:
Read the following paragraph:

Many kinds of newborn ocean animals learn to survive on their own. Mollusks, sea urchins, and starfish must fend for themselves from the moment they emerge from their eggs. Hatched from eggs left unattended, these babies receive no attention from their parents. Some fish, such as salmon, may travel thousands of miles or kilometers to lay their eggs in certain streams. Then they leave the eggs, and the baby fish that hatch must get along as best they can. Similarly, sea turtles abandon their eggs. They climb onto the beach to lay their eggs in the sand. Then they crawl right back into the sea, letting the young turtles develop by themselves. Most ocean animals do no more than lay their eggs in places where the young will be able to find food.

A question of this type would ask:
What is the main topic of the passage?

- ⬭ Ocean animals lay their eggs in the sand.
- ⬭ Newborn ocean animals are abandoned.
- ⬭ Many ocean animals are independent from birth.
- ⬭ Ocean animal babies reject nurturing.

Correct Answer: *Many ocean animals are independent from birth.* The idea is stated in the first sentence, which is also the topic sentence. The topic sentence states the main idea of the paragraph and is supported by all of the examples.
Incorrect: *Ocean animals lay their eggs in the sand.* (factually correct only for sea turtles)
Incorrect: *Newborn ocean animals are abandoned.* (factually incorrect)
Incorrect: *Ocean animal babies reject nurturing.* (factually incorrect)

- Don't pick answers that are too specific or too general.
- Some choices are factually incorrect.
- You may be asked the main idea of the entire passage or of only one paragraph.

2. DETAILS/FACTS
Look for questions such as these:

- Click on the paragraph in which the author/that best explains
- According to the passage, what, when, where, how many/which, who, why, what part, how long . . . ?
- Click on the sentence in paragraph ___ that explains/indicates/describes
- In what order does the author present
- Click on the drawing/picture that could be/shows
- Which of the following illustrations best . . . ?
- Which of the following statements is true?

EXAMPLE:
Read the following paragraph:

The armadillo is one of several small American mammals with bony plates in their upper body skin. Armadillos are found from Argentina northward to the south-central and southeastern parts of the United States. They usually eat insects, earthworms, spiders, and land snails. The animal has strong claws, which are used to dig tunnels and burrows in the ground. It uses its long, narrow tongue to lick insects. Because the armadillo has only small teeth far back in its mouth, it cannot bite in self-defense.

A question of this type would ask:
Click on the sentence in the paragraph that indicates what the armadillo could use to protect itself.

The correct sentence is highlighted.
The armadillo is one of several small American mammals with bony plates in their upper body skin. Armadillos are found from Argentina northward to the south-central and southeastern parts of the United States. They usually eat insects, earthworms, spiders, and land snails. The animal has strong claws, which are used to dig tunnels and burrows in the ground. It uses its long, narrow tongue to lick insects. Because the armadillo has only small teeth far back in its mouth, it cannot bite in self-defense.

Because the armadillo *cannot bite in self-defense,* it could use its *strong claws* to protect itself.

- Check the facts in the paragraph/passage.
- Scan the paragraph for key words related to the question.
- Look for examples.
- Look for synonyms.

3. VOCABULARY: SYNONYMS/ANTONYMS
Look for questions such as these:

- Look at the word ___ in paragraph 2. This word is closest in meaning to
- Look at the word ___ in the bold text below. Click on the word or phrase in the bold that is most nearly OPPOSITE the word _____.
- Click on the word or phrase in the bold that is closest in meaning to the word _____.
- Look at the word/expression ___ in paragraph 1. The word/expression could best be replaced by/is closest in meaning to

EXAMPLE:
A question of this type would ask:
Look at the word burrows in the text below. The word could best be replaced by

The armadillo is one of several small American mammals with bony plates in their upper body skin. Armadillos are found from Argentina northward to the south-central and southeastern parts of the United States. They usually eat insects, earthworms, spiders, and land snails. The animal has strong claws, which are used to dig tunnels and burrows in the ground. It uses its long, narrow tongue to lick insects. Because the armadillo has only small teeth far back in its mouth, it cannot bite in self-defense.

- ⬭ insects
- ⬭ traps
- ⬭ shovels
- ⬭ passages

You don't have to read the entire paragraph to answer this question. Look at the sentence. Although you may not know the word *burrows,* you see *tunnels,* a similar word and *claws* and *dig,* context clues, which can help you select the correct answer, *passages.*

- Try to eliminate one or two obviously wrong answers and then guess if you have no idea.
- Look for punctuation or phrases that might indicate a definition following a word. Definitions often follow a dash (—) or a colon (:), or phrases like *such as* and *for example.*
- Look for examples that help define a word.
- Scan the paragraph for context clues.

4. NEGATIVE ITEMS
Look for questions such as these:

- Which of the following is least accurate in describing . . . ?
- Which of the following is NOT mentioned as . . . ?
- It is NOT stated in the passage that
- Which of the following is NOT true about . . . ?
- Which of the following phrases would be LEAST likely applied to . . . ?
- All of the following are____ EXCEPT
- Which of the following is NOT a statement you would expect from . . . ?
- The author does NOT define which of the following terms?
- The author would probably use all of the following words to describe . . . EXCEPT

EXAMPLE:
Read the following paragraph:

Many kinds of newborn ocean animals learn to survive on their own. Mollusks, sea urchins, and starfish must fend for themselves from the moment they emerge from their eggs. Hatched from eggs left unattended, these babies receive no attention from their parents. Some fishes, such as salmon, may travel thousands of miles or kilometers to lay their eggs in certain streams. Then they leave the eggs, and the baby fishes that hatch must get along as best they can. Similarly, sea turtles abandon their eggs. They climb onto the beach to lay their eggs in the sand. Then they crawl right back into the sea, letting the young turtles develop by themselves. Most ocean animals do no more than lay their eggs in places where the young will be able to find food.

A question of this type would ask:
Which of the following is NOT mentioned as an animal that pays no attention to its young?

- ○ salmon
- ○ mollusks
- ○ sand dollars
- ○ turtles

To find the correct answer, scan the paragraph for all of the answer choices. The one NOT mentioned, *sand dollars,* is the correct answer.

- Check the factual information in the passage.
- Scan the passage for information that does appear.

5. PRONOUN REFERENCE

(one, it, them, he/she, they, that, its, many, the former/the latter, which)

Look for questions such as these:

Look at the word _____ in paragraph ___. Click on the word or phrase in the text that _____ refers to.

EXAMPLE:
A question of this type would ask:
Look at the word they in the paragraph. Click on the word or phrase in the paragraph that they refers to.

Many kinds of newborn ocean animals learn to survive on their own. Mollusks, sea urchins, and starfish must fend for themselves from the moment they emerge from their eggs. Hatched from eggs left unattended, these babies receive no attention from their parents. Some fishes, such as salmon, may travel thousands of miles or kilometers to lay their eggs in certain streams. Then they leave the eggs, and the baby fishes that hatch must get along as best they can. Similarly, sea turtles abandon their eggs. They climb onto the beach to lay their eggs in the sand. Then they crawl right back into the sea, letting the young turtles develop by themselves. Most ocean animals do no more than lay their eggs in places where the young will be able to find food.

The correct referent is *sea turtles,* found two sentences back.

- Look at all the nouns that are near the pronoun to find the referent word(s). BE CAREFUL. The referent USUALLY occurs BEFORE the pronoun, but not always.
- Watch out for distractors, words between the pronoun form and the referent. The pronoun and its referent always agree in gender and number.

6.
INFERENCE
Look for questions such as these:

- It can be inferred from the passage that . . .
- It is implied in the passage that . . .
- It is most likely that . . .

EXAMPLE:
Read the following paragraph:

Many kinds of newborn ocean animals learn to survive on their own. Mollusks, sea urchins, and starfish must fend for themselves from the moment they emerge from their eggs. Hatched from eggs left unattended, these babies receive no attention from their parents. Some fishes, such as salmon, may travel thousands of miles or kilometers to lay their eggs in certain streams. Then they leave the eggs, and the baby fishes that hatch must get along as best they can. Similarly, sea turtles abandon their eggs. They climb onto the beach to lay their eggs in the sand. Then they crawl right back into the sea, letting the young turtles develop by themselves. Most ocean animals do no more than lay their eggs in places where the young will be able to find food.

A question of this type would ask:
It can be inferred from the passage that

- ⬭ sea turtles spend all of their lives in the sand
- ⬭ there are some ocean animals whose parents don't ignore them
- ⬭ newborn ocean animals find food where they hatch
- ⬭ most ocean animals travel thousands of kilometers to lay their eggs

Correct Answer: *there are some ocean animals whose parents don't ignore them.* The first sentence reads *Many kinds of newborn ocean animals get along by themselves,* meaning not all. The next sentence *These ocean animals include mollusks, sea urchins, and starfish,* gives examples of which ocean animals are included in the "many" group.

Incorrect: *sea turtles spend all of their lives in the sand* (Since *sea turtles crawl right back into the sea,* they do not spend all their lives in the sand.)

Incorrect: *newborn ocean animals find food where they hatch* (*Most ocean animals do no more than lay their eggs in places where the young will be able to find food.* The sentence says *most animals,* meaning not all.)

Incorrect: *most ocean animals travel thousands of kilometers to lay their eggs* (*salmon may travel thousands of kilometers,* not most animals)

- Look at the facts in the passage. Inference questions are closely related to factual information. Deduce the answer from what has been said.
- Look for logical conclusions about ideas and/or information.

7. ADDING A SENTENCE
Look for questions such as these:

- The following sentence could be added to paragraph ___. Where would it best fit into the paragraph? Click on the square to add the sentence to the paragraph.

EXAMPLE:
A question of this type would ask:
The following sentence could be added to the paragraph.

These chambers are then used as hiding places.

The armadillo is one of several small American mammals with bony plates in their upper body skin. Armadillos are found from Argentina northward to the south-central and southeastern parts of the United States. ☐ They usually eat insects, earthworms, spiders, and land snails. ☐ The animal has strong claws, which are used to dig tunnels and burrows in the ground. ☐ It uses its long, narrow tongue to lick insects. ☐ Because the armadillo has only small teeth far back in its mouth, it cannot bite in self-defense. ☐

Where would it best fit into the paragraph? Click on the square to add the sentence to the paragraph.

The best place is: *The animal has strong claws, which it uses to dig tunnels and burrows in the ground. These chambers are then used as hiding places.* The *chambers* refer to the *tunnels and burrows* that the armadillo digs.

- Look for related words or ideas in the sentences preceding or following where the sentence could be inserted.
- Check to see if the sentence to be added presents an example that would follow a claim.
- Scan the paragraph for transition words.

8. CONCLUSION (NOT APPEARING OFTEN)
Look for questions such as these:

- The passage supports which of the following conclusions?
- The passage would most likely be assigned reading in a course on

EXAMPLE:
Read the following passage:

John James Audubon was one of the first to study and paint the birds of the United States. His lifelike paintings of birds in their natural surroundings brought him fame and fortune.

Audubon's diaries and letters created a mystery about his background and parentage, but documents indicate that he was born in 1785 in Haiti. His Haitian mother died soon after he was born, and he was taken to live in France with his father, a French sea captain.

In 1803, Captain Audubon sent his eighteen-year-old son to live near Philadelphia. There John spent a lot of his time drawing birds. In 1807, he opened a general store in Kentucky with Fernand Rozier, and married in 1808. Several business ventures with Rozier failed. While Rozier conducted their business, Audubon wandered the countryside looking for birds to draw. His business career ended in 1819 when he was jailed for debt. In order to gain freedom, he entered a plea of bankruptcy.

In 1820, he decided to publish his collection of American bird paintings. Unable to find an American publisher, he went to England and Scotland, where his pictures created a sensation. He published *Birds of America,* a work containing 435 life-sized, colored engravings. He returned to the United States in 1839, and published American editions of his bird paintings. He made his last collecting trip, along the Missouri River, in 1843. He died in 1851. Founded in 1905, the National Audubon Society, one of the oldest and largest national conservation societies, is named for John James Audubon.

A question of this type would ask:
The passage supports which of the following conclusions?

- ◯ Audubon was not appreciated in his lifetime as he is today.
- ◯ All of the 435 birds Audubon painted exist today.
- ◯ Audubon established the National Audubon Society.
- ◯ Audubon's name lives on in ways other than for his paintings.

Correct Answer: *Audubon's name lives on in ways other than for his paintings.* Because the National Audubon Society is *one of the oldest and largest conservation societies,* we can conclude that Audubon's name lives on as a result.

Incorrect: *Audubon was not appreciated in his lifetime as he is today.* (The second sentence states that his paintings *brought him fame and fortune*)

Incorrect: *All of the 435 birds Audubon painted exist today.* (There is no mention of this fact.)

Incorrect: *Audubon established the National Audubon Society.* (The last sentence *the National Audubon Society, one of the oldest and largest national conservation societies, is named for John James Audubon* states that this organization is *named for Audubon,* not that he established it.)

Look at the information in the last paragraph.

9. OVERALL ORGANIZATION (NOT APPEARING OFTEN)
Look for questions such as these:

- Which of the following best describes the organization of the passage?
- In what order does the author present

EXAMPLE:
Read the following passage:

John James Audubon was one of the first to study and paint the birds of the United States. His lifelike paintings of birds in their natural surroundings brought him fame and fortune.

Audubon's diaries and letters created a mystery about his background and parentage, but documents indicate that he was born in 1785 in Haiti. His Haitian mother died soon after he was born, and he was taken to live in France with his father, a French sea captain.

In 1803, Captain Audubon sent his eighteen-year-old son to live near Philadelphia. There John spent a lot of his time drawing birds. In 1807, he opened a general store in Kentucky with Fernand Rozier, and married in 1808. Several business ventures with Rozier failed. While Rozier conducted their business, Audubon wandered the countryside looking for birds to draw. His business career ended in 1819 when he was jailed for debt. In order to gain freedom, he entered a plea of bankruptcy.

In 1820, he decided to publish his collection of American bird paintings. Unable to find an American publisher, he went to England and Scotland, where his pictures created a sensation. He published *Birds of America,* a work containing 435 life-sized, colored engravings. He returned to the United States in 1839, and published American editions of his bird paintings. He made his last collecting trip, along the Missouri River, in 1843. He died in 1851. Founded in 1905, the National Audubon Society, one of the oldest and largest national conservation societies, is named for John James Audubon.

A question of this type would ask:
In what order does the author present the information?

- ◯ Chronologically
- ◯ Spatially
- ◯ Most important to least important
- ◯ Least important to most important

Aside from the two-sentence introduction, the facts of Audubon's life are presented in time order, or chronologically.

- Look at the topic sentence of each paragraph.
- *Chronological* means time order; look for dates and time words.
- *Spatial* order mean organization by place or direction; look for location.

10. ATTITUDE/TONE (NOT APPEARING OFTEN)
Look for questions such as these:

- The author's attitude/tone toward ____ is generally
- Which of the following best describes the tone of the passage?

Tone means the manner of expression. Is the passage angry, humorous, optimistic, sarcastic, negative, or ironic? *Attitude* means feeling. Does the author seem to feel angry, critical, positive, etc.?

EXAMPLE:
Read the following paragraph:

Would you like to have an armadillo as a pet? You'd certainly be the only one on your block to own one of these unusual creatures. There are some advantages to having an armadillo. It could eat the insects in your house. However, although you wouldn't have to worry about it biting you, it would dig up everything in your yard, creating its elaborate tunnels and burrows. It you kept it inside, its sharp claws could dig through your soft wood floors or carpets.

A question of this type would ask:
Which of the following best describes the tone of the passage?

- ⬭ Objective
- ⬭ Angry
- ⬭ Optimistic
- ⬭ Humorous

Correct Answer:	*Humorous* (The ironic humor *its sharp claws could dig through your soft wood floors or carpets* is evident. No one would want their home or yard dug up.)
Incorrect:	*Objective* (An objective paragraph would present facts about an armadillo in a straightforward manner, like the paragraph on page 275. This paragraph uses the humorous idea of owning an armadillo as a pet in order to present information about it.)
Incorrect:	*Angry* (no evidence)
Incorrect:	*Optimistic* (The passage shows both positive and negative attributes of armadillos.)

Eliminate extremes (e.g. negative). Most passages are fact, not opinion.

11. PARAGRAPH BEFORE OR AFTER (NOT APPEARING OFTEN)
Look for questions such as these:

- The paragraph preceding this essay most likely describes
- The paragraph following this passage most likely describes

These questions ask you to imagine what a paragraph before or after the passage would contain.

EXAMPLE:
Read the following passage:

John James Audubon was one of the first to study and paint the birds of the United States. His lifelike paintings of birds in their natural surroundings brought him fame and fortune.

Audubon's diaries and letters created a mystery about his background and parentage, but documents indicate that he was born in 1785 in Haiti. His Haitian mother died soon after he was born, and he was taken to live in France with his father, a French sea captain.

In 1803, Captain Audubon sent his eighteen-year-old son to live near Philadelphia. There John spent a lot of his time drawing birds. In 1807, he opened a general store in Kentucky with Fernand Rozier, and married in 1808. Several business ventures with Rozier failed. While Rozier conducted their business, Audubon wandered the countryside looking for birds to draw. His business career ended in 1819 when he was jailed for debt. In order to gain freedom, he entered a plea of bankruptcy.

In 1820, he decided to publish his collection of American bird paintings. Unable to find an American publisher, he went to England and Scotland, where his pictures created a sensation. He published *Birds of America,* a work containing 435 life-sized, colored engravings. He returned to the United States in 1839, and published American editions of his bird paintings. He made his last collecting trip, along the Missouri River, in 1843. He died in 1851. Founded in 1905, the National Audubon Society, one of the oldest and largest national conservation societies, is named for John James Audubon.

A question of this type would ask:
The paragraph following this passage most likely describes

- ⬭ The success of Audubon's publications in America
- ⬭ The activities of the National Audubon Society
- ⬭ The content of Audubon's books
- ⬭ The influence of Audubon's childhood on his work

Correct Answer: *The activities of the National Audubon Society,* the topic of the final sentence.
Incorrect: *The success of Audubon's publications in America* (factually correct, but too specific and mentioned much earlier)
Incorrect: *The content of Audubon's books* (too specific)
Incorrect: *The influence of Audubon's childhood on his work* (not mentioned; the passage mentions his drawing after age 18)

For the preceding paragraph topic, look for clues in the first line. For the paragraph following topic, look for clues in the last line.

PREPARATION AND STRATEGIES FOR THE READING SECTION

Preparation

You should prepare for the reading section by doing the following:

1. **Read for at least 30 minutes every day, preferably from a computer screen.** After a few weeks, you should notice that the time it takes to read one page has decreased.
2. **Each day, find an article in a newspaper, encyclopedia, textbook, or news magazine that is no longer than a page or 4–5 paragraphs.** Print out a copy, or make a photocopy of the article.
3. **Read the article through without a dictionary.** Then:
   a. write down 5 vocabulary words you do not know (and which you assume to be important). First try to guess the meaning. Then look the words up in the dictionary, making sure the meaning you write down is the correct one for the context. Keep your own alphabetical dictionary of new words from your readings. Refer back to your dictionary frequently. Even if these words are not on your TOEFL test, your vocabulary and therefore your speaking and writing will also improve.

   b. summarize the article into 2–3 sentences
   c. make up 5 TOEFL test-type questions (vary the 11 TOEFL test-type questions) with multiple choice answers for the passage
4. **Make sure you select a variety of reading topics (science, biography, history, etc.), and try to vary the sources you use.** If you're studying in a class, bring in your articles and TOEFL test questions for class practice.

General Strategies for the Reading Section

1. **Dismiss the directions immediately.** Don't waste any of the time you have. Make sure you feel comfortable with the directions, which are described in the beginning of this section as well as in the TOEFL Bulletin.
2. **Remember that the questions generally follow the order of the text.** The only exception is that frequently the first question asks about the purpose/main idea of the passage.
3. **Remember that you don't have to read or reread an entire paragraph to answer vocabulary and reference questions.** Because vocabulary and reference questions are bold or highlighted, you can easily find these words in the passage.
4. **Remember the section is timed, so do not spend too much time on any one question.** If you can eliminate one or two answers, make a guess and move on. Don't leave any answers blank. If time is almost up and you have one more passage, try and answer the vocabulary or reference questions since you won't have to read the entire passage to do so.
5. **You will be given paper, so you can write down a question you want to go back to before time is up, but remember it takes time to do so.**
6. **For vocabulary, factual, and reference questions, consider NOT reading the entire passage.** You can look at each question and find the place in the passage where the question is answered. Read ONLY that part carefully. Try doing this with the practice reading passages in the book to see if that works for you.
7. **Remember that although all of the passages are factually based, you don't need any previous knowledge about the subject.**
8. **It may not be easy to figure out vocabulary words in their context.** If you do NOT know a vocabulary word being tested, try and get a sense of it from the sentence or paragraph. You may recognize a word and find that the meaning in the passage is NOT the one you know.
9. **If you do finish, and there is time left, go back to the items you wrote down to check or go back to a passage you found difficult.**
10. **This section is LONG!** Your eyes may hurt from looking at a screen for over an hour. Try closing your eyes every 10–15 minutes for about 20 seconds to refresh them. Also, taking a few seconds to make a circular motion with your head will help reenergize you!

Reading Section Exercises

After each passage in this section, the number of words in the passage is given. On the TOEFL test, the average length is between 250 to 350 words. For each question below, the number in (parentheses) indicates the question type from the previous section (reference, add a sentence, etc.).

PASSAGE 1 Questions 1–4

Grandma Moses was an American painter known as a primitive painter. She started painting when she was 76 years old and remained active until near her death at age 101. She never had an art lesson. Grandma Moses painted simple but realistic scenes of rural life. These colorful and animated pictures were derived from memories of her youth in the late 1800s. Art critics have praised her work for its freshness, innocence, and humanity.

(74 words)

1. (3) Look at the word primitive in the paragraph. Click on the word or phrase in the paragraph that is closest in meaning to the word primitive.

2. (2) Which of the following statements is true?
   - ◯ Grandma Moses was instructed how to paint.
   - ◯ Grandma Moses painted for a quarter century.
   - ◯ Grandma Moses was born in the eighteenth century.
   - ◯ Grandma Moses painted in her youth.

3. (7) The following sentence could be added to the paragraph.

   Before the turn of the century, she lived on a farm in upstate New York.

   Where would it best fit into the paragraph? Click on the square to add the sentence to the paragraph.

   ☐ Grandma Moses was an American painter known as a primitive painter. She started painting when she was 76 years old and remained active until near her death at age 101. ☐ She never had an art lesson. Grandma Moses painted simple but realistic scenes of rural life. These colorful and animated pictures were derived from memories of her youth in the late 1800s. ☐ Art critics have praised her work for its freshness, innocence, and humanity. ☐

4. (6) It can be inferred from the passage that Grandma Moses was
   - ◯ senile
   - ◯ energetic
   - ◯ realistic
   - ◯ innocent

PASSAGE 2 Questions 1–7

Many anesthesiologists and psychologists have reported recent increases in the number of "awareness episodes" occurring during surgery. The greater use of narcotics and muscle relaxants to induce unconsciousness, and the corresponding decrease in the use of anesthetics, seem to be responsible for this phenomenon.

Doctors' reports indicate that even though patients may have no conscious recall of events that occurred during surgery, they can hear operating room conversations while they are "asleep" and can unconsciously incorporate such information into their behavior and attitudes toward recovery.

At the University of California Medical Center at Davis, psychologist Henry Bennett performed a carefully controlled study in which anesthetized patients received a suggestion just before being brought to consciousness. Most patients who were told to pull their ears during subsequent interviews did exactly that, even though they did not recall having received such instructions.
(141 words)

1. (1) The passage mainly discusses
   - ◯ the new methods anesthesiologists are using on their patients
   - ◯ the increased number of surgical awareness episodes patients are experiencing
   - ◯ the decreased use of anesthetics
   - ◯ the controlled study of Henry Bennett at the University of California Medical Center at Davis

2. (4) Which of the following does NOT explain the reason for the increase in surgical "awareness episodes"?
   - ◯ The increase in narcotic usage
   - ◯ The use of suggestions on anesthetized patients
   - ◯ The greater use of muscle relaxants
   - ◯ The decreased use of anesthetics

3. (5) Look at the word they in paragraph 2. Click on the word or phrase in the paragraph that they refers to.

4. (3) Look at the word subsequent in paragraph 3. The word is closest in meaning to
   - ◯ previous
   - ◯ follow-up
   - ◯ underneath
   - ◯ sequential

5. (3) Look at the word controlled in paragraph 3. The word is closest in meaning to
   - ◯ scientific
   - ◯ isolated
   - ◯ programmed
   - ◯ monitored

6. (8) The passage supports which of the following conclusions?
   - ◯ Comments made to patients during surgery will affect their recovery.
   - ◯ Anesthesiologists are trying to find ways to decrease the use of anesthetics to induce unconsciousness.
   - ◯ Patients understood why they pulled their ears during subsequent interviews.
   - ◯ Operating room conversations should be controlled.

7. (11) The paragraph following this passage most likely describes
   - ◯ experimental use of narcotics and muscle relaxants
   - ◯ limiting surgical room conversations
   - ◯ the design of a study to enhance patient recovery
   - ◯ controlled studies of patients who are not anesthetized during surgery

PASSAGE 3 Questions 1–7

The first area outside the United States to which settlers moved in substantial numbers was the province now called Texas. By 1830, eastern Texas was occupied by nearly 20,000 whites and 1,000 black slaves from the United States.

Many westerners had been disappointed when the U.S. government, in the Florida purchase treaty of 1819, accepted the Sabine River as the southwestern boundary of the

United States. By doing so, the United States surrendered whatever vague claim it had to Texas as part of the Louisiana Purchase. After winning independence from Spain in 1822, Mexico twice rejected American offers to buy this sparsely settled province; however, during the 1820s, she welcomed law-abiding American immigrants.

The first and most successful promoter of American settlement in Mexico was Stephen F. Austin, who obtained a huge land grant from the Mexican government in the 1820s and established a flourishing colony on the banks of the Brazos River. Most of the immigrants that followed Austin to what is now Texas were yeoman farmers and small landowners from the southern United States who were attracted by the rich lands suitable for cotton growing and available for a few cents an acre. Mexico restricted all immigration after 1830.
(201 words)

1. (1) What is the main topic of this passage?
   - ⬭ The influence of Mexico on settlement in Texas
   - ⬭ The geographic features of Texas
   - ⬭ The initial settlement of Texas
   - ⬭ The impact of treaties on Texas in the 1800s

2. (5) Look at the word she in paragraph 2. Click on the word or phrase in the paragraph that she refers to.

3. (4) In 1822, all of the following were true EXCEPT
   - ⬭ Mexico had already twice refused U.S. offers to buy Mexico
   - ⬭ Mexico became independent that year
   - ⬭ the Louisiana Purchase had been negotiated
   - ⬭ Texas was a populated area outside of the U.S.

4. (4) Stephen F. Austin did all of the following EXCEPT
   - ⬭ encourage newcomers to settle in Texas
   - ⬭ establish a colony on the banks of the Brazos River
   - ⬭ secure land from Mexico
   - ⬭ negotiate the Louisiana Purchase

5. (3) Look at the word successful in paragraph 3. Click on the word or phrase in the paragraph that is closest in meaning to the word successful.

6. (6) It can be inferred that Texas farmland is suitable for
   - ⬭ textile design
   - ⬭ production of raw materials for clothing
   - ⬭ food production
   - ⬭ fishing

7. (7) The following sentence could be added to paragraph 3.

   His management was so successful that by 1830 there were more than 20,000 Americans in Texas.

   Where would it best fit into the paragraph? Click on the square to add the sentence to the paragraph.

   □ The first and most successful promoter of American settlement in Mexico was Stephen F. Austin, who obtained a huge land grant from the Mexican government in the 1820s and established a flourishing colony on the banks of the Brazos River. □ Most of the immigrants that followed Austin to what is now Texas were yeoman farmers and small landowners from the southern United States who were attracted by the rich lands suitable for cotton growing and available for a few cents an acre. □ Mexico restricted all immigration after 1830. □

PASSAGE 4 Questions 1–6

Undaunted by the menacing pink tentacles of a sea anemone, a shrimp sallies forth in search of plankton and other tasty morsels. The shrimp is a parasitic guest of the larger anemone. The anemone's arms are laced with venom, but the shrimp escapes their deadly embrace by coating itself with the same material that covers its host's body. By this ingenious tactic, the tiny crustacean achieves a form of immunological camouflage; the anemone is unable to distinguish the shrimp from itself, and so it tolerates the intruder. For the shrimp, the reward for this clever disguise is twofold: protection from predators as well as a share in some of the food that the anemone catches.
(115 words)

1. (1) What is the main topic of the passage?
   - ⬭ The art of camouflage
   - ⬭ The shrimp's abilities to escape its enemies and to feed itself
   - ⬭ The similar appearance of the anemone and the shrimp
   - ⬭ The amazing world of the shrimp

2. (2) The passage explains why
   - ⬭ the shrimp benefits from its camouflage
   - ⬭ many animals need to use camouflage to survive
   - ⬭ tiny shrimp are sought by sea anemones
   - ⬭ plankton are sought by shrimp

3. (3) Look at the word camouflage in the paragraph. Click on the word or phrase that is closest in meaning to the word camouflage.

4. (5) Look at the word its in the paragraph. Click on the word or phrase that its refers to.

5. (3) Look at the phrase laced with in the passage. The phrase could best be replaced by
   - ⬭ decorated with
   - ⬭ flavored with
   - ⬭ filled with
   - ⬭ fastened with

6. (6) It can be inferred from the passage that plankton is
   - ⬭ a predator
   - ⬭ a camouflage
   - ⬭ something edible
   - ⬭ a crustacean

PASSAGE 5 Questions 1–5

Many users of personal computers have never thought twice about making copies of their favorite software programs for friends. Now a growing number of corporations and schools are doing the same thing. They are permitting, even encouraging, their employees to duplicate software rather than buy a program for each computer in the organization. Four pirated versions are made for every legitimate package sold, according to some industry estimates.
(68 words)

1. (1) Which of the following would be the most appropriate title for the passage?
   - The Growing Practice of Illegally Copying Software
   - The Increasing Use of Personal Computers at Home and at Work
   - Computer Software in School and Corporations
   - The Legalization of Duplicating Software

2. (4) According to the passage, computer software is illegally copied in all of the following places EXCEPT
   - at home
   - at schools
   - in corporations
   - in the computer industry

3. (2) For every 28 pirated versions made, how many legitimate packages are sold?
   - 4
   - 7
   - 28
   - 112

4. (3) Look at the word legitimate in the paragraph. Click on the word or phrase that is most nearly OPPOSITE the word legitimate.

5. (6) What is the implied motivation for pirating software?
   - Availability
   - Friendship
   - Speed
   - Price

PASSAGE 6 Questions 1–5

The Indian tribes of eastern North America were among the first Indians to meet English settlers. In 1621, the Indians and English celebrated a good harvest and peace together in Plymouth colony. But the good relationship did not last long. The Indians were slow to perceive that their way of life was incompatible with that of the English. They often sold their land or gave it away without realizing that it would no longer be theirs. They used the land mainly for hunting and were willing to let the English hunt on it with them. But the English cut the trees, drove out the game, and evicted the Indians. Before the Indians realized what was happening, they were outnumbered.
(119 words)

1. (2) According to the passage, what was the major downfall of the Indians?
   - Being slow to understand their differences from the English
   - Celebrating a good harvest with the English
   - Becoming outnumbered
   - Letting the English hunt on their land

2. (4) The Indians at one time did all of the following EXCEPT
   - live in eastern North America
   - give away their land
   - evict the English
   - sell their land

3. (2) According to the passage, the English
   - never paid for Indian land
   - hunted without the Indians
   - had a population that was ultimately greater than that of the Indians
   - had a lifestyle similar to that of the Indians

4. (4) The English did all of the following EXCEPT
   - cut down trees
   - drive out game
   - evict the Indians
   - use the land mainly for hunting

5. (7) The following sentence could be added to the paragraph.

   That year's celebration has come to be known as the first Thanksgiving.

   Where would it best fit into the paragraph? Click on the square to add the sentence to the paragraph.

   ☐ The Indian tribes of eastern North America were among the first Indians to meet English settlers. ☐ In 1621, the Indians and English celebrated a good harvest and peace together in Plymouth colony. ☐ But the good relationship did not last long. ☐ The Indians were slow to perceive that their way of life was incompatible with that of the English. They often sold their land or gave it away without realizing that it would no longer be theirs. They used the land mainly for hunting and were willing to let the English hunt on it with them. But the English cut the trees, drove out the game, and evicted the Indians. Before the Indians realized what was happening, they were outnumbered.

PASSAGE 7 Questions 1–6

The search for signals from intelligent beings in outer space may indeed be a roll of the dice, but after years of struggling to be taken seriously, it has become a respectable scientific endeavor. Its advocates now form an active, worldwide network of scientists who have made significant discoveries and developed techniques that could bear fruit in such diverse fields as telecommunication and theories of star formation.
(67 words)

1. (3) Look at the phrase a roll of the dice in the paragraph. The phrase could best be replaced by
   - ⬭ a game
   - ⬭ chance
   - ⬭ difficult
   - ⬭ time-consuming

2. (5) Look at the word it in the paragraph. Click on the word or phrase that it refers to.

3. (6) It can be inferred from the passage that
   - ⬭ the fields of telecommunication and theories of star formation are bearing fruit
   - ⬭ at one time, searching for signals from outer space was not taken seriously
   - ⬭ intelligent beings in outer space are communicating with a network of scientists
   - ⬭ scientists in this field of study are not found worldwide

4. (3) Look at the word endeavor in the passage. The word is closest in meaning to
   - ⬭ enlightenment
   - ⬭ enigma
   - ⬭ enemy
   - ⬭ enterprise

5. (8) The passage supports which of the following conclusions?
   - ⬭ There are intelligent beings in outer space.
   - ⬭ A network of scientists is studying theories of star formation.
   - ⬭ Not all scientists are respectable.
   - ⬭ Eventually, the study of signals from outer space may produce results in various fields.

6. (10) Which of the following best describes the tone of the passage?
   - ⬭ Humorous
   - ⬭ Sarcastic
   - ⬭ Straightforward
   - ⬭ Incredulous

PASSAGE 8 Questions 1–6

George Gallup, Jr., the man who makes and stakes his reputation on knowing what Americans think, has brought all his polling strategies together to identify and analyze what he calls future forces. Already they are shaping the form our society will assume by the end of the century. For the past several years, Gallup has sought the views of millions of Americans in the belief that broad-based polls give a corporate sense of where the country is headed, a sense that no single person possesses. He surveys the nation's youth, for example, because his polls have shown repeatedly that one's values and attitudes about life—the seeds of future actions—are formed before a person reaches the age of twenty. Gallup also seeks the opinions of a diverse group of experts—lawyers, judges, economists, business executives, artists, scientists, the clergy—to focus as sharply as possible on the future.
(145 words)

1. (1) Which of the following would be the most appropriate title for the passage?
   - ⬭ The Life of George Gallup, Jr.
   - ⬭ Predicting the Shape of American Society
   - ⬭ The Opinion of Experts
   - ⬭ Our Nation's Youth

2. (1) The passage mainly discusses George Gallup, Jr.'s life as a
   - ⬭ pollster
   - ⬭ lawyer
   - ⬭ scientist
   - ⬭ corporate executive

3. (2) Click on the sentence in the paragraph that explains why Gallup sought the opinion of young people.

4. (6) It can be inferred from the passage that George Gallup, Jr. is
   - ⬭ thorough
   - ⬭ unknown
   - ⬭ obstinate
   - ⬭ questionable

5. (2) According to the passage, Gallup would most likely seek the opinion of
   - ⬭ a factory worker
   - ⬭ a fifty-year-old
   - ⬭ a priest
   - ⬭ a prison inmate

6. (8) The passage would most likely be assigned reading in a course on
   - ⬭ sociology
   - ⬭ anthropology
   - ⬭ history
   - ⬭ politics

PASSAGE 9 Questions 1–7

On November 17, 1777, Congress finally agreed on a constitution to be presented to the state legislatures for approval or rejection. The Articles of Confederation provided for a congress much like the one existing today. Each state, whatever its size, was to have only one vote, to be cast by delegates appointed by the state legislatures. Furthermore, each state, by taxing itself, was to contribute to the common expenses of all states, according to the value of its lands. Additionally, each state was to retain "sovereignty, freedom, and independence, and every power, jurisdiction, and right" not expressly delegated to Congress. Congress was permitted to decide on issues of war and peace, appoint military and naval officers, requisition the states for soldiers and money, send and receive ambassadors, enter into treaties and alliances, establish a post office, mint, borrow, or issue money on the credit of the United States, fix weights and measures, regulate Indian affairs, and settle disputes between states.
(160 words)

1. (1) What is the main topic of the passage?
   - ⬭ The rights of states and of Congress
   - ⬭ Deciding on war and peace
   - ⬭ The history of the Articles of Confederation
   - ⬭ A comparison between the Congress of 1777 and that of today

2. (2) What is the Articles of Confederation the name of?
   - ⬭ The Congress
   - ⬭ An early constitution
   - ⬭ The state legislatures
   - ⬭ The United States

3. (4) Which of the following was Congress NOT permitted to do?
   - ⬭ Appoint military officers
   - ⬭ Send and receive ambassadors
   - ⬭ Appoint delegates to the state legislatures
   - ⬭ Establish a post office

4. (2) Click on the phrase that expresses how Congress is allowed to establish standardization for size.

5. (6) It can be inferred from the passage that
   - ⬭ each state would contribute equal amounts of money to the United States
   - ⬭ each state would have its number of votes determined by its size
   - ⬭ before November 17, 1777, no U.S. constitution existed
   - ⬭ Congress had the right to tax

6. (4) According to the passage, Congress can ratify all of the following EXCEPT
   - ⬭ peace treaties
   - ⬭ money production
   - ⬭ military appointments
   - ⬭ the number of state delegates

7. (6) It can be inferred from the passage that
   - ⬭ disputes between states could be resolved by the states involved
   - ⬭ the states would not decide on issues of war
   - ⬭ on November 17, 1777, the Constitution had not yet been approved
   - ⬭ Indian affairs would not be supervised

PASSAGE 10 Questions 1–10

Lie detectors do not detect lies. **They** record a person's physiological reactions to certain questions. Basically, the instrument records four physiological activities on a moving roll of graph paper. Two pens are driven by air-filled tubes placed around a subject's chest and stomach to record breathing movement. Another pen, connected to a blood-pressure cuff on the subject's arm, records each heartbeat and traces changes in blood pressure. The fourth pen is connected to a pair of metal electrodes attached to the fingers of one hand. This pen records changes in the electrical resistance of the skin and can indicate subtle sweating. In administering the test, examiners usually ask **neutral** questions such as birth dates and addresses in order to compare these responses with **those** from emotionally charged questions. (128 words)

1. (1) Which of the following would be the most appropriate title for the passage?
   - ⬭ The History of the Lie Detector
   - ⬭ Emotionally Charged Questions
   - ⬭ The Truth About Lie Detectors
   - ⬭ How to Assemble a Lie Detector

2. (5) Look at the word **they** in the passage. Click on the word or phrase in the paragraph that **they** refers to.

3. (4) Which of the following statements is NOT true about the fourth pen?
   - It is connected to two metal electrodes.
   - It records changes in the electrical resistance of the skin.
   - It is attached to the fingers of both hands.
   - It indicates subtle sweating.

4. (4) Which of the following is NOT needed to conduct a lie detector test?
   - Examiners
   - Four pens
   - A roll of graph paper
   - Neutral respondents

5. (4) Which of the following is NOT mentioned as a physiological reaction?
   - Breathing movements
   - Heartbeats
   - Blood-pressure changes
   - Posture differences

6. (5) Look at the word those in the paragraph. Click on the word or phrase that those refers to.

7. (6) According to the passage, what might an emotionally charged question be about?
   - A birthday
   - One's favorite color
   - A crime
   - The weather

8. (6) It can be inferred from the passage that
   - lies are detected by the test
   - one must be able to analyze reactions to a lie detector test
   - neutral questions need not be asked
   - all physiological reactions indicate lying

9. (7) The following sentence could be added to the paragraph.

   The instrument is not very sophisticated.

   Where would it best fit into the paragraph? Click on the square to add the sentence to the paragraph.

   □ Lie detectors do not detect lies. They record a person's physiological reactions to certain questions. Basically, the instrument records four physiological activities on a moving roll of graph paper. □ Two pens are driven by air-filled tubes placed around a subject's chest and stomach to record breathing movement. Another pen, connected to a blood-pressure cuff on the subject's arm, records each heartbeat and traces changes in blood pressure. The fourth pen is connected to a pair of metal electrodes attached to the fingers of one hand. This pen records changes in the electrical resistance of the skin and can indicate subtle sweating. □ In administering the test, examiners usually ask neutral questions such as birth dates and addresses in order to compare these responses with those from emotionally charged questions. □

10. (3) Look at the word neutral in the paragraph. Click on the word or phrase that is most nearly OPPOSITE the word neutral.

PASSAGE 11 Questions 1–6

The horse of 50 million years ago, called the Dawn Horse, was a little animal the size of a fox terrier. It had four toes on each front foot and three toes on each hind foot. Its toenails were little hooves. When this creature lived, there were no grasslands. Its home was the forest, where it fed on tender shoots and leaves.

There is proof that this little creature was an ancestor of the horse of today. Scientists have excavated fossils of certain animals that lived a few million years after the Dawn Horse. They found that these fossils of bigger animals than the animals of earlier times resembled both the Dawn Horse and the modern-day horse.

The horse family survived when many other animals died out because it had two advantages. The little horse was swift, as we can guess from its slim body and slender legs. It also was fairly intelligent; its skull shows that its brain was large in proportion to its body. (166 words)

1. (2) The Dawn Horse had a total of how many toes?
   - ⬭ 7
   - ⬭ 12
   - ⬭ 14
   - ⬭ 28

2. (2) According to the passage, it is assumed that the Dawn Horse was a fast runner due to its
   - ⬭ brain size
   - ⬭ similarity to the modern-day horse
   - ⬭ trim body and legs
   - ⬭ number of toes

3. (2) According to the passage, what feature of the Dawn Horse enabled the horse family to survive?
   - ⬭ It resembled the fox terrier.
   - ⬭ It ate tender shoots and leaves.
   - ⬭ It was relatively smart.
   - ⬭ It had little hooves for toenails.

4. (6) It can be inferred from the passage that
   - ⬭ three species of horse have existed
   - ⬭ the horse of 50 million years ago has survived
   - ⬭ scientists have found fossils of the Dawn Horse
   - ⬭ horses needed grasslands to survive

5. (6) It can be inferred from the passage that
   - ⬭ many contemporaries of the Dawn Horse are extinct
   - ⬭ many modern animals have 50-million-year-old ancestors
   - ⬭ after a few million years the Dawn Horse was the same size
   - ⬭ the Dawn Horse resembled a fox terrier

6. (2) Click on the drawing that could illustrate a Dawn Horse.

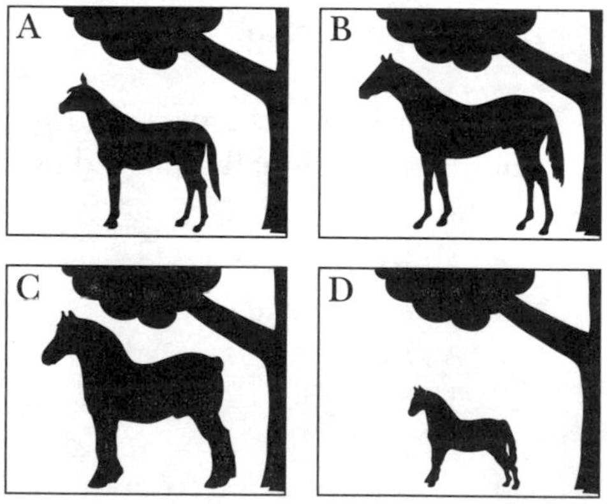

A

B

C

D

PASSAGE 12 Questions 1–9

In the not-too-distant future, instead of spending a vacation by the sea, we may be able to relax in the ocean itself. Once there, we will routinely enter private underwater crafts and zoom off to take a close-up look at the sea's mysteries.

A new creation called a Deep Rover is an acrylic, egg-shaped, underwater craft that is made in one- or two-person models. It can dive to more than half a mile beneath the surface of the sea. One can learn to operate the small sub in just a few hours. No special underwater suit is required. The vessel comes equipped with sensitive robotic arms that enable passengers to interact with the sea's environment.

At a price of $600,000, these devices will probably be out of reach for most people. However, as production increases and prices decrease, more of us should be able to purchase them. (130 words)

1. (1) Which of the following would be the most appropriate title of the passage?
   - ○ The $600,000 Dollar Underwater Suit
   - ○ Equipping the Ocean with Robotic Arms
   - ○ The Deep Rover Enables Underwater Interaction
   - ○ The Mysteries of the Seas

2. (3) Click on the word or phrase in paragraph 2 that describes the shape of the Deep Rover.

3. (2) Click on the sentence in paragraph 2 that indicates the depth to which the Deep Rover is capable of reaching.

4. (2) According to the passage, what is true about sensitive robotic arms?
   - ○ They allow passengers to remain in the sub.
   - ○ They do the diving.
   - ○ The interact with the passengers.
   - ○ They need a special suit.

5. (3) Look at the word vessel in paragraph 2. Click on the word or phrase in the paragraph that is closest in meaning to the word vessel.

6. (4) All of the following are features of the Deep Rover EXCEPT
   - ○ the ability to dive more than one mile beneath the sea
   - ○ two-person models
   - ○ sensitive robotic arms
   - ○ easily operable

7. (4) It is NOT stated in the passage that
   - ○ passengers can interact with the sea
   - ○ a special diving suit is required
   - ○ its operation can be mastered in a few hours
   - ○ it is constructed of man-made materials.

8. (5) Look at the word them in paragraph 3. Click on the word or phrase in the paragraph that them refers to.

9. (6) It can be inferred from the passage that today a purchaser of a Deep Rover would probably be
   - ○ a destitute deep-sea lover
   - ○ an ordinary citizen
   - ○ a wealthy person
   - ○ a vacationer

PASSAGE 13 Questions 1–5

The diets and practices of American Indian tribes were determined by their geographic locations. Corn prevailed as the main food in the East and South, wild rice in the Midwest, buffalo on the plains, acorns on the Pacific coast, fish further north and, in the far North, caribou and seals. Meat, whenever available, was pounded out and dried for preservation; this preparation was called *pemmican*. Another unique product was the maple sugar of the Eastern

Woodlands. For all tribes, the smoking of tobacco or other substances was limited almost entirely to social or religious ceremonies.
(93 words)

1. (1) Which of the following would be the most appropriate title for the passage?
   - ⬭ The Many American Indian Tribes
   - ⬭ How Environments Affected American Indians' Diets
   - ⬭ The Social and Religious Ceremonies of American Indians
   - ⬭ The Dietary Practices of American Indians

2. (3) Look at the word prevailed. The word could best be replaced by
   - ⬭ originated
   - ⬭ dominated
   - ⬭ domesticated
   - ⬭ subsisted

3. (2) According to the passage, which of the following statements is TRUE?
   - ⬭ American Indians never smoked tobacco.
   - ⬭ American Indians grew corn wherever they lived.
   - ⬭ All wooded areas were used for maple sugar production.
   - ⬭ American Indians raised crops suitable to their areas.

4. (6) It can be inferred from the passage that *pemmican*
   - ⬭ ensured food for the winter
   - ⬭ was a salting process
   - ⬭ was frequently done in the Midwest
   - ⬭ enabled the preservation of produce

5. (11) The paragraph following this passage most likely describes
   - ⬭ diets
   - ⬭ *pemmican*
   - ⬭ rituals
   - ⬭ maple sugar

PASSAGE 14 Questions 1–5

When is a 2,000-calorie meal fattening? It depends on what time you eat it. Dr. Franz Halberg, a professor of laboratory medicine and pathology at the University of Minnesota, probed this mystery in a study conducted a few years ago. Each day for a week, he fed six volunteers a single meal, consisting of 2,000 calories, eaten at breakfast time. Then he gave the same participants the identical 2,000-calorie meal as dinner for a week. On the breakfast-only diet, all six people lost weight. But on the dinner regimen, four of the six gained weight. Even the remaining two lost more on the breakfast diet than on the dinner diet. Dr. Halberg's conclusion is that a calorie is not the same at breakfast as it is at dinner.
(128 words)

1. (2) According to the passage, what happened on the dinner only schedule?
   - ⬭ All six people lost weight.
   - ⬭ All six people gained weight.
   - ⬭ Two people's weight stayed the same.
   - ⬭ Two-thirds of the people gained weight.

2. (4) All of the following are true EXCEPT
   - ⬭ a 2,000-meal may or may not be fattening
   - ⬭ this was not conducted this year
   - ⬭ there were 6 volunteers in Dr. Halberg's study
   - ⬭ the participants ate breakfast and dinner for a week

3. (8) The passage supports which of the following conclusions?
   - ⬭ Dr. Halberg has conducted many calorie studies.
   - ⬭ 2,000 calories a day will cause a person to gain weight.
   - ⬭ If you want to lose weight, eat only 2,000 calories a day at breakfast.
   - ⬭ The breakfasts and dinners were different meals of 2,000 calories each.

4. (3) Look at the word regimen in the paragraph. Click on the word or phrase that is closest in meaning to the word regimen .

5. (5) Look at the word it in the paragraph. Click on the word or phrase that it refers to.

PASSAGE 15 Questions 1–7

The railroad proved to be the most viable solution to the great American problem of distance. Rail transportation was fast, reliable, relatively cheap to construct, and useable even in winter. Able to go almost anywhere, even over the mountainous Allegheny barrier, the railroad defied terrain and weather. Early experiments with railroads involved the use of various kinds of power, including wind, dogs, horses, and finally, steam. The first important line was begun by the Baltimore and Ohio Company—significantly, on Independence Day in 1828. At the colorful dedication ceremony, the first stone was laid in Baltimore by Charles Carroll, then age ninety, the only surviving signer of the Declaration of Independence. But the steam locomotive for railroads, truly a declaration of independence from primitive transportation, was not, as commonly supposed, a Yankee invention. It had already been used to a limited extent in England.
(143 words)

1. (1) Which of the following would be the most appropriate title for the passage?
   - ⬭ The American Distance Problem
   - ⬭ The Life and Contribution of Charles Carroll
   - ⬭ The Initiation and Impact of the American Railroad
   - ⬭ Railroads in America and England

2. (3) Look at the phrase defied terrain in the paragraph. Click on the word or phrase that is closest in meaning to the phrase defied terrain .

3. (4) All of the following can be said about the railroad EXCEPT that it was
   - ⬭ quick
   - ⬭ somewhat inexpensive to build
   - ⬭ primitive
   - ⬭ dependable

4. (4) It is NOT stated that early power experiments with railroads included
   - ⬭ steam
   - ⬭ dogs
   - ⬭ oil
   - ⬭ horses

5. (2) According to the passage, what is known about the dedication ceremony for the first line of the Baltimore and Ohio Company?
   - ⬭ It took place through the Allegheny barrier.
   - ⬭ It coincided with America's one hundredth Independence Day.
   - ⬭ It included a survivor of the signing of the Declaration of Independence.
   - ⬭ It occurred in Ohio.

6. (5)Look at the word it in the passage. Click on the word or phrase in the paragraph that it refers to.

7. (8) The passage supports which of the following conclusions?
   - ⬭ Railroads were unreliable in difficult terrain.
   - ⬭ Americans invented the steam locomotive.
   - ⬭ Dogs and horses were necessary for railroad movement.
   - ⬭ The railroad solved America's transport problems.

PASSAGE 16 Questions 1–7

Today's space artists have more to guide them than speculation. The U.S. planetary science program sent orbiters to the moon in the late sixties, and the Mariner and Pioneer flights to Mars and Venus in the seventies. Voyager 1 and Voyager 2, the spacecrafts of the eighties, completed a grand tour of all the planets. The first two decades of planetary exploration yielded a wealth of images still being translated to canvas, including photographs from 1986, when Voyager 2 passed Uranus. The results are incomparably more realistic, and therefore more breathtaking, than the technological imaginings of the forties and fifties. Informed art reveals more than mere fantasy can.
(104 words)

1. (2) According to the passage, how long has the United State been sending orbiter flights?
   - ⬭ Since the middle of the twentieth century
   - ⬭ Since the end of the 1960s
   - ⬭ For three decades
   - ⬭ Since the 1940s

2. (3) Look at the phrase translated to canvas in the passage. The phrase is closest in meaning to
   - ⬭ explained to viewers
   - ⬭ analyzed by artists
   - ⬭ rendered as paintings
   - ⬭ interpreted to painters

3. (2) According to the passage, what happened in the forties and fifties?
   - ⬭ Realistic images of planets were produced.
   - ⬭ The planetary-science program was initiated.
   - ⬭ Space artists didn't depend on speculation.
   - ⬭ Planetary images could only be imagined.

4. (3) Look at the word imaginings in the paragraph. Click on the word that is closest in meaning to the word imaginings.

5. (4) Which of the following is NOT true?
   - ⬭ All of the planets have been photographed.
   - ⬭ Space artists in the fifties used planetary photographs.
   - ⬭ The Voyagers have yielded a wealth of images.
   - ⬭ The Voyager spacecrafts orbited the planets.

6. (7) The following sentence could be added to the passage.

   At that time one could only fantasize about what planets looked like.

   Where would it best fit into the paragraph? Click on the square to add the sentence to the paragraph.

   ☐ Today's space artists have more to guide them than speculation. The U.S. planetary science program sent orbiters to the moon in the late sixties, and the

Mariner and Pioneer flights to Mars and Venus in the seventies. Voyager 1 and Voyager 2, the spacecrafts of the eighties, completed a grand tour of all the planets. The first two decades of planetary exploration yielded a wealth of images still being translated to canvas, including photographs from 1986, when Voyager 2 passed Uranus. ☐ The results are incomparably more realistic, and therefore more breathtaking, that the technological imaginings of the forties and fifties. ☐ Informed art reveals more than mere fantasy can.

7. (9) In what order does the author present the space flights?
   - ⬭ U.S. moon orbiters, Voyager 1, Voyager 2, Mariner
   - ⬭ U.S. moon orbiters, Voyager 1, Mariner, Voyager 2
   - ⬭ U.S. moon orbiters, Mariner, Voyager 1, Voyager 2
   - ⬭ Voyager 2, Mariner, Voyager 1, U.S. moon orbiters

PASSAGE 17 Questions 1–7

When a cold air mass and a warm air mass meet, they form a zone called a front. There are two main types of fronts: cold fronts and warm fronts. In a cold front, the edge of an advancing mass of cold air moves under a mass of warm air. The warm air is forced upward, and the cold air replaces it at ground level. In a warm front, the edge of an advancing mass of warm air moves over a retreating mass of cold air. Warm air replaces the retreating cold air at ground level.

Most changes in the weather occur along fronts. The movement of fronts depends on the formation of pressure systems. Cyclones push fronts along at speeds of 20 to 32 miles (32 to 48 kilometers) per hour. Anticyclones blow into an area after a front has passed.

Cold fronts cause sudden changes in the weather. The kinds of changes depend largely on the amount of moisture in the air that is being replaced. If the air is dry, the front may bring partly cloudy weather but not precipitation. If the air is humid, large clouds may form, bringing rain or snow. The precipitation caused by most cold fronts is heavy but does not last long. Cold fronts also may bring strong winds. The passing of most cold fronts brings a sharp drop in temperature, rapidly clearing skies, and a decrease in humidity.

Warm fronts produce more gradual changes in the weather than do cold fronts. The changes depend chiefly on the humidity of the advancing warm air mass. If the air is dry, wispy clouds may form, and there will be little or no precipitation. If the air is humid, the sky becomes gray. Light, steady rain or snow may fall for several days. In some cases, heavy fog forms. Warm fronts usually have light winds. The passing of a warm front brings a sharp rise in temperature, clearing skies, and an increase in humidity.
(328 words)

1. (1) With what topic is the passage mainly concerned?
   - ⬭ Retreating masses of fronts
   - ⬭ How cyclones and anticyclones are formed
   - ⬭ Causes and effects of cold and warm fronts
   - ⬭ Predicting the weather

2. (2) According to the passage, where do most weather changes occur?
   - ⬭ Under a warm air mass
   - ⬭ At the edge of an advancing mass
   - ⬭ Along fronts
   - ⬭ At ground level

3. (2) Which of the following illustrations best depicts a cold front?

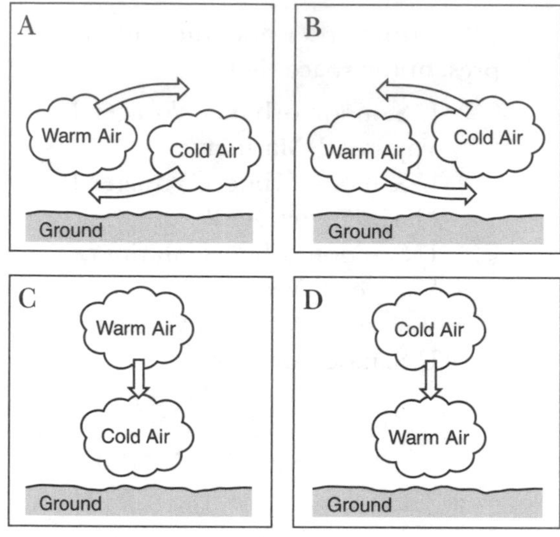

4. (2) Click on the sentence in paragraph 1 or 2 that indicates what precedes the movement of fronts.

5. (1) With what topic is paragraph 3 mainly concerned?
   - ◯ Weather changes due to cold fronts
   - ◯ The changes in weather along fronts
   - ◯ Precipitation caused by cold fronts
   - ◯ The passing of cold fronts

6. (4) A passing cold front brings all of the following EXCEPT
   - ◯ a dramatic decrease in temperature
   - ◯ heavy winds
   - ◯ increased humidity
   - ◯ clearing skies

PASSAGE 18 Questions 1–7

The development of new dyes, machinery, and textiles has greatly affected most areas of fashion, especially clothing. The style of dress has changed frequently in countries that have highly mechanized production systems.

During the 1700s, new dyes made new color combinations possible in clothes. In the late 1700s, the invention of the toothed cotton gin, the power loom, and other machines sped up the production of fabric and yarn. Industrial mass production of clothing began after the development of improved sewing machines during the mid-1800s. The production of many identical garments resulted in a more uniform clothing style for many people. Since that time, the garment industry has influenced the design of new clothing fashions.

In the early 1900s, manufacturers began to make clothing and other products from synthetic fabrics. These have become popular because they are easier to care for and less expensive than some natural fibers. In addition, people began to wear lighter weight clothing in the 1900s, following the development of more efficient heating systems.
(168 words)

1. (1) The passage mainly discusses
   - ◯ the invention of the toothed cotton gin
   - ◯ the changes in clothing in the past 300 years
   - ◯ the fashion industry and synthetic fibers
   - ◯ the development of more efficient heating systems

2. (7) The following sentence could be added to paragraph 2.

   Before that time clothes were primarily black, gray, and white.

   Where would it best fit into the paragraph? Click on the square to add the sentence to the paragraph.

☐ During the 1700s, new dyes made new color combinations possible in clothes. ☐ In the late 1700s, the invention of the toothed cotton gin, the power loom, and other machines sped up the production of fabric and yarn. ☐ Industrial mass production of clothing began after the development of improved sewing machines during the mid-1800s. The production of many identical garments resulted in a more uniform clothing style for many people. ☐ Since that time, the garment industry has influenced the design of new clothing fashions.

3. (3) Look at the word identical in paragraph 2. Click on the word or phrase in the paragraph that is closest in meaning to the word identical.

4. (5) Look at the word these in paragraph 3. Click on the word or phrase in the paragraph that these refers to.

5. (2) According to the passage, why did people begin to wear lighter-weight clothing?
   - ⬭ Because of better-heated homes and offices
   - ⬭ Due to the introduction of synthetic fabrics
   - ⬭ On account of the availability of cheaper clothing
   - ⬭ As a result of the ease in care of these items

6. (9) In what order does the author present the changes in clothing?
   - ⬭ Power loom, synthetic fabrics, improved sewing machine, new dyes
   - ⬭ Synthetic fabrics, improved sewing machine, new dyes, power loom
   - ⬭ New dyes, improved sewing machine, synthetic fabrics, power loom
   - ⬭ New dyes, power loom, improved sewing machine, synthetic fabrics

7. (8) The passage would most likely be assigned reading in a course on
   - ⬭ fashion design
   - ⬭ interior design
   - ⬭ fashion merchandising
   - ⬭ American history

PASSAGE 19 Questions 1–10

During the 1920s, the automobile profoundly changed American patterns of living. Highways significantly shortened the traveling time from cities to rural areas, thereby reducing the isolation of farm life. One farm woman, when asked why her family had an automobile but not indoor plumbing, responded that she couldn't go to town in a bathtub. Trucks allowed farmers to take more products to market more quickly and conveniently than ever before. The spread of gasoline-powered farm vehicles also reduced the need for human farm labor and thus stimulated migration to urban areas.

If the automobile changed rural life, it made an even more profound impact on life in the cities. Cities continued to grow. The 1920 census recorded more Americans living in urban areas than in rural ones for the first time. The automobile freed suburban developments from their dependence on commuter rail lines. Suburbs mushroomed; single-family houses proliferated. From 1922 through 1928, construction began on an average of 883,000 new homes each year. New home construction rivaled the auto as a major driving force behind economic growth.

From 1920 to 1930, the population of Los Angeles County more than doubled, from fewer than 1 million to 2.2 million. Los Angeles became the first large city organized around the auto. By 1925, Los Angeles counted one automobile for every three residents, twice the national average. The auto made it possible for residents to live farther from work than ever before. In the 1920s, Los Angeles developed the lowest urban population density in the United States. By 1930, about 94% of all residences in Los Angeles were single-family homes, an unprecedented figure. Due to the automobile, this young county could spread for miles and miles and not be dependent on apartment dwellings as East Coast cities had been in the previous century. Los Angeles claims title to the first modern supermarket as well as the first large shopping district designed for the automobile.
(322 words)

1. (1) Which of the following would be the most appropriate title for the passage?
   - ○ The Automobile's Impact on American Life in the 1920s
   - ○ The Birth of an American City: Los Angeles, California
   - ○ American Rural Life in the 1920s
   - ○ Commuting to Work, Los Angeles Style

2. (3) Look at the word profoundly in paragraph 1. Click on the word or phrase in the paragraph that is closest in meaning to the word profoundly.

3. (5) Look at the word ones in paragraph 2. Click on the word or phrase in the paragraph that ones refer to.

4. (3) Look at the word mushroomed in paragraph 2. Click on the word or phrase in the paragraph that is closest in meaning to the word mushroomed.

5. (3) Look at the word rivaled in paragraph 2. The word could be replaced by
   - ○ overtook
   - ○ envied
   - ○ competed with
   - ○ fought with

6. (2) According to the passage, when was the first time that more Americans lived in urban areas than in outlying areas?
   - ○ 1920
   - ○ 1925
   - ○ 1928
   - ○ 1930

7. (2) According to the passage, what was the national ratio of automobiles to residents in 1925?
   - ○ 1 to 1.5
   - ○ 1 to 3
   - ○ 1 to 6
   - ○ 3 to 1

8. (4) Which of the following is NOT true about Los Angeles?
   - ○ The first modern supermarket was built there.
   - ○ In 1920, it had the highest urban density in the U.S.
   - ○ It boasts the first shopping area designed for cars.
   - ○ It became the first large city developed around cars.

9. (7) The following sentence could be added to paragraph 3.

   A look at Los Angeles shows the automobile's pervasive impact on urban life.

   Where would it best fit into the paragraph? Click on the square to add the sentence to the paragraph.

   □ From 1920 to 1930, the population of Los Angeles County more than doubled, from fewer than 1 million to 2.2 million. Los Angeles became the first large city organized around the auto. By 1925, Los Angeles counted one automobile for every three residents, twice the national average. ☐ The auto made it possible for residents to live farther from work than ever before. ☐ In the 1920s, Los Angeles developed the lowest urban population density in the United States. By 1930, about 99% of all residences in Los Angeles were single-family homes, an unprecedented figure.

10. (10) Which of the following best describes the tone of the passage?
    - ◯ Angry
    - ◯ Positive
    - ◯ Negative
    - ◯ Amused

PASSAGE 20 Questions 1–8

One way that people can communicate with one another is by manipulating the space between them. People have a very strong sense of personal space that surrounds them and are greatly discomforted when it is invaded. Crowded subway cars, for example, may be experienced as psychologically uncomfortable, and outbreaks of aggression are more likely in crowded situations.

Edward T. Hall studied attitudes toward physical proximity in several cultures. He found that people from different cultures vary in the degree of closeness that they will tolerate from strangers or acquaintances. Americans seem to require more personal space than any other people—a distance of at least 30 to 36 inches, unless the relationship is a very intimate one. American travelers to other countries find that the inhabitants stand almost offensively close. But people in these cultures are apt to consider Americans—who are always backing away when one tries to talk to them—disdainful and rude.

Hall suggests that there are four distinct zones of private space. Intimate Distance is the zone which extends up to 18 inches from the body. It is reserved for people with whom one may have intimate physical contact. Personal Distance is the zone which extends from 18 inches to 4 feet. It is reserved for friends and acquaintances. Some physical intimacy is permitted within this zone, such as putting one's arm around another's shoulder or greeting someone with a hug, but there are limits. Social Distance is the zone which extends from 4 to 12 feet. It is maintained in relatively formal situations, such as job interviews. There is no actual physical contact within this zone. Public Distance is the zone which extends for 12 feet and beyond, and is maintained by people wishing to distinguish themselves from the general public. Speakers addressing an audience, for example, maintain this distance.
(317 words)

1. (1) With what topic is the passage mainly concerned?
    - ◯ Aggression in crowded situations
    - ◯ Cultures that consider Americans to be rude
    - ◯ Varying attitudes about private space
    - ◯ The public distance zone

2. (3) Look at the word manipulating in paragraph 1. The word is closest in meaning to
    - ◯ manhandling
    - ◯ expanding
    - ◯ limiting
    - ◯ maneuvering

3. (3) Look at the word invaded in paragraph 1. The word is closest in meaning to
   - destroyed
   - violated
   - rejected
   - conquered

4. (2) Click on the sentence in paragraph 1 that describes a specific example of what can happen when people feel mentally stressed.

5. (2) According to the passage, what offends Americans when visiting other countries?
   - Those who back away when talking
   - Those who stand too close to them
   - Those who require more personal space
   - Those who are rude

6. (6) It can be inferred from the passage that Americans would feel uncomfortable communicating with a stranger at a distance of
   - 6 inches
   - 30 inches
   - 4 feet
   - 12 feet

7. (2) According to the passage, which kind of distance would someone keep at a company meeting?
   - Intimate
   - Personal
   - Social
   - Public

8. (11) The paragraph preceding this passage most likely describes a paragraph on
   - Edward Hall
   - communication styles
   - subway research
   - cultural diversity

PASSAGE 21 Questions 1–7

As English colonists arrived in the New World, the question of where to settle was of paramount importance. The American Indians' first interactions with English colonists in the Boston area were peaceful ones. As a result, many settlers were attracted to the Boston area due to the open land that could be settled without the threat of Indian raids. William Blackstone, the first white settler, built a cottage on what is now Beacon Hill in the 1620s. In 1630, a group of about 800 Puritans led by John Winthrop founded Charlestown, now part of Boston. Later that year, Winthrop and many of the settlers crossed the Charles River and founded Boston on a peninsula that the Indians called Shawmut. Boston became the capital of Massachusetts Bay Colony in 1632.

Boston began as a tightly-knit village of craftsmen, farmers, and ministers. The settlers had been persecuted in England for their Puritan beliefs. Nevertheless, the town's leaders tried to drive out of Boston any new settlers who did not share their beliefs. Laws forbade the staging of plays and the celebration of Christmas. Because the Puritans considered cooking on Sunday a sin, many Puritan women prepared baked beans every Saturday and served them for Sunday dinner. This custom earned Boston the nickname *Beantown*.

In spite of the Puritans, Boston grew rapidly. By 1720, it was a thriving town with about 12,000 people of various political and religious beliefs. By the mid-1700s, Boston had become a leading commercial, fishing, and shipbuilding center of the American colonies. Wealthy merchants were now the town leaders, and most of the strict Puritan laws were forgotten. (269 words)

1. (1) With what topic is the passage mainly concerned?
   - ⬭ Boston from 1620 to the mid 1700s
   - ⬭ The history of the Puritans
   - ⬭ Shipbuilding in the colonies
   - ⬭ How Boston became the Beantown

2. (3) Look at the word tightly-knit in paragraph 2. The word is closest in meaning to
   - ⬭ related
   - ⬭ united
   - ⬭ mended
   - ⬭ well-constructed

3. (7) The following sentence could be added to paragraph 2.

   According to these leaders, only Puritans could vote or hold public office.

   Where would it best fit into the paragraph? Click on the square to add the sentence to the paragraph.

   ☐ Boston began as a tightly knit village of craftsmen, farmers, and ministers. The settlers had been persecuted in England for their Puritan beliefs. ☐ Nevertheless, the town's leaders tried to drive out of Boston any new settlers who did not share their beliefs. ☐ Laws forbade the staging of plays and the celebration of Christmas. Because the Puritans considered cooking on Sunday a sin, many Puritan women prepared baked beans every Saturday and served them for Sunday dinner. ☐ This custom earned Boston the nickname *Beantown.*

4. (2) Click on the sentence in paragraph 2 or 3 that shows the irony in the Puritans' behavior.

5. (4) Which of the following is NOT true about Boston?
   - ⬭ William Blackstone was its first white settler.
   - ⬭ In 1632, Boston became the capital of Massachusetts Bay Colony.
   - ⬭ By 1720, the Puritans had driven out any settlers who didn't share their beliefs.
   - ⬭ By the mid-1700s, many of the Puritan restrictions had been abandoned.

6. (11) The paragraph following this passage most likely describes
   - ⬭ why Boston's population declined in the late 1700s
   - ⬭ the changing relationship of Bostonians and American Indians
   - ⬭ life in Boston at the end of the eighteenth century
   - ⬭ a description of the abandoned Puritan laws

7. (9) In what order does the author present these occurrences?
   - ⬭ Restriction of Puritan laws, founding of Charlestown, founding of Boston, Boston's becoming a leading fishing center
   - ⬭ Founding of Charlestown, Boston's becoming a leading fishing center, founding of Boston, restriction of Puritan laws
   - ⬭ Boston's becoming a leading fishing center, founding of Charlestown, founding of Boston, restriction of Puritan laws
   - ⬭ Founding of Charlestown, founding of Boston, Boston's becoming a leading fishing center, restriction of Puritan laws

PASSAGE 22 Questions 1–3

The milk snake is a type of kingsnake that farmers once believed took milk from cows. Today, scientists know that no snake is physically able to extract milk from a cow. However, any snake might drink milk from a pail because of water content in the milk. Like other kingsnakes, the milk snake eats lizards and rodents. Milk snakes often go into barnyards to hunt for rodents that nest there. They are valuable to farmers because they eat the mice that lie in and around farm buildings.

There are many subspecies of milk snakes. The best known is the eastern milk snake. The eastern milk snake may be 4 feet long. Some other types of kingsnakes grow to be 6 feet in length. Milk snakes found in the Western and Southern United States have a pattern of rings along the entire length of their body, making them easy to recognize.
(149 words)

1. (1) What is the author's main purpose in writing this passage?
   - ⬭ To contrast milk snakes with other kingsnakes
   - ⬭ To describe the behavior and characteristics of milk snakes
   - ⬭ To scientifically classify snakes and a subspecies, kingsnakes
   - ⬭ To inform farmers of the benefits of milk snakes

2. (2) Click on the sentence in paragraph 1 that explains how milk snakes got their name.

3. (2) According to the passage, why may milk snakes drink milk?
   - ⬭ For its calcium
   - ⬭ For the water
   - ⬭ For its taste
   - ⬭ For the rodents nesting there

4. (2) Click on the drawing that could be a milk snake.

A

B

C

D

PASSAGE 23 Questions 1–4

Until a century or so ago, nearly all social life took place within the context of small primary groups: the family, the church congregation, the schoolhouse, the farm or shop, and the village community. Today the social landscape is dominated by large, impersonal organizations that influence our lives from the moment of birth. Some of these organizations are voluntary, in the sense that people may freely join them or withdraw from them. Examples include religious movements, political parties, and professional associations. Some are mandatory, in the sense that people are required to join them—for example, prisons and rehabilitation centers. Other organizations are utilitarian, in the sense that people enter them for practical reasons: they join business enterprises, for example, in order to earn a living. But whatever organizations we belong to and whatever our reasons for joining them, we spend a good part of our lives within these large, impersonal groups.
(150 words)

1. (1) The passage is about
   - organizations that impact human beings
   - joining business enterprises
   - the changing political landscape
   - withdrawing from religious movements

2. (3) Look at the word voluntary. Click on the word or phrase in the paragraph that is most nearly OPPOSITE the word voluntary.

3. (3) Look at the word utilitarian. Click on the word or phrase in the paragraph that is closest in meaning to the word utilitarian.

4. (4) All of the following are voluntary EXCEPT
   - a church affiliation
   - joining a political party
   - being incarcerated
   - membership in a teaching association

PASSAGE 24 Questions 1–7

Graphology is the study of a person's handwriting to obtain information about his or her personality. Because most scientists classify graphology as a pseudoscience, its practice is limited in the United States. However, many American business firms consult graphologists for advice about which people to hire. At least one American university—the New School for Social Research in New York City—teaches graphology as a serious diagnostic aid.

Some principles of graphology have been found to be true by legitimate scientific researchers. For example, handwriting is affected by illness, old age, and tension. But most of the broader claims of graphology lack scientific proof. For example, graphologists claim that lines slanting upward indicate enthusiasm, and that lines slanting downward indicate discouragement. A few scientific researchers have studied the relationship between handwriting and personality. It is important to distinguish their work from that of most graphologists with whom the public comes into contact. Many of these "graphoanalysis graduates" earned their degrees from schools with no official standing.

Despite the lack of evidence for the claims of graphology, some psychologists consider the study of handwriting a useful diagnostic tool. Several psychology textbooks on projective techniques include discussions of graphology. Such techniques are testing methods that obtain information about a patient's personality without asking direct questions about it.

Many psychologists have called for thorough scientific studies of graphology. However, scientific research indicates that graphology has limited value for the study of character, health, and personality.

(235 words)

1. (1) What is the main topic of the passage?
   - Whether or not to take graphology seriously
   - How to improve your handwriting
   - Writing tips when looking for a job
   - Scientific graphology studies

2. (3) Look at the word diagnostic in paragraph 1. The word could best be replaced by
   - predictive
   - scientific
   - medical
   - practical

3. (4) According to the passage, all of the following affects handwriting EXCEPT
   - disease
   - stress
   - senility
   - occupation

4. (5) Look at the word their in paragraph 2. Click on the word or phrase in the paragraph that their refers to.

5. (3) Look at the word thorough in paragraph 4. This word is closest in meaning to
   - extensive
   - continuous
   - long distance
   - potential

6. (6) It can be inferred from the passage that
   - the number of American universities teaching graphology will increase
   - graphology was more prevalent a century ago than it is today
   - graphology can be studied only at unofficial schools in the U.S.
   - scientists don't consider graphology to be a real science

7. (4) Which of the following is NOT true about graphologists?
   - They can make a hiring recommendation.
   - They look at handwriting to understand a person's personality.
   - They claim to be able to differentiate personality characteristics.
   - They determine a person's illness based on a handwriting sample.

PASSAGE 25 Questions 1–6

The Pueblo Indians are descendants of a people known as the Anasazi. Between 1000 and 1300 A.D., Pueblo culture developed throughout northern Arizona, northern New Mexico, southern Colorado, and southern Utah. By 1300, many Pueblos had moved south to the fertile valleys of the Rio Grande and its branches.

Some Pueblo Indians built villages in the valleys, and others lived in desert and mountain areas. Desert surrounded many of the valleys, and the people set up irrigation systems so they could grow crops. Pueblo women gathered berries and other foods, and the men hunted game.

Pueblo villages consisted of stone or adobe structures that resembled apartment buildings. Some families of grandparents, parents, children, aunts, and uncles lived in two or more connected dwellings.

The villages were governed by religious leaders. The Pueblos held many religious ceremonies to promote harmony and order in the universe. They believed that if harmony and order in the universe were maintained, the spirits would ensure abundant game and provide sufficient rain for their crops. Pueblo men performed kachina dances, in which they represented spirits of the earth, sky, and water. The dancers wore masks that symbolized the spirits. Most pueblos had underground chambers called kivas that were used for ceremonies and meetings.

The Pueblo Indians designed excellent pottery. They also wove beautiful baskets and cotton for their clothing.

(244 words)

1. (5) Look at the word its in paragraph 1. Click on the word or phrase in the paragraph that its refers to.

2. (2) Click on the sentence in paragraph 1 or 2 that explains how farming became possible in areas that weren't fertile.

3. (7) The following sentence could be added to paragraph 2 or 3.

   These homes had as many as four stories, and the Indians used ladders to reach the upper levels.

   Where would it best fit into the paragraph? Click on the square to add the sentence to the paragraph.

   ☐ Some Pueblo Indians built villages in the valleys, and others lived in desert and mountain areas. ☐ Desert surrounded many of the valleys, and the people set up irrigation systems so they could grow crops. Pueblo women gathered berries and other foods, and the men hunted game.

   ☐ Pueblo villages consisted of stone or adobe structures that resembled apartment buildings. ☐ Some families of grandparents, parents, children, aunts, and uncles lived in two or more connected dwellings. ☐

4. (2) Click on the sentence in paragraph 2 or 3 that indicates who lived with Pueblos in their connected homes.

5. (3) Look at the word promote in paragraph 4. This word is closest in meaning to

   - ○ advance
   - ○ suggest
   - ○ advertise
   - ○ idealize

6. (4) All of the following are TRUE about Pueblos EXCEPT

   - ○ they made excellent pottery
   - ○ they had underground chambers for ceremonies
   - ○ their women performed kachina dances
   - ○ their men hunted game

PASSAGE 26 Questions 1–7

During the 1850s and 1860s, many people began to experiment with the artistic possibilities of photography. Landscapes and architecture were popular subjects for early art photographers. In these two decades, a number of governments commissioned photographers to make visual records of important buildings and natural features in various countries. Photographs were taken of the scenery in the American West as well as many other major landmarks. Some of these pictures were remarkable not only for their technical excellence but also for the effort involved in taking them.

Some of the most dramatic photographs of the mid-1800s are battlefield scenes. The photos of the American Civil War (1861–1865) made by Mathew Brady and his assistants rank among the finest war pictures of all time.

In 1888, George Eastman, an American manufacturer, introduced the Kodak box camera. The Kodak was the first camera designed specifically for mass production and amateur use. It was lightweight, inexpensive, and easy to operate. With this invention, picture taking became a favorite pastime.

The Kodak system also eliminated the need for photographers to process their own pictures. The Kodak used a roll of gelatin-coated film that could record 100 round photographs. The plant developed the film, made prints, and then returned the camera loaded with a new roll of film. The Kodak slogan declared, "You Press the Button, We Do the Rest."
(225 words)

1. (2) Click on the phrase in paragraph 1 that indicates what the first photographers enjoyed taking pictures of.

2. (4) Which of the following is NOT a subject of commissioned photographs?
   - Important buildings
   - Landmarks
   - Famous people
   - Scenery

3. (3) Look at the word dramatic in paragraph 2. The word could best be replaced by
   - theatrical
   - striking
   - exaggerated
   - tragic

4. (2) According to the passage, who was Mathew Brady?
   - A historian
   - A photographer
   - A Civil War hero
   - A Kodak employee

5. (3) Look at the word eliminated in paragraph 4. The word is closest in meaning to
   - removed
   - heightened
   - prompted
   - pinpointed

6. (5) Look at the word their in paragraph 4. Click on the word or phrase in the paragraph that their refers to.

7. (7) The following sentence could be added to paragraph 3 or 4.

   After a roll had been used, a person sent the camera with the film inside to one of Eastman's processing plants.

   Where would it best fit into the text? Click on the square to add the sentence to the paragraph.

   In 1888, George Eastman, an American manufacturer, introduced the Kodak box camera. □ The Kodak was the first camera designed specifically for mass production and amateur use. □ It was lightweight, inexpensive, and easy to operate. □ With this invention, picture taking became a favorite pastime.

   The Kodak system also eliminated the need for photographers to process their own pictures. The Kodak used a roll of gelatin-coated film that could record 100 round photographs. □ The plant developed the film, made prints, and then returned the camera loaded with a new roll of film. □ The Kodak slogan declared, "You Press the Button, We Do the Rest." □

PASSAGE 27 Questions 1–7

Families moving to Oregon or California in the late 1840s had one main rule on the long journey west: Keep moving. They stopped for a day or two at such places as Fort Laramie or Fort Bridger in Wyoming to repair equipment and supplies. But usually the wagons halted only at noon and at nightfall. By keeping on the move, a wagon train could travel 15 or 20 miles (24 or 32 kilometers) a day. If the oxen hauling the wagons became exhausted, they were shot or simply left to die where they fell. They were replaced by animals herded behind the wagon train.

The "keep moving" rule killed many animals, but it saved many human lives. Almost all westward journeys started in spring. A spring departure gave the settlers time—if they kept moving—to get through the western mountains before the snow blocked the passes.

As long as the pioneers of the 1840s kept moving westward, the Plains Indians allowed them to pass through their hunting grounds. Some tribes guided the early pioneers, or

helped them at difficult river crossings. The Indians even supplied some wagon trains with vegetables and buffalo meat in exchange for tobacco, whiskey, or pieces of iron.
(200 words)

1. (1) With what topic is paragraph 1 mainly concerned?
   - ◯ Stopping for repairs and supplies on the move west
   - ◯ Shooting the exhausted oxen
   - ◯ The wagon train routine of the late 1840s
   - ◯ Wagon train mileage

2. (3) Look at the word halted in paragraph 1. Click on the word or phrase in the paragraph that is closest in meaning to the word halted.

3. (5) Look at the word they in paragraph 1. Click on the word or phrase in the paragraph that they refers to.

4. (5) Look at the word it in paragraph 2. Click on the word or phrase in the paragraph that it refers to.

5. (3) Look at the phrase as long as in paragraph 3. The phrase could best be replaced by
   - ◯ provided that
   - ◯ since
   - ◯ during the time
   - ◯ because

6. (5) Look at the word their in paragraph 3. Click on the word or phrase in the paragraph that their refers to.

7. (4) Which of the following is NOT true about the wagon train experience?
   - ◯ Spring departures were commonplace.
   - ◯ The wagon train stopped twice daily.
   - ◯ The Indians traded with the pioneers.
   - ◯ Oxen were buried in Indian hunting grounds.

PASSAGE 28 Questions 1–6

The greatest popular hero of the 1920s was neither an athlete nor an actor but a small-town airmail pilot named Charles Lindbergh. In 1919, a New York City hotel owner named Raymond Orteig offered $25,000 to the first aviator to fly nonstop from New York to Paris. Several pilots were killed or injured while competing for the prize. By 1927, it had still not been won. Lindbergh believed he could win if he had the right airplane. He persuaded nine St. Louis businessmen to help him finance the cost of a plane. Lindbergh then chose the Ryan Aeronautical Company of San Diego to manufacture a special plane, which he helped design. He named the plane the *Spirit of St. Louis.* On May 10–11, Lindbergh tested the plane by flying from San Diego to New York City, with an overnight stop in St. Louis. The flight took 20 hours, 21 minutes, a transcontinental record.

On May 20, Lindbergh took off in the *Spirit of St. Louis* from Roosevelt Field, near New York City, at 7:52 A.M. He landed at Le Bourget Field, near Paris, on May 21, at 10:21 P.M. after 33½ sleepless hours. In Paris, 100,000 people streamed onto the landing field to greet him. Lindbergh earned the $25,000 and the adoration of crowds on both sides of the Atlantic.

Lindbergh's heroic flight thrilled people throughout the world. He was honored with awards, celebrations, and parades. President Calvin Coolidge gave Lindbergh the Congressional Medal of Honor and the first Distinguished Flying Cross in American history.
(256 words)

1. (1) What does the article mainly discuss?
   - Heroes of the 1920s
   - The aviation accomplishments of Charles Lindbergh
   - The amazing *Spirit of St. Louis*
   - Charles Lindbergh's receiving medals from the president

2. (3) Look at the word pilot in paragraph 1. Click on the word or phrase in the paragraph that is closest in meaning to the word pilot.

3. (5) Look at the word it in paragraph 1. Click on the word or phrase in the paragraph that it refers to.

4. (2) According to the passage, what was Lindbergh's transatlantic record?
   - 10 hours, 21 minutes
   - 10–11 hours
   - 20 hours, 21 minutes
   - 33½ hours

5. (4) All of the following are true about Lindbergh EXCEPT
   - He was the first pilot to attempt a nonstop flight from New York to Paris.
   - Nine St. Louis businessmen helped him finance the cost.
   - He left from New York City on his transatlantic flight.
   - He took a transcontinental flight in preparation for his New York to Paris one.

6. (4) Which of the following is NOT mentioned as something with which Lindbergh was honored?
   - awards
   - a Congressional seat
   - parades
   - the Distinguished Flying Cross

PASSAGE 29 Questions 1–12

Several nineteenth-century inventions made printing newspapers enormously cheaper and faster. One was the invention of the linotype machine (1866), which cast rows of type directly from molten metal as needed. The other was the web press (1871), which printed simultaneously on both sides of paper. At the same time, the invention of telegraph and transoceanic cables increased the potential sources of news. Press associations like the New York Associated Press expanded greatly, and the first newspaper chains began to develop. For the first time, publishers could reach a mass audience. The first mass publisher, Joseph Pulitzer, bought the New York *World* in 1883; by the end of the century, the *World* had sold over one million copies. Another successful publisher, William Randolph Hearst, published the New York *Journal* in 1895, quickly transforming it into a sensationalistic paper.

Presenting news and features with an eye to gaining readers was the primary goal of publishers such as Pulitzer and Hearst. Catering to the public taste for lurid and intimate subject matter, they began to exploit society stories and to report scandals and murders. Reporters were encouraged to compete for scoops. Sensational headlines, colored print, pictures, and cartoons became attention-getting features of newspapers.

News articles were also geared toward mass consumption. Editors launched crusades—sometimes sincerely, but more often with an eye to sales. Muckraking campaigns—exposés of corruption and misconduct—were also launched against political bosses, trusts, bankers, and so forth. War was good press, and the threat of war was even better, so news stories became patriotic, and papers made a possible war daily fare.

Features, too, were exploited to the full, and new items began to appear, such as comic strips and columnists, household hints for wives, advice for the lovelorn, sentimental verse,

and simple short stories. Advertisements spreading over two columns broke the monotony of the page and provided revenue. Publishers also used big names to gain readers, using the promise of large salaries to attract writers of the caliber of Stephen Crane, Richard Harding Davis, and Mark Twain to work for them.
(341 words)

1. (1) What does the article mainly discuss?
   - ○ Big name authors writing for newspapers
   - ○ The evolution of newspapers
   - ○ Catering to the public taste
   - ○ The linotype machine

2. (3) Look at the word chains in paragraph 1. The word is closest in meaning to
   - ○ bonds
   - ○ restraints
   - ○ associations
   - ○ irons

3. (2) According to the passage, a sensationalistic paper
   - ○ contains many news articles
   - ○ needs to be mass produced
   - ○ responds to the public's interest in scandal
   - ○ was the first introduced in the late eighteenth century

4. (5) Look at the word they in paragraph 2. Click on the word or phrase in the paragraph that they refers to.

5. (3) Look at the word scoops in paragraph 2. The word is closest in meaning to
   - ○ excavations
   - ○ exclusive reports
   - ○ hand shovels
   - ○ color pictures and cartoons

6. (4) Which of the following is NOT mentioned at an attention-getting feature in paragraph two?
   - ○ News articles
   - ○ Cartoons
   - ○ Pictures
   - ○ Colors

7. (3) Click on the word or phrase in paragraph 3 that defines muckraking.

8. (3) Click on the word or phrase in paragraph 2 or 3 that is closest in meaning to the word crusades.

9. (3) Look at the word fare in paragraph 3. The word is closest in meaning to
   - ○ travel
   - ○ fees
   - ○ battles
   - ○ obligatory reading

10. (6) It can be inferred from the passage that new items in the newspapers appeared because of income from
    - ○ comic strips
    - ○ writers of the caliber of Steven Crane
    - ○ the increase in two-column advertisements
    - ○ fully-exploited feature stories

11. (2) Why does the author mention Mark Twain?
    - ○ To compare sensational reporting and fictional prose
    - ○ To show that famous writers wrote for papers
    - ○ To emphasize that well-known authors needed readership
    - ○ To illustrate his large salary

12. (7) The following sentence could be added to paragraph 4.

    Whereas in earlier days a reader could get through a newspaper quite rapidly, paid advertising in newspapers made the dailies significantly heftier.

    Where would it best fit into the paragraph? Click on the square to add the sentence to the paragraph.

Features, too, were exploited to the full, and new items began to appear, such as comic strips and columnists, household hints for wives, advice for the lovelorn, sentimental verse, and simple short stories. ☐ Advertisements spreading over two columns broke the monotony of the page and provided revenue. ☐ Publishers also used big names to gain readers, using the promise of large salaries to attract writers of the caliber of Stephen Crane, Richard Harding Davis, and Mark Twain to work for them. ☐

PASSAGE 30 Questions 1–10

Walt Whitman is one of the most famous American poets. His *Leaves of Grass,* a collection of poems, is considered some of the greatest lyric poetry written in English. Whitman was born in Long Island, New York, in 1819, and grew up in Brooklyn in New York City. He loved the city, especially for the cultural opportunities it afforded him. These experiences were the bedrock for Whitman's future poetic vision of an ideal society based on a foundation of fulfilled men and women.

Whitman may have started work on *Leaves of Grass* as early as 1848. The form and content of the work was so unusual for its time that he could not find a publisher, so he published a first edition at his own expense in 1855. Between 1856 and 1892, he published eight more revised and expanded editions of the collection. Whitman wrote these poems and most of his other poems in innovative free verse reminiscent of the poetry of the Old Testament and such sacred writings of India as the *Bhagavad Gita,* which Whitman may have read in translation.

Prior to the outbreak of the Civil War, the U.S. was torn by sectional discord on social, economic, and political matters. The boundless enthusiasm of the young democracy was replaced by cynicism. Whitman spent the turbulent time before the war and just after it started barely eking out a living as a newspaper editor. Coupled with his financial difficulties was the realization that *Leaves of Grass* had not achieved the success he had envisioned. Then, in 1862, his brother George, a Union soldier, was declared missing. Whitman left Brooklyn to search the military hospitals of Washington for his brother. The condition of the wounded in the military hospitals appalled him. In response, Whitman wrote poetry expressing sympathy for the suffering of both the Union and Confederate soldiers. In 1865, at the war's end, he published a small volume of his wartime poems.

After the war, Whitman lived in Washington. His poetry slowly came to be appreciated, though there continued to be those who did not like Whitman's vulgar language and what they saw as Whitman's combination of earthy details and mystical pronouncements. Whitman died in New Jersey in 1892, the year the final edition of *Leaves of Grass* was published.
(382 words)

1. (1) Which of the following would be the most appropriate title for the passage?
   - ⬭ Walt Whitman: Poet and Humanitarian
   - ⬭ The Chronicler of the Civil War
   - ⬭ Brooklyn Boy Fulfills His Dream
   - ⬭ The Old Testament Poet of the 1800s

2. (3) Look at the word afforded in paragraph 1. The word is closest in meaning to
   - ⬭ cost
   - ⬭ provided
   - ⬭ forced
   - ⬭ denied

3. (2) Click on the paragraph that discusses works which may have had an influence on Whitman's style.

4. (2) Click on the sentence in paragraph 2 which discusses Whitman's reasons for self-publishing his poetry.

5. (7) The following sentence could be added to paragraph 2.

   Other poetry was not the only influence on his work; the rhythm of Whitman's poems suggests the rise and fall of the sea that he so loved.

   Where would it best fit into the paragraph? Click on the square to add the sentence to the paragraph.

   ☐ Whitman may have started work on *Leaves of Grass* as early as 1848. ☐ The form and content of the work was so unusual for its time that he could not find a publisher, so he published a first edition at his own expense in 1855. ☐ Between 1856 and 1892, he published eight more revised and expanded editions of the collection. Whitman wrote these poems and most of his other poems in innovative free verse reminiscent of the poetry of the Old Testament and such sacred writings of India as the *Bhagavad Gita,* which Whitman may have read in translation. ☐

6. (3) Look at the word enthusiasm in paragraph 3. Click on the word or phrase in the paragraph that is most nearly OPPOSITE the word enthusiasm.

7. (3) Look at the word turbulent in paragraph 3. The word is closest in meaning to
   - ◯ calm
   - ◯ exciting
   - ◯ chaotic
   - ◯ sad

8. (3) The phrase eking out a living in paragraph 3 is closest in meaning to
   - ◯ prospering
   - ◯ surviving
   - ◯ flourishing
   - ◯ getting to the top

9. (6) It can be inferred from the passage that Whitman
   - ◯ was ambitious and on the move
   - ◯ wrote only war poems after the Civil War
   - ◯ appreciated the suffering of both Northern and Southern soldiers
   - ◯ was being rapidly promoted from one position to another

10. (10) In paragraph 4, the author
    - ◯ shares the opinion of the public
    - ◯ criticizes Whitman for his vulgar language
    - ◯ supports those who criticized Whitman
    - ◯ explains why some disliked Whitman

READING POST-TEST

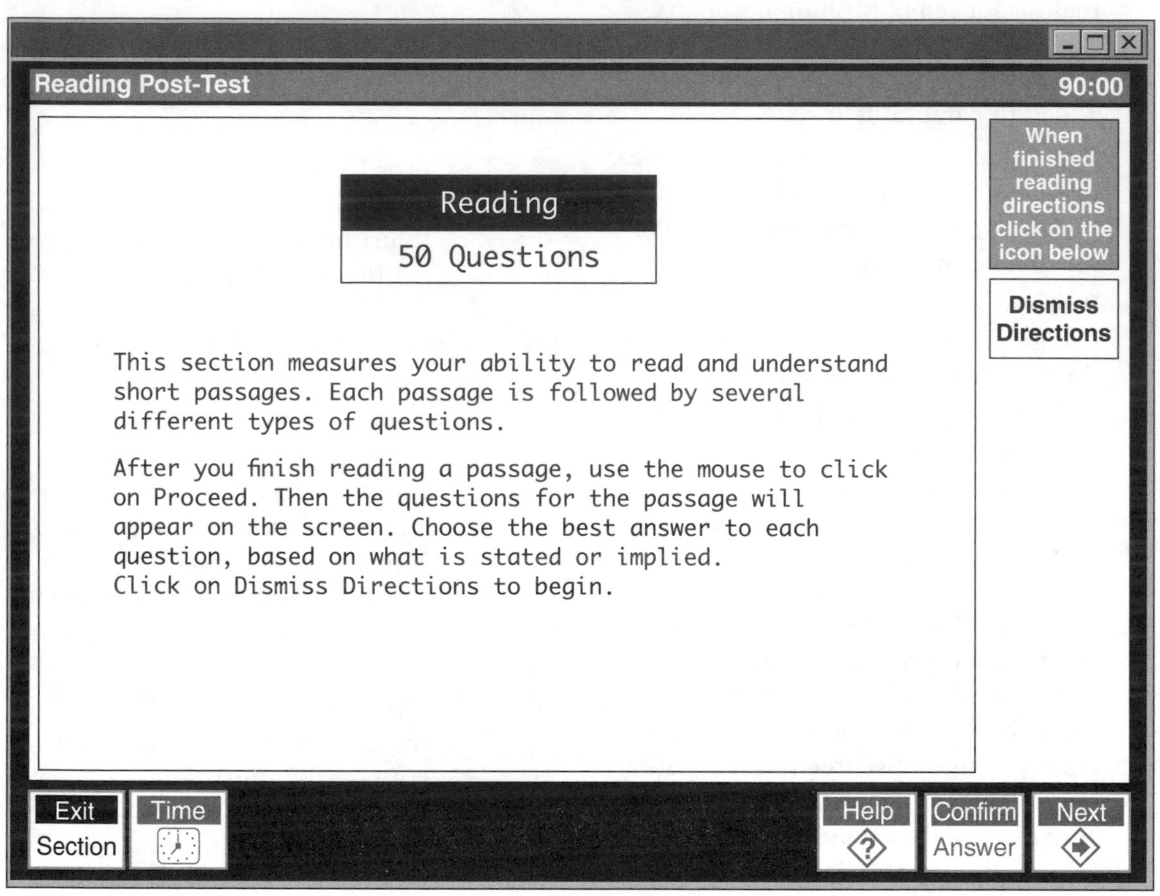

PASSAGE 1 Questions 1–12

The American game of football traces its inception to a game that resembled soccer and was played in the eastern United States around 1850. Instead of kicking a round ball into a net as is done in today's soccer games, players kicked the ball across the opposing team's goal line. Those soccer teams of the mid-1800s had 30 or more players on the field at one time; nowadays, both soccer and football teams compete with only 11 players.

As this soccerlike game became more and more popular, stricter rules were instituted, and colleges established teams. The first college game was played on November 6, 1869, in New Brunswick, New Jersey. Rutgers beat the College of New Jersey, now Princeton University, by a score of 6–4. The first game most closely resembling modern-day football took place in 1874 in Cambridge, Massachusetts, between Harvard University and a visiting team from McGill University, located in Montreal, Canada. The Canadians preferred to play rugby, an English game that allows running while holding the ball and tackling opposing players. The Harvard team wanted to play its game of soccer, advancing the ball primarily by kicking. The teams reached a compromise; they would play two games, the first using Harvard's rules and the next following McGill's rules. Harvard enjoyed McGill's game so much that the university presented it to other Eastern schools.

The new U.S. game, with its rugby-like modifications, gained acceptance. Running while holding the ball and tackling became as integral to the game as kicking. The Eastern colleges soon began to alter and improve the modified soccer game, which by then had been re-named football. One of the first football players, Walter Camp, became a pivotal force in updating the game. Under his tutelage in the 1880s, official rules—intended to increase the action and competitive nature of the game—were established. He was the primary architect of the four down system, the yardage needed to make a first down, and the center snap to the quarterback. He and Caspar Whitney, a sportswriter, initiated the tradition of selecting an all-American team, honoring the country's most outstanding college players.

More and more colleges began playing football, and football then spread beyond the East Coast. The number of players increased even more when towns formed their own teams consisting of young men who didn't attend high school or college. Rivalries between teams from different colleges, high schools, and towns continue to this day.

1. With what topic is the passage mainly concerned?
   - ◯ The origins of American football
   - ◯ The similarities and differences between soccer and football
   - ◯ Rugby's contribution to football
   - ◯ Football rules and regulations

2. Look at the word instituted in paragraph 2. The phrase is closest in meaning to
   - ◯ petitioned
   - ◯ abandoned
   - ◯ raised
   - ◯ adopted

3. Look at the word its in paragraph 2. Click on the word or phrase in the paragraph that its refers to.

4. Click on the sentence in paragraph 2 that describes the arrangement the two teams made.

5. The following sentence could be added to paragraph 3 or 4.

   As football gained in popularity in the 1880s, teams popped up in towns all over the country.

   Where would it best fit into the paragraph? Click on the square to add the sentence to the paragraph.

☐ Under his tutelage in the 1880s, official rules—intended to increase the action and competitive nature of the game—were established. ☐ He was the primary architect of the four down system, the yardage needed to make a first down, and the center snap to the quarterback. ☐ He and Caspar Whitney, a sportswriter, initiated the tradition of selecting an all-American team, honoring the country's most outstanding college players.

☐ More and more colleges began playing football, and football then spread beyond the East Coast. ☐ The number of players increased even more when towns formed their own teams consisting of young men who didn't attend high school or college. Rivalries between teams from different colleges, high schools, and towns continue to this day.

6. Look at the word architect in paragraph 3. The word is closest in meaning to
   - ⬭ builder
   - ⬭ designer
   - ⬭ principal
   - ⬭ referee

7. According to the passage, in what way does American football differ from soccer?
   - ⬭ Players run with the ball.
   - ⬭ Players advance the ball mainly by kicking it.
   - ⬭ An all-American team is selected.
   - ⬭ It is played in high schools.

8. Look at the word rivalries in paragraph 4. The word is closest in meaning to
   - ⬭ associations
   - ⬭ competitions
   - ⬭ leagues
   - ⬭ fellowships

9. According to the passage, all of the following are true EXCEPT
   - ⬭ in the 1800s, Canadians preferred rugby to soccer
   - ⬭ Walter Camp contributed changes to the game
   - ⬭ an all-American football team was selected in 1874
   - ⬭ high school and town teams played football in the 1880s

10. It can be inferred from the passage that
    - ⬭ eastern colleges were the first in the U.S. to play American football
    - ⬭ football teams always had a quarterback
    - ⬭ the Harvard-McGill football game is played annually
    - ⬭ Rutgers University was originally called the College of New Jersey

11. Click on the paragraph in which the author explains when the game got its name of "football."

12. The paragraph following this passage most likely describes
    - ⬭ a comparison between soccer and football
    - ⬭ how the game of football is played today
    - ⬭ the integration of sports into American college life
    - ⬭ scoring procedures for football games

PASSAGE 2 Questions 13–24

New methods of communication, brought about chiefly by the invention of the printing press, enabled people in fifteenth-century Europe to receive information about local and world events. For colonists starting their new lives in North America in the 1600s, however, exchanging information was more difficult. In the absence of the printed news sheets common in much of Europe, the colonists exchanged news mainly by word of mouth. A peddler or a ship captain would tell someone in Boston about something he had heard in Philadelphia. The Bostonian would then share the story with his friends and neighbors. Travelers helped spread news as well by delivering letters from family members living in different areas.

The first colonial mail deliverers, called postriders, also made it possible for people to learn about events taking place outside their immediate community. These men on horseback carried letters or messages while traveling along so-called post roads. On the way, the post-rider would hear news and share it with people he met at stopping places such as post offices and taverns. The early colonists also relied on the town crier. This "walking newspaper" stood at every corner. He read out the latest news and notified the citizens about town meetings and other future events.

During this colonial period (1607–1775), mail service operated sporadically. Until 1700, only Massachusetts, New York, and Pennsylvania had official service. In 1753, Benjamin Franklin of Pennsylvania was appointed Deputy Postmaster General to supervise the colonial postal service. Under his leadership, post offices were set up in all thirteen colonies, and there was a substantial improvement in overall service.

The next development in colonial news distribution was the newspaper. The first successful American newspaper, *The Boston News-Letter,* started publication in 1704. Newspapers came into general use after the mid-1700s, at which time the town crier largely disappeared. Newspapers in the United States multiplied significantly in the 1800s. By 1830, the country produced about one thousand papers, which focused mainly on business or political news. However, at the cost of about six cents each, a daily paper was not within a working-person's budget. The average daily wage in Philadelphia in 1830 for an artisan was $1.75 and for a laborer $1.50. In 1833, Benjamin H. Day started the *New York Sun,* the first successful penny newspaper. Its affordable price, coupled with interest stories such as crimes and weddings, spawned numerous others low-cost newspapers.

13. What is the main topic of this passage?
    - ◯ Not many people could afford newspapers in 1830.
    - ◯ Town criers were the newspapers of their day.
    - ◯ Benjamin Franklin spearheaded the colonial postal service.
    - ◯ News distribution developed rapidly throughout the colonial period.

14. It can be inferred from the passage that
    - ◯ Europeans shipped newspapers to their colonial relatives
    - ◯ colonial Americans had numerous ship captains and peddlers
    - ◯ printing presses were not operating in colonial America in the 1600s
    - ◯ citizens in Philadelphia and Boston communicated regularly

15. Click on the sentences in paragraph 2 that indicate how people would find out the schedule of community happenings.

16. Look at the word sporadically in paragraph 3. The word is closest in meaning to
    - ◯ surprisingly
    - ◯ with great difficulty

- intermittently
- regionally

17. According to the passage, where did regular mail delivery occur until 1700?
    - In all thirteen colonies
    - In Massachusetts, New York, and Pennsylvania
    - In Pennsylvania and Virginia
    - In Boston and Virginia

18. The following sentence could be added to paragraph 3.

    Franklin, an inventor and businessman, had been the postmaster of Philadelphia.

    Where would it best fit into the paragraph? Click on the square to add the sentence to the paragraph.

    □ During this colonial period (1607–1775), mail service operated sporadically. □ Until 1700, only Massachusetts, New York, and Pennsylvania had official service. □ In 1753, Benjamin Franklin of Pennsylvania was appointed Deputy Postmaster General to supervise the colonial postal service. □ Under his leadership, post offices were set up in all thirteen colonies, and there was a substantial improvement in overall service. □

19. In which year could someone buy a newspaper for a penny?
    - 1704
    - 1753
    - 1830
    - 1833

20. Look at the word each in paragraph 4. Click on the word or phrase in the paragraph that each refers to.

21. It can be inferred from the passage that
    - lowering the cost of newspapers increased revenues
    - ship captains and peddlers were wealthy individuals
    - Benjamin Franklin remained in the postal service for the rest of his life
    - working class people bought many newspapers in 1830

22. It is NOT stated in the passage that
    - the *New York Sun* cost one penny
    - travelers were among the first mail carriers in colonial times
    - town criers announced the news throughout the 1700s
    - the first successful newspaper was *The Boston News-Letter*

23. Look at the word spawned in paragraph 4. Click on the word or phrase in the paragraph that closest in meaning to the word spawned.

24. It can be inferred from the passage that
    - Benjamin H. Day started many successful newspapers
    - before Franklin became Deputy Postmaster General, mail delivery was unreliable
    - peddlers and ship captains attended town meetings
    - some laborers complained that artisans earned more money than they did

PASSAGE 3 Questions 25–36

The "dog days of summer" are periods of exceptionally hot and muggy weather that occur in July and August in the North Temperate Zone, the part of the earth's surface between the Tropic of Cancer and the Arctic Circle. The origin of the phrase describing these stifling, humid days is found in the stars.

Many centuries ago, when artificial lights and pollution did not obscure the night sky, people in different areas around the world would look into the night sky and see a group of stars; then they would connect the dots. Each civilization saw different images depending on its own culture and beliefs. The Native Americans, for example, saw pictures that were different from those seen in Asia or South America. The Big Dipper, probably the most recognizable star pattern in the sky, is not seen as a dipper in France; to the French, it is a saucepan. To the ancient Maya, it was a mythological parrot named Seven Macaw. Over 2,000 years ago, Greek astronomers saw the same patterns in the Northern sky as we see today. They named the star patterns, or constellations, after animals, mythological creatures, and gods familiar to them. The bears they saw are now called Ursa Major and Ursa Minor. The twins are known as Gemini, and the bull we know as Taurus. There are many others, including the dogs, Canis Major and Canis Minor. The brightest of the stars in the big dog, Canis Major, is Sirius. Sirius is the brightest star in the night sky.

During the summer season, the dog star Sirius rises and sets with the sun. In late July, Sirius is aligned with the sun. Therefore, the ancient Romans, Greeks, and Egyptians mistakenly assumed that Sirius's heat intensified the heat of the sun, causing hotter days on Earth. They named this hot stretch—from 20 days before and after the alignment—"the dog days." These ancient civilizations' belief that dogs were subject to spells of madness during this period may also have inspired the term. Many people became sluggish at this time of year, and the ancients blamed Sirius for their discomfort.

It is easy to understand why the ancients felt it necessary to seek out a "scientific" explanation for extreme weather. We now know, however, that the heat during the warmest period of the summer is not caused by additional radiation from the dog star.

25. The passage mainly discusses
   - ○ how the expression "dog days" originated
   - ○ the astronomical reasons for hot summer days
   - ○ how the study of astronomy developed
   - ○ why each civilization perceives star formations differently

26. Look at the word muggy in paragraph 1. Click on the word or phrase in the paragraph that is closest in meaning to the word muggy.

27. Look at the word its in paragraph 2. Click on the word or phrase in the paragraph that its refers to.

28. Click on the name in paragraph 2 of the constellation most people can identify.

29. The following sentence could be added to paragraph 3 or 4.

Actually, it is the earth's tilt toward the sun in the summer months that causes the heat.

Where would it best fit into the paragraph? Click on the square to add the sentence to the paragraph.

☐ They named this hot stretch—from 20 days before and after the alignment—"the dog days." ☐ These ancient civilizations' belief that dogs were subject to spells of madness during this period may also have inspired the term. Many people became sluggish at this time of year, and the ancients blamed Sirius for their discomfort.

☐ It is easy to understand why the ancients felt it necessary to seek out a "scientific" explanation for extreme weather. We now know, however, that the heat during the warmest period of the summer is not caused by additional radiation from the dog star. ☐

31. Look at the word they in paragraph 3. Click on the word or phrase in the paragraph that they refers to.

32. Look at the word stretch in paragraph 3. The word is closest in meaning to
    - pull of elasticity
    - a last stage of the process
    - finish line
    - continuous period

33. It can be inferred from the passage that
    - all countries experience summer "dog days"
    - every culture saw a star constellation in the shape of a dog
    - it is now more difficult to see star formations than in ancient times
    - the brightness of a star increases the heat it transmits

34. It is stated in the passage that
    - Native Americans originated the term "dog days"
    - the term "dog days" could be attributed to dogs' summertime behavior
    - pollution was a problem many centuries ago
    - ancient Greek astronomers named a constellation after a parrot

35. Click on the sentence in paragraph 3 that describes why it was thought the earth is hotter in summer.

36. Click on the drawing that could be the star formation Canis Major.

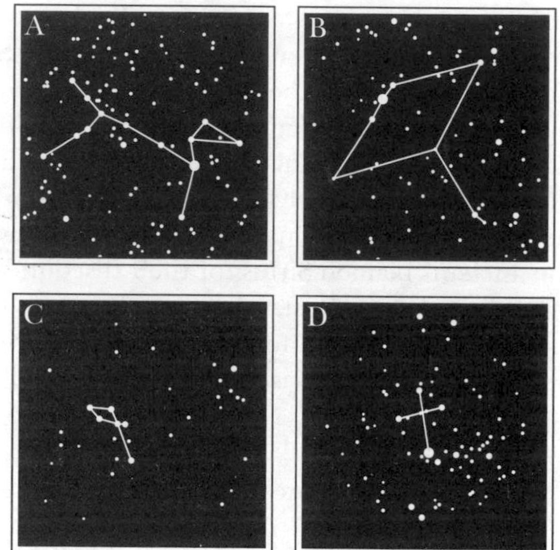

PASSAGE 4 Questions 37–50

Langston Hughes (1902–1967), the African-American poet, novelist, columnist, playwright, screenwriter, and essayist, was recognized as a great talent at an early age. Teachers and classmates marveled at Hughes's voice even when Hughes was only a teenager. Hughes's father, however, encouraged him to pursue a more practical career and agreed to pay his tuition to Columbia University in New York City if Hughes agreed to study engineering.

Hughes stayed at Columbia for only a year; meanwhile, he found Harlem, a primarily African-American neighborhood. He soon became a vital member of the Harlem arts scene. Hughes's literary work symbolizes the vitality of the Harlem Renaissance, the African-American artistic movement in the 1920s that celebrated black life and culture. Because Hughes wrote prolifically of this era, we know a great deal about it and its artists.

After traveling abroad to Africa in the 1920s, Hughes experimented with rhythmic free verse. He began using African rhythms in his poetry, mixing them with those of American blues and jazz. Due to this syncopation, his poetry differed from that of other writers. Although he has been labeled "a Harlem Renaissance poet," his fame spans more than this decade and this genre.

In 1926, Hughes returned to college, but this time he chose a black college, Lincoln University in Pennsylvania. While at Lincoln, he met a benefactor who encouraged him to write his first novel. *Not Without Laughter* was published one year after his 1929 graduation. After its publication, he continued writing poetry and began a long association with the theater. In the 1940s, he began writing a column for the African-American newspaper, *The Chicago Defender,* where he introduced his readers to a lovable and enduring character named Simple, derived from a conversation Hughes had had with a man in a Harlem bar.

Hughes never felt financially secure even though he did support himself from writing. In 1947, however, after writing lyrics for the Broadway musical "Street Scene," Hughes earned enough money to buy a house in Harlem. He continued to write; *Montage of a Dream Deferred,* one of his best-known volumes of poetry, was published in 1951. From that time until his death sixteen years later, he wrote more than twenty additional works, including plays, an autobiography, articles, scripts, and novels.

37. Which of the following would be the most appropriate title for the passage?
    - ○ The African Rhythms in Hughes's Poetry
    - ○ Langston Hughes's Character Named Simple
    - ○ Langston Hughes: More Than Just a Poet
    - ○ Finally Purchasing a House in Harlem

38. Look at the word his in paragraph 1. Click on the word or phrase in the paragraph that his refers to.

39. Look at the phrase Harlem Renaissance in paragraph 2. Click on the word, phrase, or sentence in the paragraph that defines the phrase Harlem Renaissance.

40. Look at the word prolifically in paragraph 2. The word is closest in meaning to
    - ○ artistically
    - ○ fastidiously
    - ○ devotedly
    - ○ abundantly

41. Look at the word syncopation in paragraph 3. Click on the word or phrase in the paragraph that is closest in meaning to the word syncopation.

42. Look at the word its in paragraph 4. Click on the word or phrase in the paragraph that its refers to.

43. The following sentence could be added to paragraph 4.

    Because the character Simple was humorous, Hughes was able to tackle very complex racial problems while not offending his readers.

    Where would it best fit into the paragraph? Click on the square to add the sentence to the paragraph.

    □ In 1926, Hughes returned to college, but this time he chose a black college, Lincoln University in Pennsylvania. □ While at Lincoln, he met a benefactor who encouraged him to write his first novel. *Not Without Laughter* was published one year after his 1929 graduation. □ After its publication, he continued writing poetry and began a long association with the theater. □ In the 1940s, he began writing a column for the African-American newspaper, the *Chicago Defender,* where he introduced his readers to a lovable and enduring character named Simple, derived from a conversation Hughes had had with a man in a Harlem bar. □

44. In what order did Langston Hughes spend time in the following places?
    - ○ Africa, Columbia, Lincoln University
    - ○ Columbia, Africa, Lincoln University
    - ○ Columbia, Lincoln University, Africa
    - ○ Africa, Lincoln University, Columbia

45. Look at the word lyrics in paragraph 5. The word is closest in meaning to
- ◯ screenplays
- ◯ music
- ◯ words
- ◯ reviews

46. Which of the following is NOT true about Langston Hughes?
- ◯ He died in 1967.
- ◯ He wrote the story of his life.
- ◯ He graduated from Columbia.
- ◯ He wrote even before he began college.

47. It can be inferred from the passage that
- ◯ Langston Hughes performed on Broadway
- ◯ Hughes eventually earned an engineering degree
- ◯ Hughes had a following during his lifetime
- ◯ the character Simple was autobiographical

48. Click on the paragraph that best explains how Hughes' unique type of poetry evolved.

49. Hughes wrote all of the following EXCEPT
- ◯ lyrics
- ◯ art reviews
- ◯ scripts
- ◯ columns

50. In what order did Hughes write the following?
- ◯ *Not Without Laughter*, the debut of *Simple*, lyrics for *Street Scene*, *Montage of a Dream Deferred*
- ◯ Lyrics for *Street Scene*, the debut of *Simple*, *Not Without Laughter*, *Montage of a Dream Deferred*
- ◯ *Montage of a Dream Deferred*, lyrics for *Street Scene*, *Not Without Laughter*, the debut of *Simple*
- ◯ *Not Without Laughter*, the debut of *Simple*, lyrics for *Street Scene*, *Montage of a Dream Deferred*

APPENDIXES

APPENDIX A

VERBS FOLLOWED BY GERUNDS AND INFINITIVES

These lists include the most frequently used verbs.

I. Verbs Followed by the Gerund

acknowledge	endure	postpone
admit	enjoy	practice
appreciate	escape	prevent
avoid	explain	prohibit
can't help	feel like	quit
can't stand	finish	recall
celebrate	forgive	recommend
consider	give up (stop)	regret
delay	imagine	report
deny	justify	resent
detest	keep (continue)	resist
discontinue	mention	risk
dislike	mind (object to)	suggest
dispute	miss	understand

II. Verbs Followed by the Infinitive

afford	decide	pay
agree	deserve	prepare
ask	fail	pretend
arrange	hope	refuse
attempt	hurry	request
begin	learn	seem
can't afford	manage	want
can't wait	mean	wish
choose	need	would like
consent	offer	

III. Verbs Followed by Either the Gerund or the Infinitive

begin	intend	remember
can't stand	like	start
continue	love	stop
forget	prefer	try
hate		

IV. Verbs Followed by Objects and the Infinitive

advise	force	remind
allow	hire	require
cause	invite	teach
convince	order	tell
encourage	permit	urge
forbid	persuade	warn

APPENDIX B

IRREGULAR VERBS

Base Form	Simple Past	Past Participle
be	was/were	been
beat	beat	beaten
become	became	become
begin	began	begun
bet	bet	bet
bite	bit	bitten
bleed	bled	bled
blow	blew	blown
break	broke	broken
bring	brought	brought
build	built	built
buy	bought	bought
catch	caught	caught
choose	chose	chosen
come	came	come
cost	cost	cost
cut	cut	cut
deal	dealt	dealt
dig	dug	dug
dive	dived/dove	dived
do	did	done

Base Form	Simple Past	Past Participle
draw	drew	drawn
dream	dreamed/ dreamt	dreamed/ dreamt
drink	drank	drunk
eat	ate	eaten
fall	fell	fallen
feed	fed	fed
feel	felt	felt
fight	fought	fought
find	found	found
fly	flew	flown
forbid	forbade	forbidden
forget	forgot	forgotten
freeze	froze	frozen
get	got	gotten
give	gave	given
go	went	gone
grow	grew	grown
hang	hanged/hung	hanged/hung
have	had	had
hear	heard	heard
hide	hid	hidden
hit	hit	hit
hold	held	held
hurt	hurt	hurt
keep	kept	kept
kneel	knelt	knelt
knit	knit	knit
know	knew	known
lay	laid	laid
lead	led	led
leap	leapt	leapt
leave	left	left
lend	lent	lent
let	let	let
lie (lie down)	lay	lain
light	lit	lit
lose	lost	lost
make	made	made
mean	meant	meant
meet	met	met
pay	paid	paid
put	put	put
quit	quit	quit
read	read	read
ride	rode	ridden
ring	rang	rung
rise	rose	risen
run	ran	run

Base Form	Simple Past	Past Participle
say	said	said
see	saw	seen
seek	sought	sought
sell	sold	sold
send	sent	sent
set	set	set
sew	sewed	sewn/sewed
shake	shook	shaken
shine	shone	shone
shoot	shot	shot
show	showed	shown
shrink	shrank/ shrunk	shrunk/ shrunken
shut	shut	shut
sing	sang	sung
sink	sank	sunk
sit	sat	sat
sleep	slept	slept
slide	slid	slid
speak	spoke	spoken
speed	sped	sped
spend	spent	spent
spill	spilled/spilt	spilled/spilt
spin	spun	spun
split	split	split
spread	spread	spread
spring	sprang	sprung
stand	stood	stood
steal	stole	stolen
stick	stuck	stuck
strike	struck	struck
swear	swore	sworn
sweep	swept	swept
swim	swam	swum
swing	swung	swung
take	took	taken
teach	taught	taught
tear	tore	torn
tell	told	told
think	thought	thought
understand	understood	understood
wake	woke	woken
wear	wore	worn
weave	wove	woven
weep	wept	wept
win	won	won
wind	wound	wound
write	wrote	written

TOEFL TEST I

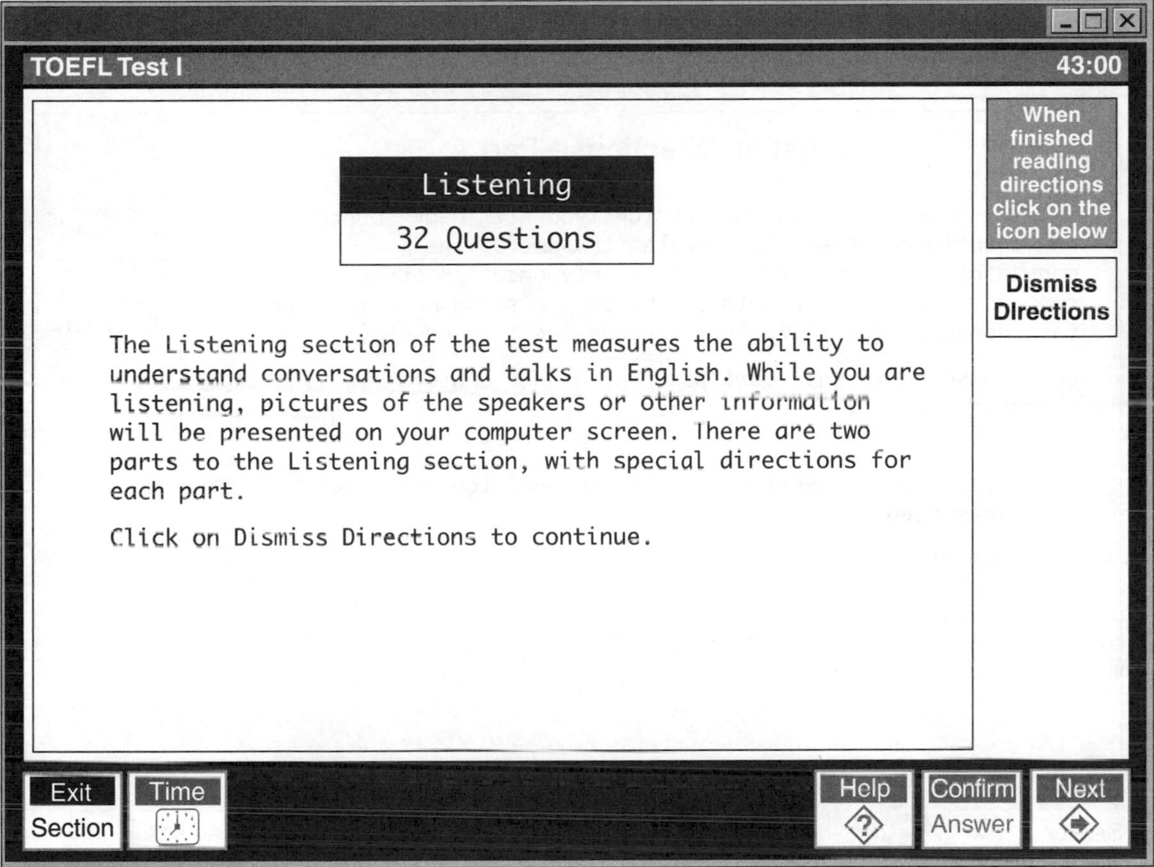
TOEFL Test I
43:00
Listening
32 Questions
The Listening section of the test measures the ability to understand conversations and talks in English. While you are listening, pictures of the speakers or other information will be presented on your computer screen. There are two parts to the Listening section, with special directions for each part.
Click on Dismiss Directions to continue.
When finished reading directions click on the icon below
Dismiss Directions
Exit Section
Time
Help
Confirm Answer
Next

See Appendix E, pages 403–406, for the transcript of the audio passages for this text.

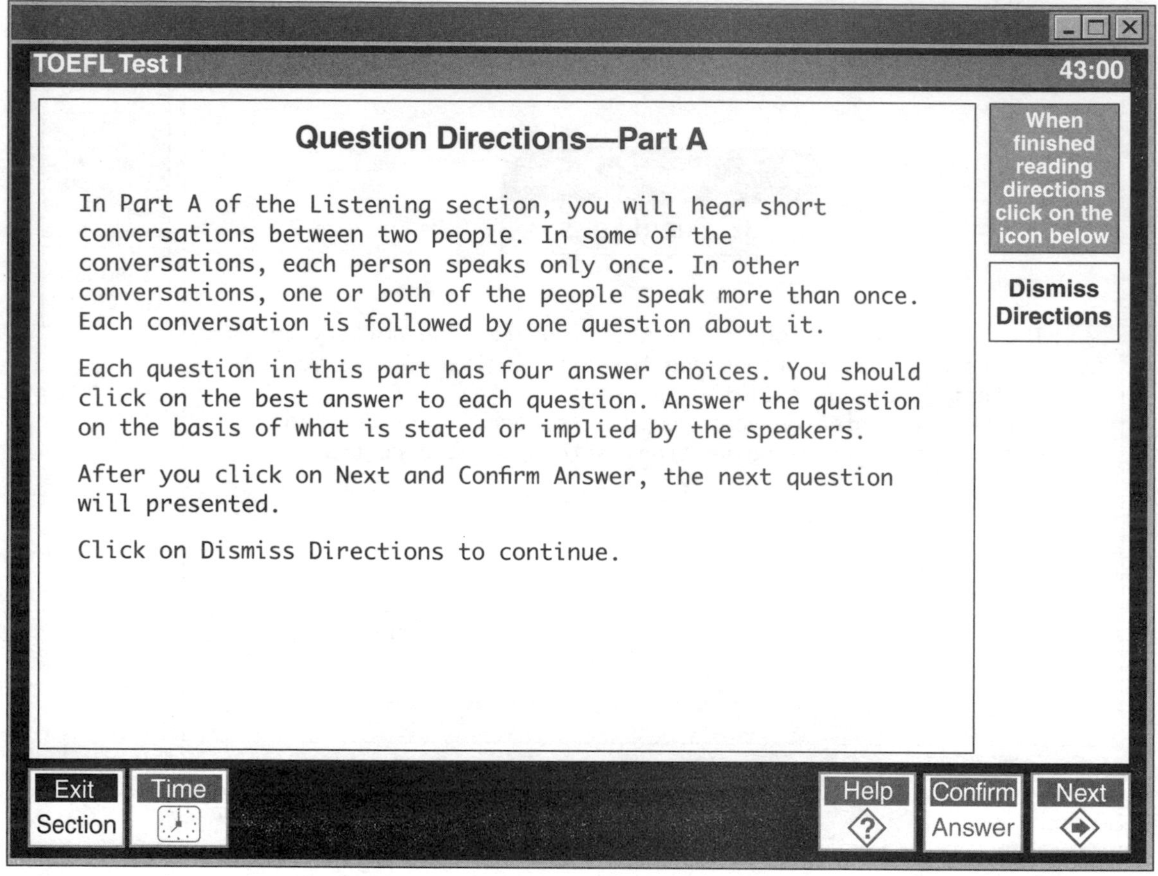
TOEFL Test I
43:00
Question Directions—Part A
In Part A of the Listening section, you will hear short conversations between two people. In some of the conversations, each person speaks only once. In other conversations, one or both of the people speak more than once. Each conversation is followed by one question about it.
Each question in this part has four answer choices. You should click on the best answer to each question. Answer the question on the basis of what is stated or implied by the speakers.
After you click on Next and Confirm Answer, the next question will presented.
Click on Dismiss Directions to continue.
When finished reading directions click on the icon below
Dismiss Directions
Exit Section
Time
Help
Confirm Answer
Next

1. What does the woman imply?
   - There will only be three or four more hot weeks.
   - She didn't know her apartment didn't have air conditioning.
   - She knew there would be so many hot days in the summer.
   - The apartment she has now doesn't have air conditioning.

2. What does the woman mean?
   - Both Tamara and Fred long for dinner.
   - Tamara and Fred messed up dinner.
   - Neither Tamara nor Fred came to dinner.
   - Tamara and Fred used to be thinner.

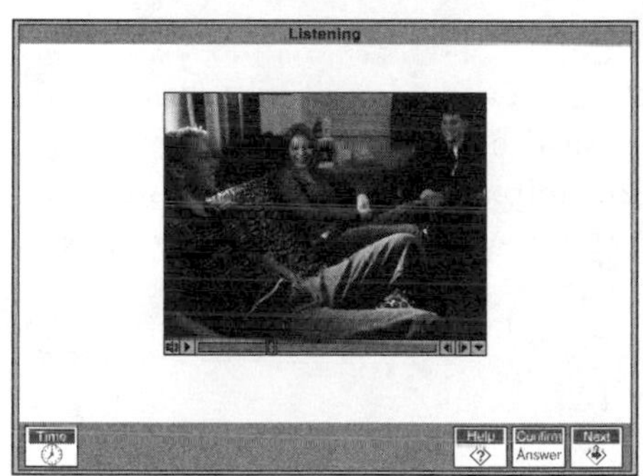

3. What does the man imply?
   - She shouldn't hate the couch.
   - She should have told him she didn't like the couch.
   - He would have told her if he had hated the couch.
   - He hates it too.

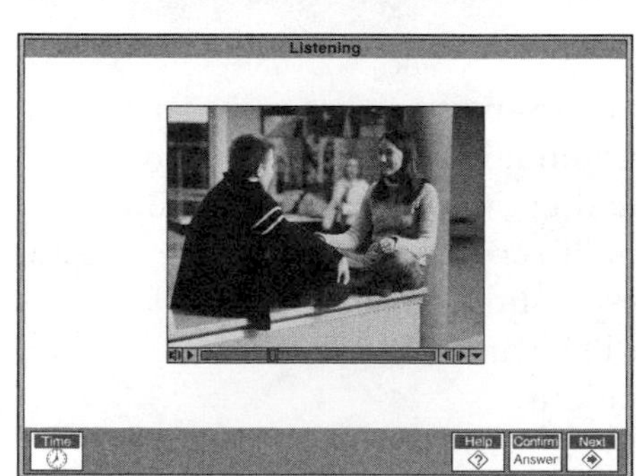

4. Where does this conversation take place?
   - In the lab
   - In the cafeteria
   - In the library
   - In the dorm

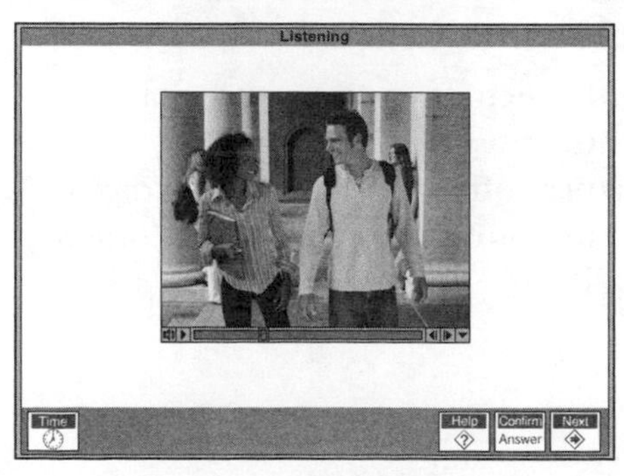

5. What does the man mean?
   - If it rains, the team will use the pool.
   - They're going by train to swim in the country.
   - The team will practice at the club swimming pool.
   - The country club pool is being repaired.

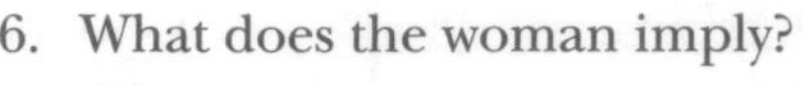

6. What does the woman imply?
   - ◯ She's got to make the 5:00 deadline.
   - ◯ She will go to the restaurant if the deadline passes.
   - ◯ She'll get to the restaurant ahead of him.
   - ◯ He should go on without her.

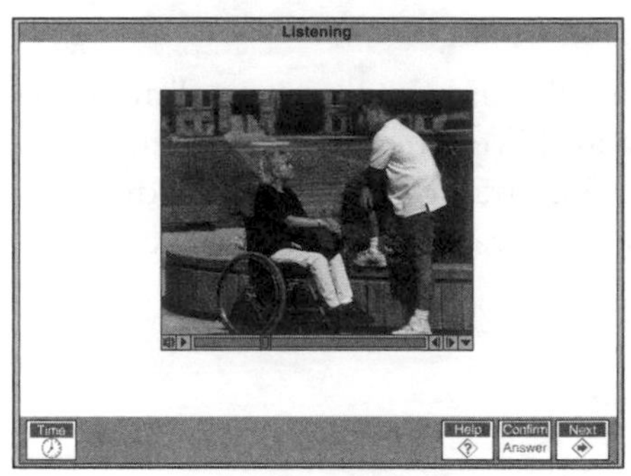

7. What does the woman mean?
   - ◯ Her computer midterm will be as long as her biology midterm.
   - ◯ She might be confused as to the length of the biology midterm.
   - ◯ Her computer midterm was very confusing.
   - ◯ Both of her midterms will be ten pages long.

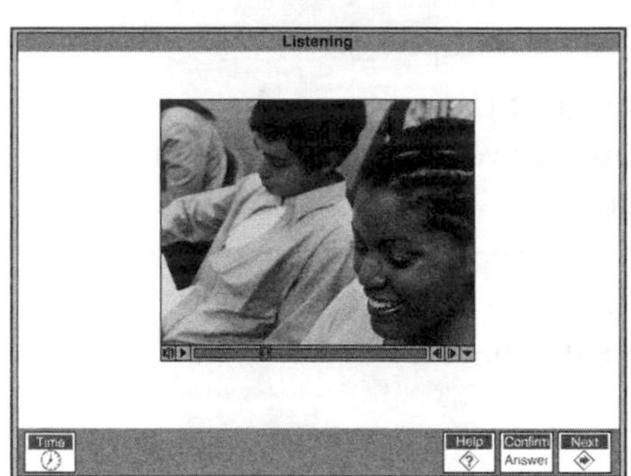

8. What does the man imply?
   - ◯ He's sitting on the edge of his seat.
   - ◯ He fell over the ledge.
   - ◯ Going for help made him more confused.
   - ◯ He's on the edge of understanding the set.

9. What does the man mean?
   - ◯ The oral presentations are voluntary.
   - ◯ If the presentation is longer than five minutes, there will be no extra credit.
   - ◯ He strongly recommends everyone give an oral presentation.
   - ◯ There will be an extra class for the presentations.

10. What does the woman mean?
   - ◯ Run to the lecture so as not to be late.
   - ◯ The lecture was delayed.
   - ◯ The lecturer often runs late in the day.
   - ◯ The lecture often goes past its scheduled time.

11. What does the man imply?
    - ◯ There were enough refreshments for the last meeting.
    - ◯ Since the cookies always get eaten, he won't get any next time.
    - ◯ He'll order more cookies for the next meeting.
    - ◯ It doesn't make a difference how many cookies he gets.

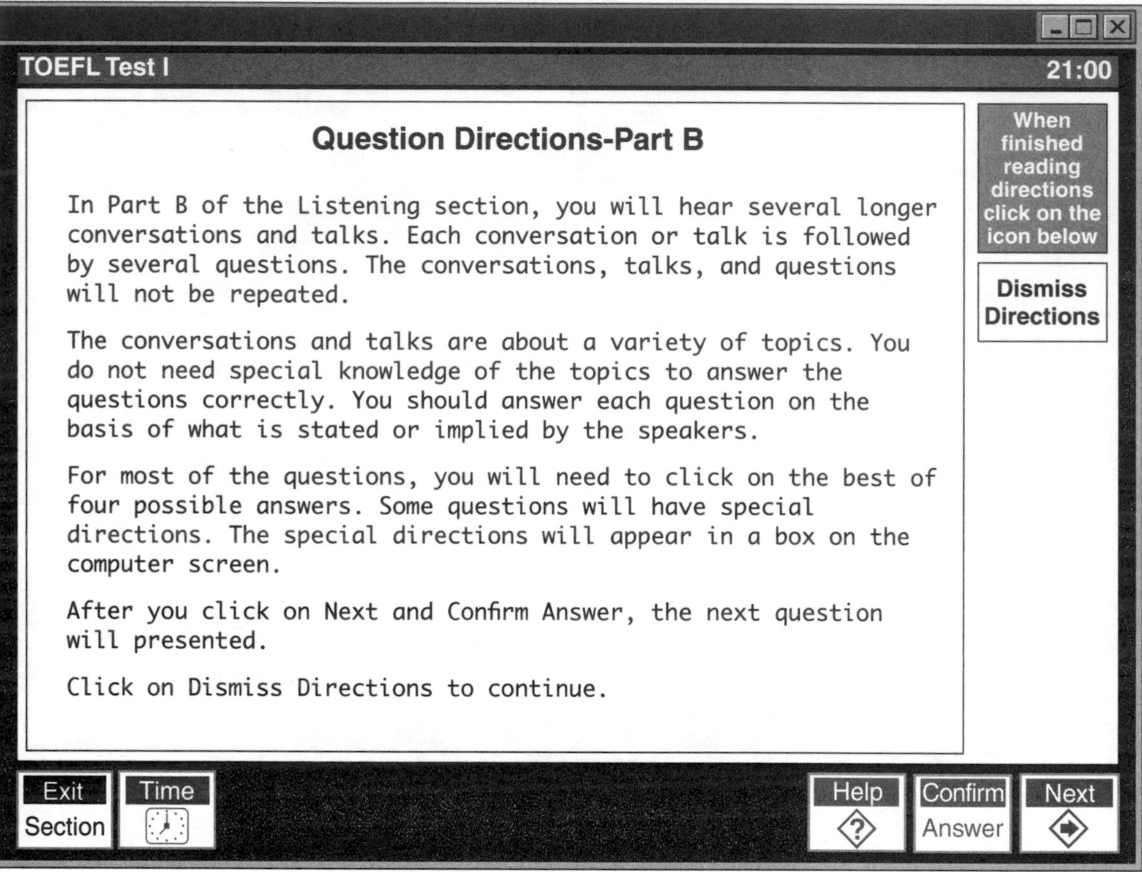
TOEFL Test I
21:00
Question Directions-Part B
In Part B of the Listening section, you will hear several longer conversations and talks. Each conversation or talk is followed by several questions. The conversations, talks, and questions will not be repeated.
The conversations and talks are about a variety of topics. You do not need special knowledge of the topics to answer the questions correctly. You should answer each question on the basis of what is stated or implied by the speakers.
For most of the questions, you will need to click on the best of four possible answers. Some questions will have special directions. The special directions will appear in a box on the computer screen.
After you click on Next and Confirm Answer, the next question will presented.
Click on Dismiss Directions to continue.
When finished reading directions click on the icon below
Dismiss Directions
Exit Section
Time
Help
Confirm Answer
Next

Questions 12–14

12. What does the man say about the student activity fee?
    - ⬭ It's no longer collected.
    - ⬭ It's voluntary.
    - ⬭ It supports campus events on weekends.
    - ⬭ It enables students to go into the city.

13. What does the man imply about Friday and Saturday nights?
    - ⬭ The college could use some new faces on weekends.
    - ⬭ Students don't participate in what's planned for them.
    - ⬭ There isn't enough money to plan programs students want to attend.
    - ⬭ Students are too tired to attend the organized programs.

14. What does the man want the woman to do?
    - ⬭ Plan new activities with him
    - ⬭ Go with him into the city on weekends
    - ⬭ Collect the student activity fee
    - ⬭ Find some new faces to be on student government

Questions 15–17

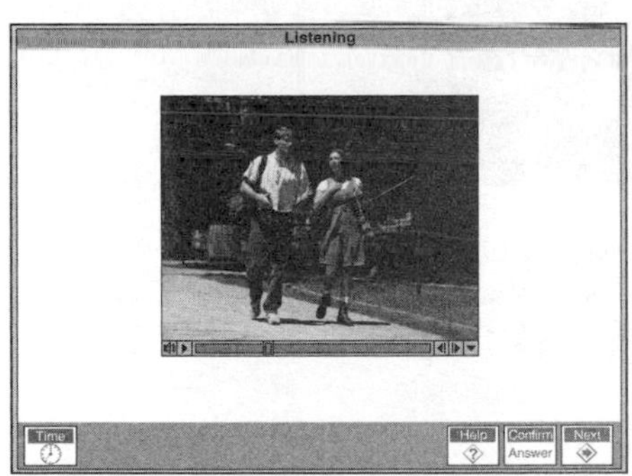

15. Where will they get the materials for the first part?
    - ⬭ From a computer
    - ⬭ In the library
    - ⬭ In the student center
    - ⬭ In class

16. What will the man do before they meet?
    - ⬭ Print the materials they need
    - ⬭ Get the sources from the library
    - ⬭ Find a big table at the student center
    - ⬭ Spread out all their materials

17. Where will they meet?
    - ⬭ In the library
    - ⬭ Over the Internet
    - ⬭ At the student center
    - ⬭ In class

Questions 18–22

Listen to a design lecture about the printmaking process.

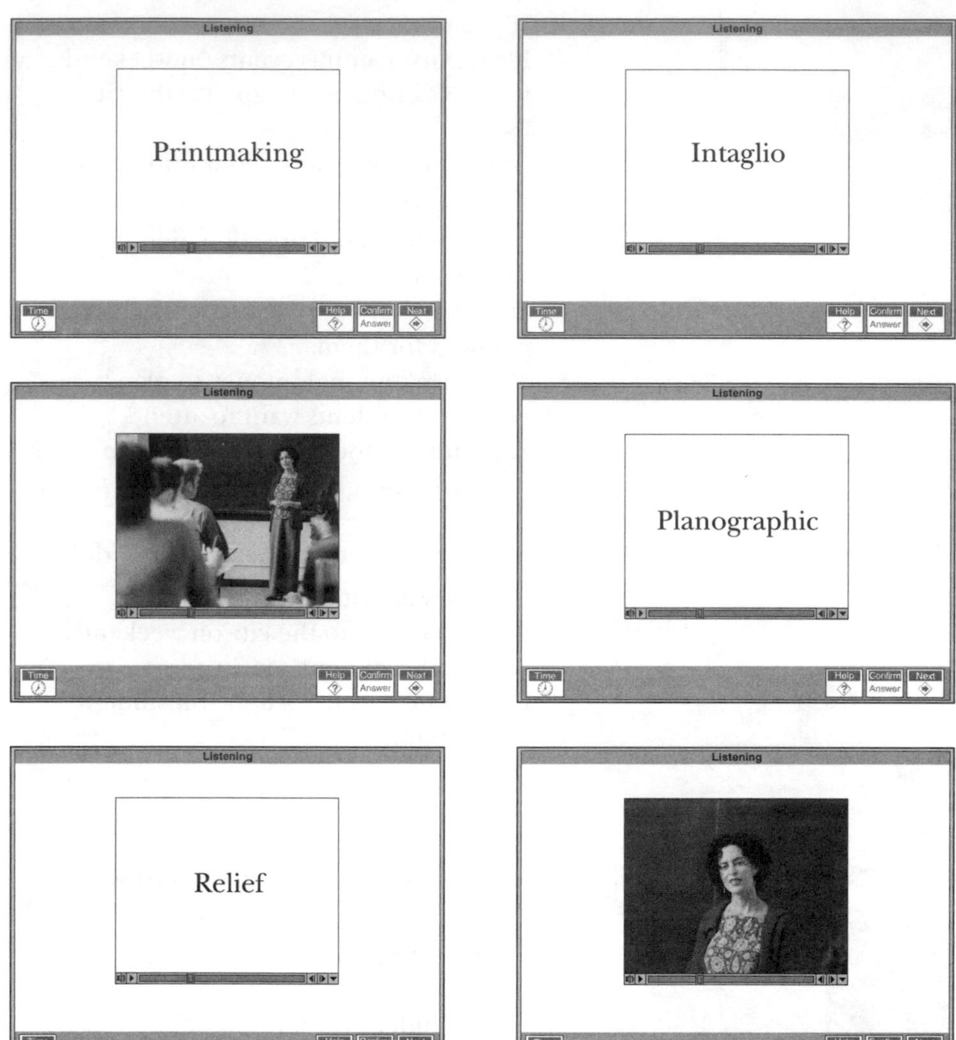

18. Which medium is used to create designs for printmaking?

Click on 2 answers.

- ☐ Stone
- ☐ Canvas
- ☐ Metal
- ☐ Paper

19. Which process leaves a platemark?

- ◯ Relief
- ◯ Intaglio
- ◯ Planographic
- ◯ Lithographic

20. What is an example of each of these types of prints?

Click on a word. Then click on the empty box in the correct column. Use each word only once.

lithographs **woodcuts** **engravings**

relief	intaglio	planographic

21. How do printmakers etch onto metal?

- ◯ With sharp tools
- ◯ With water, repulsed from a greasy image
- ◯ With platemarks
- ◯ By pressing the paper onto it

22. According to the lecture, why do printmakers go through the trouble of printmaking?

Click on 2 answers.

- ☐ They find painting too quick a process.
- ☐ They want to make many impressions of an image.
- ☐ They enjoy the slow, difficult technique.
- ☐ They enjoy the variety of effects printmaking can produce.

Questions 23–27

Listen to a discussion of a campus stamp collecting group.

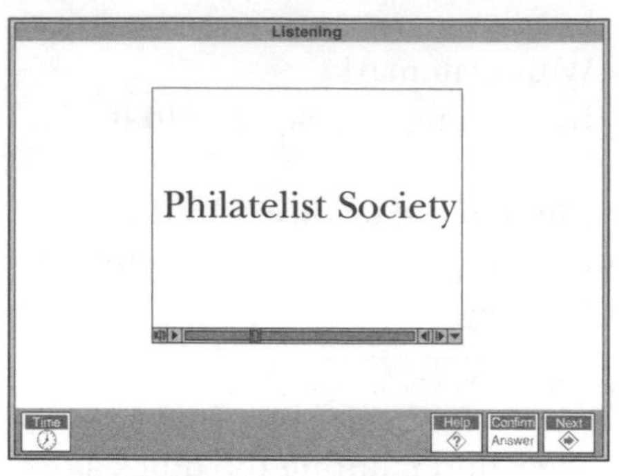

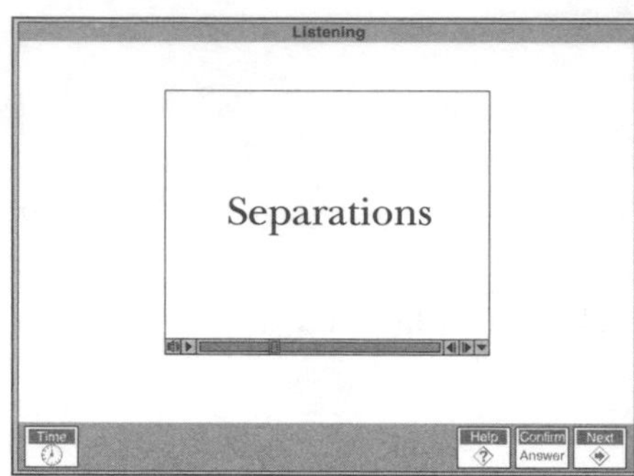

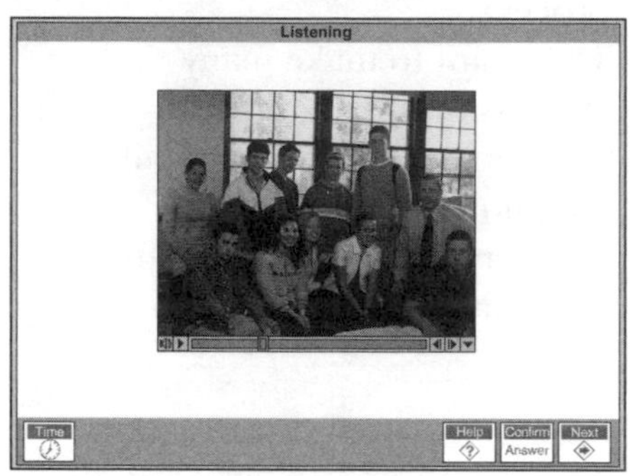

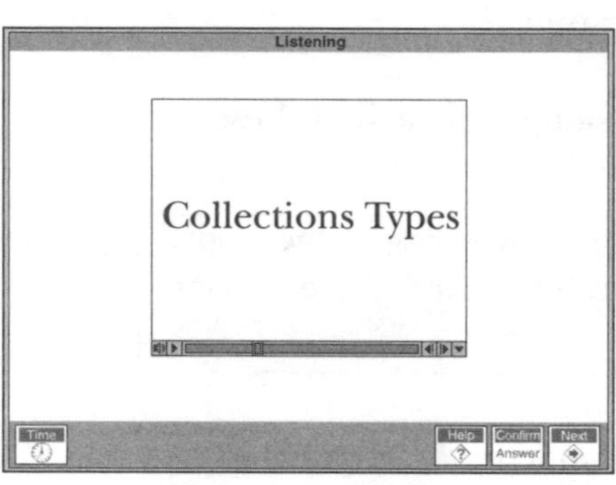

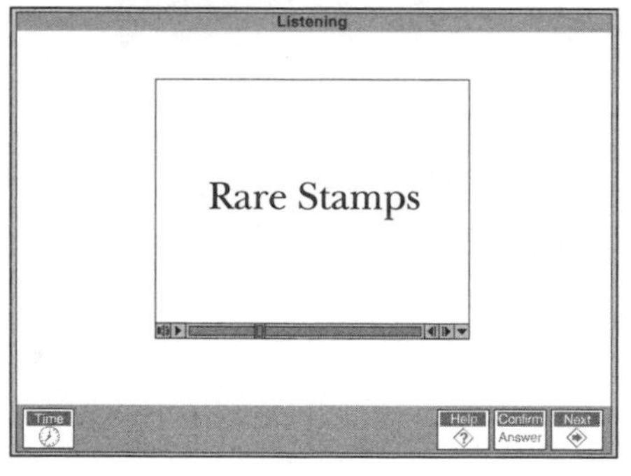

23. What is the main topic of the discussion?
    - ⬭ The contents of each section in the brochure
    - ⬭ The history of American stamp collecting
    - ⬭ Changing the name of the Campus Philatelist Society
    - ⬭ What makes a stamp rare or unusual

24. Which of these stamps would be considered as a rare stamp?

25. Based on the discussion, classify the following types of separations.

    Click on a phrase. Then click on the space where it belongs. Use each phrase only once.

roulette	**imperforate**	**perforation**
Stamps with little holes	Small cuts made by a knife	Stamps that cut apart with scissors

26. According to the discussion, which subjects would be prized as stamps?
    - ⬭ Buildings
    - ⬭ Dogs
    - ⬭ Airplanes
    - ⬭ Birds

27. When were the first U.S. stamps issued?
    - ⬭ 1847
    - ⬭ 1850
    - ⬭ 1870
    - ⬭ 1893

Questions 28–32

Listen to a lecture in a history class. The professor is talking about the California gold rush.

28. Who was Sam Brennan?
    - ⬭ A discoverer of gold
    - ⬭ A newspaperman
    - ⬭ The president
    - ⬭ A mill owner

29. What is stated in the lecture as dangers on the journey to California?

    Click on 2 answers.

    - ☐ Lack of food
    - ☐ Wild animal assaults
    - ☐ Transportation unpredictability
    - ☐ Attacks from gold seekers

30. What did people do who couldn't find a job?
    - ⬭ They tried other methods of seeking gold.
    - ⬭ They returned to where they had come from.
    - ⬭ They tried to support themselves doing other things.
    - ⬭ They fought for California's statehood.

31. What can be inferred from the lecture?
    - ⬭ Looking for gold was fraught with danger.
    - ⬭ Included in the migration were those forced to relocate.
    - ⬭ Once gold was found in California, miners searched in other states.
    - ⬭ Those who traveled to California had unrealistic expectations.

32. The professor mentions a series of events. Put them in their chronological order.

    Click on a phrase. Then click on the space where it belongs. Use each phrase only once.

    California statehood
    The president's publicizing of the gold rush
    The discovery of gold at Sutter Mill
    The migration of 90,000 people to California

    1. ________
    2. ________
    3. ________
    4. ________

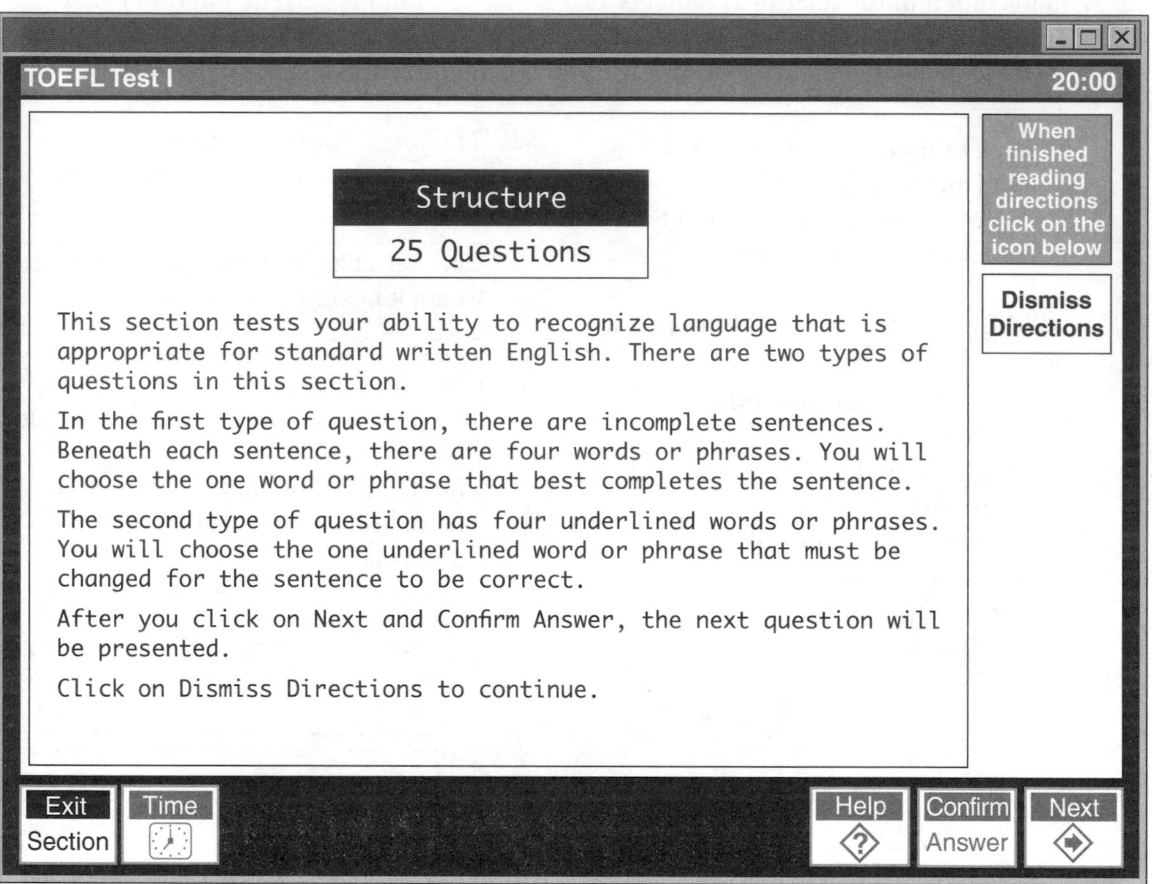
TOEFL Test I
20:00
Structure
25 Questions
This section tests your ability to recognize language that is appropriate for standard written English. There are two types of questions in this section.
In the first type of question, there are incomplete sentences. Beneath each sentence, there are four words or phrases. You will choose the one word or phrase that best completes the sentence.
The second type of question has four underlined words or phrases. You will choose the one underlined word or phrase that must be changed for the sentence to be correct.
After you click on Next and Confirm Answer, the next question will be presented.
Click on Dismiss Directions to continue.
When finished reading directions click on the icon below
Dismiss Directions
Exit Section
Time
Help
Confirm Answer
Next

1. Maurice Sendak's books *In the Night Kitchen* and *Outside Over There* describe the adventures of children which master their feelings by testing themselves in dangerous but ingenious places.

2. Woodie Guthrie had many personal misfortunes, ____ his music expressed a hopeful view of life.

   ◯ but
   ◯ therefore
   ◯ which
   ◯ so

3. Sheep are among the most important animals that people have tamed because they provide both food or clothing.

4. The bite of a tarantula is no more dangerous to people _____ the sting of a bee.

   ◯ than
   ◯ more
   ◯ like
   ◯ as is

5. Lorado Taft, an American sculptor, teacher, and writer is best remembered for *The History of American Sculpture*, ___________.

   ◯ the subject of the first book is
   ◯ which is the subject of the first book
   ◯ is the first book on the subject
   ◯ the first book on the subject

6. Whereas in the 1600s most better-quality American furniture was made in England, in the 1700s, furniture makers began producing a significant amount of furnitures in Newport, Rhode Island, Philadelphia, and other U.S. cities.

7. Tacoma, one of the largest cities in Washington, is a industrial and commercial center.

8. The majority of Saul Steinberg's thought-provoking pen-and-ink drawings _____ captions or explanations.

   ◯ have neither
   ◯ are having no
   ◯ have none
   ◯ have no

9. Talc is so soft that it can be scratched with a fingernail, and it feels soap or greasy.

10. Reptiles can alter the amount of heat their bodies absorb from the sun by changing their skins colors.

11. The body has two adrenal glands, one _________.

   ◯ on top each kidney
   ◯ top of each kidney
   ◯ kidney on top of each
   ◯ on top of each kidney

12. When a crossword puzzle is completed, each square will contain a letter that help to spell a word.

13. Tarragon is widely cultivated for their leaves and young shoots, which are used as a flavoring for vinegar.

14. In most telescopes, a lens of mirrors is used ________ an image of an object.

   ◯ to forming
   ◯ formally
   ◯ when formed
   ◯ to form

15. Teepees were home to Plains Indians who hunted the buffalo huge herds.

16. A rug makes use of variety of patterns and textures to achieve an interesting design.

17. Bella Abzug supported legislation that promotes __________, public transportation, and individual rights to privacy.
    - ⬭ job federal programs
    - ⬭ federal job programs
    - ⬭ job programs and federal
    - ⬭ programming jobs federal

18. Interferon is <u>a</u> chemical substance <u>producing</u> by the cells of human beings and <u>other</u> mammals <u>in response to</u> viral infections or certain chemicals.

19. <u>The</u> University of Illinois <u>it</u> is a <u>state-supported,</u> coeducational institution with two campuses, one <u>of which</u> is in Chicago.

20. <u>Because</u> its great popularity, television <u>has become</u> <u>a major way</u> to reach people with <u>advertising</u> messages.

21. Nitrogen is __________ that the development of low-cost nitrogen greatly affected the use of fertilizer.
    - ⬭ such an important fertilizer element
    - ⬭ so important fertilize element
    - ⬭ such a fertilizer element importance
    - ⬭ an important fertilizer element so

22. The Rio Grande, Texas's <u>longest</u> river, is <u>one of</u> longest and most <u>historic</u> rivers <u>in</u> North America.

23. __________ early anthropologists mainly studied small communities in technologically simple societies, modern-day anthropologists work in a wide-range of settings.
    - ⬭ For
    - ⬭ Despite
    - ⬭ Although
    - ⬭ Nevertheless

24. Thermodynamics is the study of <u>various</u> forms of energy and <u>its</u> conversion <u>from</u> one form into <u>other</u>.

25. _______ is made with dampened earth pressed down in building forms similar to those used for poured concrete walls.
    - ⬭ When a less common type of adobe
    - ⬭ A least common type of adobe
    - ⬭ A less common type of adobe
    - ⬭ Adobe is a less common type

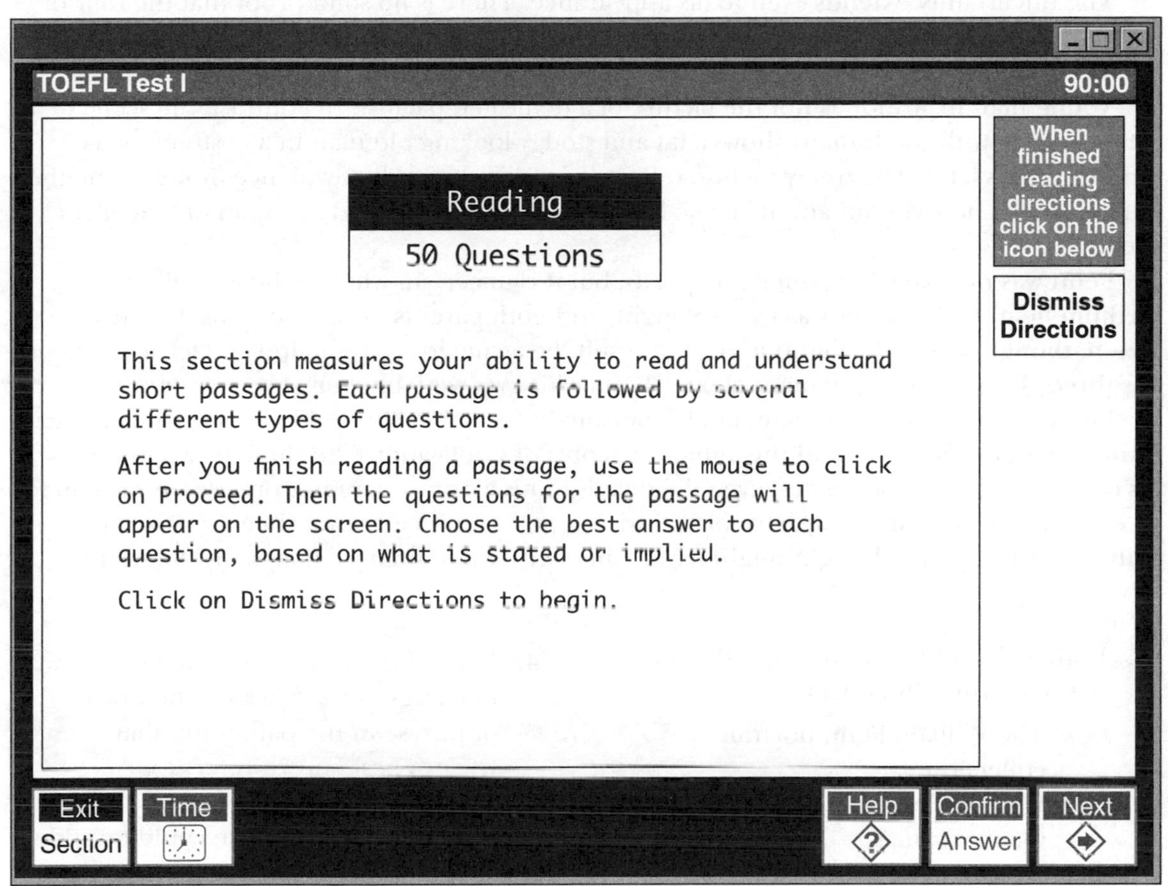
TOEFL Test I
90:00
Reading
50 Questions
This section measures your ability to read and understand short passages. Each passage is followed by several different types of questions.
After you finish reading a passage, use the mouse to click on Proceed. Then the questions for the passage will appear on the screen. Choose the best answer to each question, based on what is stated or implied.
Click on Dismiss Directions to begin.
When finished reading directions click on the icon below
Dismiss Directions
Exit Section
Time
Help
Confirm Answer
Next

PASSAGE 1 Questions 1–12

William Penn, the Quaker (1644–1718), has stirred up a fair amount of controversy. Few people during the exciting era of the Puritan Upheaval, the Cromwell Protectorate, the Stuart Restoration, and the Glorious Revolution understood him, and in many ways he remains a mystery until this day.

The uncertainty extends even to his appearance. There is no solid proof that the four or five so-called portraits of Penn were actually painted during his lifetime or by anyone who knew him well. Neither of the two best-known portrays Penn as we would expect. The portrait of a young man in armor is not the picture of a dedicated pacifist. In contrast, the scene of a treaty signing with the Indians shows a fat and stodgy-looking old man in a costume of a hundred years later. The treaty picture reflects friendliness and benevolence; however, neither portrait shows how vibrant and dynamic Penn was. He was described as a man of "excellent sweetness."

Penn was probably big-boned and portly, but it is uncertain whether he was tall or of medium height. His father was five feet eight, and both parents were stout. His hair was flaxen, though scanty throughout life, the result, he assumed, of a smallpox attack when he was three. There is no agreement about whether his eyes were blue or gray.

Penn was not a secretive man, but his personality is as much in doubt as is his appearance. Although a prolific writer and the author of scores of publications, he shed little light upon his own feelings or experiences; even the details in his writings were not precise. In recalling an event years later, time may have played tricks upon him. In all innocence, he may have written down what he thought might have happened, rather than what actually did occur.

1. With which of the following is the passage primarily concerned?
   - ⬭ The William Penn portrait collection
   - ⬭ William Penn as a reflection of Quaker values
   - ⬭ The uncertainty about Penn's demeanor and physical traits
   - ⬭ Penn's personality as evidenced in his costume and portraiture

2. Look at the word upheaval in paragraph 1. Click on the word or phrase in the paragraph that is closest in meaning to the word upheaval.

3. Look at the word armor in paragraph 2. The word is closest in meaning to
   - ⬭ vertebrate
   - ⬭ protective covering
   - ⬭ battle maneuvers
   - ⬭ military

4. Look at the phrase the two best-known in paragraph 2. Click on the word or phrase in the paragraph that the two best-known refers to.

5. The following sentence could be added to paragraph 2.

   However, Penn's armor in the portrait may be reconciled with his Quaker pacifism due to the fact that he did not become a Quaker until his twenties, shortly after posing for the portrait.

   Where would it best fit into the paragraph? Click on the square to add the sentence to the paragraph.

   The uncertainty extends even to his appearance. □ There is no solid proof that the four or five so-called portraits of Penn were actually painted during his lifetime or by anyone who knew him well. □ Neither of the two best-known portrays Penn as we would expect. □ The portrait of a young man in armor is not the picture of a dedicated pacifist.

☐ In contrast, the scene of a treaty signing with the Indians shows a fat and stodgy-looking old man in a costume of a hundred years later. ☐

6. Look at the word stout in paragraph 3. Click on the word or phrase in the paragraph that is closest in meaning to the word stout.

7. The author suggests that
   - ⬭ Penn had few acquaintances
   - ⬭ Penn may not be the subject of his portraits
   - ⬭ Penn was not the gentle, quiet man as assumed
   - ⬭ Penn dressed inappropriately for the Indian signing treaty

8. This passage would most likely be assigned reading in a course on
   - ⬭ writing
   - ⬭ art history
   - ⬭ religion
   - ⬭ American Indians

9. Click on the paragraph that describes Penn's presumed physical characteristics.

10. The author suggests that Penn may have
    - ⬭ closely resembled his father
    - ⬭ inaccurately recorded events
    - ⬭ kept many secrets
    - ⬭ played tricks with his readers

11. It can be inferred from the passage that Penn
    - ⬭ was tall
    - ⬭ kept his whereabouts hidden
    - ⬭ was a revolutionary
    - ⬭ negotiated with Indians

12. According to the passage, click on the portrait which suggests a representation of William Penn.

PASSAGE 2 Questions 13–25

If you pick up your child every time she cries, she will whimper and whine simply to get your attention. Never sleep with the baby because you will surely roll over and suffocate her. Newborn infants need rigorous schedules to be content; breastfeed only every two hours. A good mother must spend hours every day talking with her child to encourage mental development.

New parents are deluged with such advice from pediatricians, childcare experts, and just about anybody on the street who stops to peek into the carriage. What few parents realize is that most of these rules, these laws of infant care, have little scientific credibility. If proponents of a new branch of research into childcare, called ethnopediatrics, have their way, such advice may become a thing of the past. This group of anthropologists, pediatricians, and child development researchers seeks to discover exactly how different styles of parenting across the globe affect the biology, growth, health, and survival of infants. The reflexes of newborn babies the world over have been honed by millions of years of evolution. Babies instinctively know when to sleep, when to eat, and how to cry out to signal their needs. However, the way these needs are met varies widely among societies.

The researchers also aim to explain how such cultural differences come to be and how they are forged from social expectations about children. Childcare in every society aims to shape babies into the type of children—and eventually adults—valued by that culture. Although newborn babies are the same the world over, from the moment babies start interacting with their mothers, they become members of distinct, changeable, modern societies, often quite unlike those that babies once adapted to through evolution.

13. The passage mainly discusses
    - the lack of scientific credibility in parenting rules
    - new research on childrearing as a result of cultural differences
    - advice on how to be a good parent
    - shaping babies into valued members of society

14. The author includes the first paragraph in order to show
    - the difficulties of being a good parent
    - various childrearing suggestions
    - the importance of interacting with infants
    - the lack of verbal interaction with infants

15. Look at the phrase deluged with in paragraph 2. The phrase is closest in meaning to
    - deceived by
    - bombarded by
    - attacked by
    - confused by

16. According to paragraph 2, which of the following is true about the laws of infant care?
    - Laws of infant care are the same the world over.
    - These rules have little basis in science.
    - Ethnopediatrics is rewriting childcare rules.
    - Parents realize the limitations of infant care laws.

17. Click on the sentence in paragraph 2 that lists which scientists are involved with ethnopediatrics.

18. Look at the word proponents in paragraph 2. The word is closest in meaning to
    - advocates
    - opponents
    - inspectors
    - consumers

19. Look at the word their in paragraph 2. Click on the word or phrase in the paragraph that their refers to.

20. It can be inferred from the passage that the researchers will investigate all of the following except
    - ⬭ development
    - ⬭ disease
    - ⬭ heredity
    - ⬭ adaptability

21. According to the passage, what can be said about newborns?
    - ⬭ Their reflexes have remained constant throughout history.
    - ⬭ They are similar all over the world.
    - ⬭ They have their needs met in similar ways.
    - ⬭ Their survival rate depends on the parenting they receive.

22. The author's attitude toward "ethnopediatrics" is generally
    - ⬭ enthusiastic
    - ⬭ neutral
    - ⬭ hostile
    - ⬭ skeptical

23. Click on the paragraph in the passage that explains how the way infants' needs are met is relative to their societies.

24. The following sentence could be added to paragraph 2 or 3.

    For example, whether or not young boys are discouraged from crying in public depends on one's culture.

    Where would it best fit into the paragraph? Click on the square to add the sentence to the paragraph.

    □ The reflexes of newborn babies the world over have been honed by millions of years of evolution. Babies instinctively know when to sleep, when to eat, and how to cry out to signal their needs. However, the way these needs are met varies widely among societies.

    □ The researchers also aim to explain how such cultural differences come to be, and how they are forged from social expectations about children. Childcare in every society aims to shape babies into the type of children—and eventually adults—valued by that culture. □ Although newborn babies are the same the world over, from the moment babies start interacting with their mothers, they become members of distinct, changeable, modern societies, often quite unlike those that babies once adapted to through evolution. □

25. The passage following this one most likely deals with
    - ⬭ statistics on birth weights of babies born in different countries
    - ⬭ examples of childrearing in ancient cultures
    - ⬭ examples of childrearing which encourage certain culturally-valued behaviors
    - ⬭ statistics on modern society birthrates

PASSAGE 3 Questions 26–38

No one has ever seen black holes. It is not even certain that they exist, yet theorists have been enthusiastically predicting their existence ever since Einstein published his general theory of relativity in 1916. According to Einstein's theory, a black hole forms when a massive object shrinks catastrophically under its own gravitational field. It is so strong that nothing, not even light, can escape. This occurrence produces the "blackness."

After decades of searching, astronomers are now finding an increasing number of encouraging signs that black holes may exist. Definite proof of these bizarre phenomena, however, remains elusive. A minority of astronomers do not accept the black hole theory at all. The majority, however, believe there is a considerable body of evidence—admittedly indirect—which supports the existence of black holes. Getting those all important hard data will not be easy. How do you see an object that is, by definition, invisible? Moreover, black holes are extremely tiny; they pack a given mass into the least possible volume. So actually "seeing" a dark object, blotting out the light from background stars, as the moon blots out the sun in a total eclipse, is out of the question. Instead, astronomers must infer the existence of black holes indirectly from the influence of their extraordinarily strong gravity on the visible bodies that surround them.

There is, nevertheless, a way that the existence of black holes might be proved once and for all. When black holes form, they should generate vast amounts of gravity waves, which spread out like wavelets on a pond. Such "ripples" in spacetime should be detectable by gravity-wave detectors which are currently being developed.

26. What does the passage mainly discuss?
    - ○ The origins of black holes
    - ○ The difficulty in proving the existence of black holes
    - ○ Einstein's theory and its relation to black holes
    - ○ Astronomers' use of gravity-wave detectors

27. Look at the word they in paragraph 1. Click on the word or phrase in the paragraph that they refers to.

28. What is the main focus of paragraph 1?
    - ○ The definition of black holes
    - ○ The astronomers' dilemma
    - ○ Proving the existence of black holes
    - ○ Crediting Einstein with the discovery of black holes

29. Click on the word or phrase in paragraph 1 that is closest in meaning to the word definite.

30. Look at the word shrinks in paragraph 1. The word is closest in meaning to
    - ○ disappears
    - ○ blinks
    - ○ contracts
    - ○ expands

31. The following sentence could be added to paragraph 1 or 2.

    Einstein's theory proposed that gravity affects the shape of space by curving it and the flow of time by slowing it down.

    Where would it best fit into the paragraph? Click on the square to add the sentence to the paragraph.

    ☐ No one has ever seen black holes. ☐ It is not even certain that they exist, yet theorists have been enthusiastically predicting their existence ever since Einstein published his general theory of relativity in 1916. ☐ According to Einstein's theory, a black hole forms when a massive object shrinks catastrophically under its own gravitational field. It is so strong that nothing, not even light, can escape. This occurrence produces the "blackness."

☐ After decades of searching, astronomers are now finding an increasing number of encouraging signs that black holes may exist. ☐

32. According to the passage, what do the majority of astronomers believe?
   - ○ That there is direct evidence of black holes
   - ○ That the black hole theory is unacceptable
   - ○ That definite proof of black holes is out of the question
   - ○ That black holes probably exist

33. Why does the author mention the moon blotting out the sun in paragraph 2?
   - ○ To explain what the process of blotting is
   - ○ To emphasize the moon and sun's similarity to black holes
   - ○ To compare different types of seeing
   - ○ To contrast the inability of seeing black holes with seeing the moon in a total eclipse

34. Look at the phrase out of the question in paragraph 2. The phrase is closest in meaning to
   - ○ controversial
   - ○ debatable
   - ○ problematic
   - ○ impossible

35. Click on the sentence in paragraph 2 where the author explains the size of black holes.

36. Look at the word vast in paragraph 3. The word is closest in meaning to
   - ○ huge
   - ○ quick
   - ○ tangible
   - ○ powerful

37. Look at the word wavelets in paragraph 3. Click on the word or phrase in the paragraph that is closest in meaning to the word wavelets.

38. It can be inferred from the passage that
   - ○ invisible black holes may soon be visible
   - ○ the existence of black holes may soon be proved
   - ○ astronomers hope to see black holes soon
   - ○ seeing black holes is like seeing an eclipse

PASSAGE 4 Questions 39–50

A natural canal construction boom occurred in the U.S. during the 1820s and 1830s. Much of the construction occurred in what was then called "The West." For example, Ohio built the Ohio and Erie Canals linking the Ohio River to Cleveland so that farmers could transport produce directly to the East. Unfortunately, the western canal enthusiasm caused the states to overbuild. The result was that there simply wasn't enough traffic to pay for the new canals. From 1841–1842, nine states faced dangerously mounting debts and inevitably defaulted on their canal bonds. Profits were wiped out almost completely. In addition, by 1850 the railroad had emerged as an invincible competitor.

The railroads initially functioned as feeders, or branch lines, for canals. The first railroad to begin operation was the Baltimore and Ohio in 1830. Despite its potential, railroad use developed slowly. Between 1830 and 1850, only nine thousand miles of track were laid. Private capital showed mild interest, leaving the states to supply most of the building funds. The problems involved in railroad construction seemed almost insurmountable. The most commonly used metal in tracks, cast iron, proved a poor material. In addition, no standard gauge was used. The trains ejected sparks and cinders, which constituted a menace to society. Finally, engines had insufficient power to carry heavy loads over inclines. Because of the problems with railroads, shippers did not immediately switch their business to them.

The lower cost of shipping goods on canal boats also stopped shippers from switching to railroads. Additionally, certain states, such as New York, which had constructed canal systems, did not want to help fund a competitive mode of transportation. Eventually, however, land companies began to pressure the federal government to construct "trunk lines" into the West at its own expense. Much of the support for private investment in railroads came from town, county, and state governments, which not only loaned money to private investors—mainly local businessmen, merchants, and farmers—but also invested in their stock.

As a result, between 1850 and 1860 twenty thousand miles of track were laid. Railroads began to take away much of the freight business from canals, forcing many of them to fail. By 1860, railroad tracks crisscrossed every state east of the Mississippi.

39. With which of the following is the passage primarily concerned?
   - ◯ The reason for the importance of the Ohio and Erie Canal
   - ◯ Funding sources for railroad construction in the nineteen century
   - ◯ The shift from canals to railroads, 1830 to 1860
   - ◯ Problems in canal construction

40. Look at the word boom in paragraph 1. The word is closest in meaning to
   - ◯ project
   - ◯ decision
   - ◯ increase
   - ◯ crash

41. The author explains that Ohio built a canal system in order to
   - ◯ encourage canal enthusiasm
   - ◯ pay off state debts
   - ◯ ship goods to the East
   - ◯ link Cleveland to the West

42. Look at the word defaulted in paragraph 1. The word is closest in meaning to
   - ◯ paid additional money
   - ◯ failed to make a court appearance
   - ◯ continued to rely
   - ◯ stopped payment of money due

43. The author mentions New York in paragraph 3 in order to
   - ⬭ give an example of a state with a canal system
   - ⬭ compare New York with Ohio
   - ⬭ explain why certain states did not support railroad expansion
   - ⬭ demonstrate canal enthusiasm

44. Which of the following is NOT mentioned in the passage as a problem in railroad construction?
   - ⬭ Inadequate bridge engineering
   - ⬭ Safety problems
   - ⬭ Lack of engine power
   - ⬭ Lower costs of using canal boats

45. The following sentence could be added to paragraph 2.

   Understandably, passengers complained as their clothing and belongings frequently caught on fire.

   Where would it best fit into the paragraph? Click on the square to add the sentence to the paragraph.

   ☐ The railroads initially functioned as feeders, or branch lines, for canals. The first railroad to begin operation was the Baltimore and Ohio in 1830. ☐ Despite its potential, railroad use developed slowly. Between 1830 and 1850, only nine thousand miles of track were laid. Private capital showed mild interest, leaving the states to supply most of the building funds. ☐ The problems involved in railroad construction seemed almost insurmountable. The most commonly used metal in tracks, cast iron, proved a poor material. ☐ In addition, no standard gauge was used. The trains ejected sparks and cinders, which constituted a menace to society. ☐ Finally, engines had insufficient power to carry heavy loads over inclines. ☐

46. Look at the word insurmountable in paragraph 2. The word is closest in meaning to
   - ⬭ ineffective
   - ⬭ insolvable
   - ⬭ inhospitable
   - ⬭ inequitable

47. Look at the word their in paragraph 3. Click on the word or phrase in the paragraph that their refers to.

48. It can be inferred from the passage that
   - ⬭ the Federal government absorbed states' debts
   - ⬭ some states continued using cast iron
   - ⬭ growth of the railroad was due to government and private investment
   - ⬭ most farmers lived in the East

49. Look at the word them in paragraph 4. Click on the word or phrase in the paragraph that them refers to.

50. The passage supports which of the following conclusions?
   - ⬭ New York was not the only state that wanted to encourage the use of its own canal system.
   - ⬭ State governments opposed the development of the railroad system in the 1850s.
   - ⬭ Prior to 1860, the development of railroad lines took place predominantly west of the Mississippi.
   - ⬭ By 1860, the major problems involved in railroad construction had been overcome.

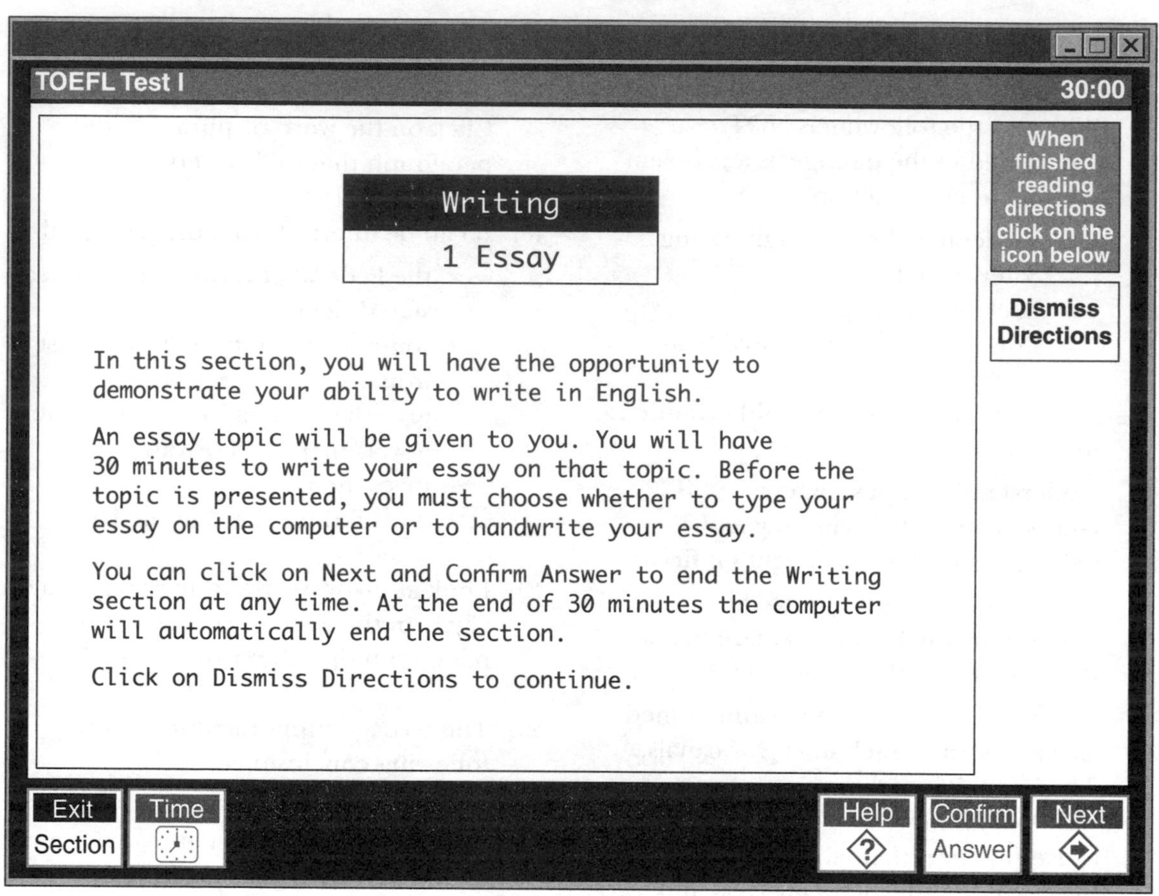
TOEFL Test I
30:00
Writing
1 Essay
In this section, you will have the opportunity to demonstrate your ability to write in English.
An essay topic will be given to you. You will have 30 minutes to write your essay on that topic. Before the topic is presented, you must choose whether to type your essay on the computer or to handwrite your essay.
You can click on Next and Confirm Answer to end the Writing section at any time. At the end of 30 minutes the computer will automatically end the section.
Click on Dismiss Directions to continue.
When finished reading directions click on the icon below
Dismiss Directions
Exit Section
Time
Help
Confirm Answer
Next

Some students prefer to prepare for tests and examinations with a study group. Others prefer to study alone. Which do you prefer? Use specific reasons and examples to support your preference.

APPENDIX D

TOEFL TEST 2

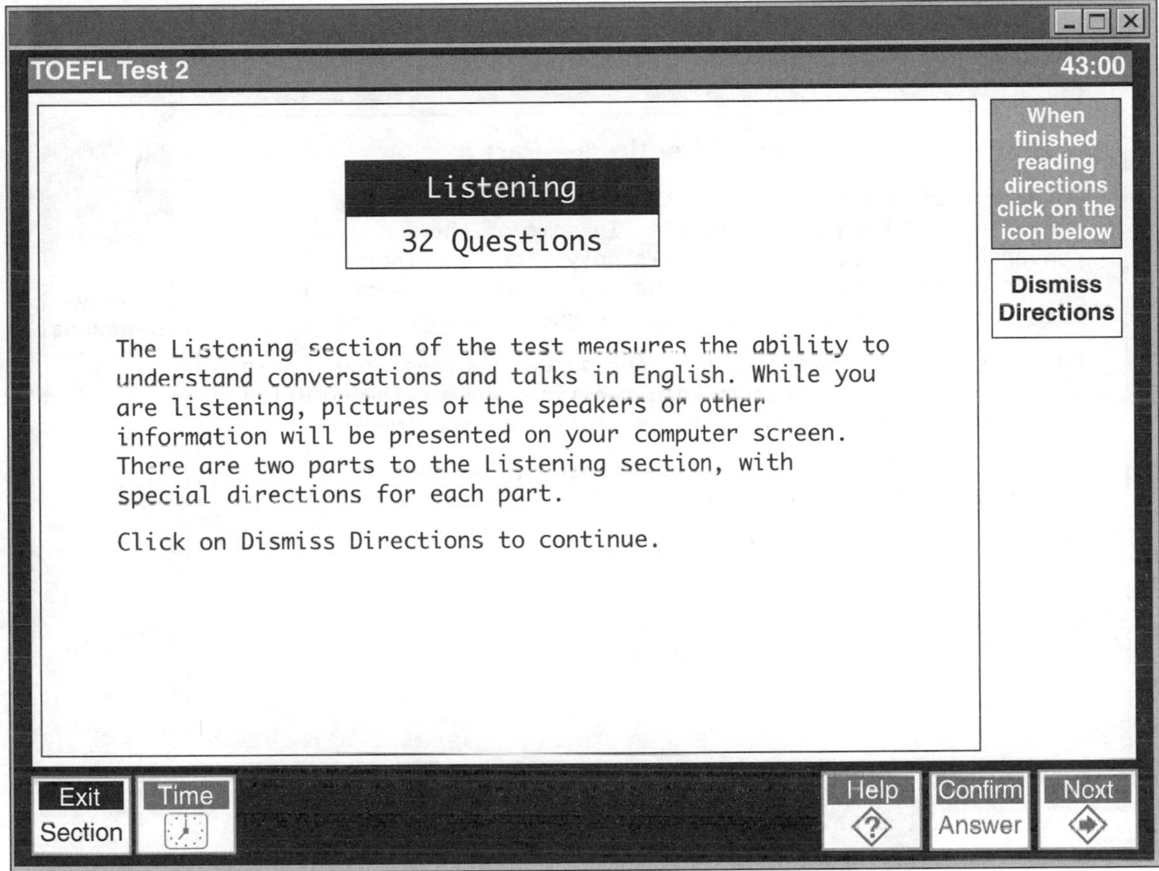
TOEFL Test 2
43:00
Listening
32 Questions
The Listening section of the test measures the ability to understand conversations and talks in English. While you are listening, pictures of the speakers or other information will be presented on your computer screen. There are two parts to the Listening section, with special directions for each part.
Click on Dismiss Directions to continue.
When finished reading directions click on the icon below
Dismiss Directions
Exit Section
Time
Help
Confirm Answer
Next

See Appendix E, pages 406–409, for the transcript of the audio passages for this text.

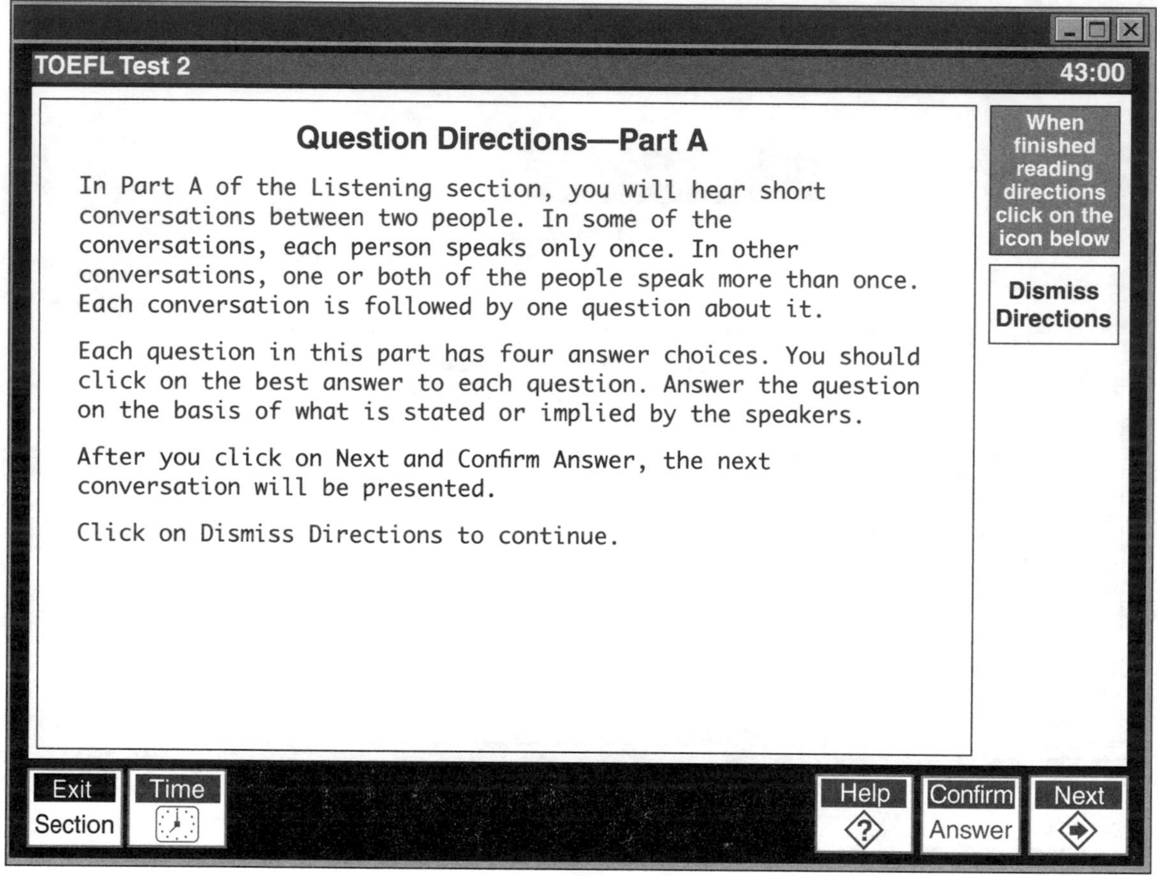

TOEFL Test 2
43:00
Question Directions—Part A
In Part A of the Listening section, you will hear short conversations between two people. In some of the conversations, each person speaks only once. In other conversations, one or both of the people speak more than once. Each conversation is followed by one question about it.
Each question in this part has four answer choices. You should click on the best answer to each question. Answer the question on the basis of what is stated or implied by the speakers.
After you click on Next and Confirm Answer, the next conversation will be presented.
Click on Dismiss Directions to continue.
When finished reading directions click on the icon below
Dismiss Directions
Exit Section
Time
Help
Confirm Answer
Next

1. What does the man mean?
   - ⬭ He didn't know where she lived, so he didn't go to see her.
   - ⬭ He knew her address, so he actually did visit her.
   - ⬭ The woman forgot to give him her address.
   - ⬭ He went to her address, but she wasn't at home.

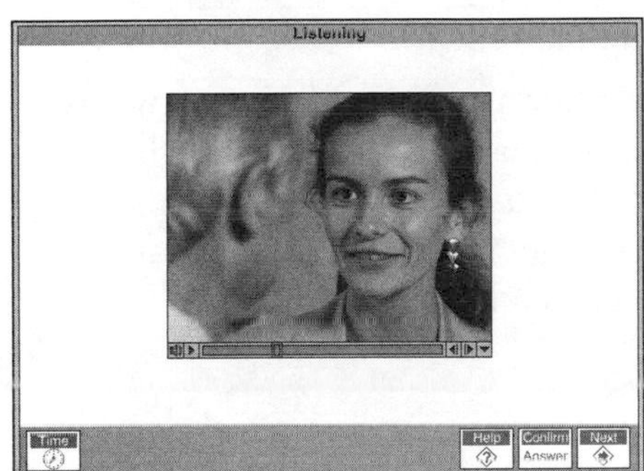

2. What will the woman probably do next?
   - ⬭ Take a careful look at the apartment
   - ⬭ Dot each line of the lease carefully
   - ⬭ Examine the document
   - ⬭ Sign the lease immediately

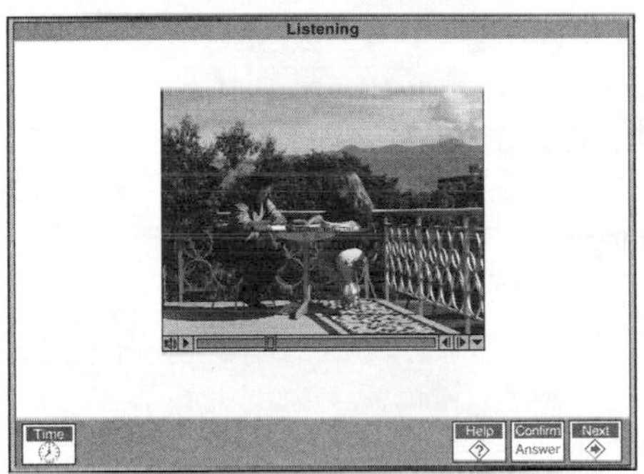

3. What does the woman imply?
   - ⬭ She changed her mind about the dorm windows.
   - ⬭ She also thinks the windows are too small.
   - ⬭ She's getting used to living in the new dorm.
   - ⬭ She thinks the colors are what make the windows look so small.

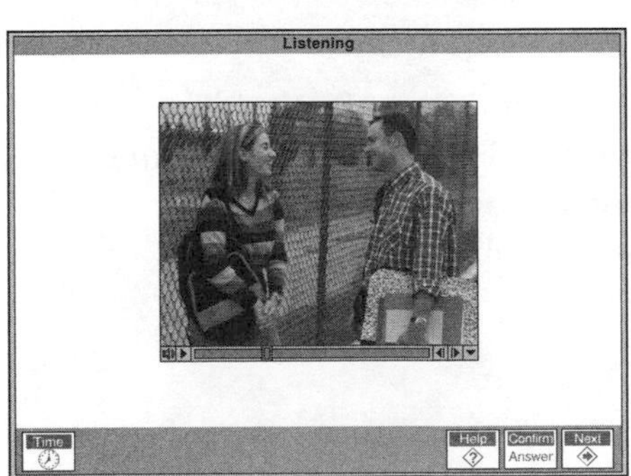

4. What does the woman mean?
   - ⬭ She has to pay the professor by check.
   - ⬭ She should make sure the professor agreed with her request.
   - ⬭ She should see if the professor is all right.
   - ⬭ She should find out if the professor checked her paper.

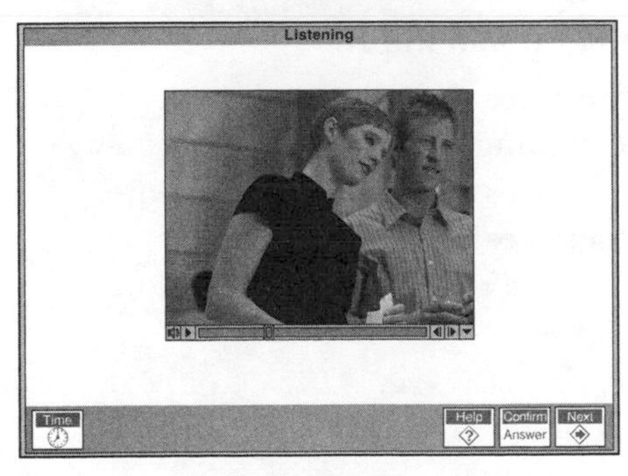

5. What does the man mean?
   - ⬭ She has already submitted her work to the judges.
   - ⬭ Anna hardly knows her ability.
   - ⬭ It's difficult to choose which of Anna's weavings is better than the rest.
   - ⬭ It's hard to know whether Anna's weavings are the best.

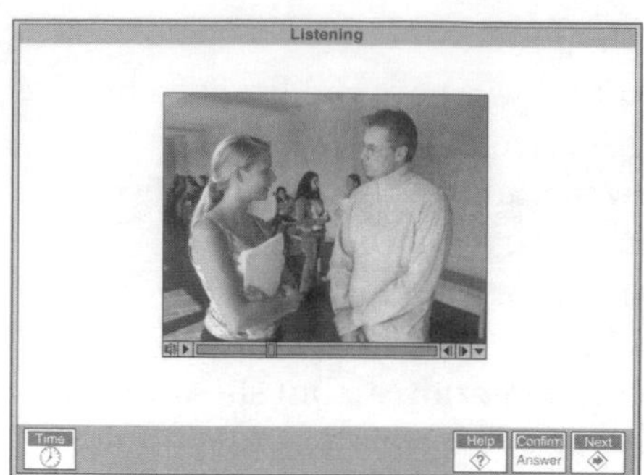

6. What does the woman imply?
   - ◯ She knows another professor teaching the course.
   - ◯ The course is strange, so maybe he shouldn't take it.
   - ◯ It's possible to take History 102 without having taken 101.
   - ◯ His only option is to take the required prerequisite.

7. What does the man mean?
   - ◯ He'll give her any piece of pie she wants.
   - ◯ She'll have a hard time deciding which school to go to.
   - ◯ She should get some scholarship money.
   - ◯ She will earn a lot of money.

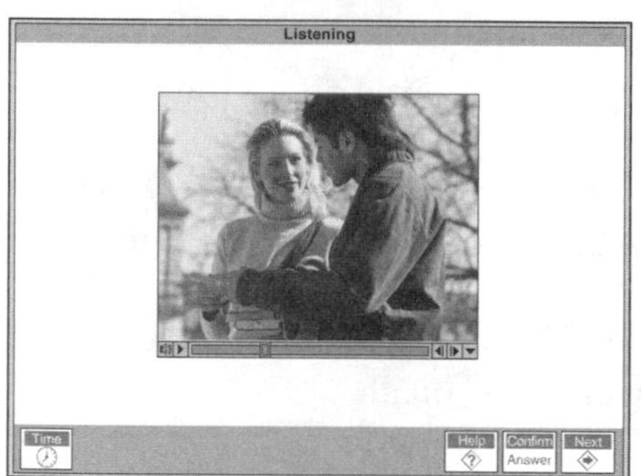

8. What will the man probably do next?
   - ◯ Cash in his frequent flier miles
   - ◯ Settle his tuition bill
   - ◯ Pay his bill in cash
   - ◯ Negotiate with the bursar's office

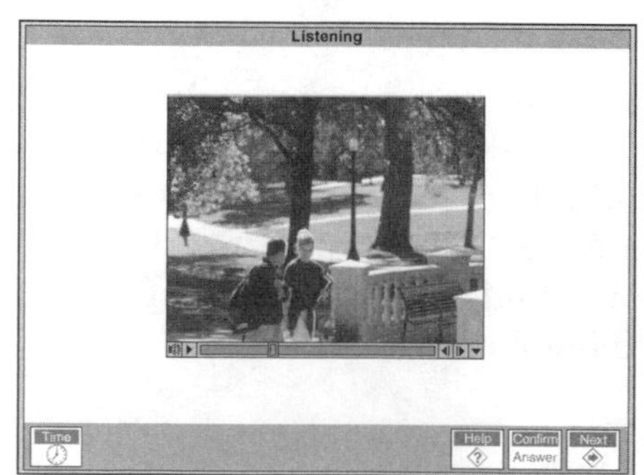

9. What does the woman mean?
   - ◯ She's not planning on graduating.
   - ◯ She's surprised about the requirement.
   - ◯ She's not a good swimmer.
   - ◯ She doesn't believe she'll be able to pass.

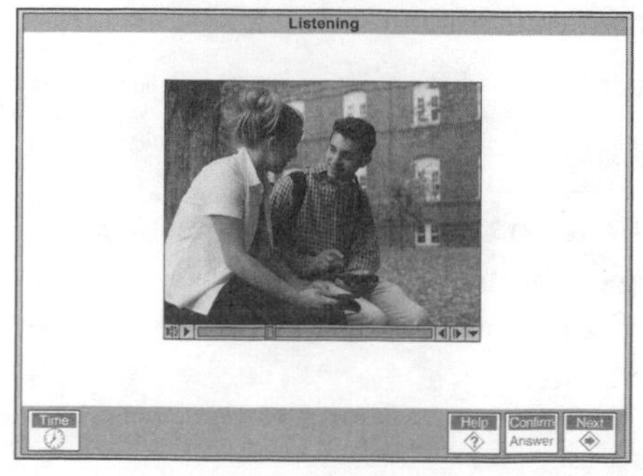

10. What does the woman imply?
   - ◯ Career services doesn't post jobs.
   - ◯ It's worth going to career services.
   - ◯ Career services will write your resume.
   - ◯ Career services is hiring.

11. What does the man imply?
    - ⬭ He'll be done by next semester.
    - ⬭ Finishing early in the day is important to him.
    - ⬭ He'll take one class after three.
    - ⬭ He wants to see what she thinks of his one class.

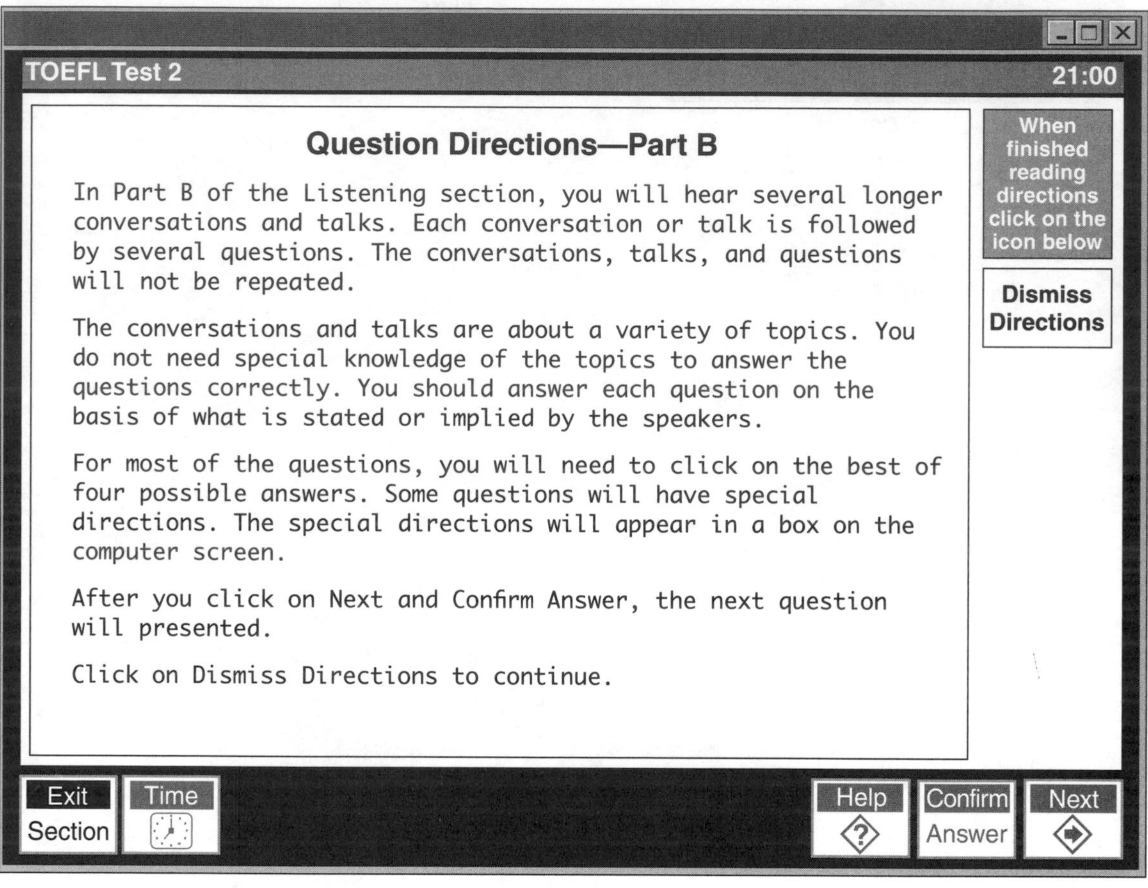
TOEFL Test 2
21:00
Question Directions—Part B
In Part B of the Listening section, you will hear several longer conversations and talks. Each conversation or talk is followed by several questions. The conversations, talks, and questions will not be repeated.
The conversations and talks are about a variety of topics. You do not need special knowledge of the topics to answer the questions correctly. You should answer each question on the basis of what is stated or implied by the speakers.
For most of the questions, you will need to click on the best of four possible answers. Some questions will have special directions. The special directions will appear in a box on the computer screen.
After you click on Next and Confirm Answer, the next question will presented.
Click on Dismiss Directions to continue.
When finished reading directions click on the icon below
Dismiss Directions
Exit Section
Time
Help
Confirm Answer
Next

Questions 12–14

12. What is the discussion mainly about?
    - ◯ Jobs that allow time to study
    - ◯ The advantages of working in the photo lab
    - ◯ Returning books to the library
    - ◯ What time to get to the job fair

13. Why does the woman not want to work as a lifeguard?
    - ◯ She wants to develop her pictures in the photo lab.
    - ◯ She can't do any of her homework while working.
    - ◯ It's too dark to see anything in the pool.
    - ◯ Since she's a photographer, she should work in the lab.

14. What will the man probably do next?
    - ◯ Develop his pictures
    - ◯ Work security at a library
    - ◯ Go to the job fair
    - ◯ Stop off at the library

Questions 15–17

15. Where is the concert?
    - ◯ At Hill Auditorium
    - ◯ At the student union
    - ◯ Off campus
    - ◯ At the music school

16. What can be inferred about the competition?
    - ◯ The orchestras must be skilled in different areas.
    - ◯ Each orchestra will play the same pieces.
    - ◯ Faculty members will compete.
    - ◯ Tickets are free only for students.

17. What will the woman probably do next?
    - ◯ Take out some money
    - ◯ Practice for the concert
    - ◯ Go with the man to the performance
    - ◯ Get herself a ticket

Questions 18–22

Listen to part of a lecture in an American history class. The lecture is on President Abraham Lincoln.

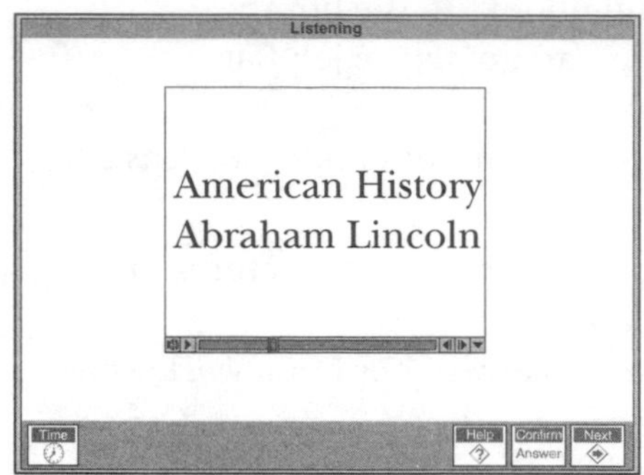

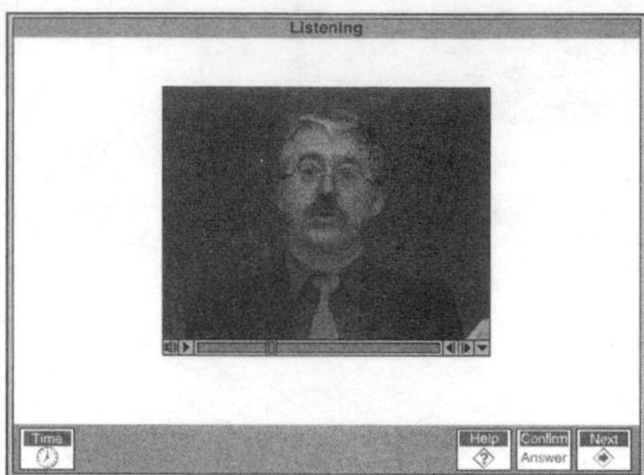

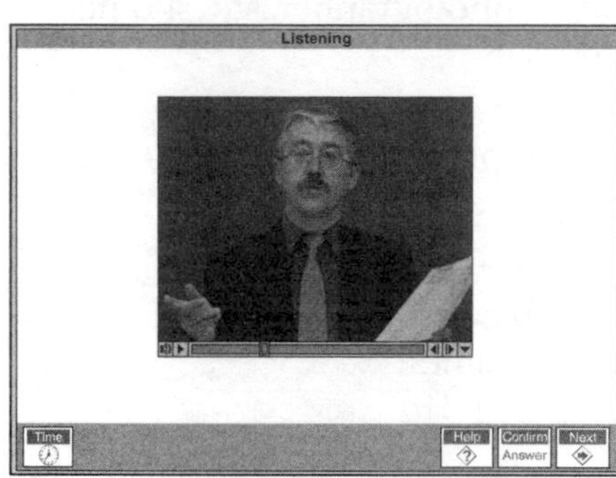

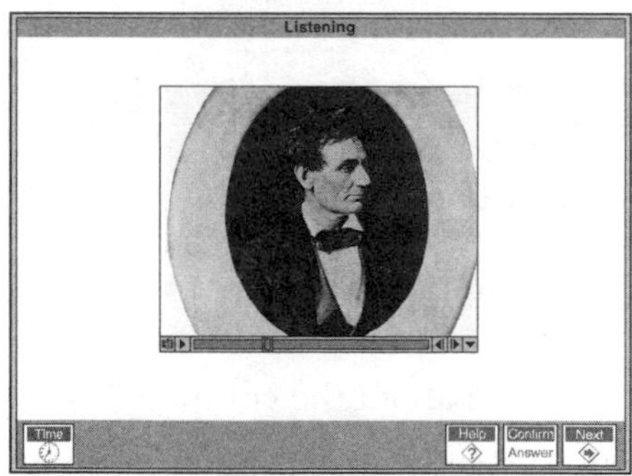

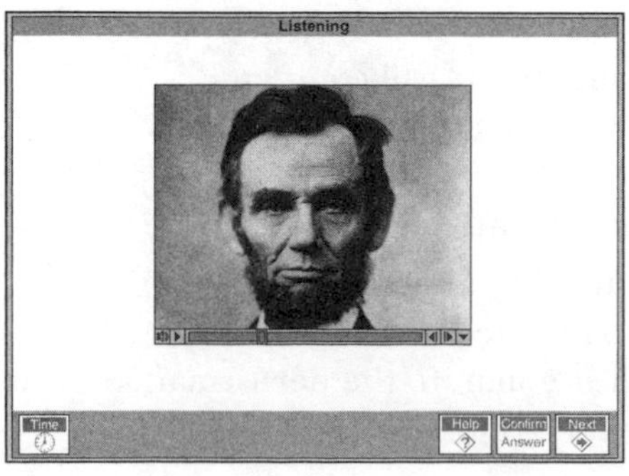

18. What is the lecture mainly about?
    - ⬭ Facial hair styles of the nineteenth century
    - ⬭ President Lincoln's close election
    - ⬭ Why Lincoln decided to grow a beard
    - ⬭ The life of Grace Bedell of New York state

19. Why does Grace suggest Lincoln grow a beard?

    Click on 2 answers.

    - ☐ To make him more popular with ladies
    - ☐ To make his face look fuller
    - ☐ To make him look older and kinder
    - ☐ So that the wives would influence their husbands' votes

20. Which picture shows Lincoln immediately after the election?

    Click on a picture.

21. When was Lincoln's Presidential inauguration?
    - ⬭ 1816
    - ⬭ 1860
    - ⬭ 1861
    - ⬭ 1862

22. In the lecture, the professor explains a historical series of events. Put the events in chronological order.

    Click on a sentence. Then click on the space where it belongs. Use each sentence only once.

    Lincoln grows whiskers.
    Grace meets Abraham Lincoln.
    Lincoln becomes President.
    Grace writes to Lincoln.

    1. ________
    2. ________
    3. ________
    4. ________

Questions 23–27

Listen to part of a discussion in a class of dental students.

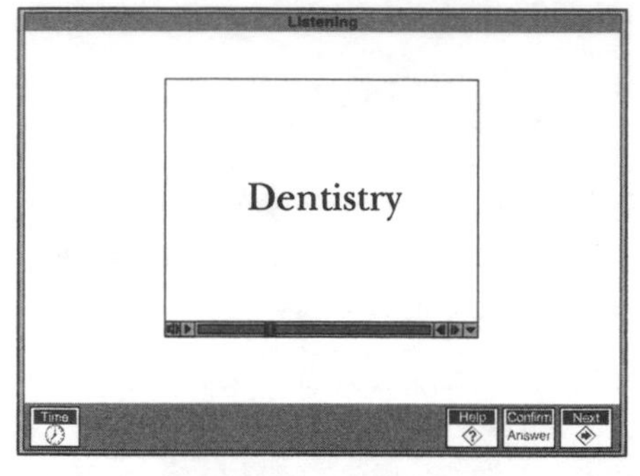

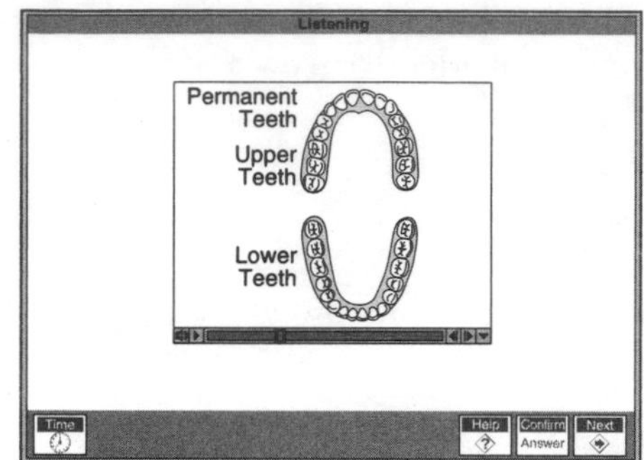

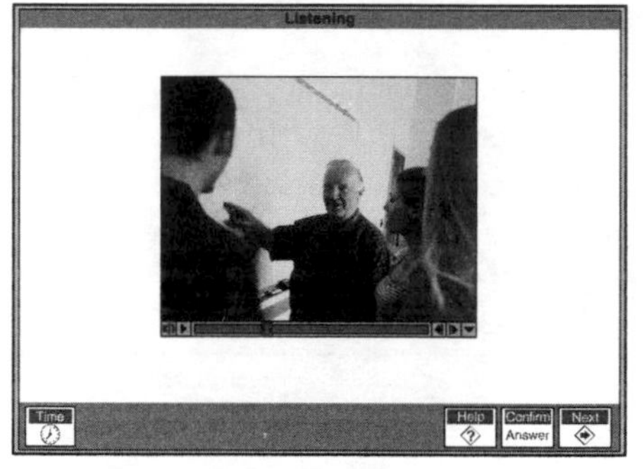

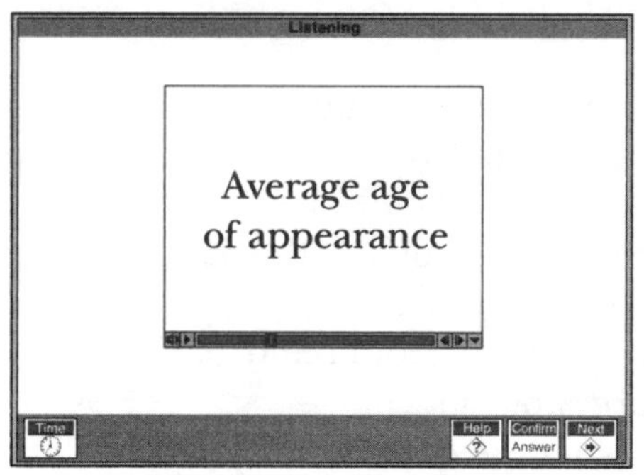

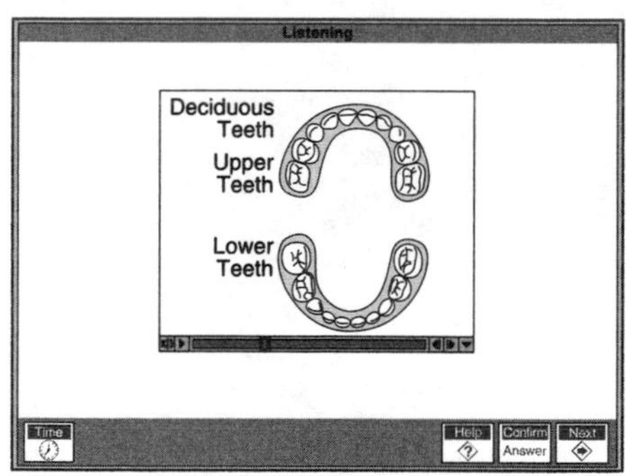

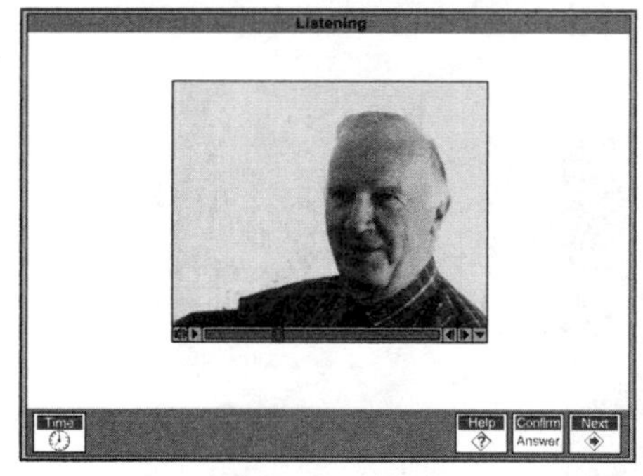

23. What is the discussion mainly about?
   - ⬭ What to do about missing teeth
   - ⬭ Exceptions to the average age of tooth development
   - ⬭ Types of teeth and age of appearance
   - ⬭ The differences between animal and human teeth

24. How old are children when they usually develop their primary or deciduous teeth?
   - ⬭ Between 9 and 20 months
   - ⬭ Between 6 months and 2 years
   - ⬭ Between 20 and 24 months
   - ⬭ Between 1 and 2 years

25. Which of the following situations happens regularly?
   - ⬭ Having two front teeth at birth
   - ⬭ Having a primary tooth removed because it never fell out
   - ⬭ Developing first permanent teeth at roughly 20 to 24 months
   - ⬭ Developing wisdom teeth between the ages of 17 and 21

26. Which of these occurrences happened to the students?

   Click on 2 answers.

   - ☐ Being born with teeth
   - ☐ Needing a tooth implant
   - ☐ Having permanent teeth that never grew in
   - ☐ Having to pull a baby tooth that never fell out

27. In the discussion, the order of permanent teeth development is discussed. Put the teeth in the order in which they appear.

   Click on a type of tooth. Then click on the space where it belongs. Use each tooth only once.

   First molars
   Central incisors
   Canines
   Lateral incisors

   1. ______
   2. ______
   3. ______
   4. ______

Questions 28–32

Listen to part of a lecture on oceanographic history.

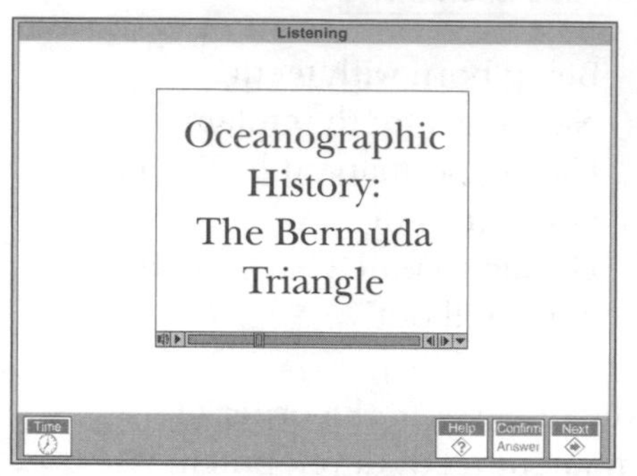

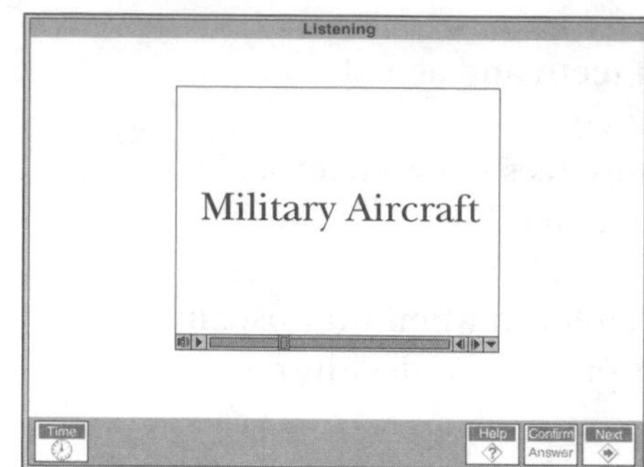

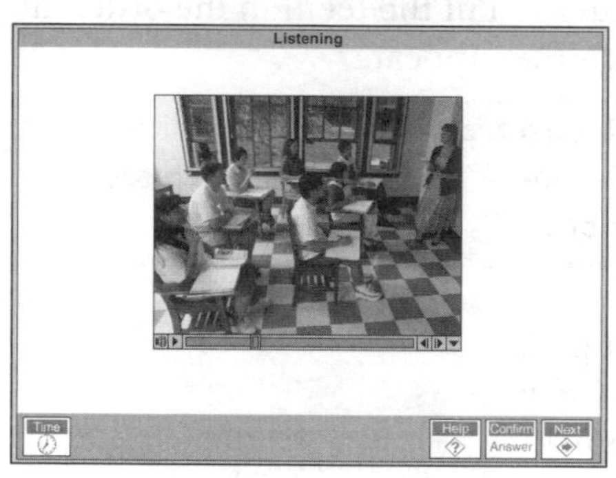

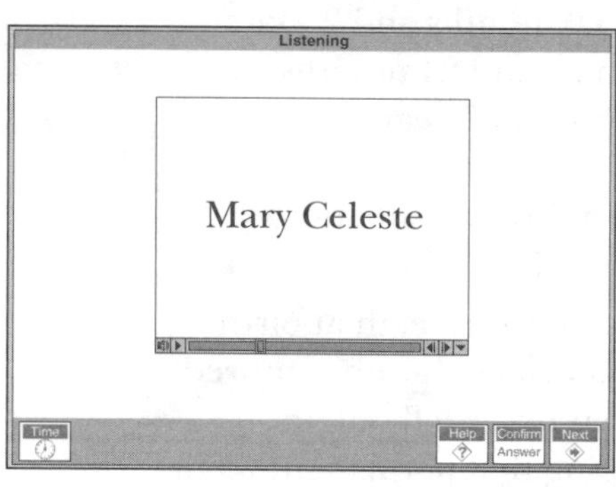

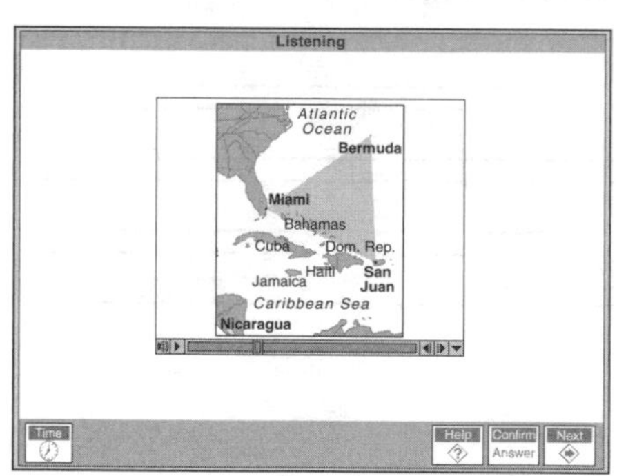

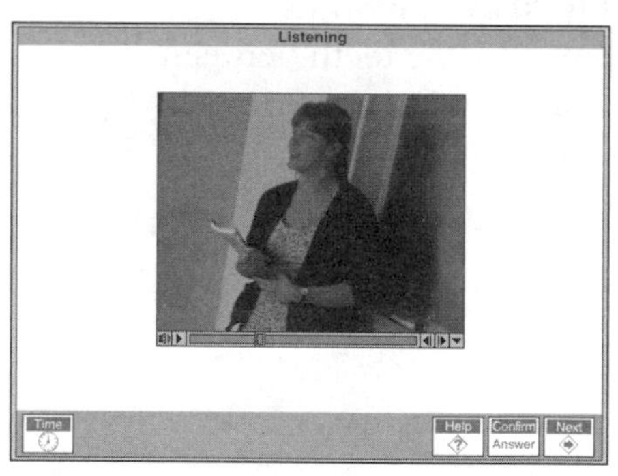

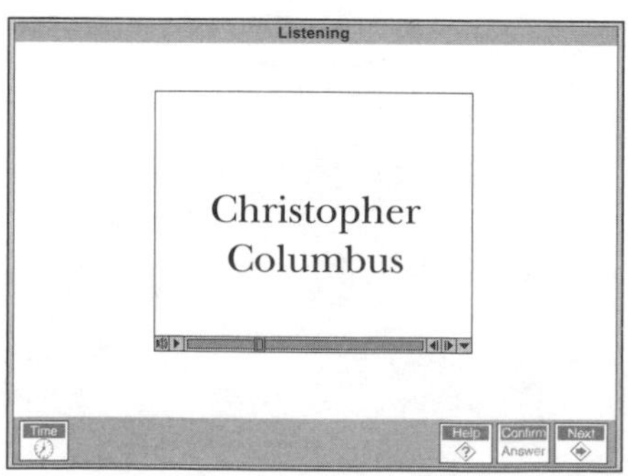

28. What does the professor mainly talk about?
    - ⬭ Christopher Columbus's connection to the Bermuda Triangle
    - ⬭ Reasons to avoid flying in the Bermuda Triangle
    - ⬭ Myths and facts about the Bermuda Triangle
    - ⬭ The expansion of the Bermuda Triangle

29. Identify the part of the map that includes the Bermuda Triangle.

    Click on the correct letter.

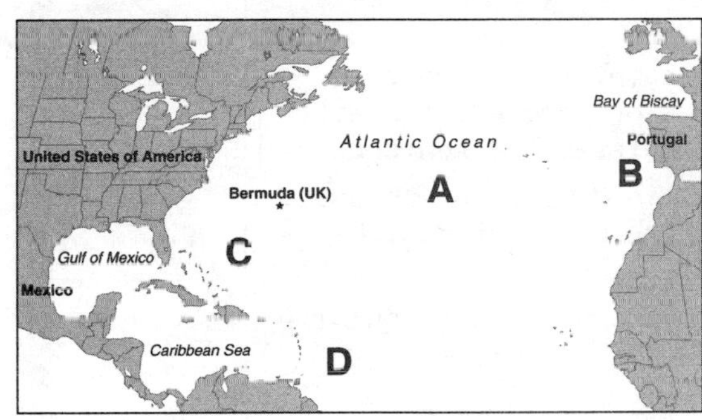

30. Which of the following is NOT mentioned as a scientific explanation for the Bermuda Triangle?
    - ⬭ Violent storms
    - ⬭ Swift ocean currents
    - ⬭ Downward air currents
    - ⬭ Very deep waters

31. What is stated in the lecture as the two major obstacles to taking the legend seriously?

    Click on 2 answers.

    - ☐ Numerous disappearances did not happen within the Bermuda Triangle region.
    - ☐ Traces of lost crafts and radio transmissions have been recovered.
    - ☐ Accidents will happen anywhere.
    - ☐ Most disappearances can be explained scientifically.

32. The professor explains a series of events. Put the events in their chronological order.

    Click on a sentence. Then click on the space where it belongs. Use each sentence only once.

    The area gets its nickname, the Bermuda Triangle.
    Bright lights and bizarre compass readings are reported.
    Six U.S. military aircraft disappear.
    The *Mary Celeste* goes off course.

    1. ______
    2. ______
    3. ______
    4. ______

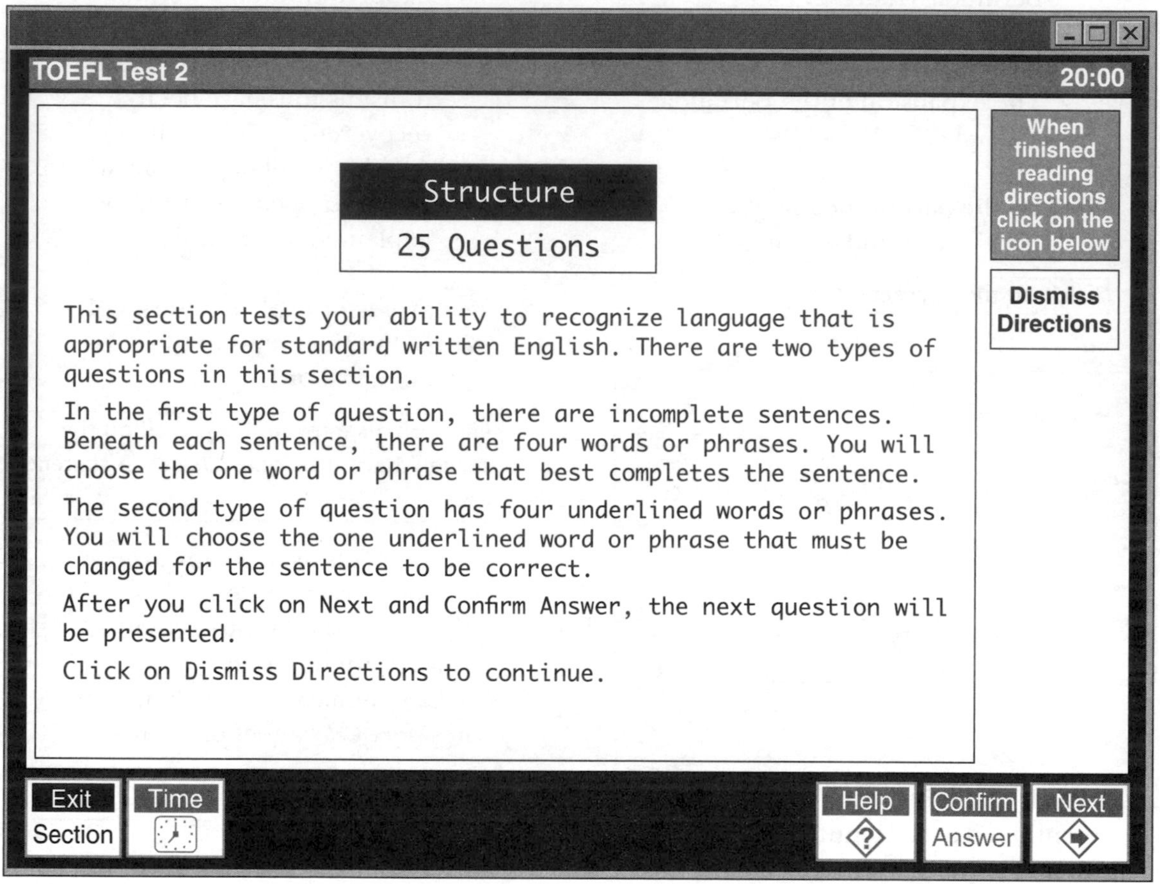
TOEFL Test 2
20:00
Structure
25 Questions
This section tests your ability to recognize language that is appropriate for standard written English. There are two types of questions in this section.
In the first type of question, there are incomplete sentences. Beneath each sentence, there are four words or phrases. You will choose the one word or phrase that best completes the sentence.
The second type of question has four underlined words or phrases. You will choose the one underlined word or phrase that must be changed for the sentence to be correct.
After you click on Next and Confirm Answer, the next question will be presented.
Click on Dismiss Directions to continue.
When finished reading directions click on the icon below
Dismiss Directions
Exit Section
Time
Help
Confirm Answer
Next

1. Since the 1940s, creativity in modern dance has centered on both U.S. dancers or dance companies.

2. Chameleons puff out their throats and the rest of its bodies to look larger in an attempt to scare away other males.

3. Animation, a motion-picture technique in which filmmakers create the illusion of motion, can to exist without relying on any type of technology.

4. _____, many people felt that America should have been named Columbus after the explorer Christopher Columbus.
   - ◯ The Revolutionary War was before
   - ◯ Before the Revolutionary War began
   - ◯ The Revolutionary War, before began
   - ◯ It was before the Revolutionary War began

5. The selection of products available through mail order companies are large and varied.

6. Crustaceans use some of their legs mainly for swimming or walking, as well as for ____ food, for fighting, or for doing other activities.
   - ◯ having caught
   - ◯ catching
   - ◯ to catch
   - ◯ catch

7. Pete Seeger is an American folk singer, musician, and composer who first gained fame _______ 1940s by singing about ordinary working people.
   - ◯ since the
   - ◯ during the
   - ◯ it was the
   - ◯ while the

8. The name "Arkansas" _________ an Indian word that means land of downstream people.
   - ◯ which comes from
   - ◯ it comes from
   - ◯ is coming from
   - ◯ comes from

9. The movie *Coffee and Cigarettes*, seventeen years in the making, consist of a series of black-and-white vignettes involving caffeine and nicotine.

10. _____, astronomy is a field in which amateurs can make significant contributions.
    - ◯ Unlike most other sciences
    - ◯ Not only most other sciences
    - ◯ However most other sciences
    - ◯ In most other sciences

11. Antennae are long, delicate sensory organs on the heads of almost all insects and most others arthropods.

12. Louis Kahn, a leading American architect of the mid-1900s, designed the British Art Center at Yale University which features creative use of concrete walls, ____, and natural light.
    - ◯ geometric shapes of simplicity
    - ◯ simple shapely geometry
    - ◯ geometry shaped simply
    - ◯ simple geometric shapes

13. Many farmers use alfalfa as a cover crop, that is, to enrich the soil and protect it on erosion.

14. Late in 1939, Orson Welles was invited to Hollywood to make a motion picture _______.
    - ◯ he chooses himself
    - ◯ his choosing by himself
    - ◯ that he could choose himself
    - ◯ that could be of his choosing himself

15. Anne Legendre Armstrong became a first woman to serve as U.S. ambassador to Great Britain.

16. The Articles of Confederation was the agreement under which the thirteen original colonies have established a government of states in 1781.

17. _____, people used beads, cocoa beans, salt, shells, stones, tobacco, and many other objects as money.
    - The past
    - Although the past
    - That in the past
    - In the past

18. By 1921, Andrew Mellon had become _____ persons in America.
    - one of the wealthiest
    - the wealthier
    - the wealthiest of one
    - one wealthiest

19. Astronauts operate spacecraft and space stations, launch and recapture satellites, and conduct engineer, medical, and scientific experiments in space.

20. Fish and other sea animals are most abundant in water whose is rich in tiny drifting plants.

21. _____ of measurement has ever equaled the metric system in simplicity.
    - Another system
    - No other system
    - No system other
    - Other systems

22. Within the limits of the wishes and needs of clients, architects can do their own personal artistic contributions.

23. Some physical anthropologists study the animals that most closely resemble human beings, included chimpanzees and other apes.

24. The luster of the fabric damask depends on the length of fibers, the closeness of weave, and the __________.
    - yarns of the uniformity
    - uniformity of yarns
    - yarns uniformity
    - uniformity yarns

25. A word-processing program allows people to type words into a computer to write articles, books, letters, reporters, and other kinds of documents.

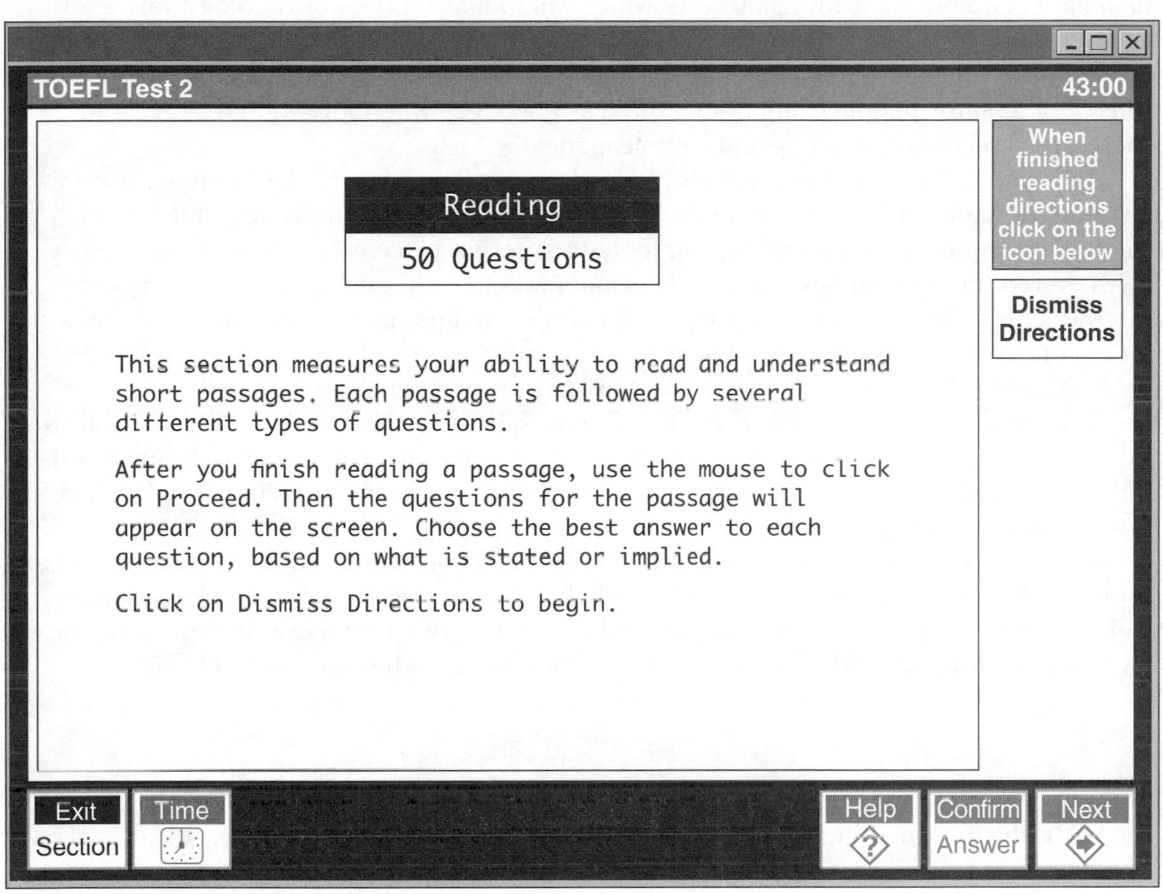
TOEFL Test 2
43:00
Reading
50 Questions
This section measures your ability to read and understand short passages. Each passage is followed by several different types of questions.
After you finish reading a passage, use the mouse to click on Proceed. Then the questions for the passage will appear on the screen. Choose the best answer to each question, based on what is stated or implied.
Click on Dismiss Directions to begin.
When finished reading directions click on the icon below
Dismiss Directions
Exit Section
Time
Help
Confirm Answer
Next

PASSAGE 1 Questions 1–12

For the past twenty years, Daniel Debouck, a Belgian plant geneticist, has been studying a type of Peruvian bean called the *nuna.* This word comes from the native Incan language, Quechua. The bean is a "lost crop of the Andes," one of the ancient crops that is relatively unknown except within the South American mountain region. Dr. Debouck believes that the *nuna* has been cultivated for 8,000 years, which would make it the world's oldest variety of bean. Because the bean could be popped open on a rock heated by a fire, it could have been grown before the technique of making clay pots was discovered. In addition, the *nuna* is well-suited as a food for people living in the Andes at 7,000 feet, where firewood is scarce and where very fast-cooking foods would have been ideal.

The ancient bean may bring rewards to modern-day Peru as well. The Peruvian government has found entrepreneurs in Japan and Spain who are interested in the *nuna.* These entrepreneurs are now doing market testing in Cuzco, a city in Southern Peru. They have covered the popped bean, which tastes and looks like a cross between popcorn and a nut, with chocolate. Tourists are testing chocolate-covered popped *nuna* beans which are set out next to peanuts in bars and in hotels.

Inspired by the *nuna* bean, James Neinhuis, a plant breeder at the University of Wisconsin's College of Agriculture and Life Sciences, has been developing a bean similar to the *nuna* with day neutrality. Plants with this characteristic can grow in the long summer days in the U.S. as well as in the shorter days of the tropics. Dr. Neinhuis envisions "Pre-Cooked Popping Beans" on supermarket shelves one day.

The *nuna* beans have been introduced at Disney's Epcot Center, where they are part of a display on lost Incan crops. Dr. Debouck is delighted and hopes that the bean he has been studying for so long may be a sign of a diversification in agriculture. He also hopes that one day it will provide native farmers and their families with a higher standard of living.

1. With which of the following is the passage primarily concerned?
   - ○ The diverse crops grown in the time of the Incas
   - ○ The research of plant geneticist Daniel Debouck
   - ○ Marketing studies in Cuzco, Peru, on nutritious snacks
   - ○ The history of the *nuna* bean and its potential as a modern-day crop

2. It can be inferred from the passage that the *nuna* bean
   - ○ may one day be better known
   - ○ is selling well at Disney's Epcot Center
   - ○ was the major source of food for ancient Peruvians
   - ○ is popular in Japan and Spain

3. Look at the word cultivated in paragraph 1. Click on the word or phrase in the paragraph that is closest in meaning to the word cultivated.

4. The passage does NOT state that
   - ○ during the time of the Incas, people lived at 7,000 feet
   - ○ there are few trees in the Andes above 7,000 feet
   - ○ the technique of making clay pots was discovered by the Incas in the 15th century
   - ○ the discovery of the technique of making clay pots influenced cooking methods among the Incas

5. Look at the word they in paragraph 2. Click on the word or phrase in the paragraph that they refers to.

6. Look at the word cross in paragraph 2. The word is closest in meaning to
   - ⬭ mixture
   - ⬭ link
   - ⬭ intersection
   - ⬭ precursor

7. Look at the phrase day neutrality in paragraph 3. The phrase refers to
   - ⬭ the appeal of the *nuna* bean as part of both a summer and a winter diet
   - ⬭ the potential appeal of the *nuna* bean to people in both the Midwestern U.S. and the tropics
   - ⬭ the ability of the *nuna* bean to grow well with varying degrees of sunlight
   - ⬭ the number of days the *nuna* beans can last on a supermarket shelf without spoiling

8. Which of the following is NOT true about Dr. Neinhuis?
   - ⬭ He works at the University of Wisconsin.
   - ⬭ He hopes to see his beans sold in supermarkets.
   - ⬭ He is marketing the beans in the tropics.
   - ⬭ He is developing a new strain of bean.

9. The following sentence could be added to paragraph 2 or 3.

   This adaptation bodes well for worldwide marketing.

   Where would it best fit into the paragraph? Click on the square to add the sentence to the paragraph.

   ☐ Tourists are testing chocolate-covered popped *nuna* beans which are set out next to peanuts in bars and in hotels.

   ☐ Inspired by the *nuna* bean, James Neinhuis, a plant breeder at the University of Wisconsin's College of Agriculture and Life Sciences, has been developing a bean similar to the *nuna* with day neutrality. Plants with this characteristic can grow in the long summer days in the U.S. as well as in the shorter days of the tropics. ☐ Dr. Neinhuis envisions "Pre-Cooked Popping Beans" on supermarket shelves one day. ☐

10. Look at the word it in paragraph 4. Click on the word or phrase in the paragraph that it refers to.

11. Look at the word native in paragraph 4. The word is closest in meaning to
    - ⬭ impoverished
    - ⬭ ambitious
    - ⬭ indigenous
    - ⬭ hard-working

12. Click on the paragraph that indicates where one can sample *nuna* beans today.

PASSAGE 2 Questions 13–25

To many people in the U.S., the buffalo, or more correctly, the bison, is part national symbol, part national pet. Buffalo have occupied the Yellowstone National Park region since the Pleistocene era, which ended 10,000 years ago. There were as many as 50 million of them on the continent before hunters reduced their numbers to a thousand or so by the last decade of the nineteenth century. Today, thanks to the efforts of conservationists and entrepreneurs who see the buffalo as a potential tourist attraction and a source of desirable meat, as many as 250,000 roam public and private lands in the U.S.

The grazing habits of the buffalo are ideally suited to the native grasses of the Great Plains. Perennial grass plants grow better where buffalo graze because the animals' sharp hoofs break up and aerate the soil, improving the ability of the soil to retain water. In addition, the buffalo can withstand the harsh winter climate of the Great Plains. The huge animals can move snow mounds aside with their great heads to find grass to eat. During blizzards, pregnant buffalo hold off delivering their young, thus ensuring their survival.

The buffalo were an important part of the religion and tradition of the Plains Indians. Additionally, buffalo meat was used for food and their hides for shelter and clothing. One Great Plains tribe, the Lakota, called themselves Pte Oyate, Buffalo Nation. According to Indian lore, buffalo were born in the Black Hills of South Dakota. There is evidence that great herds of these animals once roamed over North America between the Appalachian Mountains on the east and the Rockies on the west.

Today South Dakota is home to close to 2,000 buffalo in separate herds at Custer State Park and Wind Cave National Park. In Wyoming's Yellowstone National Park, some 3,000 buffalo range at will over two million acres of forest and mountains. In the parks where they now live, the buffalo are a major tourist attraction, yet park visitors need to be careful; the average buffalo can sprint up to 35 miles an hour, three times faster than the average tourist can run.

Buffalo meat can be found in neighborhood supermarkets. Specialty markets and mail-order firms also sell various cuts of buffalo meat, costing between $4 and $30 a pound.

13. With what topic is paragraph 1 mainly concerned?
    - ◯ The buffalo census numbers throughout history
    - ◯ Recent efforts to increase the buffalo population
    - ◯ The role of the buffalo as a tourist attraction
    - ◯ The importance of the buffalo to Native American history

14. According to the information in paragraph 1, the buffalo population was probably at its lowest point in
    - ◯ 1800
    - ◯ 1895
    - ◯ 1950
    - ◯ 1994

15. Look at the word their in paragraph 1. Click on the word or phrase in the paragraph that their refers to.

16. According to the passage, why are individuals trying to save the buffalo?
    - ◯ For religious ceremonies
    - ◯ For visitor appeal
    - ◯ For pet sales
    - ◯ For soil aeration

17. Which of the following is supported by the information in paragraph 2?
    - ◯ Buffalo destroy the habitat of waterfowl.
    - ◯ Buffalo give birth even during severe snowstorms.
    - ◯ Buffalo graze in smaller groups than cattle do.
    - ◯ Buffalo enable the ground to remain moist.

18. The following sentence could be added to paragraph 2.

    These vast grasslands extend from northern Canada to southern Texas, and from the Rocky Mountains eastward for about 400 miles.

    Where would it best fit into the paragraph? Click on the square to add the sentence to the paragraph.

    □ The grazing habits of the buffalo are ideally suited to the native grasses of the Great Plains. □ Perennial grass plants grow better where buffalo graze because the animals' sharp hoofs break up and aerate the soil, improving the ability of the soil to retain water. □ In addition, the buffalo can withstand the harsh winter climate of the Great Plains. □ The huge animals can move snow mounds aside with their great heads to find grass to eat. During blizzards, pregnant buffalo hold off delivering their young, thus ensuring their survival. □

19. Look at the word lore in paragraph 3. The word is closest in meaning to

    ○ identity
    ○ mythology
    ○ hierarchy
    ○ investigation

20. Click on the sentence in paragraph 4 that explains why visitors must be vigilant while viewing buffalo.

21. Look at the phrase at will in paragraph 4. The phrase is closest in meaning to

    ○ according to plan
    ○ freely
    ○ as stipulated in a will
    ○ as they have been trained to do

22. According to the passage, which of the following is NOT mentioned as a seller of buffalo meat?

    ○ National parks
    ○ Local markets
    ○ Catalogues
    ○ Specialty grocers

23. Click on the paragraph that explains how the presence of buffalo preserves the plants and animal life in an area.

24. According to the passage, why were buffalo important to Native Americans?

    ○ For food
    ○ For transportation
    ○ As tourist attractions
    ○ For traditional beliefs

25. According to the passage, what is the approximate number of buffalo found throughout the U.S. today?

    ○ 3,000
    ○ 4,000
    ○ 250,000
    ○ 500,000,000

PASSAGE 3 Questions 26–37

Farmers in India, as well as in countries in Central and South America, grew distinct species of the cotton plant thousands of years ago. Archaeologists have even found pieces of cotton cloth more than 4,000 years old along the Peruvian coast and in the Indus Valley. By 1500 A.D., the plant had reached the warm regions of the Americas, Eurasia, and Africa.

In the 1600s, southern American colonies began growing cotton. The colonists wove cotton into coarse cloth for their own use. Large-scale cotton growing began in the late 1700s. In the 1850s, a machine was invented to knock the hard hulls from the kernels of cottonseed, and so the cottonseed processing industry was born. In 1879, Ivory soap, made from the oil, was first produced. Around 1910 came America's first vegetable shortening, Crisco, which was made from cottonseed oil. Today, we use cottonseed oil in margarine, salad dressings, and cooking oils. Meal from the kernels is now made into fish bait, organic fertilizer, and feed for cattle. In the coming years, new uses will probably continue to be discovered for this multi-purpose plant.

Currently, cotton is the best selling fiber throughout the world. Cotton comprises 61.5% of the total retail apparel and home furnishing market, aside from carpets, in the U.S. Most of the cotton that U.S. mills spin and weave into cloth each year ends up as clothing. Cotton is frequently the fabric of choice as it absorbs color very well, and different textures can be achieved from different varieties of cotton. In addition to clothing, cotton is used in making such diverse items as bookbindings, fishnets, handbags, coffee filters, lace, tents, curtains, and diapers.

Another attribute of cotton is its endurance. For this reason, it is an important component in medical supplies. Cotton is used for bandages and sutures because it will hold up in all kinds of environments. This durability also made it the preferred material for firefighters' hoses. In the past, cotton fibers in the hoses would soak up water to prevent them from igniting. Today, however, fire hoses are usually made from synthetic materials that are cheaper and more durable than cotton. However, in some environments, natural cotton is still the requested material for hoses. For example, on U.S. Navy ships, the hoses are made of cotton since the sun tends to melt the combustible synthetic materials. In addition, recent experiments have led scientists to think that cotton may be more absorbent for cleaning up oil spills than the synthetic material currently used.

26. With which of the following is the passage primarily concerned?
    - ⬭ The historical and contemporary uses of cotton
    - ⬭ The history of the cotton textile industry
    - ⬭ The development of the edible cottonseed
    - ⬭ The shift of cotton from a textile crop to a food crop

27. Click on the sentence in paragraph 3 that indicates why cotton is a good material from which to make clothing.

28. The following sentence could be added to paragraph 3.

Cotton is a component of many items other than clothing.

Where would it best fit into the paragraph? Click on the square to add the sentence to the paragraph.

☐ Currently, cotton is the best selling fiber throughout the world. Cotton comprises 61.5% of the total retail apparel and home furnishing market, aside from carpets, in the U.S. ☐ Most of the cotton that U.S. mills spin and weave into cloth each year ends up as clothing. ☐ Cotton is frequently the fabric of choice as it absorbs color very well, and different textures can be achieved from different varieties of cotton. ☐ In addition to clothing, cotton is used in making such diverse items as bookbindings, fishnets, handbags, coffee filters, lace, tents, curtains, and diapers. □

29. Look at word **them** in paragraph 4. Click on the word or phrase in the paragraph that **them** refers to.

30. Look at the word **durability** in paragraph 4. Click on the word or phrase in the paragraph that is closest in meaning to the word **durability**.

31. For which of the following is cotton NOT generally used today?
   - ○ Hoses on U.S. Navy ships
   - ○ Bandages
   - ○ Clothing
   - ○ Oil spill clean ups

32. Look at the word **natural** in paragraph 4. Click on the word or phrase in the paragraph that is most nearly OPPOSITE the word **natural**.

33. Look at the word **combustible** in paragraph 4. The word is closest in meaning to
   - ○ breakable
   - ○ operational
   - ○ expendable
   - ○ flammable

34. Which of the following is NOT a use for cottonseed?
   - ○ Soap
   - ○ Bookbindings
   - ○ Animal food
   - ○ Vegetable shortening

35. It can be inferred from the passage that research concerning new uses of cotton
   - ○ has not yet been funded
   - ○ was not a top priority for farmers
   - ○ is an ongoing process
   - ○ will focus on the textile industry

36. Click on the paragraph that lists the edible uses of the cotton plant.

37. The passage would most likely be assigned reading in a course on
   - ○ textiles
   - ○ Naval history
   - ○ geography
   - ○ nutrition

Passage 4 Questions 38–50

Ever since their ancestors began painting animals on the walls of caves, humans have searched for surfaces on which to record their ideas. The ancient Greeks made parchment from animal skins. Mayans painted hieroglyphs on beaten mulberry bark. By pressing together wet layers of Nile grasses, the ancient Egyptians made papyrus, from which we would one day get the English word paper.

When the technique of papermaking reached Europe in the 12th century, paper was made there from plant fiber and linen rags. The early European paper lasted a long time because of its very high rag content and low tree fiber content. At the Library of Congress in Washington, D.C., we can see Saint Augustine's *City of God,* printed in 1473, which is still in excellent condition.

As a result of the demand for books and paper to print them on, following the invention of Gutenberg's printing press in the fifteenth century, the supply of good-quality rags began to dry up and papermakers began to search for new papermaking fibers. Paper printing changed very little from Gutenberg's time through the seventeenth century.

In contrast to the *City of God,* the pages on which Johann Sebastian Bach wrote his musical compositions in the 18th century have survived but are dull looking. Bach bought cheap paper, apparently because he couldn't afford anything better. The cheap paper contained proportionately more tree fiber than expensive paper did.

Still, if we look today at a book from the early years of this century, the paper will be in much worse shape than the paper Bach used two hundred years ago. Beginning in the 19th century, papermakers began making paper completely from tree fiber rather than totally or partially from rags. Tree fibers stick together because of a natural substance called lignin, which eventually oxidizes and turns the paper brown. Papermakers also began using an acid as a glaze for the paper, which explains why pages in fifty-year-old books often crumble when they are turned.

In the U.S. today, the majority of books are printed on non-acidic paper because we know now that this is the only way to ensure that the paper will survive. Unfortunately, for many of the 20 million volumes stored in the Library of Congress, it is only a matter of time before the pages become so brittle that they will disintegrate when touched. The Library is hurrying to save its treasures on microfilm or in computerized form, but it has only a few conservators to try to save its books. Because the books are decaying quickly, it is expected that only a fraction will be saved.

38. With which of the following is the passage primarily concerned?
    - ⬭ The origins of book publishing
    - ⬭ Different materials used for recording ideas
    - ⬭ The durability of paper as a function of its contents
    - ⬭ The problems facing the Library of Congress in maintaining its collection

39. The following sentence could be added to paragraph 2.

Indeed, the paper pages still look as thick and cream-colored as they did when they were printed.

Where would it best fit into the paragraph? Click on the square to add the sentence to the paragraph.

☐ When the technique of papermaking reached Europe in the 12th century, paper was made there from plant fiber and linen rags. ☐ The early European paper lasted a long time because of its very high rag content and low tree fiber content. ☐ At the Library of Congress in Washington, D.C., we can see Saint Augustine's *City of God,* printed in 1473, which is still in excellent condition. ☐

40. Look at the word technique in paragraph 2. The word is closest in meaning to
    - objectives
    - collection
    - accomplishment
    - procedure

41. In what order does the author present the events in the history of papermaking?
    - Making papyrus, printing *City of God,* using non-acidic paper, Gutenberg's invention
    - Making papyrus, Gutenberg's invention, printing *City of God,* using non-acidic paper
    - Making papyrus, printing *City of God,* Gutenberg's invention, using non-acidic paper
    - Printing *City of God,* making papyrus, Gutenberg's invention, using non-acidic paper

42. According to the passage, what causes the pages of fifty-year-old books to crumble?
    - Tree fibers
    - Acid glazes
    - Non-acidic paper
    - Lignin

43. Look at the word crumble in paragraph 5. The word is closest in meaning to
    - disintegrate
    - wrinkle
    - crease
    - fold

44. According to the passage, which of the following is NOT true about Bach?
    - His compositions survived.
    - He was a wealthy composer.
    - His compositions are two hundred years old.
    - His original works can still be seen.

45. It can be inferred from paragraph 5 that the paper that Bach used
    - had no rag content
    - was not glazed with acid
    - was totally composed of tree fiber
    - contained no lignin

46. Look at the word it in paragraph 6. Click on the word or phrase in the paragraph that it refers to.

47. How many volumes in the Library of Congress may be saved?
    - None at all
    - Very few
    - About 20 million
    - Almost all

48. What tone does the author take in the last paragraph?
    - Concerned
    - Highly optimistic
    - Neutral
    - Critical

49. It can be inferred from the passage that
    - before the eighteenth century, composers did not write down their works
    - the Library of Congress has fired many of its conservators
    - bookmakers will continue to use acid as a glaze
    - books printed today will not crumble in the future

50. The paragraph following this passage most probably describes
    - attempts to find additional conservators
    - the process of book decay
    - the contents of the books stored in the Library of Congress
    - how books are printed outside the U.S.

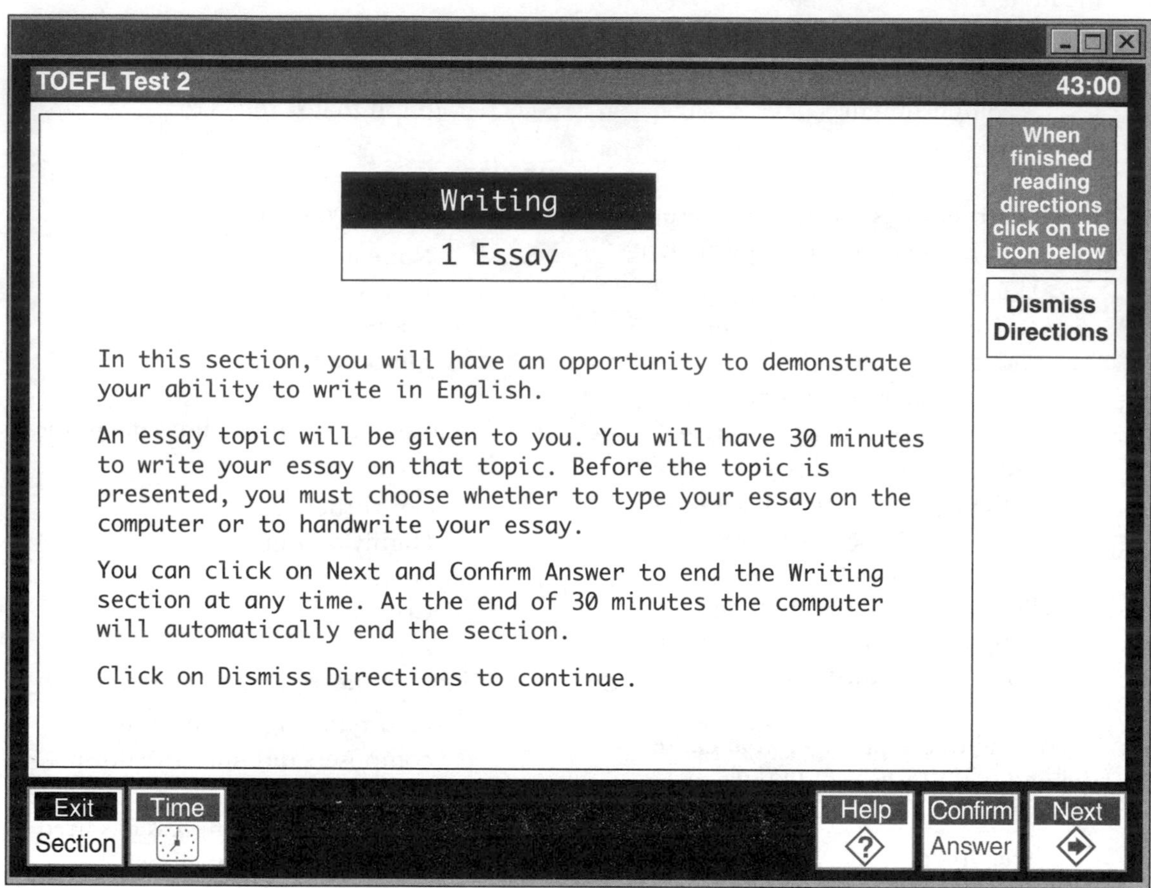
TOEFL Test 2
43:00
Writing
1 Essay
In this section, you will have an opportunity to demonstrate your ability to write in English.
An essay topic will be given to you. You will have 30 minutes to write your essay on that topic. Before the topic is presented, you must choose whether to type your essay on the computer or to handwrite your essay.
You can click on Next and Confirm Answer to end the Writing section at any time. At the end of 30 minutes the computer will automatically end the section.
Click on Dismiss Directions to continue.
When finished reading directions click on the icon below
Dismiss Directions
Exit Section
Time
Help
Confirm Answer
Next

Some people say that computers have made our lives easier. Others say that nowadays people spend so much time on their computers that they no longer do many things they used to do. Which of these two opinions do you agree with? Use specific reasons and examples to support your answer.

APPENDIX E

AUDIO SCRIPTS FOR LISTENING TESTS AND EXERCISES

LISTENING PRE-TEST

Part A

1. (Man) I haven't been able to practice for next month's performance.
(Woman) Did you forget? We have a vacation coming up and you can play all day.
(Narrator) WHAT DOES THE WOMAN MEAN?

2. (Man) I'm counting on Dan to help me write up this lab report.
(Woman) I wouldn't put all my eggs in that basket.
(Narrator) WHAT DOES THE WOMAN IMPLY?

3. (Man) Why are we splitting up into groups?
(Woman) Because the professor thinks working this way enables everyone to participate.
(Man) If you want my opinion, it's a waste of time.
(Narrator) WHAT DOES THE MAN IMPLY?

4. (Man) What time did we tell Joyce and Kenny we'd be at their house?
(Woman) 8:00. If we don't want to be late, we should call for a taxi now.
(Narrator) WHAT DOES THE WOMAN MEAN?

5. (Woman) I've had my VCR for over 20 years. It finally broke down last night, and I'd really like to fix it instead of throwing it out.
(Man) You'll never find the right part. Even if you did, it would be cheaper just to buy a new one.
(Narrator) WHAT DOES THE MAN IMPLY?

6. (Man) How am I doing in this class?
(Woman) You've been improving, but I'd still like you to repeat the course.
(Man) But all the new students will know less than I do.
(Narrator) WHAT CAN BE INFERRED FROM THIS CONVERSATION?

7. (Man) You look awful. Is everything all right?
(Woman) Not really. I cracked my tooth last week, and I've been putting off going to the dentist.
(Narrator) WHAT DOES THE WOMAN MEAN?

8. (Woman) I'll need to compare hotel prices, package deals, and transportation costs.
(Man) All the information is in our database.
(Narrator) WHERE DOES THIS CONVERSATION PROBABLY TAKE PLACE?

9. (Man) What orientation activities are you planning to go to?
(Woman) I don't want to miss the chancellor's convocation. And I'm going to the welcome night at the cafeteria to see if I want to sign up for a meal plan.
(Narrator) WHAT DOES THE WOMAN IMPLY?

10. (Man) Do you have any lectures in those new smart classrooms in Shaw Hall?
(Woman) I'm not that lucky. I hear the acoustics there are state of the art, there are giant screens around the room, and you can see and hear perfectly from any seat.
(Narrator) WHAT DOES THE WOMAN IMPLY?

11. (Woman) All I need to finish is the last chapter of my thesis.
(Man) You mean you've finished the bibliography, table of contents, and all the graphics?
(Narrator) WHAT DOES THE MAN IMPLY?

Part B

QUESTIONS 12–14

(Woman 1) Hey, Tammy. Do you want to come to the mall with me after class? I have to buy an outfit for the party my boyfriend's throwing on Friday night.
(Woman 2) Oh, Sarah. I don't think I can. My sociology paper is due tomorrow, and I've written only four pages.
(Woman 1) Well, how long does it have to be?
(Woman 2) At least six pages. It also has to have ten sources, and so far, I only have five! I think I'm going to be spending the night in the library.
(Woman 1) If you change your mind, give me a call. I'm not leaving until 4.
(Woman 2) Okay, but I really don't think I'm going to have time to come with you. If you see anything you think I'd like, let me know!

12. WHAT CAN BE INFERRED FROM THE PASSAGE?
13. WHY CAN'T TAMMY GO TO THE MALL WITH SARAH?
14. WHAT IS SARAH LIKELY TO DO AT 4?

QUESTIONS 15–17

(Man) Hi, Danielle. Did you hear that Adam Sandler is coming to speak here next Wednesday?

(Woman) Are you kidding? I love Adam Sandler! Do you know where he's speaking?

(Man) I'm not sure, but I assume it's going to be in the gym. What other place could hold such a large number of people?

(Woman) There's always the auditorium. I think it holds about two thousand.

(Man) That's true, but I think there's an a cappella concert in there on the same night. They must have found another venue.

(Woman) You're probably right. I bet they'll have it in the gym. Do you know where we can get tickets?

(Man) The student center. A friend of mine told me they have a couple hundred left.

15. WHERE WILL THE PERFORMANCE LIKELY BE HELD?
16. WHAT WILL DANIELLE PROBABLY DO NEXT?
17. WHAT CAN BE INFERRED FROM THE PASSAGE?

QUESTIONS 18–22

(Narrator) Listen to a lecture in an anthropology class on the development of speech.

(Professor) Although many species of animals lived in social groups in prehistoric times, the capacity for speech is one of the most important behavioral attributes distinguishing humans from other animals. However, the question of when the capacity for speech developed has intrigued scientists over the years.

Determining when humans acquired the ability to speak is difficult. Scientists have generally agreed that human beings capable of speech created the cave art which began to appear in Europe and Africa some 40,000 years ago. The complexity of the paintings strongly suggests their creation would have been the result of considerable cooperation requiring speech.

Now scientists at Duke University studying fossil anatomy have come up with physical evidence that humans may already have possessed the anatomical structures necessary for speech as early as 400,000 years ago.

Fossils show that by that time, human ancestors probably had the same number of these nerves leading to the muscles of the tongue as modern humans do. The number of these nerves can be estimated by studying the size of the canal at the bottom of the back of the skull. This canal houses the nerves controlling the tongue. Nerve fibers run through the canal, from the brain to the muscles of the tongue. In chimpanzees and gorillas incapable of speech, the canal is about half the size of the canal of a human. In skulls from about 400,000 years ago, the canals are already the same size as those in modern day human skulls.

Next time we'll talk about what sounds these human ancestors might have been able to produce.

18. WHAT IS ONE OF THE MOST IMPORTANT DIFFERENCES BETWEEN ANIMALS AND HUMANS?
19. APPROXIMATELY HOW LONG AGO DID CAVE ART BEGIN TO APPEAR IN EUROPE AND AFRICA?
20. WHERE IS THE CANAL THAT SCIENTISTS HAVE BEEN STUDYING TO LEARN MORE ABOUT VERY EARLY SPEECH?
21. WHICH OF THE FOLLOWING SUPPORT THE BELIEF THAT MAN WAS ABLE TO SPEAK 40,000 YEARS AGO?
22. THE PROFESSOR EXPLAINS THE ORDER OF EACH OF THESE OCCURRENCES. PUT THEM IN THEIR CHRONOLOGICAL ORDER.

QUESTIONS 23–27

(Narrator) Listen to a discussion in a fashion design class. The discussion is about weaving.

(Instructor) As you know, the craft of weaving has been practiced throughout the world for thousands of years. Many fabrics and most blankets, clothing, and rugs are woven. Today I'm going to discuss and then demonstrate the three basic kinds of weaving, and then you're all going to try it.

(Carrie) Will we be using hand looms or power looms?

(Instructor) We'll start out with hand looms, so we can better understand the process. Who knows the basic types of weaves?

(Rachel) I'm not sure what they're called, but I'm pretty sure there are three types.

(Instructor) Yes, three is the correct number. All weaves consist of two sets of threads. One set, called the warp, stretches lengthwise on a loom or frame. To make cloth, the weaver repeatedly draws a set of crosswise threads called the weft over and under the warp. The simplest and most common is the plain or tabby weave. In the odd-numbered rows of this weave, a weft thread passes under the first warp thread, over the second, and so on. In the even-numbered rows, the weft passes over the first warp, under the second, and so on.

(Joan) Sounds like a strong weave. I guess gingham is a tabby weave.

(Instructor) Yes, that's right. As well as muslin and percale. Does anyone know the second type of weave that produces sturdy cloth with raised diagonal lines?

(Carrie) I know denim and flannel are twill. These sturdy fabrics are used for work clothes and coats.

(Instructor) Yes. Each weft thread crosses two, three, or four warp threads at a time, creating extra width. This added width makes a decorative fabric that holds its shape despite repeated wear. Each row of weft threads follows the same pattern, but the pattern of each row begins slightly to the right or left of the pattern in the previous row. This technique puts a series of diagonal lines in the fabric. And who knows the third?

(Rachel) It's satin weave, isn't it?

(Instructor) Yes, it makes soft, luxurious fabrics, such as damask, sateen, and satin. Each weft spans up to 12 warps in creating a smooth, glossy finish. It is used to make formal clothes and curtains. Now let's move to the last room on the right where we'll set up the looms.

23. ACCORDING TO THE DISCUSSION, WHICH OF THE FOLLOWING IS COMMONLY WOVEN?
24. WHAT IS STATED ABOUT WEAVING?
25. WHAT ARE THE CHARACTERISTICS OF EACH OF THESE TYPES OF WEAVES?
26. HOW DOES THE SATIN WEAVE CREATE A SMOOTH FINISH?
27. WHAT WILL THE CLASS DO NEXT?

QUESTIONS 28–32

(Narrator) Listen to a lecture in an American history class. The professor is talking about the settlement of Roanoke.

(Professor) Last time we examined the reasons why a group of English families left home for America in 1587. Today we will focus on one of the mysteries of colonial history—the disappearance of the group that landed on the coastal island of Roanoke. Well, where exactly is Roanoke?

It's a small island just off the coast of what is now North Carolina. When the group landed on the island, they concluded that they could survive there. However, they were so low on supplies that several of the crew members returned to England for more. The leaders of the group left for England four days after the landing. Meanwhile, the rest of the group settled in as quickly as they could, hoping to establish themselves before the winter.

As they landed during August, they felt that they would be able to survive living off the land until the leaders returned from England. Unfortunately, the leaders were unable to return as soon as they thought they would, and the settlers were left to fend for themselves. It wasn't until three years later that the leaders were able to return with provisions.

In 1587, England was preparing to go up against the Spanish Armada, and all ships, including the one bound to return to Roanoke, were taken over to take part in the anticipated naval battle. When the leaders of the settlers finally returned to Roanoke in 1590, they found no one there. All they found was a single word carved on a tree: CROATOAN. The word seems to suggest that the local Croatoan Indian tribe had something to do with the disappearance of the settlers who may have left the Roanoke site and set out for their original destination of the Chesapeake Bay. Then again, perhaps the settlers fought with the Croatoans. Or maybe they followed them south, where today some Indians claim some of their ancestors were the settlers from Roanoke. These last two possibilities seem more likely today because of recent evidence of massive climatic changes in the area, which led to drought. The settlers might have fought with the Croatoans over food when drought brought starvation to both groups. Or, because the Croatoans were known to be friendly, the two groups may have moved out of the drought-stricken areas together to areas further south, which were not hard hit by the climate changes.

28. WHY DID THE LEADERS OF THE SETTLERS RETURN TO ENGLAND?
29. HOW SOON AFTER LANDING AT ROANOKE DID THE LEADERS OF THE GROUP RETURN TO ENGLAND?
30. WHAT MIGHT HAVE HAPPENED TO THE SETTLERS WHO DISAPPEARED FROM ROANOKE?
31. WHEN DID THE ROANOKE AREA SUFFER A TERRIBLE DROUGHT?
32. THE PROFESSOR EXPLAINS THE HISTORY OF THE ROANOKE SETTLERS AND THEIR LEADERS. PUT THESE OCCURRENCES IN THEIR CHRONOLOGICAL ORDER.

LISTENING SECTION

Part A
Exercise 1

1. (Man) Registration always takes so long.
(Woman) What bothers me is all the people who cut in line.
(Narrator) WHAT DOES THE WOMAN SAY BOTHERS HER?

2. (Man) Kate, did you make the sweater yourself?
(Woman) To tell you the truth, it's a hand-me-down from my grandmother.
(Narrator) WHAT DO WE LEARN ABOUT THE SWEATER?

3. (Woman) So, I'm not going abroad next semester.
(Man) I think the reason you didn't apply was you were afraid of being rejected.
(Woman) I think you've hit the nail on the head.
(Narrator) WHAT DOES THE WOMAN MEAN?

4. (Man) I'm really enjoying Professor Jensen's class.
(Woman) Me too.
(Man) Have you taken any other classes with him?
(Woman) O.K., enough about school. You can stop beating around the bush.
(Narrator) WHAT DOES THE WOMAN MEAN?

5. (Woman) What fabulous sunglasses!
(Man) I haven't dared to wear them in public since I got them last summer in Europe.
(Woman) You've always been ahead of the curve.
(Narrator) WHAT DOES THE WOMAN IMPLY?

6. (Man) I'm so jealous seeing how much energy you've had lately.
(Woman) Well, if you'd come with me to my aerobics class, you'd feel the same way.
(Man) I need you to take me by the hand.
(Narrator) WHAT DOES THE MAN INFER?

7. (Man) This is Doctor Ferrin's office. You had a 10:00 dentist appointment.
(Woman) Oh, I'm terribly sorry. It completely slipped my mind.
(Narrator) WHAT DOES THE WOMAN MEAN?

8. (Man) It's nice to see the sun for a change.
(Woman) Is it ever! It's been raining cats and dogs for over a week.
(Narrator) WHAT DOES THE WOMAN MEAN?

9. (Man) I have something to tell you, but I don't know how to begin.
(Woman) Well, what is it? Cat got your tongue?
(Narrator) WHAT DOES THE WOMAN IMPLY?

10. (Woman) When are you going to help me with the project?
(Man) What? You're always busy when I suggest a meeting.
(Woman) We better agree soon. It takes two to tango.
(Narrator) WHAT DOES THE WOMAN MEAN?

11. (Woman) How's the musical coming that you're in?
(Man) After a rocky start in the first few weeks, last night's rehearsal went off without a hitch.
(Narrator) WHAT DOES THE MAN MEAN?

12. (Man) Was Dr. Springer serious about inviting all of us to his department's party?
(Woman) It seemed to me he made the comment off the cuff.
(Narrator) WHAT DOES THE WOMAN MEAN?

13. (Woman) We can have the planning meeting at my apartment.
(Man) Susan, how will we all get there?
(Woman) I only live a stone's throw from the student union.
(Narrator) WHAT DOES SUSAN MEAN?

14. (Man) Are you enjoying Spanish class?
(Woman) If you had asked me last week, I probably would have said no. But slowly but surely my Spanish is improving.
(Narrator) WHAT DOES THE WOMAN SAY?

15. (Woman) What did you think about the presentation by the visiting lecturer?
(Man) I was lost. I simply couldn't follow his train of thought.
(Narrator) WHAT DOES THE MAN MEAN?

16. (Man) Are you feeling better today?
(Woman) Thanks for asking. It seems to me my headache is finally going away.
(Narrator) WHAT DOES THE WOMAN SAY?

Exercise 2

1. (Man) Do you know how to check flight arrivals on line?
(Woman) Give me the flight number, and I'll do it for you.
(Man) It's Flight 211 from San Diego.
(Woman) Hey, Flight 211 was canceled.
(Narrator) WHAT DOES THE WOMAN MEAN?

2. (Man) Have you seen Kathy's new red car?
(Woman) She was lucky. She got it on sale from the dealer before he closed down.
(Narrator) WHAT HAPPENED TO THE CAR DEALER?

3. (Man) Sam had better hurry if he wants to get the assignment in before Friday.
(Woman) He always puts things off until the last minute.
(Narrator) WHAT CAN BE INFERRED ABOUT SAM?

4. (Woman) What do you think of my idea?
(Man) I can't come up with a better one, Julie.
(Narrator) WHAT DOES THE MAN THINK?

5. (Man) How did Jeremy build his reputation in such a short time?
(Woman) He started his company with almost no money, and this year all his hard work has paid off.
(Narrator) WHAT DO WE LEARN ABOUT JEREMY?

6. (Man) Are you going to Jackie's going away party?
(Woman) Yeah. Aren't you?
(Man) If you give me some money, I'll get a gift from the two of us.
(Woman) Sorry. I went in on a gift with friends from her softball team.
(Narrator) WHAT DOES THE WOMAN MEAN?

7. (Man) Isn't payday this Friday?
(Woman) Am I ever looking forward to getting paid.
(Narrator) WHAT DOES THE WOMAN MEAN?

8. (Man) Was that Professor Jason with twin babies?
(Woman) I wasn't sure if he's the father or the grandfather. But someone told me he and his wife put off having children until their forties.
(Narrator) WHAT DOES THE WOMAN MEAN?

9. (Woman) You'll never guess who I ran into on the subway.
(Man) Let me guess. Was it someone famous?
(Woman) Sort of. My advisor.
(Narrator) WHAT DOES THE WOMAN MEAN?

10. (Man) Toby, I'm going on vacation for two weeks, and I'm worried about my plants.
(Woman) No problem. I'll look after them.
(Narrator) WHAT DOES THE WOMAN IMPLY?

11. (Man) What are you doing at the League so late?
(Woman) Oh, I locked myself out of my room, and I have to wait until my roommate gets back.
(Narrator) WHAT DOES THE WOMAN MEAN?

12. (Woman) I haven't seen Henry in any of my classes for a while.
(Man) Someone in my history class told me he dropped out last month.
(Narrator) WHAT DOES THE MAN MEAN?

13. (Woman) Will you be joining us later?
(Man) I need to catch up on the work I missed.
(Narrator) WHAT CAN BE SAID ABOUT THE MAN?

Exercise 3

1. (Woman) I wish all of your friends were as nice as Michael.
(Man) Not everyone has such a good friend.
(Narrator) WHAT DO WE LEARN FROM THE CONVERSATION?

2. (Man) So, are you or aren't you moving someplace closer to campus?
(Woman) I wish we were. Our house has been on the market since July.
(Narrator) WHAT DOES THE WOMAN MEAN?

3. (Woman) I thought you knew I go to my parents' beach house each August.
(Man) I just wish you had told me your vacation plans sooner.
(Narrator) WHY IS THE MAN UPSET?

4. (Man) I wish I hadn't transferred out of your biology section, Judy.
(Woman) Remember? You thought it was going to be too hard.
(Man) Now I realize I would have learned so much more.
(Narrator) WHAT DOES THE MAN SAY?

5. (Woman) If you're in a hurry, you can take the subway. If you want to sightsee, take a bus.
(Man) Actually I don't have to be at the conference until noon.
(Narrator) WHAT WILL THE MAN PROBABLY DO?

6. (Man) What's taking so long?
(Woman) I want to get the waitress's attention to tell her I put her tip on the credit card.
(Man) If we don't see her, we'll tell the hostess.
(Narrator) WHAT DOES THE MAN IMPLY THE HOSTESS WILL DO?

7. (Man) I understand that only the dean can sign my withdrawal form.
(Woman) If you can come back in the morning, the dean will be able to see you.
He's all booked up this afternoon.
(Narrator) WHAT WILL THE DEAN BE ABLE TO DO?

8. (Man) Where will graduation be held if it's raining on Sunday?
(Woman) It looks like it'll be outside, come rain or shine.
(Narrator) WHAT DOES THE WOMAN MEAN?

9. (Woman) Why don't you see if the professor will let you into his class?
(Man) I know it's already full. I heard many students are asking for her permission to take the class.
(Woman) If you don't ask, you'll never know.
(Narrator) WHAT DOES THE WOMAN IMPLY?

10. (Man) Is Dr. White your thesis advisor?
(Woman) I wish I had picked someone else. It turns out he isn't an expert in my field.
(Man) Is it too late to switch?
(Narrator) WHAT DOES THE MAN WANT TO KNOW?

Exercise 4

1. (Man) Did you hear that David flunked the final?
(Woman) I'm surprised. He's the star pupil in the class.
(Narrator) WHAT DOES THE WOMAN MEAN?

2. (Woman) Carol made up for the time she missed by working overtime.
(Man) Oh. That's why she worked the weekend shift.
(Narrator) WHAT DID CAROL DO?

3. (Woman) What does John do with all the milk?
(Man) He sells it to the same people who buy his wool.
(Woman) It's hard to believe someone with a PhD is a shepherd.
(Narrator) WHAT CAN BE INFERRED ABOUT JOHN?

4. (Man) The college is planning to drop the language requirement for science majors.
(Woman) Wouldn't you know it! I just finished the language sequence.
(Narrator) WHAT CAN BE INFERRED ABOUT THE WOMAN?

5. (Woman) Why do you always forward me those silly e-mails?
(Man) Guess I was wrong. I thought you got a kick out of them.
(Narrator) WHAT DOES THE MAN MEAN?

6. (Man) Did you hear Bill hurt his back in the last hockey game?
(Woman) Oh. That explains why I saw him at health services.
(Narrator) WHAT DOES THE WOMAN IMPLY?

7. (Man) So I'll get back to you later.
(Woman) Excuse me, I couldn't help overhearing your conversation. Are you THE Professor Rankin?
(Narrator) WHAT DOES THE WOMAN MEAN?

8. (Woman) Would you be able to take a look at the graphics I'm working on for the exhibition?
(Man) Wow! You did all these? You've really come a long way.
(Narrator) WHAT DOES THE MAN MEAN?

9. (Man) What? You invited the Millers for dinner AGAIN? It seems like they were here last week.
(Woman) What are you talking about? It's been over a year since they were here.
(Narrator) WHAT DOES THE WOMAN IMPLY?

10. (Woman) Do you have to get special permission to look at the rare manuscripts?
(Man) I just had to get a note from my professor saying I needed information for my research.
(Woman) That's all? I thought it would be nearly impossible.
(Narrator) WHAT DOES THE WOMAN MEAN?

Exercise 5

1. (Man) I'm getting a busy signal each time I dial the operator.
(Woman) That's strange. The same thing is happening to me.
(Narrator) WHAT DOES THE WOMAN MEAN?

2. (Woman) I dozed off for most of the seminar.
(Man) It almost put me to sleep, too.
(Narrator) WHAT HAPPENED TO THE MAN?

3. (Man) I'd like to drive. It would save us some time.
(Woman) OK. Then I think we should park the car downtown.
(Man) Yeah, but I don't know where we can.
(Narrator) WHAT IS BEING DISCUSSED?

4. (Man) I read in the paper that the novel you're reading is excellent.
(Woman) I've also read some negative reviews.
(Narrator) WHAT CAN BE LEARNED FROM THE CONVERSATION?

5. (Man) Let's choose a topic for our group's in-class debate.
(Woman) Good idea. I think we have to tell the professor by Friday.
(Man) By Friday? I don't think so. I thought he said a week from Friday.
(Narrator) WHAT DOES THE MAN BELIEVE?

6. (Woman) It's so dark in here I can hardly read the menu.
(Man) I know what you mean. Here, you can borrow my glasses.
(Woman) It's not my eyes. It's the light.
(Narrator) WHAT DOES THE WOMAN IMPLY?

7. (Woman) I can hardly tell Jennifer and Jessica apart.
(Man) I know. But their looks is about the only thing they have in common.
(Narrator) WHAT DOES THE MAN MEAN?

8. (Man) Gail, I just got your messages.
(Woman) Where have you been? I've been trying you for days.
(Man) I've been around.
(Woman) I beg to differ. I've dialed your number a thousand times.
(Narrator) WHAT DOES THE WOMAN IMPLY?

9. (Woman) Do you have change for a dollar? I'm low on quarters.
(Man) Oh, finally joining us at the laundromat?
(Woman) What are you talking about? I practically live here.
(Narrator) WHAT DOES THE WOMAN IMPLY?

10. (Man) The history lectures have been so interesting this semester.
(Woman) Have they ever! I wish she had been my high school history teacher.
(Narrator) WHAT DOES THE WOMAN MEAN?

11. (Woman) You should have finished the book before it was due.
(Man) You can say that again. Now I'll have to pay a huge fine.
(Narrator) WHAT WILL THE MAN HAVE TO DO?

Exercise 6

1. (Woman) Did you study for the exam?
(Man) I couldn't. I lent my notes to someone in the class who promised to return them days ago.
(Woman) Next time, don't be so nice.
(Narrator) WHAT DOES THE WOMAN IMPLY?

2. (Man) Did you have a leisurely vacation?
(Woman) I haven't rested a bit. I've been jogging, weightlifting, and trying to get back into shape.
(Narrator) WHAT HAS THE WOMAN BEEN DOING?

3. (Man) You can have it mailed or take it with you.
(Woman) I don't have much time; just put it in a bag.
(Narrator) WHAT DOES THE WOMAN WANT TO DO WITH HER PURCHASE?

4. (Woman) Do you want to go someplace quieter so we can talk?
(Man) What did you say? I couldn't hear you.
(Narrator) WHAT DOES THE MAN MEAN?

5. (Man) What do you think about the new players?
(Woman) I don't want to talk about football anymore. Every time I think the team will win, I'm disappointed.
(Narrator) WHAT DOES THE WOMAN MEAN?

6. (Woman) I've just found out there won't be a final exam in calculus.
(Man) Yeah. He's going to average all the tests we've taken.
(Woman) Then I've got nothing to worry about.
(Narrator) WHAT CAN BE INFERRED ABOUT THE WOMAN?

7. (Man) I thought we were going to meet for coffee.
(Woman) What a morning! I was running late, and I didn't have a second to call you.
(Narrator) WHAT DOES THE WOMAN MEAN?

8. (Man) The only kind of animal our dorm allows is birds.
(Woman) So are you going to buy one?
(Man) Yeah, except I have no idea what kind to get.
(Woman) Don't look at me. I can't tell a parrot from a peacock.
(Narrator) WHAT DOES THE WOMAN IMPLY?

9. (Man) Why are you taking composition for international students?
(Woman) Because I'm not American.
(Man) I can't believe you weren't born in America.
(Narrator) WHAT DOES THE MAN IMPLY?

10. (Woman) Did you know that all the professor's notes can be downloaded?
(Man) Yeah. When I was sick, I e-mailed the professor, and she told me to download the lectures I missed.
(Woman) Some students now think they can skip class. They don't realize how helpful the discussions are.
(Narrator) WHAT DOES THE WOMAN BELIEVE?

11. (Woman) Isn't there anything I could do improve my grade, professor?
(Man) Nope. Nothing. Extra credit projects were due last Friday.
(Narrator) WHAT DOES THE PROFESSOR IMPLY?

12. (Man) Did you read the fantastic reviews about the play we're going to see?
(Woman) Everyone has been raving, even the critic from the Sunday Times.
(Man) I can't wait.
(Narrator) HOW DO THEY FEEL ABOUT THE PLAY?

Exercise 7

1. (Woman) Do you have a phone? I need to check in with the office.
(Man) Help yourself to the phone in the kitchen.
(Narrator) WHAT DOES THE MAN OFFER?

2. (Man) I hear there are several vacancies in the new high rise downtown.
(Woman) Would you keep your eye out for a one-bedroom apartment for me?
(Narrator) WHAT DOES THE WOMAN REQUEST THE MAN DO?

3. (Man) Even though you're not crazy about my friends, I'd like to host a party next Saturday.
(Woman) Okay, but I think you should make all the arrangements.
(Man) So, is that a yes?
(Narrator) WHAT DOES THE WOMAN SUGGEST THE MAN DO?

4. (Woman) Where can I write you this summer?
(Man) While I'm at summer school in Boston, you can write me at my brother's address. He'll forward the mail.
(Narrator) WHERE CAN THE WOMAN WRITE THE MAN?

5. (Man) What color should we paint the walls?
(Woman) It makes no difference to me.
(Man) Then would you mind blue? I think it would look good in here.
(Narrator) WHAT DOES THE MAN REQUEST?

6. (Man) I had to miss my class on Monday because I was sick. I don't want to fall behind in my work.
(Woman) Why don't you stay after tomorrow's lecture, and we can discuss what you missed?
(Narrator) WHAT DOES THE WOMAN SUGGEST?

7. (Man) Oh no. I forgot to bring my umbrella downstairs.
(Woman) Here's mine. My hat will keep my hair dry.
(Narrator) WHAT DOES THE WOMAN MEAN?

8. (Man) Can you help me find Building 10? I'm late for a placement test.
(Woman) Follow me. That's where I'm heading as well.
(Narrator) WHAT WILL THE MAN PROBABLY DO?

9. (Man) Would it be OK if I brought my roommate to the party?
(Woman) Of course. The more the merrier.
(Narrator) WHAT DOES THE WOMAN IMPLY?

10. (Woman) Those muffins look delicious. May I have one?
(Man) Be my guest. I brought them in for the meeting, and no one touched them.
(Narrator) WHAT DOES THE MAN MEAN?

11. (Man) Where should we meet?
(Woman) We can stay here after class or go to the library.
(Man) Let's go straight to the library after class.
(Narrator) WHAT DOES THE MAN SUGGEST?

12. (Man) Is it time for dinner yet? I'm so hungry.
(Woman) The cafeteria doesn't open for an hour! Why don't we have a snack? Come with me to the machines.
(Narrator) WHAT DOES THE WOMAN SUGGEST THEY DO?

13. (Woman) I'll have lots of free time next semester, and I'm thinking of taking up writing.
(Man) I know a perfect space. You could use the old desk in the attic.
(Narrator) WHAT DOES THE MAN SUGGEST?

14. (Man) Every time I log onto the campus website my computer crashes.
(Woman) Haven't you heard? The site has some kind of virus. It would be best to stay away from it.
(Narrator) WHAT DOES THE WOMAN MEAN?

Exercise 8

1. (Woman) Should we get Ed a CD for his birthday?
(Man) Just because he's a composer doesn't mean he likes only to listen to music.
(Narrator) WHAT DID THE MAN MEAN?

2. (Woman) Do you have Dana's number in California?
(Man) Not yet. She promised she'd give it to me as soon as she gets a cell phone. I can give it to you once I know it.
(Narrator) WHAT CAN BE CONCLUDED FROM THE CONVERSATION?

3. (Man) Can you fix our pipes as soon as possible?
(Woman) It all depends on whether I finish the drains at the apartment building where I'm working.
(Narrator) WHAT WILL THE WOMAN DO FIRST?

4. (Man) I'm so tired I think I'll go home now. You shouldn't work so hard.
(Woman) I have to stay up until I finish the story for the morning edition.
(Narrator) WHAT WILL THE WOMAN DO?

5. (Man) I'm going to the cafeteria. Do you want to come along?
(Woman) I've got to keep my eye on the new workers during lunch.
(Man) Then I'll see you later.
(Narrator) WHAT WILL THE WOMAN BE DOING?

6. (Man) Would you like me to bring you some coffee for a break?
(Woman) Could you wait just a while? I'm trying to finish this report before the meeting.
(Narrator) WHAT DOES THE WOMAN WANT?

7. (Man) Did you make a reservation on the 7:00 flight?
(Woman) I thought you wanted to take the 6:00 one. Do you want me to change it?
(Narrator) WHAT DID THE WOMAN DO?

8. (Man) Why are you rushing to class?
(Woman) If we don't get there early, we won't get one of the front row seats in the auditorium.
(Narrator) WHAT DOES THE WOMAN SUGGEST THEY DO?

9. (Man) How about going to see the movie at the student center tonight?
(Woman) Well, I really ought to review my sociology notes before the midterm.
(Narrator) WHAT DOES THE WOMAN IMPLY?

10. (Woman) Do you remember how to get to the bursar's office?
(Man) I think it's somewhere in Angell Hall. Why don't you ask someone there?
(Woman) Well, I need to get there before it closes, so I'll check the campus directory.
(Narrator) WHAT WILL THE WOMAN PROBABLY DO?

11. (Woman) I told our group members you'd join us as soon as you could.
(Man) Let me just finish the paper I'm working on for tomorrow. I won't need more than an hour.
(Narrator) WHAT WILL THE MAN PROBABLY DO FIRST?

Exercise 9

1. (Woman) Were you able to catch the president's speech Saturday at the union?
(Man) I had to miss it. I was fixing up my office.
(Narrator) WHAT IS THE PROBABLE RELATIONSHIP OF THE SPEAKERS?

2. (Man) Housewares are on the second floor.
(Woman) After we pick out a gift, we have to get it wrapped on the first floor.
(Narrator) WHAT ARE THE SPEAKERS DOING?

3. (Man) Did Rob show you his photos from the last trip?
(Woman) Looking at them, I could see myself skiing in the Alps.
(Narrator) WHAT DID THE WOMAN DO?

4. (Man) I heard Ann inherited a lot of money.
(Woman) Her uncle was quite generous in his will.
(Narrator) WHAT HAPPENED TO ANN?

5. (Woman) The hours are 9 to 12, Monday through Friday.
(Man) Are there any paid vacation days?
(Narrator) WHAT ARE THESE TWO TALKING ABOUT?

6. (Man) How come you weren't at the recitation this morning?
(Woman) I'd written down NEXT Tuesday.
(Man) Don't forget next week it's back to Thursdays.
(Narrator) WHAT DID THE MAN SAY?

7. (Man) My internship begins the first of the month.
(Woman) How much time will you spend working each week?
(Man) It depends on how much they'll need me. Some weeks more than others.
(Narrator) WHAT DOES THE MAN TELL THE WOMAN?

8. (Man) Can we stop at the closest cash machine? I need to take out some money.
(Woman) There's no need. This dinner is my treat.
(Narrator) WHAT DOES THE WOMAN MEAN?

9. (Woman) Do you know how I can change my advisor?
(Man) You can download a change of advisor form from the academic section on the website.
(Woman) Then what do I do with it?
(Narrator) WHAT DOES THE WOMAN WANT TO KNOW?

10. (Woman) I'll be at the produce section in aisle 2.
(Man) Meet me at the express check-out counter in ten minutes.
(Narrator) WHERE DID THIS CONVERSATION TAKE PLACE?

11. (Man) Where did Mary Ann get that new outfit?
(Woman) She had a tailor remake an old skirt and jacket of hers.
(Narrator) WHERE DID MARY ANN GET THE OUTFIT?

12. (Man) I'd like five rolls, a pound of cookies, and a birthday cake.
(Woman) Do you want the cake decorated?
(Narrator) WHERE DOES THIS CONVERSATION TAKE PLACE?

Exercise 10

1. (Woman) Let's grab a bite before the movie they're showing in class tonight.
(Man) I'd rather eat afterwards.
(Woman) I'm hungry now, but I'll wait.
(Narrator) WHAT HAS THE WOMAN DECIDED TO DO?

2. (Man) The baby crying next door kept me up all night.
(Woman) She must be sick.
(Man) Well, now I don't feel so hot either.
(Narrator) WHAT DOES THE WOMAN CONCLUDE?

3. (Man) Just as I left for school, I realized I forgot the rough draft we'll need for class.
(Woman) What a shame. Now you won't be able to exchange papers.
(Narrator) WHAT DOES THE WOMAN MEAN?

4. (Man) Can you walk to class from your dorm on North Campus?
(Woman) Are you kidding? The bus takes thirty minutes when there's no traffic.
(Man) You must have to get up before the roosters.
(Narrator) WHAT DOES THE MAN IMPLY?

5. (Man) So are you going to change your major?
(Woman) It's too late now. I should have listened to my teacher's advice.
(Narrator) WHAT HAS THE WOMAN CONCLUDED?

6. (Man) Does that child in the striped shirt look familiar to you?
(Woman) I've never seen him before, but he must be a Jackson.
(Narrator) WHAT DOES THE WOMAN MEAN?

7. (Man) How can we set up the room for the reception? There are only ten chairs here.
(Woman) Uh-oh . . . I saw Christine take the rest of the chairs with her.
(Narrator) WHAT DOES THE WOMAN MEAN?

8. (Man) I'm just about finished with my thesis. Can you recommend anyone to proof it for me?
(Woman) Well, I used Cheryl. But I hesitate to recommend her. She has a unique style of proofreading.
(Narrator) WHAT DOES THE WOMAN MEAN?

9. (Man) What will you do after graduation?
(Woman) I don't know whether or not to go out on my own or work for a large company.
(Narrator) WHAT COULD THE WOMAN DO?

10. (Woman) Someone left an accounting book in class today.
(Man) Maybe the person put his or her name on it.
(Woman) There's no name, but look at the drawings all over it. There's only one person I know who's this artistic.
(Narrator) WHAT DID THE WOMAN CONCLUDE?

11. (Woman) Where should we get something to eat?
(Man) The choices are the union, the cafeteria, the supermarket, or my apartment.
(Woman) I don't want to cook and clean up, so it's between the union and the cafeteria.
(Narrator) WHAT DOES THE WOMAN IMPLY?

12. (Man) If I buy the textbook, then I get a free copy of the newspaper every day, right?
(Woman) That's right. You fill out this card and it'll be delivered daily for 12 weeks.
(Man) Oh . . . so it's only 12 weeks.
(Narrator) WHAT DOES THE MAN CONCLUDE?

13. (Man) The audition for the school musical is tomorrow.
(Woman) I think I'm too nervous to try out.
(Narrator) WHAT IS THE WOMAN'S PROBLEM?

14. (Man) My friend Emily has an extra ticket for the concert.
(Woman) What's she asking?
(Man) I'm not sure. Probably less than she paid.
(Narrator) WHAT DOES THE MAN IMPLY?

Part B
Exercise 11

QUESTIONS 1–3

(Woman) Hi, Mark! Why are you here an hour early?
(Man) I wanted to review my notes one last time. What about you?
(Woman) This is the time my car pool gets to school every day. What kind of format do you think the test will have?
(Man) I wouldn't be surprised to find an essay question on it. Make sure you include lots of facts. For sure there'll be some multiple-choice questions because they're easier to correct.
(Woman) I hope not. Multiple-choice tests always get me mixed up, especially biology ones. And biology is my major!
(Man) So why are you taking this course? I'm a history major, so this economics course was a requirement for me.

1. WHY DID MARK ARRIVE EARLY?
2. WHAT SUBJECT IS THE EXAM TESTING?
3. WHAT DOES MARK ADVISE THE WOMAN?

QUESTIONS 4–6

(Woman) And on the right you'll see the new student center.
(Man) Do you know what time it closes?
(Woman) Midnight during the week, and 2 AM on weekends.
(Man) Could we go in? I'd like to see the facilities.
(Woman) Actually, it's not part of the official tour. Once we're done, you can go back and see it. It's open to the public.
(Man) I'll do that. Since I'll be commuting, I want to make sure there will be some place comfortable where I can hang out between classes.
(Woman) Oh. There are lots of places for commuters. All the cafeterias are open to non-resident students at a reasonable charge. You can go to the League, the Union, and of course any of the libraries.

4. WHY DOES THE MAN WANT TO SEE THE STUDENT CENTER?
5. WHY DID THE TOUR NOT GO INSIDE THE STUDENT CENTER?
6. WHAT WILL THE MAN PROBABLY DO AFTER THE TOUR?

QUESTIONS 7–8

(Man) What do you do with your used books at the end of the term?
(Woman) I usually sell them back to the bookstore.
(Man) They don't give you much money for them. What do you get? 2 dollars for an 80 dollar book?
(Woman) That's an exaggeration, but it's convenient since it's right on campus.

(Man) Well, I've started selling mine over the Internet. I can give you the site, and you get a five-dollar credit just for signing up.

(Woman) Thanks. Please give me that address. I'll take a look at it, but I probably won't sell mine that way. You have to mail the books yourself.

7. WHY DOES THE WOMAN SELL HER BOOKS TO THE BOOKSTORE?
8. WHAT WILL THE WOMAN PROBABLY DO NEXT?

QUESTIONS 9–11

(Woman) Pat, do you know who's making the assignments for the TAs next semester?

(Man) I think Brian is doing it again. Why?

(Woman) Well, I've been a TA for 3 semesters in American History now, and I wanted to teach something different.

(Man) I know what you mean. After 2 semesters of Ancient Civilizations, I switched to twentieth century Europe! What a difference!

(Woman) Since I'm not sure what I'm going to write my dissertation on, I figured I'd better get a feel for some other disciplines.

(Man) You should get in touch with Brian. I know the recommendations have to be in to the department chair by the first of the month.

(Woman) Thanks. I think working with Professor Halpern and teaching her sections of Women in American History would be fascinating.

9. WHAT WILL THE WOMAN PROBABLY DO NEXT?
10. WHAT DID THE MAN MOST RECENTLY TEACH?
11. WHY DOESN'T THE WOMAN WANT TO TEACH THE SAME COURSE AGAIN?

QUESTIONS 12–14

(Man) Dr. Martin, are you my academic advisor this semester?

(Woman) Yes. I'll be keeping all the students I had last term. What can I do for you?

(Man) Well, I'm thinking about transferring. I want to make sure what I'm taking will transfer.

(Woman) Let me pull up your transcript. Here it is. I see you're taking introductory courses. That should be fine. Most universities will transfer these. It's the upper level courses that most schools want you to take with them.

(Man) I plan to stay here for the spring term and transfer next fall.

(Woman) When you come to see me to preregister, bring the catalogues of the schools you're considering. They should spell out their transfer policies.

(Man) Great. See you in November.

12. WHAT DOES DR. MARTIN THINK THE MAN SHOULD DO NEXT?
13. WHEN WILL THE MAN PROBABLY TRANSFER?
14. WHAT DOES DR. MARTIN IMPLY?

QUESTIONS 15–17

(Woman) Do you think everyone in the class knows Dr. Roberts will be retiring as soon as the term ends?

(Man) He's mentioned it several times. Seems like he's really looking forward to it.

(Woman) I know the university is planning a big night-time reception, but that'll be mainly for faculty. I'd like our class to do something special.

(Man) What did you have in mind?

(Woman) Remember he told us how much he enjoys gardening? I thought we could get him some exotic plants and seeds for his garden.

(Man) Sounds like a plan. I've got everyone's e-mail address in the class. How much of a donation should I ask for?

15. WHAT WILL THE MAN PROBABLY DO NEXT?
16. WHAT IS THE UNIVERSITY PLANNING FOR DR. ROBERTS?
17. WHAT DOES THE WOMAN SAY ABOUT DR. ROBERTS?

QUESTIONS 18–19

(Man) What are you doing over Thanksgiving?

(Woman) I'm going home to see my family. What about you?

(Man) I'm not sure. I didn't realize the dorms would be closed, and I have to be out of my room by 1:00 on Wednesday.

(Woman) You can come with me for the holiday. Just be prepared for my chatty relatives and lots of football.

(Man) Thanks so much. I really had no idea what to do. And don't worry; when my family gets together, I can never get a word in edgewise.

18. WHAT WILL THE MAN PROBABLY DO OVER THANKSGIVING?
19. WHAT DO THE MAN AND WOMAN HAVE IN COMMON?

QUESTIONS 20–22

(Man) Do you know anyone who's ever gotten a ride that was posted on the ride board?

(Woman) Oh, you mean the board in the student center? How does that work?

(Man) Students post where they're driving and how many passengers they can take. The board is divided into regions. Say if I'm looking for a ride to Chicago, I check Chicago and the date.

(Woman) Where are you going?

(Man) To Tennessee.

(Woman) It would certainly be much faster than taking a bus and certainly cheaper than flying. Do you know anyone who's ever used it?

(Man) My freshman roommate got a ride home for Spring Break that way. There were three other passengers and they paid for the gas and tolls. I don't know . . . it makes me a little bit nervous. But I figured I could meet the person first and see how I felt.

20. WHAT WILL THE MAN PROBABLY DO NEXT?
21. HOW DOES THE MAN FEEL ABOUT DRIVING WITH SOMEONE HE DOESN'T KNOW?
22. WHAT DOES THE MAN SAY ABOUT HIS FRESHMAN ROOMMATE?

QUESTIONS 23–24

(Man) (Knock, knock) Carly, are you in your room? It's your R.A.

(Woman) Oh, hi. Come in.

(Man) Carly, I'm sure you're aware that it's finals week, and that every dorm has a 24-hour quiet policy. That means no loud music and no loud noise at any time. We've had several complaints about your room.

(Woman) Are you sure it was my room? I don't even have a CD player, let alone a TV set.

(Man) Well, we could have the wrong room, but I've got 3 different complaints about C-305.

(Woman) Well, that explains it. You're in C-405.

23. WHY DOES THE MAN STOP BY CARLY'S ROOM?
24. WHAT DID THE MAN DO?

QUESTIONS 25–27

(Woman) Coach Neumer, hi, I'm a transfer student and wanted to know if I could try out for the swim team.

(Man) Actually, we have a full roster, but I'd still like to see your times and your strokes. Can you come to the practice tomorrow?

(Woman) Sure. At what time?

(Man) From 4 to 6 at the Blodgett Pool. First, tell me about your swimming.

(Woman) Well, I've been swimming on a private team since I was six, and my high school team won the state championship. My best stroke is butterfly, and I swam at nationals the last three years.

(Man) Why didn't you contact me earlier about the team?

(Woman) To be honest, I wasn't sure if I wanted to swim again this year. Last year I had a hard time keeping up with my school work.

25. WHEN SHOULD THE WOMAN GO TO PRACTICE?
26. WHY IS THE WOMAN UNSURE ABOUT SWIMMING AGAIN?
27. WHAT DOES THE COACH WANT THE WOMAN TO DO NEXT?

QUESTIONS 28–29

(Man) Excuse me. Are you Ms. Howard, the bursar?

(Woman) Yes. Can I help you with something?

(Man) I hope you can help me. I can't register online. My last name is Root, and my first name is Ian.

(Woman) Just a minute. Let me pull up your file. It's because you owe $4,000 in tuition.

(Man) Can you double check? That's impossible. I know my parents transfered the money. Actually I think I have a copy of the bank transfer in my room.

(Woman) Unfortunately, we have no record. Can you bring that documentation back to this office before 5 today? If you can't find it, I suggest you double check with your parents.

28. WHAT IS THE PROBLEM?
29. WHAT WILL THE MAN PROBABLY DO NEXT?

QUESTIONS 30–32

(Woman) Excuse me, I'm new on campus, and I'm looking for the computer technology center.

(Man) Do you mean the place where you can work on computers or the place where they can fix your computer?

(Woman) Unfortunately the latter.

(Man) Too bad. You take a right at the library. Continue two blocks, and it's next to the admissions office.

(Woman) Could you repeat that one more time?

(Man) Sure. Take a right at the library, and after two blocks you'll see the admissions office. It's next door. Why don't you pick up a copy of the student handbook at the admissions office. It's got the location of every office on campus.

(Woman) Thanks a lot.

30. WHAT IS THE WOMAN LOOKING FOR?
31. WHAT CAN YOU SAY ABOUT THE DIRECTIONS?
32. WHERE IS THE PLACE THAT FIXES COMPUTERS?

Exercise 12

QUESTIONS 1–5

(Narrator) Listen to a discussion in a philosophy class on Brook Farm.

(Professor) Remember we're leaving for Brook Farm this Saturday at 8:30 A.M. It should take us about four hours to get there.

(Karen) But Professor? I know I read it burned down.

(Professor) Yes, that's partially correct. The central building burned down in 1846, and all that remains of the community which we're studying is cellarholes.

(Jarred) Well, if all that's left are some cellarholes, what are we going to see there?

(Professor) Good question. As you know, Brook Farm, the most celebrated American Utopian society, lasted for six years, from 1841 until 1847. We'll be able to get a sense of the rolling hills and surrounding nature which influenced the community. From there we'll go on to Salem, to the house of Nathaniel Hawthorne who lived at Brook Farm in the 1840s.

(Heather) How many people actually lived at Brook Farm?

(Professor) They began with 15. They had 200 acres with four buildings. But the land was ill-suited for farming, and they lacked water power for industry. Nevertheless, they attempted various agricultural and industrial projects, for these members of Brook Farm embraced physical labor as well as amusement. Each member worked several hours every day on the farm. The work allowed them to be close to nature. And so the Brook Farm members developed a philosophy encompassing literature, religion, and social issues. After work was done and dinner served, there was plenty of time for music, dancing, card playing, dramatic readings, costume parties, sledding, and skating.

(Karen) Excuse me. We studied how the transcendentalists believed that the physical world is secondary to the spiritual world. I'm a little mixed up about their need to work.

(Professor) Well, they wanted to be financially self-sufficient. Secondarily, they believed that one learns about the physical world through one's senses and understanding. Working is part of the physical world. In addition to the physical world, one learns about the world of the spirit through another power, called reason. They defined reason as the independent and intuitive capacity to know what is absolutely true.

(Jarred) I have an unrelated question. I don't understand what I read about a phalanx.

(Professor) One of the Brook Farm members was influenced by a French philosopher who claimed that universal harmony could be reached if a society numbered 1800. A society of that number was called a phalanx. Although Brook Farm was incorporated into a phalanx in 1844, they never had more than 120 members.

(Heather) So what happened to these philosophers after 1847?

(Professor) They abandoned Brook Farm, and their numbers remained quite small. However, their writings greatly influenced American intellectual history and literature. That'll be all for today's class. Make sure you read Chapter 3 before Saturday, and bring with you drawing paper, a notebook, and comfortable clothing.

1. WHAT IS THE DISCUSSION MAINLY ABOUT?
2. WHAT IS STATED IN THE DISCUSSION ABOUT NATHANIEL HAWTHORNE?
3. ACCORDING TO THE DISCUSSION, WHICH OF THE FOLLOWING IS NOT MENTIONED AS CHARACTERISTIC OF THE BROOK FARM PHILOSOPHY?
4. WHAT ARE THE NUMBERS OF EACH OF THE FOLLOWING?
5. THE EVENTS WHICH OCCURRED AT BROOK FARM WERE DISCUSSED. PUT THEM IN THE CORRECT CHRONOLOGICAL ORDER.

QUESTIONS 6–10

(Narrator) Listen to a discussion in an engineering class. The discussion is on windmills.

(Professor) As many of you know, man has used wind power as a natural source of energy for centuries. The first windmills probably originated in the seventh century in what is today Iran. These windmills had sails that revolved around a vertical axis. They were used chiefly to grind grain. By the 12th century, windmills had spread to Europe, probably by Crusaders returning from the wars in the Holy Land. The early mills were quite small, and we can see some of their details from mediaeval manuscripts, stained glass, and carved representations.

(Erica) Did those early European windmills also use sails?

(Professor) No, good question. About that time, inventors discovered that windmills produced more power if the sails or blades turned on a horizontal shaft.

(Donald) Isn't that the principle of Dutch windmills?

(Professor) Exactly. As we can see in this picture, this discovery led to the development of Dutch windmills. These windmills were widely used in the Netherlands to drain water from the land. They had four long arms with cloth sails or wooden slats or shutters mounted on them.

(Lee) When did American windmills become popular? Last summer I saw hundreds of them on Cape Cod.

(Professor) During the 1800s and 1900s, many American windmills were built throughout the United States to pump water and generate electricity. The wheels of early American windmills had numerous curved blades of wood or steel, and were mounted on horizontal shafts. A vane on the end of the shaft opposite the wheel moved the wheel to face the wind.
During the 1930s, the U.S. government started building a large number of central generating plants to bring electricity to rural areas. Thus, the use of windmills to produce electricity declined.

(Donald) My parents told me that in the 1970s there was a renewed interest in windmills.

(Professor) Can anyone explain why?

(Lee) Was it related to the oil shortages?

(Professor) Precisely. In the 70s, shortages of oil for generating electricity led to renewed interest and research in wind power. Since that time, the U.S. government has sponsored the building and testing of a number of wind turbines. One type has two long propellerlike blades, and can generate more than two megawatts of electricity in moderate wind. Researchers have also developed the Darrieus wind turbine. This device resembles an eggbeater, with two or three long curved blades attached to a vertical shaft. Lee, you mentioned Cape Cod. Does anyone know which countries are leading the way today in windmill experimentation and production?

(Erica) I've heard about New Zealand.

(Professor) Yes, they've just recently jumped on the bandwagon. That leads to your assignment for tomorrow. Research the five leading countries that are utilizing wind power and compare and contrast the various windmill types, expenditures, and results.

6. WHAT DOES THE PROFESSOR MAINLY TALK ABOUT?
7. IDENTIFY WHICH PICTURE REPRESENTS A DUTCH WINDMILL.
8. BASED ON THE PROFESSOR'S DESCRIPTION, CLASSIFY EACH OF THE FOLLOWING DESCRIPTIONS.
9. THE PROFESSOR EXPLAINS THE ORDER IN WHICH COUNTRIES DEVELOPED WINDMILLS. PUT THESE COUNTRIES IN THEIR HISTORICAL ORDER, FROM FIRST TO MOST RECENT.
10. WHAT IS THE ASSIGNMENT FOR THE NEXT CLASS?

QUESTIONS 11–15

(Narrator) Listen to a discussion about the architect Frank Lloyd Wright.

(Professor) Today we're going to be viewing and discussing various buildings designed by Frank Lloyd Wright that characterize the different stages of his evolution as an architect. Let's begin with the first home Wright designed in 1889. It actually was his own home in Oak Park, Illinois.

(Greg) Wow! It's surfaced with wood shingles. I think of Wright as using cement and stucco.

(Professor) Yes, the home is shingles and brick. Remember it was 1889, and he had just begun to work. By 1896, his first distinctive style, known as Prairie Style, evolved.

(Matthew) Was the Willits' House the first one of its kind?

(Professor) Yes, you can see in this picture that the spaces inside the home expand into the outdoors through porches and terraces. Because of their low, horizontal form, the homes seem

	to grow out of the ground. The effect was emphasized by his use of wood and other materials as they appear in nature. The home was built in 1901.
(Matthew)	I've been to the Robie House in Chicago. Isn't that a Prairie Style home as well?
(Professor)	Yes, that's correct. I'm glad you've seen it because this 1906 home is considered his best expression of the Prairie structure. It looks like a series of horizontal layers floating over the ground. We'll move to some of his nonresidential designs now. The Unity Temple, completed in 1908 in Oak Park, Illinois, is one of the first significant American architectural statements in poured concrete. In most earlier concrete buildings, concrete is covered with some other materials. We're going to jump a decade to his next significant development. Is anyone here from California?
(Amy)	I am. I know you'll want to discuss his textile-block houses. I live near the Samuel Freeman house in Los Angeles.
(Professor)	Lucky you. During the 1920s, Wright designed several houses in southern California that are noted for the use of precast concrete blocks. The patterns of the blocks vary for each project. It looks like we'll only be able to get through the 1920s today. The last project I want to discuss is the Imperial Hotel complex, built from 1915–1922 in Tokyo. Unfortunately, the hotel was demolished in 1968.
(Greg)	Wasn't the entrance lobby reconstructed in Nagoya?
(Professor)	That's right. But let's get back to the hotel first. The Imperial Hotel was Wright's major work in Japan. He made liberal use of soft lava, or Oya stone. The hotel's floating foundation permitted it to survive, with little damage, the great earthquake of September 1, 1923, which destroyed most of Tokyo. As Tokyo's land values rose following World War II, the hotel was torn down. However, the entrance lobby was dismantled and taken to Nagoya. It's now an architectural museum. For next class, finish reading the chapter on Wright, paying particular attention to the Johnson Wax Building, the Guggenheim Museum, and his summer Wisconsin home, Taliesin, as well as Taliesin West in Arizona.

11. ACCORDING TO THE PROFESSOR, WHAT IS CHARACTERISTIC OF THE PRAIRIE STYLE?
12. WHAT IS CHARACTERISTIC OF EACH OF THESE BUILDINGS?
13. WHAT IS STATED ABOUT SOUTHERN CALIFORNIAN WRIGHT HOUSES?
14. WHAT IS NOT STATED ABOUT THE IMPERIAL HOTEL?
15. THE PROFESSOR MENTIONS THE COMPLETION DATE FOR EACH OF THESE BUILDINGS. PUT THE ORDER IN WHICH THEY WERE CONSTRUCTED IN THEIR HISTORICAL ORDER.

QUESTIONS 16–20

(Narrator)	Listen to a discussion in an American history class. They are discussing the American flag.
(Professor)	Does anyone know the names the American flag was once called?
(Teddy)	Didn't some people used to call it the *Star Spangled Banner,* like our national anthem?
(Professor)	You're right.
(Jamie)	I've heard it referred to as *Old Glory.*
(Professor)	Also correct. The most popular name is *The Stars and Stripes,* based on its design. At the start of the Revolutionary War in 1775, the American flag had a British flag in the upper left corner. But after the Declaration of Independence in 1777, the British flag was no longer appropriate as part of the American flag. On June 4, 1777, the Continental Congress resolved that "the Flag of the United States be 13 stripes alternating red and white, with 13 white stars in a blue field." But there was no official arrangement for the stars. The most popular design had alternating rows of 3, 2, 3, 2, and 3 stars. Another flag with 13 stars in a circle was rarely used at that time.
(Lauren)	Is that the flag Betsy Ross made?
(Professor)	In 1870, William Canby claimed that his grandmother, Betsy Ross, a Philadelphia seamstress, had made the first United States flag. Although she made flags during the Revolutionary War, most historians, myself included, do not support Canby's claim.
(Teddy)	I have a question. Why did the 1775 flag incorporate the British flag if the colonists were already fighting for independence?
(Professor)	Actually, the colonists did not at first seek full independence, so the Union Jack, another name for the British flag, remained in the American flag because there was still a connection to England. By

1794, two new states had joined the Union. Congress decided to add two stars and two stripes to the flag. It ordered a 15-stripe flag used after May 1, 1795. The stars appeared in five rows, three to a row. Americans carried this flag in the War of 1812.

(Lauren) But doesn't our flag today have only 13 stripes?

(Professor) Exactly. As more states came into the Union, Congress realized that a new star and a new stripe for each state would make the flag too cluttered. Samuel Chester Reid, a navy captain, proposed a flag of 13 stripes, one for each of the original colonies, and a star for each state. Congress accepted the idea because it could then change the number of stars easily. On April 4, 1818, it set the number of stripes at 13 again. It ordered a new star to be added to the flag on the July 4th after a state joined the Union.

(Teddy) How was it determined how the stars would be arranged?

(Professor) I was getting to that. When Congress changed the stripes back to 13, it did not say how the stars were to be arranged. Flagmakers used various designs. The Great Star Flag of 1818 had its 20 stars arranged in the form of a five-pointed star. In the years that followed, various presidents sometimes proclaimed new arrangements for the stars when a new state entered the Union. In some cases, the army and navy worked out the new designs. In some cases, no official action was ever taken. President Lincoln refused to have the stars for southern states removed from the flag even though the South had its own flag. No government official decided on the design of the 46-star flag, used from 1908 to 1912. Presidential orders fixed the positions of the stars in 1912 for 48 stars, in 1959 for 49, and in 1960 for 50.

16. WHAT IS THE DISCUSSION MAINLY ABOUT?
17. WHAT IS STATED IN THE DISCUSSION ABOUT THE AMERICAN FLAG?
18. WHO DECIDED ON THE DESIGN OF THE 46-STAR FLAG, USED FROM 1908 TO 1912?
19. WHEN DOES A NEW STAR GET ADDED TO THE AMERICAN FLAG?
20. THE PROFESSOR MENTIONS SEVERAL DIFFERENT FLAG CONFIGURATIONS. PUT THESE EVENTS IN THEIR HISTORICAL ORDER.

Exercise 13

QUESTIONS 1–4

(Narrator) Listen to part of a lecture in a biology class.

(Professor) Good morning, class. Yesterday, we spoke about chromosomes, the part of a cell that contains genetic information. As we said, all humans have 23 pairs, and the only difference between men and women is in one of those 23 pairs, called the sex chromosome. For the 23rd chromosome pair, women have two X chromosomes, while men have an X and a Y.

Today we will discuss why some disorders, like colorblindness, occur more often in men than in women. When a disorder is caused by a mutation, or change, on one of the 22 regular chromosomes, also called autosomes, the disorder will appear as often in men as in women, ignoring other possible factors. But when a disorder occurs because of a mutation on the X chromosome, men are more likely to be affected.

Why would a change on the X chromosome affect men more than woman if women have two Xs and men only have one? A disorder like colorblindness is caused when a cell is missing the gene to create a protein to differentiate between colors. This gene regularly appears on the X chromosome. If a woman inherits two X chromosomes, one without the gene and one with the gene, she will still be able to differentiate between colors, because she had one copy of the gene, which is enough. However, a man only has one X chromosome. If that one is missing the gene, he will not be able to see the difference between certain colors.

Because of the difference in the genetics of men and women, disorders such as colorblindness affect men more often. These disorders are called sex-linked because they are linked to the sex chromosomes. Other disorders that work this way are hemophilia, a blood-clotting disorder, and muscular dystrophy, in which muscle tissue is lost.

For next class, read chapter 27, paying particular attention to recent developments in gene replacement therapies.

1. WHAT DOES THE PROFESSOR MAINLY TALK ABOUT?
2. WHAT WILL HAPPEN WHEN MUTATIONS OCCUR IN ONE OF THE REGULAR 22 CHROMOSOMES?
3. WHAT CAUSES COLORBLINDNESS?
4. WHICH OF THESE DISORDERS IN NOT MENTIONED AS A DISORDER LINKED TO THE SEX CHROMOSOME?

QUESTIONS 5–9

(Narrator) Listen to part of a lecture in a criminology class.

(Professor) One of the newest tools used by police and other experts in solving crimes is called forensic science, or forensics, meaning the use of science and technology to investigate and establish facts in criminal or civil courts of law.

One especially important tool in forensics is DNA analysis. Since every cell in the human body contains a person's DNA, a drop of blood or a single strand of hair is enough to provide a DNA sample. The specialist then compares a DNA sample from a crime scene to the DNA of a suspect using a method called gel electrophoresis. Electrophoresis is the separation of fragments using an electric field.

The DNA fragments are produced by cutting both DNA samples, one from the crime scene and one from the suspect, into smaller pieces, using proteins called "restriction enzymes." If the DNA samples belong to the same person, the pieces should all be the same size.

To compare the size of the pieces, scientists insert the two samples into a gel, made out of a material called agarose, which is purified from algae. Then they run an electric current through the solution liquid surrounding the gel. DNA is negatively charged, so it is attracted to the positively charged end of the gel. Smaller DNA pieces move more slowly through the gel. When the current is turned off, the scientists can compare the distance the different pieces have traveled, and see if the two DNA samples match.

This procedure is very, very accurate, especially if repeated a number of times using different restriction enzymes to reduce the possibility that change contributed to the similarity. However, one limitation of this method is that it can only confirm or eliminate a suspect. Scientists cannot yet use DNA to determine a person's identity; they need to have a sample from a suspect to which to compare the DNA.

5. WHAT DOES THE PROFESSOR MAINLY TALK ABOUT?
6. WHAT IS TRUE ABOUT DNA?
7. WHAT IS GEL ELECTROPHORESIS?
8. WHAT ARE THE CHARACTERISTICS OF EACH OF THE FOLLOWING?
9. ACCORDING TO THE PASSAGE, WHEN IS DNA ANALYSIS VERY ACCURATE?

QUESTIONS 10–14

(Narrator) Listen to part of a lecture in a meteorology class. The professor is talking about the El Niño weather pattern.

(Professor) The term El Niño, which is Spanish for Christ child, was originally used by fishermen along the coasts of Ecuador and Peru to refer to a warm ocean current that typically appears around Christmastime and lasts for several months. Fish are less abundant during these warm intervals, so fishermen often take a break to repair their equipment and spend time with their families. In some years, however, the water is especially warm and the break in the fishing season persists into May or even June. Over the years, the term El Niño has come to be reserved for these exceptionally strong warm intervals that not only disrupt the fishing routines of the fishermen, but also bring heavy rains.

During the past 40 years, nine El Niños have affected the South American coast. Most of them raised water temperatures not only along the coast, but also at the Galapagos Islands and in a belt stretching 5000 miles across the equatorial Pacific. The strong ones, like the El Niño of 1982–83, left an imprint upon the local weather and marine life, as well as on climatic conditions around the globe.

Before the flood waters from the record breaking 1982–1983 El Niño event had fully receded, farmers in Peru were already beginning to worry that sea-surface temperatures might drop below normal the following year, bringing drought and crop failures. It was at this time that the Peruvian government decided to develop a program to forecast future climate swings.

The first task was to make a forecast for the next rainy season, which was expected to occur in early 1984. Information available in early November, 1983, indicated that the climatic conditions in the equatorial Pacific were near normal and were likely to remain so through the rainy season, producing favorable conditions for agriculture. This information was conveyed to numerous organizations and to the Minister of Agriculture, who incorporated it into the planning for the 1983–1984 growing season. The forecast proved to be correct, and the harvest was an abundant one. Since that time, forecasts of the upcoming rainy season have been issued each November based on observations of winds and water temperatures in the tropical Pacific region and the output of numerical prediction models. The forecasts are presented in terms of four possibilities, the first having the greatest probability of occurring, and the remainder in descending order: (1) a weak El Niño with a slightly wetter than normal growing season, (2) near normal conditions, (3) a full blown El Nino with flooding, and (4) cooler than normal waters offshore, with higher than normal chance of drought.

Once the forecast is issued, farmers' representatives and government officials meet to decide on the appropriate combination of crops to plant in order to maximize the overall yield. Rice and cotton, two of the primary crops grown in northern Peru, are highly sensitive to the quantities and timing of rainfall. Rice thrives in wet conditions during the growing season followed by drier conditions during the ripening phase. Cotton, with its deeper root system, can tolerate drier weather. Hence, a forecast of El Niño weather might induce farmers to plant more rice and less cotton than in a year without El Niño.

10. WHAT DOES THE PROFESSOR MAINLY TALK ABOUT?
11. WHAT DOES THE TERM EL NIÑO MEAN TODAY?
12. WHAT IS TRUE ABOUT PERUVIAN EL NIÑO FORECASTS SINCE THE 1983–1984 SEASON?
13. WHICH OF THE FOLLOWING HAVE THE HIGHEST PROBABILITY OF OCCURRING ACCORDING TO FORECASTS?
14. ACCORDING TO THE PROFESSOR, WHAT MIGHT PERUVIAN FARMERS DO IF EL NIÑO IS FORECAST?

QUESTIONS 15–19

(Narrator) Listen to part of a lecture in an anatomy class. The professor is discussing the left-brained, right-brained theory.

(Professor) Today I'm going to present an overview of the parts of the brain and the function of each. The three main divisions are the cerebrum, the cerebellum, and the brain stem. We'll focus today on the cerebrum and briefly discuss the popular "left-brained, right-brained" theory.

The cerebrum, the large, rounded structure of the brain occupying most of the cranial cavity, makes up about 85% of the weight of the human brain. Behind the forehead is the frontal lobe, the part of the brain responsible for speech, body movement and coordination, as well as planning and consciousness. Under it is the temporal lobe, which is also responsible for speech in addition to hearing. Behind the temporal lobe is the occipital lobe, which is responsible for vision and reading. Above the temporal lobe and between the frontal and occipital lobe is the parietal lobe, which is responsible for touch interpretation and body position. I repeat, the frontal lobe, which many refer to as the "left-brain," as well as the temporal lobe, commonly referred to as the "right brain," both control speech.

This fact contradicts the left-brained, right-brained theory although the theory is established firmly in popular culture. According to this theory, if we draw an imaginary line down the brain, and call the forehead side the left hemisphere, and call the back of the head side the right hemisphere, each hemisphere has specialized, unique functions. Proponents of this theory contend that the left hemisphere controls language, analysis, and logic, whereas the right hemisphere is the more creative, problem solving, and intuitive half. Many proponents try to classify a person as "right-brained" or "left-brained," suggesting that the two hemispheres do not work together in the same person, and thus, can be considered independent. According to these theorists, artists are "right-brained" and accountants are "left-brained."

However, opponents to this theory, including almost all scientists, base their arguments on the fact that when surgery is performed to disconnect the two sides, each side can still function well, although not perfectly. Moreover, the fact that the two hemispheres differ in purpose indicates that they must integrate activities. Therefore, opponents argue, the resulting processes must be different from and even greater than the processes of either hemisphere alone.

What I'd like you to do for next class is to research the left-brained, right-brained theory and bring in any evidence you can find which supports this theory, be it experimental or theoretical.

15. WHAT IS THE LECTURE MAINLY ABOUT?
16. WHICH OF THE FOLLOWING PARTS OF THE ILLUSTRATION IS THE TEMPORAL LOBE?
17. ON WHAT DO THE OPPONENTS OF THE LEFT-BRAINED, RIGHT-BRAINED THEORY BASE THEIR ARGUMENTS?
18. ACCORDING TO THE LEFT-BRAINED, RIGHT-BRAINED THEORISTS, WHICH OF THE FOLLOWING PROFESSIONS WOULD BE CONSIDERED LEFT-BRAINED?
19. WHAT IS THE ASSIGNMENT FOR THE NEXT CLASS?

LISTENING POST-TEST

Part A

1. (Man) Could you recommend one of your desserts? They all look so good.
   (Woman) Our most popular dessert is the chocolate cake, but my favorite is the strawberry cheesecake.
   (Man) That's right up my alley.
   (Narrator) WHAT WILL THE MAN PROBABLY DO?

2. (Woman) I've been looking for a printer like yours.
   (Man) I never could have bought it if the computer store downtown weren't having its blowout sale.
   (Narrator) WHAT DOES THE MAN MEAN?

3. (Man) Are you taking the bus to the company retreat?
   (Woman) No, I'll be driving. Want a ride?
   (Man) Only if I can chip in on the expenses.
   (Narrator) WHAT DOES THE MAN MEAN?

4. (Woman) Can you believe how much reading we have this week for our history class?
   (Man) That's nothing. My literature class has just as much reading plus two papers due this week.
   (Narrator) WHAT DOES THE MAN IMPLY?

5. (Man) Could I have the sports section of your newspaper?
   (Woman) The one on the chair? It's not mine, but no one's been reading it since I got here.
   (Narrator) WHAT DOES THE WOMAN IMPLY?

6. (Woman) I have to pick up Alice's sister at the airport, and all I know is she'll be wearing a red dress.
   (Man) Oh. I saw her picture on Alice's desk. She looks just like her.
   (Narrator) WHAT DOES THE MAN IMPLY?

7. (Man) Do you have black and white film?
   (Woman) Yes, will you be using it indoors or outdoors?
   (Man) It all depends. Primarily outdoors.
   (Narrator) WHERE DOES THIS CONVERSATION TAKE PLACE?

8. (Woman) Will you be meeting with a professor while you're doing your off-campus internship?
   (Man) I'm afraid it's sink or swim. I'll be on my own the whole time.
   (Narrator) WHAT DOES THE MAN IMPLY?

9. (Woman) What comes in each dorm room?
   (Man) A bed, a desk and an attached lamp, a chair, a mirror, and a wastebasket.
   (Woman) That's it? I wish I'd known to bring my own sheets and blankets.
   (Narrator) WHAT DOES THE WOMAN IMPLY?

10. (Man) Does everyone have to take the writing seminar assessment?
    (Woman) The catalogue says only students who received a letter have to.
    (Man) Well, I didn't get a letter.
    (Narrator) WHAT DOES THE MAN IMPLY?

11. (Man) Excuse me. Could I get the official copy of my high school transcript

	back that I submitted with my undergraduate application?
(Woman)	Oh, I'm sorry. Once we receive a transcript, it can't leave our office.
(Man)	I can't believe it! I don't see how I can get another one.
(Narrator)	WHAT'S THE MAN'S PROBLEM?

Part B

QUESTIONS 12–14

(Man)	Hey, Charlotte. Are you going to the football game on Saturday?
(Woman)	No, Tim. I'm not a big football fan. Why, are you going?
(Man)	Of course! We're playing Penn State, and it should be a really good game. Both teams are undefeated, and this game will decide who gets to go to the league championships.
(Woman)	Well, that sounds like it could be exciting. What time does the game start? And how much are the tickets?
(Man)	At 2, but it's good to get there at least an hour early. Everyone likes to hang out before the game actually begins. And tickets are free with your student ID; you just have to pick them up at the stadium by the end of the day today.
(Woman)	I'm glad I ran into you. I think my first football game will be this weekend!

12. WHAT WILL CHARLOTTE PROBABLY DO NEXT?
13. WHAT CAN BE INFERRED ABOUT TIM?
14. WHY DOES TIM SUGGEST GETTING TO THE GAME EARLY?

QUESTIONS 15–17

(Woman)	Hey, Craig. How did you do on the philosophy quiz?
(Man)	It was a complete disaster, Alison. I got a C minus. How 'bout you?
(Woman)	It wasn't so bad. I got a B plus, but philosophy is my major.
(Man)	I get the feeling that most of the students in our class are philosophy majors. I'm a physics major, and most of what the professor says is way over my head.
(Woman)	Have you thought about getting a tutor? I had one last semester, and she really helped me with my econ class.
(Man)	Really? Do they tutor everything? Even philosophy and psychology? Where can I get one?
(Woman)	Just go to the Academic Success Center. It's on the first floor of College Hall.

15. WHY DID ALISON DO BETTER ON THE QUIZ THAN CRAIG?
16. WHAT IS CRAIG'S MAJOR?
17. WHAT DOES ALISON ADVISE CRAIG TO DO?

QUESTIONS 18–22

(Narrator)	Listen to a lecture in an art history class. The professor is talking about Mary Cassatt.
(Professor)	On the screen is a portrait of Mary Cassatt, painted by another Impressionist painter and friend, Edgar Degas. Mary Cassatt is one of the best-loved American Impressionists. She was born in 1844 to a middle class family in Pittsburgh, Pennsylvania. As a child, she lived in Pittsburgh, Philadelphia, and Europe. When she was very young, she decided to become an artist. Her family was opposed to the idea, but this did not stop her from entering the Pennsylvania Academy of Fine Arts, where she studied for four years. During the late 1860s, she studied in Europe—in Spain, Italy, and France. It was in France that she finally found an environment where she could work and learn from other artists. She had grown tired of the traditional style that she had studied, and the new movement of Impressionism appealed to her. The qualities of her work that were typically Impressionist were her use of light colors, her visible brushstrokes, and her choice of day to day subject matter. Let's look at a painting Cassatt did during this period. Notice the subject matter. It's of people doing something very ordinary, two women sitting having tea together. It's entitled *Afternoon Tea Party.* She also painted women quietly reading or writing letters. She became particularly well known for her paintings of peaceful, loving moments shared by mothers and their young children. She often used her family members as models. She painted the people of her day, engaged in daily life. Look at this picture, entitled *The Bath,* which shows how she used flat, delicate colors and strong, clear lines. Like her French impressionist friends, she used light, bright colors and sketchy brushstrokes to create the effect of what the eye sees at a glance.

In the late 1890s, she created a series of beautiful prints. In their strong outlines and flattened, simplified shapes, these prints show the influence of woodcuts by Japanese artists.

18. WHAT IS STATED ABOUT MARY CASSATT'S FAMILY?
19. WHEN DID MARY CASSATT DECIDE TO BECOME AN ARTIST?
20. WHAT IS TYPICAL OF IMPRESSIONIST PAINTING?
21. WHAT KIND OF PEOPLE DID MARY CASSATT PAINT?
22. WHICH WORK OF ART IS PROBABLY BY MARY CASSATT?

QUESTIONS 23–27

(Narrator) Listen to a discussion in a history class. The discussion is about the Great Depression.

(Professor) Okay, class. I hope everyone read pages 35 to 70 for today's discussion.
And, as you know, there's a quiz on Friday on the Great Depression.

(Jim) Actually, I have a question about the quiz. When exactly did the Great Depression start?

(Professor) The start of the Great Depression can be traced back to the stock market crash of October, 1929, often referred to as "Black Thursday."

(Valerie) Why would a stock market crash trigger a depression?

(Professor) People and corporations lost a lot of money in the stock market. Then the banks failed, and people lost their savings.

(Isaac) Was there a lot of unemployment?

(Professor) Yes. Millions of people were out of work, and long lines began to form outside of soup kitchens in American cities because people couldn't afford to buy food.

(Jim) Couldn't the government do anything about it?

(Professor) The government tried to help. After President Franklin Delano Roosevelt was elected in 1932, he created the New Deal, which tried to help Americans affected by the Depression. As part of the New Deal, Roosevelt established the Works Project Administration, or WPA, in 1935. The WPA sponsored many projects for the unemployed, ranging from construction to art.

(Valerie) But there probably weren't that many artists who worked with the WPA, were there?

(Professor) Actually over 5,000 artists produced over 225,000 works of art during the years of the WPA. Everything from murals to sculpture was commissioned by the government.

(Isaac) Did everything end up in museums?

(Professor) No, not at all. In fact, most of the artwork was displayed in public places, for everyone to see and enjoy.

(Valerie) What other kinds of projects did the WPA sponsor?

(Professor) Believe it or not, they built golf courses, swimming pools, and even a bath house! But I think we've gotten a bit off topic. None of this is going to be on your quiz!

23. WHAT IS THE ASSIGNMENT FOR FRIDAY?
24. WHICH OF THE FOLLOWING IS MENTIONED AS BEING BUILT BY THE WPA?
25. THE PROFESSOR MENTIONS A SERIES OF EVENTS. PUT THEM IN THEIR CHRONOLOGICAL ORDER.
26. ACCORDING TO THE PROFESSOR, WHAT WERE THE EFFECTS OF THE GREAT DEPRESSION ON THE AMERICAN ECONOMY?
27. WHAT ARE THE CHARACTERISTICS OF EACH OF THESE TERMS?

QUESTIONS 28–32

(Narrator) Listen to part of a talk in a genetics class.

(Professor) Probably the most well-known genetic breakthrough was made by James Watson and Francis Crick in the 1960s. They were awarded the Nobel Prize in Medicine in 1962 for their discovery of the double-helix structure of DNA and its replication process. Now, can you think of the name of any woman who has been honored by the Nobel committee in the area of medicine related to genetics? If you can't, it's not surprising. Can you think of the names of any well-known female scientists? The name Marie Curie should come to mind for her co-discovery of radioactivity in the nineteenth century. As the twentieth century progressed, more and more women entered the scientific realm, breaking the traditional females roles of Western European and U.S. society. One such woman, whose name you should know, was Barbara McClintock, winner of the Nobel Prize for medicine in 1984.

McClintock chose a scientific career even as an undergraduate at Cornell University in 1919, and in the face of social criticism and tremendous intellectual challenges, she established herself among the great geneticists of the twentieth century.

In the twenties and thirties, scientists were just gaining awareness of the connection between cellular phenomena as seen through a microscope and heredity. McClintock's discoveries came from the study of corn at the cellular level. This study is known as maize cytogenics.

In 1931, she showed that chromosomes can break, yet during the formation of egg or sperm, they can rejoin in a different configuration. In 1951, she claimed that certain genes, mobile genes, can change their position on the chromosomes of cells. This claim was supported by the observation that nearby genes were affected by the presence or absence of such cells. In addition, the mobility occurred in different places in the cells of different corn plants.

In 1984, McClintock was recognized by the Nobel committee for her discovery of mobile genes.

28. WHAT DOES THE PROFESSOR MAINLY TALK ABOUT?
29. WHAT IS STATED IN THE LECTURE ABOUT BARBARA MCCLINTOCK?
30. ACCORDING TO THE LECTURE, WHAT DID MCCLINTOCK STUDY?
31. WHAT CAN BE INFERRED ABOUT CORN PLANTS?
32. THE PROFESSOR DISCUSSES A SERIES OF EVENTS. PUT THE EVENTS IN THEIR CHRONOLOGICAL ORDER.

TOEFL TEST 1

Part A

1. (Woman) I thought we only got 3 or 4 really hot weeks in the summer.
   (Man) I know that's what I told you, but it seems like every week this summer has been hotter than the one before.
   (Woman) If I had known, I would have taken the apartment with air conditioning.
   (Narrator) WHAT DOES THE WOMAN IMPLY?
2. (Man) I'm not sure that everyone knew that tonight's dinner was an hour earlier than usual.
   (Woman) Yeah, I noticed both Tamara and Fred missed dinner.
   (Narrator) WHAT DOES THE WOMAN MEAN?
3. (Woman) I've always hated this couch.
   (Man) Really? Why didn't you just say so?
   (Narrator) WHAT DOES THE MAN IMPLY?
4. (Woman) Have you seen the disk I was using in the lab?
   (Man) I remember you had it in your hand when you left the lab.
   (Woman) Yeah, me too. But then we had lunch in the cafeteria and went to the library. We've been back in the dorm for hours.
   (Narrator) WHERE DOES THIS CONVERSATION TAKE PLACE?
5. (Man) I need to send a mass mailing to everyone on the swim team.
   (Woman) I can do it; I have everyone's e-mail address. What's the message?
   (Man) We'll train at the country club pool until ours is repaired.
   (Narrator) WHAT DOES THE MAN MEAN?
6. (Man) Will you be ready to leave by 5:00?
   (Woman) I've got to make today's deadline. You go on ahead, and I'll meet you at the restaurant.
   (Narrator) WHAT DOES THE WOMAN IMPLY?
7. (Man) How many pages is the biology midterm going to be?
   (Woman) Was it ten? Maybe I'm mixed up with my computer midterm.
   (Narrator) WHAT DOES THE WOMAN MEAN?
8. (Woman) How are you doing on the last problem set?
   (Man) I went for extra help, but now I'm even more confused. It's put me right over the edge.
   (Narrator) WHAT DOES THE MAN IMPLY?
9. (Man) The oral presentation should be no longer than five minutes.
   (Woman) Excuse me. Does everyone have to give an oral presentation?
   (Man) Only if you want extra credit.
   (Narrator) WHAT DOES THE MAN MEAN?
10. (Man) I'm going to sit in the back row and on the aisle, so I can dash out of here as soon as he finishes.
    (Woman) Good idea; his lectures frequently run late.
    (Narrator) WHAT DOES THE WOMAN MEAN?
11. (Man) Did you hear anyone complain about our last club meeting?
    (Woman) I did hear some grumbling about a lack of refreshments.

(Man)	It seems that no matter how many cookies we order, there's never enough.
(Narrator)	WHAT DOES THE MAN IMPLY?

Part B

QUESTIONS 12–14

(Man)	I thought I'd volunteer for student government.
(Woman)	We could use some new faces and some new activities.
(Man)	Yeah, I'm really tired of nothing happening on campus over the weekend.
(Woman)	That's the problem with suburban colleges. Students go into the city on the weekends.
(Man)	Supposedly our activity fee goes for weekend events, but they're talking about stopping them because no one ever goes. I want to try to organize some programs that'll keep people here on Friday and Saturday nights.
(Woman)	Great idea. I promise I'll come to your events!
(Man)	Well . . . I was hoping you'd work with me.

12. WHAT DOES THE MAN SAY ABOUT THE STUDENT ACTIVITY FEE?
13. WHAT DOES THE MAN IMPLY ABOUT FRIDAY AND SATURDAY NIGHTS?
14. WHAT DOES THE MAN WANT THE WOMAN TO DO?

QUESTIONS 15–17

(Woman)	What time do you want to meet to go over our class presentation?
(Man)	Does 4:00 tomorrow work for you?
(Woman)	Actually, 5:00 is better. Before we meet, I'll go on the Internet and print out the electronic reserve articles we need for the first part.
(Man)	OK. And I can go to the library and get the books we need for the second part.
(Woman)	Good. Where should we meet?
(Man)	I always like working in the student center. We can talk without disturbing anyone else, and they've got those big tables where we can spread out our materials.
(Woman)	Sounds like a plan. Call me if you're going to be late.

15. WHERE WILL THEY GET THE MATERIALS FOR THE FIRST PART?
16. WHAT WILL THE MAN DO BEFORE THEY MEET?
17. WHERE WILL THEY MEET?

QUESTIONS 18–22

(Narrator) Listen to a design lecture about the printmaking process.

(Professor) Today we are going to discuss the process of making original prints.

There are three main categories of prints: relief, intaglio, and planographic. Although each category entails a different process, all use matrixes of either wood, stone, or metal as a means of transfering an ink design to paper.

Let's begin with relief prints, which typically involve wooden blocks. A matrix is created by cutting away any surface area that is not meant to show up in the final design. After applying ink to the raised surface of the matrix, the printmaker presses it onto a sheet of paper to create a print. Popular examples of relief prints are woodcuts and wood engravings.

To make an intaglio print, an opposite process occurs. The printmaker creates a matrix by cutting a design into a surface. The cutaway part forms the design that is printed on the paper. After the ink is pressed into the recessed area, the surface is wiped clean. Then, under pressure, the ink is transferred to the paper. This process leaves a platemark, the sign of an intaglio print. Popular examples are engravings and etchings.

To make a planographic print, a print is made from a flat matrix of stone or metal whose surface is covered by a grease crayon or greasy ink. Water, which is repelled by the greasy surface, is washed onto the surface, and then ink, which the greasy images holds, is applied to the surface. A press transfers the image onto paper. A popular example is lithographs.

As you can see, the printmaking process is complex and time-consuming. Printmakers must use caution while using sharp tools to carve lines onto the matrix and acid to burn away unwanted sections. What makes printmaking desirable is that matrixes can be used to create multiple images of a single design. In addition, printmakers can experiment with color and shading by varying the inking of the matrix. Ultimately, printmaking renders visual effects that differ from painting or sketching, justifying such a detailed process.

18. WHICH MEDIUM IS USED TO CREATE DESIGNS FOR PRINTMAKING?
19. WHICH PROCESS LEAVES A PLATEMARK?
20. WHAT IS AN EXAMPLE OF EACH OF THESE TYPES OF PRINTS?
21. HOW DO PRINTMAKERS ETCH ONTO METAL?
22. ACCORDING TO THE LECTURE, WHY DO PRINTMAKERS GO THROUGH THE TROUBLE OF PRINTMAKING?

QUESTIONS 23–27

(Narrator) Listen to a discussion of a campus stamp collecting group.

(Jesse) The September meeting of the Campus Philatelist Society is now called to order.

(Joey) I'm worried about our dwindling numbers. Maybe if we call ourselves the stamp collection society, we'll get new members.

(Kevin) I agree with Joey. But as we don't have much time today, let's discuss what's on the agenda for today's meeting: presenting and evaluating the contents for each section of our new brochure.

(Jesse) Did you all bring your sections?

(All) Yeah.

(Joey) I'll start. My section includes rare and unusual stamps. I brought prints of famous rare stamps, including a U.S. airmail stamp from 1918 which has an inverted center, and a French series from 1870 in which one of the stamps was accidentally printed upside down.

(Kevin) My section deals with separations. The first stamps were not perforated, so they had to be cut apart with scissors. The common term for this process is imperforate. Here is an example of an imperforate issued in France in the 1850s. Eventually, stamps were made easy to separate through two methods. First, small holes, or perforations, were punched between rows of stamps. A second method, known as roulette, relied on small cuts made by a knife.

(Eric) I've been working on collection types. I have samples from collections made up exclusively of birds, railroads, ships, or stamps of only one color that are prized all around the world. It's interesting that collectors from different countries value the same collections.

(Danielle) My section is on the history of American stamp collecting. In 1847, the U.S. post office issued its first two stamps, bearing portraits of George Washington and our first postmaster general, Benjamin Franklin. The first U.S. commemorative stamps, honoring famous events, were issued in 1893, celebrating the four-hundredth anniversary of the discovery of America.

(Jesse) Well, everybody, you've done a great job, and we're right on schedule. Please give me your original pages, and I'll take everything to the printer. The booklets will be assembled by next month's meeting. See you the first of next month. Same time, same place. Be prepared to discuss changing our group name and to make plans for distributing our brochure.

23. WHAT IS THE MAIN TOPIC OF THE DISCUSSION?
24. WHICH OF THESE STAMPS WOULD BE CONSIDERED A RARE STAMP?
25. BASED ON THE DISCUSSION, CLASSIFY THE FOLLOWING TYPES OF SEPARATIONS.
26. ACCORDING TO THE DISCUSSION, WHICH TYPE OF COLLECTION WOULD BE PRIZED?
27. WHEN WERE THE FIRST U.S. STAMPS ISSUED?

QUESTIONS 28–32

(Narrator) Listen to a lecture in a history class. The professor is talking about the California gold rush.

(Professor) Today I'll be discussing the California gold rush, especially how the gold rush shaped the state of California. We can say that the gold rush began on January 24, 1848, when a man named James Marshall discovered gold at Sutter's Mill, near San Francisco. But it took another man, Sam Brennan, a San Francisco newspaperman and entrepreneur, to create a frenzy about Marshall's discovery. The informational dam burst on May 14, 1848, when Brennan published an article in his San Francisco newspaper about the gold strike. His newspaper was shut down shortly thereafter because even his own employees had caught the fever and headed for the hills. This excitement would lead to the biggest voluntary migration in the history of the world. The people who participated in this migration to find gold in 1849 were the so-called "49ers."

In the late 1840s, California wasn't even an American state yet, but it already had a reputation as a land full of people who came seeking adventure and riches. After Marshall's discovery was further publicized by President James Polk in his annual message to Congress in December, 1848, the mass migration truly began. In 1849, over 90,000 people would make the often dangerous journey to California, by land and by sea, to try their luck at discovering gold for themselves. Ultimately, hundreds of thousands of people would travel to California as part of the "gold rush."

The routes people traveled to California were often fraught with danger. Not only were weather conditions unpredictable, especially through the Rockies, but there was always the possibility of fatal illness, malnutrition, or attacks from wild animals. Just making it to California was an achievement in itself. However, once there, many people found that the availability of riches had been overstated. There were so many people looking for gold that it was difficult, if not impossible, for most people to find anything at all. But many of them stayed in California and tried to make a living doing other things.

Indeed, the mass migration into California helped its case for American statehood. Only two years after the gold rush began, California was admitted to the union as the thirty-first state.

28. WHO WAS SAM BRENNAN?
29. WHAT IS STATED IN THE LECTURE AS DANGERS ON THE JOURNEY TO CALIFORNIA?
30. WHAT DID PEOPLE DO WHO COULDN'T FIND A JOB?
31. WHAT CAN BE INFERRED FROM THE LECTURE?
32. THE PROFESSOR MENTIONS A SERIES OF EVENTS. PUT THEM IN THEIR CHRONOLOGICAL ORDER.

TOEFL TEST 2

Part A

1. (Woman) I heard you were up in Maine this summer. Why didn't you stop by?
(Man) If I had known your address, I would have visited you.
(Narrator) WHAT DOES THE MAN MEAN?

2. (Man) Just sign on the dotted line, and the apartment is all yours.
(Woman) If you don't mind, I'd like to read the lease through carefully.
(Narrator) WHAT WILL THE WOMAN PROBABLY DO NEXT?

3. (Man) Did you see how small the windows are on the new freshman dorm on Vassar Street?
(Woman) I didn't like them at first either. Now I think they're rather distinctive, with all the different colors.
(Narrator) WHAT DOES THE WOMAN IMPLY?

4. (Man) Are you sure the professor said you could have an extension on your paper?
(Woman) I thought so. I guess I better check with him right away.
(Narrator) WHAT DOES THE WOMAN MEAN?

5. (Woman) I can't believe this exhibit includes only student work.
(Man) Have you seen Anna's weavings? They're all so good it's hard to decide which is best, but she can submit only one for judging.
(Narrator) WHAT DOES THE MAN MEAN?

6. (Man) It says in the catalogue that you need History 101 before you can take 102.
I don't understand why because each course covers different material.
(Woman) I know. It seems strange to me too. But I heard you can get the professor to override the prerequisite.
(Narrator) WHAT DOES THE WOMAN IMPLY?

7. (Man) If you get into every grad school you've applied to, where do you think you'll go?
(Woman) It all depends on how much money each school gives me.
(Man) You certainly deserve a piece of the pie.
(Narrator) WHAT DOES THE MAN MEAN?

8. (Man) Do you know if I can pay with a credit card at the bursar's office?
(Woman) Racking up those frequent flier miles, huh?
(Man) Actually, I don't have any cash, and my tuition bill is due today.
(Narrator) WHAT WILL THE MAN PROBABLY DO NEXT?

9. (Woman) Is it true everyone has to pass a swimming test in order to graduate?
(Man) Don't worry. You only have to do one lap.

(Woman) I can't believe they still make everyone do this!
(Narrator) WHAT DOES THE WOMAN MEAN?

10. (Man) Have you stopped by career services yet?
(Woman) Yeah, they're great. They edit resumes, do practice interviews, and post a surprisingly large number of available jobs.
(Narrator) WHAT DOES THE WOMAN IMPLY?

11. (Man) What do you think about this schedule for next semester?
(Woman) Let me see. Are you sure you want to have three classes in a row?
(Man) That way I can be done every day by one.
(Narrator) WHAT DOES THE MAN IMPLY?

Part B

QUESTIONS 12–14

(Man) Are you going to the campus job fair?
(Woman) Yeah, I was hoping to get a job working security in one of the libraries.
(Man) That looks like a great job. You just look in people's bags. Most of the time you can sit and do homework.
(Woman) Exactly. I've been a lifeguard on campus, but while you're sitting there guarding, you're not allowed to do anything else—even if no one's in the pool. I was also a monitor in the photo lab where it's too dark to do any reading.
(Man) But if you're a photographer, you can develop your pictures for free.
(Woman) Right, except I'm not. So do you want to go to the fair now?
(Man) I'll probably see you there. I've got to return a book to the library first.

12. WHAT IS THE DISCUSSION MAINLY ABOUT?
13. WHY DOES THE WOMAN NOT WANT TO WORK AS A LIFEGUARD?
14. WHAT WILL THE MAN PROBABLY DO NEXT?

QUESTIONS 15–17

(Man) Are you going to the concert tonight?
(Woman) I hadn't heard about it. Who's playing?
(Man) It's the competition of all the student orchestras on campus. They'll be judged on originality, performance, and difficulty.
(Woman) Oh that sounds fabulous. Where are they playing?
(Man) At Hill Auditorium at 8.
(Woman) I'd love to go. I just don't have any money right now.
(Man) You're in luck. You can pick up a complimentary ticket before 6 at the student union.

15. WHERE IS THE CONCERT?
16. WHAT CAN BE INFERRED ABOUT THE COMPETITION?
17. WHAT WILL THE WOMAN PROBABLY DO NEXT?

QUESTIONS 18–22

(Narrator) Listen to part of a lecture in an American history class. The lecture is on President Abraham Lincoln.

(Professor) In 1860, both Abraham Lincoln and William H. Seward sought the presidency of the United States. The campaign was particularly fierce in New York. William H. Seward, the former governor of the state of New York had a good reputation as a statesman and well-respected businessman, whereas Lincoln, from Illinois, was less well-known. However, Mr. Lincoln also had many supporters. Surprisingly enough, eleven-year-old Grace Bedell, from the town of Westfield, proved to be one of Lincoln's most influential supporters. After listening to adult conversations about the candidates and looking at photographs of the two men, Grace felt that Lincoln could win the nomination by improving his appearance.

In her mind, Lincoln could win the nomination by growing a full beard. She reasoned that most ladies like whiskers and would urge their husbands to vote for Lincoln if he had a beard. Grace wrote Lincoln with her suggestion. Through the kindness of one of his secretaries, her letter reached Lincoln, touching him deeply. He responded to Grace's letter, explaining that growing a beard so late in the campaign might seem like a publicity stunt. A week later, however, he changed his mind.

One year later, Lincoln left his home in Illinois, bound for the White House to start his new job as president. Along the way, he related the incident to a group of followers and said he would like to see his young admirer. His train trip took him through New York State, stopping briefly in Westfield on February 16. Grace, with her family, was waiting to see Lincoln when his train stopped, and the little girl was lifted up to meet the future president. "You see, my dear," he said, "I let these grow for you. Perhaps you made me President."

18. WHAT IS THE LECTURE MAINLY ABOUT?
19. WHY DOES GRACE SUGGEST LINCOLN GROW A BEARD?
20. WHICH PICTURE SHOWS LINCOLN IMMEDIATELY AFTER THE ELECTION?
21. WHEN WAS LINCOLN'S PRESIDENTIAL INAUGURATION?
22. IN THE LECTURE, THE PROFESSOR EXPLAINS A HISTORICAL SERIES OF EVENTS. PUT THE EVENTS IN CHRONOLOGICAL ORDER.

QUESTIONS 23–27

(Narrator) Listen to part of a discussion in a class of dental students.

(Professor) In the last class, we concluded our overview of animal teeth, and today we turn our attention to human teeth. Humans normally develop the 20 primary or deciduous teeth, or what's commonly called baby teeth, and 32 permanent teeth. The primary teeth, which begin to form before a child is born, usually push through the gums between the ages of 6 months and 2 years. Central incisors commonly appear when the child is 6 to 7 months old, followed by the lateral incisors at about 7 to 9 months of age, first molars at about 12 to 14 months, canines from 16 to 20 months, and second molars at roughly 20 to 24 months.

(Chris) I didn't get any baby teeth until I was almost two and a half. My parents were freaking out.

(Vicky) What about me? I actually had two front teeth in my mouth when I was born!

(Professor) These occurrences can happen. You have to remember the information I am giving you is based on averages. The two of you happen to fall outside the average. To continue, the permanent teeth begin to break through the gums at about 6 or 7 years. By the age of 13 years, they usually replace all of the primary teeth.

(Tina) Wait a minute! I had a baby tooth that had to be pulled out because it never fell out. The permanent one grew in over it.

(Professor) That's truly rare. And there are some adults who have one or two permanent teeth that never grow in. They aren't even inside their gums. But to continue on with our averages. . . . The first molars are the first permanent teeth to appear, followed by the central incisors at 6 to 8 years, lateral incisors at 7 to 9 years, canines and premolars at from 9 to 12 years, and second molars at about 11 to 12 years. The third molars, or wisdom teeth, which erupt at approximately 17 to 21 years of age, complete the set of teeth. The ages the permanent teeth appear may vary widely from one individual to another.

(Chris) Can we go back to what you mentioned earlier? What happens to someone who is missing a tooth or two, say in the front?

(Professor) The field of tooth implants, which we'll cover next week, has come up with miraculous alternatives for people who lack a full set of teeth.

23. WHAT IS THE DISCUSSION MAINLY ABOUT?
24. HOW OLD ARE CHILDREN WHEN THEY USUALLY DEVELOP THEIR PRIMARY OR DECIDUOUS TEETH?
25. WHICH OF THE FOLLOWING SITUATIONS HAPPENS REGULARLY?
26. WHICH OF THESE OCCURRENCES HAPPENED TO THE STUDENTS?
27. IN THE DISCUSSION, THE ORDER OF PERMANENT TEETH DEVELOPMENT IS DISCUSSED. PUT THE TEETH IN THE ORDER IN WHICH THEY APPEAR.

QUESTIONS 28–32

(Narrator) Listen to part of a lecture on oceanographic history.

(Professor) One of the most enduring mysteries of modern times, the Bermuda Triangle, has fascinated the U.S. public since the 1940s. But are the reports of missing ships and airplanes scientifically accurate? Is it really true that the 440,000 square mile triangle, whose three corners touch Florida, Bermuda, and Puerto Rico, literally swallows ships and aircraft? Does it really have mystical properties, or have historical facts been distorted or inaccurately reported? Looking at some of the most famous incidents attributed to this triangle, also known as the Devil's Triangle, historical researchers and scientists have found that the mysteries of the Bermuda Triangle, so named in 1964, are more fiction than fact.

The first reports of strange phenomena in this area of the southwestern Atlantic date as far back as 1492 when Christopher Columbus sailed into the area. Columbus's journal entry dated October 11, 1492, contains an account of a malfunctioning compass and the presence of strange lights in the sky, including a "great flame of fire" which crashed into the ocean. Though they sound too incredible to be true, these events can be scientifically explained. First, it is quite reasonable to believe that the compass malfunction was the result of the discrepancy between true north and magnetic north. Second, the lights that appeared to be in the sky were actually reflections of lights from land. Finally, the "great flame of fire" may well have been a meteor falling into the sea.

In the end, many mysterious disappearances aren't mysterious at all. Swift ocean currents and sudden unexpected storms or downward air currents provide strong scientific evidence for previously unexplained phenomena. In addition, many maritime disasters attributed to the Bermuda Triangle didn't occur anywhere near the area. The most exaggerated of these tales is that of the lost ship the *Mary Celeste,* which went off course in 1892, and was eventually found near the coast of Portugal.

It seems that many maritime disasters and disappearances have been attributed to the Bermuda Triangle. The most compelling tale of mysterious happenings in the Bermuda Triangle centers around the disappearance of six U.S. military aircraft in 1945. A squadron of five bombers on a routine training mission was lost. The sixth plane, a search plane, was lost as well. However, these incidents also have less than mysterious explanations. The squadron most likely went off course as result of malfunctioning navigational equipment, poor weather, inexperienced pilots, and a squadron commander who was unfit to fly. Once the squadron commander became disoriented, he may have led the squadron north and east instead of south and west, which explains why no wreckage was ever found. If the planes ran out of fuel past the continental shelf of the Atlantic, the planes could have sunk to a depth of 30,000 feet below the surface of the sea. As for the search plane, an examination of naval records shows that the plane exploded about 20 seconds after taking off. In other words, the plane never made it into the area known as the Bermuda Triangle. It seems that none of the aircraft disappeared as the result of mysterious phenomena.

28. WHAT DOES THE PROFESSOR MAINLY TALK ABOUT?
29. IDENTIFY THE PART OF THE MAP THAT INCLUDES THE BERMUDA TRIANGLE.
30. WHICH OF THE FOLLOWING IS NOT MENTIONED AS A SCIENTIFIC EXPLANATION FOR THE BERMUDA TRIANGLE?
31. WHAT IS STATED IN THE LECTURE AS THE TWO MAJOR OBSTACLES TO TAKING THE LEGEND SERIOUSLY?
32. THE PROFESSOR EXPLAINS A SERIES OF EVENTS. PUT THE EVENTS IN THEIR CHRONOLOGICAL ORDER.

ANSWER KEY

SECTION ONE: LISTENING

Pre-Test

PART A

1. He'll soon have time to get ready.
2. She wouldn't rely on Dan.
3. He'd rather not divide into groups.
4. To avoid being late, it's best to call for a taxi immediately.
5. Replacing the machine would cost less than repairing the old one.
6. The man doesn't want to repeat the course.
7. She still hasn't gone to see the dentist.
8. At a travel agency
9. She may be signing up for a cafeteria meal plan.
10. Her classrooms aren't up to date.
11. He's surprised that she's completed all but the final chapter.

PART B

12. It isn't 4 o'clock yet.
13. She needs to complete her assignment.
14. Go to the mall
15. The gymnasium
16. Get a ticket for the performance
17. There are still tickets left to see Adam Sandler.
18. Humans have the capacity for speech.
19. 40,000 years ago
20. In the skull
21. Evidence of cooperative behavior, The appearance of cave art
22. 1. Social groups without the ability to speak
    2. The first skulls with canals the same size as modern skulls
    3. The appearance of cave art
    4. The study of fossil anatomy
23. Rugs, Clothing
24. Both hand looms and power looms can be used. Crossing 2, 3, or 4 warp threads at a time creates extra width.
25. sturdy/twill glossy/satin simplest/tabby
26. By each weft spanning up to 12 warps
27. Get the looms ready
28. To get more supplies
29. Three years later
30. Maybe they fought with the Indians., Maybe they followed the Croatoans south.
31. In the late 16th century
32. 1. Arriving in 1587
    2. Leaders returning to England
    3. Taking British ships for the Spanish Armada
    4. Finding the word "Croatoan"

Part A

EXERCISE 1

1. People who don't wait their turn
2. Kate's grandmother used to wear it.
3. That she agrees with the man.
4. Get right to the point
5. The man is fashionable.
6. He wants her to make him go.
7. She forgot all about it.
8. It's been pouring.
9. The man finds it hard to speak.
10. They need to cooperate.
11. The rehearsal was perfect.
12. Dr. Springer was speaking informally.
13. Susan lives close to the student union.
14. Her Spanish is gradually getting better.
15. He couldn't understand what the lecturer said.
16. It looks like her headache is stopping.

EXERCISE 2

1. Flight 211 was called off.
2. He went out of business.
3. He never finishes assignments early.
4. He thinks Julie's idea is the best.
5. Jeremy's efforts have been worthwhile.
6. She contributed money to a gift.
7. She's eagerly awaiting getting her money.
8. They postponed having a family.
9. She bumped into her advisor.
10. She'll take care of his plants.
11. She doesn't have the key to her room.
12. Henry no longer attends college.
13. He is behind in his work.

EXERCISE 3

1. The man feels lucky to have Michael as a friend.
2. The house has been for sale since July.
3. Because he didn't know the woman's intentions
4. He's sorry he didn't stay in Judy's class.
5. Get on a bus
6. Tell the waitress about the tip
7. Meet with the man the next day
8. Graduation will be outside no matter the weather.
9. He can't get in if he doesn't try.
10. If she can choose a different advisor

EXERCISE 4

1. David is the best student in the class.
2. Worked over the weekend
3. He raises sheep.
4. She's a science major.
5. He thought she enjoyed what he sent her.
6. When she saw Bill, she didn't know what was wrong.

7. She is surprised who he is.
8. That her work has really improved
9. It's been a very long time since the Millers visited.
10. She thought it would be really difficult to get authorization.

EXERCISE 5

1. She can't reach the operator either.
2. He felt sleepy during the seminar.
3. The man doesn't know where to park the car.
4. Reactions to the book have been varied.
5. They have another week to decide.
6. She doesn't need glasses.
7. Jennifer and Jessica don't act alike.
8. He hasn't been at home much.
9. She's always washing her clothes.
10. Her high school teacher wasn't as good as her current one.
11. Pay the library penalty

EXERCISE 6

1. It's not a good idea to let others use your notes.
2. Exercising
3. She'll take it with her because she's in a hurry.
4. The man couldn't understand what she said.
5. She doesn't want to discuss the game.
6. She must have done well on the tests.
7. She didn't have time to meet him.
8. She knows nothing about birds.
9. She seems to be American.
10. Students benefit from attending class.
11. She shouldn't have missed the deadline.
12. They're excited about it.

EXERCISE 7

1. That she feel free to make a call
2. Be on the lookout for an apartment for her
3. Arrange everything
4. At his brother's home
5. That they select the color blue
6. That they meet the next day
7. The man should borrow her umbrella.
8. Go with her to the test
9. The party will be more fun with lots of people.
10. She should take a muffin.
11. That they go directly to the library
12. Eat something
13. She do her writing at home
14. Don't try to get on the college website.

EXERCISE 8

1. Composers like things other than music.
2. The man doesn't have Dana's phone number yet.
3. Complete her current project
4. Continue working
5. She'll be supervising the new employees.
6. To have coffee later
7. She made a reservation for the 6:00 flight.
8. Arrive before class starts
9. She knows she shouldn't go.
10. Look up the office location
11. Complete the paper

EXERCISE 9

1. They're colleagues.
2. Buying a present
3. She imagined herself skiing.
4. Ann received money from a relative.
5. A part-time job
6. The next recitation will be on the regular day.
7. His schedule will vary.
8. She'll be paying for dinner.
9. Where she'll take her completed form
10. In a supermarket
11. She had an old one remade.
12. At a bakery

EXERCISE 10

1. Eat after the film
2. His neighbor's baby is ill.
3. No one else can read the man's paper.
4. The woman must wake up really early.
5. Not listening to the teacher was a mistake.
6. That boy resembles other Jacksons.
7. There won't be enough chairs.
8. Cheryl's proofreading may not be effective.
9. Be independent
10. She knows who the book belongs to.
11. Going to the supermarket or his apartment will necessitate cooking.
12. He thought he'd be getting the paper free for longer than twelve weeks.
13. She may be too scared to audition.
14. Emily's willing to take a loss.

Part B

EXERCISE 11

1. He wanted to go over his notes.
2. Biology
3. To be very specific
4. He might be spending time there.
5. It's not included in the visit.
6. He'll make sure he likes the student center.
7. It's in a good location.
8. Check out the site the man mentioned
9. Speak to Brian
10. Twentieth Century Europe
11. She wants to explore other fields.
12. Get catalogues from other schools
13. Next fall
14. Transfer policies vary from school to school.
15. Get in touch with everyone in the class
16. A large party
17. He informed the class of his hobby.
18. He'll accompany the woman.
19. Talkative family members
20. Check out the ride listings
21. Somewhat scared
22. He got a ride from someone he didn't know.
23. To make sure her room isn't so noisy
24. He went to the wrong room.
25. From 4 to 6
26. It's difficult to go to school and swim.
27. Come to practice

28. The school has no record of his family's having paid.
29. Bring his paperwork to the bursar
30. The place that repairs computers
31. They had to be repeated.
32. Next to the admissions office

EXERCISE 12

1. The Brook Farm Utopian experiment
2. He lived at Brook Farm in the 1840s. His house is located in Salem.
3. Political
4. A Phalanx/1800
   Brook Farm's Acreage/200
   The Greatest Number of Residents/120
5. 1. Brook Farm opened.
   2. Brook Farm incorporated as a phalanx.
   3. The central building burned down.
   4. Brook Farm closed.
6. The evolution of windmills
7. B (picture of windmill with shutters)
8. Iranian windmills/sails
   Dutch windmills/four long arms
   American windmills/curved blades of wood or steel
9. 1. Iran
   2. Netherlands
   3. U.S.A.
   4. New Zealand
10. To analyze windmill usage where it is most popular
11. The homes seem to grow out of the ground., It is Wright's first unique style.
12. Wright's house/ shingles and brick
    Robie House/ low, horizontal form
    Unity Temple/ poured concrete
13. They are made of precast concrete blocks., There are different block patterns on each house.
14. It was severely damaged in the Tokyo earthquake of 1923.
15. 1. The Wright House in Oak Park
    2. The Robie House
    3. The Southern California houses
    4. The Imperial Hotel
16. Arranging and rearranging the American flag
17. At one time there was a star and stripe for each state.
18. No one in government
19. On the July 4 after a state enters the union
20. 1. A flag with a British flag in the upper left-hand corner
    2. A flag with 13 stars in a circle
    3. A flag with 15 stripes
    4. A flag with 20 stars in a five-pointed star

EXERCISE 13

1. The relation of the sex chromosome to some disorders in men.
2. Men and women will develop disorders at the same rate.,
   Other possible factors may influence the development of disorders.
3. A cell is missing a gene
4. Blood type mismatches
5. The DNA processes used in crime solving
6. Smaller DNA pieces move more slowly through gel., DNA is negatively charged.
7. The division of fragments utilizing an electric field
8. electrophoresis/fragment separation
   restriction enzymes/proteins
   agarose/material purified from algae
9. When electrophoresis is repeated using different restriction enzymes
10. Forecasting El Niño
11. Periods of warm weather coupled with much rain
12. Forecasts are based on wind observations and water temperatures.
13. A weak El Niño with a slightly wetter than normal growing season
14. Plant more rice and less cotton
15. Demythologizing the left-brained, right-brained theory
16. B (picture of temporal lobe)
17. When the two brain hemispheres are disconnected, each side can still function.
18. An accountant, a mathematician
19. Find experimental or theoretical support of the left-brained, right-brained theory

Post-Test

PART A

1. Order the cheesecake
2. He got the printer for a good price.
3. He'll give her money for gas.
4. He has much more work for his literature class.
5. The man should feel free to read the paper.
6. The woman won't have a problem recognizing Alice's sister.
7. At a camera shop
8. If he's going to make it, he'll do it by himself.
9. She'll have to get bedding.
10. He won't be taking the writing test
11. He doesn't know how to get an official record.

PART B

12. Pick up a ticket to the game
13. He's been to football games before.
14. People enjoy themselves at the stadium then.
15. Alison is majoring in the subject.
16. Physics
17. Stop by the Academic Success Center
18. They were opposed to her decision to become an artist., They were middle class.
19. When she was still a child
20. Day-to-day subject matter, Use of light colors
21. Her family, The people of her day
22. D (picture of mother and child)
23. To prepare for the quiz
24. Golf courses, A bath house
25. 1. Stock Market Crash
    2. Great Depression
    3. Election of Franklin Delano Roosevelt
    4. Establishment of Works Project Administration
26. Millions of people were out of work., People lost their savings.
27. New Deal/Plan to help Americans affected by the Depression
    WPA/Sponsored projects for the unemployed

Black Thursday/stock market crash of Oct. 1929

28. The lifework and accomplishments of Barbara McClintock
29. She decided to become a scientist while in college., She pioneered the field of maize cytogenetics.
30. The way corn inherits its traits, How chromosomes break and join together
31. The mobile gene's location on a chromosome can vary.
32. 1. McClintock attends Cornell University
    2. McClintock shows that chromosomes can break and join together differently.
    3. McClintock announces her discovery of mobile genetic elements.
    4. McClintock receives the Nobel Prize.

SECTION TWO: STRUCTURE

Pre-Test

1. much *should be* many (*people* is a count noun)
2. but (coordinating conjunction showing contrast)
3. In the (prepositional phrase before independent clause)
4. drawing up *should be* to draw up (use infinitive after *permitting*)
5. drafts *should be* draft (subject-verb agreement—*scientists* is plural)
6. the largest (superlative form)
7. or *should be* and (both . . . and)
8. especially valuable (adverb + adjective)
9. usefulest *should be* useful (superlative form)
10. Despite of *should be* Despite (no such form)
11. among *should be* between (word choice for two things)
12. as well as (only phrase that grammatically works before phrase *for those of animals*)
13. another *should be* other (plural adjective form before *materials*)
14. Latex (subject needed before verb, *is*)
15. call themselves (verb needed, then reflexive pronoun)
16. who succeeded (adjective clause: relative pronoun + verb)
17. finding *should be* found (passive form)
18. are looking *should be* look (present simple for facts)
19. Although *shouldn't be in sentence* (cause and effect connector; *although* could work *grammatically* if *because* weren't in sentence)
20. is highly sought (passive, agrees with noncount noun, *furniture*)
21. to maintain *should be* maintain (no infinitive follows modal, *must*)
22. entirety *should be* entire (adjective form before compound noun)
23. the name John F. Kennedy gave to his program (appositive + deleted adjective clause: without *that*)
24. Each state (subject needed, adjective + noun)
25. accountant *should be* accounting (parallel form with advertising, not the person noun)

EXERCISE 1

1. delivers *should be* delivered (action completed in the past)
2. was having *should be* has (fact)
3. married (action completed in *1956*)
4. wild violets grow (fact, subject + verb)
5. weighed *should be* weighs (fact)
6. develops *should be* developed (action completed in the past)
7. praises the virtues (explanation of a written text)
8. arose (action completed in *1794*)
9. kicking *should be* kicks (fact)
10. consists of five vowels (fact, phrasal verb + object)
11. sets *should be* set (action completed in *1937*)
12. a telephoto lens magnifies (fact, subject + verb)
13. worked (action completed in 1920s)
14. entering *should be* enter (fact)
15. designing *should be* designed (action completed)

16. focuses attention on	(explanation of a written text)		
17. has begun	*should be*	began	(simple past for action completed *in 1861*)
18. assign	(fact)		
19. has	(fact		
20. to be	*should be*	are	(fact)
21. asking	*should be*	asked	(action completed)
22. occurs	(fact)		
23. generated	*should be*	generates	(fact)
24. led	(simple past for action completed *in 1950*)		
25. satisfying	*should be*	satisfy	(fact)

EXERCISE 2

1. has reached	(present perfect)		
2. say	*should be*	said	(past participle with present perfect)
3. begun	*should be*	have begun	(present perfect)
4. have used	(present perfect)		
5. is being	*should be*	has been	(present perfect, no progressive with "be" verb)
6. has	*should be*	have	(to agree with plural subject, *beings*)
7. for	*should be*	since	(specific time)
8. invented	(simple past for action completed *in 1709*)		
9. have used	*should be*	used	(simple past for action completed *in the 1950s and 1960s*)
10. has increased	(present perfect)		
11. have relied	*should be*	had relied	(past perfect, happening before *the Greek philosophers sought*)
12. will be	*should be*	will have been	(future perfect, with By the year 2076)

ESSAY EXERCISE 1

1. When I was in junior high, I often **cleaned** our bathroom.
2. When I study by myself, I may never know the answer. (omit *am*) OR When I am **studying**. . . .
3. If you're **learning** boxing, it's always better if there's a teacher with you. OR If you **learn** . . .
4. Requiring hard work **made** me be responsible when I was in high school.
5. Moving to the countryside last year **enabled** us to enjoy nature.
6. When I was in high school, I **listened** to my friends' advice.
7. In 1995, I **decided** to visit China.
8. I enjoy when a large number of my family **is** in the same place.
9. I think when all my dreams come true, I **am** going to be happy.
10. In my country, everybody has to go to school **for** sixteen years.
11. I **heard** there are a lot of beautiful places in China.
12. I think no matter **who you're with,** the most important thing is to have fun.

ACTIVE/PASSIVE EXERCISE 1

1. The jewels were stolen by one of the servants.
2. More letters could have been written to their parents.
3. The animals are fed twice a day (by us).
4. *CAN'T BE PASSIVE* (no direct object)
5. We were invited to the movies by her.
6. *CAN'T BE PASSIVE* (no direct object)
7. The test was taken by us on Friday.
8. The song was sung by one of the students.
9. Literature is taught by Professor Scott in the fall.
10. The meat is frozen by the grocer every day.

ACTIVE/PASSIVE EXERCISE 2

1. The enemy captured the prisoners.
2. The class is doing the exercises.
3. He could have done the homework in ten minutes.
4. The teacher teaches the lesson on Fridays.
5. People who live outside the city don't use the museum.
6. Creole was spoken by the students before they came to Miami.
7. Our club holds meetings on Fridays.
8. Latin is no longer spoken by Romans.
9. My roommate always forgets the key.
10. By the time I was called, I had already filled out my application.

EXERCISE 3

1. it is used	(passive)		
2. built in 1772	(*which was* is deleted)		
3. has dipped	*should be*	has been dipped	(passive)
4. is normally played	(passive)		
5. is called	(passive)		
6. are raised	(passive)		
7. to form	*should be*	formed	(passive)
8. was born	(passive)		
9. was noted	(passive)		
10. is found	(passive)		
11. drawing was practiced	(passive)		
12. locate	*should be*	located	(passive, past participle needed)
13. has been verified	(passive)		
14. is award	*should be*	is awarded	(passive, past participle needed)
15. to be examined	(passive)		
16. are made of	(passive)		
17. feed	*should be*	fed	(passive, *that are* deleted)
18. women were not granted	(passive)		
19. devising	*should be*	devised	(passive, *that were* deleted)
20. is protected	*should be*	are protected	(passive agreement)
21. distant objects can be brought	(passive, subject + verb)		
22. heard	*should be*	be heard	(passive)
23. was invented	(passive)		
24. are producing	*should be*	are produced	(passive, past participle needed)
25. founding	*should be*	found	(passive)

ESSAY EXERCISE 2

1. I **grew up** in the countryside.
2. I have **spent** a lot of time with only one or two close friends.
3. Traditional schools are **based** on the idea that learning with a teacher is best.
4. Cities where universities are **found** usually have a higher standard of living.
5. Only good students **are** admitted to universities in my country, so many students don't have a chance to improve their lives.
6. Changes are **being made** to my university.
7. If a new university **is built** in my hometown, students will have good and bad experiences.
8. England **uses** English. OR English **is used** in England.
9. High level students **apply** to medical and dental schools.
10. If I study with a teacher, I can **understand** my problems.

EXERCISE 4

1. is	(verb)	
2. led the way	(action verb + direct object)	
3. comes	(simple present verb)	
4. it	*should be omitted*	(double subject)
5. It takes	(missing subject + verb)	
6. the crested peacock	(missing subject)	
7. he	*should be omitted*	(double subject)
8. each line consists	(missing subject + verb)	
9. an international reputation	(direct object)	
10. is	(simple present verb)	
11. was the first American officer	(linking verb + noun)	
12. he	should be omitted	(double subject)
13. will destroy	(action verb, active voice)	
14. are found	(passive voice)	
15. a leading figure	(linking verb + noun)	
16. The United States has	(subject + verb)	
17. John Singer Sargent	(missing subject)	
18. Nurses with special training	(missing subject)	
19. they	*should be omitted*	(double subject)
20. consider	(verb)	

21.	The Louisiana Purchase	(missing subject)	
22.	<u>it</u>	*should be omitted*	(double subject)
23.	showed his mastery	(action verb + direct object)	
24.	<u>developed</u>	*should be*	have developed (present perfect)
25.	<u>is</u>	*should be omitted*	(*uses* is simple present form)

NOUN CLAUSE EXERCISE

1.	Q: Why is she transferring?	NC: Please tell me why she is transferring.
2.	Q: Where does her friend live?	NC: Please remind me where her friend lives.
3.	Q: What kind of computer does Rose's mother have?	NC: Do you know what kind of computer Rose's mother has?
4.	Who is Tom's roommate?	NC: I don't know who Tom's roommate is.
5.	Q: How much did that textbook cost?	NC: Tell me how much that textbook cost.

ADJECTIVE CLAUSE EXERCISE

1. Karen went to see a friend **whose** father is the president of the college.
2. Montpelier, **which has six months of winter,** is the capital city of Vermont.
3. I had an interesting talk with two students, both of **whom** are from Turkey.
4. In my house I have all kinds of paintings, most of **which** are from the twentieth century.
5. Friends are people **who/that** choose to spend time together.
6. The exam **that/which** began at ten will end at midnight.
7. My economics professor will let me take my final exam after vacation for **which** I am very grateful.
8. I would never marry a man **whose** religion is different from mine.

ADVERB CLAUSE EXERCISE

Answers will vary.

1. She lived in France so that she could learn French.
   because she loved French food.
   whereas her twin sister lived in Australia.
2. I sold all my furniture even though I need it.
   as soon as I moved to a larger apartment. after I moved to Texas.
3. They're going to take the TOEFL test if there's any open times this month.
   wherever they can.
   so many times that they'll feel prepared.
4. I'm going to the party in order that I can meet some new people.
   after I wash my hair.
   unless I find something better to do.

EXERCISE 5

1.	<u>what</u>	*should be*	that	(wrong trigger word for noun clause)
2.	its low price	(*because* + noun phrase, dep. clause missing subject)		
3.	As it orbits the sun	(dependent adverb clause to indicate time)		
4.	whose	(*whose* before noun, *tales* to indicate possession)		
5.	<u>Whichever</u>	*should be*	Although	(wrong trigger word for noun clause)
6.	as long as he lived	(dependent adverb clause)		
7.	meaning	(substitution for *that mean,* reduced adverb clause)		
8.	Because the moon is so near the Earth	(adverbial dependent clause)		
9.	Because of its importance	(*Because of* + noun phrase)		
10.	<u>However</u>	*should be*	Although	(wrong trigger word for adverbial clause)
11.	Although pure aluminum	(dependent adverb clause)		
12.	whose coloring	(*whose* before noun, coloring; relative pronoun shows possession)		
13.	<u>but</u>	*should be*	that	(wrong trigger word for adjective clause)
14.	In spite of its usefulness	(*In spite of* + noun)		
15.	a	(article before appositive)		
16.	that human nature is	(dependent adjective clause, adjective follows)		
17.	<u>them</u>	*should be*	whom	(after preposition, *of,* use *which*)

18. they grow	(dependent adjective clause, relative pronoun, *that* not needed because subject, *they* precedes verb)		
19. their	(possessive pronoun before subject, *branches*)		
20. because of	(precedes noun phrase)		
21. where Colonial brick houses line	(dependent adjective clause)		
22. what they now know	(dependent noun clause following preposition, *of*)		
23. <u>that</u>	*should be*	as	(*as . . . as*/adverbial clause)
24. who pioneered	(dependent adjective clause)		
25. he considers	(subject + verb following *what* in dependent noun clause)		

EXERCISE 6

1. <u>or</u>	*should be*	and	(both . . . and)
2. either could not or would not	(either . . . or)		
3. either	(either . . . or)		
4. <u>neither</u>	*should be*	nor	(neither . . . nor)
5. <u>either</u>	*should be*	both	(both . . . and)
6. both the husband and the wife	(both . . . and)		
7. <u>and</u>	*should be*	or	(either . . . or)
8. <u>either</u>	*should be*	neither	(neither . . . nor)
9. <u>either</u>	*should be*	both	(both . . . and)
10. <u>or</u>	*should be*	and	(both . . . and)

SUBJECT/VERB AGREEMENT EXERCISE

1. has	11. love
2. hope	12. is
3. is	13. is
4. is	14. is
5. is	15. are
6. are	16. are
7. has	17. is
8. is	18. aren't
9. is	19. is
10. is	20. is

EXERCISE 7

1. <u>drafts</u>	*should be*	draft	(agrees with *scientists*)
2. <u>help</u>	*should be*	helps	(agrees with singular, *letter*)
3. <u>extends</u>	*should be*	extend	(agrees with plural, *wings*)
4. <u>lives</u>	*should be*	live	(verb agrees with plural, *people*)
5. <u>is</u>	*should be*	are	(*a number of* is plural)
6. <u>are</u>	*should be*	is	(math facts are singular)
7. <u>produce</u>	*should be*	produces	(gerund subject, *knitting*, is singular)
8. <u>are</u>	*should be*	is	(languages are singular)

ESSAY EXERCISE 3

1. Trading products **has** different advantages than paying money.
2. A big city usually **has** a large population and serious pollution.
3. If half of the students **choose** a traditional school, they won't have teachers.
4. Establishing new universities **is** not always a good thing.
5. Each of these ways **is** pretty good.
6. My sister together with my parents **lives** in the countryside.
7. There **is** in Eastern European countries a serious problem: pollution.
8. In my country measles **is** still a big health concern.
9. The Chinese **love** to visit their Great Wall.
10. I'd like to visit Argentina because Spanish **is** spoken there.

EXERCISE 8

1. <u>teeths</u>	*should be*	teeth	(spelling)
2. <u>leafs</u>	*should be*	leaves	(spelling)

3. hundred of	*should be*	hundreds of	(plural quantity word before *of*)
4. ant	*should be*	ants	(plural after *two*)
5. much	*should be*	many	(modifier for count noun, *paintings*)
6. foots	*should be*	feet	(spelling)
7. source	*should be*	sources	(*a variety of* + plural count noun)
8. lamps	*should be*	lamp	(singular count noun after *a*)
9. program	*should be*	programs	(plural because *an* not present)
10. type	*should be*	types	(plural because *a* not present)
11. clothes	*should be*	cloth	(singular to agree with *is*)
12. sea	*should be*	seas	(plural after *two*)
13. household	*should be*	households	(plural after *7.4 million*)
14. adult	*should be*	adults	(plural because *an* not present)
15. area	*should be*	areas	(plural because *an* not present)
16. cities	*should be*	city	(after *the seventh largest*, singular)
17. theory	*should be*	theories	(*a number of* + plural)
18. figure	*should be*	figures	(plural after *many*)
19. women	*should be*	woman	(singular after *Every*)
20. Pharmacist	*should be*	Pharmacists	(plural to agree with *fill*)

ARTICLE EXERCISE

1. the . . . an	11. A . . . an . . . a . . . a
2. the . . . the . . . the	12. an . . . a . . . a
3. the . . . the	13. a . . . an . . . a . . . the
4. a . . . the	14. a . . . the
5. the . . . a . . . a	15. the . . . a . . . the
6. a . . . an . . . the . . . the	16. an . . . 0
7. the . . . the	17. an . . . a . . . a
8. an . . . an	18. the . . . a
9. a . . . a . . . an	19. a . . . an
10. The . . . a . . . a . . . the	20. 0 . . . the

EXERCISE 9

1. the	*should be*	a	(nonspecific)
2. a	*should be*	an	(before vowel sound)
3. of a day	*should be*	of the day	(specific)
4. a	*should be*	an	(before vowel sound)
5. the	*should be*	a	(nonspecific)
6. an	*should be*	a	(before consonant sound)
7. the	*should be*	a	(nonspecific before count noun)
8. largest group	*should be*	the largest group	(*the* before superlative)
9. a	*should be*	an	(before vowel sound)
10. the	*should be omitted*		(not specific)
11. a	*should be*	the	(*the* before superlative)
12. mineral	*should be*	a mineral	(singular count noun)
13. United States	*should be*	the United States	(always starts with *the*)
14. the	*should be*	a	(singular count noun, not specific)
15. the astronomer	*should be*	a	(singular count noun, not specific)
16. a	*should be*	an	(before vowel sound)
17. the	*should be omitted*	(general, not specific, before noncount noun)	
18. end	*should be*	the	(specific time)
19. a	*should be*	the	(*the* before superlative)
20. a	*should be*	an	(before vowel sound)

ESSAY EXERCISE 4

1. I agree with **the** view that all students should have access to higher education.
2. I prefer to study following **a** teacher's lectures.
3. I cannot understand what a **good student is**.
4. If there is **a** poor man who is a genius, should the university accept him?
5. I prefer to have a teacher because if I just learn by myself, maybe I will make **a** mistake.
6. When I was **a** high school student, my hometown had only one university.
7. NO ERROR
8. As you know, Venezuela was **a** Spanish colony.
9. There is a saying that nature is **a** teacher.
10. First, those who like to spend time with close friends can do many things in **a** short time.
11. I need to find **a** job now, so I prefer to spend time with a number of friends.
12. It is very important to me that everyone who is an expert give me advice.
13. When I was a child, my mother always told me that I could not cook without **an** adult supervisor.
14. They just want **a** degree to enter some good company.
15. However, they had good grades in high school.
16. My family decided to move because they wanted to give us **a** better environment and larger space to enjoy ourselves.
17. If I do not know the answer to something, maybe I can find **a** book in order to help me.
18. **A** teacher will teach you if you're using **the** wrong posture, or using **the** wrong hand.

PREPOSITION EXERCISE

1. with . . . of
2. for . . . on
3. in . . . in
4. in . . . in
5. of . . . of
6. by . . . since
7. from . . . without
8. by . . . of
9. by . . . above
10. of . . . of
11. by . . . of
12. except
13. After . . . against
14. on . . . during
15. In . . . to
16. Because of
17. alike . . . like
18. because . . . Because of
19. unlike
20. because of . . . Because

EXERCISE 10

1. on top	*should be*	on top of
2. on	*should be*	in
3. in	*should be*	from
4. among	*should be*	between
5. according of	*should be*	according to
6. In addition	*should be*	In addition to
7. based in	*should be*	based on
8. from	*should be*	at
9. Alike	*should be*	Unlike
10. at	*should be*	on
11. to	*should be*	into
12. during	*should be*	from
13. capable in	*should be*	capable of
14. shown for	*should be*	shown at
15. In	*should be*	On
16. in place	*should be*	in place of
17. depending	*should be*	depending on
18. among	*should be*	between
19. in	*should be*	at
20. consist in	*should be*	consist of
21. depends the	*should be*	depends on
22. to	*should be*	from
23. account of	*should be*	on account of
24. throughout	*should be*	through
25. for	*should be*	since

ESSAY EXERCISE 5

1. I think that information technology is useful **for** two reasons.
2. Human beings have become skillful people by listening **to** many things.
3. Because new students will come to my community, people living in my community may interact **with** these new people.
4. When I was a child, I grew up **in** the countryside.
5. I think children should be required to help with household tasks as soon as they are able because parents can give their children some knowledge.
6. **In** my experience, when I was in junior high, I often cleaned our bathroom.
7. In order to establish a new university, the government has to look **for** areas to build the necessary buildings.
8. In my community there are two educational institutions **at** a high level.
9. NO ERRORS
10. When you are with a large number of friends, you can do many activities together, like going **on** a trip.
11. I used to always be with two of my friends. Do you think I was happy **at** that time?
12. We need to belong **to** a society.
13. They can speak **to/with** each other all the time.
14. I like to share my happiness **on** this special day.
15. I always had fun **at** my birthday parties.

GERUND/INFINITIVE EXERCISE

1. swimming
2. me to go
3. to play
4. waiting
5. crossing
6. to live
7. them to speak
8. being
9. arriving
10. giving
11. repeating

EXERCISE 11

1. <u>to inferring</u>	*should be*	to infer	(infinitive form)
2. <u>seeing</u>	*should be*	to see	(infinitive form after *allow*)
3. <u>to playfully</u>	*should be*	to play	(infinitive form after *encouraged*)
4. <u>grow</u>	*should be*	to grow	(infinitive form after *needed*)
5. <u>to advancing</u>	*should be*	to advance	(infinitive form after *work*)
6. <u>to spend</u>	*should be*	spending	(gerund form after *enjoy*)
7. <u>to visualize</u>	*should be*	visualizing	(gerund form after *imagine*)
8. <u>growing</u>	*should be*	to grow	(infinitive form after *help*)
9. <u>design</u>	*should be*	designing	(gerund after preposition, *in*)
10. <u>spending</u>	*should be*	to spend	(infinitive form after *enable*)

PARTICIPLE EXERCISE

1. satisfying Copley Place	satisfied customers
2. frightened children	frightening clowns
3. exhausted swimmers	exhausting races
4. the boring article	the bored students
5. the confusing new traffic patterns	the confused drivers
6. the interesting recipe	the interested cook
7. the damaged forest	the damaging fire
8. the tired hikers	the tiring trip
9. the surprised test taker	the surprising score
10. the distracted professor	the distracting conversation

EXERCISE 12

1. <u>troubling</u>	*should be*	troubled	(the *man* is troubled by . . .)
2. <u>celebrating</u>	*should be*	celebrated	(the *example* is celebrated by . . .)
3. <u>included</u>	*should be*	including	(they are including . . .)
4. <u>existed</u>	*should be*	existing	(the *buildings* are existing)
5. <u>sparkled</u>	*should be*	sparkling	(*the lakes* are sparkling)
6. <u>imitated</u>	*should be*	imitating	(the *poems* are imitating . . .)
7. <u>Twinkled</u>	*should be*	twinkling	(the *stars* are twinkling)
8. <u>depressed</u>	*should be*	depressing	(the *topics* are depressing)
9. <u>associating</u>	*should be*	associated	(He is associated with O.Henry)
10. <u>giving</u>	*should be*	given	(Her *name* was given to her)
11. <u>connected</u>	*should be*	connecting	(*the plan* is connecting)
12. <u>applying</u>	*should be*	applied	(the *paint* is applied *with a brush*)
13. <u>dying</u>	*should be*	dyed	(the articles are dyed by/with henna)
14. <u>televising</u>	*should be*	televised	(the *debates* were televised)
15. <u>heating</u>	*should be*	heated	(the *gold* is heated by the *fire*)

ESSAY EXERCISE 6

1. I'm **interested** in the evolution of those people.
2. Studying without a teacher would be **boring**.
3. I really miss **being** with my close friends in my country.
4. Children should be required **to help** with the household tasks.
5. It is **located** in the center of town.
6. I can't wait **to return** to see my hometown's new university.
7. If I could visit a country for two weeks, I'd visit Thailand because I've been hoping **to go** there for many years.
8. I enjoy **living** in a university town.
9. When I stopped **wearing** my school uniform every day, I felt like an adult.
10. I can't wait **to visit** Spain because I want to see a bullfight.

EXERCISE 13

1. <u>can to</u>	*should be*	can	(no *to* following *can*)
2. <u>have reach</u>	*should be*	have to reach	(modal form is *have to*)
3. <u>grown</u>	*should be*	grow	(modal, *can* + base form)
4. <u>might to</u>	*should be*	might	(no *to* following *might*)

5. may advanced	*should be*	may advance	(modal, *may* + base form)
6. can leading	*should be*	can lead	(modal, *can* + base form)
7. using	*should be*	use	(modal, *used to* + base form)
8. can to	*should be*	can	(modal, *can* + base form)
9. may be drop	*should be*	may drop	(modal, *may* + base form)
10. painting	*should be*	paint	(modal, *would* + base form)

ESSAY EXERCISE 7

1. If I had the opportunity to visit any country in the world, I would probably **choose** Spain.
2. Education should remain as an undergraduate major.
3. My mother told me that I could not cook without adult supervision because I would **burn** myself.
4. Not being able to pay the tuition might **affect** my studying.
5. We could easily **understand** each other.
6. I must graduate next spring.
7. Sometimes I would like just **to** be with one or two of my friends.

PRONOUN EXERCISE

1. its	*should be*	his	(to agree with *Lincoln*)
2. his	*should be*	her	(to agree with *the woman, Marianne*)
3. its	*should be*	their	(to agree with *plants*)
4. its	*should be*	their	(to agree with *farmers*)
5. one's	*should be*	our	(to agree with *we*)
6. they	*should be omitted*	(double subject)	
7. themselves	*should be*	itself	(to agree with *civilization*)
8. himself	*should be*	he	(subject form)
9. them	*should be*	it	(to agree with pumpkin)
10. its	*should be*	their	(to agree with substances)

EXERCISE 14

1. them	*should be*	themselves	(reflexive)
2. it	*should be omitted*	(double subject)	
3. called their	*should be*	called a	(no reason for possessive pronoun)
4. its	*should be*	their	(to agree with *kinds*)
5. their	*should be*	its	(to agree with *celebration*)
6. its	*should be*	their	(to agree with *creatures*)
7. their	*should be*	its	(to agree with *porcelain*)
8. them	*should be*	their	(possessive pronoun before noun, *products*)
9. him	*should be*	his	(possessive pronoun before noun, *patent*)
10. its	*should be*	their	(to agree with caterpillars)
11. it	*should be*	its	(possessive pronoun before noun, *crystallization*)
12. himself	*should be*	herself	(to agree with *woman*)
13. their	*should be*	its	(to agree with *The Postal Service*)
14. it	*should be omitted*	(double subject)	
15. his	*should be*	its	(to agree with object, *origin*)
16. his	*should be*	their	(to agree with *hardness,* a thing, not a person)
17. them	*should be*	it	(to agree with *Taconite*)
18. them	*should be*	themselves	(reflexive)
19. it	*should be*	them	(to agree with *Gorillas*)
20. them	*should be*	they	(subject form)
21. them	*should be*	themselves	(reflexive form)
22. their	*should be*	its	(to agree with subject, *Tarragon*)
23. theirs	*should be*	themselves	(reflexive form)
24. them	*should be*	themselves	(reflexive)
25. their	*should be*	its	(to agree with singular noun, *company*)

ESSAY EXERCISE 8

1. It helps people to get rid of something they don't want instead of throwing **it** away.
2. Everybody has to do what **she is/he is/one is** told to do.
3. In some countries, teenagers have jobs while **they** are students.
4. Between you and **me,** it's not a good idea to build a high school in my community.
5. I think universities should give more money to **their** libraries than to sports.
6. My best friend watches television all the time and doesn't spend enough time on **her** homework.
7. I thought I knew a lot about the United States because I had seen many of **its** advertisements.
8. If I were to choose my roommate by myself, I might pick someone just like **me.**
9. The invention of the telephone has enabled people in very remote areas of my country to feel less isolated.
10. **My best friend and I** went to ten countries together last summer.

***TAKE/MAKE/DO* EXERCISE**

1. take
2. do
3. make
4. making
5. took
6. do
7. take
8. do
9. make
10. take
11. do
12. do
13. make
14. took
15. take
16. take
17. make
18. do
19. take
20. make

EXERCISE 15

1. take	*should be*	make
2. did	*should be*	made
3. Doing	*should be*	Making
4. does	*should be*	makes
5. doing	*should be*	making
6. do	*should be*	take
7. did	*should be*	took
8. making	*should be*	doing
9. make	*should be*	do
10. take	*should be*	make

EXERCISE 16

1. half only	*should be*	only half	(adverb + noun)
2. climates temperate	*should be*	temperate climates	(adjective + noun)
3. World Old	*should be*	Old World	(adjective + noun)
4. what the information is	(noun clause: signal word, noun + verb)		
5. which by	*should be*	by which	(preposition + signal word)
6. an entertaining picture of upper-class life	(a + adj + noun, preposition + adjective + noun)		
7. science horticultural	*should be*	horticultural science	(adjective + noun)
8. the length of time that it takes	(noun phrase + adjective clause, *that it takes*)		
9. after shortly	*should be*	shortly after	(adverb + adjective)
10. woods useful	*should be*	useful woods	(adjective + noun)
11. reached yet	*should be*	yet reached	(adverb + verb)
12. early the	*should be*	the early	(article, the + adjective)
13. each line consists	(adjective + noun + verb)		
14. famous became	*should be*	became famous	(linking verb + adjective)
15. has brought to light	(present perfect +preposition + noun)		
16. polyps coral	*should be*	coral polyps	(adjective + noun)
17. cowboy sad	*should be*	sad cowboy	(adjective + compound noun *cowboy songs*)
18. people several days to shovel	(*some* + noun, *people* + direct object, *several days to shovel*)		
19. painter portrait	*should be*	portrait painter	(adjective, *portrait* before noun, *painter*)
20. Neither the page size	(parallel with nor + noun)		

EXERCISE 17

1. going	*should be omitted*		(parallel: all preposition + noun)
2. legal	*should be*	law	(noun, not adjective)
3. for dividing	*should be*	divide	(parallel: all infinitive forms)
4. great	*should be*	greatly	(adverb + verb, *influenced*)
5. billions	*should be*	billion	(adjective + noun, *dollars*)
6. commercial	*should be*	commercially	(adverb + adjective, *successful*)
7. farm	*should be*	farming	(the occupation)
8. photographically	*should be*	photographic	(adjective before noun, *plate*)
9. sell	(parallel: both base forms)		
10. carpet	*should be*	carpeted	(adjective + noun, *floors*)
11. specifically	(adverb + verb, *designed*)		
12. involuntarily	should be	involuntary	(adjective + noun, *intake*)

13. imaginative (adjective + noun, *dances*)
14. juicy *should be* juice (noun + verb *provides*)
15. speed (parallel: both nouns)
16. honest *should be* honesty (noun after preposition)
17. companionship (noun after action verb, *provide*)
18. major *should be* majority (not person noun)
19. probably (adverb + verb, *made*)
20. cleaning *should be* cleanest (parallel: all superlative forms)

EXERCISE 18

1. working *should be* work (noun, not gerund form)
2. an important concern (an + adjective + noun)
3. naturally *should be* natural (adjective + noun, *treasure*)
4. discoverer *should be* discovery (not person form, noun)
5. significant *should be* significantly (adverb after verb, *contributed*)
6. uniformity of yarns (parallel: noun + preposition + noun)
7. annually *should be* annual (adjective + compound noun, *garden flowers*)
8. yellow spots (adjective + noun)
9. psychologists (parallel : occupation, like *psychiatrists*)
10. incredible *should be* incredibly (adverb + adjective + noun)
11. poets *should be* poems (not person form, noun)
12. minerals *should be* mineral (adjective + noun)
13. wide *should be* widely (adverb + verb)
14. buys *should be* buyers (parallel: occupation noun, like *sellers*)
15. increasing *should be* increase (parallel: infinitive like *to improve*)
16. noise *should be* noisy (adjective + noun)
17. government (direct object noun)
18. famous *should be* fame (verb, *achieved* + direct object)
19. attractive (adjective + compound noun)
20. vocal *should be* voice (preposition + noun)

INVERTED WORD ORDER EXERCISE

1. Nowhere do we find . . . (negative beginning)
2. In the drawer are the . . . (introductory prepositional phrase)
3. Here are the final numbers. (sentence beginning with *here*)
4. Were you prepared (conditional sentence)
5. . . . than do those . . . (comparison ending)
6. . . . were questions (introductory prepositional phrase)
7. did I answer (*only* + time expression)
8. I have no interest in going and neither does Steve. (comparison ending)
9. Rarely does it snow . . . (negative beginning)
10. There are my students . . . (sentence beginning with *there*)

EXERCISE 19

1. has it become (*only* + time expression)
2. has the mathematical theory of games (comparison ending)
3. than did (negative beginnings)
4. are electronic switches (negative beginning)
5. Not only do the tides (negative beginning)
6. exists the network (introductory prepositional phrase)
7. had it not been (conditional sentence)
8. are hard rocks (comparison ending)
9. Had (conditional sentence)
10. have breeders developed (only + time expression)

OTHER EXERCISE

1. other
2. Others
3. the others
4. the other
5. another
6. Another Another Others Others the others

COMPARATIVE/SUPERLATIVE EXERCISE

1. faster
2. more difficult
3. worst
4. less
5. farther
6. as well

EXERCISE 20

1. most sure	*should be*	surest	(superlative form, 1-syllable)
2. those of the domestic marketer	(comparing *activities* with *those*)		
3. the more difficult	(the comparative (*er*), the comparative (*the more*)		
4. one of the greatest	(superlative)		
5. a longer history	(comparative)		

EXERCISE 21

1. well	*should be*	well as	(complete the comparative)
2. made up	*should be*	made up of	(missing preposition)
3. interest	*should be*	interest in	(missing preposition)
4. others	*should be*	other	(adjective before noun, *materials*)
5. Much	*should be*	Many	(many before count noun, *people*)
6. Alike	*should be*	Unlike	(preposition before noun, *fibers*)
7. more heavier	*should be*	heavier	(incorrect comparative form)
8. like	*should be*	alike	(adjective needed after linking verb, *look*)
9. that	*should be*	which	(after preposition, *through*, use *which*)
10. most oldest	*should be*	oldest	(incorrect superlative form)
11. most famousest	*should be*	most famous	(incorrect superlative form)
12. While in	*should be*	During	(preposition before noun, *century*)
13. less	*should be*	least	(incorrect superlative form)
14. most popularest	*should be*	most popular	(incorrect superlative form)
15. most worst	*should be*	worst	(incorrect superlative form)
16. more securer	*should be*	more secure	(incorrect comparative form)
17. larger	*should be*	largest	(superlative form)
18. finding	*should be*	are finding	(missing word)
19. three	*should be*	the three	(incorrect superlative form)
20. more easy	*should be*	easier	(incorrect comparative form)
21. as	*should be*	than	(incorrect comparative form)
22. fascinated	*should be*	fascinating	(wrong word, active participle needed)
23. Underneath	*should be*	under	(wrong word, preposition needed)
24. more popular	*should be*	most popular	(incorrect superlative form)

ESSAY EXERCISE 9

Answers may vary.

1. **Another** thing is **the** many special experiences from school.
2. I agree **that** children **should** grow up in the countryside
3. Maybe it's because we have different opinions. (omit **of**)
4. Despite **living** in a big city, I like the quiet of the countryside.
5. I prefer to spend time with **a** number of friends.
6. Others choose to spend time **with** a large number of friends.
7. Usually I like to enjoy activities that do not involve a lot of time to prepare. Then it is easy to commit **to** one or two people.
8. I enjoy spending time with one or two **close lifelong friends.**
9. People are not the same **with/as** each other. OR People are not **alike.**

10. In China there are a lot of people **who** speak Mandarin.
11. If I have good teachers, they can help me **with** my problems.
12. We need to belong **to a** society which we call school, and we also need to communicate.
13. **Although** it was not an advanced course, I learned a lot.
14. Now I'm a student **like** my children.
15. When children can help to do tasks, they will learn what responsibilities are. (omit **that**)
16. They don't have a good time together because her roommate complains **to/about** her all the time.
17. People living in my community may interact **with** these new people, and social relations may increase.
18. But, on the other hand, my community has a high **growth** rate.
19. If the community were **bigger,** we would feel better.
20. What happens to you may be totally different **than** what happens to your family or friends.

Post-Test

1. as we know it	(*as* + subject + active verb + pronoun, *it*)		
2. a	*should be*	an	(before vowel sound)
3. Thanksgivings	*should be*	Thanksgiving	(adjective before noun, *feasts*)
4. but	(coordinating conjunction showing contrast)		
5. that have a warm climate	(adjective clause)		
6. have hypnotized	*should be* have been hypnotized		(passive)
7. them	*should be*	it	(to agree with noncount noun, *time*)
8. elegant	*should be*	elegance	(noun after adjective, *sleek*)
9. hundreds of thousands	(plural form before *of*)		
10. wrote	*should be*	written	(passive)
11. An American illustrator	(appositive)		
12. On the average	(prepositional phrase before independent clause)		
13. fiction science	*should be*	science fiction	(word order, noun after adjective)
14. served	(missing verb in adjective clause)		
15. because of	*should be*	because	(preceding subject, *it* + verb, *changes*)
16. such a civilized plant	(correct word order)		
17. at	*should be*	in	(preposition error)
18. study	(present simple for facts)		
19. journalism	*should be*	journalist	(occupation form of the noun)
20. the first	(superlative form)		
21. variety	*should be*	a variety of **OR** various	(before noun, *angles,* both choices are correct)
22. where the majority of people lived	(adjective clause, relative pronoun + subject + verb)		
23. it could hold	(reduced adjective clause, without *that* + subject + verb)		
24. others	*should be*	other	(adjective before noun, *employees*)
25. wide	*should be*	widely	(adverb + verb)

Writing the Essay

BRAINSTORMING EXERCISE

Answers will vary.

THESIS STATEMENT EXERCISE

Answers will vary. Here are some possibilities.

1. Although playing games is fun, it's more fun when your team wins.
2. Because I've always lived in an apartment building, I think it would be more interesting to live in a traditional house for a change.
3. Although some people say zoos have no useful purposes, I've been impressed with how children become more animated when seeing animals.
4. Even though my high school did not require students to study art and music, I wish my high school experience had been more well-rounded.
5. Although I usually listen to music for background noise, I become more relaxed listening to music when I'm feeling bad.
6. Although teenagers may see themselves as adults, it's only when one lives alone that one becomes more of an adult.

7. I might want to build my own home on a piece of land, but I know it would be more beneficial for my community to build a park on that space.

INTRODUCTION EXERCISE

Answers will vary. Here are some possibilities.

1. It doesn't give any specifics.
2. A better introduction, but which games specifically?
3. Too specific to be an introduction.
   What makes this introduction different?
   More developed, leaves the reader wanting to read on, doesn't get too specific with the details.

INTRODUCTION AND THESIS STATEMENT EXERCISE

Answers will vary. Here are some possibilities.

1. We see thousands of advertisements every day: in newspapers, on television, on the Internet, on billboards. Although occasionally I may learn about a product that I don't know about that might improve my life, I sometimes am seduced by advertising to buy things that I don't really need.
2. I live in a technologically advanced country. We no longer rely on animals for farming or transportation as we once did. If I were to choose the most important animal in my country I would select dogs because they provide companionship to so many people that would otherwise be lonely.
3. A building that special meaning to me is the Museum of Fine Arts in Boston, Massachusetts. I grew up in Boston and fondly remember running among the mummies with my visiting cousins and many years later taking my children there for enrichment classes. Today whenever I have time, I steal away for a few hours and revisit familiar treasures and discover new masterpieces.

COMBINING AGREE/DISAGREE EXERCISE

Answers will vary. Here are some possibilities.

1. One or two friends: you can know them better, they like the same things you do
   A large number of friends: you'll never be bored, you'll talk about many different things
   Thesis statement: Although some people enjoy being with a large number of friends who keep them from being bored, I prefer to spend more quality time with one or two friends.
2. All students: some students mature only when they're in college, society needs all of its members to be educated
   Good students only: because it's so expensive to educate students, only the good ones deserve it, good students have proven already that they can handle the pressures of college
   Thesis statement: Many people in my country contend that only good students should be allowed to attend university; however, I'm convinced that students who didn't do well in high school should be given another chance if they so desire.
3. Outdoors: healthier, chance to interact with nature
   Indoors: not polluted, quieter
   Thesis statement: Even though some of my friends spend all of their free time on nature walks and camping, I prefer the quiet and tranquility of being indoors.
4. Should do: go beyond comfort zone to experience something new, learn more
   Shouldn't do: stressful, life is too short
   Thesis statement: I have complained about doing some activities in my life that I don't enjoy; nevertheless, these very activities have enriched my life.
5. By hand: unique, creative
   Machine: cheaper, saves time
   Thesis statement: Even though the objects I cherish the most in my life—an oil painting done my best friend and a sweater my grandmother knit—are hand-made, I realize that it's too expensive and too time-consuming to decide that all of my clothes and furniture should be hand-made.

TOPIC SENTENCE AND SUPPORTING DETAILS EXERCISE 1

PART I.

1. TS: A SP: B
2. TS: A SP: B
3. TS: B SP: A
4. TS: A SP: B
5. TS: A SP: B
6. TS: A SP: B
2. TS: B SP: A
3. TS: B SP: A
4. TS: A SP: B
5. TS: A SP: B

PART II.

Answers will vary. Here are some possibilities.

1. Young children learn cooperation and other life lessons through playing.
   Young children discover the world through play.
2. Children learn most easily when they're young.
   If children learn study habits while young, they'll always find studying to be easy.

TOPIC SENTENCE/SUPPORTING DETAILS EXERCISE 2

1. A 2. B 3. A 4. B

TRANSITION EXERCISE 1

Answers will vary. Here are some possibilities.

1. I'm one of those persons who loves to be in a large group of friends.
2. I can't think of any benefits that zoos provide to either the animals or the visitors.
3. from the earliest years, teachers and parents should encourage game playing.
4. the teachers can get suggestions of things they could do differently.
5. a shopping center would bring thousands of cars, creating traffic jams and causing pollution.
6. my inability to teach myself.
7. the Earth has no more room for all the items I discard to make room for new purchases.

8. I decided to take the TOEFL test and apply for admission to an American university.
9. I enjoy modern art and music.
10. art and music enhance one's creativity, which can be applied to every field.

TRANSITION EXERCISE 2

1. c. 2. a. 3. a. 4. b. 5. a.

TRANSITION EXERCISE 3

Answers will vary. Here are some possibilities.

1. . . . .semester although I . . .
2. . . . homework, whereas my
3. . . . buses; moreover, I had . . .
4. . . . had; hence, I signed . . .
5. . . . essays; moreover, I'm

CONCLUSION EXERCISE

Answers will vary. Here are some possibilities.

1. Although a movie is usually spectacular and engrossing, when I read a book my imagination transports me to another world which I often prefer to watching a film.
2. Whenever I look for a new apartment, I first ask how many rooms the place has.
3. I can think of a dozen countries I would love to visit, but the one at the top of the list is Australia.
4. Some of my friends are satisfied with their lives; others seem to be always searching.
5. The first time I saw the commercial with the Japanese monkey listening to its Sony Walkman, I thought to myself "what a clever designer"!
6. I like my school, the teachers, the curriculum, and my classmates; however, I hate having to wear a uniform.
7. I was surprised to hear that some American students choose what they study, for I believe that experienced educators should make curricular decisions.
8. When I think back to family crises and times of tragedy, our being able to laugh together has made difficult times easier.
9. Instead of being judgmental about the practices of different cultures, it's more fun to try and adjust to what each culture deems acceptable when one is a visitor.
10. My eighty-year-old mother seems to be sixty because she's always trying something new, whether it is using a computer or doing yoga.

SENTENCE VARIETY EXERCISE

Answers will vary. Here are some possibilities.

1. I had to wear a uniform every single day, and you have no idea how much I hated it.
2. I've lived in five different countries, always trying to dress and act like the native people.
3. Although some people learn better from a manual or a teacher, I'm the kind of person who learns by doing, such as when I learned to ride a bicycle.
4. In contrast to what I've heard about some institutions in the United States, in my country teachers at the university level don't care whether or not students come to class.
5. Unfortunately my high school soccer team never won even one game.
6. Although I like to be alone during the week, I look forward to going out with my many friends on the weekend.
7. Maybe because I grew up in a modern twenty-two-story apartment building, I want to live in a traditional house.
8. Although I could never afford to visit Australia, I'd certainly like to visit there.
9. Some people like to listen to music when they're sad; whereas others like to listen when they're in a good mood.
10. Because my hometown is so small and boring, it doesn't even have a movie theater!

TITLE EXERCISE 1

Answers will vary.

TITLE EXERCISE 2

Answers will vary. Here are some possibilities.

1. Athletics Bring in the Money
2. Thousand of Cars and Tons of Pollution
3. A Room of My Own
4. Day Care Centers for the Elderly
5. The Championship Women's Soccer Team
6. Happy Children, Happy Adults
7. The Class I Never Missed
8. Study English and Expand Your Horizons
9. Esther: My Best Friend, My Companion, My Dog

SENTENCE ERROR EXERCISE 1

Here are some possible fragment and run on corrections.

1. F . . . .watch, go to a good jeweler.
2. RO . . . easy because it . . .
3. F . . . .quiet is hard to find.
4. F . . . trip is a good idea.
5. S
6. RO . . . apartment, but I . . .
7. F There are twelve . . .
8. S
9. S
10. R . . . directions, so she . . .

SENTENCE ERROR EXERCISE 2

Here are some possible fragment and run on corrections.

1.	F	First, people who
2.	S	
3.	F	friends, it is fun.
4.	RO	example. When . . .
5.	RO	there. I hope
6.	RO	Spain. I think
7.	S	
8.	F	something is a mistake
9.	F	problems, I call a friend.
10.	F	There are two . . .
11.	F	. . . better than computers?
12.	RO	countryside. I think . . .
13.	F	kitchen, I screamed.
14.	F	They learned a lot through . . .
15.	F	it, I ask someone.
16.	S	
17.	S	
18.	F	They took a summer job even though
19.	F	beautifully, I help other people and know . . .
20.	S	

NOUN ENDINGS	EXAMPLES	YOUR EXAMPLES
• ness	happiness	*sadness, shyness*
• (i)ty	community	*university, solidarity*
• th	width	*length, breadth*
• sion, tion	position	*information, registration*
• ism	Buddhism	*schism, impressionism*
• ure	architecture	*erasure, closure*
(ure can also indicate a verb)		
• ment	repayment	*government, enjoyment*
(ment can also indicate a verb)		
• ude	gratitude	*solitude, magnitude*
• ence, ance	independence	*governance, credence*
• ship	friendship	*internship, leadership*
• ery, ary,ory	cemetery	*memory, bribery*
(ery, ary can also indicate an adjective)		
• hood	neighborhood	*sisterhood, brotherhood*
• phy, gy, try	philosophy	*biology, geometry*
• inct/ct	precinct	*instinct, district*
• ess	address	*duress, stress*
(ess can also indicate a verb)		

PEOPLE NOUN ENDINGS

• ist, yst	chemist	*artist, analyst*
• er,or	doctor	*sailor, dancer*
• ess	hostess	*princess, stewardess*
• ian	librarian	*magician, vegetarian*
• ic	medic	*comic, cynic*
(ic can also indicate adjectives)		
• eur	voyeur	*entrepreneur, voyeur*
• ant, ent	correspondent	*immigrant, claimant*
(ant, ent can also indicate adjectives)		
• ect, ict	suspect	*architect, derelict*
(ect can also indicate verbs)		

VERB ENDINGS

• ize, yze	criticize	*memorize, theorize*
• ate, ete	refrigerate	*create, complete*
(ate can also indicate adjectives)		
• ify	identify	*quantify, magnify*
• uish, ish	distinguish	*flourish, finish*
(ish can also indicate adjectives)		
• en	lengthen	*widen, broaden*
• ute	dilute	*commute, compute*
(ute can also be an adjective)		
• ure	endure	*insure, capture*
• ose	oppose	*depose, suppose*
• ulge	indulge	*bulge, deluge*
• ict, uct	predict	*conflict, deduct*
• erse, earse	converse	*rehearse, traverse*
• end, ond	pretend	*correspond, respond*
• use	enthuse	*diffuse, confuse*
• erve	deserve	*preserve, serve*
• uce	produce	*reduce, introduce*
• ess	address	*redress, compress*
• uade, ade	persuade	*dissuade, degrade*
• ote	promote	*demote, connote*
• ave	behave	*engrave, save*
• age	encourage	*discourage, barrage*
• ect	reflect	*dissect, connect*
• ame	inflame	*tame, rename*
• ment	experiment	*compliment*
• oy	destroy	*employ, annoy*

ADJECTIVE ENDINGS

• ly	lovely	*friendly, neighborly*
(usually-*ly* signifies an adverb, but some nouns+- *ly* = adjectives)		
• less	careless	*useless, hopeless*
• ful	useful	*beautiful, careful*
• al	usual	*casual, mutual*
• ish	foolish	*selfish, sheepish*
• y	crazy	*sunny, happy*
• ary, ory	scary	*momentary, sedentary*
• ic	heroic	*energetic, athletic*
• ble, ible, able	incredible	*teachable, inflatable*
• ive, tive	passive	*successive, repetative*
• ant, ent	dependant	*resplendant, independent*
• ing, ed	interesting	*bored, frightening*
• ous, ious	religious	*serious, copious*
• ate, ete, ute	ornate	*obsolete, resolute*

WORD FORM EXERCISE

Some forms have other options.

creation	**creator**	create	**creative**
symbol	**XXXXX**	**symbolize**	**symbolic**
communication	**communicator**	**communicate**	communicative
art	**artist**	**XXXXX**	**artistic**
prediction	**predictor**	predict	**predictable**
execution	**executive**	execute	**executive**
correspondence	**correspondent**	**correspond**	**corresponding**
suspicion	**suspect**	**suspect**	suspicious
therapy	**therapist**	**XXXXX**	**therapeutic**
analysis	analyst	analyze	**analytic**
diagnosis	**diagnostician**	**diagnose**	**diagnostic**
education	**educator**	**educate**	educational
manipulation	**manipulator**	**manipulate**	**manipulative**
science	scientist	**XXXXX**	**scientific**
development	**developer**	**develop**	**developed**
competition	**competitor**	compete	**competitive**
immigration	immigrant	**immigrate**	XXXXX
popularity	XXXXX	popularize	**popular**

PARALLELISM EXERCISE 1

Answers may vary. Here are some possibilities.

1. The apartment was beautiful, expensive, and **spacious.**
2. If you're going to use this recipe, you'll need a pepper, **an** onion, and **a** tomato.
3. Our teacher is interesting: she plays piano, writes poetry, and **paints watercolors.**
4. I always have **sung** and always will sing in the shower.
5. Please turn down the television or go to sleep.
6. Michael hopes his dedication, ability, and **consideration** will help him get the job.
7. Daniel is a happy child and a **sound sleeper**.
8. Jodie Foster is a great actress and **a good director**.
9. The books on the top shelf are older than **those on** the bottom shelves.
10. At the University of Pennsylvania, morning classes are far more popular than the afternoon **ones.**

PARALLELISM EXERCISE 2

Answers may vary. Here are some possibilities.

1. I was in favor of either *painting the walls purple* or ***leaving them alone.***
2. Matt found what he needed in the desk: *a ruler, a pen,* and ***an old exam.***
3. The square was crowded with young tourists *studying their guidebooks, eating lunches from backpacks,* and ***taking pictures of each other.***
4. Moving to a new apartment means I'll have to *decide what to keep, what to give away,* and ***what to sell.***
5. During our coffee break we ate blueberry muffins that were *small* but ***delicious.***
6. The hats and coats were piled everywhere: *on the bed, on the chairs,* and even ***on the floor.***
7. Bonnie knew neither *what to say in her letter of application* nor ***how to express herself effectively.***
8. *Either the government will ban smoking in public buildings* or ***the people will revolt.***
9. Molly walked *across the square* and ***into the library.***
10. In the morning newspaper I *read that plans for a second airport are being considered* and ***noticed that the governor is opposed to the idea.***

PARALLELISM EXERCISE 3

Answers may vary. Here are some possibilities.

1. Life is **simpler** and more convenient than **for** people who lived in the past.
2. I think neither spending time with one or two friends nor **being with** a large number of friends is preferable to being alone.
3. Some people say it is easy to get into but difficult to graduate **from** U.S. colleges or universities.
4. If the community would be bigger, it would be more comfortable and **convenient.**
5. A teacher can tell you what **is wrong** or which **way is better.**
6. I like to visit a lot of different foreign countries and to spend my time with the people there.
7. It helps people to get rid of something they don't want instead of throwing it away. **They should** give it to someone who needs and wants it.
8. I don't have to worry if the goods are **either** damaged or not worth anything.
9. The boss must decide **either** to hire new employees or retrain the current ones.
10. The unemployment figures for those under twenty-five in Manila is larger than **those in** Singapore.

PARALLELISM EXERCISE 4

Answers may vary. Here are some possibilities.

1. After a day at the beach, the children came home tired, sunburned, and **hungry.**
2. Larry Bird was a quick, skillful, and **energetic** basketball player.

3. A good writer edits her work slowly, carefully, and **regularly**.
4. The English composition course contains short stories, a novel, and **poetry**.
5. When you write an essay, you should check each verb for **agreement,** tense, and form.
6. The airline allows passengers to take one, two or **three** suitcases.
7. My mother has been a waitress, a secretary, and **a teacher**.
8. My uncle spoke **with humor** and kindness.
9. I am hot, dirty, and **thirsty**.
10. The flavor of the strawberry yogurt is better than **the flavor of** the peach.

PARALLELISM EXERCISE 5

Answers may vary. Here are some possibilities.

1. We want to have a flower garden, but we don't know where to begin, how to proceed, or **which flowers to plant**.
2. The summer of 1950 was as hot **as,** if not hotter than any other in the last century.
3. I **know neither** what kind of computer he uses nor where he bought it.
4. I am afraid **of** and excited about taking the TOEFL.
5. Jared has sent resumes to graphic design firms in **both** Taipei and Hong Kong.
6. Chris is an affectionate husband, a dutiful son, and **a kind father**.
7. The shape of the rock, **the length,** and the color reminds me of a small elephant.
8. He danced gracefully, rhythmically, and **easily**.
9. Judy is a gifted woman: a biologist, **a carpenter,** and **a cook**.
10. Your job consists of arranging the books, cataloging the new arrivals, and **alphabetizing the brochures**.

PUNCTUATION EXERCISE

1. Although Yutaka was absent, she e-mailed me for the homework.
2. There are three sections on the TOEFL exam: listening, structure, and reading
3. I improved my writing ability because I write **two** essays a day.
4. I got autographs from my three favorite movie stars: Meryl Streep, Jodie Foster, and Robin Williams.
5. Jean-Claude has taken several English classes; therefore, he is confident about his writing ability.
6. Luis Carlos, a Mexican, didn't want to take a class with **seven** other Mexicans.
7. Maria Paula, who comes from Colombia, explained in her essay why she prefers to live in a dorm.
8. Carmen's daughter was sick, so Carmen took her to the doctor.
9. CORRECT
10. CORRECT
11. After Diana came to one class, she never appeared again.
12. Luis speaks several languages: Portuguese, Spanish, English, and Italian.
13. I arrived on time for the test; however, I forgot my passport.
14. CORRECT
15. Bravo! If I call your name, you passed the entrance examination.

Student Essays

TOPIC 1

#1/A
Score: 3
Noticeably inappropriate choice of words or word forms
Accumulation of errors in sentence structure and/or usage
Good use of specifics; inadequate introduction, no background given; conclusion not related to the essay; not formatted correctly

#1/B
Score: 4
Adequately organized and developed
Uses some details to support a thesis
Adequate but inconsistent facility with syntax and usage
Good examples; too repetitive; numerous preposition, plural errors

#1/C
Score: 5
Is generally well-organized and developed
Demonstrates some syntactic variety and range of vocabulary
Very good examples; introduction needs work— don't just repeat the prompt; some awkward phrasing

#1/D
Score: 4
Contains some errors that occasionally obscure meaning
Adequately organized and developed
Good vocabulary but repeats prompt too many times; specific examples needed; article errors

#1/E
Score: 4
Adequately organized and developed
Good length and specifics; numerous errors lower this score, including those of prepositions, pronouns, spelling, articles, word choice, and plurals

#1/F
Score: 3
Noticeably inappropriate choice or words or word forms
Good conclusion; numerous errors lower this score, including those of subject-verb agreement, prepositions, plurals, and word choice

#1/G
Score: 3
Long, but an accumulation of errors in sentence structure and usage
Good length; numerous errors lower this score, including those of spelling, word choice, prepositions, and sentence fragments

#1/H
Score: 5.5
Well organized and developed
Demonstrates syntactic variety and appropriate word choice
Addresses some parts of the task more effectively than others
Well-developed; conclusion needs development

#1/I
Score: 6
Effectively addresses the writing task
Demonstrates syntactic variety and appropriate word choice
Uses clearly appropriate details
A very effective essay—does everything right

#1/J
Score: 4.5
Displays some syntactic variety and range of vocabulary
Contains some errors that occasionally obscure meaning
Good length and examples; errors lower this score including those of subject-verb agreement and word choice

TOPIC 2

#2/A
Score: 4
Close to becoming a 5, but still has inconsistent facility with syntax and usage
Has some errors that occasionally obscure meaning
Very good specifics; some basic errors keep this essay from getting a higher score, including those of articles, subject-verb agreement, and plurals

#2/B
Score: 4
Close to becoming a 5, but has some errors that occasionally obscure meaning
Very good specifics but introduction needs development; numerous errors lower this score, including those of run-on sentences, word choice, missing subject, prepositions, and spelling

#2/C
Score: 4.5
Uses some details to support a thesis
Inconsistent facility with syntax and usage
Very good specifics and interesting use of a proverb; errors lower this score, including those of double subject, spelling, and run-on sentences

#2/D
Score: 3
An accumulation of errors in sentence structure and usage.
A variety of examples, but introduction and conclusion lack development; numerous errors lower this score, including those of word choice, spelling, and prepositions

#2/E
Score: 4
Uses some details to support a thesis and illustrate an idea
Inconsistent facility with syntax and usage
Very good specifics but lacking introduction and conclusion; numerous errors lower this score, including those of basic spelling and apostrophes

#2/F
Score: 2
Serious underdevelopment
Little detail
Serious and frequent errors in sentence structure and usage
Way too short; numerous errors lower this score, including those of fragments, participles, prepositions, articles, and verb tenses

#2/G
Score: 3
Almost a 4, but lacks development
Accumulation of errors in sentence structure and usage
Don't use informal language in essays, such as "gonna"; numerous errors lower this score, including those of word order and word choice

#2/H
Score: 4
Contains some errors that occasionally obscure meaning
Is adequately organized and developed except Par. 3 which has an organizational shift
Interesting introduction and specifics; numerous errors lower this score, including those of spelling, articles, apostrophes, participles, word order, and contractions

#2/I
Score: 4.5
Becoming a 5—demonstrates fluency with vocabulary and syntax
Adequately organized and developed
A variety of specifics; effective conclusion ending with a question; errors lower this score, including those of count/non-count nouns and subject-verb agreement

#2/J
Score: 5
Is generally well organized and developed
Uses details to support a thesis/illustrate ideas
Wonderful specifics and examples; a few grammatical errors, including subject-verb agreement

TOPIC 3

#3/A
Score: 4
Close to becoming a 5, but still has inconsistent facility with syntax and usage

Good specifics; numerous errors lower this score, including those of word choice and phrasing throughout

#3/B
Score: 3
Noticeably inappropriate word choice or word forms
Accumulation of errors in sentence structure and usage
Good specifics; numerous errors lower this score, including those of spelling, word choice, verb forms, sentence fragments, and subject-verb agreement

#3/C
Score: 4
Interesting ideas, but inconsistent facility with syntax and usage
Contains errors that occasionally obscure meaning
Compelling introduction; numerous errors lower this score, including those of articles, plurals, and awkward phrasing

#3/D
Score: 2.5
Inadequate development
Accumulation of errors in sentence structure and usage
Needs more than one paragraph—way too short; numerous errors lower this score, including those of subject-verb agreement, pronouns, and spelling

#3/E
Score: 2
Underdevelopment
Noticeably inappropriate choice of words or word forms
Frequent errors in sentence structure and usage
Single sentences aren't paragraphs—way too short; incorrect word choice throughout

#3/F
Score: 5.5
Uses details to support thesis and ideas
Addresses some parts of the task more effectively than others
Very good examples; syntax/usage is adequate, but a little short; more developed introduction and conclusion would have made this essay a 6

#3/G
Score: 5.5
Although there are a few errors, in general demonstrates syntactic variety and appropriate word choice
Displays consistent facility in the use of language
Well-organized and well-argued; a weak paragraph 4 and paragraphs without indentations keep this essay from being a 6

#3/H
Score: 0
Merely copies the topic
No essay here. Try never to copy the prompt anywhere in the essay.

#3/I
Score: 4
Adequately developed and organized
Uses some details to support thesis/illustrate idea
Inconsistent facility with syntax and usage
Good specifics; restate the arguments in the conclusion—don't say "the reasons above show"; numerous errors lower this score including those of count/non-count nouns, and prepositions

#3/J
Score: 3.5
Inconsistent facility with syntax and usage
Uses some details to support thesis/illustrate idea
Good examples; numerous errors lower this score, including those of spelling, comparatives, word choice, and abbreviations

TOPIC 4

#4/A
Score: 3.5
Adequate length
Accumulation of errors in sentence structure and usage
Good specifics but needs to be organized into paragraphs; numerous errors lower this score, including those of articles, prepositions, word form, participles, and verbs

#4/B
Score: 5
Generally well-organized and developed
Displays facility in the use of the language
Some syntactic variety and range of vocabulary
Effective use of a question as a topic sentence; don't copy title from the prompt

#4/C
Score: 2
Accumulation of serious errors in sentence structure and usage
Serious and frequent errors in sentence structure and usage
Lack of development
Too short; numerous errors lower this score, including those of spelling, word order, verbs, fragments, and word choice

#4/D
Score: 3
Accumulation of errors in sentence structure and usage
Noticeably inappropriate choice of words or word forms
Indent paragraphs—needs multiple paragraphs and more development; numerous errors lower this score, including those of verbs, word choice, articles, and word form

#4/E
Score: 5.5
Almost a 6, is generally well organized and developed, but some errors with syntax and usage
Well-argued with specifics, but short paragraphs and a lack of transitions keep this essay from being a 6

#4/F
Score: 1.5
Severe and persistent writing errors
Somewhat incoherent
Too short; illogical sentence connections

#4/G
Score: 4.5
Adequately developed and organized
Contains some errors that occasionally obscure meaning
Good specifics; incomplete and illogical conclusion; errors lower this score, including those of capitalization, spelling, prepositions, and word choice

#4/H
Score: 6
Demonstrates syntactic variety and appropriate word choice
Displays facility in the use of language
A very effective essay—does everything right

#4/I
Score: 4.5
Adequately organized and developed
Uses some detail to support thesis and illustrate ideas
Contains some errors that occasionally obscure meaning
Inconsistent facility with syntax and usage
Good use of questions; errors lower this score, including those of subject-verb agreement, articles, and verb tenses

#4/J
Score: 4.5
Inconsistent facility with syntax and usage
Meaning occasionally obscured
Good paragraph development, focus and length; errors lower this score, including those of word choice, word form, articles, and prepositions

TOPIC 5

#5/A
Score: 3.5
Accumulation of errors in usage but good conclusion
Good specifics, but no introduction; undeveloped paragraph 2; numerous errors lower this score, including those of word choice and word form

#5/B
Score: 4
Adequately organized and developed
Inconsistent facility with syntax and usage
Good specifics; numerous errors lower this score, including those of subject-verb agreement, plurals, and prepositions

#5/C
Score: 4
Contains errors that occasionally obscure meaning
Inconsistent facility with syntax and usage
Uses details to support thesis and illustrate ideas
Good specifics but paragraphs need indentation; no real introduction; numerous errors lower this score, including those of articles, word choice, and prepositions

#5/D
Score: 3
Accumulation of errors in sentence structure and usage
Noticeably inappropriate choice or words and word forms.
Good examples, but inadequate paragraph development—don't end the essay with only a sentence; numerous errors lower this score, including those of word choice, articles, verbs, and prepositions

#5/E
Score: 3.5
Accumulation of errors in sentence structure and usage
Good examples, but incomplete introduction; paragraphs need indentation; numerous errors lower this score, including those of sentence fragments and word choice

#5/F
Score: 5
Displays facility and range of vocabulary
Generally well-developed and organized
Good specific examples; numerous spelling and count/noncount noun errors

#5/G
Score: 2
Serious underdevelopment
Serious and frequent errors in sentence structure and usage
Ends too abruptly; numerous errors lower this score, including those of count/noncount nouns, spelling, subject-verb agreement, and word choice

#5/H
Score: 2
Serious underdevelopment
Serious and frequent errors in sentence structure and usage
Little detail
Numerous errors lower this score, including those of word form, subject-verb agreement, fragments, spelling, and missing words

#5/I
Score: 3.5
Uses some details to support thesis and illustrate ideas
An accumulation of errors in sentence structure and usage
Good examples, but undeveloped conclusion; numerous errors lower this score, including those of subject-verb agreement, spelling, and articles

#5/J
Score: 4.5
Close to becoming a 5, but inconsistent facility with syntax and usage
Undeveloped conclusion; errors lower this score, including those of plurals, spelling, and prepositions

TOPIC 6

#6/A
Score: 4
Adequate but inconsistent facility with syntax and usage
Contains some errors that occasionally obscure meaning
Adequately organized and developed

Good specifics and organization; numerous errors lower this score, including those of plurals, articles, and verb errors

#6/B
Score: 2.5
Inadequate organization and development
Noticeably inappropriate choice of words and word forms
Serious and frequent errors
Talk about your own country—when you personalize your writing, it's much more persuasive; numerous errors lower this score, including those of word forms, word choice, and subject-verb agreement

#6/C
Score: 2.5
Inadequate development and organization
Accumulation of serious errors in sentence structure and usage
Develop introduction; numerous errors lower this score, including those of verb tenses, spelling, word choice, word form, articles, plurals, count/ non-count nouns, prepositions, and word order

#6/D
Score: 2.5
Inadequate development and organization
Accumulation of serious errors in sentence structure and usage
Develop introduction and conclusion; numerous errors lower this score, including those of spelling, capitalization, plurals, word choice, prepositions, and articles

#6/E
Score: 4
Addresses the writing topic adequately but slights parts of the task
Inconsistent facility with syntax and usage
Good title, don't use informal language in essays, such as "wanna", develop paragraphs more; occasional errors, including those of subject-verb agreement and word form

#6/F
Score: 4.5
Addresses some parts of the task more effectively than others
Displays facility in the use of the language
Almost no errors with syntax or usage, but the length and lack of development prevent it from receiving a higher score

#6/G
Score: 6
Effectively addresses the task
Demonstrates syntactic variety and appropriate word choice
Good use of a question in the conclusion; well-argued and developed throughout

#6/H
Score: 2
Serious underdevelopment
Serious and frequent errors in sentence structure and usage
Little detail
Almost no errors with syntax or usage, but the length and lack of development prevent it from receiving a higher score

#6/I
Score: 5.5
Generally well developed and organized
Displays facility in the use of the language
Alternative organization (with numbering), but it works because points are developed in paragraph form with complete sentences

#6/J
Score: 4
Adequate but inconsistent facility with syntax and usage
Adequately organized and developed
Good conclusion; numerous errors lower this score, including those of phrasing and word choice

TOPIC 7

#7/A
Score: 4
Although the student didn't finish the majority of the essay, is adequately organized and developed
Inconsistent facility with syntax and usage
Weak introduction which restates the prompt; numerous errors lower this score, including those of word-choice, articles, and plurals

#7/B
Score: 4
Contains some errors that occasionally obscure meaning
Inconsistent facility with syntax and usage
Interesting examples; numerous errors lower this score, including those of word form, count/noncount nouns, articles, verbs, and capitalization

#7/C
Score: 2
Serious disorganization and underdevelopment
Serious and frequent errors in sentence structure and usage
Organize the essay into paragraphs—then organize each paragraph by ideas

#7/D
Score: 3
Accumulation of errors in sentence structure and usage
Noticeably inappropriate choice of words or word forms
Examples from personal experience work well; numerous errors lower this score, including those of plurals, prepositions, fragments, word form, and word choice

#7/E
Score: 6
Effectively addresses the task
Demonstrates syntactic variety and appropriate word choice
Consistent facility in the use of language
Impressive length and development

#7/F
Score: 4.5
Inconsistent facility with syntax and usage
Good title, details, length; errors lower this score, including those of verb tenses, capitalization, count/non-count nouns, and prepositions

#7/G
Score: 2
Serious problem with focus
Serious disorganization and underdevelopment.
Frequent errors in sentence structure and usage
Underdeveloped; numerous errors lower this score, including those of pronouns, count/non-count nouns, and word choice

#7/H
Score: 2.5
Insufficient details to support or illustrate generalizations
Accumulation of errors in sentence structure and usage
Most of the sentences don't make sense

#7/I
Score: 3.5
Close to becoming a 4, but accumulation of errors in sentence structure and usage
Good length, good questions, and good examples; numerous errors lower this score, including those of spelling, word choice, verbs, articles, and plurals

#7/J
Score: 4
Adequately organized and developed
Uses some details to support thesis/illustrate idea
Good use of question in introduction; numerous errors lower this score, including those of word choice, spelling, participles, plurals, and word form

TOPIC 8

#8/A
Score: 3.5
Inconsistent facility with syntax
Accumulation of errors in sentence structure and usage
Title from the prompt doesn't add anything; numerous errors lower this score, including those of spelling, articles, subject-verb agreement, word choice, plurals, and comparatives

#8/B
Score: 4.5
Inconsistent facility with syntax and usage
Contains some errors that occasionally obscure meaning
Uses details to illustrate an idea
Good details, but a thin introduction; almost a 5 but has some awkward phrasings

#8/C
Score: 3
Slights parts of the writing task
Contains some errors that occasionally obscure meaning
Underdeveloped introduction and conclusion; numerous errors lower this score, including those of comparative/superlative, word form, and run-on sentences

#8/D
Score: 6
Effectively addresses the writing task
Demonstrates syntactic variety and range of vocabulary
Although there are problems with the introduction, the essay is strong; occasional unobtrusive word choice errors

#8/E
Score: 2.5
Frequent errors in sentence structure and usage
Underdeveloped; numerous errors lower this score, including those of articles, word choice, prepositions, subject-verb agreement, and verbs

#8/F
Score: 4
Contains some errors that occasionally obscure meaning
Uses some details to support thesis and illustrate ideas
Adequate but inconsistent facility with syntax and usage
Good specifics; numerous errors lower this score, including those of articles, word form, and word choice

#8/G
Score: 4
Undeveloped conclusion
Inconsistent facility with syntax and usage
Good examples, lack of focus in last body paragraph; numerous errors lower this score, including those of subject-verb agreement, word choice, and plurals

#8/H
Score: 4
Inconsistent facility with syntax and usage
Adequately developed and organized
Good specifics, but conversational tone doesn't work well, inadequate introduction; numerous errors lower this score, including those of word choice and phrasing

#8/I
Score: 5
Generally well-organized and developed
Demonstrates some syntactic variety and range of vocabulary
Essay flows and has substantial examples; errors lower this score, including those of subject-verb agreement, articles, word choice, and word form

#8/J
Score: 5.5
Displays facility in the range of vocabulary
Almost a 6
Uses details to support thesis/illustrate ideas
Alternative design listing points before the paragraphs keeps essay from being a 6

TOPIC 9

#9/A
Score: 4
A weak 4, but uses details to support thesis and illustrate idea
Inconsistent facility with syntax and usage
Good examples, but thin introduction and conclusion; numerous errors lower this score including those of phrasing and word choice

#9/B
Score: 4
A weak 4
Uses details to support thesis and illustrate ideas
Inconsistent facility with syntax and usage
Good specifics, but repeats phrase "children should be required . . . " too many times—leaves the reader feeling writer hasn't said much

#9/C
Score: 5
Although the he/she, him/her really gets in the way, the essay is generally well-organized and developed
Demonstrates some syntactic variety and range of vocabulary
Good specifics, don't use he/she, his/her—pluralize everything (children/they/them/their)

#9/D
Score: 5
Displays consistent facility in the use of language
Demonstrates syntactic variety and appropriate word choice
Although only 2 paragraphs, includes a variety of examples and reads fluently—too short to be a 6

#9/E
Score: 4
Adequately organized and developed
Inconsistent facility with syntax and usage
Good specifics, but underdeveloped conclusion; numerous errors lower this score, including those of word choice, prepositions, and subject-verb agreement

#9/F
Score: 4.5
Adequately organized and developed
Inconsistent facility with syntax and usage
Interesting points, but underdeveloped introduction and conclusion and too many "!"s; errors lower this score, including those of word choice, plurals, and phrasing

#9/G
Score: 3.5
Contains errors that occasionally obscure meaning
Inconsistent facility with syntax and usage
Uses some details to support thesis/illustrate ideas
Good length; numerous errors lower this score, including those of run-ons, plurals, subject-verb agreement, verb form, and tense

#9/H
Score: 5
Is generally well organized and developed
Displays facility in the use of the language
Uses details to support thesis/illustrate idea
Very good specifics, but underdeveloped conclusion; errors lower this score, including those of word choice and plurals

#9/I
Score: 4
Inconsistent facility with syntax and usage
Uses some details to support thesis/illustrate ideas
Good details; numerous errors lower this score, including those of word choice, articles, word order, word form, and plurals

#9/J
Score: 4
Inconsistent facility with syntax and usage
Adequately organized and developed
Good length, underdeveloped conclusion; numerous errors lower this score, including those of verb form, plurals, non-count nouns, word form, and word choice

SECTION THREE: READING

Pre-Test

1. Jim Fixx and the Jogging Craze
2. speed
3. exhausting
4. weekend tennis
5. fad
6. *The Complete Book of Running*
7. become popular
8. trumpeted=proclaimed
9. **Joggers, even presidents and movie stars, became familiar sights on jogging paths and highways.** In addition, Fixx proclaimed that jogging was good for everything from losing weight to increasing concentration.
10. leader
11. He designed a sneaker and exercise clothing line.
12. wrote more than one book
13. the words jogging and running are interchangeable
14. The history of the Erector set
15. He set up a magic trick supply company.
16. He realized that by using miniature girders, gears, and motors like those he saw on the railway project, his product could be used for much more sophisticated designs.
17. ideal
18. Even children who played with their Erector sets every day realized the number of building possibilities was limitless.
19. revolutionary
20. achievements
21. **Searching for other materials, Gilbert developed wooden girders.** Back in full production in 1950, he came out with the Amusement Park set, which had an impressive merry-go-round.
22. Roller coasters
23. 1913

24. paragraph 3
25. original Erector sets have increased in value
26. The Adaptation of the House Finch
27. wild
28. domestic birds *OR* house finches
29. impressive
30. had glamorous appeal
31. Instead of paying hefty fines, they released the birds into the city streets when confronted by law enforcement.
32. prohibited
33. restraining
34. To be sold in New York City
35. instructive example
36. **The birds experienced exponential growth in the wild because of the species' high fertility rate, which had decreased in captivity.** Their total number in North America is estimated at more than a billion, with a substantial percentage east of the Mississippi River.
37. a different example of environmental adaptation
38. The History of the American Log Cabin
39. frame houses
40. built=assembled
41. Swedish, German, Scotch-Irish
42. round, hewn on two sides, and squared
43. cut
44. logs
45. Bark
46. Glass was too expensive.
47. **Daniel Boone and Andrew Jackson are others.** The belief that one may begin life humbly and become President of the United States still rings true.
48. plain
49. the early English colonists built the first log cabins
50. animal skins were accessible to settlers

Reading Exercises

PASSAGE 1

1. primitive=simple
2. Grandma Moses painted for a quarter century.
3. **Before the turn of the century, she lived on a farm in upstate New York.**
   Art critics have praised her work for its freshness, innocence, and humanity.
4. energetic

PASSAGE 2

1. the increased number of surgical awareness episodes patients are experiencing
2. The use of suggestions on anesthetized patients
3. patients
4. follow-up
5. monitored
6. Comments made to patients during surgery will affect their recovery.
7. the design of a study to enhance patient recovery

PASSAGE 3

1. The initial settlement of Texas
2. Mexico
3. Mexico had already twice refused U.S. offers to buy Mexico
4. negotiate the Louisiana Purchase
5. successful=flourishing
6. production of raw materials for clothing
7. **His management was so successful that by 1830 there were more than 20,000 Americans in Texas.**
   Mexico restricted all immigration after 1830.

PASSAGE 4

1. The shrimp's abilities to escape its enemies and to feed itself
2. the shrimp benefits from its camouflage
3. camouflage=disguise
4. the shrimp
5. filled with
6. something edible

PASSAGE 5

1. The Growing Practice of Illegally Copying Software
2. in the computer industry
3. 7
4. pirated
5. Price

PASSAGE 6

1. Being slow to understand their differences from the English
2. evict the English
3. had a population that was ultimately greater than that of the Indians
4. use the land mainly for hunting
5. **That year's celebration has come to be known as the first Thanksgiving.**
   But the good relationship did not last long.

PASSAGE 7

1. chance
2. The search (for signals from intelligent beings in outer space)
3. at one time, searching for signals from outer space was not taken seriously
4. enterprise
5. Eventually, the study of signals from outer space may produce results in various fields.
6. Straightforward

PASSAGE 8

1. Predicting the Shape of American Society
2. pollster
3. He surveys the nation's youth, for example, because his polls have shown repeatedly that one's values and attitudes about life—the seeds of future actions—are formed before a person reaches the age of twenty.
4. thorough
5. a priest
6. sociology

PASSAGE 9

1. The rights of states and of Congress
2. An early constitution
3. Appoint delegates to the state legislatures
4. fix weights and measures
5. before November 17, 1777, no U.S. constitution existed
6. the number of state delegates
7. the states would not decide on issues of war

PASSAGE 10

1. The Truth About Lie Detectors
2. Lie detectors
3. It is attached to the fingers of both hands.
4. Neutral respondents
5. Posture differences
6. responses
7. A crime
8. one must be able to analyze reactions to a lie detector test
9. **The instrument is not very sophisticated.** Two pens are driven by air-filled tubes place around a subject's chest and stomach to record breathing movement.
10. emotionally charged OR charged

PASSAGE 11

1. 14
2. trim body and legs
3. It was relatively smart.
4. three species of horse have existed
5. many contemporaries of the Dawn Horse are extinct
6. D (horse the size of a fox terrier dog)

PASSAGE 12

1. The Deep Rover Enables Underwater Interaction
2. egg-shaped
3. It can dive to more than half a mile beneath the surface of the sea.
4. They allow passengers to remain in the sub.
5. vessel=craft
6. the ability to dive more than one mile beneath the sea
7. a special diving suit is required
8. these devices
9. a wealthy person

PASSAGE 13

1. How Environments Affected American Indians' Diets
2. dominated
3. American Indians raised crops suitable to their areas.
4. ensured food for the winter
5. rituals

PASSAGE 14

1. Two-thirds of the people gained weight.
2. the participants ate breakfast and dinner for a week
3. If you want to lost weight, eat only 2,000 calories a day at breakfast.
4. regimen=diet
5. a calorie

PASSAGE 15

1. The Initiation and Impact of the American Railroad
2. defied terrain=Able to go almost anywhere
3. primitive
4. oil
5. It included a survivor of the signing of the Declaration of Independence.
6. the steam locomotive for railroads
7. The railroad solved America's transport problems.

PASSAGE 16

1. Since the end of the 1960s
2. rendered as paintings
3. Planetary images could only be imagined.
4. imaginings=fantasy
5. Space artists in the fifties used planetary photographs.
6. **At that time one could only fantasize about what planets looked like.**
   Informed art reveals more than mere fantasy can.
7. U.S. moon orbiters, Mariner, Voyager 1, Voyager 2

PASSAGE 17

1. Causes and effects of cold and warm fronts
2. Along fronts
3. A (warm air going under cold air)
4. The movement of fronts depends on the formation of pressure systems.
5. Weather changes due to cold fronts
6. increased humidity
7. moisture=precipitation

PASSAGE 18

1. the changes in clothing in the past 300 years
2. **Before that time clothes were primarily black, gray, and white.** In the late 1700s, the invention of the toothed cotton gin, the power loom, and other machines sped up the production of fabric and yarn.
3. identical=uniform
4. synthetic fabrics
5. Because of better-heated homes and offices
6. New dyes, power loom, improved sewing machine, synthetic fabrics
7. fashion design

PASSAGE 19

1. The Automobile's Impact on American Life in the 1920s
2. profoundly=significantly
3. areas
4. mushroomed=proliferated
5. competed with
6. 1920
7. 1 to 6
8. In 1920, it had the highest urban density in the U.S.

9. **A look at Los Angeles shows the automobile's pervasive impact on urban life.** From 1920 to 1930, the population of Los Angeles County more than doubled, from fewer than 1 million to 2.2 million.
10. Positive

PASSAGE 20

1. Varying attitudes about private space
2. maneuvering
3. violated
4. Crowded subway cars, for example, may be experienced as psychologically uncomfortable, and outbreaks of aggression are more likely in crowded situations.
5. Those who stand too close to them
6. 6 inches
7. Social
8. communication styles

PASSAGE 21

1. Boston from 1620 to the mid 1700s
2. united
3. **According to these leaders, only Puritans could vote or hold public office.** Laws forbade the staging of plays and the celebration of Christmas.
4. Nevertheless, the town's leaders tried to drive out of Boston any new settlers who did not share their beliefs.
5. By 1720, the Puritans had driven out any settlers who didn't share their beliefs.
6. Life in Boston at the end of the eighteenth century
7. Founding of Charlestown, founding of Boston, Boston's becoming a leading fishing center, restriction of Puritan laws

PASSAGE 22

1. To describe the behavior and characteristics of milk snakes
2. The milk snake is a type of kingsnake that farmers once believed took milk from cows.
3. For the water
4. A (picture of snake with rings)

PASSAGE 23

1. organizations that impact human beings
2. mandatory
3. utilitarian=practical
4. being incarcerated

PASSAGE 24

1. Whether or not to take graphology seriously
2. predictive
3. occupation
4. graphoanalysis graduates
5. extensive
6. scientists don't consider graphology to be a real science
7. They determine a person's illness based on a handwriting sample.

PASSAGE 25

1. Rio Grande
2. Desert surrounded many of the valleys, and the people set up irrigation systems so they could grow crops.
3. **These homes had as many as four stories, and the Indians used ladders to reach the upper levels.** Some families of grandparents, parents, children, aunts, and uncles lived in two or more connected dwellings.
4. Some families of grandparents, parents, children, aunts, and uncles lived in two or more connected dwellings.
5. advance
6. their women performed kachina dances

PASSAGE 26

1. Landscapes and architecture were popular subjects for early art photographers.
2. Famous people
3. striking
4. A photographer
5. removed
6. photographers
7. **After a roll had been used, a person sent the camera with the film inside to one of Eastman's processing plants.** The plant developed the film, made prints, and then returned the camera loaded with a new roll of film.

PASSAGE 27

1. The wagon train routine of the late 1840s
2. halted=stopped
3. oxen
4. The "keep moving" rule
5. provided that
6. Plains Indians
7. Oxen were buried in Indian hunting grounds.

PASSAGE 28

1. The aviation accomplishments of Charles Lindbergh
2. pilot=aviator
3. the prize
4. 33 1/2 hours
5. He was the first pilot to attempt a nonstop flight from New York to Paris.
6. a Congressional seat

PASSAGE 29

1. The evolution of newspapers
2. associations
3. responds to the public's interest in scandal
4. publishers (such as Pulitzer and Hearst)
5. exclusive reports
6. News articles
7. exposes of corruption and misconduct (against political bosses, trusts, bankers, and so forth)
8. campaigns
9. obligatory reading
10. the increase in two-column advertisements
11. To show that famous writers wrote for papers

12. **Whereas in earlier days a reader could get through a newspaper quite rapidly, paid advertising in newspapers made the dailies significantly heftier.** Publishers also used big names to gain readers, using the promise of large salaries to attract writers of the caliber of Stephen Crane, Richard Harding Davis, and Mark Twain to work for them.

PASSAGE 30

1. Walt Whitman: Poet and Humanitarian
2. provided
3. paragraph 2
4. The form and content of the work was so unusual for its time that he could not find a publisher, so he published a first edition at his own expense in 1855.
5. Between 1856 and 1892, he published eight more revised and expanded editions of the collection. Whitman wrote these poems and most of his other poems in innovative free verse reminiscent of the poetry of the Old Testament and such sacred writings of India as the *Bhagavad Gita,* which Whitman may have read in translation. **Other poetry was not the only influence on his work; the rhythm of Whitman's poems suggests the rise and fall of the sea that he so loved.**
6. cynicism
7. chaotic
8. surviving
9. appreciated the suffering of both Northern and Southern soldiers
10. explains why some disliked Whitman

Post-Test

1. The origins of American football
2. adopted
3. The Harvard team
4. The teams reached a compromise; they would play two games, the first using Harvard's rules and the next following McGill's rules.
5. **As football gained in popularity in the 1880s, teams popped up in towns all over the country.** The number of players increased even more when towns formed their own teams consisting of young men who didn't attend high school or college.
6. designer
7. Players run with the ball.
8. competitions
9. an all-American football team was selected in 1874
10. eastern colleges were the first in the U.S. to play American football
11. paragraph 3
12. how the game of football is played today
13. News distribution developed rapidly throughout the colonial period.
14. printing presses were not operating in colonial America in the 1600s
15. The early colonists also relied on the town crier. This "walking newspaper" stood at every corner. He read out the latest news and notified the citizens about town meetings and other future events.
16. intermittently
17. In Massachusetts, New York, and Pennsylvania
18. **Franklin, an inventor and businessman, had been the postmaster of Philadelphia.** Under his leadership, post offices were set up in all thirteen colonies, and there was a substantial improvement in overall service.
19. 1833
20. a daily paper
21. lowering the cost of newspapers increased revenues
22. town criers announced the news throughout the 1700s
23. spawned=produced
24. before Franklin became Deputy Postmaster General, mail delivery was unreliable
25. how the expression "dog days" originated
26. muggy=humid
27. Each civilization
28. star patterns
29. The Big Dipper
30. We now know, however, that the heat during the warmest period of the summer is not caused by additional radiation from the dog star. **Actually, it is the earth's tilt toward the sun in the summer months that causes the heat.**
31. The ancient Romans, Greeks, and Egyptians
32. continuous period
33. it is now more difficult to see star formations than in ancient times
34. the term "dog days" could be attributed to dogs' summertime behavior
35. Therefore, the ancient Romans, Greeks, and Egyptians mistakenly assumed that Sirius's heat intensified the heat of the sun, causing hotter days on Earth.
36. A (picture of a dog formation)
37. Langston Hughes: More Than Just a Poet
38. Langston Hughes
39. the African-American artistic movement in the 1920s that celebrated black life and culture
40. abundantly
41. rhythms
42. *Not Without Laughter*
43. In the 1940s, he began writing a column for the African-American newspaper, the *Chicago Defender,* where he introduced his readers to a lovable and enduring character named Simple, derived from a conversation Hughes had had with a man in a Harlem bar.
    Because the character Simple was humorous, Hughes was able to tackle very complex racial problems while not offending his readers.
44. Columbia, Africa, Lincoln University
45. words
46. He graduated from Columbia.
47. Hughes had a following during his lifetime
48. paragraph 3
49. art reviews
50. *Not Without Laughter,* the debut of *Simple,* lyrics for *Street Scene, Montage of a Dream Deferred*

TOEFL TEST 1

Section 1

1. The apartment she has now doesn't have air conditioning.
2. Neither Gail nor Fred came to dinner.
3. She should have told him she didn't like the couch.
4. In the dorm
5. The team will practice at the club swimming pool.
6. He should go on without her.
7. She might be confused as to the length of the biology midterm.
8. Going for help made him more confused.
9. The oral presentations are voluntary.
10. The lecture often goes past its scheduled time.
11. It doesn't make a difference how many cookies he gets.
12. It supports campus events on weekends.
13. Students don't participate in what's planned for them.
14. Plan new activities with him
15. From a computer
16. Get the sources from the library
17. At the student center
18. Stone, Metal
19. Intaglio
20. lithographs/planographic
    woodcuts/relief
    engravings/intaglio
21. With sharp tools
22. They want to make many impressions of an image./They enjoy the variety of effects printmaking can produce.
23. The contents of each section in the brochure
24. (picture of the upside down stamp) B
25. roulette/small cuts made by a knife
    imperforate/stamps that cut apart with scissors
    perforation/stamps with little holes
26. birds
27. 1847
28. A newspaperman
29. Lack of food, Wild animal assaults
30. They tried to support themselves doing other things.
31. Those who traveled to California had unrealistic expectations.
32. 1. The discovery of gold at Sutter Mill
    2. The president's publicizing of the gold rush
    3. The migration of 90,000 people to California
    4. California becomes a state

Section 2

1. which	*should be*	who	(wrong relative pronoun)
2. but	(coordinating conjunction showing contrast)		
3. or	*should be*	and	(both . . . and)
4. than	(use with comparative form)		
5. the first book on the subject	(appositive)		
6. furnitures	*should be*	furniture	(non-count noun)
7. a	*should be*	an	(before vowel sound *industrial*)
8. have no	(correct verb tense/form and *no* before nouns)		
9. soap	*should be*	soapy	(adjective form)
10. skins	*should be*	skin	(adjective form)
11. on top of each kidney	(expression is *on top of* + noun)		
12. help	*should be*	helps	(to agree with *a letter*)
13. their	*should be*	its	(to agree with singular *tarragon*)
14. to form	(infinitive form is needed)		
15. buffalo huge	*should be*	huge buffalo	(word order, adjective+ noun)
16. variety	*should be*	a variety	(*variety* is a count noun)
17. federal job programs	(adjective + compound noun)		
18. producing	*should be*	produced	(past participle needed for passive structure in reduced adjective clause)
19. it	*shouldn't be in sentence*		(double subject error)
20. Because	*should be*	Because of	(before noun phrase)
21. such an important fertilizer element			(such an + adj + compound noun)
22. one of	*should be*	one of the	(*the* before superlative)
23. Although	(dependent clause indicating contrast)		
24. other	*should be*	another	(pronoun, not adjective form)
25. A less common type of adobe	(Subject, *adobe*, preceded by comparative form)		

Section 3

1. The uncertainty about Penn's demeanor and physical traits
2. upheaval=revolution
3. protective covering
4. portraits
5. **However, Penn's armor in the portrait may be reconciled with his Quaker pacifism due to the fact that he did not become a Quaker until his twenties, shortly after posing for the portrait.** In contrast, the scene of a treaty signing with the Indian shows a fat and stodgy-looking old man in a costume of a hundred years later.
6. stout=portly
7. Penn may not be the subject of his portraits.
8. art history
9. paragraph 3
10. inaccurately recorded events
11. negotiated with Indians
12. (picture in armor)D
13. new research on childrearing as a result of cultural differences
14. various childrearing suggestions
15. bombarded by
16. These rules have little basis in science.
17. This group of anthropologists, pediatricians, and child development researchers seeks to discover exactly how different styles of parenting across the globe affect the biology, growth, health, and survival of infants.
18. advocates
19. proponents
20. heredity
21. They are similar all over the world.
22. neutral
23. paragraph 3
24. **For example, whether or not young boys are discouraged from crying in public depends on one's culture.** Although newborn babies are the same the world over, from the moment babies start interacting with their mothers, they become members of distinct, changeable, modern societies, often quite unlike those that babies once adapted to through evolution.
25. examples of childrearing which encourage certain culturally-valued behaviors
26. The difficulty in proving the existence of black holes
27. black holes
28. The definition of black holes
29. definite=certain
30. contracts
31. **Einstein's theory proposed that gravity affects the shape of space by curving it and the flow of time by slowing it down.** According to Einstein's theory, a black hole forms when a massive object shrinks catastrophically under its own gravitational field.
32. That black holes probably exist
33. To explain what the process of blotting is
34. impossible
35. Moreover, black holes are extremely tiny; they pack a given mass into the least possible volume.
36. huge
37. wavelets=ripples
38. the existence of black holes may soon be proved
39. The shift from canals to railroad, 1830 to 1860
40. increase
41. ship goods to the East
42. stopped payment of money due
43. explain why certain states did not support railroad expansion
44. Inadequate bridge engineering
45. **Understandably, passengers complained as their clothing and belonging frequently caught on fire.** Finally, engines had insufficient power to carry heavy loads over inclines.
46. insolvable
47. private investors
48. growth of the railroad was due to government and private investment
49. canals
50. New York was not the only state that wanted to encourage the use of its own canal system.

TOEFL TEST 2

Section 1

1. He didn't know where she lived, so he didn't go to see her.
2. Examine the document
3. She changed her mind about the dorm windows.
4. She should make sure the professor agreed with her request.
5. It's difficult to choose which of Anna's weavings is better than the rest.
6. It's possible to take History 102 without having taken 101.
7. She should get some scholarship money.
8. Settle his tuition bill
9. She's surprised about the requirement.
10. It's worth going to career services.
11. Finishing early in the day is important to him.
12. Jobs that allow time to study
13. She can't do any of her homework while working.
14. Stop off at the library
15. At Hill Auditorium
16. The orchestras must be skilled in different areas.
17. Get herself a ticket
18. Why Lincoln decided to grow a beard
19. To make him more popular with ladies, So that the wives would influence their husbands' votes
20. B (picture in beard)
21. 1861
22. 1. Grace writes to Lincoln.
    2. Lincoln grows whiskers.
    3. Lincoln becomes President.
    4. Grace meets Abraham Lincoln.
23. Types of teeth and age of appearance
24. Between 6 months and 2 years
25. Developing wisdom teeth between the ages of 17 to 21
26. Being born with teeth, Having to pull a baby tooth that never fell out
27. 1. Central incisors
    2. Lateral incisors

3. First molars
4. Canines

28. Myths and facts about the Bermuda Triangle
29. C
30. Very deep waters
31. Numerous disappearances did not happen within the Bermuda Triangle region, Most disappearances can be explained scientifically
32. 1. Bright lights and bizarre compass readings are reported.
    2. The *Mary Celeste* goes off course.
    3. Six US military aircraft disappear
    4. The area gets its nickname, the Bermuda Triangle.

Section 2

1. or	*should be*	and	(both . . . and))
2. its	*should be*	their	(to agree with *chameleons*)
3. to exist	*should be*	exist	(modal *can* is not followed by *to*)
4. Before the Revolutionary War began			(dependent clause)
5. are	*should be*	is	(to agree with *selection*)
6. catching	(gerund, to be parallel with *swimming*, etc.)		
7. during the	(preposition needed before *1940s*)		
8. comes from	(simple present tense to state a fact)		
9. consist	*should be*	consists	(to agree with *the movie*)
10. Unlike most other sciences	(preposition needed)		
11. others	*should be*	other	(adjective form needed before noun, *anthropods*)
12. simple geometric shapes	(parallel structure, adjective *simple* before *geometric shapes*)		
13. on	*should be*	from	(incorrect preposition)
14. that he could choose himself	(adjective clause)		
15. a	*should be*	the	(*the first*, specific woman)
16. has established	*should be*	established	(simple past with specific date, *1781*)
17. In the past	(prepositional phrase showing time)		
18. one of the wealthiest	(correct word order, *one* + *of the* + superlative, *wealthiest*)		
19. engineer	*should be*	engineering	(adjective, to be parallel with *medical*, and *scientific*)
20. whose	*should be*	which	(subject relative pronoun)
21. No other system	(No + adjective + noun)		
22. do	*should be*	make	(*make* a contribution)
23. included	*should be*	including	(active participle)
24. uniformity of yarns	(noun+ of + noun, to be parallel with *length*, etc.)		
25. reporters	*should be*	reports	(object noun not person noun, to be *parallel with books, etc.)*

Section 3

1. The history of the *nuna* bean and its potential as a modern-day crop
2. may one day be better known
3. cultivated=grown
4. the technique of making clay pots was discovered by the Incas in the 15th century
5. entrepreneurs
6. mixture
7. the ability of the *nuna* bean to grow well with varying degrees of sunlight
8. He is marketing the beans in the tropics.
9. **This adaptation bodes well for world-wide marketing.** Dr. Neinhuis envisions "Pre-Cooked Popping Beans" on supermarket shelves one day.
10. the bean
11. indigenous
12. paragraph 2
13. Recent efforts to increase the buffalo population
14. 1895
15. buffalo
16. For visitor appeal
17. Buffalo enable the ground to remain moist.
18. **These vast grasslands extend from northern Canada to southern Texas, and from the Rocky Mountains eastward for about 400 miles.** Perennial grass plants grow better where buffalo graze because the animals' sharp hoofs break up and aerate the soil, improving the ability of the soil to retain water.
19. mythology
20. In the parks where they now live, the buffalo are a major tourist attraction, yet park visitors need to be careful; the average buffalo can sprint up to 35 miles an hour, three times faster than the average tourist can run.
21. freely
22. National parks
23. paragraph 2

24. For traditional beliefs
25. 250,000
26. The historical and contemporary uses of cotton
27. Cotton is frequently the fabric of choice as it absorbs color very well, and different textures can be achieved from different varieties of cotton.
28. **Cotton is a component of many items other than clothing.** In addition to clothing, cotton is used in making such diverse items as bookbindings, fishnets, handbags, coffee filters, lace, tents, curtains, and diapers.
29. hoses
30. durability=endurance
31. Oil spill clean ups
32. synthetic
33. flammable
34. Animal food
35. is an ongoing process
36. paragraph 2
37. textiles
38. The durability of paper as a function of its contents
39. At the Library of Congress in Washington, D.C., we can see Saint Augustine's *City of God,* printed in 1473, which is still in excellent condition. **Indeed, the paper pages still look as thick and cream-colored as they did when they were printed.**
40. procedure
41. Making papyrus, printing *City of God,* Gutenberg's invention, using nonacidic paper
42. Acid glazes
43. disintegrate
44. He was a wealthy composer.
45. was not glazed with acid
46. The Library of Congress
47. Very few
48. Concerned
49. books printed today will not crumble in the future
50. attempts to find additional conservators